UNDERSTANDING SALES AND LEASES OF GOODS

William H. Lawrence
Professor of Law
University of San Diego

William H. Henning
R.B. Price Professor of Law
University of Missouri-Columbia

D1537469

LEGAL TEXT SERIES

MATTHEW BENDER

QUESTIONS ABOUT THIS PUBLICATION?

For questions about the **Editorial Content** appearing in these volumes or reprint permission, please call:

Mike Bruno, J.D., at .... 1-800-252-9257 Ext. 2518
Outside the United States and Canada please call .... (212) 448-2000

For assistance with replacement pages, shipments, billing or other customer service matters, please call:

Customer Services Department at .... (800) 833-9844
Outside the United States and Canada, please call .... (518) 487-3000
Fax number .... (518) 487-3584

For information on other Matthew Bender publications, please call
Your account manager or .... (800) 223-1940
Outside the United States and Canada, please call .... (518) 487-3000

Library of Congress Cataloging-in-Publication Data

Lawrence, William H.
    Understanding sales and leases of goods / William H. Lawrence, William H. Henning
    p.   cm. — (Legal Text Series)
    ISBN 0-8205-2864-1
    1. Sales—United States 2. Industrial equipment leases—United States
    I. Henning, William H. 1947-. II. Title. III. Series.
KF915.L395   1996
346.73'072—dc20
[347.30672]   95-18149

MATTHEW BENDER & CO., INC.
EDITORIAL OFFICES
2 Park Avenue, New York, NY 10016-5675 (212) 448-2000
201 Mission St., San Francisco, CA 94105-1831 (415) 908-3200

PREFACE

This book is designed exclusively as a student text. Although it covers both sales and leases of goods, the primary focus is on Article 2—on sales of goods. The decision to pursue this approach is based in part on recognition that several commercial law courses will continue to be based almost entirely on sales. Even courses that address leases of goods under Article 2A generally will continue their major emphasis on sales of goods. Thus, concentrating primarily on sales will best meet the needs of the student.

The decision to make the main emphasis sales of goods is also based on the need to develop an efficient method of presentation. Much of Article 2A on leases is based on Article 2 as a statutory analogue.[1]

With respect to those provisions in the two Articles that are comparable, the text will be primarily concerned with the sales perspective. The case law is quite well-developed with respect to Article 2, and Article 2 case law is often beneficial in interpreting comparable provisions that have been incorporated into Article 2A. These comparable provisions in Article 2A are cross-referenced to facilitate their access. The major discussion devoted to lease transactions will focus on provisions that deviate from the statutory analogue. Most importantly, the text will discuss the differences in the nature of lease and sales transactions that elicited from the drafters unique statutory approaches.

The organization of the subject matter is also designed to correlate nicely with that of a general contracts course. This approach recognizes that, at some institutions, the treatment of sales and leases of goods is included as part of a contracts course.

The Table of Contents includes the basic UCC section numbers for both Articles 2 and 2A. It does not include all of the relevant Code sections, but only the most fundamental provisions relating to the topics. This approach should aid students because they can find relevant discussion by either the subject or the basic Code section number. The Index and the Table of Statutes and

---

[1] See § 1.04 *supra*.

Authorities will enable a more detailed search. The use of the section numbers in the Table of Contents should also facilitate the book's integrated approach to sales and leases.

More detailed treatment of the subject areas can be found in earlier works by the authors. Each of the authors of this text has also written a more specialized volume published by Warren Gorham & Lamont that is intended for practitioners. These volumes are W. Henning and G. Wallach, *The Law of Sales Under the Uniform Commercial Code* (rev. ed. 1992 & 1993 Supp.) and W. Lawrence and J. Minan, *The Law of Personal Property Leasing* (1993 & 1994 Supp.). Although this text has drawn on those prior works to some extent, their greater scope and depth of coverage should be helpful to students who wish to pursue certain aspects of the subject in greater detail.

Professor Lawrence gratefully acknowledges the support provided by the General Research Fund of the University of Kansas. Professor Henning gratefully acknowledges the support provided by the Robert L. Cope Faculty Research Fellowship and the Gary A. Tatlow Research Fellowship.

September 1995

William H. Lawrence
William H. Henning

SUMMARY CONTENTS

PREFACE, *v*

CHAPTER 1   THE UNIFORM COMMERCIAL CODE, *1*

CHAPTER 2   THE AGREEMENT PROCESS, *19*

CHAPTER 3   THE REQUIREMENT OF A WRITING, *51*

CHAPTER 4   SOURCES OF CONTRACT TERMS, *75*

CHAPTER 5   WARRANTY, *119*

CHAPTER 6   RISK OF LOSS, *169*

CHAPTER 7   PERFORMANCE AND BREACH, *187*

CHAPTER 8   REMEDIES OF BUYERS AND LESSEES, *251*

CHAPTER 9   REMEDIES OF SELLERS AND LESSORS, *277*

CHAPTER 10   THIRD-PARTY INTERESTS, *305*

TABLE OF CASES, *TC–1*
TABLE OF STATUTES, *TS–1*
INDEX, *I–1*

CONTENTS

CHAPTER 1 THE UNIFORM COMMERCIAL CODE

§ 1.01 Brief History of Commercial Law Prior to the Uniform Commercial Code, 1

§ 1.02 Initial Promulgation of the Uniform Commercial Code, 2

§ 1.03 Scope of Article 2 [2–102], 3

[A] Sales, 3

[1] Direct Application, 3

[2] Application by Analogy, 5

[B] Goods, 6

[C] Hybrid Transactions, 7

§ 1.04 Promulgation of Article 2A, 8

§ 1.05 Scope of Article 2A [2A–102], 10

[A] Lease Defined [2A–103(1)(j)], 10

[1] Generally, 10

[2] Distinguishing Sales, 11

[3] Distinguishing Secured Transactions [1–201(37)], 11

[B] Finance Leases [2A–103(1)(g)], 13

[C] Consumer Leases [2A–103(1)(e)], 16

§ 1.06 Supplementing Provisions of the Uniform Commercial Code [1–103], 17

CHAPTER 2 THE AGREEMENT PROCESS

§ 2.01 Contract Formation in General [2–204; 2A–204], 19

§ 2.02 Offer, 22

§ 2.03 Acceptance [2–206; 2A–206], 23

[A] Generally, 23

[B] Countering the Unilateral Contract Trick, 25

§ 2.04 Firm Offers [2–205; 2A–205], 26

§ 2.05 The Battle of the Forms [2–207], 28

[A] Introduction, 28

[B] The Basic Rule, 29

[1] Definite Expressions of Assent, 29

[2]   Written Confirmations 33

[C]   "Between Merchants", 34

[1]   Materiality, 35

[2]   "Additional" and "Different" Terms, 38

[D]   Expressly Conditional Expressions of Acceptance, 39

[1]   Language Creating an Expressly Conditional Acceptance, 39

[2]   Consequences of an Expressly Conditional Acceptance, 41

§ 2.06   Modification [2–209; 2A–208], 43

[A]   Consideration, 43

[B]   Modifications and the Statute of Frauds, 45

[1]   Applying the Code's Statute of Frauds to Modifications, 45

[2]   Private Statutes of Frauds, 47

[3]   Waiver and Estoppel, 47

CHAPTER 3   THE REQUIREMENT OF A WRITING

§ 3.01   The Statute of Frauds: A Brief History, 51

§ 3.02   The Code's General Statute of Frauds Provision [1–206], 52

§ 3.03   Specific Statute of Frauds Provisions [2–201(1); 2A–201(1)], 54

[A]   The Writing Requirement, 55

[B]   The Signature Requirement, 56

[C]   Sufficient to Show a Contract, 57

[D]   The Quantity Term, 59

[E]   Terms Describing the Goods and Duration—Leases, 60

§ 3.04   Statutory Exceptions: The Written Confirmation Rule [2–201(2)], 61

[A]   Contents of the Written Confirmation, 62

[B]   The Merchant Requirement, 63

§ 3.05   Statutory Exceptions: Exceptions Based on Equitable Principles [2–201(3); 2A–201(4)], 64

[A]   Specially Manufactured Goods [2–201(3)(a); 2A–201(4)(a)], 65

[B]   Admissions in Judicial Proceedings [2–201(3)(b); 2A–201(4)(b)], 67

[C] Goods Accepted or Payment Made [2–201(3)(c);
2A–201(4)(c)], *68*

§ 3.06 Nonstatutory Exceptions: Equitable and Promissory
Estoppel, *71*

§ 3.07 The Effects of Noncompliance, *73*

CHAPTER 4 SOURCES OF CONTRACT TERMS

§ 4.01 Introduction, *75*

§ 4.02 The Parol Evidence Rule, *76*

[A] Common Law, *76*

[B] The Code's Formulation of the Rule [2–202; 2A–202], *77*

[C] Finality, *79*

[D] Completeness, *79*

[1] Common Law, *79*

[2] The Code Test, *81*

[E] Contradiction and Consistency, *82*

[F] The Effect of a Merger Clause, *84*

[G] Terms That Can Be Proved Notwithstanding a Complete
Writing, *85*

[1] Supplementation Through Usage of Trade, Course
of Dealing, and Course of Performance, *85*

[2] Invalidating Causes, *86*

[3] Conditions Precedent, *87*

[4] Interpretation, *88*

[H] Reformation as an Alternative Approach, *89*

§ 4.03 The Special Roles of Trade Usage, Course of Dealing,
and Course of Performance [1–205; 2–208; 2A–207], *90*

[A] Usage of Trade Defined, *90*

[B] Course of Dealing Defined, *91*

[C] Course of Performance Defined, *92*

[D] The Code's Hierarchy of Terms, *93*

§ 4.04 The Process of Interpretation, *96*

[A] The Plain Meaning Rule, *96*

[B] Aids in the Process of Interpretation, *97*

§ 4.05 Implied-in-Law Terms [Gap-Fillers], *99*

[A] Open and Deferred Price Terms [2–305], *99*

[B] Delivery and Payment Terms Generally, *101*

  [1] Place of Delivery [2–308], *102*

  [2] Time for Performance [2–309], *102*

  [3] Shipment and Destination Contracts [2–503; 2–504], *104*

  [4] Payment Terms [2–310; 2–511; 2–513], *105*

  [5] Payment by Check [2–507; 2–511], *107*

[C] Open Quantity Terms (Output and Requirements Contracts) [2–306], *108*

§ 4.06 Supereminent Principles, *110*

[A] Unconscionability [2–302; 2A–108], *110*

  [1] Procedural and Substantive Unconscionability, *112*

  [2] Unconscionability in a Commercial Context, *115*

  [3] Forms of Relief Available, *116*

  [4] Additional Consumer Protection—Leases, *116*

[B] The Duty of Good Faith [1–203; 1–201(19); 2–103(1)(c); 2A–103(2)], *117*

CHAPTER 5 WARRANTY

§ 5.01 Warranties in General, *119*

§ 5.02 Types of Warranties, *120*

[A] Express Warranties [2–313; 2A–210], *120*

  [1] The Affirmation of Fact/Opinion Dichotomy, *120*

  [2] Description, *122*

  [3] Sample or Model, *124*

  [4] Basis of the Bargain, *126*

[B] The Implied Warranty of Merchantability Generally [2–314; 2A–212], *130*

  [1] "Merchant with Respect to Goods of That Kind", *131*

  [2] The Standard of Merchantability, *132*

[C] The Implied Warranty of Fitness for a Particular Purpose [2–315; 2A–213], *136*

  [1] "Reason to Know", *136*

  [2] Particular Purpose, *137*

  [3] Reliance by the Buyer, *138*

[D] The Warranties of Title and Against Infringement
[2–312; 2A–211], *139*

§ 5.03 Warranty Disclaimers [2–316; 2A–214], *141*

[A] Disclaiming Express Warranties, *141*

[B] Disclaiming the Implied Warranties of Merchantability
and Fitness, *142*

[1] Disclaimers Using "Safe-Harbor" Language, *142*

[2] Disclaimers Using Other Language, *144*

[3] Inspection of the Goods, *145*

[4] Post-Contracting Disclaimers, *146*

[C] Disclaimers and Unconscionability, *148*

§ 5.04 Modification or Impairment of Rights and Remedies
[2–719; 2A–503], *148*

[A] Substituted Remedy Clauses, *148*

[1] "Expressly Agreed to Be Exclusive", *149*

[2] Failure of Essential Purpose, *150*

[B] Clauses Limiting or Excluding Consequential Damages,
152

[C] Substituted Remedy Clauses and Clauses Limiting
Consequential Damages in Combination, *153*

§ 5.05 Defenses Based on the Claimant's Conduct, *154*

§ 5.06 Privity, *157*

[A] Strict Liability in Tort: A Brief Comparison, *157*

[B] Horizontal Privity, *159*

[C] Vertical Privity, *161*

[D] Express Warranties, *162*

[E] Finance Lessee as Beneficiary of Supply Contract
[2A–209], *163*

§ 5.07 The Statute of Limitations [2–725, 2A–506], *164*

§ 5.08 Cumulation and Conflict of Warranties [2–317; 2A–215],
167

CHAPTER 6 RISK OF LOSS

§ 6.01 Introduction, *169*

Part A: Sales

§ 6.02 In the Absence of Breach [2–509], *170*

[A] Express Agreement, *170*

[B]   Shipment by Carrier, *172*

[C]   Goods Held by a Bailee, *174*

[D]   All Other Cases, *176*

§ 6.03   In the Event of Breach [2–510], *177*

[A]   Buyer's Right to Reject, *177*

[B]   Buyer's Revocation of Acceptance, *178*

[C]   Breach by the Buyer, *180*

Part B: Leases

§ 6.04   General Rule [2A–219(1)], *181*

§ 6.05   Exceptions, *181*

[A]   Applicability, *181*

[1]   Express Agreement, *182*

[2]   Finance Leases [2A–219(1)], *182*

[B]   When Risk Passes, *183*

[1]   In the Absence of Default [2A–219(2)], *183*

[2]   In the Event of Default [2A–220], *184*

CHAPTER 7   PERFORMANCE AND BREACH

§ 7.01   Obligations of the Parties [2–301], *187*

Part A: Buyer Responses to Tender of Delivery

§ 7.02   Overview, *188*

§ 7.03   Acceptance, *188*

[A]   Methods of Acceptance [2–606; 2A–515], *188*

[1]   Statement, *189*

[2]   Silence, *190*

[3]   Conduct, *191*

[B]   Consequences of Acceptance [2–607; 2A–516], *194*

[1]   Rejection and Revocation, *195*

[2]   Obligation to Pay, *195*

[3]   Notification, *196*

[4]   Burden of Proof, *197*

§ 7.04   Rejection, *198*

[A]   Perfect Tender Rule [2–601; 2A–509(1)], *198*

[B]   Procedural Aspects [2–602; 2A–509(2)], *199*

[1]   Timeliness, *200*

[2] Notice Contents, *201*

[3] Rights and Duties of Buyer, *202*

[C] The Cure Limitation [2–508; 2A–513], *203*

[1] Time During Which to Cure, *204*

[2] Seasonable Notification, *206*

[3] Reasonable Grounds to Believe, *207*

[4] Money Allowance, *210*

[5] Conforming Tender, *211*

[6] Consensual Cure, *214*

[D] The Good-Faith Limitation [1–203], *215*

[E] The Installment Contract Exception [2–612; 2A–510], *216*

[F] The Shipment Contract Exception [2–504], *218*

§ 7.05 Revocation of Acceptance [2–608; 2A–517], *219*

[A] The Right, *220*

[1] Limited Circumstances, *220*

[2] Subjective Standard of Substantial Impairment, *221*

[B] Procedural Aspects, *223*

[C] Cure, *224*

[D] Wrongful Revocation, *226*

[E] Revocation and Privity, *227*

[F] Compensation for Use of Goods, *227*

[G] Irrevocable Promises in Finance Leases [2A–407], *228*

Part B: Breach or Default

§ 7.06 Sale of Goods, *229*

[A] Breach by Seller [2–711], *229*

[B] Breach by Buyer [2–703], *230*

§ 7.07 Lease of Goods, *230*

[A] Default, *230*

[B] Default by Lessor [2A–508], *232*

[C] Default by Lessee [2A–523], *232*

Part C: Prospective Impairment of Expectations

§ 7.08 General, *232*

§ 7.09 Anticipatory Repudiation [2–610; 2A–402], *233*

[A] What Constitutes Repudiation, *233*

[B] Options of the Aggrieved Party, *234*

[C] Retraction [2–611; 2A–403], *235*

[D] Installment Contracts [2–612(3); 2A–510(2)], *236*

§ 7.10 Demand for Assurances of Performance [2–609; 2A–401], *238*

[A] The Right, *238*

[B] Effect of the Demand, *240*

Part D: Excuse

§ 7.11 Fundamental versus Incidental, *241*

§ 7.12 Casualty to Identified Goods [2–613; 2A–221], *242*

§ 7.13 Substituted Performance [2–614; 2A–404], *243*

§ 7.14 Commercial Impracticability [2–615; 2A–405], *244*

[A] Excuse, *244*

[1] Nonoccurrence of a Basic Assumption, *245*

[2] Governmental Regulation, *247*

[3] Resulting Commercial Impracticability, *248*

[B] Duties of the Seller, *250*

CHAPTER 8 REMEDIES OF BUYERS AND LESSEES

§ 8.01 General, *251*

[A] Cumulation of Remedies, *252*

[B] Time Value of Money, *252*

Part A: Monetary Remedies

§ 8.02 Recovery of Payments Made [2–711(1); 2A–508(1)(b)], *253*

§ 8.03 Cover [2–712; 2A–518], *254*

[A] The Substitute, *254*

[B] The Cover Formula, *257*

[C] Leases, *258*

§ 8.04 Market Price/Contract Price Differential [2–713; 2A–519(1),(2)], *259*

[A] Election, *260*

[B] Selecting the Market, *261*

[1] Place, *261*

[2] Time, *263*

§ 8.05 Damages When Buyer Accepts the Goods [2–714; 2A–519(3),(4)], *264*

[A] Recovery of Ordinary Loss, *265*

[B] Breach of Warranty, *265*

[1]   The Standard Formula, *265*

[2]   Time and Place to Measure Value, *267*

[3]   Special Circumstances, *267*

§ 8.06   Incidental and Consequential Damages [2–715; 2A–520], *268*

[A]   Incidental, *269*

[B]   Consequential, *269*

Part B: Nonmonetary Damages

§ 8.07   Cancellation [2–711(1); 2A–508(1)(a)], *273*

§ 8.08   Specific Performance [2–716; 2A–521], *273*

CHAPTER 9   REMEDIES OF SELLERS AND LESSORS

Part A: Monetary Remedies

§ 9.01   Resale [2–706; 2A–527], *277*

[A]   Sales, *277*

[B]   Leases, *280*

[C]   Comparing Sales, Leases, and Secured Transactions, *281*

§ 9.02   Contract Price/Market Price Differential [2–708(1); 2A–528(1)], *283*

[A]   The Measure, *283*

[B]   Determining the Market, *284*

[1]   Sales, *284*

[2]   Leases, *285*

§ 9.03   Lost Profits [2–708(2), 2A–528(2)], *286*

§ 9.04   Action for Price or Rent [2–709; 2A–529], *288*

[A]   Limited Applicability, *288*

[1]   Accepted Goods, *288*

[2]   Goods Lost or Damaged, *289*

[3]   Goods Not Readily Resalable, *290*

[B]   Recovery of Rent, *291*

§ 9.05   Incidental Damages [2–710; 2A–530], *292*

§ 9.06   Injury to Lessor's Residual Interest [2A–532], *294*

Part B: Nonmonetary Remedies

§ 9.07   Cancellation [2–703(f), 2A–523(1)(a)], *295*

§ 9.08   Withholding Delivery [2–703(a), 2A–523(1)(c)], *295*

§ 9.09   Retaking Possession [2–702(2), 2A–525], *296*

[A] Seller, *296*

[B] Lessor, *298*

Part C: Liquidated Damages

§ 9.10 Sales [2–718(1)], *299*

§ 9.11 Leases [2A–504], *302*

CHAPTER 10 THIRD-PARTY INTERESTS

§ 10.01 Assignment and Delegation, *305*

[A] Sales [2–210], *305*

[B] Leases [2A–303], *308*

§ 10.02 Priorities, *310*

[A] Subsequent Buyers or Lessees [2–403; 2A–304; 2A–305], *310*

[1] Derivative Title, *310*

[2] Bona Fide Purchasers, *311*

[3] Ordinary Course of Business, *312*

[B] Secured Parties [9–307(1); 9–301(1)(c); 2A–307], *312*

[C] Other Creditors [2–403(2); 2A–306; 2A–307(2)(c); 2A–308], *313*

Table of Cases, *TC–1*
Table of Statutes, *TS–1*
Index, *315*

CHAPTER

1

The Uniform Commercial Code

§ 1.01 BRIEF HISTORY OF COMMERCIAL LAW PRIOR TO THE UNIFORM COMMERCIAL CODE

The earliest regulation of commerce was provided through custom rather than law.[1] The practices of merchants were the dominant source for the standards governing commercial disputes. The institutions and personnel needed to resolve those disputes also developed through commercial activities rather than governmental action. The Law Merchant evolved as customary law by merchants and for merchants.

When exchanges of products began to develop in medieval Europe, trading custom was localized. With the expansion of trade boundaries to include even exchanges of goods with merchants from Asia and Africa, the Law Merchant developed during the 12th and 13th centuries to reflect a more universal custom of merchants. Trading markets and fairs based on unfettered principles of free trade became established in European locations. These markets were mutually beneficial to all parties: the merchants enjoyed the profits, the local rulers collected taxes, and the community attained increased employment and desired goods from other locations. The universality of the Law Merchant meant that it was based on customs of trading practice that were common to all nationalities.

---

[1] For an excellent and much more thorough explanation, *see* L. Trakman, *The Law Merchant: The Evolution of Commercial Law* (1983).

The Law Merchant was truly merchants' law rather than a regulatory scheme imposed as an exercise of local or regional sovereign authority. Values were determined in accordance with commercial custom as reflected in dynamic trade relationships. Even the methods of resolving disputes reflected practical needs of commerce. Separate tribunals considered commercial disputes. The judges selected were usually merchants who could apply their experience and understanding of mercantile customs. The adjudication of disputes often occurred at the markets or ports themselves, with procedures kept informal to promote prompt decisions.

The emergence of national interests and the expansion of trading areas prevented true universality of the Law Merchant, resulting in its incorporation into national legal systems. On the European continent, the essentials of the Law Merchant were basically codified into commercial codes. The initial influence of the Law Merchant was considerably diminished in England, where it was largely subjugated to the strict proceedings of the common law. Trade custom lost much of its role as a source of commercial law.

The continued vitality of the Law Merchant in international trade and England's position as a world trading power meant that the English courts could not ignore custom completely. Lord Mansfield recognized commercial realities and successfully sought to free commercial law from many of the common law restraints. The essential objective was to allow commercial law to reflect commercial practices. Tremendous advances were made in this respect, but the English experience has often been characterized by formal methods required to establish trade custom.

The Law Merchant re-emerged as a more powerful influence in the United States. Trade practices have been recognized as a primary source of U.S. commercial law, and legal rules in the area have generally been premised on business practices. The constraints of formality have also been rejected in American law. Current commercial legislation, particularly the Uniform Commercial Code (UCC), continues these traditions. The UCC recognizes trade usages and courses of dealing; it does not follow the English approach of requiring custom to have been established since time immemorial to be effective.

§ 1.02 INITIAL PROMULGATION OF THE UNIFORM COMMERCIAL CODE

The Uniform Commercial Code was not the initial codification of commercial law in the United States. The National Conference of Commissioners on Uniform State Laws (NCCUSL) sponsored several uniform acts that encompassed areas of commercial law. The Uniform Sales Act, drafted by Professor

Samuel Williston, was promulgated in 1906 and was ultimately adopted by about two-thirds of the states.

Interest in commercial law reform became pronounced by 1940. The various uniform acts were no longer sufficient. Commercial law practices and activities had changed, leaving the acts inadequate to resolve new issues. Uniformity among the states was also undercut by the failure of some states to enact some of the acts and by differing approaches taken in various enacting jurisdictions. The National Conference of Commissioners on Uniform State Laws sponsored a bold plan to prepare a single commercial code. The American Law Institute agreed in 1944 to co-sponsor the project, and Professor Karl Llewellyn was appointed as the Chief Reporter.

The first Official Text of the Code was promulgated in 1951. It consisted of nine Articles, including Article 2 on sales. Although Pennsylvania in 1953 became the first state to enact the Code, further enactments bogged down when the legislature and governor in New York referred it to the New York State Law Revision Commission. Based on recommendations of the New York Commission and other authorities, the Editorial Board for the Code studied and revised it. State enactments followed quickly after the promulgation of the 1962 Official Text. By 1968, all of the states except Louisiana,[2] as well as the District of Columbia and the Virgin Islands, had adopted the Code.

The advance of time and the evolution of new business practices have led the Editorial Board to undertake a revision of Article 2. Under the leadership of Professor Richard E. Speidel of Northwestern University as the Reporter for the project, the revision process is currently under way. The first draft of the revision was presented at the 1994 annual meeting of the NCCUSL. Following refinement of the draft and final approval by the sponsoring bodies, the revision will be promulgated and available for adoption by state legislatures.

§ 1.03   SCOPE OF ARTICLE 2 [2–102]

[A]   Sales

[1]   Direct Application

The scope provision of Article 2 states that the Article "applies to transactions in goods," with the only stated exception being transactions in the form

---

[2]   Louisiana enacted some of the other articles of the UCC. Adhering to its French civil law tradition, Louisiana has not enacted Article 2.

of sales that are intended to operate only as security transactions.[3] The range of applicable transactions appears to be very broad. Additional transactions in goods include leases, bailments, gifts, storage, and transit of goods. The range of these transactions in goods certainly extends beyond the scope suggested by the short title of Article 2, "Uniform Commercial Code—Sales."[4] The scope of Article 2 is restricted to transactions involving sales of goods through the language of the substantive provisions of Article 2. Most of the provisions are written in terms of "contract for sale,"[5] "sale,"[6] "buyer,"[7] or "seller."[8] Section 2–106(1) further states that "[i]n this Article unless the context otherwise requires 'contract' and 'agreement' are limited to those relating to the present or future sale of goods."[9]

Despite the fact that none of these terms can apply to any transactions other than sales, some courts have ignored the substantive sections and held that transactions in goods other than sales are also within the scope of Article 2.[10] Most courts, however, have restricted the direct application of Article 2 to sales.[11] A sale is a distinct transaction that is easy to ascertain under Article 2. It is defined to consist "in the passing of title from the seller to the buyer for a price."[12] The signature feature of a sale is that the seller does not retain any tie to the goods upon completing his or her performance. Most of the provisions of Article 2 apply irrespective of the location of title to the goods.[13] Basing

---

[3]   UCC § 2–102.

[4]   UCC § 2–101.

[5]   " 'Contract' for sale includes both a present sale of goods and a contract to sell goods at a future time." UCC § 2–106(1).

[6]   "A 'sale' consists in the passing of title from the seller to the buyer for a price." UCC § 2–106(1).

[7]   " 'Buyer' means a person who buys or contracts to buy goods." UCC § 2–103(1)(a).

[8]   " 'Seller' means a person who sells or contracts to sell goods." UCC § 2–103(1)(d).

[9]   The comments undercut any attempt to give an expansive construction to the reference to context in order to apply Article 2 directly to transactions other than the sale of goods. " 'Contract for sale' is used as a general concept throughout this Article, but the rights of the parties do not vary according to whether the transaction is a present sale or a contract to sell unless the Article expressly so provides." UCC § 2–106, Comment 1.

[10] Murphy v. McNamara, 27 UCC Rep. Serv. 911 (Conn. Super. Ct. 1979) (applied unconscionability provision to a lease of goods); Owens v. Patent Scaffolding Co., 354 N.Y.S.2d 778, 14 UCC Rep. Serv. 610 (Sup. Ct. 1974), rev'd on other grounds, 376 N.Y.S.2d 948, 18 UCC Rep. Serv. 699 (App. Div. 1975) (applied warranty and statute of limitations provisions to a lease).

[11] Cases denying direct applicability of Article 2 to contracts for the lease of goods include W. R. Weaver Co. v. Burroughs Corp., 580 S.W.2d 76, 27 UCC Rep. Serv. 64 (Tex. Civ. App. 1979); Bona v. Graefe, 264 Md. 69, 285 A.2d 607, 10 UCC Rep. Serv. 47 (Md. Ct. App. 1972).

[12] UCC § 2–106(1).

[13] UCC § 2–401.

issues such as the allocation of risk of loss on the moment of passing of title, which was the approach under the Uniform Sales Act,[14] proved to be too complicated and uncertain under prior law and was thus largely abandoned as the relevant determinant in Article 2. The essence of a sale nevertheless continues to be the passing of title from the seller to the buyer for a price.

[2] Application by Analogy

Some of the provisions of Article 2, even though directly applicable only to sales, might be applied by analogy to other types of transactions. Application by analogy is not, however, a magic wand that simply dispenses with the scope limitations. An appropriate base for the analogy must be established before a court should apply a statute by analogy.[15] Two basic approaches have been followed in applying Article 2 by analogy. Some courts have addressed the policies that support individual Code sections to determine whether they also apply to the transaction in question. In *Baker v. City of Seattle*,[16] the court refused to uphold the liability disclaimer provision on the rental of a golf cart. It applied provisions of Article 2 on the grounds that such provisions state public policy with respect to disclaimers of liability in commercial transactions.[17] Other courts have applied Article 2 by analogy only when the transaction in question is analogous to a sale. The court in *Glenn Dick Equipment Co. v. Galey Construction, Inc.*,[18] stated, ''[w]e will use Article 2 as 'a premise for reasoning only when the case involves the same considerations that gave rise to the Code provisions and an analogy is not rebutted by additional antithetical considerations.' ''[19] It determined that the same considerations that supported the creation of implied warranties in a sales transaction were present in the lease in the case before it: the lessor was a merchant specializing in both sales and leases of goods, the lessor placed the goods into the stream of commerce, and the lessee relied on the lessor's expertise.

The court in *Wivagg v. Duquesne Light Co.*[20] similarly concluded that the policies underlying the implied warranty of merchantability would be

---

14 Uniform Sales Act § 22.

15 For an excellent discussion of argument by analogy with respect to the Code, *see* Murray, *Under the Spreading Analogy of Article 2 of the Uniform Commercial Code*, 39 Fordham L. Rev. 447 (1971).

16 79 Wash. 2d 198, 484 P.2d 405, 9 UCC Rep. Serv. 226 (1971).

17 The court applied sections 2–316(2) and 2–719(3). *See also* W. E. Johnson Equip. Co. v. United Airlines, Inc., 238 So. 2d 98, 8 UCC Rep. Serv. 533 (Fla. 1970) (warranty of fitness for a particular purpose imposed because public policy requires consumers who lease to be given protection equivalent to consumers who purchase).

18 97 Idaho 216, 541 P.2d 1184, 18 UCC Rep. Serv. 340 (1975).

19 541 P.2d at 1190, 18 UCC Rep. Serv. at 348, citing Note, *The Uniform Commercial Code as a Premise for Judicial Reasoning*, 65 Colum. L. Rev. 880, 888 (1965).

20 73 Pa. D. & C. 2d 694, 20 UCC Rep. Serv. 597 (1975).

furthered if the warranty were applied to a public utility that provided electricity service. It found the basis for liability grounded in the social policies that support the imposition of liability on entities that make or market defective products. The court emphasized that the utility was in complete control of the electricity service until its entry into the plaintiff's building, so that the consumer could not have protected itself against a power surge that caused a fire. In addition, the superior position of the utility to absorb the resulting loss further justified imposing enterprise liability that underlies the implied warranty of merchantability.

[B]   Goods

Even with respect to sales transactions, Article 2 is limited to sales of goods. "Goods" are defined as "all things (including specially manufactured goods) which are moveable at the time of identification to the contract for sale other than money in which the price is to be paid, investment securities (Article 8) and things in action."[21] Essentially, goods are any form of tangible, personal property whose value is ascertained by its own physical properties. Real property is excluded, as is intangible personal property, such as contract rights or patents. Personal property that is reified in the form of indispensable paper, such as negotiable instruments or negotiable documents, is tangible and moveable in the form of a writing, but its actual value is ascertained by the rights embodied in the writing. A negotiable instrument, which includes checks and promissory notes, has value because of the obligation to pay money that it evidences.[22] A negotiable document, which could be a bill of lading or a warehouse receipt, establishes title to the goods covered, so its value is based on the value of the goods.[23] The value of goods, on the other hand, is based on the attributes of the goods themselves.

The reference to identification in the definition of goods is included in recognition that parties sometimes enter a contract for the sale of goods that have not yet been produced.[24] Goods must be moveable at the time of their identification to the contract. Before any interest in goods can pass from the seller to the buyer, the goods must be both existing and identified.[25] Identification occurs essentially at the earliest point in time when the specific goods that the

---

[21]   UCC § 2–105(1). " 'Goods' also includes the unborn young of animals and growing crops and other identified things attached to realty as described in the section on goods to be severed from realty (Section 2–107)." *Id.*

[22]   Negotiable instruments are covered under Article 3 of the UCC.

[23]   Negotiable documents are covered under Article 7 of the UCC and, in some cases of interstate commerce, under federal law.

[24]   "Goods which are not both existing and identified are 'future' goods. A purported present sale of future goods or of any interest therein operates as a contract to sell." UCC § 2–105(2).

[25]   UCC § 2–105(2).

seller will tender to the buyer in fulfillment of the contract are so designated. When the buyer selects the specific goods at the time of contract formation, identification occurs.[26] The parties might contract, however, for goods that the seller has yet to mass produce. Identification might not result until the distant delivery date, at which time the specific units for delivery to the buyer are selected for the first time from the seller's subsequently manufactured stock of goods.[27]

[C] Hybrid Transactions

The most difficult aspect of the scope provision is to determine the applicability of Article 2 to hybrid transactions. These contracts involve a sale of goods, but they include additional categories of transactions as well. For example, a contract can include both a sale of goods and a service. Hybrid transactions are illustrated by the contract in *Cumberland Farms, Inc. v. Drehan Paving & Flooring Co.*[28] to sell and install bricks and the contract in *Federal Express Corp. v. Pan American World Airways, Inc.*[29] to sell aircraft and provide the initial training for the crews. Another type of hybrid transaction involves the sale of other items together with a sale of goods. The contract in *Dehahn v. Innes*[30] included the sale of both goods and real property, whereas *Dravo Corp. v. White Consolidated Industries, Inc.*[31] involved the sale of goods and intangibles.

To determine whether a hybrid transaction is within the scope of Article 2, most courts apply the primary purpose test. If the court determines that the sale of goods was the primary or dominant purpose motivating the parties to enter the contract, the entire contract is governed by Article 2. Conversely, if the sale of goods aspect of the contract is considered secondary to the overall transaction, Article 2 is held not to cover any part of the agreement. Applying this test, the court in *Bonebrake v. Cox*[32] found that Article 2 applied to the sale of used bowling alley equipment and lane beds, even though the contract also involved substantial amounts of labor to install the

---

[26] In the absence of explicit agreement, identification occurs
    (a) when the contract is made if it is for the sale of goods already existing and identified. UCC § 2–501(1)(a).

[27] In the absence of explicit agreement, identification occurs
    (b) if the contract is for the sale of future goods other than those described in paragraph (c), when goods are shipped, marked or otherwise designated by the seller as goods to which the contract refers. UCC § 2–501(1)(b).

[28] 25 Mass. App. 530, 520 N.E.2d 1321, 7 UCC Rep. Serv. 2d 747 (1988).

[29] 623 F.2d 1297, 29 UCC Rep. Serv. 778 (8th Cir. 1980).

[30] 356 A.2d 711, 19 UCC Rep. Serv. 407 (Me. 1976) (sale of heavy road-building equipment and a gravel pit).

[31] 602 F. Supp. 1136, 40 UCC Rep. Serv. 362 (W.D. Pa. 1985) (sale of business included drawings that represented ideas and an agreement not to compete for five years).

[32] 499 F.2d 951, 14 UCC Rep. Serv. 1318 (8th Cir. 1974).

goods.[33] In contrast, the court in *Cork Plumbing Co. v. Martin Bloom Associates, Inc.*[34] found that the materials supplied were only incidental in a plumbing construction contract that required the contractor to assemble and connect different plumbing materials into a completed system.[35] Courts have often focused on the percentage of the total contract price that could be allocated to the purchase of the goods in applying the primary purpose test.[36] Other courts have indicated that the primary purpose of a hybrid transaction is controlled by the intent of the parties.[37]

Some courts determine the applicability of Article 2 to a hybrid transaction by separating out the sale of goods aspect and applying Article 2 only to that part of the transaction. Thus, in *Foster v. Colorado Radio Corp.*,[38] the court applied Article 2 to a contract for the sale of a radio station as a going concern only insofar as the sale covered office equipment and furnishings. The bulk of the assets under the contract, covering items such as the license, goodwill, real estate, and transmission equipment, were not goods. Most jurisdictions have not followed this approach.[39] Even though the goods in a transaction are severable, these courts stress that the parties did not contemplate severance, but rather a transaction in which the various elements were combined.[40]

§ 1.04 PROMULGATION OF ARTICLE 2A

The initial UCC project understandably did not include lease of goods transactions because leasing activity was relatively insignificant during the late

---

[33] *See also* Neibarger v. Universal Cooperatives, Inc., 439 Mich. 512, 486 N.W.2d 612, 18 UCC Rep. Serv. 2d 729 (1992) (installation and servicing obligations were incidental to the sale of automatic milking system).

[34] 573 S.W.2d 947, 25 UCC Rep. Serv. 1245 (Mo. Ct. App. 1978).

[35] *See also* Geotech Energy Corp. v. Gulf States Telecommunications & Information Systems, Inc., 788 S.W.2d 386, 12 UCC Rep. Serv. 2d 41 (Tex. Ct. App. 1990) (installation of telephone system and creation of software to customize it predominated).

[36] Baker v. Compton, 455 N.E.2d 382, 38 UCC Rep. Serv. 10 (Ind. Ct. App. 1983) (predominant purpose measured in part by relationship of cost of the goods to the total contract price); Monetti, S.P.A. v. Anchor Hocking Corp., 931 F.2d 1178, 14 UCC Rep. Serv. 2d 706 (7th Cir. 1991) (contemplated sales volume outweighed intangibles sold in exclusive distributorship agreement).

[37] Urban Indus. of Ohio, Inc. v. Tectum, Inc., 81 Ohio App. 3d 768, 612 N.E.2d 382, 20 UCC Rep. Serv. 2d 1193 (1992); Standard Structural Steel Co. v. Debron Corp., 515 F. Supp. 803, 32 UCC Rep. Serv. 393 (D. Conn. 1980).

[38] 381 F.2d 222, 4 UCC Rep. Serv. 446 (10th Cir. 1967).

[39] Insul-Mark Midwest, Inc. v. Modern Materials, Inc., 612 N.E.2d 550, 21 UCC Rep. Serv. 2d 219 (Ind. 1993) (bifurcation approach followed by a lower court is rejected in favor of the "predominant thrust" test).

[40] Field v. Golden Triangle Broadcasting, Inc., 451 Pa. 410, 304 A.2d 689, 12 UCC Rep. Serv. 1037 (1973) (sale of two radio stations as a going concern); McClanahan v. American Gilsonite Co., 494 F. Supp. 1334, 30 UCC Rep. Serv. 21 (D. Colo. 1980) (sale of a crude oil refinery).

1940s and the 1950s. Leasing of personal property simply was not sufficiently developed to be included in a project codifying commercial law.

The modern leasing industry is entirely different. Approximately one-third of new capital invested in equipment in this country is now invested through leasing.[41] Business leasing of equipment grew twice as fast as overall business investment in equipment during the 1980s.[42] The leasing of personal property has become a significant economic activity both nationally and internationally.[43]

The law of personal property leasing did not keep pace with the growth of leasing activity. It was found in scattered fragments in the ancient law of bailments, isolated statutory provisions, arguments by analogy to Article 2 and real property law, and private agreements between the contracting parties. The need for a comprehensive body of law to govern the transactions became increasingly apparent.

Following an initial study by the American Bar Association in 1980, the National Conference of Commissioners on Uniform State Laws (NCCUSL) appointed a Drafting Committee in 1982.[44] The Drafting Committee responded with the Uniform Personal Property Leasing Act. It was later decided to incorporate the new act into the UCC, so the drafting committee revised the act into new Article 2A. Article 2A was promulgated with approval of the Permanent Editorial Board in March 1987. This new article was the first expansion of subject matter within the scope of the Uniform Commercial Code since the Code was originally promulgated in 1951.

Article 2A is based in large part on Article 2 and to a lesser extent on Article 9. Unlike the drafters of other articles of the Code, the drafters of Article 2A did not have a predecessor statute on which they could base their work. They wisely decided, therefore, to draw on Articles 2 and 9 to the extent that their provisions are compatible with lease transactions,[45] but to deviate from the statutory analogues when necessary.[46] Article 2 was used as the primary analogue

---

[41] U.S. Dep't of Commerce, *U.S. Industrial Outlook 1993—Equipment Leasing* 53–1 (1992).

[42] U.S. Dep't of Commerce, *U.S. Industrial Outlook 1990—Equipment Leasing* 56–1 (1989).

[43] An international convention was adopted in final form in 1988. UNIDROIT, Convention on International Financial Leasing, App. I, 27 *Int'l Legal Materials* 931 (1988).

[44] A more extensive discussion of the initial development of Article 2A is provided in A. Boss, *The History of Article 2A: A Lesson for Practitioner and Scholar Alike,* 39 Ala. L. Rev. 575 (1988).

[45] For a discussion of the major policy decisions facing the drafters, including the decision to use statutory analogues, *see* W. Lawrence & J. Minan, *Resolved: That the Kansas and Other State Legislatures Should Enact Article 2A of the Uniform Commercial Code,* 39 U. Kan. L. Rev. 95 (1990).

[46] The differences are highlighted in W. Lawrence & J. Minan, *Deviations from the Statutory Analogues: The New U.C.C. Article 2A,* 40 U. Kan. L. Rev. 531 (1992).

because of the similarity of many aspects of sales and lease transactions, the bilateral nature of both types of transactions, and the desire of the drafters to perpetuate the freedom of contract principle embodied in Article 2.[47] The drafters, however, did not deviate from the analogues to the full extent necessary to differentiate lease transactions. The California State Bar Association Committee prepared a preliminary draft report that identified several areas in which the text of Article 2A needed revisions to better conform to lease transactions.[48] The drafters were reluctant to reopen debate on the text and simply made explanatory changes in the Official Comments. The California Committee rejected this inadequate approach,[49] and California ultimately enacted a version of Article 2A with several revisions.

Recognizing that a number of states were prepared to follow California's lead, the NCCUSL relented and proposed amendments to the text of Article 2A that reflected much of the California criticism.[50] Final approval of the amendments followed in December 1990. Thirty-nine states and the District of Columbia had enacted Article 2A as of March 1994.[51]

§ 1.05   SCOPE OF ARTICLE 2A [2A–102]

[A]   Lease Defined [2A–103(1)(j)]

[1]   Generally

Scope is established much more directly in Article 2A than it is in Article 2. The scope section simply states that the article "applies to any transaction,

---

[47] "This codification was greatly influenced by the fundamental tenet of the common law as it has developed with respect to leases of goods: freedom of the parties to contract." UCC § 2A–101, Comment (Relationship of Article 2A to Other Articles).

[48] Preliminary Draft Report of the Uniform Commercial Code Committee of the Business Law Section of the State Bar of California on Proposed California Commercial Code Division 10 (Article 2A) (May 18, 1987).

[49] Report of the Uniform Commercial Code Committee of the Business Law Section of the State Bar of California on Proposed California Commercial Code Division 10 (Article 2A) (Dec. 18, 1987).

[50] NCCUSL Amendments to Uniform Commercial Code Article 2A, Leases (with Drafting Notes)(July 13–20, 1990).

[51] Article 2A has been enacted in Alabama, Alaska, Arizona, Arkansas, California, Colorado, Delaware, Florida, Georgia, Hawaii, Idaho, Illinois, Indiana, Kansas, Kentucky, Maine, Michigan, Minnesota, Missouri, Montana, Nebraska, Nevada, New Hampshire, New Mexico, North Carolina, North Dakota, Ohio, Oklahoma, Oregon, Pennsylvania, Rhode Island, South Dakota, Tennessee, Texas, Utah, Virginia, Washington, Wisconsin, Wyoming, and the District of Columbia.

regardless of form, that creates a lease."[52] The definition of lease limits applicability to leases of goods.[53] The range of applicable transactions extends from the rental of a tool or a punch bowl for a few hours to sophisticated leases of industrial equipment for a number of years.[54] Article 2A defines a lease as "a transfer of the right to possession and use of goods for a term in return for consideration, but a sale or retention of a security interest is not a lease."[55] The definition thus requires two determinations: That the appropriate type of transfer has been made and that the result is neither a sale nor a secured transaction. Additional code provisions defining these other transactions therefore must also be consulted.

[2] Distinguishing Sales

A sale is easy to distinguish from a lease. A sale transfers title to the goods from the seller to the buyer.[56] The seller does not retain any ties to the goods. If the buyer does not pay for the goods, the seller has an action for the price but does not have the right to pursue the goods themselves.[57] A lessee acquires only the right to the use and enjoyment of the goods for a limited period of time. Title to the goods does not pass; rather, the seller retains it in the form of a residual interest in the goods. The goods revert back to the lessor at the end of the lease term. The lessor can recover the goods sooner if the lessee breaches during the term of the lease.

[3] Distinguishing Secured Transactions [1–201(37)]

The essential characteristics of secured transactions and leases are also easy to distinguish. A secured party who retains a security interest in goods sold essentially passes conditional title to the buyer/debtor; the buyer can retain the goods if the payment obligations are satisfied. In the event of default, the secured party can repossess the goods.[58] Generally, however, the secured party must dispose of the goods and apply the proceeds to the outstanding indebtedness.[59] Any surplus proceeds belong to the buyer/debtor.[60] A seller's retained security interest is thus only a limited contingent interest. A lessor, on the other hand, always retains a residual interest in the leased goods. A lessor can also retake the goods following a default by the lessee.[61] Unlike the secured

---

[52] UCC § 2A–102.
[53] UCC § 2A–103(1)(j).
[54] UCC § 2A–102, Comment.
[55] UCC § 2A–103(1)(j).
[56] UCC § 2–106(1).
[57] For a limited exception to this principle, see § 9.09[A], infra.
[58] UCC § 9–503.
[59] UCC § 9–504(1).
[60] UCC § 9–504(2).
[61] UCC § 2A–525(2). For discussion of this provision, see § 9.09[B], infra.

party, however, the lessor is not required to dispose of the goods and need not distribute any proceeds of disposition to the lessee.[62]

Distinguishing leases from secured transactions in actual practice has proved to be a more difficult endeavor. The issue has led to some of the most pervasive litigation under the Code.[63] The greater similarity of attributes of these two transactions, compared with leases and unconditional sales, contributes to the problem. Even more responsible is the fact that, for a variety of reasons related to taxes, accounting, or bankruptcy, parties sometimes disguise a secured transaction to appear in the form of a lease. Inadequate legal standards have also played a significant role. The original Code definition of "security interest" includes a sentence directed toward distinguishing sales and secured transactions.[64] It has proved to be woefully inadequate.[65]

With the promulgation of Article 2A, the drafters also extensively amended the Article 1 definition of security interest.[66] The resulting definition is extremely long and complex, but it does provide an effective definition based on functional considerations. Rather than continuing the approach of the predecessor definition of relying on the unworkable central standard of the intent of the parties, the new definition focuses on the economics of the transaction. The basic economic reality of a lease is that the lessor has retained a meaningful residual interest. The new definition thus is directed toward a determination of whether the terms of the transaction actually compensate the purported lessor for the residual interest, as well as for the use of the goods during the lease term.

The revised definition includes a two-part test for determining a security interest. The first part of the test provides that "a transaction creates a security interest if the consideration the lessee is to pay the lessor for the right to possession and use of the goods is an obligation for the term of the lease not subject to termination by the lessee."[67] When the lessee can terminate the lease, the lessor clearly retains the residual interest in the leased goods and the lessee is not obligated for the term of the lease. The transaction thus creates a true lease and not a security interest.

If the lessee is not allowed under the terms of the agreement to terminate the transaction, a security interest is created if any of the factors enumerated in the second part of the two-part test is present. One of these factors is that

---

62   UCC § 2A–527. For discussion of this provision, see § 9.01[B], infra.

63   See the extensive case law citations in W. Lawrence & J. Minan, The Law of Personal Property Leasing 2–6 to 2–21 (1993).

64   UCC § 1–201(37) (last sentence) (original version).

65   For a critique of the inadequacies of the original definition, see W. Lawrence & J. Minan, The Law of Personal Property Leasing 2–15 to 2–21 (1993).

66   UCC § 1–201(37)(1987).

67   UCC § 1–201(37)(second para.).

the original term of the lease equals or exceeds the remaining economic life of the goods. The economic reality of such a transaction is that the purported lessor has not retained any residual interest in the goods, but rather has sold the goods and retained a security interest in them against the outstanding payment of installments. Under an agreement that extends to the end of the economic life of the goods, the consideration paid compensates the purported lessor for the full economic interest in the goods. When the lessee cannot terminate the agreement, the lessee is contractually bound to pay this full measure of compensation. The lack of any meaningful residual interest means that a transaction is a disguised lease, which is recognized for the security interest that it really is.

The practical effect is precisely the same if a lessee who cannot terminate the lease is bound to renew the lease to the end of the economic life of the goods or is bound to become the owner of the goods. The lessee is contractually obligated to pay for the remaining economic life of the goods, leaving no residual interest in the purported lessor. These factors, therefore, are sufficient to satisfy the second part of the test in the revised definition.

The remaining factors of the second part of the test address the role of options. They cover the circumstances in which a lessee, upon compliance with the terms of the lease, has the option to become the owner of the goods or to renew the lease for the remaining economic life of the goods. If the lessee can exercise either option for no additional consideration or for only nominal consideration, the transaction is not a true lease but is rather a security interest. The purported rental payments in such a transaction obviously compensated the lessor not only for the lessee's use of the goods during the lease term but also for the residual value that remained in the goods following the lease term. Despite the labels applied by the parties to the transaction, the economic reality is that a lessor willing to allow the lessee to retain the goods for nominal or even no additional consideration has not retained any meaningful residual interest. Conversely, the lessor has retained the requisite interest for a true lease when the lessee must pay more than nominal additional consideration in order to exercise an option to purchase the goods or to renew the lease until the end of the goods' economic life.

[B] Finance Leases [2A–103(1)(g)]

The lessor serves a unique role in some lease transactions. Rather than supplying the lessee with goods from an inventory maintained by the lessor, the lessor sometimes serves merely as a financing conduit, facilitating the lessee's acquisition of the goods from a supplier. The lessor in these transactions is comparable to a purchase-money secured party who finances a buyer/debtor's acquisition of goods by lending the buyer the purchase price and retaining a security interest in the goods. In the lease transaction, the lessor purchases or leases goods that the lessee desires and in turn leases or subleases the goods to the lessee.

Because lease agreements of this type result in a tripartite relationship, they do not fit into the statutory analogue of Article 2. They pose several special circumstances that cannot be resolved through the bipartite provisions of the Sales Article. On the other hand, these leases are quite significant in modern commercial transactions. They cover approximately 88 percent of the total original cost of leased equipment.[68]

The drafters of Article 2A recognized the importance of these leases. They designated them "finance leases" and included several provisions throughout Article 2A to deal with them. Several of these provisions represent some of the most significant departures from the statutory analogue.

To qualify as a finance lease under Article 2A, an agreement must, in addition to qualifying as a true lease,[69] satisfy three specific requirements.[70] First, the lessor cannot participate in selecting, manufacturing, or supplying the goods. The essential function of the finance lessor is to facilitate the finance lessee's acquisition of the goods from the supplier, rather than having anything to do with supplying the goods. Consequently, the finance lessee selects the desired goods. The finance lessor enters into a supply agreement with the supplier and then enters into a separate lease agreement with the finance lessee. The supplier often ships the goods directly to the finance lessee.

Isolating the finance lessor from direct participation in selecting or supplying the goods prompts the finance lessee to look directly to the manufacturer or supplier for recourse if there are problems with the goods. Article 2A relieves a finance lessor of any liability for implied warranties of quality with respect to the goods, and such a lessor is unlikely to extend express warranties with respect to goods that he or she did not supply. The lack of involvement in selecting and supplying the goods provides the basis for relieving finance lessors from this warranty responsibility.[71]

The second requirement in Article 2A for a lease to qualify as a finance lease is that the finance lessor's acquisition of the goods must be "in connection with the lease."[72] This means that the lessor cannot acquire goods from a supplier and

---

[68] U.S. Dep't of Commerce, *U.S. Industrial Outlook 1993 — Equipment Leasing* 52–2 (1992). The leasing in this study does not include short-term equipment rentals from retail outlets. The leases in the study are longer-term operating leases in which equipment is leased directly from a lessor's inventory without the lessor playing a role as a financing intermediary.

[69] *See* § 1.05[A] *supra*.

[70] UCC § 2A–103(1)(g).

[71] UCC § 2A–103, Comment (g).

[72] UCC § 2A–103(1)(g)(ii).

then later decide to lease them. It thus further restricts the finance lessor to a financing function and further ensures that the finance lessee dealt with the supplier and will look to the supplier for satisfaction of any products liability claims.

The final requirement for a finance lease is that one of four stated methods must be used to give the lessee advance notification of applicable warranties and promises by the supplier. Since a finance lessee will have to turn to the supplier, rather than the finance lessor, with respect to any dissatisfaction with the goods, this requirement is designed to apprise the finance lessee of the extent of available warranties. The requirement is logical because the supplier's contract is with the finance lessor rather than the finance lessee, and the finance lessee might not otherwise be adequately informed about available warranties against the supplier.

In addition to eliminating warranties that otherwise would apply to a finance lessor, Article 2A includes other provisions that are needed to further the tripartite relationship envisioned in a finance lease. A finance lessee is expected to turn to the supplier for warranty protection, but the absence of contractual privity between the finance lessee and the supplier poses a conceptual obstacle to any warranty claim asserted by a finance lessee. This obstacle is overcome in Article 2A through a provision that makes the finance lessee the beneficiary of any promises and warranties that are extended to the finance lessor in the supply agreement.[73] This provision effectively gives the finance lessee a direct cause of action against the manufacturer or supplier for a breach of warranty.

A finance lessee does lose something in exchange for the benefit of becoming a beneficiary of third-party promises and warranties. If the finance lease is not also a consumer lease,[74] the lessee's promises under the lease contract "become irrevocable and independent upon the lessee's acceptance of the goods."[75] This provision deprives a lessee of any right to set off rents due under the lease, even though the goods are nonconforming. It has the effect of an express "hell or high water" clause,[76] which makes the party against whom it operates irrevocably committed to perform its obligations. A finance lessor is simply the financial conduit through which the finance lessee acquires goods

---

[73] "The benefit of a supplier's promises to the lessor under the supply contract and of all warranties, whether express or implied, including those of any third party provided in connection with or as part of the supply contract, extends to the lessee to the extent of the lessee's leasehold interest under a finance lease related to the supply contract, but is subject to the terms of the warranty and of the supply contract and all defenses or claims arising therefrom." UCC § 2A–209(1).

[74] See § 1.05[C] infra.

[75] UCC § 2A–407(1).

[76] The clause is so called because of its initial use in ship charter contracts.

from the supplier. Once the finance lessee accepts the goods, any complaints are between it and the supplier. The finance lessor is thus entitled to the rent payments, irrespective of any problems the finance lessee may subsequently experience.

[C]   Consumer Leases [2A–103(1)(e)]

Most of the drafting of Article 2 was accomplished in the late 1940s, long before the consumer protection movement that developed during the 1960s. Consequently, it is not surprising that Article 2 contains very few provisions that could be characterized as consumer-oriented in tone.

Even though, by the time Article 2A was drafted, consumer protection was a much greater concern, the drafters faced a major policy decision. They ultimately decided to adhere for the most part to the Article 2 statutory analogue, but to add a sprinkling of provisions with a consumer protection orientation. Because of political implications, they wisely chose not to make wholesale additions. State legislatures have always been free to enact any consumer protection measures they consider appropriate. Although some states have enacted extensive protection measures,[77] others have declined to pursue this option. The drafters were concerned that the addition of several consumer protection measures in Article 2A could create problems integrating those provisions with more general consumer protection measures in some states. Even more problematic, they feared it could result in legislative rejection of the entire Article in jurisdictions that had not previously adopted comparable consumer protection measures.[78] Except for the few modest extensions included in Article 2A, the ultimate policy choice of the extent of consumer protection is thus left to the individual discretion of each state.

Article 2A includes a definition of "consumer lease" that draws heavily on the definition in the federal Consumer Leasing Act.[79] "Consumer lease" is defined to mean "a lease that a lessor regularly engaged in the business of leasing or selling makes to a lessee who is an individual and who takes under the lease primarily for a personal, family or household purpose[, if the total payments

---

[77] *See* California Song–Beverly Consumer Warranty Act, Cal. Civ. Code §§ 1790–1795.8; Ann. Cal. Codes, Civil §§ 1790–1795.8 (1985) and (Supp. 1992); Kansas Consumer Protection Act, Kan. Stat. Ann. §§ 50–623 to 50–644 (1983 & Supp. 1991). Eleven states have enacted the Uniform Consumer Credit Code (UCCC), which includes several provisions of consumer protection. UCCC (revised Official Text with Comments), 7A ULA 1 (1974).

[78] *See* F. Miller, *Consumer Leases Under Uniform Commercial Code Article 2A*, 39 Ala. L. Rev. 957, 962 (1988).

[79] 15 U.S.C. § 1667(1)(1982).

to be made under the lease contract, excluding payments for options to renew
or buy, do not exceed $_____]."[80]

§ 1.06   SUPPLEMENTING PROVISIONS OF THE UNIFORM COMMERCIAL CODE [1–103]

Articles 2 and 2A are not the exclusive sources of the law of sales and leases
of goods. An important provision in Article 1 recognizes the continuing via-
bility of general principles of law and equity. It provides in its entirety as
follows:

> Unless displaced by the particular provisions of this Act, the principles
> of law and equity, including the law merchant and the law relative to
> capacity to contract, principal and agent, estoppel, fraud, misrepresen-
> tation, duress, coercion, mistake, bankruptcy, or other validating or in-
> validating cause shall supplement its provisions.[81]

The Code was drafted against the existing backdrop of the common law.
Many of the provisions of Articles 2 and 2A were adopted to change the
common-law approach or at least to provide a consistent approach to certain
issues on which some jurisdictions varied. Unless a Code provision displaces
a principle of law or equity, however, those principles are equally relevant to
transactions covered by the Code. Sale and lease transactions in particular draw
heavily on the common law of contracts.

Many essential aspects of contract law are covered only partially or not at
all in Articles 2 and 2A. The drafters did not intend to change the law in these
omitted areas, so the Code draws on the common law for continued applicability. Students of Articles 2 and 2A should note the interplay of the Code provisions with other principles of law and equity.

---

[80] UCC § 2A–103(1)(e). The language in brackets is provided for states that wish to impose
a monetary limitation to qualify as a consumer transaction.
[81] UCC § 1–103. The listing provided in this section is not exhaustive. UCC § 1–103, Comment 3.

CHAPTER

2

The Agreement Process

§ 2.01   CONTRACT FORMATION IN GENERAL [2–204; 2A–204]

As late as the first half of this century, contract formation was seen as a rigid process. It usually required communications between the parties that took the form of an offer and an acceptance. The offer had to address certain material terms in an unambiguous fashion. The acceptance had to mirror the offer perfectly and be communicated using the same medium as that chosen by the offeror. The court had to be able to pinpoint the precise moment of contract formation. Offers were freely revocable unless the offeree gave consideration for the privilege of having the offer held open (thereby creating an option contract), and modification agreements required separate consideration. The Statute of Frauds, when applicable, imposed a detailed writing requirement, and the parol evidence rule made supplementation of written contracts difficult.

By the time the Code was first promulgated, many progressive jurisdictions had begun to relax this formalism, and Article 2 greatly accelerated this trend. Section 2–204 tells us that "[a] contract for sale of goods may be made in any manner sufficient to show agreement, including conduct of both parties which recognizes the existence of such a contract"[1] and that "[a]n agreement sufficient to constitute a contract for sale may be found even though the moment of its making is undetermined."[2] The idea that an agreement can be found solely by

---

[1]   UCC § 2–204(1). § 2A–204(1) is comparable.
[2]   UCC § 2–204(2). § 2A–204(2) is comparable.

looking at the conduct of the parties allows us, in appropriate cases, to dispense with the necessity of a formal offer and acceptance.[3]

Although an agreement based solely on conduct is possible, it is also relatively rare. In most cases, the courts will still have to search for an offer and an acceptance, but here, also, the rules have been relaxed. The Code does not define an "offer" and, therefore, defers to some extent to the common law. Nevertheless, as we shall see in the next section, the offer need not address as wide a range of terms as would have been required at common law. While the offeror is still the master of the offer and can insist on a particular method of acceptance, an ambiguous offer is to "be construed as inviting acceptance in any manner and by any medium reasonable in the circumstances."[4] Hence the offeree can ordinarily accept either by making a return promise or by commencing the requested performance. When a promissory acceptance is given, it need not be transmitted using the same medium as that selected by the offeror. Further, the acceptance no longer need mirror the offer to be effective.[5]

Section 2–204(3) lets us fill a variety of gaps that may have been left open in the formation process. It states that:

> Even though one or more terms are left open a contract for sale does not fail for indefiniteness if the parties have intended to make a contract and there is a reasonably certain basis for giving an appropriate remedy.

Article 2 further facilitates contract formation by identifying the "reasonably certain basis" for a variety of standard terms. This process, called "gap-filling," is discussed in detail in another section of the book.[6] In sum, the drafters created provisions that come into play when the parties have reached basic agreement on the outlines of their contract but have not nailed down all the details.

Even the idea of contract itself has been altered by Article 2. The Code differentiates between the "agreement" of the parties and their "contract." The "agreement" refers to "the bargain of the parties in fact as found in their language or by implication from other circumstances including course of dealing

---

[3] The ability to form contracts based solely on conduct is reinforced by UCC § 2–207(3), discussed in § 2.05[D] *infra.*

[4] UCC § 2–206(1)(a).

[5] UCC § 2–207.

[6] *See* § 4.05 *infra.*

or usage of trade or course of performance."[7] The idea of this is that parties do not enter contracts in a vacuum; they do so in a particular setting, and they make a variety of assumptions based on that setting. If, for example, both parties are members of a trade and goods are always delivered on 30 days' credit within that trade, the agreement of the parties will, unless they expressly agree to the contrary, contain a credit term. The drafters of the Code elevated the surrounding circumstances to an exalted position in the contract formation process.[8] The agreement, then, contains the terms that the parties have expressly assented to, plus a variety of other terms drawn from the context within which the parties are operating (often called implied-in-fact terms).

The "contract," by contrast, means "the total legal obligation which results from the parties' agreement as affected by this Act and any other applicable rules of law."[9] The contract—the total set of enforceable obligations—may not include all of the terms of the agreement. Some of them may have been excluded through the parol evidence rule or one of its corollaries, or rendered unenforceable via the unconscionability doctrine. The contract may include terms that are not part of the agreement—the gap-filling, implied-in-law provisions referred to above.

Finally, as we shall see, in certain situations offers are irrevocable without an option contract, and modifications are enforceable without separate consideration. The writing required to satisfy the Statute of Frauds is considerably less detailed than its non-Code counterpart, and the parol evidence rule has been liberalized to make it easier to supplement final writings.

All in all, the process of contract formation under the Code looks very different from its antecedents; it has had a profound influence on the Second Restatement and, therefore, development of the common law.[10] The Code's

---

[7] UCC § 1–201(3).

[8] *See, e.g.,* UCC § 1–102(2)(b), which states that one of the purposes underlying the Code is "to permit the continued expansion of commercial practices through custom, usage and agreement of the parties."

[9] UCC § 1–201(11).

[10] All is not new under the Code. Contract formation is still based on objective manifestations of assent rather than the subjective intent of the parties. *See, e.g.,* Computer Network Ltd. v. Purcell Tire & Rubber Co., 747 S.W.2d 669, 6 UCC Rep. Serv. 2d 642 (Mo. Ct. App. 1988) (buyer who signed written agreement to purchase 21 computers held to that quantity notwithstanding evidence of subjective intent to purchase one computer for each of its 15 stores).

philosophy was perhaps best expressed in *Kleinschmidt Division of SCM Corp. v. Futuronics, Inc.,*[11] where the New York Court of Appeals stated that:

> The basic philosophy of the sales article of the Uniform Commercial Code is simple. Practical business people cannot be expected to govern their actions with reference to nice legal formalisms. Thus, when there is basic agreement, however manifested and whether or not the precise moment of agreement may be determined, failure to articulate that agreement in the precise language of a lawyer, with every difficulty and contingency considered and resolved, will not prevent formation of a contract.[12]

§ 2.02　Offer

As seen in the previous section, the Code defers to many of the common-law rules regarding offers (although, given the existence of gap-fillers, not to the rule requiring that the offeror express all material terms). For example, advertisements, circulars, and price quotes still are generally not viewed as offers.[13] Further, a number of cases have held that a reservation in a communication requiring further approval by the sender makes it an invitation to deal rather than an offer.[14] Perhaps the most that can be said about offers is that courts interpreting the Code will continue to follow the common law.

Section 24 of the Second Restatement provides the best available definition of an offer:

> An offer is the manifestation of willingness to enter into a bargain, so made as to justify another person in understanding that his assent to that bargain is invited and will conclude it.

The Code does contain one special provision on "firm offers" that will be discussed separately.[15]

---

[11] 41 N.Y.2d 972, 395 N.Y.S.2d 151, 363 N.E.2d 701, 21 UCC Rep. Serv. 422 (1977).

[12] *Id.*, 41 N.Y.2d at 973, 363 N.E.2d at 701, 21 UCC Rep. Serv. at 423. The court went on to affirm the trial court's ruling that there was not enough evidence of assent to satisfy even the Code's minimal requirements.

[13] *See, e.g.,* Master Palletizer Sys., Inc. v. T.S. Ragsdale Co., 725 F. Supp. 1525, 11 UCC Rep. Serv. 2d 1125 (D. Colo. 1989) (price quote sent to buyer); Corinthian Pharmaceutical Sys., Inc. v. Lederle Laboratories, 724 F. Supp. 605, 11 UCC Rep. Serv.2d 463 (S.D. Ind. 1989) (price list circulated among prospective buyers).

[14] *See, e.g.,* McCarty v. Verson Allsteel Press Co., 89 Ill. App. 3d 498, 411 N.E.2d 936, 30 UCC Rep. Serv. 440 (1980) (clause requiring approval by home office prevented seller's proposal from being an offer); Brown Mach. v. Hercules, Inc., 770 S.W.2d 416, 9 UCC Rep. Serv. 2d 480 (Mo. Ct. App. 1989).

[15] *See* § 2.04 *infra.*

§ 2.03   ACCEPTANCE [2–206; 2A–206]

[A]   Generally

The offeror has always had the power to impose an exclusive method of acceptance, but if the offeror failed to do so, the pre-Code common-law courts had to decide whether the offer invited acceptance by full performance (creating a unilateral contract) or by return promise (creating a bilateral contract). Further, a return promise had to be communicated using the same medium as that selected by the offeror for communicating the offer. An offeree who selected the wrong method or medium did not create a contract.

The Code effects a radical change. Unless the language or the circumstances make it clear that the offeror is insisting on an exclusive method of acceptance, the offeree can accept in any manner that is reasonable under the circumstances.[16] An offeree who chooses to accept by making a return promise can also do so by way of any reasonable medium.[17] Functionally, most offerees will accept either by making a return promise or by beginning the requested performance. A return promise still must be communicated to be effective,[18] and the common law's "mailbox rule" still makes promissory acceptances effective upon dispatch.[19] Ordinarily, beginning performance will be a reasonable alternative.[20] The effect of commencing performance will be to bind both parties—that is, the offeror will be bound because an acceptance has occurred, and the offeree will be bound because the conduct signifies an intent to render complete performance.[21]

Even though the offeree's conduct in beginning performance is treated as a return promise, it does not have to be communicated to be effective. The reason should be obvious. If we encourage offerees to begin work quickly by treating their conduct as an acceptance, we must also preclude the offeror from revoking once that performance has begun. This approach has the benefit of protecting the offeree's reasonable reliance, but it creates problems for the offeror, who may need to know whether to seek performance elsewhere. Section 2–206(2), which is designed to protect the offeror, states, "[w]here the beginning of performance is a reasonable mode of acceptance an offeror who is not

---

[16]   UCC §§ 2–206(1)(a), 2A–206(1).

[17]   *Id.*

[18]   *See* Restatement (Second) of Contracts § 56.

[19]   *See* Restatement (Second) of Contracts § 63. Of course, the common law permits the offeror to dispense with the mailbox rule and insist that the acceptance not be effective until received.

[20]   *See* UCC § 2–206(2), and Comment 3; § 2A–206(2).

[21]   The Code does not specify this result, but it is consistent with Restatement (Second) of Contracts § 62(2).

notified of acceptance within a reasonable time may treat the offer as having lapsed before acceptance." Article 2A is comparable.[22]

In effect, then, the Code balances the interests of the parties. The offeree is encouraged to perform, and once he or she begins, the offeror cannot revoke. Nevertheless, the offeree should notify the offeror within a reasonable time so that the offeror knows that full performance can be expected in due course. If the offeree waits too long to send the notice, the offeror is off the hook. Conceptually, it is as if the beginning of performance creates a bilateral contract, with the offeror's duty to perform subject to a condition precedent: notification of acceptance by the offeree within a reasonable time following the beginning of performance.[23]

Suppose, for example, that on Tuesday the seller receives an order for equipment that will need to be specially manufactured. That same day the seller begins work on the equipment, but the seller has not yet notified the buyer when, on Friday, the buyer calls and revokes. During the conversation, the seller insists on going through with the contract and tells the buyer that performance has begun. On these facts, the seller's conduct amounts to an acceptance, and the buyer's revocation is ineffective. The only issue is whether the three-day delay in giving notice was unreasonable. The cases to date give little guidance in determining what is a reasonable time, but surely the courts will want to protect an offeror who, after waiting for a response, enters into a binding contract with a third party.

The Comments invite the courts to follow common-law precedents that render offers irrevocable in certain situations.[24] Suppose, for example, that one party relies on an offer in a way that does not amount to beginning performance.[25] The classic case involves a contractor who receives an offer to sell

---

[22]   UCC § 2A–206(2).

[23]   The offeree may not have to take affirmative steps to notify the offeror. UCC § 1–201(26) tells us that a person has received notification when the facts come to his or her attention.

[24]   UCC § 2–206, Comment 3.

[25]   If the beginning of performance operates as an acceptance, the offeree does not need the protection provided by this approach. The offer is irrevocable because acceptance has occurred, and all the offeree needs to do is give timely notification to the offeror.

Article 2 does not deal directly with the consequences of beginning performance when the offeror has insisted on full performance as the exclusive method of acceptance (the common law's unilateral contract). Under Restatement (Second) of Contracts § 45, beginning performance would create an option contract, permitting the offeree to walk away from the deal but precluding the offeror from revoking. Restatement (Second) of Contracts § 54(2) imposes on the offeree in this situation a notification requirement that is similar to that set forth in UCC § 2–206(2). Section 2–206, Comment 3 invites the courts to follow this approach.

equipment from a subcontractor and then uses that offer in computing a project bid. If the contractor is awarded the project and the subcontractor revokes, the contractor may suffer a loss, but his or her reliance does not constitute the beginning of performance.

While there are some early cases to the contrary,[26] later cases[27] and the Second Restatement[28] use the doctrine of promissory estoppel to create what is in effect an option contract—that is, the offer cannot be revoked pending timely acceptance by the offeree. Thus, upon being awarded the project, the contractor has the power to accept until such time as the offer lapses.

[B]   Countering the Unilateral Contract Trick

Article 2 further implements its policy of permitting an offeree to accept in any reasonable fashion by addressing a specific fact situation. It provides that:

> [a]n order or other offer to buy goods for prompt or current shipment shall be construed as inviting acceptance either by a prompt promise to ship or by the prompt or current shipment of conforming or non-conforming goods, but such a shipment of non-conforming goods does not constitute an acceptance if the seller seasonably notifies the buyer that the shipment is offered only as an accommodation to the buyer.[29]

---

[26] *See, e.g.,* James Baird Co. v. Gimbel Bros., 64 F.2d 344 (2d Cir. 1933). In that case, Judge Learned Hand refused to deviate from the standard common-law rule making offers revocable until acceptance. Among other reasons, Judge Hand stated that the contractor could have protected itself by entering into an option contract with the subcontractor. In an option contract, the offeree pays the offeror to keep the offer open. Nothing in Article 2 prevents parties from using option contracts. As an alternative, the offeree could insist on a "firm offer," a concept that is discussed in § 2.04 *infra*.

[27] *See, e.g.,* Drennan v. Star Paving Co., 51 Cal. 2d 409, 333 P.2d 757 (1958); Jenkins & Boiler Co., Inc. v. Schmidt Iron Works, Inc., 36 Ill. App. 3d 1044, 344 N.E.2d 275, 19 UCC Rep. Serv. 425 (1976); Montgomery Indus. Int'l v. Thomas Constr. Co., 620 F.2d 91 (5th Cir. 1980).

A few cases, primarily in Massachusetts, have held that the contractor's mere use of the bid amounts to an acceptance, creating a contract subject to the condition that the contractor be awarded the project. *See, e.g.,* Loranger Constr. Corp. v. E. F. Hauserman, 376 Mass. 757, 384 N.E.2d 176 (1978). Chicopee Concrete Serv., Inc. v. Hart Eng'g Co., 20 Mass. App. 315, 479 N.E.2d 748, 42 UCC Rep. Serv. 375 (1985) involved a novel twist on this theme. The *Chicopee* court held that the contractor's use of the bid created a contract because the contractor had given the seller assurances that its services would be needed, which caused the seller to expand its facilities in anticipation of performing.

[28] *See* Restatement (Second) of Contracts § 87(2).

[29] UCC § 2–206(1)(b).

This provision prevents sellers from using what came to be called the "unilateral contract trick." Under pre-Code law, the seller could ship nonconforming goods in response to an offer and then wait to see what happened. If the buyer accepted the goods, a contract resulted, with the seller as offeror of the nonconforming goods and the buyer as offeree. If the buyer brought suit instead, the seller could avoid liability by denying the existence of a contract because shipping nonconforming goods was not the act of acceptance requested by the buyer.

Under Article 2, the shipment of nonconforming goods amounts to an acceptance (unless the seller notifies the buyer that the shipment is being made as an accommodation) of the buyer's offer. Accordingly, the same act that creates the contract also amounts to a breach.

The impact of the provision can be illustrated by the facts of *Corinthian Pharmaceutical Systems, Inc. v. Lederle Laboratories*.[30] The buyer in *Corinthian* offered to purchase 1,000 vials of vaccine at the seller's listed price one day before a price increase was due to take effect. The seller shipped 50 vials along with a letter stating that, as an accommodation, the buyer could have those vials for the old price, but the balance would have to be paid for at the new price. When the buyer sued for breach, the court sided with the seller. After all, the seller's nonconforming shipment[31] had been accompanied by a letter stating that it was being sent as an accommodation. Accordingly, nothing the seller had done amounted to an acceptance. Had the seller not sent the letter, its nonconforming shipment would have operated as an acceptance of the buyer's offer, obligating the seller to sell the full 1,000 vials at the old price. While *Corinthian Pharmaceutical* is not directly on point because it involved a nonconforming tender rather than nonconforming goods, the principle involved is the same.

§ 2.04   FIRM OFFERS [2–205; 2A–205]

At common law, offers are freely revocable, even if the offeror has promised not to revoke, and even if the revocation is made in bad faith.[32] The rationale for this strange rule is that the offeror's promise to leave the offer open is typically unsupported by independent consideration.

---

30   724 F. Supp. 605, 11 UCC Rep. Serv. 2d 463 (S.D. Ind. 1989).

31   The seller's shipment was nonconforming because of UCC § 2–307. Absent agreement by the parties to the contrary, the seller must deliver all the goods in a single lot rather than in installments.

32   Even under the Code, the duty of good faith does not extend to the contract formation stage. See discussion in § 4.06[B] *infra*.

The common law developed two basic responses to this doctrine. First came the option contract, wherein the offeree gives consideration to keep the offer open.[33] More recently, courts have begun to use promissory estoppel to make offers irrevocable.[34] Nothing prevents these devices from being used by parties operating within the scope of Articles 2 and 2A.

The Code, however, gives parties yet another option. It provides for what are called "firm offers":

> An offer by a merchant to buy or sell goods in a signed writing which by its terms gives assurances that it will be held open is not revocable, for lack of consideration, during the time stated or if no time is stated for a reasonable time, but in no event may such period of irrevocability exceed three months; but any such term of assurance on a form supplied by the offeree must be separately signed by the offeror.[35]

The Code gives the firm offer much the same effect as the seal at common law. Promises made under seal were enforceable absent consideration, with the seal providing evidence of the promisor's seriousness of purpose. The Code has abolished the seal for sales and leases of goods,[36] but offers can be made irrevocable by following the specified format.

A firm offer must, of course, in the first instance, constitute an offer.[37] In addition, the offeror must be a merchant,[38] the offer must be in a signed writing,[39] and the writing must give assurances that it will be held open.[40] These requirements are quite clear and have generated relatively little litigation.

Three months is the maximum period of irrevocability. A firm offer can establish a date for lapse that is more than three months in the future, and the

---

33 Even nominal consideration will suffice. *See, e.g.*, Board of Control v. Burgess, 45 Mich. App. 183, 206 N.W.2d 256 (1973). Restatement (Second) of Contracts § 87(1) goes even further, stating that an offer is irrevocable when a writing signed by the offeror recites a separate consideration.

34 *See* discussion in § 2.03[A] *supra.*

35 UCC § 2–205. § 2A–205 is comparable.

36 UCC §§ 2–203, 2A–203.

37 *See* discussion in § 2.02 *supra.*

38 *See* discussion in § 3.04[B] *infra.*

39 *See* discussion in § 3.03[A] *infra.*

40 The writing must do more than merely state that an offer exists. *See, e.g.*, Ivey's Plumbing & Elec. Co. v. Petrochem Maintenance, Inc., 463 F. Supp. 543, 26 UCC Rep. Serv. 621 (N.D. Miss. 1978) (no language of irrevocability); Lowenstern v. Stop & Shop Companies, 32 UCC Rep. Serv. 414 (Mass. Super. 1981) (a "raincheck" issued by a store allowing customer to purchase item at a later date constituted a firm offer).

offeree can accept until lapse occurs. However, the offer becomes revocable after three months.[41] When the signed offer gives assurances that it will be held open but does not establish a definite time period, it is irrevocable for a reasonable time. The courts have given little guidance here,[42] although surely the most important factors are the volatility of the product's price and the degree to which the goods may become unavailable to the seller.

§ 2.05   THE BATTLE OF THE FORMS [2–207]

[A]   Introduction

At common law, a purported "acceptance" that does not precisely mirror the terms of the offer is treated as a counteroffer—a rejection of the original offer coupled with a new offer by the original offeree.[43] This approach might have worked reasonably well at a time when communications were relatively short and one party could be expected to read everything proposed by the other. It is unworkable in a marketplace increasingly given to the use of standardized forms.[44]

The mirror-image rule led to abuses by sellers. For example, suppose on one hand the buyer sends a purchase order form (the offer) calling for future delivery, and the seller responds with a standard acknowledgment form that does not precisely mirror the offer. If the price of the goods rises before the delivery date, the seller is free to back out. The seller is, in effect, allowed to speculate at the buyer's expense.

---

[41] UCC § 2–205, Comment 3. *See also* Mid-South Packers, Inc. v. Shoney's, Inc., 761 F.2d 1117, 41 UCC Rep. Serv. 38 (5th Cir. 1985); Loranger Plastics Corp. v. Incoe Corp., 670 F. Supp. 145, 5 UCC Rep. Serv. 2d 58 (W.D. Pa. 1987).

[42] *See, e.g.*, Lowenstern v. Stop & Shop Companies, 32 UCC Rep. Serv. 414 (Mass. Super. 1981) (court gave no convincing rationale for holding that store's raincheck was irrevocable for 15 days).

[43] *See* Restatement (Second) of Contracts § 39. Perhaps the most graphic example of the rule is Poel v. Brunswicke-Balke-Collender Co., 216 N.Y. 310, 110 N.E.2d 619 (1915), where a buyer of rubber accepted the seller's offer and added that the seller had to send back a prompt acknowledgment. The court held that this addition made the acceptance conditional, converting it into a counteroffer.

[44] *See generally*, Murray, *The Chaos of the "Battle of the Forms": Solutions*, 39 Vand. L. Rev. 1307 (1986); Baird & Weisberg, *Rules, Standards, and the Battle of the Forms: A Reassessment of §* 2–207, 68 Va. L. Rev. 1217 (1982); Brown, *Restoring Peace in the Battle of the Forms: A Framework for Making Uniform Commercial Code § 2–207 Work*, 69 N.C. L. Rev. 893 (1991).

Suppose now, on the other hand, that the goods are delivered and accepted by the buyer. The exercise of dominion over the goods will amount to an acceptance of the terms on the seller's form.[45] The rule is advantageous to the seller, who typically sends the last form. For this reason the mirror-image doctrine is sometimes called the "last-shot" rule. Of course, the buyer arguably could read the seller's form and object to anything contained in it, but having purchasing agents spend their time poring over fine print is simply not efficient.

As we shall see, one of the assumptions underlying the Code's approach is that each party will focus on certain "dickered" terms, such as the description of the goods, price, and quantity, but will not read anything else contained in the other party's form.[46] The Code dispenses with the last-shot rule and replaces it with what might be called a "first-shot" rule: the party that sends the offer (the first legally effective form) has a decided advantage in shaping the ultimate terms of the agreement.

The Code has been somewhat successful in ending the abuses of the last-shot rule, but, as we shall see, it has created a whole host of new problems. The applicable section of Article 2 is poorly drafted, and virtually no aspect of this area is free from conflicting court decisions. The confusion is so great that the drafters of Article 2A, who closely modeled their product on Article 2, would have no part of the "battle of the forms."

[B]   The Basic Rule

[1]   Definite Expressions of Assent

Section 2–207(1), which sets out the basic rule, states in full that:

A definite and seasonable expression of acceptance or a written confirmation which is sent within a reasonable time operates as an acceptance even though it states terms additional to or different from those offered or agreed upon, unless acceptance is made expressly conditional on assent to the additional or different terms.

This section deals with two different types of communications: an expression of acceptance and a written confirmation. The written confirmation presupposes that a contract has already been formed, perhaps during a telephone conversation, and the issue is the effect of the confirmation on the agreed terms.

---

[45] *See* Restatement (Second) of Contracts § 69(2).

[46] *See, e.g.*, American Parts Co., Inc. v. American Arbitration Ass'n, 8 Mich. App. 156, 154 N.W.2d 5, 6 UCC Rep. Serv. 119 (1967); Daitom, Inc. v. Pennwalt Corp., 741 F.2d 1569, 39 UCC Rep. Serv. 1203 (10th Cir. 1984).

Discussion of written confirmations, and discussion of the language following the comma in the statute, will be deferred to later. The word "seasonable" merely refers to the fact that an acceptance must occur before the offer lapses.

Now reread the section, leaving out the material just mentioned. It provides that "A definite . . . expression of acceptance . . . operates as an acceptance even though it contains terms additional to or different from those offered. . . ." This provision stands the common law's mirror-image rule on its head. An expression that does not mirror the offer nevertheless operates as an acceptance, not a counteroffer. Obviously, a "definite expression of acceptance" is not the same as a common-law acceptance. What is it, then?

The consensus seems to be that a "definite expression of acceptance" is a commitment to go forward with the deal on the same dickered terms as those that have been offered, but there is an inherent problem in defining what we mean by "dickered." In some transactions, the parties will have had preliminary negotiations, and the dickered terms will be those that were sufficiently important to have been expressly raised and discussed. In other cases, however, the first communication will be the offer, which may be on a standard form that covers a wide range of topics, some material and some minor. Dickered terms will undoubtedly be material, but clearly, there can be material terms that are not dickered terms. The Comments specify that a definite expression of acceptance can contain a warranty disclaimer and that such a term is material for purposes of section 2–207(2)(b).[47] That statement would make no sense if warranty disclaimers were considered dickered terms. In the final analysis, the court may have to decide which terms are sufficiently important to be classified as dickered terms, and this determination will no doubt vary from court to court.[48]

If, as to the dickered terms, the offeree's form differs from the offeror's form, the offeree's communication should be treated as a common-law counteroffer, not a definite expression of acceptance.[49] For example, suppose the offeror sends a purchase order offering to buy a Jaguar for $50,000. The offeree sends back a confirmation form indicating a willingness to sell a Mercedes for

---

[47] UCC § 2–207, Comment 4. We will discuss this issue further in § 2.05[C][1] *infra*.

[48] *Contrast* Southern Idaho Pipe & Steel Co. v. Cal-Cut Pipe & Supply, Inc., 98 Idaho 495, 567 P.2d 1246, 22 UCC Rep. Serv. 25 (1977) (second form, which differed as to delivery date, operated as an acceptance), *with* Alliance Wall Corp. v. Ampat Midwest Corp., 17 Ohio App. 3d 59, 477 N.E.2d 1206, 41 UCC Rep. Serv. 377 (1984) (second form, which differed as to delivery date, did not operate as an acceptance).

[49] *See, e.g.*, Dubrofsky v. Messer, 1981 Mass. App. Div. 55, 31 UCC Rep. Serv. 907 (1981) (difference as to quantity); Alliance Wall Corp. v. Ampat Midwest Corp., 17 Ohio App. 3d 59, 477 N.E.2d 1206, 41 UCC Rep. Serv. 377 (1984) (difference as to delivery date).

$60,000. Surely no one would argue that the seller has expressed agreement to a contract on the buyer's terms.

When an offer is followed by a definite expression of acceptance, the second communication operates as an acceptance, meaning that a contract is formed on the offeror's terms. This "first-shot" result gives the offeror a significant advantage. An offeree who wants to avoid this result must read the offer and insist that it be modified before sending an expression of acceptance.

Suppose, for example, that the buyer sends the seller a purchase order (an offer) setting forth the subject matter, price, and quantity. The order also specifies that the buyer will make payment 30 days after delivery. The seller responds with an acknowledgment form that mirrors the offer's dickered terms but indicates that payment is due on delivery. The seller's form also states that all disputes will be resolved through binding arbitration. When the date for delivery arrives, the seller refuses to turn over the goods because the buyer fails to tender payment. The buyer then covers elsewhere at a higher price and sues the seller for breach. The seller asks the court to order that the matter be arbitrated. Was a contract formed, and if so, what are its terms?

The Code states that, in this example, the seller's form operates as an acceptance even though it contains one term that differs from those set out in the buyer's offer (the payment term) and another that is in addition to what the buyer expressed (the arbitration term). It should result in a contract on the buyer's terms. The seller is not entitled to arbitration, and the buyer did not breach by failing to tender payment (although, as we shall see in the next few paragraphs, some courts have failed to analyze this latter point correctly). The buyer should recover for the damages flowing from the seller's breach in failing to turn over the goods.

What happened to the seller's terms? The additional term simply evaporated. The first sentence of section 2–207(2) provides that "[t]he additional terms are to be construed as proposals for addition to the contract." In effect, the seller asked the buyer for a modification, and the buyer did not assent.

What about the different term? This issue is more complex and has led to a split in the cases and commentary. Some courts have held that the different terms cancel each other out, reasoning that to hold otherwise would be to take the offeror's first-shot advantage to an extreme.[50] These courts often cite Comment 6 to section 2–207, which states, "Where clauses on confirming forms conflict each party must be assumed to object to a clause of the other conflicting

---

[50] *See, e.g.*, Daitom, Inc. v. Pennwalt, Inc., 741 F.2d 1569, 39 UCC Rep. Serv. 1203 (10th Cir. 1984); Gardner Zemke Co. v. Dunham Bush, Inc., 115 N.M. 260, 850 P.2d 319, 20 UCC Rep.

with one on the confirmation sent by himself." This analysis, while representing the majority view, is inconsistent with the apparent sense of the statute and the Comments. Section 2–207(1) deals with both definite expressions of acceptance and written communications that purport to confirm terms already agreed upon. Comment 6 applies only to written confirmations, not to definite expressions of acceptance.[51] The plain language of section 2–207(1) states that a definite expression of acceptance operates as an acceptance even though it contains terms that differ from those of the offer. The only thing it can be an acceptance *of* is the offer.

The cases that refuse to follow the majority's approach frequently rely on Comment 3 to section 2–207, which indicates that the drafters intended for different terms to be treated the same as additional terms.[52] These courts have assumed that the drafters simply made a drafting error. This assumption may be correct, or another possibility may hold the interpretive key. The first sentence of section 2–207(2) performs a dual function: it looks back to the basic rule of section 2–207(1), and it introduces the "between merchants" rule of section 2–207(2). As applied to section 2–207(1), giving additional and different terms the same treatment is sensible. Both types of terms are proposals for addition to the contract, and both are inoperative absent assent. As applied to the "between merchants" rule, however, it may make sense to treat additional and different terms differently. This topic is explored further in the discussion of the between-merchants rule.[53]

Suppose the buyer sends a merchant seller a purchase order that is silent as to the quality of the goods. The seller responds with an acknowledgment that mirrors the buyer's offer, except that it disclaims the implied warranty of merchantability. The seller then sends the goods, which the buyer accepts and uses. When the goods prove defective, the buyer sues for breach of the implied warranty and the seller seeks shelter behind the disclaimer. Under section 2–207(1), the seller has accepted the buyer's offer, and under section 2–207(2) the disclaimer is nothing more than a proposal for addition to the contract.[54] The

---

Serv. 2d 842 (1993). In our hypothetical case, the gap would be filled by UCC § 2–310(a), which calls for payment on delivery. The seller would prevail, but not because of the language on his or her form.

[51] *Cf.* Gardner Zemke Co. v. Dunham Bush, Inc., 115 N.M. 260, 850 P.2d 319, 20 UCC Rep. Serv. 2d 842 (1993).

[52] *See, e.g.,* Mead Corp. v. McNally-Pittsburgh Mfg. Corp., 654 F.2d 1197, 35 UCC Rep. Serv. 368 (6th Cir. 1981).

[53] *See* § 2.05[C][2] *infra.*

[54] This example is not designed to raise issues involving the "between merchants" rule. The seller is a merchant here in order to invoke the implied warranty of merchantability. *See* UCC § 2–314. Even if the buyer were also a merchant, the analysis would probably be the same. See discussion in § 2.05[C][1] *infra.*

seller cannot argue successfully that the buyer accepted the seller's terms by exercising dominion over the goods. Such reasoning would make section 2–207 indistinguishable from the common law's last-shot rule, which it was clearly designed to supplant. The buyer should not be deemed to have assented to the seller's proposal absent an expression of that assent.[55]

While the Code has solved some of the problems created by the last-shot rule, its first-shot approach has created its own set of problems. In *Technographics, Inc. v. Mercer Corp.*,[56] for example, the seller sent the buyer a price quotation on a form that clearly disclaimed implied warranties and consequential damages. The buyer responded with an order form that was silent on these matters, and the seller delivered the equipment. When issues of quality arose, the court concluded that the seller's disclaimers were ineffective. The seller's price quotation was an invitation to deal, and the buyer's purchase order was the offer. The seller's delivery of the machine was a definite expression of acceptance, forming a contract on the buyer's terms. The result would have been the same if the seller had acknowledged the buyer's offer with another form reiterating its disclaimers.

The decision is defensible given the language of section 2–207, but it is troubling. What could the seller have done? It could have converted its price quotation into an offer, giving it the first shot. Another approach would have been to insist on the buyer's express assent to its terms before sending the goods. The safest way to secure this assent would have been to respond to the buyer's purchase order with another form reiterating the disclaimers and containing a signature block for the buyer's assent to the seller's terms. Had the seller refused to deliver the goods until it received the signed acknowledgment, it would no doubt have prevailed.[57]

[2]   Written Confirmations

Section 2–207(1) also provides that "a written confirmation . . . operates as an acceptance even though it states terms additional to or different from . . . those agreed upon." This statement is problematic. A written confirmation can be sent only after the parties have already reached an agreement, as during a telephone conversation. Once the parties agree on certain basic terms and manifest an intent to be bound, the Code supplies a variety of "gap-fillers" to flesh

---

[55] *See, e.g.*, Twin Disc, Inc. v. Big Bud Tractor, Inc., 772 F.2d 1329, 41 UCC Rep. Serv. 1627 (7th Cir. 1985).

[56] 777 F. Supp. 1214, 16 UCC Rep. Serv. 2d 1035 (M.D. Pa. 1991).

[57] A third possibility is suggested by the decision in *Graham Hydraulic Power, Inc. v. Stewart & Stevenson Power, Inc.*, 797 P.2d 835, 12 UCC Rep. Serv. 2d 658 (Colo. Ct. App. 1990), discussed in the text at note 71 *infra*.

out their contract.[58] These gap-fillers are provisions that come into play in the absence of agreement to the contrary. Thus, when a written confirmation is sent, a full-blown contract already exists and it is nonsensical to say that the confirmation operates as an acceptance.

What, then, is the effect of the confirmation? It is similar to the function of the definite expression of acceptance discussed in the preceding subsection. To the extent that the confirmation contains terms additional to the prior agreement, they are treated as proposals for addition to the contract. They become operative only if the recipient expressly assents to them. With regard to different terms, the drafting of section 2–207(2) again creates a problem. Perhaps the different terms simply drop out. The better approach, however, is to treat them as proposals also. After all, a proposal for addition to the contract cannot become effective unless the other party expressly assents.

Each party might send a confirmation form that covers a topic not discussed when the parties reached agreement, such as a requirement to arbitrate any disputes. In such a case, each party should be assumed to have assented to the other's proposal to arbitrate. Keeping such a provision out of the contract would not be justified.

Perhaps the most important issues involving written confirmations arise in the context of the "between merchants" rule, discussed in the next subsection.

[C]   "Between Merchants"

The "between merchants" rule of section 2–207(2) modifies the basic approach that prevents additional (or different) terms from being effective absent assent by the other party. If both parties are merchants,[59] some terms contained in a definite expression of acceptance or a written confirmation become part of the contract automatically.

Not every term comes in automatically. If the offer expressly states that acceptance must be on its terms, the rule does not come into play.[60] The same is true if the term is material,[61] or if the recipient objects to it, either before the form containing the term is received or within a reasonable time thereafter.[62] Thus a term can become part of the contract automatically only if it is nonmaterial and if the other party does not object to it. Consequently, the between

---

[58] For a discussion of the Code gap-fillers, see § 4.05 *infra*.

[59] For purposes of UCC § 2–207, the term "merchant" should have the same meaning as in UCC § 2–201(2). See discussion of that topic in § 3.04[B] *infra*.

[60] UCC § 2–207(2)(a).

[61] UCC § 2–207(2)(b).

[62] UCC § 2–207(2)(c).

merchants rule is a minor exception to the basic rules. If both parties are merchants and a term does not automatically enter the contract, its impact should be analyzed under the basic rules described in the preceding subsections.

[1]   Materiality

What terms are "material" for purposes of section 2–207(2)? The Comments provide some guidance by stating that a clause materially alters a contract if it would "result in surprise or hardship if incorporated without express awareness by the other party."[63] They go on to give the following examples of material terms:[64]

- a clause disclaiming implied warranties of merchantability or fitness;
- a clause requiring a different guaranty of quantity than that provided by a trade usage;
- a clause giving the seller a right to cancel if the buyer fails to pay an invoice; and
- a clause requiring that complaints be made within a time period shorter than that which is customary or reasonable.

The Comments also give the following examples of nonmaterial clauses:

- a *force majeure* clause;
- a clause setting a reasonable time for complaints;
- a clause giving the seller reasonable credit terms; and
- a clause limiting the buyer's right of rejection for defects that fall within trade tolerances for acceptance with adjustment.[65]

The meaning and importance of "surprise" and "hardship" are not entirely clear, and two different approaches seem to be emerging. One approach is illustrated by the decision in *Dale R. Hornung Co. v. Falconer Glass Industries, Inc.*[66] The buyer, a glazing subcontractor on an office building project, ordered glass from the seller by phone. Before shipment, the seller sent a written confirmation, with a clause excluding consequential damages. When the glass proved defective, the buyer sued to recover the consequential losses incurred.

Hornung held that for a clause to be effective under section 2–207(2), it must cause neither hardship nor surprise. The decision reasoned that "surprise"

---

[63] UCC § 2–207, Comment 4.

[64] *Id.*

[65] UCC § 2–207, Comment 5. The last example is troubling. Terms derived from a trade usage are already a part of the agreement. *See* UCC § 1–201(3), and the discussion in § 4.03 *infra*.

[66] 730 F. Supp. 962, 11 UCC Rep. Serv. 2d 536 (S.D. Ind. 1990). *See also* Trans-Aire Int'l, Inc. v. Northern Adhesive Co., 882 F.2d 1254, 9 UCC Rep. Serv. 2d 878 (7th Cir. 1989).

refers to whether the clause would catch the buyer unaware. The court found that the buyer should not have been surprised because clauses excluding consequential damages are fairly common in the industry.[67]

The *Hornung* court then stated that "hardship" refers to whether enforcement of the clause would impose a substantial economic detriment on the nonassenting party. Under this test, any clause that shifts a substantial economic risk from one party to another is material. The court found that excluding consequential damages would cause the buyer to suffer a hardship, and it refused to enforce the clause. The court noted that the seller could have separately negotiated its limitation prior to shipping the glass.

A different approach was adopted by the Seventh Circuit Court of Appeals in *Union Carbide Corp. v. Oscar Mayer Foods Corp.*[68] Union Carbide, which had been selling plastic sausage casings to Oscar Mayer, had printed on the back of its invoices a clause requiring the buyer to indemnify it for all sales tax liability. Eventually, the Illinois tax authorities held that the seller owed additional sales taxes, and the issue for the Seventh Circuit was the enforceability of the indemnification clause. The decision, authored by Judge Posner, held that the only relevant test for materiality is surprise. If the term is so unusual that it would come as a surprise to the other party, we ought not presume that party's assent. Hardship results as a consequence of surprise, and is not a separate criterion. If a term is so routine that it does not cause surprise, assent can be presumed, and any hardship that it causes is legally insignificant unless it reaches such a level that it gives rise to a claim of commercial impracticability. Ultimately, the court found that the clause in question came as a surprise to the buyer, precluding its liability for the additional taxes.

An example of a clause that has routinely been viewed as nonmaterial is one requiring the buyer to pay interest on past-due accounts.[69] On the other hand, warranty disclaimers are almost always seen as material,[70] although one decision is to the contrary. In *Graham Hydraulic Power, Inc. v. Stewart & Stevenson*

---

[67] Apparently, the practice of excluding consequential damages was not so common that it rose to the level of a trade usage. Had it done so, it would have been part of the contract from the outset.

[68] 947 F.2d 1333, 16 UCC Rep. Serv. 2d 46 (7th Cir. 1991).

[69] *See, e.g.*, Advance Concrete Forms, Inc. v. McCann Constr. Specialties Co., 916 F.2d 412, 12 UCC Rep. Serv. 2d 1047 (7th Cir. 1990); Southwest Concrete Prod. v. Gosh Constr. Corp., 215 Cal. App. 3d 134, 263 Cal. Rptr. 387, 10 UCC Rep. Serv. 2d 73 (1989).

[70] *See, e.g.*, USEMCO, Inc. v. Marbro Co., Inc., 60 Md. App. 351, 483 A.2d 88, 39 UCC Rep. Serv. 1600 (1984); Boese-Hilburn Co. v. Dean Mach. Co., 616 S.W.2d 520, 31 UCC Rep. Serv. 830 (Mo. Ct. App. 1981).

Power, Inc.,[71] the parties held preliminary discussions regarding the sale of hydraulic pumps, and the seller gave the buyer a copy of its warranty disclaimer form. After the buyer sent its purchase order (the offer), the seller sent an acknowledgment that disclaimed implied warranties. When the pumps proved to be defective, the court found that the seller's disclaimer, in context, caused neither hardship nor surprise and was, therefore, nonmaterial. Since both parties were merchants, the disclaimer became part of the contract automatically. While somewhat unusual, the result seems appropriate given the circumstances. The buyer was aware of the seller's terms, and allowing the buyer to avoid the risk because of a mechanical application of section 2–207 would have violated the spirit of that section.

As the *Graham Hydraulic Power* case shows, the issue of materiality is one of fact and is best decided on a case-by-case basis. Inconsistencies in the courts' approaches are inevitable.[72] While some cases hold that certain types of clauses, such as arbitration clauses, are material as a matter of law,[73] the better reasoned decisions have adopted the case-by-case approach, focusing primarily on the degree to which the term at issue is used within the relevant industry.[74]

Two straightforward illustrations show the effect of materiality on the between merchants rule. Suppose the buyer places a purchase order for a particular product and the order states that payment is due 30 days after delivery. The seller responds with an acknowledgment form that requires the buyer to pay interest if its payment is late and that also disclaims warranties. The seller's response is a definite expression of acceptance, and the parties' forms create a contract on the buyer's terms. Nonmaterial terms become part of the contract; material terms are treated as mere proposals. The probable result here is that the seller's interest clause will be enforced and its disclaimer clause will not.

Now assume that the parties agreed by telephone on the subject matter, quantity, price, and credit terms. The buyer sends a written confirmation calling for arbitration, and the seller sends a written confirmation with an interest clause and a warranty disclaimer. Again, the interest clause will probably

---

[71] 797 P.2d 835, 12 UCC Rep. Serv. 2d 658 (Colo. App. 1990).

[72] *Compare* Burbic Constr. Co., Inc. v. Cement Asbestos Prod. Co., Inc., 409 So. 2d 1, 32 UCC Rep. Serv. 1406 (Ala. 1982) (limited-remedy clause nonmaterial); *with* Transamerica Oil Co. v. Lynes, Inc., 723 F.2d 758, 37 UCC Rep. Serv. 1076 (10th Cir. 1983) (limited-remedy clause material).

[73] *See, e.g.*, Windsor Mills, Inc. v. Collins & Aikman Corp., 25 Cal. App. 3d 987, 101 Cal. Rptr. 347, 10 UCC Rep. Serv. 1020 (1972).

[74] Valmont Indus., Inc. v. Mitsui & Co. (USA), Inc., 419 F. Supp. 1238, 20 UCC Rep. Serv. 626 (D. Neb. 1976) (court should consider industry practices in deciding materiality of arbitration clause). If the industry practice is sufficiently widespread, it becomes part of the agreement through implication.

become part of the contract and the disclaimer clause will not. The arbitration clause will be a closer question, but the analysis remains the same. If the clause is nonmaterial, it is in; if material, it is just a proposal.

[2] "Additional" and "Different" Terms

The examples at the end of the preceding subsection are easy because the terms at issue are "additional" rather than "different." Suppose, however, the buyer sends a purchase order that expressly states that interest will not be paid on any payments made within 60 days after their due date (a grace period). The seller responds with an acknowledgment form that calls for interest on all late payments. Under section 2–207(1), the form will qualify as a definite expression of acceptance even though it contains a different term.

Ordinarily, terms like the seller's are viewed as nonmaterial, and had the term been merely additional, it would have become part of the contract automatically. However, the first sentence of section 2–207(2) refers only to "additional" terms; arguably, different terms never come in automatically.[75] The seller's term would be analyzed under the basic rules, not the between merchants rule.[76] Since the buyer did not expressly assent to it, the seller's term would be ineffective.

A different approach is suggested by the Comments, which state that:

Whether or not additional or different terms will become part of the agreement depends upon the provisions of subsection (2). If they are such as materially to alter the original bargain, they will not be included unless expressly agreed to by the other party. If, however, they are terms which would not so change the bargain they will be incorporated unless notice of objection to them has already been given or is given within a reasonable time.[77]

This comment suggests that section 2–207(2) contains a drafting error and that it should be equally applicable to additional and different terms. A number of courts have followed this line of reasoning.[78] Going back to our example, a majority of courts would apply the basic rules and side with the buyer. The minority would apply the between merchants rule and make the seller's term part of the contract automatically.

---

[75] The majority of courts have concluded that different terms are not within the scope of § 2–207(2). *See, e.g.,* the cases set forth in note 50 *supra.*

[76] *See* text accompanying notes 50–53 *supra.*

[77] UCC § 2–207, Comment 3.

[78] *See, e.g.,* Mead Corp. v. McNally-Pittsburgh Mfg. Corp., 654 F.2d 1197, 35 UCC Rep. Serv. 368 (6th Cir. 1981).

The majority appears to have the better side of this issue. The idea here is a simple one. Innocuous provisions—ones that are not likely to be objectionable to the other party—ought to be enforced. However, when the term at issue is likely to be objectionable, it ought not come in absent express assent. Surely a term is objectionable if the other party has gone to the trouble of drafting a contrary provision. The original offer should be seen as a continuing objection, thus invoking section 2–207(2)(c).

The same issue, of course, can arise with written confirmations. If one party sends a confirmation that differs from what the parties expressly agreed to, the majority analysis set forth above should be used to preclude the term from becoming effective. If each party sends a confirmation and their terms differ, each confirmation should be viewed as a continuing objection to the other and neither party's term should be enforced.[79]

This analysis suggests that, the Comments notwithstanding, the drafters did not make a mistake when they excluded different terms from the between merchants rule. The first sentence of section 2–207(2) performs two functions: it leads into the between merchants rule, and it refers back to the basic rules.[80] To the extent that they are used in the context of the basic rules, additional and different terms should not be distinguished. After all, section 2–207(1) refers to both kinds of terms, and no term can become effective without the assent of the other party. The between merchants rule, however, should apply only to additional terms. Different terms should never become part of the contract automatically. This bifurcated approach represents the best approach to resolving an extraordinarily difficult problem of statutory interpretation.

[D]   Expressly Conditional Expressions of Acceptance

The exception provision of section 2–207(1) states that a definite expression of acceptance operates as an acceptance "unless acceptance is expressly made conditional on assent to the additional or different terms." The provision is incongruous: the drafters assumed that the offeror would not read the offeree's standard form, yet they created a mechanism that allows the offeree to escape the impact of the first-shot rule by including specific language. The two basic issues in this area concern the language that triggers the clause and the impact of its being triggered.

[1]   Language Creating an Expressly Conditional Acceptance

The first major case to address the first issue was the infamous *Roto-Lith, Ltd. v. F.P. Bartlett & Co, Inc.*[81] The case presented one of the classic problems

---

[79] UCC § 2–207, Comment 6.
[80] See text accompanying notes 52–53 *supra*.
[81] 297 F.2d 497, 1 UCC Rep. Serv. 73 (1st Cir. 1962).

that section 2–207 was designed to remedy. The buyer had sent a purchase order for goods that was silent as to quality, and the seller had responded with an acknowledgment disclaiming implied warranties. The seller then sent the goods, which the buyer accepted and used. When the goods proved defective, the buyer asserted the implied warranty of merchantability and the seller raised the disclaimer as a defense.

The proper analysis would have been to treat the seller's acknowledgment as a definite expression of acceptance, forming a contract on the buyer's terms. The disclaimer could not come in automatically under the merchant rule because it was material, so it should have been treated as a proposal for addition to the contract. The buyer's conduct did not amount to assent to that proposal, so the disclaimer should have dropped out. Thus, the buyer should have prevailed. This result, of course, is inconsistent with the common law's mirror-image rule.

The court apparently could not conceive that the drafters had effected such a radical change. It held that since the disclaimer was material, it triggered the conditional acceptance clause of section 2–207(1). It also held that a response that comes within that clause operates as a common-law counteroffer. According to the opinion, the buyer had accepted the seller's counteroffer by using the goods.

Roto-Lith stands for the proposition that any response that materially differs from the offer should be treated like a counteroffer. Such an approach essentially reinstates the last-shot rule. The court ignored the fact that the last clause of section 2–207(1) requires that the seller's communication be *"expressly made conditional"*[82] on assent to its terms and that the form used by the seller had contained no language insisting that the final contract reflect its terms. The court also ignored the Comments, which state that a disclaimer should be considered material for purposes of the between-merchants rule.[83] The Comments make no sense if every materially different response is treated like a counteroffer. Fortunately, the commentary and cases have resoundingly rejected *Roto-Lith.*

Most cases since *Roto-Lith* have made it difficult for a party to invoke the expressly conditional acceptance clause. The standard was set in *Dorton v. Collins & Aikman Corp.,*[84] where the court held that the phrase "The acceptance of

---

[82] Emphasis supplied.

[83] UCC § 2–207, Comment 4.

[84] 453 F.2d 1161, 10 UCC Rep. Serv. 585 (6th Cir. 1972). *See also* Reaction Molding Technologies, Inc., 588 F. Supp. 1280, 38 UCC Rep. Serv. 1537 (E.D. Pa. 1984); Step-Saver Data Sys., Inc. v. Wyse Technology, 912 F.2d 643, 12 UCC Rep. Serv. 2d 343 (3d Cir. 1990). *But see* Construction Aggregates, Inc. v. Hewitt-Robins, Inc., 404 F.2d 505, 6 UCC Rep. Serv. 112 (7th Cir. 1968) (seller's acknowledgment, which stated that final contract was "pred-

your order is subject to all the terms & conditions on the face and reverse side hereof, including arbitration" did not make a seller's response expressly conditional. According to the court, the condition must be "directly and distinctly stated rather than implied or left to inference."[85] The words "subject to" did not clearly reveal that the seller was unwilling to proceed with the transaction without being assured of the buyer's assent to its terms.

[2]   Consequences of an Expressly Conditional Acceptance

The court in *Roto-Lith* held that a response of an offeree who successfully invoked section 2–207(1)'s expressly conditional acceptance clause operated as a common-law counteroffer. While the language of section 2–207(1) does not mandate this result,[86] it seems reasonable based on an analogy to the common law.[87] After all, if the original offeror expressly assents to the terms set forth in the offeree's response, a contract should certainly be formed on those terms. And if the original offeror fails to expressly assent but the goods are never shipped, no contract should result.

What if the seller sends an expressly conditional acceptance and then ships the goods, which the buyer uses? If, as the court in *Roto-Lith* held, the buyer's conduct constitutes assent to each term in the seller's counteroffer, we will have allowed the seller, by careful drafting, to reinstate the mirror-image rule. Since much of the rationale for section 2–207 is that the offeror will not read the offeree's form, such a result is unacceptable. The proper analysis is to conclude that, under the circumstances, the counteroffer cannot be accepted by any method other than an expression of assent.[88] Accordingly, the conduct of the parties makes it clear that a contract exists, but neither party has accepted the other's offer. The terms of the resulting contract are dictated by section 2–207(3), which is sometimes referred to as the "knock-out" rule. That subsection states in full that:

> Conduct by both parties which recognizes the existence of a contract is sufficient to establish a contract for sale although the writings of the parties do not otherwise establish a contract. In such case the terms of

---

icated on the following clarifications, additions or modifications to the [buyer's] order" was expressly conditional).

[85] *Id.*, 453 F.2d at 1168, 10 UCC Rep. Serv. at 594 (citing *Webster's Third International Dictionary's* definition of "express").

[86] The express language of UCC § 2–207(1) does nothing more than make it clear that an expressly conditional acceptance does not operate as an acceptance. ("A definite . . . expression of acceptance . . . operates as an acceptance . . . *unless*. . . ." (Emphasis supplied.)

[87] *See* UCC § 1–103.

[88] UCC § 2–206(1) provides some support for this analysis. It states that an offer (presumably including a counteroffer) can be accepted by any reasonable method *"[u]nless the language or circumstances"* (emphasis supplied) indicate otherwise.

the particular contract consist of those terms on which the writings of the parties agree, together with any supplementary terms incorporated under any other provisions of this Act.

In other words, the terms of the contract are the terms on which the writings agree, plus any other terms supplied by other provisions of the Code. The parties' forms are likely to agree on the dickered terms, and they may by coincidence agree on other terms, such as arbitration or interest on late payments. To the extent that the terms do not agree, they fall out. A clear majority of recent decisions has adopted this knock-out analysis.[89]

The terms supplied by the Code clearly include the standard gap-fillers. Do they also include implied-in-fact terms derived from trade usage, course of dealing, or course of performance? The court in *Dresser Industries, Inc. v. The Gradall Co.*[90] answered this question in the affirmative. The buyer had bought a series of engines. Each sale was initiated by a purchase order from the buyer, and each purchase order specified that the buyer would have the benefit of all implied warranties plus a 15-month express warranty. The seller had consistently responded with acknowledgments that disclaimed all implied warranties and gave a one-year express warranty. Each acknowledgment was expressly conditioned on the buyer's assent.

When litigation arose over a problem that had developed in one engine between the twelfth and fifteenth months after sale, the court applied section 2–207(3). The buyer, of course, argued that the resulting contract could be supplemented only by standard Code gap-fillers because it would receive the benefit of the implied warranty of merchantability. The court, however, sided with the seller, which wanted to show that the series of purchases established a course of dealing, since the buyer had been aware of its terms of sale for a long time, and that, under a relevant trade usage, buyers generally adopted the seller's warranty terms.[91] Given the importance of implied-in-fact terms in the Code scheme and the fact that they are more likely to reflect the parties' real expectations than the standard gap-fillers, the decision in *Dresser* seems correct.

---

[89] *See, e.g.*, McJunkin Corp. v. Mechanicals, Inc., 888 F.2d 481, 10 UCC Rep. Serv. 2d 712 (6th Cir. 1989); Diamond Fruit Growers, Inc. v. Krack Corp., 794 F.2d 1440, 1 UCC Rep. Serv. 2d 1073 (9th Cir. 1986); Step-Saver Data Sys., Inc. v. Wyse Technology, 912 F.2d 643, 12 UCC Rep. Serv. 2d 343 (3d Cir. 1990). The analysis also applies where the offeree rejects the buyer's offer, but the goods are subsequently shipped and used.

[90] 956 F.2d 1442, 18 UCC Rep. Serv. 2d 43 (9th Cir. 1992). *See also*, Daitom, Inc. v. Pennwalt Corp., 741 F.2d 1569, 39 UCC Rep. Serv. 1203 (10th Cir. 1984). *Contra* C. Itoh & Co. v. Jordan Int'l Co., 552 F.2d 1228, 21 UCC Rep. Serv. 353 (7th Cir. 1977) (supplementation under UCC § 2–207(3) limited to standardized Code gap-fillers).

[91] Warranties can be established by implication from a course of dealing or trade usage. *See* UCC § 2–314(3).

While using section 2–207(3) is preferable to reverting to the mirror-image rule, the parties must be aware of its impact and plan accordingly. In particular, sellers should be wary of the following situation. Suppose the seller sends the buyer an offer that clearly disclaims implied warranties. The buyer responds with an acknowledgment form that is silent as to warranties but does not mirror the seller's offer. The buyer's acknowledgment states that acceptance is expressly conditioned on assent to its terms. The seller then ships the goods, which the buyer uses. When the goods prove defective, the buyer can argue that the writings of the parties did not create a contract but that their conduct did. Applying the knock-out rule, the seller's disclaimer drops out and the buyer is left with the Code's gap-fillers on quality—the implied warranties. The seller who wants to insist on a disclaimer must be aware that it cannot be certain of prevailing, either as the offeror or the offeree, if it relies on its standard forms. The only way to be sure of the disclaimer's validity is to raise it during the negotiations and then refuse to ship the goods unless the buyer expressly assents.

§ 2.06   MODIFICATION [2–209; 2A–208]

[A]   Consideration

Parties to a contract frequently find it necessary to modify their understandings in order to meet changing circumstances, but the common law made such modifications difficult. Under the pre-existing duty rule, a promise modifying a contract needed new consideration to be binding. *Lingenfelder v. Wainwright Brewery Co.*[92] demonstrates the problem this rule was designed to address. The defendant hired an architect to supervise the construction of a brewery. The architect was also the president of a company that sold refrigeration equipment, and when he learned that the refrigeration subcontract had been given to a competitor, he walked off the job. He returned only after the defendant's president promised additional compensation. When the defendant later reneged, the architect sued. In holding for the defendant, the court stated, "To permit plaintiff to recover under such circumstances would be to offer a premium upon bad faith, and invite men to violate their most sacred contracts that they may profit by their own wrong."[93]

While the pre-existing duty rule led to the right result in *Lingenfelder*, it also made it harder for parties facing genuine hardships to enter into good-faith modifications. As a result, the courts began to look for ways to avoid its application. Some courts found that the original contract had been rescinded first

---

[92]   103 Mo. 578, 15 S.W. 844 (1891).
[93]   103 Mo. at 582, 15 S.W. at 848.

and that the subsequent "modification" was in fact a new contract with new consideration.[94] Others found that the promisee's duties had been altered in some trivial way and enforced the modification on the basis of this nominal consideration.[95] A rule is seriously flawed when the courts have to resort to fictions to avoid its harsh impact, and the Second Restatement has abandoned the consideration requirement for some contracts that are not fully performed on either side.[96] While the Second Restatement represents an improvement, it does not go far enough. It does not deal with modifications of contracts that are fully executed on one side, and it invites courts to engage in speculation about what circumstances the parties ought to have anticipated.

The Code eliminates the consideration requirement for modifications. It provides simply that "[a]n agreement modifying a contract within this Article needs no consideration to be binding."[97]

The Comments address the potential abuses of this approach as follows:

> However, modifications made thereunder must meet the test of good faith imposed by this Act. The effective use of bad faith to escape performance on the original contract terms is barred, and the extortion of a "modification" without legitimate commercial reason is ineffective as a violation of the duty of good faith. Nor can a mere technical consideration support a modification made in bad faith.[98]

The Code appropriately shifts the focus from the application of a rule of form to an inquiry into the underlying rationale for the modification.[99] Despite what the Comments say, however, about imposing the Code's obligation of good faith, the stated obligation is more expansive than any good-faith obligation included directly in the codification.[100] It is objective in its thrust, and its application is not limited to merchants. Although stated only in the Comment, its inherent logic is persuasive for its application in Article 2 modification cases and as the basis for a common-law standard that more adequately addresses the potential abuse-of-power problems in these types of cases.

---

[94] *See, e.g.*, Schwartzreich v. Bauman-Basch, Inc., 231 N.Y. 196, 131 N.E. 887 (1921).

[95] *See, e.g.*, Jaffray v. Davis, 124 N.Y. 164, 26 N.E. 351 (1891).

[96] Restatement (Second) of Contracts § 89 provides that "[a] promise modifying a duty under a contract not fully performed on either side is binding (a) if the modification is fair and equitable in view of circumstances not anticipated by the parties when the contract was made; or (b) to the extent provided by statute; or (c) to the extent that justice requires enforcement in view of material change of position in reliance on the promise."

[97] UCC § 2–209(1).

[98] UCC § 2–209, Comment 2.

[99] *See generally*, Hillman, *Policing Contract Modifications Under the UCC: Good Faith and the Doctrine of Economic Duress*, 64 Iowa L. Rev. 849 (1979).

[100] The codified provisions on good faith are discussed in § 4.06[B] *infra*.

[B]   Modifications and the Statute of Frauds

The drafters were concerned that abandoning the pre-existing duty rule would make it too easy for a dissatisfied party to invent a modification.[101] Accordingly, they subjected modifications to Article 2's Statute of Frauds, and they sanctioned the creation of private Statutes of Frauds—contractual provisions requiring that modifications be evidenced by a signed writing. They also provided a mechanism—waiver—for circumventing these rules. Section 2–209(2) through (5) states in full:

> (2) A signed agreement which excludes modification or rescission except by a signed writing cannot be otherwise modified or rescinded, but except as between merchants such a requirement on a form supplied by the merchant must be separately signed by the other party.

> (3) The requirements of the statute of frauds section of this Article (Section 2–201) must be satisfied if the contract as modified is within its provisions.

> (4) Although an attempt at modification or rescission does not satisfy the requirements of subsection (2) or (3) it can operate as a waiver.

> (5) A party who has made a waiver affecting an executory portion of the contract may retract the waiver by reasonable notification received by the other party that strict performance will be required of any term waived, unless the retraction would be unjust in view of a material change of position in reliance on the waiver.

These provisions have led to great confusion and uncertainty, as will be shown in the ensuing discussion.

[1]   Applying the Code's Statute of Frauds to Modifications

Under section 2–209(3), the requirements of section 2–201, Article 2's basic Statute of Frauds provision, must be satisfied "if the contract as modified is within its provisions." This provision presents difficult problems of interpretation. Perhaps the section applies only when a modification brings a contract within the Statute of Frauds for the first time. An example would be a modification raising the price term to $500 or more. Such an interpretation is implausible because it would, as a practical matter, limit application of the section to relatively insignificant contracts. Another possibility is that the section applies whenever a modification calls for the purchase of additional goods costing $500 or more. The text, which refers to the "contract as modified" rather than the modification itself, suggests otherwise.

---

[101] UCC § 2–209, Comment 3.

Another, more plausible interpretation is that a signed writing is not necessary unless the modification changes the quantity term. The text supports this approach. Section 2–209(3) does *not* expressly state that all the terms of a modification must be in a signed writing; it simply says that section 2–201 must be satisfied. Quantity is the only term mandated by section 2–201.[102] All other terms can be proved by extrinsic evidence. If the parties modified the price but not the quantity, a new writing that reiterated the quantity term but omitted any reference to price would satisfy section 2–201. Why, then, require a new writing at all? The problem with (or, some might say, the benefit of) this approach is that it renders section 2–209(1) inapplicable to the vast majority of modifications.

The most common approach has been for courts to impose a writing requirement for modifications that is more stringent than section 2–201's requirements for the original contract. Courts following this approach have held that all the essential terms of the modification must be expressed with reasonable certainty in a signed writing,[103] a standard similar to that adopted by the Second Restatement.[104] This approach finds some support in the Comments, which state, "Modification for the future cannot therefore be conjured up by oral testimony if the price involved is $500 or more since such modification must be shown at least by an authenticated memo."[105] A broad application of section 2–209(3) is consistent with the drafters' desire to substitute a formal writing requirement for the common law's formal consideration requirement.

If the signed writing requirement is not met, are the exceptions set out in section 2–201(2) and (3) available to the party seeking to enforce the modification?[106] Since section 2–209 does not refer to any specific subsection of 2–201, the answer should be yes. In *Starry Construction Co., Inc. v. Murphy Oil USA, Inc.*,[107] the parties initially agreed to a contract for the sale of 20,000 tons of asphalt cement oil and then changed the quantity to 25,000 tons. Six months later, Iraq invaded Kuwait. The buyer, concerned about the seller's ability to

---

[102] See the discussion of Article 2's writing requirement in § 3.03 *infra*.

[103] *See, e.g.*, In re Atkins, 139 B.R. 39, 19 UCC Rep. Serv. 2d 18 (Bankr. M.D. Fla. 1992) (alleged agreement modifying the financing aspects of the contract unenforceable); Cooley v. Big Horn Harvestore Sys., Inc., 767 P.2d 740, 7 UCC Rep. Serv. 2d 1051 (Colo. Ct. App. 1988) (alleged agreement by seller to broaden its warranty liability unenforceable); Symbol Technologies, Inc. v. Sonco, Inc., 36 UCC Rep. Serv. 402 (E.D. Pa. 1983) (oral modification of term "net 30 days" unenforceable).

[104] *See* Restatement (Second) of Contracts § 131(c) (writing must state "with reasonable certainty the essential terms of the unperformed promises").

[105] UCC § 2–209, Comment 3.

[106] These exceptions are discussed in §§ 3.04 and 3.05 *infra*.

[107] 785 F. Supp. 1356, 17 UCC Rep. Serv. 2d 353 (D. Minn. 1993), *aff'd*, 986 F.2d 503 (8th Cir. 1993).

perform, sent the seller a signed confirmation of the modification. The seller later breached and raised the Statute of Frauds as a defense. The court held that the written confirmation exception of section 2–201(2) can be used to satisfy section 2–209(3), but that the buyer's confirmation had not been sent within a reasonable time after the modification. Accordingly, the modification was unenforceable.

[2] Private Statutes of Frauds

Parties frequently provide that their contracts cannot be modified except by a signed writing, and section 2–209(2) validates such "private Statute of Frauds" clauses. It requires that the clause be contained in a signed writing, but it does not say which party needs to sign the writing. Analogizing to section 2–201, the clause should be enforced if the agreement has been signed by the party seeking to avoid enforcement of the oral modification. An added layer of protection applies when a merchant provides the original contract form and later seeks to enforce a private Statute of Frauds provision against a consumer. The clause is unenforceable unless the consumer has separately signed the contract at the place where the clause appears.[108]

[3] Waiver and Estoppel

While sections 2–209(2) and (3) create hurdles for a party seeking to enforce an oral modification, sections 2–209(4) and (5) suggest that the doctrine of waiver provides a way around those hurdles. Waiver is, however, a notoriously elusive concept. Historically, the term referred to a voluntary relinquishment of the right to assert a condition, usually a relatively minor one. For example, an owner might waive the right to an architect's certificate as a condition to the release of a progress payment. If the condition being waived was a material part of the agreed exchange, the parties were in effect entering into a modification, and consideration was required.[109] Further, where a purported waiver had the effect of increasing the duties of the waiving party, there was really a modification, not a waiver.[110]

---

[108] *See, e.g.,* Knoxville Rod & Bearing, Inc. v. Bettis Corp. of Knoxville, Inc., 672 S.W.2d 203, 39 UCC Rep. Serv. 415 (Tenn. Ct. App. 1984).

[109] *See* Restatement (Second) of Contracts § 84(1). Numerous decisions hold that a waiver of a material condition must be supported by consideration. *See, e.g.,* Rennie & Laughlin, Inc. v. Chrysler Corp., 242 F.2d 208 (9th Cir. 1957). The Code dispenses with the consideration requirement for modifications but is silent with regard to waivers. Waivers affecting material conditions are really modifications, notwithstanding the terminology used by the courts, and consideration should not be required.

[110] *See, e.g.,* Nat'l Utility Service, Inc. v. Whirlpool Corp., 325 F.2d 779 (2d Cir. 1963) (a party cannot by waiver create in itself an obligation where none previously existed).

Conditions can be waived in several ways. For example, a party may express in advance an intent not to enforce a condition. Such a waiver can be retracted until the time for the condition has passed or the other party has materially relied on the waiver. Another example, called an "election," occurs when a party proceeds to perform, knowing that performance has been excused by the failure of a condition. A waiver by election cannot be retracted. Finally, a party who acts without regard to a condition may nevertheless be estopped to enforce it.[111] In *Universal Builders, Inc. v. Moon Motor Lodge, Inc.*,[112] for example, an owner asked a contractor to do work not called for in the original plans. The court held the owner liable for payment, notwithstanding a clause requiring that all modifications be contained in a signed writing.

While the preceding analysis seems logical and orderly, the cases are not. Many common-law courts use the waiver doctrine indiscriminately, applying it to situations that conceptually should be viewed as modifications. If the court characterizes the parties' conduct as a modification, it must refuse to enforce the modification in the absence of consideration. If, instead, it uses the term "waiver," it can avoid this requirement. Further, when there are repeated occasions for performance, characterizing conduct as a waiver allows the original contract term to be reinstated for the future, whereas characterizing it as a modification does not.

This preference for waiver rather than modification finds expression in section 2–208 of the Code, which states that a "course of performance shall be relevant to show a waiver or modification of any term inconsistent with such course of performance."[113] The Comments then express a preference "in favor of 'waiver' whenever such construction, plus the application of the provision on the reinstatement of rights waived (see Section 2–209), is needed to preserve the flexible character of commercial contracts and to prevent surprise or other hardship."[114]

Section 2–209(4) states that an attempt at modification "can" operate as a waiver, but it does not define when it should occur. Suppose the seller agrees to a particular delivery date and then, after encountering difficulties, requests an extension. The contract contains a private Statute of Frauds clause.[115] The buyer grants the extension orally, and the seller relies by ceasing what had been frantic efforts to meet the original date. The parties have orally agreed to a modification, but has the buyer waived the private Statute of Frauds provision?

---

[111] Waiver by estoppel can enter the Code through either UCC § 2–209 or § 1–103.

[112] 430 Pa. 550, 244 A.2d 10 (1968).

[113] UCC § 2–208(3). This provision is expressly subordinated to the provisions of § 2–209.

[114] UCC § 2–208, Comment 3.

[115] The analysis would be the same without the private Statute of Frauds clause if the modification fell within the scope of UCC § 2–209(3).

One early case held that waiver could not apply unless the private Statute of Frauds provision had been addressed directly.[116] In other words, the buyer had to say something like "I hereby waive our agreement on modifications being in writing, and I also agree to your requested extension." This approach is unreasonable. Parties who agree to oral modifications are unlikely to take the time to address the problem of the Statute of Frauds, and an overly technical insistence on formalities can work a substantial injustice.

Wisconsin Knife Works v. National Metal Crafters[117] represents a more realistic approach. The buyer was purchasing spade-bit blanks that were to be manufactured into finished spade bits pursuant to a contract with a private Statute of Frauds clause. When the seller failed to make timely delivery, the buyer sued for damages. The seller claimed that the buyer had by its conduct agreed to a new delivery schedule, and the buyer raised section 2–209(2) as a defense. Writing for the majority, Judge Posner held that an attempted modification acts as a waiver of section 2–209(2) only if there has been reliance. The opinion states:

> The path of reconciliation with subsection (4) is found by attending to its precise wording. It does not say that an attempted modification "is" a waiver; it says that "it can operate as a waiver." It does not say in what circumstances it can operate as a waiver; but if an attempted modification is effective as a waiver only if there is reliance, then both §§ 2–209(2) and 2–209(4) can be given effect. Reliance, if reasonably induced and reasonable in extent, is a common substitute for consideration in making a promise legally enforceable, in part because it adds something in the way of credibility to the mere say-so of one party.[118]

If there has been no reliance, a waiver, whether express or inferred from conduct, affecting an executory part of the contract can be retracted.[119] The limitation in section 2–209(5) to executory terms suggests that the Code recognizes waiver by election. That is, a party who proceeds to perform even though he or she is aware that performance has been excused by failure of a condition is deemed to have waived the condition irrevocably.

---

[116] C.I.T. Corp. v. Jonnet, 3 UCC Rep. Serv. 321 (Pa. C.P. 1965), *aff'd*, 419 Pa. 435, 214 A.2d 620, 3 UCC Rep. Serv. 968 (1965).

[117] 781 F.2d 1280, 42 UCC Rep. Serv. 830 (7th Cir. 1986). *See also* Thomas Knutson Shipbuilding Corp. v. George W. Rogers Constr. Co., 6 UCC Rep. Serv. 323 (N.Y. Sup. Ct. 1969).

[118] 781 F.2d at 1287, 42 UCC Rep. Serv. at 837.

[119] UCC § 2–209(5). *See also* Double-E Sportswear Corp. v. Girard Trust Bank, 488 F.2d 292, 13 UCC Rep. Serv. 577 (3d Cir. 1973) (whether notice of retraction is reasonable is an issue of fact).

CHAPTER

3

The Requirement of a Writing

§ 3.01   THE STATUTE OF FRAUDS: A BRIEF HISTORY

The Statute of Frauds has been a part of our legal tradition since it was first enacted by Parliament in 1677. At that time parties could not testify on their own behalf, and judges had little control over arbitrary jury verdicts. A litigant had every reason to suborn perjured testimony to the effect that the other party had been overheard making a binding commitment.[1] This state of affairs led to the passage of the original "Act for Prevention of Frauds and Perjuries."[2] Section 17 placed certain sales of goods within the scope of the act. Section 4 referred to five other classes of contracts.

During the more than three centuries of its existence, the Statute of Frauds has won widespread praise and generated more than its share of criticism.[3] Certainly, the original conditions that contributed to its passage have changed: parties are competent to testify, and judges have a host of mechanisms available to control runaway juries. In England, the statute came to be viewed as an

---

[1]   *See* E.A. Farnsworth *Contracts* § 6.1 (2d ed. 1990); 6 W. Holdsworth, *History of English Law* 379–397 (1924).

[2]   Stat. 29 Car. 2, c. 3

[3]   Two classic law review articles stated the arguments for and against the statute over 60 years ago, and the arguments have changed little since that time. The article supporting the statute is Vold, *The Application of the Statute of Frauds Under the Uniform Sales Act*, 15 Minn. L. Rev. 391 (1931). The article urging repeal is Willis, *The Statute of Frauds—a Legal Anachronism*, 3 Ind. L.J. 427 (1928).

anachronism, and in 1954 all but the suretyship provision and the land provision were repealed.[4] The statute retains much of its original vigor in the
United States, although many exceptions have sprung up over the years. The
modern justification for the statute is aptly described in the following note,
which precedes section 110 of the Restatement (Second) of Contracts:

> In general, the primary purpose of the statute is presumed to be evi-
> dentiary, to provide reliable evidence of the existence and terms of the
> contract, and the classes of contracts covered seem for the most part to
> have been selected because of importance or complexity. Historical re-
> cords provide no evidence that the draftsmen had a cautionary pur-
> pose, but the Statute serves such a purpose at least in the cases covered
> by the suretyship and marriage provisions. The land contract provi-
> sion, together with formal requirements for the conveyance of land,
> performs a channeling function; it has helped to create a climate in
> which parties often regard their agreements as tentative until there is
> a signed writing. These additional functions have sometimes been re-
> flected in judicial decisions and have played a part in discussion of the
> desirability of repeal.

Opponents of the Statute counter these points by arguing that, now that the
procedural conditions prevalent in the seventeenth century have changed, the
statute actually serves to promote fraud by encouraging parties seeking to
avoid liability to perjure themselves. They argue that juries today are well-
equipped to determine the truth or falsity of one party's claim that an oral contract was created.

§ 3.02   THE CODE'S GENERAL STATUTE OF FRAUDS PROVISION [1–206]

The basic Statute of Frauds for Article 2 is set out in section 2–201(1), which
requires a signed writing for any contract for the sale of goods where the price
is $500 or more. Section 2A–201(1)(a) requires a writing for leases, but the
threshold monetary value is raised to $1,000.[5] These sections are not the Code's
only statutes of frauds. Section 8–319 creates a Statute of Frauds for the sale of
securities; section 9–203 does likewise for secured transactions. There are also
writing requirements for letters of credit[6] and for goods sold on sale or return.[7]

---

4   Grunfeld Law Reform (Enforcement of Contracts) Act, 1954, 2 & 3 Eliz. 2, c. 34.
5   The $1,000 measure is for total payments to be made under the lease, and excludes pay-
    ments for options to renew or buy. UCC § 2A–201(1)(a).
6   UCC § 5–104.
7   UCC § 2–326(4). *See* Consolidated Foods Corp. v. Roland Foods, Inc., 13 UCC Rep. Serv.
    245 (D.C. Super. Ct. 1973) (an oral agreement adding a right to return goods subject to a
    contract for sale is invalid).

These provisions encompass contracts for the sale of a wide variety of assets, but they do not cover all forms of personal property. For example, they do not cover the sale of the goodwill of a business. Section 1–206 provides a "gap-filler" Statute of Frauds for sales of personal property not covered by the Code's other provisions. It states that a contract for the sale of personal property is not enforceable "beyond five thousand dollars in amount or value of remedy unless there is some writing which indicates that a contract for sale has been made between the parties at a defined or stated price, reasonably identifies the subject matter, and is signed by the party against whom enforcement is sought."

This provision has been applied to the sale of a limited partnership,[8] the sale of a loan portfolio,[9] and the sale of a business that included an office lease and equipment.[10] This last example raises a difficult problem of scope. When the sale of a business includes both tangible and intangible assets, does it fall within section 1–206 or is it governed by section 2–201? The courts have generally approached this problem by determining which aspect of the sale predominates.[11]

Section 1–206 differs from section 2–201 in some important respects. First, as will be explained, section 2–201 does not require that the signed writing contain a price term. This requirement is explicit in section 1–206. Second, section 2–201 states simply that an oral contract for the sale of goods for $500 or more is not enforceable (either affirmatively or by way of defense), whereas section 1–206 contains a curious phrase that makes an oral contract for the sale of personalty unenforceable (again, affirmatively or defensively) "beyond five thousand dollars in amount or value of remedy." By stating the value of the remedy, section 1–206, unlike any other Statute of Frauds provision, appears to make certain contracts partially enforceable. Thus, a party seeking to enforce an oral contract for the sale of personalty not covered by the more specific Statute of Frauds provisions can introduce evidence of the agreement and recover damages for breach in an amount up to, but not beyond, $5,000.[12]

---

8   In re Bicoastal Corp., 117 B.R. 696, 12 UCC Rep. Serv. 2d 638 (Bankr. M.D. Fla. 1990) (oral contract unenforceable despite plaintiff's reliance in declining other offers).

9   Dairyland Fin. Corp. v. Federal Intermediate Credit Bank, 852 F.2d 242, 6 UCC Rep. Serv. 2d 622 (7th Cir. 1988).

10 Beldengreen v. Ashinsky, 139 Misc. 2d 766, 528 N.Y.S.2d 744, 6 UCC Rep. Serv. 2d 1053 (Civ. Ct. 1987).

11 See, e.g., Wikler v. Mar-Van Indus., Inc., 39 Pa. D.&C. 3d 136, 2 UCC Rep. Serv. 2d 1190 (Pa. Ct. C.P. 1984) (contract not within UCC § 1–206 where 98 percent of the value was related to tangible goods); Olympic Juniors, Inc. v. David Crystal, Inc., 463 F.2d 1141, 10 UCC Rep. Serv. 1138 (3d Cir. 1972) (contract within § 1–206).

12 See, e.g., Olympic Juniors, Inc. v. David Crystal, Inc., 463 F.2d 1141, 10 UCC Rep. Serv.

§ 3.03   SPECIFIC STATUTE OF FRAUDS PROVISIONS [2–201(1); 2A-201(1)]

The basic Statute of Frauds for Article 2 is stated in section 2–201(1) as follows:

> Except as otherwise provided in this section a contract for the sale of goods for the price of $500 or more is not enforceable by way of action or defense unless there is some writing sufficient to indicate that a contract for sale has been made between the parties and signed by the party against whom enforcement is sought or his authorized agent or broker. A writing is not insufficient because it omits or incorrectly states a term agreed upon but the contract is not enforceable under this paragraph beyond the quantity of goods shown in the writing.

Although comparable to this provision, section 2A–201(1) includes some variations that are necessary to accommodate leases.

Section 2–201(1) does not require that all the terms of the agreement be in the writing.[13] It does not even require that all express terms be in the writing. All that is explicitly required for an effective writing is a skeletal note that contains the following elements:

1. the signature of the party against whom enforcement is sought (or his or her authorized agent or broker);

2. sufficient information to identify the parties and show that a contract for sale exists between them; and

3. a quantity term.

1138 (3d Cir. 1972); In re Bicoastal Corp., 117 B.R. 696, 12 UCC Rep. Serv. 2d 638 (Bankr. M.D. Fla. 1990).

[13] The Code's writing requirement should be contrasted with the common-law requirement for contracts within other Statute of Frauds classifications. Restatement (First) of Contracts § 207 required that the writing contain "the terms and conditions of all the promises constituting the contract and by whom and to whom the promises are made." Restatement (Second) of Contracts § 131 requires that the writing state the essential terms of the unperformed promises. In other words, the First Restatement required that the details of all the promises (whether performed or unperformed) be in the writing, while the Second Restatement is satisfied by a writing that establishes the broad outlines of the unperformed promises even if it omits the details. Both of these approaches require far more information than does UCC § 2–201(1). *See, e.g.,* AP Propane, Inc. v. Sperback, 157 A.D. 2d 27, 555 N.Y.S.2d 211, 12 UCC Rep. Serv. 2d 35 (App. Div. 1990), *aff'd,* 77 N.Y.2d 886, 568 N.Y.S.2d 908, 571 N.E.2d 78 (1991) (Code displaces other law requiring that terms like price be contained in the writing).

In a lease transaction, the writing must also contain a description of the goods leased and the lease term.[14]

In the absence of a Statute of Frauds, oral contracts are enforceable. A party seeking enforcement would prove its terms by introducing evidence (oral testimony, correspondence, etc.) of any express understandings plus evidence (trade usage, course of dealing, or course of performance) of any terms to be inferred from the surrounding circumstances. The other party would be free to refute this evidence, and ultimately the fact-finder would determine the existence and scope of the agreement. The agreement would then be supplemented with any necessary Code gap-fillers (implied-in-law terms).[15] If a memorandum that complies with the Code's minimal requirements is introduced, the bar of the Statute of Frauds is lowered and the parties are free to prove the terms of the contract by introducing extrinsic evidence, as described above.[16]

The production of a sufficient writing does not of itself establish that the parties entered into an enforceable contract. Even though the bar of the statute has been lowered, the defendant can still introduce evidence to show that, despite the writing, the parties never in fact reached a binding agreement. For example, the fact that the seller introduces a memorandum apparently indicating the sale of a certain quantity of goods does not preclude the buyer from attempting to show that the memorandum represents a misunderstanding on the seller's part.

The elements of a sufficient writing are discussed in the ensuing subsections.

[A]   The Writing Requirement

Consistent with the common law, the writing need not appear on a single document. Several writings can be combined to satisfy section 2–201(1).[17] For example, the buyer's signed offer to purchase a particular quantity of goods

---

[14] UCC § 2A–201(1)(b).

[15] This process is discussed in § 2.01 *supra*.

[16] If the writing that satisfies the Statute of Frauds is also a final writing for purposes of the parol evidence rule, extrinsic evidence may be excluded. See § 4.02[C] *infra*. Also, UCC § 2–201(1) limits the use of extrinsic evidence to vary the writing's quantity term. See § 3.03[D] *infra*.

[17] *See, e.g.*, Waltham Truck Equip. Corp. v. Massachusetts Equip. Co., 7 Mass. App. 580, 389 N.E.2d 753, 26 UCC Rep. Serv. 613 (1979) (three writings combined to satisfy statute); Nebraska Builders Prods. Co. v. Industrial Erectors, Inc., 239 Neb. 744, 478 N.W.2d 257, 16 UCC Rep. Serv. 2d 568 (1992) (several letters considered together); Azevedo v. Minister, 86 Nev. 576, 471 P.2d 661, 7 UCC Rep. Serv. 1281 (1970) (multiple accounting statements sent by seller held sufficient). *Contra*, Songbird Jet Ltd., Inc. v. Amax, Inc., 581 F. Supp. 912, 38 UCC Rep. Serv. 431 (S.D.N.Y. 1984) (decision based on pre-Code law).

might not be sufficient to overcome the buyer's Statute of Frauds defense.[18] However, a written acceptance from the seller would cure this deficiency. The two writings in combination show that a contract exists, and the offer contains the quantity term and the buyer's signature. For another example, an unsigned writing could indicate that a contract had been entered into, and the requisite signature could be found on a check given by the buyer to the seller as a down payment.[19]

When multiple writings are used, are sufficient internal cross-references necessary to show their relationship to the same transaction, or can this connection be shown by extrinsic evidence? Pre-Code courts split on this issue, and, not surprisingly, the split continues. The court in *West Central Packing, Inc. v. A.F. Murch Co.*[20] allowed the jury to consider any combination of writings, while the court in *Horn & Hardart Co. v. Pillsbury Co.*[21] insisted that the writing showing that a contract existed had to be signed and that any unsigned writings used to satisfy the other requirements had to show on their face that they were part of the same transaction.

Pre-Code law did not require that the writing be approved by both parties. Indeed, one party could prepare a file memo after reaching an oral understanding and, if the memo was produced during discovery, it could be used against its author. In some states, a party could even show that a sufficient memo existed at one time but disappeared.[22] These approaches should not be any less effective under Articles 2 and 2A.

[B]   The Signature Requirement

Under section 2–201(1), an effective writing must be signed by the party to be charged. The Code treats the concept of "signed" broadly to include "any symbol executed or adopted by a party with present intention to authenticate

---

[18] The authorities are split regarding the sufficiency of a signed offer. See discussion in § 3.03[C] *infra*.

[19] A check, standing alone, might be sufficiently complete to satisfy the statute. Also, the check could constitute a payment that would bring the contract within an exception to the statute. *See* UCC § 2–201(3)(c).

[20] 109 Mich. App. 493, 311 N.W.2d 404, 32 UCC Rep. Serv. 1361 (1981). *See also*, Migerobe, Inc. v. Certina USA, Inc., 924 F.2d 1330, 14 UCC Rep. Serv. 2d 59 (5th Cir. 1991) (there must be a sufficiently strong connection to suggest that the writings relate to the same transaction).

[21] 703 F. Supp. 1062, 8 UCC Rep. Serv. 2d 354 (S.D.N.Y. 1989).

[22] *Cf.* Sebasty v. Perschke, 404 N.E.2d 1200, 29 UCC Rep. Serv. 39 (Ind. Ct. App. 1980) (proof of lost confirming memorandum admissible for merchant seeking to use UCC § 2–201(2)).

[handwritten: Cts have been liberal in construing this provision]

a writing."[23] The courts have been quite liberal in construing this provision. For example, a letterhead has been held to satisfy the signature requirement,[24] as have a typed name,[25] a hand-printed name at the top of a memorandum,[26] a company name on a sales brochure,[27] the minutes of a board of directors meeting,[28] and even a tape recording.[29] In *Procyon Corp. v. Components Direct, Inc.*,[30] a buyer that directed its bank to issue a letter of credit was bound by the bank's signature. Obviously, the symbol must identify the party seeking to avoid enforcement. The courts nevertheless have had little difficulty in trivializing the signature requirement.

[C]　Sufficient to Show a Contract

Article 2 requires that the writing "be sufficient to indicate that a contract for sale has been made between the parties,"[31] but the Comments are confusing with regard to the required level of specificity. On the one hand, the Comments state, "[a]ll that is required is that the writing afford a basis for believing that the offered oral evidence rests on a real transaction."[32] This suggests that the writing must make it more probable than not that the parties reached an agreement. The same Comment, however, goes on to state that the contract must "evidence a contract for the sale of goods."[33] This appears to create a certainty standard under which, looking at the face of the writing alone, one would conclude with certainty that a contract had been made. Not surprisingly, the confusion in the Comments has led to a split of authority in the courts.

---

[23]　UCC § 1–201(39).

[24]　*See, e.g.,* Automotive Spares Corp. v. Archer Bearings Co., 382 F. Supp. 513, 15 UCC Rep. Serv. 590 (N.D.Ill. 1974); First Valley Leasing, Inc. v. Goushy, 795 F. Supp. 693, 19 UCC Rep. Serv. 2d 1002 (D.N.J. 1992). This approach is supported by UCC § 1–201, Comment 39.

[25]　*See, e.g.,* A & G Constr. Co., Inc. v. Reid Bros. Logging Co., Inc., 547 P.2d 1207, 19 UCC Rep. Serv. 37 (Alaska 1976).

[26]　*See, e.g.,* Southwest Eng'g Co. v. Martin Tractor Co., 205 Kan. 684, 473 P.2d 18, 7 UCC Rep. Serv. 1288 (1970) (interpreting UCC § 1–206).

[27]　*See, e.g.,* Barber & Ross Co. v. Lifetime Doors, Inc., 810 F.2d 1276, 3 UCC Rep. Serv. 2d 41 (4th Cir. 1987), *cert. denied,* 484 U.S. 823, 108 S. Ct. 86, 98 L. Ed. 2d 48 (1987).

[28]　Modern Mach. v. Flathead County, 202 Mont. 140, 656 P.2d 206, 36 UCC Rep. Serv. 395 (1982).

[29]　*See, e.g.,* Ellis Canning Co. v. Bernstein, 348 F. Supp. 1212, 11 UCC Rep. Serv. 443 (D. Colo. 1972).

[30]　203 Cal. App. 3d 409, 249 Cal. Rptr. 813, 6 UCC Rep. Serv. 2d 655 (Cal. Ct. App. 1988).

[31]　UCC § 2–201(1). Article 2A is consistent. § 2A–201(1)(b).

[32]　UCC § 2–201, Comment 1.

[33]　*Id.*

Many courts have held that the statute cannot be satisfied by an offer,[34] an application,[35] a proposal,[36] or a statement that a future contract is intended.[37] The language of the Code, which seems to require that the writing show that a contract presently exists,[38] supports these decisions. Courts adopting this approach have held that the writing cannot be supplemented by testimony of oral understandings to show that the parties later reached an agreement, since doing so would create the risk of perjury that led to adoption of the statute in the first place.[39] For example, the recipient of a signed offer would not be permitted to introduce evidence of an oral acceptance.[40] The court in *Smith Packing Co. v. Quality Pork International, Inc.*[41] failed to fully understand the nature of the evidence to be excluded. The court refused to admit testimony showing that the party who signed an otherwise sufficient writing was acting as the defendant's agent. The decision is wrong. Once a sufficient writing is produced, the barrier of the statute is lowered. Nothing in section 2–201(1) requires that the signer's authority be apparent from the face of the writing.

Other courts, relying on common-law precedents,[42] have held that the statute can be satisfied by a writing that does not explicitly demonstrate the existence of a contract.[43] These courts have the better argument. The Code drafters clearly intended to relax the writing requirement, and they did not likely intend to require a more explicit showing that a contract exists than was required at common law.[44] The correct approach is illustrated by *Barber & Ross*

---

[34] *See, e.g.,* Howard Constr. Co. v. Jeff-Cole Quarries, Inc., 669 S.W.2d 221, 37 UCC Rep. Serv. 1040 (Mo. Ct. App. 1983); Conaway v. 20th Century Corp., 491 Pa. 189, 420 A.2d 405, 29 UCC Rep. Serv. 1387 (1980).

[35] *See, e.g.,* McClure v. Duggan, 674 F. Supp. 211, 5 UCC Rep. Serv. 2d 925 (N.D. Tex. 1987).

[36] *See, e.g.,* Oakley v. Little, 49 N.C. App. 650, 272 S.E.2d 370, 30 UCC Rep. Serv. 675 (1980) (note outlining a proposed sale held insufficient); Arcuri v. Weiss, 198 Pa. Super. 506, 184 A.2d 24, 1 UCC Rep. Serv. 45 (1962) (writing stated that agreement was tentative).

[37] *See, e.g.,* John H. Wickersham Eng'g & Constr., Inc. v. Arbutus Steel Co., 1 UCC Rep. Serv. 49 (Pa. Ct. C.P. 1962) (writing stated intent to award contract).

[38] *See* UCC § 2–201(1) (writing must be sufficient to show that a contract *"has been* made" [emphasis supplied]).

[39] *See, e.g.,* Bazak Int'l Corp. v. Mast Indus., Inc., 73 N.Y.2d 113, 538 N.Y.S.2d 503, 535 N.E.2d 633, 7 UCC Rep. Serv. 2d 1380, 82 A.L.R. 4th 689 (1989).

[40] A written acceptance could be introduced to show that the two writings, taken together, satisfy the statute. See the discussion of multiple writings in § 3.03[A] *infra.*

[41] 167 A.D.2d 875, 561 N.Y.S.2d 970, 13 UCC Rep. Serv. 2d 698 (App. Div. 1990).

[42] *See, e.g.,* Tymon v. Linoki, 16 N.Y.2d 293, 213 N.E.2d 661 (1965) (signed offer to sell land sufficient in action against offeror). *See also* Restatement (Second) of Contracts § 133, Illustration 2; § 131, Comment f.

[43] *See, e.g.,* General Matters, Inc. v. Penny Products, Inc., 651 F.2d 1017, 31 UCC Rep. Serv. 1556 (5th Cir. 1981).

[44] *See, e.g.,* Monetti, S.P.A. v. Anchor Hocking Corp., 931 F.2d 1178, 14 UCC Rep. Serv. 2d 706 (7th Cir. 1991) (suggesting that, notwithstanding the verb tense chosen by the drafters, it is unlikely that they would weaken the writing requirement generally yet strengthen it in this respect).

Co. v. Lifetime Doors, Inc.[45] The seller sent the buyer sales literature promising that the seller would be able to meet all of the buyer's demands for doors if the buyer would agree to purchase exclusively from the seller. The buyer was permitted to introduce evidence showing that the parties later reached an oral agreement. The court held that the writing was sufficient to lower the bar of the statute because, citing the Comments, it provided "a basis for believing that the offered oral evidence rests on a real transaction."

[D] The Quantity Term

Virtually all of the cases have held that section 2–201(1) requires a written quantity term,[46] but nothing in the statute itself mandates this result. The language relied on by the courts is the last sentence of section 2–201(1), which states that "[a] writing is not insufficient because it omits or incorrectly states a term agreed upon but the contract is not enforceable under this paragraph beyond the quantity of goods shown in such writing."[47]

All this sentence really indicates is that if the writing contains a quantity term, the party seeking enforcement cannot enforce a contract for a greater quantity. The statute does not expressly state that the writing must indicate a quantity.[48] Nevertheless, this distinction has largely been lost on the courts, and as a practical matter the party seeking enforcement must show that the writing makes reference to a particular quantity. The courts' approach finds support in the Comments, which state, "The only term which must appear is the quantity term which need not be accurately stated but recovery is limited to the amount stated."[49] Quantity may be expressed in terms of output or requirements,[50] and a letter indicating that a dealership agreement existed was

---

[45] 810 F.2d 1276, 3 UCC Rep. Serv. 2d 41 (4th Cir. 1987). *See also* Impossible Elec. Techniques, Inc. v. Wackenhut Protective Systems, Inc., 669 F.2d 1026, 33 UCC Rep. Serv. 806 (5th Cir. 1982) (permitting evidence of oral understanding to be introduced to connect purchase order to contract).

[46] *See, e.g.*, Ivey's Plumbing & Elec. Co. v. Petrochem Maintenance, Inc., 463 F. Supp. 543, 26 UCC Rep. Serv. 621 (N.D. Miss. 1978); Alabama Great Southern R.R. Co. v. McVay, 381 So.2d 607, 29 UCC Rep. Serv. 767 (Miss. 1980); Columbus Trade Exch., Inc. v. AMCA Int'l Corp., 763 F. Supp. 946, 15 UCC Rep. Serv. 2d 51 (S.D. Ohio 1991).

[47] Article 2A contains a comparable limitation. UCC § 2A–201(3).

[48] Only a few courts have picked up on this distinction. *See, e.g.*, Great Northern Packaging, Inc. v. General Tire and Rubber Co., 154 Mich. App. 777, 399 N.W.2d 408, 3 UCC Rep. Serv. 2d 51 (1986); Advent Sys., Ltd. v. Unisys Corp., 925 F.2d 670, 13 UCC Rep. Serv. 2d 669 (3d Cir. 1991) (dictum suggests that UCC § 2–201(1) does not require a quantity term).

[49] UCC § 2–201, Comment 1.

[50] *See, e.g.*, Riegle Fiber Corp. v. Anderson Gin Co., 512 F.2d 784, 16 UCC Rep. Serv. 1207 (5th Cir. 1975) ("all acceptable cotton" grown on a specified amount of acreage held sufficient); Marion Square Corp. v. Kroger Co., 873 F.2d 72, 8 UCC Rep. Serv. 2d 913 (4th Cir. 1989) (all equipment at a stated location held sufficient). Output and requirement contracts are discussed generally in § 4.05[C] *infra*.

sufficient even though it was totally silent as to quantity because a dealership is, by definition, a requirements contract.[51]

Section 2–201(1) makes it clear that a contract will not be enforced beyond the quantity shown in the writing, which is illustrated in *Ivey's Plumbing & Electric Co. v. Petrochem Maintenance, Inc.*,[52] where the seller unsuccessfully argued that the parties had actually agreed on five units when the writing indicated a quantity of two. Conversely, if the writing had stated five, the Statute of Frauds would not have prevented one of the parties from arguing that it was a mistake and that the actual agreement was for two units.[53]

[E]   Terms Describing the Goods and Duration—Leases

In addition to the quantity term, Article 2A requires the writing to "describe the goods leased and the lease term."[54] Because a lease gives a lessee the right to use the goods for a period of time, duration is as crucial to a lease transaction as quantity. Article 2A therefore treats the duration term the same as it does the quantity term: the contract is not enforceable beyond the duration shown in the writing.[55] In addition to providing evidence of the goods that are to be returned to the lessor at the end of the lease term, the requirement that the goods be described serves a function comparable to Article 9's requirement that a security agreement include a description of the collateral.[56] The description identifies the affected property for purposes of third-party claims, as well as the relationship of the parties to the transaction. Article 2A is consistent with Article 9 in providing that the description of the goods or the lease term is sufficient "whether or not it is specific, if it reasonably identifies what is described."[57]

---

[51]   *See* Seaman's Direct Buying Service v. Standard Oil Co., 36 Cal.3d 752, 206 Cal. Rptr. 354, 686 P.2d 1158, 39 UCC Rep. Serv. 46 (1984). *See also* Jo-Ann, Inc. v. Alfin Fragrances, Inc., 731 F. Supp. 149, 11 UCC Rep. Serv. 2d 782 (D.N.J. 1989) (implied obligation to use best efforts in exclusive distributorship held to satisfy requirement for a quantity term).

[52]   463 F. Supp. 543, 26 UCC Rep. Serv. 621 (N.D. Miss. 1978).

[53]   If the written memorandom qualified as a final writing for purposes of the parol evidence rule, any extrinsic evidence of a different quantity would be excluded except for the purpose of showing that the writing should be reformed. Just because a writing satisfies the Statute of Frauds does not mean that it is also final for purposes of invoking the parol evidence rule. A final writing requires the parties to agree on the form of expression. A written memo may be no more than one party's recollection of a conversation.

The parol evidence rule is discussed in general in § 4.02 *infra*. The requirements for a final writing are discussed in § 4.02[B], and the use of reformation to overcome the rule is discussed in § 4.02[H].

[54]   UCC § 2A–201(1)(b).

[55]   UCC § 2A–201(3).

[56]   UCC § 9–203(1)(a).

[57]   UCC § 2A–201(2) (based on § 9–110).

§ 3.04   STATUTORY EXCEPTIONS: THE WRITTEN CONFIRMATION RULE [2–201(2)]

The Code contains several statutory exceptions to the writing requirement. The first is exclusive to Article 2. There is nothing similar to it at common law, and the drafters of Article 2A chose not to replicate it.[58] The exception, which represents a significant loosening of the signature requirement, is stated in section 2–201(2) as follows:

> Between merchants if within a reasonable time a writing in confirmation of the contract and sufficient against the sender is received and the party receiving it has reason to know its contents, it satisfies the requirements of subsection (1) against such party unless written notice of objection to its contents is given within 10 days after it is received.

Put simply, a writing that would satisfy the Statute of Frauds as to the merchant who signed it can also satisfy the statute as to another merchant who has not signed it. Merchants who fail to read their mail do so at their peril.

The written confirmation rule was designed to remedy the following problem. Suppose the buyer calls the seller and places an order for future goods that falls within section 2–201(1). The seller will frequently respond with a written confirmation of the order and be bound, but the buyer, who has signed nothing, is not bound and can now speculate at the seller's expense. If the market price rises, the buyer enforces the contract. If it falls, the buyer refuses to accept the goods and raises the Statute of Frauds if the seller attempts to enforce the contract. The written confirmation rule prevents the buyer from playing this game.

The Code does not make the contents of the written confirmation binding on the recipient. Section 2–201(2) specifies that the effect of a written confirmation is to satisfy the requirements of section 2–201(1) as against the recipient, preventing that party from raising the Statute of Frauds. The recipient is still free to introduce extrinsic evidence to show that in fact no contract was ever formed or that a contract was created but its terms differ significantly from those contained in the confirmation.[59] Terms in the confirmation may become part of the contract under the rules of section 2–207,[60] but nothing in section 2–201 makes them effective.

---

[58] The exception in UCC § 2–201(2) is based on one party sending a written confirmation of the contract to the other party. The drafters of Article 2A considered this exception superfluous in the leasing context because of the very limited observance of the practice in the leasing industry. *See* UCC § 2A–201, Comment.

[59] The recipient would not be able to show a quantity term beyond that stated in the confirmation.

[60] See discussion of the "battle of the forms" in § 2.05 *supra*.

At least one court lost sight of this distinction. In *Milltex Industries Corp. v. Jacquard Lace Co., Ltd.*,[61] a seller of unfinished textiles sent the buyer a confirmation letter showing that the parties had agreed on a price of $4.50 per pound. The buyer, who had failed to object to the confirmation, argued that the parties had in fact agreed on $4.15 per pound. The court held that the buyer's failure to object meant that it had acquiesced to the seller's price. The decision is wrong.[62] The buyer's failure to object did no more than preclude the buyer from using the Statute of Frauds as a defense. Nothing in the Code precludes the buyer from introducing extrinsic evidence of the parties' real agreement on price.[63]

The mailbox rule does not apply to written confirmations. Confirmations must be received to be effective, and the recipient can avoid the effect of a confirmation by sending a written objection within 10 days following receipt. The time of receipt can be an issue, so the Code provides guidance on this point.[64]

[A] Contents of the Written Confirmation

To satisfy section 2–201(2), a written confirmation must be "sufficient against the sender." This requirement means that the confirmation must contain enough detail to prevent the sender from successfully raising the Statute of Frauds as a defense. In other words, it must meet all the requirements of section 2–201(1) with respect to the sender. Thus, section 2–201(2) will not bind the recipient unless the sender is also bound.

An element that has been frequently litigated under the written confirmation rule is the section 2–201(1) requirement that the writing indicate the existence of a contract for the sale of goods.[65] In *Kline Iron & Steel Co., Inc. v. Gray*

---

[61] 557 So. 2d 1222, 12 UCC Rep. Serv. 2d 44 (Ala. 1990).

[62] For a decision that reached the correct result on this issue, see Pacific Western Resin Co. v. Condux Pipe Sys., Inc., 771 F. Supp. 313, 16 UCC Rep. Serv. 2d 38 (D. Or. 1991).

[63] Two possible alternative approaches have some superficial appeal for the seller, but each fails ultimately. First, under the battle of the forms, the price term in the seller's confirmation does not become part of the contract automatically because it is material. *See* UCC § 2–207(2)(b), and the discussion in § 2.05[C][1] *supra*. Second, the parol evidence rule does not preclude the buyer from introducing extrinsic evidence of a different price because the seller's confirmation does not qualify as a final writing. *See* § 2–202, and the discussion in § 4.02[A], n. 11, *infra*.

[64] UCC § 1–201(26) states that "[a] person 'receives' a notice or notification when (a) it comes to his attention; or (b) it is duly delivered at the place of business through which the contract was made or at any other place held out by him as the place for receipt of such communications." *See also* Thompson Printing Mach. Co. v. B.F. Goodrich Co., 714 F.2d 744, 36 UCC Rep. Serv. 737 (7th Cir. 1983) (receipt occurs even if mailroom personnel mishandle confirmation).

[65] This requirement is discussed in § 3.03[C] *supra*.

Communications Consultant, Inc.,[66] the seller's written confirmation requested the buyer to sign and return it. The court held that this request indicated that no contract existed until the buyer complied. The *Kline* decision is troubling because it puts the sender of the confirmation in a bind. Due to the "battle of the forms," a party sending a written confirmation can reasonably ask the other party to sign and return it because compliance will bind the other party to any different or additional terms contained in the confirmation.[67] The court in *Busby, Inc. v. Smoky Valley Bean, Inc.*[68] recognized the dilemma and held that a mere request that the recipient sign and return a written confirmation does not prevent it from being effective under section 2–201(2).

The *Busby* decision advances the better analysis. The court in *Kline* appears to have confused the written confirmation rule with the relatively rare situation in which the parties intend that there be no binding contract until each party signs a writing.[69] Nothing in *Kline* suggests that the parties were still engaged in preliminary negotiations at the time the written confirmation was sent. Nevertheless, to avoid confusion the safest approach would be to have the confirmation form first state that it is confirming an existing contract and then state that the signature is requested for the sole purpose of indicating assent to additional and different terms.

At least one court has suggested that a written confirmation must have additional language that expressly states that it is a confirmation.[70] For example, it might state "This will confirm" or words to that effect. Such a requirement goes well beyond the language of section 2–201(2), and it was properly rejected by the New York Court of Appeals in *Bazak International Corp. v. Mast Industries, Inc.*[71]

[B]   The Merchant Requirement

Section 2–201(2) applies only when both parties are merchants, but courts should be careful in handling this issue. The term "merchant" is defined to include both someone who deals in the particular goods involved in the transaction and someone who "by his occupation holds himself out as having

---

[66]   715 F. Supp. 135, 9 UCC Rep. Serv. 2d 858 (D.S.C. 1989).

[67]   *See* discussion in § 2.05[B][2] *supra.*

[68]   767 F. Supp. 235, 15 UCC Rep. Serv. 2d 438 (D. Kan. 1991).

[69]   *See* Restatement (Second) of Contracts § 27.

[70]   *See* Trilco Terminal v. Prebilt Corp., 167 N.J. Super. 449, 400 A.2d 1237 (1979) (dictum).

[71]   73 N.Y.2d 113, 538 N.Y.S.2d 503, 535 N.E.2d 663, 7 UCC Rep. Serv. 2d 1380, 82 A.L.R.4th 689 (1989).

knowledge or skill peculiar to the practices or goods involved in the transaction."[72] The Comments explain the "practices" involved in a written confirmation situation as follows:

> Sections 2–201(2), 2–205, 2–207 and 2–209 rest on normal business practices which are or ought to be typical of and familiar to any person in business. For purposes of these sections almost every person in business would, therefore, be deemed to be a "merchant" under [the definition] since the practices involved in the transactions are non-specialized business practices such as answering mail.[73]

In other words, the term "merchant" is a flexible term and can mean different things in different contexts. When a hospital orders a computer and receives a written confirmation from the seller, it is a merchant and can be bound by section 2–201(2). When that same hospital later sells the computer as a used good, it is probably not a merchant for purposes of imposing the implied warranty of merchantability[74] since it has no particular expertise in computer products.[75]

§ 3.05   Statutory Exceptions: Exceptions Based on Equitable Principles [2–201(3); 2A–201(4)]

Articles 2 and 2A contain three statutory exceptions to the basic writing requirement of their respective Statutes of Frauds. Each of these exceptions is predicated on equitable considerations. The exceptions are discussed in the ensuing subsections.

Application of the exceptions poses a unique problem in the context of Article 2A. Enforcement of a lease is dependent upon knowing the duration of the lease, and the Article 2A Statute of Frauds thus requires that the writing must include such a provision in order to be sufficient. The duration of the lease will not always be apparent, however, when the statutory exceptions are applied. The drafters solved this problem by adding the following provision in Article 2A:

> The lease term under a lease contract referred to in [the statutory exception provision] is:
>
> (a) if there is a writing signed by the party against whom enforcement is sought or by that party's authorized agent specifying the lease term, the term so specified;

---

[72]   UCC § 2–104(1).
[73]   UCC § 2–104, Comment 2.
[74]   UCC § 2–314.
[75]   See UCC § 2–104, Comment 2. See also American Plastic Equip., Inc. v. CBS, Inc., 886 F.2d 521, 9 UCC Rep. Serv. 2d 848 (2d Cir. 1989).

(b) if the party against whom enforcement is sought admits in that party's pleading, testimony, or otherwise in court a lease term, the term so admitted; or

(c) a reasonable lease term.[76]

[A]   Specially Manufactured Goods [2–201(3)(a); 2A–201(4)(a)]

The first of the statutory exceptions, with its genesis in the concept of estoppel, is for specialty goods. Section 2–201(3)(a) states that no writing is required:

[i]f the goods are to be specially manufactured for the buyer and are not suitable for sale to others in the ordinary course of the seller's business and the seller, before notice of repudiation is received and under circumstances which reasonably indicate that the goods are for the buyer, has made either a substantial beginning of their manufacture or commitments for their procurement.

Article 2A states equivalent terms in the leasing context.[77]

The fact that the seller has begun to perform is taken as sufficient corroborative evidence that a contract exists, and the seller's reliance is protected by enforcement of the contract.[78] The exception is akin to the "part performance" rule for contracts transferring interests in realty.[79]

The key point is that the seller's reliance cannot be protected by resort to the marketplace. Since the goods are not suitable for sale to others, the seller's only recourse absent this provision would be to scrap them, undoubtedly at a significant sacrifice. With the protection of section 2–201(3)(a), the seller will have an adequate remedy. If the buyer repudiates while the goods are unfinished, the seller can pursue a lost-profit recovery.[80] If the buyer's breach occurs after the goods have been finished, the seller can recover the contract price.[81] Determining the level of reliance necessary to invoke the exception can be

---

[76] UCC § 2A–201(5).

[77] UCC § 2A–201(4)(a).

[78] A restitutionary cause of action would not work here because the buyer has not received a benefit.

[79] *See* Restatement (Second) of Contracts § 129.

[80] *See* UCC § 2–708(2) and the discussion in § 9.03 *infra*. The seller would not ordinarily be able to finish the goods and then sue for the price under UCC §§ 2–703(e) and 2–709(1)(b) because of the lack of a market for them.

[81] *See* UCC § 2–709(1)(b) and the discussion in § 9.04[A][3] *infra*.

tricky.[82] In *Chambers Steel Engraving Corp. v. Tambrands, Inc.*,[83] the seller alleged that the buyer had repudiated a contract for the purchase of at least 20 embossing machines. The seller argued that its reliance in building a complete prototype was sufficient to invoke the exception for specialty goods. The court held that the reliance was insufficient, stating that at least some evidence that funds had been expended on the actual goods to be sold was required.

The decision in *Chambers* is correct since a buyer might refuse to enter into a contract after examining a prototype. However, the court relied on a troubling precedent in reaching its conclusion. In *Epprecht v. IBM Corp.*,[84] a seller that had begun work on 7,000 parts tried to show that it had a contract for a total of 50,000 parts. The court held that the seller could recover for the 7,000 parts but not for the remaining 43,000. The decision is troubling because the court was, in effect, reading section 2–201(1)'s quantity term limitation into section 2–201(3)(a). However, section 2–201(3)(a) by its terms dispenses with the requirements of section 2–201(1).[85] Once there has been sufficient reliance to drop the bar of the Statute of Frauds, there is no reason why the parties should not be as free to introduce evidence regarding quantity as they are to introduce evidence regarding any other term, such as price.

As indicated above, a seller seeking to use the statutory exception must show that the goods are peculiar to the buyer and are not suitable for sale to another party in the normal course of the seller's business. In *Smith-Scharff Paper Co. v. P. N. Hirsch & Co. Stores, Inc.*,[86] for example, the statutory exception was clearly satisfied when the seller manufactured paper bags imprinted with the buyer's logo. By contrast, the court in *Jones v. Wide World of Cars, Inc.*[87] correctly held that a limited-production, high-quality sports car was suitable for sale to others and refused to enforce an alleged oral contract against the buyer. The key here is whether the goods can be rendered marketable to others with only minor alterations or whether wholesale changes are necessary.[88]

---

[82]   The issue is a question of law for the judge. *See, e.g.*, Chambers Steel Engraving Corp. v. Tambrands, Inc., 895 F.2d 858, 10 UCC Rep. Serv. 2d 1152 (1st Cir. 1990).

[83]   *Id.*

[84]   36 UCC Rep. Serv. 391 (E.D. Pa. 1983).

[85]   UCC §§ 2–201(3)(b) and (c) also contain quantity limitations. This makes the absence of such a limitation in § 2–201(3)(a) all the more conspicuous.

[86]   754 S.W.2d 298, 7 UCC Rep. Serv. 2d 38 (Mo. Ct. App. 1988).

[87]   820 F. Supp. 132, 21 UCC Rep. Serv. 2d 27 (S.D.N.Y. 1993).

[88]   *See, e.g.*, Impossible Elec. Techniques, Inc. v. Wackenhut Protective Systems, Inc., 669 F.2d 1026, 33 UCC Rep. Serv. 806 (5th Cir. 1982).

[B]   Admissions in Judicial Proceedings [2–201(3)(b); 2A–201(4)(b)]

At one time, a defendant could admit entering into a contract with the plaintiff but still raise the technical defense of the Statute of Frauds. This "laughing defendant" approach made a mockery of the statute's policy of preventing fraud. A party could use it as a positive instrument for the perpetration of fraud.

Section 2–201(3)(b) overturns the laughing defendant rule by creating an exception to the writing requirement:

[i]f the party against whom enforcement is sought admits in his pleading, testimony or otherwise in court that a contract for sale was made, but the contract is not enforceable under this provision beyond the quantity of goods admitted.

Article 2A includes a comparable exception in the lease context.[89]

What types of admissions are sufficient to satisfy the statute? The exception refers to an admission that "a contract" was made, but the existence of a contract is an ultimate conclusion to be drawn by the jury. The defendant who is asked whether he or she entered into a contract with the plaintiff might answer in the negative even while admitting the existence of underlying facts[90] from which the jury could conclude that a contract had been reached. The admission of those underlying facts is all that is necessary to overcome the writing requirement.[91]

Clearly, a voluntary admission in a pleading or on the witness stand in court will suffice to meet the exception. What about an involuntary admission elicited under cross-examination? Notwithstanding some pre-Code authority to the contrary,[92] it now appears settled that such involuntary admissions will satisfy the statute.[93]

---

[89]   UCC § 2A–201(4)(b).

[90]   *E.g.*, that the parties had engaged in a certain conversation or certain conduct.

[91]   *See, e.g.*, Quaney v. Tobine, 236 Kan. 201, 689 P.2d 844, 40 UCC Rep. Serv. 37 (1984); Lewis v. Hughes, 276 Md. 247, 346 A.2d 231, 18 UCC Rep. Serv. 52 (1975).

[92]   Lewis v. Hughes, 276 Md. 247, 346 A.2d 231, 18 UCC Rep. Serv. 52 (1975), contains an excellent discussion of the issue and an extensive listing of the authorities.

[93]   *See, e.g.*, Harvey v. McKinney, 221 Ill. App. 3d 140, 581 N.E.2d 786, 16 UCC Rep. Serv. 2d 1003 (1991); Lewis v. Hughes, 276 Md. 247, 346 A.2d 231, 18 UCC Rep. Serv. 52 (1975).

With one caveat, admissions contained in depositions, affidavits, responses to interrogatories or requests to admit also satisfy the statute.[94] Purely procedural admissions, such as the negative inference to be drawn from a failure to respond to a request to admit, do not qualify.[95] An affirmative statement by the defendant is required.

Perhaps the most intriguing question presented by this section is the extent to which the trial judge should allow the plaintiff to pursue discovery, or even go to trial, in an attempt to force the defendant to admit the existence of the contract. Suppose the defendant raises the Statute of Frauds as an affirmative defense and then files a motion for summary judgment. In response to the motion, the plaintiff asks the judge for an opportunity to depose the defendant in the hope of gaining a useful admission. Most courts will allow the plaintiff this opportunity,[96] although some authority to the contrary persists.[97]

Should a plaintiff whose discovery attempts fail be allowed to go to trial in order to cross-examine the defendant on the witness stand? On this issue, both the courts and commentators have split.[98] The argument favoring trial is that a defendant is most likely to admit the truth when faced with the majesty of the courtroom setting. The argument against is based on efficiency. A trial is unlikely to produce any results that discovery has not yielded, yet the defendant will have been forced to go to the expense of mounting a courtroom defense and the resources of the judicial system will have been needlessly utilized.

[C]   Goods Accepted or Payment Made [2–201(3)(c); 2A–201(4)(c)]

The third statutory exception states that no writing is required "with respect to goods for which payment has been made and accepted or which have

---

[94] *See, e.g.,* Oskey Gasoline & Oil Co. v. Continental Oil Co., 534 F.2d 1281, 19 UCC Rep. Serv. 61 (8th Cir. 1976) (deposition); Jackson v. Meadows, 153 Ga. App. 1, 264 S.E.2d 503, 28 UCC Rep. Serv. 990 (1980) (affidavit attached to motion for summary judgment).

[95] *See, e.g.,* Anthony v. Tidwell, 560 S.W.2d 908, 23 UCC Rep. Serv. 561 (Tenn. 1977) (inference drawn from filing motion to dismiss rather than raising affirmative defense insufficient to invoke UCC § 2–201(3)(b)).

[96] *See, e.g.,* Migerobe, Inc. v. Certina USA, Inc., 924 F.2d 1330, 14 UCC Rep. Serv. 2d 59 (5th Cir. 1991) (plaintiff entitled to enough discovery to determine whether defendant has internal documents that would satisfy the statute).

[97] *See, e.g.,* Triangle Mkt'g, Inc. v. Action Indus., Inc., 630 F. Supp. 1578, 1 UCC Rep. Serv. 2d 36 (N.D. Ill. 1986).

[98] The cases requiring trial appear to be more numerous. *See, e.g.,* Franklin County Coop. v. MFC Services, 441 So. 2d 1376, 37 UCC Rep. Serv. 1465 (Miss. 1983). *Contra,* Farmland Service Coop., Inc. v. Klein, 196 Neb. 538, 244 N.W.2d 86, 19 UCC Rep. Serv. 1063 (1976).

been received and accepted.''[99] The concept here is simple: a buyer's receipt and acceptance of goods or a seller's receipt and acceptance of payment constitutes sufficient corroborative evidence of a contractual relationship to allow elimination of the usual writing requirement. Of course, either party is still free to show that no contract really exists—for example, the buyer might try to show that a gift was intended—but the showing will be an uphill struggle.

· Under the Uniform Sales Act, part performance took away the entire Statute of Frauds defense, just as it still does in contracts for the transfer of an interest in real estate.[100] Under Article 2, part performance renders the contract enforceable only as to the quantity of goods accepted by the buyer, or the quantity for which the seller has received payment. In *Howard Construction Co. v. Jeff-Cole Quarries, Inc.*,[101] for example, the seller delivered base rock, for which it was paid. The buyer then sought to prove that the oral agreement also called for the seller to deliver asphaltic rock. The court correctly held that the statutory exception did not lower the bar of the Statute of Frauds for rock that was neither delivered nor paid for.

A problem arises repeatedly when buyers make a partial payment towards the purchase of a single, indivisible item. In *Lockwood v. Smigel*,[102] the buyer made a $100 down payment and later sued for breach of an oral contract to sell a 1961 Rolls-Royce Silver Shadow for $11,400. The court held that the partial payment entirely satisfied the Statute of Frauds. The court reasoned that the seller's acceptance of the money indicated that a contract existed, and the fact that the asset was indivisible precluded a dispute over quantity.

Receipt of goods can indicate a bailment rather than a contract for sale. That possibility created a difficult issue for the Nebraska Supreme Court in *Joseph Heiting & Sons v. Jacks Bean Co.*,[103] where a grain elevator regularly purchased some beans for its own use and received other beans as bailee, storing them for the producers. When it was sued by a producer for failing to pay for beans that it had allegedly purchased, the elevator raised the Statute of Frauds as a defense and argued that its receipt of the beans amounted to a mere bailment. The producer argued that by taking and keeping the beans, the elevator had lost the protection of the Statute of Frauds, and that it could make its bailment argument to the jury.

---

[99] UCC § 2-201(3)(c). The exception in Article 2A differs somewhat, as is explained in the text.

[100] *See* Restatement (Second) of Contracts § 129.

[101] 669 S.W.2d 221, 37 UCC Rep. Serv. 1040 (Mo. Ct. App. 1983).

[102] 18 Cal. App.3d 800, 96 Cal. Rptr. 289, 9 UCC Rep. Serv. 452 (1971). *See also* Sedmark v. Charlie's Chevrolet, Inc., 622 S.W.2d 694, 31 UCC Rep. Serv. 851, 26 A.L.R.4th 284 (Mo. Ct. App. 1981); W. I. Snyder Corp. v. Caracciolo, 373 Pa. Super. 486, 541 A.2d 775, 7 UCC Rep. Serv. 2d 993 (1988) (partial payment may be made with goods rather than money).

[103] 236 Neb. 765, 463 N.W.2d 817, 13 UCC Rep. Serv. 2d 336 (1990).

The Court remanded the case for further hearings, instructing the trial judge to focus on three factors: 1) whether the beans were out of the producer's control;[104] 2) whether the elevator exercised complete control; and 3) whether the particular beans could be returned to the producer.[105] In other words, the trial judge was instructed to make a preliminary determination as to whether the transaction looked more like a sale or a bailment. If it looked like a sale, the elevator could not use the Statute of Frauds because of its receipt and acceptance of the beans, although it could still try to convince the jury that, despite appearances, the parties had agreed to a bailment. If looked like a bailment, then the statute created a complete defense, and the producer could gain nothing more than the return of its beans (after paying for their storage).

Perhaps the court made too much of the issue. The Comments state:

The overt actions of the parties make admissible evidence of the other terms of the contract necessary to a just apportionment. This is true even though the actions of the parties are not inconsistent in themselves with a different transaction such as a consignment for resale or a mere loan of money.[106]

In other words, the mere fact that the elevator operator received and kept the beans should have been sufficient to lower the bar of the statute. The operator could then have tried to convince the jury that the agreement was in fact a bailment rather than a sale, presumably focusing on the factors discussed by the court.

Article 2A deviates from the statutory analogue by excluding the Article 2 exception for goods for which payment has been made and accepted.[107] The drafters reasoned that "[u]nlike a buyer in a sales transaction, the lessee does not tender payment in full for goods delivered, but only payment of rent for one or more months."[108] They concluded that rent payments were not a sufficient substitute for a signed writing.

This reasoning is unpersuasive. As the *Lockwood* case discussed previously so ably demonstrates, partial payment for the purchase of an indivisible item has been upheld as sufficient under the Article 2 exception because it meets the underlying objective of providing corroborative evidence of a sale while

---

[104] For example, the producer might have received a warehouse receipt giving it continuing control over the beans (or a fungible portion of commingled beans).

[105] It appeared that the beans had been commingled and, therefore, could not be returned.

[106] UCC § 2–201, Comment 2.

[107] The exception is retained for goods that have been received and accepted by the lessee. UCC § 2A–201(4)(c).

[108] UCC § 2A–201, Comment.

avoiding a dispute over the quantity of goods sold. When limited to a single item, an advance payment of rent serves precisely the same objective.

§ 3.06   NONSTATUTORY EXCEPTIONS: EQUITABLE AND PROMISSORY ESTOPPEL

Equitable estoppel, or estoppel *in pais*, has traditionally been viewed as an exception to the Statute of Frauds. More recently, many courts have also begun to accept promissory estoppel as an exception. An equitable estoppel generally requires a misrepresentation or concealment of existing facts, whereas promissory estoppel requires a promise regarding future facts. In either case, reasonable reliance by the party seeking to use the doctrine is a prerequisite.

Common-law courts have been quite strict about the facts that will support an equitable estoppel, requiring the plaintiff to show that the defendant made one of the following affirmative representations: 1) that the Statute of Frauds had been satisfied; 2) that the defendant would prepare a signed writing in the future; or 3) that the Statute of Frauds would not be used as a defense.[109]

The common-law courts that accept promissory estoppel often require a great deal of reliance. In one of the early cases utilizing the doctrine, the California Supreme Court held that to overcome the Statute of Frauds, the promisee's reliance must amount to an unconscionable injury.[110] Section 139 of the Second Restatement explicitly recognizes promissory estoppel as an exception to the Statute of Frauds, but it suggests that the promisee's reliance must be "definite and substantial"[111] and that other remedies, such as cancellation and restitution, must be insufficient to mitigate the harm.[112]

Despite a number of cases to the contrary, the trend seems to be to permit equitable or promissory estoppel to be used to overcome the Code's Statute of Frauds. The courts that have permitted the use of estoppel have cited section 1–103, which states that, unless displaced by the Code, common-law and equitable doctrines supplement its provisions.

A prime example is *R. S. Bennett & Co. v. Economy Mechanical Industries, Inc.*,[113] where the plaintiff, who wanted to sell equipment to be used in a water

---

[109] Even though the second and third affirmations amount to promises of future conduct, the courts lumped them in with equitable estoppel. *See* Restatement of Contracts § 178, Comment f.

[110] Monarco v. Lo Greco, 35 Cal. 2d 621, 220 P.2d 737 (1950).

[111] *See* Restatement (Second) of Contracts § 139(2)(b).

[112] *See* Restatement (Second) of Contracts § 139(2)(a).

[113] 606 F.2d 182, 27 UCC Rep. Serv. 345 (7th Cir. 1979).

reclamation project, made initial offers to three general contractors who were bidding on the project. Just before the bidding deadline, the plaintiff told each contractor that it would reveal a lower price if the contractor agreed to buy from it in the event the contractor was awarded the project. Each contractor agreed, but when the defendant won the project it refused to deal with the plaintiff, who then brought suit. The plaintiff argued that if the defendant had not agreed to buy from it, it would never have revealed the lower price and another contractor would have won the competition and purchased the equipment from it. Even though the Illinois Supreme Court had ruled some 25 years earlier that promissory estoppel could not be used to overcome the Statute of Frauds,[114] the Seventh Circuit Court of Appeals concluded that the use of promissory estoppel had become so commonplace that the Illinois Supreme Court, if faced with the issue again, would change its mind.[115]

Despite the trend, a number of courts still have held that the Code's Statute of Frauds, because it specifies three equity-based exceptions, has displaced supplemental common-law and equitable doctrines.[116] Even among those courts that have accepted the doctrines, some confusion persists as to the factors that will support its invocation. For example, in *Columbus Trade Exchange, Inc. v. AMCA Int'l Corp.*,[117] the court indicated that it was receptive to the use of promissory estoppel but that the plaintiff had not shown that it had suffered such an injury that failure to enforce the contract would amount to a manifest inequity.[118] The court gave little indication of what it would have considered sufficient, although it did cite section 139 of the Second Restatement with approval. Another, somewhat older example is *Sacred Heart Farmers Cooperative v. Johnson*,[119] where the court held that to work an estoppel the conduct must be unconscionable or akin to fraud.

---

[114] *See* Ozier v. Haines, 411 Ill. 160, 103 N.E.2d 485 (1952).

[115] Most of the recent opinions have accepted estoppel-based arguments. *See, e.g.*, Adams v. Petrade Int'l, Inc., 754 S.W.2d 696, 7 UCC Rep. Serv. 2d 369 (Tex. Civ. App. 1988); Massey v. Hardcastle, 753 S.W.2d 127, 7 UCC Rep. Serv.2d 661 (Tenn. Ct. App. 1988); Allen M. Campbell Co. v. Virginia Metal Indus., 708 F.2d 930, 36 UCC Rep. Serv. 384 (4th Cir. 1983).

[116] *See, e.g.*, Futch v. James River—Norwalk, Inc., 722 F. Supp. 1395, 10 UCC Rep. Serv. 2d 684 (S.D. Miss. 1989); Golden Plains Feedlot, Inc. v. Great W. Sugar Co., 588 F. Supp. 985, 39 UCC Rep. Serv. 785 (D.S.D. 1984); Renfroe v. Ladd, 701 S.W.2d 148, 42 UCC Rep. Serv. 547 (Ky. Ct. App. 1985).

[117] 763 F. Supp. 946, 15 UCC Rep. Serv. 2d 51 (S.D. Ohio 1991).

[118] *See also* Hoffman v. Boone, 708 F. Supp. 78, 9 UCC Rep. Serv. 2d 474 (S.D.N.Y. 1989) (insufficient injury even though prospective buyer of painting traveled from Florida to New York three times to finalize the contract and passed up the opportunity to buy other paintings).

[119] 305 Minn. 324, 232 N.W.2d 921, 17 UCC Rep. Serv. 901 (1975).

Notice that the court in *Columbus Trade Exchange* focused on the degree of harm, while the court in *Sacred Heart* focused on the culpability of the promisor. Obviously, a great deal remains to be settled with regard to this issue.

§ 3.07   THE EFFECTS OF NONCOMPLIANCE

Noncompliance with the Statute of Frauds generally renders a contract unenforceable. This consequence is different from declaring the contract void. Unenforceability refers to the lack of a remedy. In the words of the Second Restatement:

> Where a contract within the Statute of Frauds is not enforceable against the party to be charged by an action against him, it is not enforceable by a set-off or counterclaim in an action brought by him, or as a defense to a claim by him.[120]

The difference between voidness and unenforceability is significant. A void contract is an oxymoron—the contract does not exist for any purpose. By contrast, a contract that is unenforceable may later become enforceable, through either the creation of a complying memorandum, part performance, estoppel, or judicial admissions. The distinction has another important consequence. A party who has bestowed a benefit upon another may seek a restitutionary remedy,[121] and evidence of an unenforceable contract is admissible to show that the plaintiff did not bestow the benefit as a gift or as an officious intermeddler.[122]

Finally, the Statute of Frauds is generally viewed as an affirmative defense, meaning that it must be pleaded or it will be considered waived. If it is properly raised, the party seeking to overcome the statute will have the burden of showing that the statute has been satisfied by either producing a conforming writing or showing that the defendant's conduct brings the contract within one of the exceptions discussed in the preceding sections.

---

[120] Restatement (Second) of Contracts § 138.

[121] *See* Restatement (Second) of Contracts § 375; Restatement of Restitution § 108.

[122] *See* Restatement (Second) of Contracts § 143, Comment a, Illustration 1. See also A. Corbin, 2 *Contracts*, § 279 (rev. ed. 1960) for a discussion of other contexts in which the distinction is significant.

CHAPTER

4

Sources of Contract Terms

§ 4.01 INTRODUCTION

A contract's terms may have been agreed to by the parties, either expressly or by implication from the surrounding circumstances (implied-in-fact),[1] or they may have been injected into the contract by operation of law (implied-in-law).[2] Express terms are those the parties have articulated, either orally or in writing. Implied-in-fact terms are derived from either the status or the conduct of the parties. A term may be implied from a trade usage of which both parties are, or should be, aware; it may be implied from a course of dealing between the parties on prior contracts; or it may be implied from a course of performance between the parties on the contract in question.

If the parties' intent cannot be ascertained from their expressions or from the surrounding circumstances, the Code may provide a term as a matter of law. Such implied-in-law terms are commonly referred to as "gap-fillers." In effect, the Code creates a default contract for the parties that becomes operative in the absence of an agreement to the contrary. Prior to the creation of these gap-fillers, courts frequently found that agreements lacking such terms as

---

[1] An "agreement' is "the bargain of the parties in fact as found in their language or by implication from other circumstances including course of dealing or usage of trade or course of performance. . . . " UCC § 1–201(3). This definition should be compared with the definition of "contract" in note 2 *infra*. The distinction between "agreement" and "contract" is discussed in § 4.03[D] *infra* and in Chapter 2 on contract formation. *See* § 2.01 *supra*.

[2] The term "contract" refers to "the total legal obligation which results from the parties' agreement as affected by this Act and any other applicable rules of law." UCC § 1–201(11).

price, time and place of delivery, and time for payment were too indefinite to be enforced.

§ 4.02 THE PAROL EVIDENCE RULE

[A] Common Law

Subject to the limitations imposed by the Statute of Frauds, contracts need not be written to be enforceable. Nevertheless, parties frequently choose to reduce some or all of their understandings to written form, and when they do the parol evidence rule limits their ability to introduce evidence of terms not reflected in the writing. Because an understanding of the Code's version of the rule requires some familiarity with the rule's long and tortured common-law history, references to the common law will be intertwined with our discussion of the Code.

The parol evidence rule has been stated many ways,[3] but the following is a working statement of the common-law rule:

> When parties to a contract have reduced their agreement to a writing which they intend to be a final expression of at least some of their understandings, they may not introduce evidence of prior oral or written terms, or contemporaneous oral terms, that contradict the writing. They may, however, attempt to supplement the writing by introducing evidence of consistent additional terms. If they intend that the writing be both final and complete, even evidence of consistent additional terms will be excluded.

This statement creates some terminology problems. A writing is considered final when the parties have gone beyond the negotiating stage and have agreed that the language represents at least some of their understandings with respect to the contract. The Second Restatement uses the term "partial integration" to refer to a writing that is final but not complete.[4] A writing is complete (or, in the language of the Second Restatement, a "complete integration"[5]) when the parties intend for it to represent *all* of their understandings with respect to the contract. The terms "contradict" and "consistent" also create definitional problems, which will be dealt with in later sections.[6]

---

[3] *See, e.g.,* Restatement of Contracts §§ 237, 240; Restatement (Second) of Contracts §§ 210, 213; A. Corbin, 3 *Contracts* § 573 (rev. ed. 1960); S. Williston, 4 *Contracts* § 631 (3d ed. 1961); J. Wigmore, 9 *Evidence* § 2425 (3d ed. 1940).

[4] Restatement (Second) of Contracts § 210(2).

[5] Restatement (Second) of Contracts § 210(1).

[6] See §§ 4.02[E], 4.03[D] *infra*.

The term "parol evidence rule" is misleading in several respects. The word "parol," for example, means oral, but the parol evidence rule can exclude evidence of both oral and written understandings. Further, the rule is not a rule of evidence but operates instead as a rule of substantive law. In general, a rule of evidence deals with the appropriate method of proving a question of fact, and evidence is excluded if it is not relevant, is subject to serious credibility problems, or is susceptible to misuse by the jury. The parol evidence rule, by contrast, excludes extrinsic evidence on policy grounds even when it meets the ordinary tests for admissibility. The adoption of a final writing operates to discharge those understandings that are excluded by the rule.[7] In effect, the writing has superseded the understandings.

The parol evidence rule has the effect of elevating the written word to a preferred status, thereby eliminating risks of perjury and fading memories. Since it excludes evidence of extrinsic understandings (meaning understandings not reflected in the writing), the rule allows judges to control juries by keeping out evidence that they consider to be suspect in some way.[8] As we shall see, however, it often does so at the expense of the true agreement of the parties, and to that extent it can subvert the goal of fairly adjudicating a particular dispute. The tension between these policy goals has led to such inconsistent results that some commentators have despairingly concluded that the parol evidence rule lacks the certainty necessary to make it a "rule."[9]

[B] The Code's Formulation of the Rule [2–202; 2A–202]

Section 2–202 states in its entirety:

> Terms with respect to which the confirmatory memoranda of the parties agree or which are otherwise set forth in a writing intended by the parties as a final expression of their agreement with respect to such terms as are included therein may not be contradicted by evidence of any prior agreement or of a contemporaneous oral agreement but may be explained or supplemented

---

7   Restatement (Second) of Contracts § 213 states the proposition as follows:
  (1) A binding integrated agreement discharges prior agreements to the extent that it is inconsistent with them.
  (2) A binding completely integrated agreement discharges prior agreements to the extent that they are within its scope.

8   *See* McCormick, *The Parol Evidence Rule as a Procedural Device for the Control of the Jury*, 41 Yale L.J. 365 (1932).

9   *See, e.g.*, Broude, *The Consumer and the Parol Evidence Rule: Section 2–202 of the Uniform Commercial Code*, 1970 Duke L.J. 881, 884 ("even these leading academic commentators cannot agree about what the rule is, what it purports to exclude, and what evidence may be admitted despite its restrictions").

(a) by course of dealing or usage of trade (section 1–205) or by course of performance (section 2–208); and

(b) by evidence of consistent additional terms unless the court finds the writing to have been intended also as a complete and exclusive statement of the terms of the agreement.

The substance of section 2A-202 is identical.

Before proceeding further, a few brief points are in order. Under the Code a final writing includes "terms with respect to which the confirmatory memoranda of the parties agree." This is a reference to the "battle of the forms" provisions of section 2–207.[10] For example, suppose the buyer and the seller reach agreement over the telephone and each then sends a confirmatory memorandum to the other. The memoranda will inevitably go beyond the issues discussed by the parties, but they are clearly operative to the extent that they mirror each other. If each memorandum contains an arbitration clause, for example, disputes will be arbitrated. The parol evidence rule would preclude either party from introducing evidence showing that they had orally agreed not to arbitrate.[11]

Notice also that the statute refers to both explaining and supplementing final writings. The term "explained" refers to problems of interpretation, which will be considered separately from the parol evidence rule.[12] For now, our focus is on the process of supplementation. Further, ignore clause (a) for the moment, since it refers to a special kind of problem that will also be addressed separately.[13]

With these points in mind, look at the statute again. It really contains a very simple statement of the traditional rule: if a writing is final, it cannot be contradicted by evidence of any *prior* agreement (including both oral and written

---

[10] Article 2A deletes any provision comparable to UCC § 2–207.

[11] Where the confirmatory memoranda do not agree, the extent to which their provisions are operative is governed by UCC § 2–207, which is discussed in § 2.05 *supra*. If one party's provisions are operative by virtue of that section, the other party should be free to introduce extrinsic evidence to show that the parties in fact agreed on something different, even something contradictory. Since the memoranda do not agree, the parties have not mutually assented to a particular form of expression. *See, e.g.*, BNE Swedbank, S.A. v. Banker, 794 F. Supp. 1291, 20 UCC Rep. Serv. 2d 35 (S.D.N.Y. 1992)(parol evidence rule inapplicable where the only writing was a confirmatory memorandum sent by one party); Airstream, Inc. v. CIT Financial Services, Inc., 111 Idaho 307, 723 P.2d 851, 2 UCC Rep. Serv. 2d 816 (1986), *app. after remand*, 115 Idaho 569, 768 P.2d 1302 (1986).

[12] See § 4.04 *infra*.

[13] See § 4.02[G][1] *infra*.

agreements) or any *contemporaneous* oral agreement,[14] but it can be supplemented by evidence of consistent additional terms. If the court finds that the writing is also complete and exclusive, all supplementation is precluded.

[C] Finality

The first step in determining whether to invoke the parol evidence rule is to ascertain whether the parties have adopted a particular writing as a final expression of at least part of their agreement. One party may have made a memorandum of an oral agreement, but it will not be considered final even if it is sufficient to satisfy the Statute of Frauds.[15] The reason is that the other party never assented to the form of expression used in the writing. Likewise, the parties may have exchanged various writings during the course of their negotiations, and a draft advanced by one party but not assented to by the other will not be considered final.

Without a final writing, either party is free to introduce evidence tending to show that the parties agreed to certain terms. The jury will then determine the scope of the contract as an issue of fact. While the question of finality turns on the intent of the parties and is therefore an issue of fact, it will be decided by the trial judge.[16]

[D] Completeness

[1] Common Law

A final writing can still be supplemented by evidence of consistent additional terms, so the next step in the inquiry is to determine whether the writing is also complete. If the writing is obviously skeletal in nature, the judge can easily find that it is only a partial integration. The difficult issues arise when the writing appears complete on its face. The Code's test for completeness can be understood only in light of its common-law antecedents.

An early common-law approach, commonly referred to as the "four corners" doctrine, involved a two-step process. The judge first would look at the

---

[14] Evidence of contemporaneous writings can always be introduced, even if the writings are contradictory. The writings must be read as a whole, and if the jury cannot interpret them in a manner that renders them consistent, it will have to choose which writing best expresses the actual agreement of the parties.

[15] *See* note 11 *supra*.

[16] *See* Restatement (Second) of Contracts § 209(2) and Comment c. UCC § 2–202 is silent on this point, but it expressly allocates the issue of completeness to the court. Unless the court also handles the issue of finality, the evidence that may ultimately have to be excluded will be heard by the jury.

writing to see whether it appeared complete. If the judge concluded that it did, the next step was to presume that it *was* complete. Neither party could convince the court that what they actually intended was a partial integration.

Even under this restrictive approach, a party was free to show that the agreement represented by the writing was not the only contract between the parties. No matter how complete it may appear, a writing can cover only so much ground. For example, a writing covering the sale of a wagon could not preclude one party from trying to show that the parties had also orally agreed to the sale of a shotgun. An independent contract with a separate subject matter and a separate consideration would not be affected by the writing.

Suppose, however, that the writing referred to the sale of a wagon for $100, and the buyer wanted to show that the seller had orally agreed to replace the wheels for an extra $25. Should this understanding, which is really collateral to the main contract, be treated as if it were truly independent, thereby clearing the path for the introduction of extrinsic evidence? Over time, a series of tests has developed to determine this issue.

One of the most influential "collateral contract" cases is *Mitchill v. Lath*,[17] where the buyer of a farm wanted to show that the seller had orally agreed to remove an unsightly icehouse that he owned and that was located on another piece of land. This agreement, of course, was not mentioned in the writing, which appeared complete on its face; nor was it supported by a separate consideration. Nevertheless, the court held that the evidence was admissible if the term was one that a reasonable person "would not ordinarily be expected to embody in the writing."[18]

Ultimately, a majority of the court concluded that a reasonable person would have included the proffered oral term in the writing, and the buyer lost. Nevertheless, the case is noteworthy because it created the possibility that evidence of a collateral agreement, not supported by a separate consideration, might be admissible to supplement the terms of an apparently complete writing.

The Second Restatement has built on the *Mitchill* decision. Section 216(2) states that a writing is not completely integrated if it "omits a consistent additional agreed term which is (a) agreed to for a separate consideration, or (b) such a term as in the circumstances might naturally be omitted from the writing." Thus, with separate consideration, the only inquiry is consistency. Without separate consideration, the reasonable person test must be applied.

---

[17]   247 N.Y. 377, 160 N.E. 646, 68 A.L.R. 239 (1928).
[18]   *Id.*, 247 N.Y. at 381, 160 N.E. at 647.

This provision is not operative, however, if the writing contains an effective merger clause.[19]

Before we go on, note that the *Mitchill* test turns on the *presumed* intent of a mythical "reasonable person" rather than the *actual* intent of the parties. That is, it operates as a rule of form, not a test of credibility. Under the *Mitchill* test, a judge who believes that the parties actually agreed on an omitted term can still keep the evidence from the jury if he or she concludes that a reasonable person would not have omitted the term from the writing. This raises a subsidiary issue: what information should the judge consider in deciding what a reasonable person would have done?

In many of the early cases, the judge looked only at the writing before applying the reasonable person test. Other judges listened to evidence of the general circumstances surrounding the contract (the status and sophistication of the parties, their purposes in entering into the transaction, etc.) but refused to listen to evidence regarding the disputed term itself (how it first came up, why it wasn't included in the writing, etc.). Both of these approaches were criticized by Professor Corbin[20] on the ground that a judge can hardly decide what a reasonable person would have done without listening to evidence of all the surrounding circumstances. For example, suppose the omitted term was an afterthought that the parties, who were not sophisticated in legal matters and were not represented by counsel, agreed to after the writing had been prepared but before it had been signed. Surely these facts should be relevant in deciding whether a reasonable person would have gone to the effort of modifying the writing. Corbin's criticism finds expression in the Second Restatement, which states that "a writing cannot of itself prove its own completeness, and wide latitude must be allowed for inquiry into circumstances bearing on the intention of the parties."[21]

[2] The Code Test

Section 2–202 of the Code does not contain a test for completeness. Scanning down the statute, however, it appears that the first question for the judge is whether "the writing [was] intended by the parties as a final expression of their agreement with respect to such terms as are included therein." If so, the writing may be supplemented by evidence of consistent additional terms, unless the court finds that the writing is complete. By stating affirmatively that evidence is admissible absent a finding of completeness, the statute suggests that there should not be a presumption of completeness.

---

[19] Merger clauses will be discussed in § 4.02[F] *infra*.

[20] A. Corbin, *supra* note 3, at § 582.

[21] Restatement (Second) of Contracts, § 210 Comment b.

The Comments support this analysis, stating that the Code rejects "any assumption that because a writing has been worked out which is final on some matters, it is to be taken as including all the matters agreed upon."[22] The structure of the statute and the Comments appear to reject the four corners approach, under which writings that appeared complete were presumed to be complete.[23]

Comment 3, which provides further clues about the appropriate test, states as follows:

> Under paragraph (b) consistent additional terms, not reduced to writing, may be proved unless the court finds that the writing was intended by both parties as a complete and exclusive statement of all the terms. If the additional terms are such that, if agreed upon, they would certainly have been included in the document in the view of the court, then evidence of their alleged making must be kept from the trier of fact.

Unless the term would "certainly" have been included in the writing, extrinsic evidence goes to the jury. This standard must be contrasted with the *Mitchill* and Second Restatement tests, which ask whether the term would "naturally" have been omitted. Since "certainly" refers to a narrower range of conduct than "naturally," it must be assumed that the drafters intended to liberalize the parol evidence rule and allow additional evidence to flow to the jury.

It is unclear what evidence the judge should consider in applying the "certainly" test, although Corbin's analysis, as reflected in the Second Restatement, seems to be the most appropriate. Surely the judge should listen to all the evidence, including the evidence that may ultimately be excluded from the jury, before deciding whether a reasonable person would certainly have included the disputed term in the writing.[24]

[E]   Contradiction and Consistency

A partial integration cannot be contradicted by evidence of extrinsic understandings, but it can be supplemented by evidence of consistent additional

---

[22] UCC § 2–202, Comment 1(a).

[23] *See, e.g.,* Northwest Cent. Pipeline Corp. v. JER Partnership, 943 F.2d 1219, 16 UCC Rep. Serv. 2d 1004 (10th Cir. 1991) (§ 2–202 creates a presumption that a writing is not fully integrated unless the court makes an explicit finding to the contrary); Century Ready-Mix Co. v. Lower & Co., 770 P.2d 692, 10 UCC Rep. Serv. 2d 705 (Wyo. 1989), *app. after remand,* 816 P.2d 795 (1991) (Code eliminates any presumption of completeness).

[24] *See, e.g.,* Alaska Northern Dev., Inc. v. Alyeska Pipeline Serv. Co., 666 P.2d 33, 36 UCC Rep. Serv. 1527 (Alaska 1983), *cert. denied* 464 U.S. 1041, 104 S. Ct. 706, 79 L. Ed.2d 170 (1984).

terms. What is a contradiction, and when is an additional term consistent? The first major case to wrestle with these issues under the Code was *Hunt Foods & Industries v. Doliner*.[25] The case actually involved a contract for the sale of stock rather than goods, but the court nevertheless applied section 2–202.

The plaintiff corporation wanted to buy the defendant's controlling stock in another corporation and the parties had agreed on the price when circumstances forced a temporary recess in the negotiations. Before the recess, the seller executed a writing giving the buyer an option on the stock at the agreed price. The writing did not disclose any conditions to exercise of the option, but when the buyer attempted to do so the seller argued that the parties had agreed that it could be exercised only if the seller received an offer from a third party.

In deciding that the alleged condition did not contradict the writing and was not inconsistent with it, the court stated, "To be inconsistent the term must contradict or negate a term of the writing. A term or condition which has a lesser effect is provable."[26] Under this analysis, contradiction and inconsistency are equated, and extrinsic evidence is admissible unless a term that is expressed in the writing is directly negated. The *Hunt Foods* analysis was a dramatic contrast with many pre-Code cases, which typically held that to be consistent, the proffered term could not even vary the terms of the writing, much less contradict them.[27] A number of the early decisions applying the Code adopted the *Hunt Foods* approach.[28]

Hunt Foods represents the extreme, as most subsequent cases have been less hostile to the parol evidence rule. The emerging approach seems to be the "reasonable harmony" test, first articulated in *Snyder v. Herbert Greenbaum & Associates*.[29] In *Snyder*, the buyer of carpeting tried to show through a course of dealing that it had a right to cancel the contract unilaterally. The court held that even though the contract was silent on cancellation, thus eliminating direct contradiction of an express term, the proffered understanding was not consistent because it was not in reasonable harmony with the writing. Obviously, a highly subjective standard like "reasonable harmony" gives judges great discretion, and, not surprisingly, the test has now been adopted by a number of courts.[30]

---

[25] 26 A.D.2d 41, 270 N.Y.S.2d 937, 3 UCC Rep. Serv. 597 (1966).

[26] *Id.*, 26 A.D.2d at 43, 270 N.Y.S.2d at 940.

[27] Surprisingly, the Restatement (Second) of Contracts provides no guidance on this issue. Section 215 states that a partial integration cannot be contradicted, and Comment b to that section states that whether there is a contradiction depends on whether the proffered term is consistent or inconsistent with the writing.

[28] *See, e.g.*, Ace Supply, Inc. v. Rocky-Mountain Mach. Co., 96 Idaho 183, 525 P.2d 965, 15 UCC Rep. Serv. 324 (1974)(court admitted buyer's evidence that apparently unconditional sale of tractor was in fact conditioned on seller's inability to find another buyer).

[29] 38 Md. App. 144, 380 A.2d 618, 22 UCC Rep. Serv. 1104 (1977).

[30] *See, e.g.*, ARB, Inc. v. E-Sys., Inc., 663 F.2d 189, 30 UCC Rep. Serv. 949 (D.C. Cir. 1980);

Problems of inconsistency also arise between express terms and terms derived from a trade usage, course of dealing, or course of performance. While section 2–202(a) does not contain an explicit consistency requirement, most courts have read in such a requirement by reference to sections 1–205(4) and 2–208(2). These issues will be discussed in a later section.[31]

[F]   The Effect of a Merger Clause

In deciding whether a final writing is also complete, the judge is, of course, looking for the intent of the parties. Suppose that a clause in the contract explicitly states that the writing represents the complete understanding of the parties. If such a clause, commonly called a merger clause, is given effect, the writing cannot be supplemented by evidence of consistent additional terms. At one time, merger clauses were routinely enforced without further analysis, and that is still true in commercial contracts between merchants of relatively equal bargaining strength. In other cases, however, merger clauses have lost much of their vitality.

In *Luther Williams, Jr., Inc. v. Johnson*,[32] the court held that a merger clause was not conclusive evidence of the parties' intent to have a completely integrated writing, and it admitted evidence of an oral condition precedent to the contract in question.[33] A number of other courts have seized on this analysis to invalidate merger clauses.[34] Although these decisions do not usually invoke doctrines such as duress, bad faith, and unconscionability, the clauses are clearly being invalidated for similar reasons.

While this analysis is most common in consumer cases, it is by no means limited to that category. For example, the court in *Sierra Diesel Injection Serv., Inc. v. Burroughs Corp.*[35] invalidated a merger clause on a preprinted form contract between a sophisticated corporation and a small business being run by family members who lacked a college education.[36]

Alaska Northern Dev., Inc. v. Alyeska Pipeline Serv. Co., 666 P.2d 33, 36 UCC Rep. Serv. 1527 (Alaska 1983), *cert. denied* 464 U.S. 1041, 104 S. Ct. 706, 79 L. Ed. 2d 170 (1984).

[31]   *See* § 4.03[D] *infra*.

[32]   229 A.2d 163 (D.C. Ct. App. 1967).

[33]   For an explanation of how many courts admit evidence of an oral condition precedent even if the merger clause is effective, *see* § 4.02[G][3] *infra*.

[34]   *See, e.g.,* Seibel v. Layne & Bowler, Inc., 56 Or. App. 387, 641 P.2d 668, 33 UCC Rep. Serv. 893 (1982); Morgan v. Stokely-Van Camp, Inc., 34 Wash. App. 801, 663 P.2d 1384, 36 UCC Rep. Serv. 1535 (1983). *See also* Restatement (Second) of Contracts § 216, Comment e (suggesting that boilerplate merger clauses should not be enforced).

[35]   890 F.2d 108 (9th Cir. 1989).

[36]   *Cf.* Ray Martin Painting, Inc. v. Ameron, Inc., 638 F. Supp. 768, 1 UCC Rep. Serv. 2d 713 (D. Kan. 1986)(court upheld merger clause, but only after explicitly finding that corporations had relatively equal bargaining strength).

[G] Terms That Can Be Proved Notwithstanding a Complete Writing

Even if the court finds that a writing is intended to be both final and complete, extrinsic evidence of certain terms can still be introduced. The most important situations are discussed below.

[1] Supplementation Through Usage of Trade, Course of Dealing, and Course of Performance

Evidence of a trade usage or course of dealing is most commonly used to aid in the process of interpreting ambiguous terms, but it can also be used to supplement a writing by adding terms to it. Section 2–202(a) makes it clear that evidence of supplemental terms derived from these sources can be introduced even if there is a final writing—indeed, even if there is a complete writing insulated by an effective merger clause. Notice that under section 2–202(b), a writing can be supplemented by evidence of consistent additional terms (drawn from sources other than those listed in section 2–202(a)) unless the court finds that the writing is complete. Section 2–202(a) does not include a completeness test, and the omission was not an oversight. Terms derived from implied-in-fact sources are the background music for the agreement—that is, the parties implicitly rely on them even if they are not articulated. Comment 2 to section 2–202 makes this clear by stating that:

> Such writings are to be read on the assumption that the course of prior dealings between the parties and the usages of trade were taken for granted when the document was phrased. Unless carefully negated they have become an element of the meaning of the words used.

In other words, if the parties want to preclude supplementation through course of dealing and usage of trade, the writing itself must contain an effective clause stating that such sources are out of bounds. For example, the court in *Madison Industries, Inc. v. Eastman Kodak Co.*[37] enforced such a clause and excluded evidence that the term "right of first refusal" in the writing had a particular meaning within the industry.

Although section 2–202(a) also refers to course of performance, the discussion has thus far omitted that source. This is because a course of performance by definition cannot occur until after the parties have reached their initial agreement, and (aside from use as an aid in interpretation) this source is most often used to show either a waiver or modification.[38] The parol evidence rule does not apply to evidence of agreements waiving or modifying the terms of a

---

[37] 243 N.J. Super. 578, 581 A.2d 85, 13 UCC Rep. Serv. 2d 325 (1990).
[38] UCC § 2–208(3).

writing, and thus it normally makes no sense to talk about the parol evidence rule's impact on a course of performance.[39] Section 2–202 applies to attempts to explain a writing's terms as well as to attempts to supplement them, and it is in the context of interpretation that the reference to course of performance makes the most sense.

For the moment, we will defer giving detailed definitions of trade usage, course of dealing, and course of performance. That discussion will come in the ensuing section of this chapter,[40] section 4.03, which also examines the problems that arise when there is an apparent clash between a writing's express terms and a proffered implied-in-fact term.[41]

[2] Invalidating Causes

The parol evidence rule precludes the introduction of certain evidence for the purpose of supplementing a writing. That same evidence, however, may be used to show that the contract represented by the writing is avoidable. The parol evidence rule does not apply to attempts to avoid the contract by introducing extrinsic evidence that would prove an invalidating cause. Although the Code does not address this issue, the Second Restatement makes it clear that extrinsic evidence is admissible to show "illegality, fraud, duress, mistake, lack of consideration or other invalidating cause."[42] One of the other invalidating causes that could be used under the Code is unconscionability.

The most commonly used exception is based on fraud. For example, in *Latham & Associates, Inc. v. William Raveis Real Estate, Inc.*,[43] the buyer of two computer systems was permitted to introduce evidence of certain express warranties made by the seller and not reflected in the writing. The buyer's rationale for introducing the warranty evidence was to show the court that the seller had deliberately misrepresented its expertise in developing the systems. The states vary a great deal regarding the degree of scienter necessary to invalidate a contract through the fraud exception.

Suppose the buyer in *Latham & Associates* had wanted to introduce evidence of the oral express warranties in order to make them part of the contract,

---

[39] It is possible to reach agreement and then establish a course of performance before the parties bother to write up their understanding. In such a case, UCC § 2–202(a) tells us that evidence of the course of performance is admissible to supplement the writing unless it contradicts one of the writing's terms.

[40] See § 4.03[A]–[C] *infra*.

[41] See § 4.03[D] *infra*.

[42] Restatement (Second) of Contracts § 214(d).

[43] 218 Conn. 297, 589 A.2d 337, 14 UCC Rep. Serv. 2d 394 (1991).

thereby giving it an affirmative cause of action for damages.[44] This claim would have raised the parol evidence rule, and the judge would have had to use the traditional analysis to decide whether to admit the evidence.

A party who wants to recover affirmatively for misrepresentations should consider bringing the action in tort rather than in contract, thereby avoiding the parol evidence rule altogether. *Keller v. A. O. Smith Harvestore Products, Inc.*[45] represents an extreme example of this approach. There, the Colorado Supreme Court, on certification from the Tenth Circuit Court of Appeals, held that a merger clause does not bar a claim in tort based on an innocent misrepresentation. Many states do not even accept a negligent promissory misrepresentation as a basis for a claim in tort, much less an innocent misrepresentation. The *Keller* decision sparked a strong dissent from a judge who worried, with some reason, that it projected tort concepts too far into the traditional realm of contract law.

Extrinsic evidence can also be used to prove other invalidating causes. The Second Restatement uses an example in which a buyer and a seller enter into a completely integrated agreement for the sale of rifles. Extrinsic evidence would be admissible to show that the buyer had promised to buy the rifles to foment a rebellion, thereby making the contract illegal.[46] Although extreme, the example illustrates the point well.

[3]   Conditions Precedent

Let's return briefly to *Luther Williams, Jr., Inc. v. Johnson,*[47] described in section 4.02[F] above dealing with merger clauses. There, the court found that the merger clause was ineffective and permitted introduction of extrinsic evidence of an oral condition precedent. Many, perhaps most, courts would have permitted the evidence to be introduced even if the merger clause had been effective. The rationale is that a condition precedent operates much like an invalidating cause.[48] In other words, since the condition precedent prevents the parties' duties from becoming enforceable, the evidence is being used to invalidate the writing rather than to supplement it.[49]

The Code is not as conducive to this argument as the common law. Notice that section 2–202(b) precludes supplementation by consistent additional

---

[44] In the actual case, the buyer recovered the purchase price. This is consistent with the restitutionary remedy typically available in cases of contract avoidance.

[45] 819 P.2d 69, 15 UCC Rep. Serv. 2d 733 (Colo. 1991).

[46] Restatement (Second) of Contracts § 214, Comment c, Illustration 6.

[47] 229 A.2d 163 (D.C. Ct. App. 1967).

[48] *See* § 4.02[G][2] *supra* for a discussion of other invalidating causes.

[49] *See* Restatement (Second) of Contracts § 217.

"terms" where the writing is complete, and the word "term" means "that portion of an agreement that relates to a particular matter."[50] It is hard to argue that a condition precedent is not just another term for purposes of the parol evidence rule.[51] Despite this analysis, numerous common-law decisions and a few decisions under the Code permit extrinsic evidence of a condition precedent.[52]

Presumably, additional language in a merger clause specifying that there are no conditions precedent would be effective, assuming the merger clause is enforced by the court. Of course, evidence of an inconsistent condition precedent will not be admitted, and if a writing specifies a number of conditions it will be difficult for one party to convince the judge that there was, in fact, an additional one.

[4] Interpretation

The parol evidence rule does not preclude the introduction of extrinsic evidence for the purpose of explaining ambiguities in a writing. The rule applies to attempts to supplement a writing; when the parties have included a term, attempts to resolve ambiguities within that term do not amount to supplementation.

The line between interpretation and supplementation can be a very thin one, and how the judge views the issue can determine the outcome. If the judge concludes that the issue involves interpretation, extrinsic evidence is admissible. If the issue concerns supplementation, the same evidence may be excluded because of the parol evidence rule. Obviously, a party seeking to introduce extrinsic evidence will want to be able to argue that the issue is really one of interpretation.

The borderline between interpretation and supplementation was explored in *Alaska Northern Development, Inc. v. Alyeska Pipeline Service Co.*[53] The buyer entered into a written agreement to buy all of the seller's inventory of Caterpillar parts "subject to the final approval of the [seller's] owner committee." Later, the seller's committee refused to approve the sale for reasons unrelated

---

50 UCC § 1–201(42).

51 *See* Deck House, Inc. v. Scarborough, Sheffield & Gaston, Inc., 139 Ga. App. 173, 228 S.E.2d 142, 20 UCC Rep. Serv. 278 (1976).

52 *See, e.g.,* Ace Supply, Inc. v. Rocky-Mountain Mach. Co., 96 Idaho 183, 525 P.2d 965, 15 UCC Rep. Serv. 324 (1974). It should be noted that the court could have decided the *Hunt Foods* case, discussed in § 4.02[E] *supra,* on this basis.

53 666 P.2d 33, 36 UCC Rep. Serv. 1257 (Alaska 1983), *cert. denied* 464 U.S. 1041, 104 S. Ct. 706, 79 L. Ed. 2d 170 (1984).

to price. The buyer then sought to prove the existence of an extrinsic understanding pursuant to which the owner's committee could disapprove the sale
only if it concluded that the contract price was unfair. The court concluded that
the issue was one of supplementation because the meaning being asserted by
the buyer—that the committee's discretion was limited—was not one to which
the language of the writing was reasonably susceptible.

The process of interpretation will be discussed in an ensuing section.[54] For
now, the important point is that extrinsic evidence introduced to show meaning
is not precluded by the parol evidence rule.

[H]   Reformation as an Alternative Approach

In certain situations, a party faced with a completely integrated writing
may be able to convince the court that the writing should be reformed to show
the true intent of the parties. The predicate for this approach is that the parties
agreed on the disputed term but that a mistake was made in transcription.[55]
The theory is that the protection of the parol evidence rule is not necessary,
since a contract cannot be reformed without "clear and convincing" evidence
of the mistake.

Intershoe, Inc. v. Bankers Trust Co.[56] is a case in which the theory, had it been
pursued, might have been effective. The parties agreed to exchange Italian lira
for American dollars, and the defendant sent a written confirmation indicating
that it would buy the lira. The plaintiff's agent signed and returned the confirmation. Later, the plaintiff attempted to prove that the defendant was supposed
to be the seller, not the buyer. Not surprisingly, the court excluded this testimony since it directly contradicted a term in the writing.

Had the plaintiff sought reformation, it might have prevailed. Perhaps it
could have shown a course of dealing in which it was always the buyer and
defendant the seller. This course of dealing would have been inadmissible
under a parol evidence analysis since it contradicted an express term of the
writing, but it might have provided the court with the clear and convincing
evidence necessary for reformation.[57]

---

[54] *See* § 4.04 *infra.*
[55] *See, e.g.,* Stephenson v. Ketchikan Spruce Mills, Inc., 412 P.2d 496 (Alaska 1966).
[56] 77 N.Y.2d 517, 569 N.Y.S.2d 333, 571 N.E.2d 641, 14 UCC Rep. Serv. 2d 1 (1991).
[57] While evidence of a course of dealing may be used to supplement a complete writing, it
      may not be used to contradict the express terms of the writing. *See, e.g.,* General Plumbing
      & Heating, Inc. v. American Air Filter Co., Inc., 696 F.2d 375, 35 UCC Rep. Serv. 364 (5th
      Cir. 1983).

§ 4.03   THE SPECIAL ROLES OF TRADE USAGE, COURSE OF DEALING, AND COURSE OF PERFORMANCE [1–205; 2–208; 2A–207]

We have already seen that a final writing can be supplemented by terms that are implied from trade usage, course of dealing and, perhaps, course of performance.[58] This section looks more closely at the Code's definition of these sources. It then examines the problems that arise when terms derived from various sources are inconsistent.

[A]   Usage of Trade Defined

The Code defines a usage of trade as "any practice or method of dealing having such regularity of observance in a place, vocation or trade as to justify an expectation that it will be observed with respect to the transaction in question."[59] At its core, the idea is really quite simple: if you engage in a business, you ought to be aware of the customs used by others in that business.

How deeply rooted must a trade usage be? The Comments state that the Code has abandoned the ancient English tests for "custom" and that a party seeking to take advantage of a trade usage need not prove that it is " 'ancient or immemorial,' 'universal' or the like."[60] They go on to state that new usages can be proved, along with usages "currently observed by the great majority of decent dealers, even though dissidents ready to cut corners do not agree."[61] Of course, the usage must have enough "regularity of observance" to "justify an expectation that it will be observed."[62] Obviously, this is a flexible standard that leaves the fact-finder with considerable discretion.[63] Further flexibility is suggested by Comment 9 to section 1–205, which states that:

In cases of a well established line of usage varying from the general rules of this Act where the precise amount of the variation has not been worked out into a single standard, the party relying on the usage is entitled, in any event, to the minimum variation demonstrated.

---

58   *See* § 4.02[G][1] and note 39 *supra.*

59   UCC § 1–205(2).

60   UCC § 1–205, Comment 5. The common-law tests for establishing a "custom" were quite stringent. *See generally* Levie, *Trade Usage and Custom Under the Common Law and the Uniform Commercial Code,* 40 N.Y.U. L. Rev. 1101 (1965).

61   UCC § 1–205, Comment 5.

62   UCC § 1–205(2).

63   The Code allocates determinations about the existence and scope of a trade usage to the trier of facts. If the usage is a part of a written trade code that requires interpretation, the meaning of the code is an issue for the judge. UCC § 1–205(2).

The definition of trade usage includes practices in a "place" as well as in a "vocation or trade,"[64] and it is effective against parties who are members of the vocation or trade or who are or should be aware of the usage. A trade usage can thus be effective against a party who is not a member of the particular trade, a fact that was demonstrated in *Nanakuli Paving & Rock Co. v. Shell Oil Co., Inc.*[65] Shell supplied asphalt to Nanakuli, which was a paving contractor on the island of Oahu. The contract provided that the price of asphalt would be Shell's posted price at the time of delivery, but Nanakuli tried to show that it was common on Oahu for parties selling supplies to paving contractors to offer "price protection." If effective, this usage would have limited Shell to the price in effect at the time Nanakuli entered into its contracts with third parties.

Shell was apparently the only asphalt supplier on Oahu, so Nanakuli could not show a usage in the asphalt supply business. It did, however, show that parties supplying other types of materials, such as aggregate rock, to paving contractors granted price protection, and it successfully argued that Shell should have been aware of the practices within the paving business on Oahu. The Comments support this result, stating, "[t]he language used [by the parties] is to be interpreted as meaning what it may fairly be expected to mean to parties involved in the particular commercial transaction *in a given locality* or in a given vocation or trade."[66]

The Code does not allocate the burden of proving a trade usage, but it surely must fall on the party who would benefit from its existence.[67] A party seeking to establish a trade usage must give the other party sufficient notice to avoid unfair surprise.[68] Unlike course of dealing and course of performance, establishing a trade usage is almost certain to require expert testimony.[69]

[B]   Course of Dealing Defined

A course of dealing is "a sequence of previous conduct between the parties which is fairly to be regarded as establishing a common basis of understanding for interpreting their expressions and other conduct."[70] Again, the idea is quite

---

[64]   UCC § 1–205(2).

[65]   664 F.2d 772, 32 UCC Rep. Serv. 1025 (9th Cir. 1981).

[66]   UCC § 1–205, Comment 4 (emphasis supplied).

[67]   *See, e.g.,* MortgageAmerica Corp. v. American Nat'l Bank, 651 S.W.2d 851, 36 UCC Rep. Serv. 1710 (Tex. Ct. App. 1983); Coleman v. Dupree, 1994 WL 8614 (Tex. Ct. App.).

[68]   UCC § 1–205(6). *See, e.g.,* Western Int'l Forest Prods., Inc. v. Boise Cascade Corp., 63 Or. App. 475, 665 P.2d 1231 (1983)(plaintiff precluded from introducing evidence of a trade usage because no advance notice given to defendant).

[69]   *See, e.g.,* Western Indus., Inc. v. Newcor Canada, Ltd., 739 F.2d 1198, 38 UCC Rep. Serv. 1458 (7th Cir. 1984).

[70]   UCC § 1–205(1).

simple: a party to a current contract has reason to expect that its terms will be consistent with the terms of previous contracts with the same party.

The existence of a course of dealing would seem to be a question of fact for the jury, although the Code is silent on this point.[71] The proof will typically come from a party's own experiences, and no expert testimony is necessary.

How extensive does a course of dealing have to be before it becomes legally significant? The Code does not say, but the word "course" suggests more than one previous contract between the parties. The same issue arises with regard to course of performance, and the Comments to section 2–208 provide that a single occasion does not constitute a course of performance.[72] The Comments to section 1–205 equate course of dealing and course of performance, requiring a "sequence of conduct" for each.[73] The major difference between the two concepts is that a course of dealing involves a sequence of conduct between the parties prior to the contract in question, and a course of performance involves a sequence of conduct *under* the contract in question.

[C] Course of Performance Defined

A course of performance is established when "the contract for sale involves repeated occasions for performance by either party with knowledge of the nature of the performance and opportunity for objection to it by the other."[74] As indicated in the previous section, more than one occasion for performance is required,[75] and even then the courts are often reluctant to find a course of performance. For example, in *John P. Saad & Sons v. Nashville Thermal Transfer Corp.*,[76] the court refused to find that the buyer's repeated pattern of accepting nonconforming oil in an installment contract amounted to a course of performance.

---

[71] Arguably, since the existence of a trade usage is expressly assigned to the jury, silence with regard to a course of dealing implies that it is an issue for the judge. This argument is weak. The existence of a trade usage is allocated to the jury in order to establish a contrast with the issue of interpretation of a trade code, which is assigned to the judge. UCC § 1–205(2).

[72] UCC § 2–208, Comment 4. *See, e.g.,* Nanakuli Paving & Rock Co. v. Shell Oil Co., 664 F.2d 772, 32 UCC Rep. Serv. 1025 (9th Cir. 1981); Palmer v. Idaho Peterbilt, Inc., 102 Idaho 800, 641 P.2d 346, 33 UCC Rep. Serv. 827 (1982).

[73] UCC § 1–205, Comment 2.

[74] UCC § 2–208. The substance of the definition in Article 2A is identical. § 2A–207(1).

[75] *See* Nanakuli Paving & Rock Co. v. Shell Oil Co., Inc., 664 F.2d 772, 32 UCC Rep. Serv. 1025 (9th Cir. 1981).

[76] 715 S.W.2d 41 (Tenn. 1986). *Contra,* Lancaster Glass Corp. v. Phillips ECG, Inc., 835 F.2d 652, 5 UCC Rep. Serv. 2d 1306 (6th Cir. 1987)(pattern of accepting nonconforming installments established a course of performance).

When one party regularly performs in a certain manner but the other party repeatedly objects, there is no course of performance.[77] Likewise, there is no course of performance when the nonperforming party is mistaken as to the requirements of the contract.[78] As with trade usage and course of dealing, the burden of proof should be on the party who will benefit from the evidence, and the existence of a course of performance should be a question of fact for the jury.

[D]   The Code's Hierarchy of Terms

The discussion in Chapter 2[79] showed that the "agreement" of the parties is their bargain in fact, and it consists of their express understandings plus those derived from trade usage, course of dealing, and course of performance.[80] The "contract" of the parties is something very different. The contract is "the total legal obligation which results from the parties' agreement as affected by this Act and any other applicable rules of law."[81] The contract may contain more or fewer terms than the agreement. If the agreement does not address a particular issue, the Code's gap-fillers may come into play and add enforceable terms to the contract. If part of the agreement cannot be proved because of the parol evidence rule, or is unenforceable because of some other doctrine such as unconscionability, the contract will not contain that part.

As was also discussed previously, a writing can be supplemented by evidence of an implied-in-fact term, notwithstanding the parol evidence rule.[82] Likewise, an agreement not represented by a final writing may contain implied-in-fact terms. Section 1–205(3) makes this explicit for trade usage and course of dealing. Section 2–208(1) is less clear on this point, referring only to the process of interpretation, but Section 2–208(3) permits evidence of a course of performance to be used to show a waiver or modification, and the definition of agreement[83] refers to terms derived from a course of performance. Thus, undoubtedly, an agreement's terms can be drawn from all three sources.

What happens, however, when terms drawn from different sources conflict? Section 2–202 indicates that the express terms of a writing cannot be directly contradicted by implied-in-fact terms, but beyond that it provides no

---

[77] *See, e.g.*, A & G Constr. Co. v. Reid Bros. Logging Co., 547 P.2d 1207, 19 UCC Rep. Serv. 37 (Alaska 1976).

[78] *See, e.g.*, Kern Oil & Refining Co. v. Tenneco Oil Co., 792 F.2d 1380, 1 UCC Rep. Serv. 2d 651 (9th Cir. 1986), *cert. denied*, 480 U.S. 906, 107 S. Ct. 1349, 94 L. Ed. 2d 520 (1987).

[79] *See* § 2.01 *supra.*

[80] UCC § 1–201(3).

[81] UCC § 1–201(11).

[82] *See* § 4.02[G][1] *supra.*

[83] UCC § 1–201(3).

guidance. Section 1–205(3) permits a trade usage or course of dealing to "supplement or qualify" the terms of an agreement. The word "qualify" suggests that such terms can cut back on express terms, but it does not explain where to draw the line. Section 2–208 likewise provides no useful guidance. As might be expected, the approach of the courts has been inconsistent.

The Code does contain two other provisions that are relevant to our inquiry. Sections 1–205(4) and 2–208(2) create what might be called a hierarchy of terms. Section 1–205(4) states that:

> The express terms of an agreement and an applicable course of dealing or usage of trade shall be construed wherever reasonable as consistent with each other; but when such construction is unreasonable express terms control both course of dealing and usage of trade and course of dealing controls usage of trade.

Section 2–208(2) then adds course of performance to the hierarchy, placing it below express terms but above course of dealing and trade usage.

In one respect, this hierarchy makes perfect sense. The purpose of the inquiry should be to ascertain the intent of the parties with respect to their present agreement. Express terms represent the best evidence of intent, followed by a course of performance. A course of dealing is somewhat more attenuated because it deals with past conduct, but it is more relevant than a trade usage because it deals with the conduct of *these parties* rather than that of the average person within the trade.

Despite the common sense of the hierarchy, the language of the statutes and practical problems of application make this a particularly thorny area. When, for example, does "qualification" cross over into "inconsistency"? Surely we have to allow evidence of an inconsistent course of performance to override an express term when the conduct is sufficiently entrenched to amount to a waiver or modification.

One of the earliest cases in this area was *Division of Triple T Services, Inc. v. Mobil Oil Corp.*[84] The plaintiff, who was leasing a gasoline station, wanted to show a trade usage that precluded termination by the lessor except for cause, notwithstanding a written provision that the lease would "terminate at the end of any current period (original or renewal) by notice from either party to the other, given not less than 90 days prior to such termination."[85] The court refused to admit the evidence, relying on the Code's hierarchy. The result is undesirable. The writing did not expressly state that the lease was terminable at

---

[84] 60 Misc. 2d 720, 304 N.Y.S.2d 191, 6 UCC Rep. Serv. 1011 (Sup. Ct. 1969), *aff'd*, 34 A.D.2d 618, 311 N.Y.S.2d 961 (1970).

[85] *Id.*, 60 Misc. 2d at 722, 304 N.Y.S.2d at 194, 6 UCC Rep. Serv. at 1014.

will; it was simply silent on that point. Evidence of the parties' intent should displace the Code's hierarchy. The decision did not establish a satisfactory test for determining consistency, and it did not explain why the alleged usage did more than qualify the right to terminate.

In *Columbia Nitrogen Corp. v. Royster Co.*,[86] the Fourth Circuit Court of Appeals took a more liberal approach. A written contract set out the quantity of phosphate to be delivered and the price, which was subject to escalation if certain market conditions occurred but was not subject to decline. When the market price fell, the buyer refused to accept the stated quantity, arguing that under a trade usage and course of dealing the quantity term was a mere projection. The Fourth Circuit reversed the trial judge, holding that the proffered evidence was consistent with the contract. The court stressed the fact that the writing did not exclude evidence of implied-in-fact terms and that it was silent as to price declines. The court noted that the Code assigns to such terms "unique and important roles" and stated that "overly simplistic and overly legalistic interpretation of a contract should be avoided."[87]

A case that arguably permits a trade usage to contradict an express term is *Nanakuli Paving & Rock Co. v. Shell Oil Co., Inc.*[88] The written contract called for the price of asphalt to be Shell's posted price at the time of delivery. After Shell raised its prices, Nanakuli tried to show that under a trade usage, Shell should have given it "price protection." This protection would require Shell to sell asphalt to Nanakuli at the price in effect at the time Nanakuli bound itself to perform paving work for third parties. The court concluded that this usage merely qualified the express term, but since Nanakuli was unlikely to order asphalt unless it had a binding contract with a third party, it is hard to escape the conclusion that the Court permitted a direct contradiction of the writing. In effect, the contract as interpreted called for the price to be the posted price at the time Nanakuli contracted with a third party, not the posted price at the time of delivery.

The law in this area is difficult to summarize. While there is no consistency in judicial attitudes toward "consistency," the trend indicates that courts are becoming far more receptive to the introduction of extrinsic evidence that significantly qualifies the meaning of what are otherwise clear, unambiguous written terms.

---

[86] 451 F.2d 3, 9 UCC Rep. Serv. 977 (4th Cir. 1971).

[87] *Id.*, 451 F.2d at 10, 9 UCC Rep. Serv. at 987. *See also* Modine Mfg. Co. v. North E. Indep. School Dist., 503 S.W.2d 833, 14 UCC Rep. Serv. 317 (Tex. Ct. App. 1973) (6 percent deviation from express quantity term permitted under trade usage); Heggblade-Marguleas-Tenneco, Inc. v. Sunshine Biscuit, Inc., 59 Cal. App. 3d 948, 131 Cal. Rptr. 183, 19 UCC Rep. Serv. 1067 (1976)(trade usage used to show that fixed quantity term was a mere estimate).

[88] 664 F.2d 772, 32 UCC Rep. Serv. 1025 (9th Cir. 1981).

§ 4.04   THE PROCESS OF INTERPRETATION

The discussion moves now from issues involved in identifying a contract's terms to those involved in interpreting ambiguous terms. When the parties are unable to agree on interpretation, the court might adopt the meaning proffered by one of the parties, refuse to enforce the contract on the ground that the parties failed to reach an enforceable agreement, fill the gap with a reasonable rule based on external commercial factors, or it might adopt an artificial rule of interpretation.

[A]   The Plain Meaning Rule

Of course, all of this presupposes an ambiguity, and many courts have refused to find ambiguity, notwithstanding the arguments of one of the parties, because of a doctrine called the "plain meaning rule." A court relying on this rule will exclude any extrinsic evidence that might help shed light on a term's meaning because the judge believes the term has a single meaning that is so obvious and universal that it cannot be refuted. The plain meaning rule can be applied to any contract, oral or written.

The plain meaning rule has been condemned by most scholars,[89] who argue that even an apparently unambiguous term can have an unusual secondary meaning in a particular factual context. Perhaps the most succinct statement of this attitude comes from *Pacific Gas and Electric Co. v. G. W. Thomas Drayage & Rigging Co.*,[90] where Judge Traynor wrote that:

> When a court interprets a contract on this basis, it determines the meaning of the instrument in accordance with the ". . . extrinsic evidence of the judge's own linguistic education and experience." The exclusion of testimony that might contradict the linguistic background of the judge reflects a judicial belief in the possibility of perfect verbal expression. . . . This belief is a remnant of a primitive faith in the inherent potency and inherent meaning of words." [Citations omitted].[91]

Judge Traynor went on to state that the judge should not automatically permit extrinsic evidence of meaning to reach the jury.[92] The judge should first screen the evidence, and "[i]f the court decides, after considering this evidence, that the language of a contract is 'fairly susceptible of either one of the two

---

[89] *See, e.g.,* A. Corbin, *supra* note 3, at § 542; S. Williston, *supra* note 3, at §§ 600A, 609, 629; Patterson, *The Interpretation and Construction of Contracts,* 64 Colum. L. Rev. 833 (1964).

[90] 69 Cal. 2d 33, 69 Cal. Rptr. 561, 442 P.2d 641 (1968).

[91] *Id.,* 69 Cal. 2d at 36–37, 69 Cal. Rptr. at 563, 442 P.2d at 643.

[92] In some states, the issue of interpretation, although a question of fact, is treated as an issue of law for the judge.

interpretations contended for . . .' extrinsic evidence relevant to prove either of such meanings is admissible.''[93] The Second Restatement is in accord.[94]

The plain meaning rule may be undergoing a bit of a revival. In *Trident Center v. Connecticut General Life Insurance*,[95] Judge Kozinski argued that the uncertainty created by Judge Traynor's approach makes it difficult to decide cases on summary judgment, which leads to an increase in costly commercial litigation. He stated some of his objections this way:

> If one side is willing to claim that the parties intended one thing but the agreement provides for another, the court must consider extrinsic evidence of possible ambiguity. If that evidence raises the specter of ambiguity where there was none before, the contract language is displaced and the intention of the parties must be divined from self-serving testimony offered by partisan witnesses whose recollection is hazy from passage of time and colored by their conflicting interests. . . . We question whether this approach is more likely to divulge the original intention of the parties than reliance on the seemingly clear words they agreed upon at the time. [Citation omitted].[96]

Despite the protestations of the scholars, many courts using both the common law and the Code have been reluctant to give up a device as powerful as the plain meaning rule.[97]

[B] Aids in the Process of Interpretation

Section 2–202 makes it clear that trade usage, course of dealing, and course of performance may be introduced to explain the terms of a final writing, and the Comments reject at least some aspects of the plain meaning rule by stating that the Code rejects "[t]he requirement that a condition precedent to the admissibility of evidence specified in paragraph (a) is an original interpretation by the court that the language used is ambiguous.''[98]

---

[93] Pacific Gas and Electric Co. v. G. W. Thomas Drayage & Rigging Co., 69 Cal.2d 33, 40, 69 Cal. Rptr. 561, 565–566, 442 P.2d 641, 645–646 (1968). *See also* text supporting note 53 *supra*.

[94] Restatement (Second) of Contracts § 212, Comment b.

[95] 847 F.2d 564 (9th Cir. 1988).

[96] *Id.* at 569.

[97] *See, e.g.*, Paragon Resources, Inc. v. Nat'l Fuel Gas Distr. Corp., 723 F.2d 419, 37 UCC Rep. Serv. 1482 (5th Cir. 1984); Western Beef, Inc. v. Compton Inv. Co., 611 F.2d 587 (5th Cir. 1980).

[98] UCC § 2–202, Comment 1(c). Comment 1(b), which is also relevant, rejects the premise that language should be interpreted according to legal constructs as opposed to commercial realities.

Taken at face value, this language would preclude even Judge Traynor's limited screening role for the judge,[99] but the courts do not appear to be going this far. The Code also rejects the plain meaning rule when a party attempts to introduce evidence from an implied-in-fact source to interpret the terms of an agreement that has not been reduced to a final writing.[100]

The reference to the "intent of the parties" means their manifest intent, not their subjective intent. Thus, when each party has adopted a different meaning for a particular term, the court may choose to adopt the analysis set forth in section 201(2) of the Second Restatement:

> Where the parties have attached different meanings to a promise or agreement or a term thereof, it is interpreted in accordance with the meaning attached by one of them if at the time the agreement was made (a) that party did not know of any different meaning attached by the other, and the other knew the meaning attached by the first party; or (b) that party had no reason to know of any different meaning attached by the other, and the other had reason to know the meaning attached by the first party.

While the language used in the Second Restatement is somewhat confusing, the concept is relatively simple. The provision refers to three levels of understanding (or lack thereof). If we use a particular form of expression, I may have no reason to know your meaning, I may have reason to know your meaning, or I may actually know your meaning. The same is true for you with regard to my meaning. Neither of us should be permitted to take unfair advantage of the other, so if I know your meaning but you don't know mine, the court should adopt your meaning. By going ahead with the contract knowing that you are either confused or unaware of our different meanings, I am trying to take unfair advantage of you. Similarly, if I have reason to know your meaning and you have no reason to know mine, the court should adopt your meaning. Even if I am not consciously trying to take advantage of you, I am still the more culpable party.

If we are both on the same level and the term is material, then neither party will be bound by the meaning attached by the other.[101] The court will either have to avoid the contract because of a lack of mutual assent[102] or will have to supply a meaning. The most logical source for this meaning is a course of performance acquiesced in by one of the parties after contract formation.[103] Absent a course of performance, the Second Restatement suggests that the term may

---

[99] *See* text supporting notes 92–93 *supra*.

[100] UCC § 1–201, Comment 1 supports this approach, although it is not entirely clear on the point.

[101] *See* Restatement (Second) of Contracts § 201(3).

[102] *See* Restatement (Second) of Contracts § 20.

[103] *See* UCC § 2–208(1).

be interpreted according to its most common meaning,[104] it may be construed against the drafter,[105] or it may be interpreted in a manner that serves the public interest.[106] A complete discussion of the aids used in the interpretation process is beyond the scope of this book.

Under section 201 of the Second Restatement, what evidence should be considered in deciding whether, at the time of contracting, one party knew or had reason to know the meaning attached by the other? Surely relevant evidence would come from their actual expressions during the course of their negotiations and any course of performance, course of dealing, or trade usage.[107]

§ 4.05   Implied-in-Law Terms [Gap-Fillers]

At common law, failure to agree on a material term frequently meant that the courts would not enforce an agreement. Article 2 represents a dramatic shift from that approach. Recognizing that parties frequently reach agreement during a relatively short exchange (a phone conversation, for example), the drafters of Article 2 created what can best be understood as a default contract. If the parties intend to be bound but have not agreed on certain common terms (either expressly or by implication from the surrounding facts), the Code often will supply those terms. Those terms, which are implied-in-law, have come to be known as "gap-fillers." The remainder of this section is devoted to a discussion of some of the most important gap-fillers. Treatment of the single most important gap-filler, the implied warranty of merchantability (filling the gap as to the quality of the goods), will be reserved for the next chapter.[108]

[A]   Open and Deferred Price Terms [2–305]

Section 2–305, which supplies a missing price term, provides in full as follows:

(1) The parties if they so intend can conclude a contract for sale even though the price is not settled. In such a case the price is a reasonable price at the time for delivery if
  (a) nothing is said as to price; or

---

[104] Restatement (Second) of Contracts § 202(3). This choice should not be mistaken for the plain meaning rule. It is a rule of construction that is used after the court listens to all the extrinsic evidence and concludes that it is not persuasive in ascertaining the parties' intent. A judge applying the plain meaning rule would jump directly to this approach without listening to the extrinsic evidence.

[105] Restatement (Second) of Contracts § 206.

[106] Restatement (Second) of Contracts § 207.

[107] See UCC § 1–205(3). Remember the discussion of the Code's hierarchy of terms in § 4.03[D] *supra*. A similar hierarchy is set out in Restatement (Second) of Contracts § 203(b).

[108] See § 5.02[B] *infra*.

(b) the price is left to be agreed by the parties and they fail to agree; or
(c) the price is to be fixed in terms of some agreed market or other standard as set or recorded by a third person or agency and it is not so set or recorded.
(2) A price to be fixed by the seller or by the buyer means a price for him to fix in good faith.
(3) When a price left to be fixed otherwise than by agreement of the parties fails to be fixed through fault of one party the other may at his option treat the contract as cancelled or himself fix a reasonable price.
(4) When, however, the parties intend not to be bound unless the price be fixed or agreed and it is not fixed or agreed there is no contract. In such a case the buyer must return any goods already received and if unable to do so must pay their reasonable value at the time of delivery and the seller must return any portion of the price paid on account.

Obviously, this provision addresses a host of related issues. The absence of an agreement on a term as important as price may well indicate that the parties never went beyond the negotiating stage, and a court should not supply a price term unless it is convinced that the parties intended to be bound.[109] Of course, the most obvious indication of an intent to be bound would be delivery of the goods by the seller and acceptance by the buyer. Short of such a showing, the court will no doubt be influenced by a desire to protect any significant, reasonable reliance by one of the parties.

It is relatively rare for the parties to fail even to address the issue of price, and when they do, each party is likely to be gambling on a favorable market shift before the delivery date. If the contract is completely silent as to price, the court will fill the gap with a "reasonable price." Ordinarily, this standard means the market price,[110] although the term is not limited to market equivalence. When the goods are so unusual as to preclude an objective method for measuring the market, the contract will most likely fail for indefiniteness.[111]

Parties frequently discuss price without setting a specific amount. They may, for example, agree to agree on the price in the future (deferred pricing),

---

[109] This observation restates the basic principle of UCC § 2–204(3), which makes intent to be bound a prerequisite to gap-filling. *See, e.g.,* In re BTS, Inc., 104 B.R. 1009, 11 UCC Rep. Serv. 2d 444 (Bankr. W.D. Mo. 1989)(court should not supply price in the absence of evidence that the parties intended to go forward with the deal); D. R. Curtis Co. v. Mathews, 103 Idaho 776, 653 P.2d 1188, 35 UCC Rep. Serv. 1425 (App. 1982)(court must find intent to be bound before supplying missing price term).
[110] *See, e.g.,* Spartan Grain & Mill Co. v. Ayers, 517 F.2d 214, 17 UCC Rep. Serv. 693 (5th Cir. 1975); Alamo Clay Prods., Inc. v. Gunn Tile Co., 597 S.W.2d 388, 29 UCC Rep. Serv. 31 (Tex. Ct. App. 1980).
[111] UCC § 2–204(3).

or they may establish some mechanism for determining the price such as a trade journal or a neutral third party. Prior to the Code, most courts held that agreements to agree on material terms were unenforceable,[112] and they also generally refused to enforce agreements establishing a pricing mechanism if the mechanism failed to produce a result.[113]

Section 2–305(1)(b) and (c) explicitly reverses such decisions, but before the court fills the gap with a reasonable price, it must make a separate determination that the parties intended to remain bound notwithstanding the failure.[114] When the parties have a longstanding relationship and their pricing procedure fails, or when one of the parties has made a significant investment that cannot be recouped if the contract fails to be enforced, the court should not hesitate to fill the gap if it has an objective basis for doing so. When, however, the contract is purely executory and neither side has relied to any significant degree, the best result is for the court to void the contract and allow the parties to go their own ways. Of course, the parties are free to draft clauses expressing their intent whether a gap should be filled.

[B] Delivery and Payment Terms Generally

The starting point for understanding the duties of the parties with respect to delivery and payment is section 2–301, which states:

The obligation of the seller is to transfer and deliver and that of the buyer is to accept and pay in accordance with the contract.

Thus, delivery and payment are essential duties of sellers and buyers respectively.

Parties often make explicit arrangements regarding delivery and payment, negating the need for gap-fillers. Where they are located in the same community, for example, they may specify that the seller is to drop off the goods or that the buyer will pick them up. When they are in different locations, they may expressly adopt one of several common methods of shipment. Some of these methods are known by a sort of commercial shorthand, like "F.O.B." Sections 2–319 and 2–320 flesh out the standard meaning of such expressions, but these are express terms, not gap-fillers.

---

[112] *See, e.g.,* Taller & Cooper v. Illuminating Elec. Co., 172 F.2d 625 (7th Cir. 1949)(deferred pricing mechanism unenforceable for lack of mutuality of obligation).

[113] *See, e.g.,* Interstate Plywood Sales Co. v. Interstate Container Corp., 331 F.2d 449 (9th Cir. 1949)(contract held unenforceable when price-setting mechanism based on prices at five mills failed due to closure of some of the mills).

[114] UCC § 2–305(4).

When the parties fail to reach agreement, the Code provides a variety of gap-fillers covering such matters as place of delivery, time for performance, terms of shipment, and method of payment. The most important of these gap-fillers are discussed in the ensuing subsections.

[1] Place of Delivery [2–308]

Section 2–308(a) specifies that the place for delivery is deemed to be the seller's place of business or, if none exists, the seller's residence. In other words, the norm is that the buyer will pick up the goods. Where the parties at the time of contracting know that the goods are physically located at some place other than the seller's business or residence, then that place becomes the place for delivery.[115] This situation often occurs because the goods are in the hands of a bailee. The Comments clarify that the seller must take whatever steps are necessary to make certain the bailee will release the goods to the buyer.[116]

[2] Time for Performance [2–309]

Unless the parties (or some other provision of the Code) specify otherwise, the time for any action required of either party under their contract is deemed to be a reasonable time. A reasonable time for delivery by the seller will vary depending upon a variety of factors, including the "nature, purpose and circumstances"[117] of the transaction. For example, if the contract involves complex goods that require special manufacture, the seller must be given sufficient preparation time. If the seller knows that the buyer has a particular need for the goods, delivery must be in time to allow the buyer to make use of them.

Since a "reasonable time" for delivery provides the seller with a great deal of flexibility, the seller needs to make certain that the buyer is in a position to receive the goods. Section 2–503(1), which deals with tender generally, requires that the seller "put and hold conforming goods at the buyer's disposition and give the buyer any notification reasonably necessary to enable him to take delivery." This means that the tender must occur at a reasonable hour of the day[118] and that the seller must keep the goods available for a sufficient time to enable the buyer to take possession of them.[119] The buyer has the concomitant responsibility of furnishing facilities that are reasonably suited to receiving the goods.[120]

---

[115] UCC § 2–308(b).
[116] UCC § 2–308, Comment 2.
[117] UCC § 2–309, Comment 1.
[118] UCC § 2–503(1)(a).
[119] *Id.*
[120] UCC § 2–503(1)(b).

Section 2–503(1) imposes an explicit notification requirement on the seller, but the Comments suggest that *both* parties have a responsibility to continue communicating with one another in good faith during the "reasonable time" between contracting and delivery.[121] The seller, for example, must at some point give the buyer a specific delivery date so that the buyer can prepare to receive the goods. A failure to do so would preclude the seller from treating a good faith rejection by the buyer as a breach.

Likewise, the buyer cannot just let what appears to be a reasonable time for delivery go by and then cancel the contract. The buyer needs to let the seller know that the time for delivery is expiring so that the seller can attempt to respond. Silence by either party can be treated as a course of conduct "enlarging the reasonable time for tender or demand for performance."[122] At some point, the parties may be deemed to have abandoned the contract.[123]

Following this theme of flexibility, the Comments state that a party who gives reasonable notification to the other does not do so at his or her peril.[124] If, for example, the buyer notifies the seller that delivery is due by June 1, a seller who believes that this date is unreasonably early cannot simply cancel the contract in the hope that a court will agree and hold that the buyer's demand amounted to a breach. The seller must communicate his or her concerns to the buyer and attempt to work out an alternative date. "Only when a party insists on undue delay or on rejection of the other party's reasonable proposal is there a question of flat breach under the present section."[125] Where one party notifies the other of a proposed delivery date, silence by the other will be viewed as acquiescence.[126]

Suppose the seller makes, or offers to make, an unreasonably early delivery. Clearly, the buyer who rejects such a delivery is not in breach since the delivery does not conform to the contract.[127] Is the seller in breach? The Comments suggest not, stating that such conduct by sellers should be "read under this Article as expressions of desire or intention, requesting the assent or acquiescence of the other party, not as final positions which may amount without more to breach. . . ."[128] In other words, if the buyer rejects an early delivery, the seller should be allowed to back off and try again at the appropriate time.

---

[121] UCC § 2–309, Comment 5.
[122] UCC § 2–305, Comment 5.
[123] *Id.*
[124] UCC § 2–309, Comment 6.
[125] UCC § 2–309, Comment 6.
[126] *Id.*
[127] *Cf.* UCC § 2–601.
[128] UCC § 2–309, Comment 4.

[3]   Shipment and Destination Contracts [2–503; 2–504]

When the parties are not in physical proximity, the contract will frequently call for the seller to send the goods to the buyer, usually by common carrier. The responsibilities of the parties in such cases are often a combination of express terms and gap-fillers. The basic Code gap-filler with regard to delivery requires that the buyer pick up the goods from the seller.[129] Thus, the provisions discussed in this subsection are not relevant unless the contract requires, or at least authorizes, the seller to send the goods to the buyer.

The parties often use a sort of commercial shorthand to designate the manner in which the goods will be sent. For example, the contract may say "F.O.B. seller's city" or "F.O.B. buyer's city." These (and other)[130] express terms invoke two related concepts—the "shipment contract" and the "destination contract." A shipment contract is one in which "the seller is required or authorized to send the goods to the buyer and the contract does not require him to deliver them at a particular destination. . . . "[131] For example, the designation "F.O.B. seller's city" means that the parties have agreed to a shipment contract. A destination contract occurs where "the seller is required to deliver at a particular destination. . . . " The designation "F.O.B. buyer's city" creates a destination contract. Of course, the contract may simply state that the goods will be shipped to the buyer without using any of the standard shorthand designations. In such a case, a shipment contract is presumed.[132]

Classification as a shipment or destination contract has important consequences. In a shipment contract, the seller is required to:

(a) put the goods in the possession of such a carrier and make such a contract for their transportation as may be reasonable having regard to the nature of the goods and other circumstances of the case;

(b) obtain and promptly deliver or tender in due form any document necessary to enable the buyer to obtain possession of the goods or otherwise required by the agreement or by usage of trade; and

(c) promptly notify the buyer of the shipment.[133]

---

[129] *See* UCC § 2–308, discussed in § 4.05[B][1] *supra.*

[130] A complete discussion of the various delivery terms is beyond the scope of this work.

[131] UCC § 2–504.

[132] *See* UCC § 2–503, Comment 5. *Cf.* National Heater Co., Inc. v. Corrigan Co. Mechanical Contractors, Inc., 482 F.2d 87, 13 UCC Rep. Serv. 78 (8th Cir. 1973) (designation "$275,640.00 Total Delivered to Rail Siding" overcomes presumption of shipment contract).

[133] UCC § 2–504.

A seller who has borne the expense and risk associated with fulfilling these responsibilities has properly tendered the goods and his or her duties are largely at an end.[134] The risk of loss shifts to the buyer,[135] meaning that if the goods are damaged in transit, the buyer will have to pay the contract price and then pursue the carrier to recoup the loss.[136]

The seller's responsibilities under a destination contract do not end until the seller is able to "put and hold conforming goods at the buyer's disposition and give the buyer any notification reasonably necessary to enable him to take delivery."[137] The risk of loss will not pass until the goods are tendered to the buyer at the designated destination.[138]

Of course, the parties can agree on the terms of shipment down to the most minute detail, but if they fail to do so, the Code states that "specifications or arrangements relating to shipment are at the seller's option."[139] Thus, the seller can select the carrier and the route so long as the selection is made in good faith and in conformity with the limits established by commercial reasonableness.[140]

[4]   Payment Terms [2–310; 2–511; 2–513]

At its simplest, the Code's gap-filler on payment is quite straightforward. Under section 2–310(a), payment is due "at the time and place at which the buyer is to receive the goods even though the place of shipment is the place of delivery." This means that cash is due when the goods are physically delivered to the buyer, and so credit must be bargained for. The last clause of section 2–310(a) refers to shipment contracts, where delivery technically occurs when the seller turns the goods over to the carrier. The buyer generally has a right to inspect the goods before making payment, so payment need not be made upon delivery to a common carrier in a distant city.[141]

---

[134] *Cf.* UCC § 2–503(2); § 2–504, Comment 1. Unless the contract calls for the buyer to make payment before inspecting the goods [§§ 2–513(3), 2–512(1)], the seller must make certain that the buyer has an opportunity to inspect the goods prior to making payment. *See* §§ 2–310(b), 2–513(1).

[135] UCC § 2–509(1)(a).

[136] Risk of loss issues are discussed in § 6.02 [B] *infra.*

[137] UCC § 2–503(1), (3).

[138] UCC § 2–509(1)(b).

[139] UCC § 2–311(2). In cases where the seller cannot make a proper delivery without being provided certain information, such as the name of a ship, the duty to provide that information is placed on the buyer. *See* §§ 2–319(1)(c), (3).

[140] UCC § 2–311(1).

[141] UCC § 2–513(1) provides that the buyer has the right, before payment or acceptance, to inspect the goods "at any reasonable place and time and in any reasonable manner. When

When the seller turns the goods directly over to the buyer, the seller's duty to deliver and the buyer's duty to pay are treated as concurrent conditions.[142] Thus, the seller must at a minimum make a conforming tender[143] of conforming goods before the buyer can be found in breach for failure to pay. Likewise, the buyer must be ready, willing, and able to tender payment before the seller can be found in breach for failure to properly deliver.[144] This system protects both the seller, who need not part with the goods before payment has been made, and the buyer, who need not part with payment before having a chance to inspect. If the buyer refuses to make the payment, even though justified, the seller cannot be required to part with the goods. Of course, if the buyer's refusal was justified by the seller's breach, the seller will be liable for compensatory damages.

When the goods are to be delivered by carrier to the buyer's distant location, the Code provides the parties with substantially the same level of protection. The buyer ordinarily will have an opportunity to inspect the goods before making payment, but the carrier will not release the goods until that payment has been made.[145]

The buyer can bargain away the right to inspect the goods prior to making payment. The typical rationale for doing so is that the documents that will allow the buyer to take the goods from the carrier are expected to arrive while the goods are still in transit.[146] For example, the seller may have obtained a negotiable bill of lading and indorsed it to the buyer,[147] or a nonnegotiable bill of lading (typically called a straight bill of lading) might name the buyer as consignee.[148] Since possession of these documents provides the means by which

---

the seller is required or authorized to send the goods to the buyer, the inspection may be after their arrival."

[142] *See* UCC §§ 2–301, 2–507(1), 2–511(1).

[143] *See generally* UCC § 2–503(1).

[144] Of course, an anticipatory repudiation would excuse either party from this condition. *See* UCC § 2–610 and the discussion in § 7.09 *infra*.

[145] The seller can obtain documents of title that require the carrier to obey the seller's orders with regard to delivery. Of course, the most important order for the seller is that delivery be withheld until proper payment has been made.

[146] *See* UCC § 2–513(3)(b). Payment is also due prior to inspection when the goods are delivered C.O.D. *See* § 2–513(3)(a). When the buyer has agreed to pay against documents but the parties have also agreed that the payment need not occur until after the goods have arrived, the buyer may inspect them prior to making the payment. § 2–513(3)(b). This provision does not apply if the goods merely happen to arrive prior to payment. § 2–513, Comment 5.

[147] Under UCC § 7–303(1)(a), the carrier must follow instructions given by the holder of a negotiable bill of lading.

[148] Under UCC § 7–403(1) the carrier must deliver the goods to the person named in the bill of lading.

the buyer gains access to the goods, the seller will want to be paid before giving them to the buyer.[149] The buyer loses the right to inspect the goods before making payment. Once they arrive, the buyer can inspect them and, if they are defective, still reject them.[150] Of course, the buyer will then have to pursue the seller for a refund.

[5]   Payment by Check [2–507; 2–511]

What if the buyer tenders a check rather than cash? Section 2–511(2) states that the tender is sufficient if it is "made by any means or in any manner current in the ordinary course of business. . . . " Absent unusual circumstances, payment by check would satisfy this test and constitute an appropriate tender. Section 2–511(2) allows the seller, however, to refuse the tender and demand payment in cash, in which case the buyer is entitled to "any extension of time reasonably necessary to procure it."

The title acquired by a buyer who pays by check is conditional, and the seller is entitled to reclaim the goods (usually by replevin) if the check is dishonored.[151] Prior to the Code, payment by check was considered the same as payment in cash for purposes of the "cash sale" doctrine. Under this doctrine, the transfer of title to the buyer was considered void (as opposed to voidable) if the check was dishonored, which meant that the goods could also be replevied from third parties, even bona fide purchasers who acquired them from the buyer. The rationale behind the rule was that the seller intended to give up title to the goods only if the cash payment was forthcoming.

The cash sale doctrine at common law stood in contrast to the "credit sale" doctrine. In a credit sale, the seller clearly did intend to transfer title to the buyer in exchange for a promise, so the buyer's title was voidable rather than void. This distinction meant that a subsequent bona fide purchaser could acquire full title.

The Code does away with the distinction between cash and credit sales as applied to subsequent transferees from the buyer. Under the Code, the buyer in either situation can transfer full title to a good-faith purchaser.[152] The Code

---

[149] The documents typically include a bill of lading and a draft to be paid (or, in some instances where the buyer has obtained credit, accepted) by the buyer. They are frequently forwarded to the buyer through banking channels. That is, the seller's bank forwards the documents to a bank in the buyer's city, and this bank notifies the buyer that the documents have arrived. The bank then gives the documents to the buyer upon payment (or acceptance) of the draft.

[150] UCC § 2–512(2).

[151] UCC § 2–511(3).

[152] UCC §§ 2–403(1)(b) and (c).

does, however, make some distinctions between a cash and a credit sale. In a credit sale, the buyer must have been insolvent upon receiving the goods and the seller must give notice of an intent to reclaim within 10 days after receipt.[153] In a cash sale (including payment by check), the buyer need not be insolvent. If the check is dishonored, the seller may reclaim the goods. The 10-day limit for giving notice also is not applied, although the Comments originally indicated that a 10-day limit should be imposed by analogy.[154] A number of courts followed this suggestion,[155] although others declined to read such a limitation into the text of the Code.[156] The Comments have now been revised to state that "[t]here is no specific limit for a cash seller to exercise the right of reclamation."

[C]   Open Quantity Terms (Output and Requirements Contracts) [2–306]

A requirements contract is one in which a buyer agrees to purchase all of his or her requirements for particular goods from the seller. An output contract is one in which the buyer agrees to purchase all of the seller's output of particular goods. Historically, these types of contracts were often invalidated for two reasons: lack of mutuality of obligation, and indefiniteness as to quantity. Even before enactment of the Code, however, most common-law courts had come around to the view that these contracts had great utility and ought to be enforced. The problems with mutuality and indefiniteness were resolved by resort to the doctrine of good faith. These contracts are clearly enforceable today under section 2–306.

Despite the general enforceability of these contracts, the lack of a specific quantity term can still present problems. For example, suppose a buyer in a requirements contract is purchasing a particular product for use in a manufacturing process. When the market price for the goods rises, the buyer suddenly begins ordering more of the product than can be used in order to sell the excess on the spot market. Under pre-Code law, a court no doubt would have considered the buyer's order excessive under the good-faith doctrine. A court today would reach the same result under section 2–306(1), which states:

---

[153] UCC § 2–702(2). The seller has a further reasonable time to make demand if the buyer has made a written misrepresentation of solvency within three months prior to delivery.

[154] UCC § 2–507, Comment 3.

[155] *See, e.g.*, Szabo v. Vinton Motors, 630 F.2d 1, 29 UCC Rep. Serv. 737 (1st Cir. 1980); Holiday Rambler Corp. v. First Nat'l Bank & Trust, 723 F.2d 1449, 37 UCC Rep. Serv. 1553 (10th Cir. 1983).

[156] *See, e.g.*, Burk v. Emmick, 637 F.2d 1172, 29 UCC Rep. Serv. 1489 (8th Cir. 1980); Citizens Bank v. Taggart, 143 Cal. App.3d 318, 191 Cal. Rptr. 729, 36 UCC Rep. Serv. 529 (1983).

A term which measures the quantity by the output of the seller or the requirements of the buyer means such actual output or requirements as may occur in good faith, except that no quantity unreasonably disproportionate to any stated estimate or in the absence of a stated estimate to any normal or otherwise comparable prior output or requirements may be tendered or demanded.

Notice that the Code goes well beyond good faith in policing the appropriate quantity. In the example posed, the buyer's demand would have violated the duty of good faith because the buyer was in effect appropriating a business opportunity that had been implicitly allocated to the seller under their agreement. The buyer's demand might also have been stricken if it was unreasonably disproportionate to stated estimates or past orders.

The courts have struggled with the "unreasonably disproportionate" standard. A seller in a requirements contract should understand that risk is involved. If, for example, the buyer's business falls off, the seller will be selling fewer goods. If the buyer's business suddenly takes off, the seller may be called upon to provide goods in excess of production capacity. In either case, the buyer's demands are consistent with actual requirements and with good faith. Nevertheless, in either case, the new demands may be disproportionate to the seller's actual expectations.

A number of courts have differentiated between situations in which the buyer's demands increase and those in which they decrease. When they decrease, these courts have effectively read the "unreasonably disproportionate" limitation out of the Code,[157] relying solely on good faith to police the transactions.[158] The idea seems to be that the buyer is likely to have a valid business reason for a decrease and the good faith doctrine will protect the seller in the rare case to the contrary.

With the unexpected increase, the seller may be caught off guard, unable either to expand capacity in a short period of time or to purchase the excess on the spot market. Many courts have been sympathetic with sellers in such cases and have bound the buyer by both the doctrine of good faith and the requirement of reasonable proportionality. In analyzing this latter requirement, the

---

[157] *See, e.g.,* R. A. Weaver & Assocs. v. Asphalt Construction, Inc., 587 F.2d 1315, 25 UCC Rep. Serv. 388 (D.C. Cir. 1978); Empire Gas Corp. v. American Bakeries Co., 840 F.2d 1333, 5 UCC Rep. Serv. 2d 545 (7th Cir. 1988); Atlantic Track & Turnout Co. v. Perini Corp., 989 F.2d 541, 20 UCC Rep. Serv. 2d 426 (1st Cir. 1993)(output contract).

[158] UCC § 2–306, Comment 2 suggests that the buyer cannot curtail demands in order to cut his or her losses on the requirements contract itself. The reduction must be related to the buyer's market for the finished product.

New York Court of Appeals in *Orange and Rockland Utilities v. Amerada Hess Corp.*[159] suggested that the following factors be considered:

(1) the amount by which the requirements exceed the contract estimate; (2) whether the seller had any reasonable basis on which to forecast or anticipate the requested increase; (3) the amount, if any, by which the market price of the goods in question exceeded the contract price; (4) whether such an increase in market price was itself fortuitous; and (5) the reason for the increase in requirements.[160]

While eliminating the disproportionality requirement in cases of a decrease in quantity does violence to the language of the Code, it appears to have become the trend in both requirements and output contracts.[161]

§ 4.06 SUPEREMINENT PRINCIPLES

While freedom of contract generally prevails under the Code, that freedom is constrained in several respects. For example, section 1–102(3) states:

The effect of provisions of this Act may be varied by agreement, except as otherwise provided in this Act and except that the obligations of good faith, diligence, reasonableness and care prescribed by this Act may not be disclaimed by agreement but the parties may by agreement determine the standards by which the performance of such obligations is to be measured if such standards are not manifestly unreasonable.

The two most important limitations on freedom of contract, unconscionability and good faith, are discussed below.

[A] Unconscionability [2–302; 2A–108]

Historically, doctrines like misrepresentation (including fraud) and duress were considered sufficient to protect contracting parties, but occasional cases

---

[159] 397 N.Y.S.2d 814, 59 A.D.2d 110, 22 UCC Rep. Serv. 310, 96 A.L.R.3d 1263 (1977).

[160] *Id.,* 397 N.Y.S.2d at 818–819, 59 A.D.2d at 115–116.

[161] *See, e.g.,* Atlantic Track & Turnout Co. v. Perini Corp., 989 F.2d 541, 20 UCC Rep. Serv. 2d 426 (1st Cir. 1993).

of gross unfairness did not fit squarely within the black letter of these doctrines. The need to adjudicate such cases fairly gave rise to the concept of
unconscionability.[162]

This kind of "policing" of contracts by the courts has become more
common since the advent of standard-form contracts, particularly when they
are offered to relatively unsophisticated customers on a take-it-or-leave-it
basis. Because customers do not assent to the terms on these forms but rather
are forced to adhere to them, the term "contract of adhesion" was coined to
describe such forms. The courts were particularly likely to intervene when an
entire industry began using such forms, essentially precluding customers from
negotiating better terms by shopping around.

Despite increased use of the unconscionability doctrine, common-law
courts often expressed reservations about it. It involved, after all, departing
from traditional notions of *caveat emptor* and freedom of contract. By explicitly
recognizing the doctrine, the Code seems to have spurred the courts to overcome this reluctance.[163] Section 2–302 states in its entirety:

> (1) If the court as a matter of law finds the contract or any clause of the
> contract to have been unconscionable at the time it was made the court
> may refuse to enforce the contract, or it may enforce the remainder of
> the contract without the unconscionable clause, or it may so limit the
> application of any unconscionable clause as to avoid any unconscion-
> able result.

> (2) When it is claimed or appears to the court that the contract or any
> clause thereof may be unconscionable the parties shall be afforded a
> reasonable opportunity to present evidence as to its commercial setting,
> purpose and effect to aid the court in making the determination.

Article 2A includes comparable provisions.[164]

---

[162] The earliest reference to the doctrine seems to have been by Lord Hardwicke in *Earl of
Chesterfield v. Janssen*, 2 Ves. Sen. 125, 28 Eng. Rep. 82 (Ch. 1750). The development of the
doctrine at common law is discussed in Spanogle, *Analyzing Unconscionability Problems*,
117 U. Pa. L. Rev. 931 (1969).
   Two classic law review articles have had a significant influence on the development
of the doctrine under the Code. *See* Ellinghaus, *In Defense of Unconscionability*, 78 Yale L.J.
757 (1969), and Leff, *Unconscionability and the Code—The Emperor's New Clause*, 115 U. Pa.
L. Rev. 485 (1967).

[163] Only California failed to adopt UCC § 2–302. The state nevertheless recognizes the doctrine and applies it to sales cases. *See, e.g.,* Carboni v. Arrospide, 2 Cal. App. 4th 76, 2 Cal.
Rptr. 2d 845, 16 UCC Rep. Serv. 2d 584 (Cal. Ct. App. 1991) (applying Cal. Civ. Code §
1670.5, a virtual reproduction of UCC § 2–302, to sales cases).

[164] UCC § 2A–108(1), (3).

Several aspects of these provisions are notable. Either party can raise the issue of unconscionability, or the court can raise it *sua sponte*.[165] The issue should be decided by the judge rather than the jury,[166] and once the issue has been raised, the court should hold a hearing to resolve it. The best discussion of the factors to be considered by the court at the hearing comes from *Johnson v. Mobil Oil Corp.*[167] These factors include the parties' relative age, status, intelligence, business sophistication, and bargaining power. The degree to which the party with greater bargaining strength has explained the suspect term, the intrinsic fairness of the term, and the availability of alternatives in the marketplace are also important.

The doctrine applies only to terms that are unconscionable at the time of contract formation. Thus, the doctrine should be viewed as an invalidating cause, much like the related doctrines of misrepresentation and duress. Issues related to the performance stage are dealt with under the doctrine of good faith, which by its terms has no application to the contract formation stage.[168]

Finally, one of the most important areas to which the doctrine has been applied is the area of product warranties. The discussion of unconscionability in that context will be deferred until the next chapter.[169]

[1] Procedural and Substantive Unconscionability

What makes a particular term unconscionable? The mere fact that a term is contained in a standard form does not render it unenforceable. Standard forms represent an efficient method of doing business, and the courts generally enforce their terms. An attitude still prevails, after all, that one should read and understand a document before signing it.

The Comments provide the courts with some guidance on the meaning of unconscionability:

> The basic test is whether, in the light of the general commercial background and the commercial needs of the particular trade or case, the clauses involved are so one-sided as to be unconscionable under the circumstances existing at the time of the making of the contract. Subsection (2) makes it clear that it is proper for the court to hear evidence upon these questions. The principle is the prevention of oppression and

---

[165] *See, e.g.*, Maxon Corp. v. Tyler Pipe Indus., Inc., 497 N.E.2d 570, 3 UCC Rep. Serv. 2d 52 (Ind. Ct. App. 1986)(issue raised by court *sua sponte*).

[166] UCC § 2–302, Comment 3.

[167] 415 F. Supp. 264, 20 UCC Rep. Serv. 637 (E.D. Mich. 1976).

[168] *See* UCC § 1–203, which states, "Every contract or duty within this Act imposes an obligation of good faith in its *performance or enforcement*." (Emphasis supplied.)

[169] *See* § 5.03[C] *infra*.

unfair surprise [citation omitted] and not of disturbance of allocation of risks because of superior bargaining power.[170]

Obviously, the key principle seems to be that some terms are so one-sided as to cause oppression and unfair surprise, but many one-sided terms are to be enforced as the product of normal bargaining and risk allocation. Where do we draw the line?

Many courts have resolved the problem by dividing general unconscionability into two categories, procedural and substantive, and requiring that each be present before the doctrine can be successfully invoked. As the discussion below explains, procedural unconscionability addresses concern over unfair surprise, while substantive unconscionability deals with one-sidedness.

Procedural unconscionability refers to problems that taint the bargaining process. Evidence of procedural unconscionability includes gross inequality of bargaining power (typically exemplified by a lack of intelligence and/or sophistication on the part of the buyer),[171] creation by the seller of an atmosphere of haste, the use of high-pressure sales tactics, the use of confusing language, the use of small print, and the presence of a relationship that allows one party to exert undue influence. Procedural unconscionability deprives a party of any "meaningful choice"[172]

Substantive unconscionability refers to terms that are so grossly unfair and one-sided that they shock the conscience of the court. Without procedural problems, the suspect term is almost certainly the product of normal risk allocation, even if it is one-sided. Without a substantive problem, the court has no reason to use this particular doctrine.

Numerous cases have discussed procedural and substantive unconscionability, although not always in those terms. In *Williams v. Walker-Thomas Furniture Co.*,[173] the buyer was a welfare recipient who had purchased a significant number of consumer items from the seller over a period of years. Each item was purchased on a secured, installment basis, and each installment sales contract signed by the buyer contained what was referred to as a "cross-collateral" clause. This clause allowed each of the buyer's payments to be credited on a pro rata basis to each item purchased, so that even though she had given the

---

[170] UCC § 2–302, Comment 1.

[171] Of course, either party can make a claim of unconscionability, but the buyer or lessee most often asserts the doctrine against the seller or lessor respectively.

[172] This oft-repeated term comes from Judge Skelly Wright's opinion in the celebrated case of Williams v. Walker-Thomas Furniture Co., 350 F.2d 445, 449, 2 UCC Rep. Serv. 955, 958 (D.C. Cir. 1965) (applying Code by analogy).

[173] *Id.*

seller enough money to pay for her earlier purchases many times over, the seller was able to retain her security interest in even those early items. The court emphasized the buyer's lack of sophistication and criticized the seller for displaying the clause in fine print. The court also noted that the very concept underlying the clause is so difficult that the average consumer could not understand it. Finally, the court stressed the unfairness of a term that allowed the seller to repossess items for which the buyer had given the seller the full price.

Serious unconscionability of both the procedural and substantive varieties is obvious in the *Williams* case, but that combination is not always present. Sometimes the procedural unconscionability is slight, sometimes the substantive unconscionability is slight, sometimes both are slight, or sometimes one is missing. What relative weight should the court give to these factors? Many courts have followed a line of analysis first articulated in *Funding Systems Leasing Corp. v. King Louie International, Inc.*[174] The court in that case concluded that while both procedural and substantive unconscionability must be present for relief to be granted, a sliding scale should be used: gross procedural unconscionability coupled with slight substantive unconscionability, or vice versa, would suffice. A few courts have gone even further, indicating that a term can be so harsh that relief is appropriate even though procedural unconscionability is lacking altogether.[175]

Can the price term be successfully attacked as substantively unconscionable? Certainly it can be argued that price is always the product of ordinary bargaining and, no matter how unsophisticated, the buyer should be able to understand the price term and seek out alternatives. Nevertheless, a few cases have held that the price term can be unconscionable. For example, in *Jones v. Star Credit Corp.*[176] the buyers, who were welfare recipients, agreed to purchase a freezer worth a maximum of $300 for a total price, including interest and

---

[174] 597 S.W.2d 624 (Mo. Ct. App. 1979). *See also* Tacoma Boatbuilding, Inc. v. Delta Fishing Co., 28 UCC Rep. Serv. 26 (W.D. Wash. 1980).

[175] *See, e.g.*, Gillman v. Chase Manhattan Bank, N.A., 73 N.Y.2d 1, 537 N.Y.S.2d 787, 534 N.E.2d 824, 7 UCC Rep. Serv. 2d 945, 15 A.L.R.5th 1039 (1988)(applying unconscionability to an Article 9 secured transaction).

[176] 59 Misc. 2d 189, 298 N.Y.S.2d 264, 6 UCC Rep. Serv. 76 (Sup. Ct. 1969). Other cases holding that the price term can be unconscionable include American Home Improvement, Inc. v. MacIver, 105 N.H. 435, 201 A.2d 886, 2 UCC Rep. Serv. 235, 14 A.L.R.3d 324 (1964); Murphy v. McNamara, 36 Conn. Supp. 183, 416 A.2d 170, 27 UCC Rep. Serv. 911 (1979). Virtually all of the cases declaring a price term unconscionable were decided before 1980. *See* Horowitz, *Reviving the Law of Substantive Unconscionability: Applying the Implied Covenant of Good Faith and Fair Dealing to Excessively Priced Consumer Credit Contracts,* 33 UCLA L. Rev. 940 (1986)(surveying the cases and urging a shift from unconscionability to a good faith analysis).

credit life and property insurance, of over $1,200. Aspects of procedural un-conscionability were also clearly present. The buyers were unsophisticated, and the salesman came to their home and apparently applied significant pressure. The court found that the price term was unconscionable and in effect reformed the term by allowing the buyers to keep the freezer with no further obligation even though they had paid only around $600.

[2]   Unconscionability in a Commercial Context

Courts applying the unconscionability doctrine often stress the status of the parties. Application of the doctrine is most common when the seller is a merchant and the buyer is a consumer. It is virtually never successfully asserted when both parties are merchants with relative equality of bargaining strength.[177]

Use of the doctrine appears to be on the rise, however, when both parties are merchants but are unequal in their bargaining strength. In that context, the courts have focused on whether the disadvantaged party could have read and understood the suspect clause, whether that party had any meaningful alternatives readily available in the marketplace, and perhaps most importantly, whether the clause bears a reasonable relationship to the risks associated with the party seeking to enforce it.[178]

As might be expected, the cases in the commercial context have focused heavily on the procedural aspects of the transaction. Of course, the terms at issue are one-sided, but tolerance of one-sided terms seems to be greater outside the consumer area. This attitude is a natural outgrowth of our general reluctance to upset the risk-allocation system adopted by commercial entities. Several of the cases have involved indemnification clauses in fine print, not separated by headings from other portions of a long, standard-form contract.[179] Many other cases have involved disclaimers of consequential damages, a topic that will be discussed separately in the next chapter.[180]

---

[177] See, e.g., Royal Indem. Co. v. Westinghouse Elec. Co., 385 F. Supp. 520, 15 UCC Rep. Serv. 631 (S.D.N.Y. 1974)(court refused even to listen to plaintiff's argument that a particular term had not been read and understood).

[178] See, e.g., Geldermann & Co. v. Lane Processing, Inc., 527 F.2d 571, 18 UCC Rep. Serv. 294 (8th Cir. 1975); Johnson v. Mobil Oil Corp., 415 F. Supp. 264, 20 UCC Rep. Serv. 637 (E.D. Mich. 1976).

[179] See, e.g., Weaver v. American Oil Co., 257 Ind. 458, 276 N.E.2d 144 (1971); Maxon v. Tyler Pipe Indus., Inc., 497 N.E.2d 570, 3 UCC Rep. Serv. 2d 52 (Ind. Ct. App. 1986). See generally Mallor, Unconscionability in Contracts Between Merchants, 40 Sw. L.J. 1065 (1986).

[180] See § 5.04[B] infra.

[3] Forms of Relief Available

Articles 2 and 2A explicitly permit the courts to strike an entire contract because of unconscionability or to strike the offending term and enforce the rest of the contract.[181] These options suggest that unconscionability can be used only defensively, not as a vehicle for the affirmative recovery of damages.[182] Nevertheless, a court that strikes an unconscionable clause can still proceed to award damages for breach of the remaining portion of the contract.[183] Also, conduct by a party attempting to enforce an unconscionable clause might constitute a breach of the duty of good faith, for which monetary damages are available.[184]

Although not expressly sanctioned by the Code, some courts have used unconscionability to reform the terms of a contract. In the *Jones*[185] case discussed above, the court reformed the price term of a contract downward from $1,200 to $600. Although not decided under the Code, a similar result was reached in *Vockner v. Erickson*,[186] where the court lowered the amount of installment payments due under a land sales contract.

[4] Additional Consumer Protection—Leases

Article 2A adds some provisions on unconscionability beyond those provided in the statutory analogue.[187] In each instance, these additions apply only with respect to a consumer lease.[188] One of these provisions empowers a court to grant appropriate relief if a lease contract or a clause in the contract was induced by unconscionable conduct.[189] Procedural unconscionability is thus sufficient for a court to grant relief in the absence of any substantive unconscionability, at least in the case of a consumer lease. Article 2A also allows courts to grant appropriate relief if the unconscionable conduct occurred in the collection of a claim that arose from a lease contract.[190]

---

[181] UCC §§ 2–302(1), 2A–108(1).

[182] *See, e.g.,* Cowin Equip. Co. v. General Motors Corp., 734 F.2d 1581, 38 UCC Rep. Serv. 1565 (11th Cir. 1984).

[183] *See, e.g.,* Langemeier v. Nat'l Oats Co., Inc., 775 F.2d 975, 41 UCC Rep. Serv. 1616 (8th Cir. 1985).

[184] *Cf.* Best v. United States Nat'l Bank, 303 Or. 557, 739 P.2d 554, 4 UCC Rep. Serv. 2d 8, 73 A.L.R.4th 1009 (1987).

[185] Jones v. Star Credit Corp., 59 Misc. 2d 189, 298 N.Y.S.2d 264, 6 UCC Rep. Serv. 76 (Sup. Ct. 1969).

[186] 712 P.2d 379 (Alaska 1986).

[187] These additional provisions are based on Uniform Consumer Credit Code § 5.108(1),(2),(6), 7A U.L.A. 167, 169.

[188] For a discussion of consumer leases, *see* § 1.05[C] *supra.*

[189] UCC § 2A–108(2)

[190] *Id.*

Another provision unique to Article 2A deals with attorney's fees. A court that finds unconscionability in a consumer lease is required to award reasonable attorney's fees to the lessee.[191] This provision recognizes that a successful lessee will be excused from performing if the court cancels the contract but will often not be entitled to damages. An award of attorney's fees protects a consumer lessee by covering the cost of legal representation to press the unconscionability claim. To counter the tendency to assert clearly unwarranted claims, Article 2A also requires courts to award attorney's fees to a lessor against whom a consumer lessee asserts a claim of unconscionability that the lessee knows to be groundless.[192]

[B]   The Duty of Good Faith [1–203; 1–201(19); 2–103(1)(c); 2A–103(2)]

Contract law in this century has increasingly come to recognize a general obligation to deal in good faith. This concept finds expression in section 1–203 of the Code, which states very simply that "Every contract or duty within this Act imposes an obligation of good faith in its performance or enforcement." Unlike the related doctrine of unconscionability, which presents issues to be decided by the judge, the determination of whether a party has acted in good faith is generally understood as a factual inquiry that is within the province of the jury.[193]

This section does not impose a duty of good faith in negotiating a contract—only in performing or enforcing one. The duty is an implied-in-law obligation that arises from the contract itself. Conceptually, therefore, the duty cannot exist during the negotiating stage. Problems that occur during negotiations must be handled under other doctrines, such as misrepresentation, duress, and unconscionability.

While section 1–203 establishes a broad principle, the Code gives courts very little guidance, and this omission is deliberate. The section's short Comment notes that particular sections of the Code reiterate the duty of good faith in specific contexts,[194] and then goes on to say:

The concept, however, is broader than any of these illustrations and applies generally, as stated in this section, to the performance or enforcement of every contract or duty within this Act.

---

[191] UCC § 2A–108(4)(a).

[192] UCC § 2A–108(4)(b).

[193] See, e.g., Banner Iron Works, Inc. v. Amax Zinc Co., 621 F.2d 883 (8th Cir. 1980).

[194] Examples include options to accelerate at will [UCC § 1–208]; the right of cure [§ 2–508]; and the failure of presupposed conditions [§ 2–615].

As we shall see, it is almost impossible to articulate a detailed standard for determining when the duty has been breached.

The Code gives the term "good faith" both a general definition and a specific definition for merchants operating within the scope of Articles 2 and 2A. The general definition is "honesty in fact in the conduct or transaction concerned."[195] This definition creates a purely subjective standard. Good faith means subjective honesty. It can be best understood in contrast to bad faith, which must involve a subjective intent to take advantage of another in some dishonest fashion.

The specific definition of good faith for merchants is "honesty in fact and the observance of reasonable commercial standards of fair dealing in the trade."[196] This definition incorporates the subjective honesty standard of the general definition and adds an objective component—whether the merchant's conduct would be considered fair and reasonable by the average member of the trade.

Commentators have pointed out a moralistic tone to the duty of good faith. Terms such as honesty and fairness are themselves highly subjective and can only be understood as imposing some level of morality on contracting parties.[197] This minimum morality requires that each party avoid conduct that prevents the other from substantially realizing the bargained-for benefit.

Good faith can best be understood by employing an "excluder"[198] analysis. It excludes certain specific forms of bad conduct but beyond that has no particular meaning. Thus, good faith can only be understood in context, and most of the discussion of good faith in this book is reserved for other sections.[199]

---

[195] UCC § 1–201(19)

[196] UCC § 2–103(1)(c). This definition is cross-referenced for Article 2A. UCC § 2A–103(2).

[197] *See generally* Farnsworth, *Good Faith Performance and Commercial Reasonableness Under the Uniform Commercial Code*, 30 U. Chi. L. Rev. 666 (1963); Burton, *Good Faith Performance of a Contract Within Article 2 of the Uniform Commercial Code*, 67 Iowa L. Rev. 1 (1981); Summers, *The General Duty of Good Faith — Its Recognition and Conceptualization*, 67 Cornell L. Rev. 810 (1982).

[198] This term was first used in Summers, *"Good Faith" in General Contract Law and the Sales Provisions of the Uniform Commercial Code*, 54 Va. L. Rev. 195 (1968). Summers' analysis was further developed in his law review article cited in note 197 *supra*.

[199] *See, e.g.,* § 2.06 *supra* (contract modification); § 7.14[A][1] *infra* (failure of presupposed condition); § 7.04 *infra* (rejection of goods); and § 7.09 *infra* (anticipatory repudiation).

CHAPTER

5

Warranty

§ 5.01 WARRANTIES IN GENERAL

Article 2 covers several basic types of warranties: express warranties, implied warranties of merchantability, implied warranties of fitness, and implied warranties of title and against infringement. Warranties can arise through a course of dealing or usage of trade,[1] as well as through express agreement and by operation of law.

Warranty liability is a type of strict liability. If the goods are not of merchantable quality, for example, the reason for the failure is irrelevant. If they fail to live up to the seller's express representations regarding quality, lack of negligence on the seller's part is no defense. The buyer need only prove that the goods were nonconforming at the time the risk of loss passed.[2] Of course,

---

[1] Article 2A is largely comparable, although it adds an implied warranty of quiet possession and deletes the implied warranty of title.

[2] An excellent statement of the Code's strict liability approach can be found in *Vlases v. Montgomery Ward & Co., Inc.*, 377 F.2d 846, 4 UCC Rep. Serv. 164 (3d Cir. 1967), where the buyer of diseased chickens sought to recover for breach of the implied warranty of merchantability. In response to the seller's argument that it was blameless, the court stated as follows:

> The entire purpose behind the implied warranty sections of the Code is to hold the seller responsible when inferior goods are passed along to the unsuspecting buyer. What the Code requires is not evidence that the defects could or should have been uncovered by the seller but only that the goods upon delivery were not of merchantable quality. . . . The gravamen here is not so much with what precautions

the buyer must also prove that any damages he or she has sustained were proximately caused by the breach. Even if the goods were defective, the seller may raise a number of affirmative defenses. The seller may argue that the warranty was disclaimed or that the buyer failed to give proper notice, lacked privity, or assumed the risk.

§ 5.02 TYPES OF WARRANTIES

[A] Express Warranties [2–313; 2A–210]

Express warranties can arise in three ways. First, an affirmation of fact or a promise by the seller or the lessor that relates to the goods and becomes part of the basis of the bargain creates a warranty that the goods will conform to the affirmation or promise.[3] Second, a description of the goods that becomes part of the basis of the bargain creates a warranty that the goods will conform to the description.[4] Third, a sample or model that becomes part of the basis of the bargain creates a warranty that the goods will conform to the sample or model.[5]

[1] The Affirmation of Fact/Opinion Dichotomy

By lumping together affirmations of fact and promises,[6] the drafters repudiated a line of older cases that limited express warranties to situations in which the seller used words of promise. This repudiation is set forth explicitly in section 2–313(2), which states as follows:

> It is not necessary to the creation of an express warranty that the seller use formal words such as "warrant" or "guarantee" or that he have a specific intention to make a warranty, but an affirmation merely of the value of the goods or a statement purporting to be merely the seller's opinion or commendation of the goods does not create a warranty.

Article 2A contains a comparable provision.[7] This approach is based on the realistic appraisal that buyers and lessees are just as likely to be affected by a seller's or lessor's statements of fact with respect to the goods offered for sale

---

were taken by the seller but rather with the quality of the goods contracted for by the buyer.

377 F.2d at 849–50, 4 UCC Rep. Serv. at 168–69.

3   UCC §§ 2–313(1)(a); 2A–210(1)(a).
4   UCC §§ 2–313(1)(b); 2A–210(1)(b).
5   UCC §§ 2–313(1)(c); 2A–210(1)(c).
6   UCC §§ 2–313(1)(a); 2A–210(1)(a).
7   UCC § 2A–210(2).

or lease as they are by direct promises or guarantees stated by sellers and lessors.

Differentiating between affirmations of fact and statements of opinion is often difficult, and disputes are inevitably resolved on a case-by-case basis. The courts have been unable to develop a workable test, but the following generalizations may be helpful in borderline cases. First, the more a statement can be empirically tested, the more likely it is to be an affirmation of fact. Second, as the discrepancy in sophistication between seller and buyer increases, statements by the seller are more likely to be seen as warranties. Third, if the statement is made in the context of other statements of fact, it is likely to take on their coloring and give rise to warranty liability. Fourth, statements made during final negotiations are more likely to be viewed as warranties than statements made in advertising or in preliminary discussions.

In the leading case of *Interco, Inc. v. Randustrial Corp.*,[8] the buyer resurfaced its warehouse floor with Sylox, a floor covering manufactured by the seller. The product proved to be an impediment to warehouse traffic rather than an expedient because the floor shifted more than the covering could tolerate. The buyer argued that the following language from the seller's sales catalog created an express warranty: "Sylox is a hard yet malleable material which bonds firm to wood floors for smooth and easy hand-trucking. *Sylox will absorb considerable flex without cracking* and is not softened by spillage of oil, grease or solvents." (Emphasis supplied). The seller, of course, characterized the language as a mere statement of opinion. At trial, the jury returned a verdict for the seller.

The appellate court concluded that the seller's statement was an affirmation of a particular fact—that Sylox would absorb a considerable amount of flex—rather than a statement of the seller's opinion. Noting that the buyer had no particular expertise in the field of floor coverings, the court stated, "An important factor is whether the seller assumes to assert a fact of which the buyer is ignorant or whether the seller merely expresses an opinion on which the buyer may be expected to have an opinion and be able to express his own judgment."[9] The court nevertheless affirmed the jury's verdict. Even though the seller's statement constituted an express warranty, it was too imprecise to be defined as a matter of law. It was the jury's job to determine whether the Sylox conformed to the warranty, and from the evidence presented the jury could

---

[8]   533 S.W.2d 257, 19 UCC Rep. Serv. 464 (Mo. Ct. App. 1976). The case demonstrates that express warranties can arise from prebargaining advertising. *See also* Crest Container Corp. v. R. H. Bishop Co., 111 Ill. App. 3d 1068, 67 Ill. Dec. 727, 445 N.E.2d 19, 35 UCC Rep. Serv. 1498 (1982) (catalog); Keith v. Buchanan, 173 Cal. App. 3d 13, 220 Cal. Rptr. 392, 42 UCC Rep. Serv. 386 (1985) (advertising).

[9]   533 S.W.2d at 263, 19 UCC Rep. Serv. at 471.

have concluded that the flex in the warehouse floor was more than considerable and thus more than the product was warranted to handle.

By contrast, the court in *Sessa v. Riegle*[10] found that the seller's statement that a racehorse was "sound" was merely a statement of opinion. The court was influenced by the fact that the buyer was a sophisticated horseman who had the horse inspected before sale by another, even more sophisticated expert. Further, the statement was made in the context of other statements that were obviously the seller's opinion, such as "the horse is a good one" and "you will like him." The statement regarding soundness fell within the penumbra of the seller's other statements and took on their coloring. In other cases, similar statements made to less sophisticated buyers have given rise to warranty liability.[11]

Balog v. Center Art Gallery—Hawaii, Inc.[12] is another illustration of the degree to which the relative sophistication of the parties bears on the outcome. The seller, an art dealer, represented that a painting was an original work by Salvador Dali. The court noted that a sophisticated buyer would have understood this as a statement of opinion but concluded that given the actual buyer's lack of expertise, it constituted an express warranty.

The Code gives explicit protection to sellers who make statements regarding the value of goods.[13] In *Daughtrey v. Ashe*,[14] for example, the court held that a seller's appraisal of a diamond ring for insurance purposes was merely an opinion. The seller's statement in the same appraisal that the diamond was "v.v.s." quality, one of the highest ratings used by gemologists, was held to be an affirmation of fact.

[2]   Description

When language that describes the goods becomes part of the basis of the bargain, the seller warrants that the goods conform to the description. In *Best*

---

10   427 F. Supp. 760, 21 UCC Rep. Serv. 745 (E.D. Pa. 1977).

11   *See, e.g.,* Slyman v. Pickwick Farms, 15 Ohio App. 3d 25, 472 N.E.2d 380, 39 UCC Rep. Serv. 1630 (1984) (veterinarian's statement to the crowd at an auction that a racehorse was "sound" was an affirmation of fact); Yuzwak v. Dygert, 144 A.D.2d 938, 534 N.Y.S.2d 35, 7 UCC Rep. Serv. 2d 731 (1988) (court denied seller's motion for summary judgment where seller stated that a horse was a good one for children).

12   745 F. Supp. 1556, 12 UCC Rep. Serv. 2d 962 (D. Haw. 1990).

13   UCC §§ 2–313(2); 2A–210(2).

14   243 Va. 73, 413 S.E.2d 336, 16 UCC Rep. Serv. 2d 294 (1992). *See also* Hall v. T. L. Kemp Jewelry, Inc., 71 N.C. App. 101, 322 S.E.2d 7, 39 UCC Rep. Serv. 1648 (1984). *But see* Goldman v. Barnett, 793 F. Supp. 28, 18 UCC Rep. Serv. 2d 55 (D. Mass. 1992) (whether dealer's appraisal of paintings constituted an express warranty was an issue of fact).

Buick, Inc. v. Welcome,[15] for example, a consumer traded in a Mercedes on the
purchase of a new car. The consumer told the dealer that the Mercedes was a
1970 model when in fact it was a 1968 model. When the dealer sought damages
for the discrepancy, the court found that the consumer had made an express
warranty by description. Similarly, the court in *Hill Aircraft & Leasing Corp. v.
Simon*[16] found that the description "Aero Commander, N–2677B, Number 135,
FAA, Flyable" created a warranty that the aircraft could be fully certified under
FAA regulation 135.

To what extent does a description incorporate a representation regarding
the quality of the goods? For example, does a seller's statement that the product
is a used automobile mean that the car will actually run? In many cases, the
implied warranty of merchantability will supply the quality requirement, but
the implied warranty may have been disclaimed. The Comments encourage the
courts to reject an overly literal reading of warranty disclaimers, stating:

> A contract is normally a contract for the sale of something describable
> and described. A clause generally disclaiming "all warranties, express
> or implied" cannot reduce the seller's obligation with respect to such
> description and therefore cannot be given literal effect under Section
> 2–316.
>
> This is not intended to mean that the parties, if they consciously
> desire, cannot make their own bargain as they wish. But in determining
> what they have agreed upon good faith is a factor and consideration
> should be given to the fact that the probability is small that a real price
> is intended to be exchanged for a pseudo-obligation.[17]

Thus, a used-car dealer who disclaims all implied warranties but describes
the product as an automobile may be found to have created an express warranty of quality that is consistent with, although not higher than, the standard
of merchantability.

The approach suggested by the Comments was rejected in *Tacoma Boatbuilding Co., Inc. v. Delta Fishing Co., Inc.*[18] The buyer purchased a marine engine
that malfunctioned and argued that the seller's description of the product as a
"marine engine" created an express warranty that it would work to propel a
boat across the water. The court found that the seller had delivered a product

---

[15] 18 UCC Rep. Serv. 75 (Mass. App. Div. 1975). *See also* American Honda Motor Co., Inc. v.
    Boyd, 475 So. 2d 835, 41 UCC Rep. Serv. 410 (Ala. 1985) (seller liable for breach of express
    warranty where car described as new had been damaged in transit); Adam Metal Supply,
    Inc. v. Electrodex, Inc., 386 So. 2d 1316, 30 UCC Rep. Serv. 178 (Fla. Ct. App. 1980) (de-
    scription of aluminum by brand name created an express warranty).

[16] 122 Ga. App. 524, 177 S.E.2d 803, 8 UCC Rep. Serv. 474 (1970).

[17] UCC § 2–313, Comment 4.

[18] 28 UCC Rep. Serv. 26 (W.D. Wash. 1980).

that conformed to the description even though it was not of merchantable quality and held further that the seller's disclaimer of the implied warranty of merchantability was effective. The court noted that the buyer would have a cause of action if the engine had in fact been a "wooden box." It is not clear how the *Tacoma Boatbuilding* court would have reacted if the seller had provided the buyer with a marine engine shell containing a mechanism of such little value that it could not be repaired. As a matter of policy, however, courts should be prepared to protect buyers in situations that fall short of the court's wooden-box example.

Although express warranties created through description or through promises or statements of fact can overlap in some cases, a significant factor distinguishes the two categories. Unlike express warranties created through promises or statements of fact, a description does not have to be made by the seller to the buyer. As long as the description becomes part of the basis of the bargain, its source is irrelevant.[19] Commonly, a buyer describes the goods by placing an order with a seller. If the seller responds by delivering goods, an express warranty is created.[20]

[3]   Sample or Model

Express warranties by sample or model arise whenever the seller provides the buyer with an example of the goods. The Comments indicate that a sample must be drawn from the goods to be sold, while a model is not drawn from those goods.[21] By providing the buyer with a sample or model, the seller warrants that the goods will not be of lesser quality than the example.[22] When the buyer is purchasing goods in bulk, this warranty can be more valuable than the implied warranty of merchantability. The implied warranty requires only that fungible goods be of "fair average quality."[23] A sample or model can bind the seller to a higher standard by requiring the goods to have characteristics comparable to those of the sample or model shown.

---

[19] Autzen v. John C. Taylor Lumber Sales, Inc., 280 Or. 783, 572 P.2d 1322, 23 UCC Rep. Serv. 304 (1977) (inadequate defense for seller to assert that survey of boat hull was conducted by a third party and thus statements were made by someone other than the seller); Miles v. Kavanaugh, 350 So. 2d 1090, 22 UCC Rep. Serv. 911 (Fla. Dist. Ct. App. 1977) (description by appraiser became an express warranty when used in the sales negotiations).

[20] Klein v. Sears Roebuck & Co., 733 F.2d 1421, 41 UCC Rep. Serv. 1233 (4th Cir. 1985) (buyer specified need for mower that would be safe on his rolling lawn).

[21] UCC § 2–313, Comment 6.

[22] *Id.*

[23] UCC § 2–314(2)(b).

The Comments suggest that the seller be given more leeway when using a model than when using a sample:

> If the sample has been drawn from an existing bulk, it must be regarded as describing values of the goods contracted for unless it is accompanied by an unmistakable denial of such responsibility. If, on the other hand, a model of merchandise not on hand is offered, the mercantile presumption that it has become a literal description of the subject matter is not so strong, and particularly so if modification on the buyer's initiative impairs any feature of the model.[24]

For example, wine drawn from a larger supply that is available for sale and shown to the buyer would be a sample,[25] but a miniaturized version of the goods to be sold would be a model.[26] Because the sample is part of the actual goods available for sale, it logically should be perceived as more inclusive concerning the attributes of the goods represented.

Like warranties based on a description of the goods, warranties that arise by sample or model raise questions of scope. The Comments indicate the nature of the issue.

> [T]here is no escape from the question of fact. . . . [I]n mercantile experience the mere exhibition of a "sample" does not of itself show whether it is merely intended to "suggest" or to "be" the character of the subject-matter of the contract. The question is whether the seller has so acted with reference to the sample as to make him responsible that the whole shall have at least the values shown by it. The circumstances aid in answering this question.[27]

This distinction could lead parties to dispute whether an express warranty was created by sample or model, or, conceding the creation of the warranty, which attributes are included within its scope.

The express warranty created by sample or model does not amount to a warranty that the goods will be fit for the buyer's intended use. In *Trans-Aire*

---

24 UCC § 2–313, Comment 6. *See also* Blockhead, Inc. v. Plastic Forming Co., Inc., 402 F. Supp. 1017, 18 UCC Rep. Serv. 636 (D. Conn. 1975) (presumption that model is a literal description of the goods is not strong).

25 Regina Grape Prods. Co. v. Supreme Wine Co., 357 Mass. 631, 260 N.E.2d 219, 7 UCC Rep. Serv. 1168 (1970).

26 Mileham & King, Inc. v. Fitzgerald, 33 UCC Rep. Serv. 208 (D.C. Super. 1982) (model of window shutters).

27 UCC § 2–313, Comment 6. *See also* Kopper Clo Fuel, Inc., v. Island Lake Coal Co., 436 F. Supp. 91, 22 UCC Rep. Serv. 1117 (E.D. Tenn. 1977) (sample shown only as representative and thus not an express warranty).

International, Inc. v. Northern Adhesive Co., Inc.,[28] the seller sent the buyer samples of its adhesive, which the buyer intended to use to install fabric in recreational vehicles. The buyer then purchased a quantity of the adhesive, but it failed to perform the task. Because the final product was consistent with the sample, the express warranty was not breached.

[4]   Basis of the Bargain

An express warranty cannot be created unless the affirmation or promise, description, or sample or model becomes "part of the basis of the bargain." This requirement stands in contrast to the corresponding provision in Article 2's predecessor, the Uniform Sales Act, which stated, "Any affirmation of fact or any promise by the seller relating to the goods is an express warranty if the natural tendency of such affirmation or promise is to induce the buyer to purchase the goods, and if the buyer purchases the goods relying thereon."[29] The Code drafters consciously deleted all references to reliance and substituted the phrase "basis of the bargain," but they did not attempt to define the phrase.

Most courts have treated the basis-of-the-bargain provision as a liberalized reliance requirement. In other words, merely by showing that he or she was aware of the seller's statements at the time the sale was consummated, the buyer is able to shift the burden of proving nonreliance to the seller.[30] This analysis is consistent with the Comments, which state:

> The present section deals with affirmations of fact by the seller, descriptions of the goods or exhibitions of samples, exactly as any other part of a negotiation which ends in a contract is dealt with. No specific intention to make a warranty is necessary if any of these factors is made part of the basis of the bargain. In actual practice affirmations of fact made by the seller about the goods during a bargain are regarded as part of the description of those goods; hence no particular reliance on such statements need be shown in order to weave them into the fabric of the agreement. Rather, any fact which is to take such affirmations, once made, out of the agreement requires clear affirmative proof.[31]

---

[28] 882 F.2d 1254, 9 UCC Rep. Serv. 2d 878 (7th Cir. 1989).

[29] Uniform Sales Act § 12.

[30] Some courts still incorrectly place the burden of pleading and proving reliance on the buyer. *See, e.g.,* Williams v. Beechnut Nutrition Corp., 185 Cal. App. 3d 135, 229 Cal. Rptr. 605, 2 UCC Rep. Serv. 2d 1252 (1986); Thomas v. Amway Corp., 488 A.2d 716, 40 UCC Rep. Serv. 836 (R.I. 1985); Stang v. Hertz Corp., 490 P.2d 475, 9 UCC Rep. Serv. 794 (N.M. Ct. App. 1972), *aff'd on this point,* 497 P.2d 732, 10 UCC Rep. Serv. 1010 (N.M. 1972).

[31] UCC § 2–313, Comment 3.

Sylvia Coal Co. v. Mercury Coal & Coke Co.[32] illustrates how the presumption of reliance can be rebutted. The seller gave the buyer a sample of coal but stressed that the coal to be delivered would be of inferior quality. This language negated any reliance by the buyer and prevented the sample from rising to the level of an express warranty.[33]

Suppose the buyer is unaware of the seller's affirmations until after the sale is consummated. Does ignorance prevent them from becoming part of the basis of the bargain? The decisions have generally favored sellers,[34] but a few courts have sided with buyers on the theory that the Code eliminates the reliance requirement altogether.

For example, in *Winston Industries, Inc. v. Stuyvesant Insurance Co., Inc.*[35] a consumer purchased a mobile home that proved to be defective. The buyer admitted that he had been unaware of the manufacturer's express warranty until after the breach, but the court upheld his claim nonetheless. The court was more concerned with what the seller thought was being sold than with what the buyer thought he was purchasing. The rationale for this approach is that two buyers, each of whom pays the same price for the same product, should receive the same warranty protection from a merchant seller. The seller's responsibilities should not be contingent on what the particular buyer has read or heard.

Other buyer-oriented courts have taken different approaches. In *Massey-Ferguson, Inc. v. Laird,*[36] the buyer sued even though the seller's express warranty was not delivered to him until after the sale. The buyer prevailed because he had been aware before the sale that the manufacturer gave express warranties. The fact that he was unaware of the precise nature of the warranty was not fatal to his claim. Suppose, however, that the buyer in *Massey-Ferguson* had

---

[32] 156 S.E.2d 1, 4 UCC Rep. Serv. 650 (W. Va. 1967).

[33] *See also* Alan Wood Steel Co. v. Capital Equip. Enterprises, Inc., 39 Ill. App. 3d 48, 349 N.E.2d 627, 19 UCC Rep. Serv. 1310 (1976) (extremely low purchase price paid for used crane rebutted reliance on description of "75 ton Brownhoist" as indicating that the crane would lift 75 tons).

[34] *See, e.g.,* Ciba-Geigy Corp. v. Alter, 309 Ark. 426, 834 S.W.2d 136, 20 UCC Rep. Serv. 2d 448 (1992) (seller's advertising could not create an express warranty when buyer was unaware of it); Terry v. Moore, 448 P.2d 601 (Wyo. 1968) (post-sale statement by seller of well-drilling equipment regarding production capacity was unenforceable); Schmaltz v. Nissen, 431 N.W.2d 657, 7 UCC Rep. Serv. 2d 1061 (S.D. 1988) (merchant seller of seeds was not liable when buyer admitted he had not read the language on the seed bags before consummating the sale).

[35] 317 So. 2d 493, 17 UCC Rep. Serv. 924 (Ala. Ct. App. 1975). *See also* Villalon v. Vollmering, 676 S.W.2d 220, 39 UCC Rep. Serv. 80 (Tex. Ct. App. 1984); Jensen v. Seigel Mobile Homes Group, 105 Idaho 189, 668 P.2d 65, 35 UCC Rep. Serv. 804 (1983).

[36] 432 So. 2d 1259, 36 UCC Rep. Serv. 437 (Ala. 1983).

been totally unaware of the warranty's existence until after the sale. A few courts would still have found in his favor on the theory that the contract had been modified. This rationale finds support in the following statement from the Comments:

> The precise time when words of description or affirmations are made or samples are shown is not material. The sole question is whether the language or samples or models are fairly to be regarded as part of the contract. If language is used after the closing of the deal (as when the buyer when taking delivery asks and receives an additional assurance), the warranty becomes a modification, and need not be supported by consideration if it is otherwise reasonable and in order (section 2–209).[37]

The modification approach is problematic. Section 2–209 applies to "[a]n *agreement* modifying a contract" (emphasis supplied), and it is difficult to conceptualize a post-sale comment as an "agreement" absent consideration or reliance.[38] A slightly different but more palatable approach involves an expansive reading of the word "bargain." In contrast to a "contract," which is usually formed at a particular time, the term "bargain" can encompass an ongoing consensual relationship between the parties. Affirmations by the seller during the course of this relationship therefore qualify as part of the basis of the expanded bargain.[39]

The argument is diminished if the affirmations are made long after the deal has been consummated. In such cases, the buyer with the best chance is one who has relied on the seller's expressions. For example, the buyer in *Downie v. Abex Corp.*[40] testified that he refrained from making safety modifications to the goods because of the seller's post-sale representations. The court found for the buyer on the theory that the contract had been modified.[41]

---

[37] UCC § 2–313, Comment 7.

[38] *See, e.g.,* Hrosik v. J. Keim Builders, 37 Ill. App.3d 352, 345 N.E.2d 514, 19 UCC Rep. Serv. 472 (1976) (post-sale affirmations require new consideration to be binding).

[39] *See, e.g.,* Autzen v. John C. Taylor Lumber Sales, Inc., 280 Ore. 783, 572 P.2d 1322, 23 UCC Rep. Serv. 304 (1977) (seller's post-sale statement that a boat's hull was "very sound" was part of the parties' ongoing relationship as seller and buyer). *See generally* Murray, *Basis of the Bargain: Transcending Classical Concepts,* 66 Minn. L. Rev. 283 (1982).

[40] 741 F.2d 1235, 39 UCC Rep. Serv. 427 (10th Cir. 1984). *See also* Bigelow v. Agway, Inc., 506 F.2d 551, 15 UCC Rep. Serv. 769 (2d Cir. 1974) (farmer prevailed after relying on seller's statement that hay could be baled safely after being sprayed with seller's product).

[41] In some cases, an alternative approach may be available. Under section 2–314(2)(f), goods are not of merchantable quality if they fail to "conform to the promises or affirmations of fact made on the container or label if any." The implied warranty of merchantability is discussed in § 5.02[B] *infra.* Unless this implied warranty is effectively disclaimed, a disappointed buyer can enforce affirmations made on the container or label without having to prove that they became part of the basis of the bargain. *See, e.g.,* Farmers Union Coop. Gin v. Smith, 9 UCC Rep. Serv. 823 (Okla. Ct. App. 1971).

Another illustrative case is *Autzen v. John C. Taylor Lumber Sales, Inc.*[42] The buyer and seller agreed to terms on the sale of a 50-foot wooden boat. The seller insisted that it would have a survey conducted on the boat to determine its soundness. The survey results, passed on to the buyer, indicated that the boat was "very sound" and "should be well suited for its intended purpose." To the contrary, the buyer encountered problems and discovered extensive dry rot and insect infestation. The seller appealed a verdict returned in favor of the buyer for a claim based on breach of an express warranty.

Part of the seller's argument on appeal was that the survey could not have been part of the basis of the bargain because it was not provided until after the parties had entered their contract. The appellate court indicated that the seller improperly confused the concepts of bargain and contract, and explained how the survey could have been part of the basis of the bargain between the parties.

> At the time Buyer was first informed of the Huhta survey results, he had not yet taken possession of the boat. While this description did not induce the actual formation of the contract, the jury might have found that it did induce and was intended by the Seller to induce Buyer's satisfaction with the agreement just made, as well as to lessen Buyer's degree of vigilance in inspecting the boat prior to acceptance.[43]

As well as distinguishing between reliance and the basis of the bargain as a requirement for the creation of an express warranty, courts should also be aware that representations through statements, descriptions, or samples or models do not have to be the primary basis of the bargain between the parties. They must simply be "*part* of the basis of the bargain." A buyer can be influenced by multiple inducements to enter into a bargain and remain pleased with it through complete performance of all of the obligations. If the transaction is pursued and completed at least in part on the basis of the pertinent representations, those representations become express warranties.[44]

Courts also should be aware that the distinction between express warranties and mere sales talk or puffing that is indicated in section 2–313(2) does not create a new test, but rather simply restates the basis-of-the-bargain requirement. The Comments stress the correlation between the two subsections.

> Concerning affirmations of value or a seller's opinion or commendation under subsection (2), the basic question remains the same: What statements of the seller have in the circumstances and in objective judgment become part of the basis of the bargain?[45]

---

[42]   280 Or. 783, 572 P.2d 1322, 23 UCC Rep. Serv. 304 (1977).
[43]   572 P.2d at 1325–26.
[44]   R. Nordstrom, *Handbook on the Law of Sales* 208 (1970).
[45]   UCC § 2–313, Comment 8.

Subsection (2) excludes only "an affirmation *merely* of the value of the goods or a statement purporting to be *merely* the seller's opinion or commendation of the goods." At some point the seller's representations shade out from being *merely* his or her opinion and become an express warranty.[46] The point at which this transformation occurs is when those representations become part of the basis of the bargain. The law should be primarily interested in protecting the reasonable expectations of the buyer under all the circumstances of the transaction.

[B]   The Implied Warranty of Merchantability Generally [2–314; 2A–212]

The implied warranty of merchantability is created by section 2–314. Because of its singular importance, the section is set forth here in its entirety:

(1) Unless excluded or modified (Section 2–316), a warranty that the goods shall be merchantable is implied in a contract for their sale if the seller is a merchant with respect to goods of that kind. Under this section the serving for value of food or drink to be consumed either on the premises or elsewhere is a sale.

(2) Goods to be merchantable must be at least such as
- (a) pass without objection in the trade under the contract description; and
- (b) in the case of fungible goods, are of fair average quality within the description; and
- (c) are fit for the ordinary purposes for which such goods are used; and
- (d) run, within the variations permitted by the agreement, of even kind, quality and quantity within each unit and among all units involved; and
- (e) are adequately contained, packaged, and labeled as the agreement may require; and
- (f) conform to the promises or affirmations of fact made on the container or label, if any.

(3) Unless excluded or modified (Section 2–316) other implied warranties may arise from course of dealing or usage of trade.

Article 2A contains a comparable provision.[47]

This section discusses the circumstances that give rise to the implied warranty of merchantability and the standard to be applied in such circumstances.

---

[46]   R. Nordstrom, *Handbook on the Law of Sales* 219 (1970). Young & Cooper, Inc. v. Vestring, 214 Kan. 311, 521 P.2d 281, 14 UCC Rep. Serv. 916 (1974).

[47]   UCC § 2A–212. The warranty is not made by a finance lessor.

Defenses of the seller, such as disclaimer, lack of privity, and assumption of the risk, are discussed later in this chapter.

[1]   "Merchant with Respect to Goods of That Kind"

The implied warranty of merchantability overturns the common-law doctrine of *caveat emptor*,[48] but it does not apply to all sales. It arises only when the seller is a particular type of merchant—one who deals in goods of the kind that are at issue. The Code defines the term "merchant,"[49] but it does not define "merchant with respect to goods of that kind." The Comments provide some help, indicating that "this qualification restricts the implied warranty to a much smaller group than everyone who is engaged in business and requires a professional status as to particular kinds of goods."[50]

Clearly a manufacturer is a merchant,[51] but what about a seller further down the chain of distribution? The Comments suggest that the issue turns on the quantity of such goods sold by the particular seller.[52] Sellers who make only isolated sales of the product are not merchants for purposes of section 2–314 even though they may qualify as merchants for purposes of the Statute of Frauds or the battle of the forms.[53] For example, in *Cohen v. Hathaway*[54] the defendants, commercial fishermen, sold their boat to the plaintiff. The boat proved to be defective, but the court held that the defendants were not in the business of selling fishing boats and did not make the implied warranty of merchantability.

As the *Cohen* case illustrates, sellers have a better chance of avoiding liability when the goods are equipment rather than inventory,[55] but equipment sellers have occasionally been classified as merchants and inventory sellers have occasionally escaped liability. In *Ferragamo v. Massachusetts Bay Transportation Authority*,[56] the seller of used trolley equipment was found to be a merchant because it made such sales on a regular basis. By contrast, the seller in

---

48   The phrase means "let the buyer beware."

49   UCC § 2–104(1). This definition is discussed in § 3.04[B] *supra*.

50   UCC § 2–104, Comment 2.

51   *See, e.g.*, Valley Iron & Steel Co. v. Thorin, 278 Or. 103, 562 P.2d 1212, 21 UCC Rep. Serv. 760 (1977) (foundry operator was merchant even though it was for the first time manufacturing a special tool for the buyer).

52   UCC § 2–314, Comment 3.

53   See UCC § 2–104, Comment 2.

54   95 F. Supp. 575, 39 UCC Rep. Serv. 857 (D. Mass. 1984).

55   *See, e.g.*, Siemen v. Alden, 34 Ill. App. 3d 961, 341 N.E.2d 713, 18 UCC Rep. Serv. 884 (1975) (sawmill that sold saw not a merchant); Allen v. Nicole, Inc., 172 N.J. Super. 442, 412 A.2d 824, 28 UCC Rep. Serv. 982 (1980) (carnival operator who sold defective ride not a merchant).

56   395 Mass. 581, 481 N.E.2d 477, 41 UCC Rep. Serv. 304 (1985).

Czarnecki v. Roller[57] was not a merchant even though he had sold five yachts over a period of several years. The court was undoubtedly influenced by the fact that the seller was an individual selling yachts that he had used for consumer purposes.

In *Storey v. Day Heating & Air Conditioning Co.*,[58] the seller avoided liability for selling a defective condensate pump even though it clearly qualified as inventory. The court stressed that there was nothing in the record to show that the defendant regularly sold such pumps, but the jury may have been influenced more by the fact that the seller had replaced the pump on an emergency basis while the buyer was on vacation and had not charged the buyer for its time.

Cases involving farmers and ranchers have given the courts considerable trouble, although most of the decisions have held such parties to be merchants.[59] Care must be exercised in this area, however, because a number of states have enacted nonuniform amendments to the Code insulating farmers and ranchers from merchant status.[60]

[2] The Standard of Merchantability

Section 2–314(2) establishes six minimum standards of merchantability, the most important of which requires that the goods be "fit for the ordinary purposes for which such goods are used. . . ."[61] The seller need not tender the best possible goods under this standard, but a product must be able to perform the ordinary tasks for which it is manufactured. In contrast to an express warranty, which can be breached with a perfect product if the seller has overpromised its capabilities, the implied warranty of merchantability cannot be breached unless the product is defective in some way.[62] Consistent with the kinds of defects that give rise to strict liability in tort,[63] liability can be predicated on design defects, defects in the manufacturing process, or defects in the instructions given to the buyer.

---

[57] 726 F. Supp. 832, 11 UCC Rep. Serv. 2d 829 (S.D. Fla. 1989).

[58] 319 So. 2d 279, 17 UCC Rep. Serv. 1208 (Ala. Ct. App. 1975).

[59] *See, e.g.*, Fear Ranches, Inc. v. Berry, 470 F.2d 905, 12 UCC Rep. Serv. 27 (10th Cir. 1972); Dotts v. Bennett, 382 N.W.2d 85, 42 UCC Rep. Serv. 1273 (Iowa 1986). *But see* Sparks v. Stich, 135 A.D.2d 989, 522 N.Y.S.2d 707, 5 UCC Rep. Serv. 2d 922 (1987) (farmers were not merchants in transaction involving sale of their house and 17 cows even though they regularly raised and sold such animals).

[60] *See, e.g.*, Kan. Stat. Ann. § 82–2–316 (1983), overturning the result in *Musil v. Hendrich*, 6 Kan. App. 2d 196, 627 P.2d 367, 31 UCC Rep. Serv. 432 (1981).

[61] UCC § 2–314(2)(c).

[62] *See, e.g.*, Costilla v. Aluminum Co. of America, 836 F.2d 1444, 4 UCC Rep. Serv. 2d 1056 (5th Cir. 1987).

[63] *See* Restatement (Second) of Torts § 402A. Warranty liability is broader than strict liability

The most common defect is a flaw in the manufacturing process. In *Fredrick v. Dryer*,[64] for example, the buyer recovered for breach of the implied warranty of merchantability when the mobile home that he purchased proved to be a "lemon." The roof leaked, the doors would not latch, the electrical wiring was installed incorrectly, and the plumbing did not work. The merchantability standard is also breached, however, when the defect stems from a design error. In *Valley Iron & Steel Co. v. Thorin*,[65] for example, the buyer was a retail dealer in forestry equipment and wanted to carry a line of hoedads, tools used to plant seedlings. The manufacturer, a foundry that had never produced a hoedad before, recommended that the tool be made of iron. The hoedads broke easily, producing a large volume of complaints, but hoedads subsequently manufactured from steel by a different foundry proved satisfactory. The manufacturer was held accountable for the design flaw.

Even if the goods are properly designed and manufactured, they are not of merchantable quality if the seller's failure to give adequate instructions to the buyer results in harm. In *Hayes v. Ariens Co.*,[66] for example, a buyer recovered for his personal injuries because the manufacturer failed to warn of the dangers of removing clogged snow from a snowblower without turning the motor off. And in *Stephens v. G. D. Searle & Co.*,[67] the court held that a prescription-drug manufacturer can be liable for failing to warn of the side effects of its products.

Goods are not defective merely because they will not perform the task for which they were purchased. In *Computerized Radiological Services v. Syntex Corp.*,[68] for example, radiologists who had purchased an X-ray scanner complained that it was unfit to perform body scans. The machine, which was not defective, had been designed to perform head scans only. The court held that the machine was of merchantable quality, but it found for the radiologists under the implied warranty of fitness.[69]

---

in tort. Tort liability is predicated on personal injury or property damage, whereas a seller may be liable in warranty for purely economic losses. Further, warranty law does not require that the product be unreasonably dangerous.

[64]   257 N.W.2d 835, 23 UCC Rep. Serv. 55 (S.D. 1977).

[65]   278 Or. 103, 562 P.2d 1212, 21 UCC Rep. Serv. 760 (1977).

[66]   391 Mass. 407, 462 N.E.2d 273, 38 UCC Rep. Serv. 48 (1984).

[67]   602 F. Supp. 379, 40 UCC Rep. Serv. 441 (E.D. Mich. 1985).

[68]   595 F. Supp. 1495, 40 UCC Rep. Serv. 49 (E.D.N.Y. 1984).

[69]   *See also* Fiddler's Inn, Inc. v. Andrews Dist. Co., Inc., 612 S.W.2d 166, 31 UCC Rep. Serv. 1277 (Tenn. Ct. App. 1980) (implied warranty of merchantability not breached when buyer ordered heating units that were too small to keep buyer's rooms warm). The implied warranty of fitness, which is discussed in § 5.02[C] *infra*, can be breached even though the product is not defective.

Even though a product causes harm, it is merchantable if its quality is consistent with that of other goods of the same class. In *Webster v. Blue Ship Tea Room*,[70] for example, the plaintiff was injured by a fish bone in her fish chowder. The court, siding with the seller, adopted a "foreign/natural" test and concluded that a buyer who is injured by a substance that is natural to the food cannot recover for breach of the implied warranty of merchantability. The buyer would have prevailed if she had been injured by a stone that had fallen into the soup.

Recently, a number of courts have abandoned the foreign/natural test in favor of a standard based on consumer expectations. In *Johnson v. CFM, Inc.*,[71] a consumer became ill after drinking a cup of coffee that contained excessive grounds. The consumer recovered even though grounds are a natural product of coffee because the concentration level exceeded the expectations of the reasonable consumer. The buyer did not fare as well in *Morrison's Cafeteria of Montgomery, Inc. v. Haddox*,[72] where the court ruled as a matter of law that a one-centimeter fish bone in a fish fillet was not inconsistent with consumer expectations.

The Comments indicate that the implied warranty of merchantability should be applied to used goods,[73] and most courts have done so.[74] Of course, the standard applied must be appropriate for used goods, and less is expected of used than of new goods. Thus, the seller may be able to avoid liability by showing that the product failed due to normal wear and tear.[75] On the other hand, buyers have recovered by tracing the failure to a design or manufac-

---

[70] 347 Mass. 421, 198 N.E.2d 309, 2 UCC Rep. Serv. 161 (1964).
[71] 726 F. Supp. 1228, 10 UCC Rep. Serv. 2d 1195 (D. Kan. 1990). *See also* Goodman v. Wenco Management, 100 N.C. App. 108, 394 S.E.2d 832, 13 UCC Rep. Serv. 2d 106 (1990) (consumer who chipped tooth on bone in hamburger recovered because size of bone exceeded consumer expectations).
[72] 431 So. 2d 975, 35 UCC Rep. Serv. 1074 (Ala. 1983).
[73] UCC § 2–314, Comment 3. *See also* § 2–314, Comment 7, which states, "In case of doubt as to what quality is intended, the price at which a merchant closes a contract is an excellent index of the nature and scope of his obligation under the present section." This suggests that a buyer who pays a rock-bottom price should have low expectations regarding quality.
[74] Only in Texas and Alabama have the courts held that section 2–314 is inapplicable to a merchant's sale of used goods. *See, e.g.*, Valley Datsun v. Martinez, 587 S.W.2d 485, 26 UCC Rep. Serv. 331 (Tex. Ct. Civ. App. 1979); Osborn v. Custom Truck Sales and Serv., 562 So. 2d 243, 12 UCC Rep. Serv. 2d 664 (Ala. 1990).
[75] *See, e.g.*, Carey v. Woburn Motors, Inc., 29 UCC Rep. Serv. 1228 (Mass. Ct. App. 1980) (seller not responsible when used car broke down 29 days after purchase since failure was consistent with normal wear and tear).

turing defect,[76] or by demonstrating that the product was exposed to excessive wear and tear for its age.[77]

Most of the reported cases have been decided under the "ordinary purposes" standard, but the other standards set forth in section 2–314(2) occasionally come into play. Under section 2–314(2)(a), for example, the goods must pass without objection in the trade under the contract description. This standard is illustrated by *Delano Growers' Cooperative Winery v. Supreme Wine Co., Inc.*,[78] where the seller of California sweet wine incurred liability for selling wine that failed to meet industry standards due to the presence of too much purple nectar. Under section 2–314(2)(b), fungible goods must be of fair average quality, and in *T. J. Stevenson & Co., Inc. v. 81,193 Bags of Flour*,[79] the buyer recovered when flour was found to contain an excessive level of beetle infestation. Either of these cases could have been decided under the basic standard of section 2–314(2)(c).

Section 2–314(2)(e) requires that the goods be adequately contained, packaged, and labeled. Thus, buyers have recovered when bottles have exploded,[80] when the product has broken during shipment,[81] when misleading labeling has made resale difficult,[82] and when inadequate labeling of cartons has caused confusion over the brand of appliances contained within.[83]

Finally, section 2–314(2)(f) requires that the product conform to any promises or affirmations of fact on the container or label. This theory is particularly useful to a buyer who failed to read the label prior to consummating the sale and is precluded from using express warranty theory to enforce the representations on the label.[84]

---

[76] *See, e.g.*, Whittle v. Timesavers, Inc., 614 F. Supp. 115, 42 UCC Rep. Serv. 126 (W.D. Va. 1985). *But see* Fuquay v. Revels Motors, Inc., 398 So. 2d 1238, 30 UCC Rep. Serv. 494 (Fla. Ct. App. 1980) (latent defects in used goods not actionable because sellers of used goods, unlike sellers of new goods, lack the ability to influence manufacturers to make safe products).

[77] *See, e.g.*, Testo v. Dunmire Oldsmobile, Inc., 16 Wash. App. 39, 554 P.2d 349, 20 UCC Rep. Serv. 54 (1976) (used car failed within 200 miles of purchase and evidence showed that it had been raced by previous owner).

[78] 393 Mass. 666, 473 N.E.2d 1066, 40 UCC Rep. Serv. 93 (1985).

[79] 629 F.2d 338, 30 UCC Rep. Serv. 865 (5th Cir. 1980). The court actually relied on UCC § 2–314(2)(a), but § 2–314(2)(b) would have provided a more appropriate basis for the holding since it explicitly applies to fungible goods.

[80] *See, e.g.*, Seigel v. Giant Food, Inc., 20 Md. App. 611, 318 A.2d 874, 14 UCC Rep. Serv. 892 (1974).

[81] *See, e.g.*, Standard Brands Chemical Indus., Inc. v. Pilot Freight Carriers, Inc., 65 Misc. 2d 1029, 319 N.Y.S.2d 457, 9 UCC Rep. Serv. 422 (Sup. Ct. 1972).

[82] *See, e.g.*, Agricultural Services Ass'n v. Ferry-Morse Seed Co., 551 F.2d 1057, 21 UCC Rep. Serv. 443 (6th Cir. 1977).

[83] *See, e.g.*, Carnes Constr. Co. v. Richards & Conover Steel & Supply Co., 10 UCC Rep. Serv. 797 (Okla. Ct. App. 1972).

[84] *See* text accompanying notes 36–37 *supra*. *See also* UCC § 2–314, Comment 10.

[C]   The Implied Warranty of Fitness for a Particular Purpose [2–315; 2A–213]

The implied warranty of fitness for a particular purpose can be made by any seller, not just a merchant,[85] but it is much narrower in its application than the implied warranty of merchantability. It requires that the seller, at the time of contracting, have reason to know 1) of the particular purpose for which the buyer will be using the goods, and 2) that the buyer is relying on the seller's skill or judgment to select or furnish the goods.[86] These requirements are discussed below.

[1]   "Reason to Know"

For the implied warranty of fitness to arise, the seller must have reason to know of the buyer's intended use and of the buyer's reliance on the seller's expertise. "Reason to know" is not a defined term, but it clearly contemplates situations in which the seller lacks actual knowledge. The Comments explain the term as follows:

> Whether or not this warranty arises in any individual case is basically a question of fact to be determined by the circumstances of the contracting. Under this section the buyer need not bring home to the seller actual knowledge of the particular purpose for which the goods are intended or of his reliance on the seller's skill and judgment, if the circumstances are such that the seller has reason to realize the purpose intended or that the reliance exists.[87]

In most cases, the buyer simply tells the seller about his or her particular needs. For example, in *Computerized Radiological Services v. Syntex Corp.*,[88] a group of radiologists told the seller they needed a machine for body scans. The seller breached the implied warranty of fitness when it supplied a machine that performed only head scans. In other cases, the seller may lack actual knowledge but be charged with reason to know. In *Agricultural Services Association v. Ferry-Morse Seed Co.*,[89] for example, the buyer purchased a quantity of seeds that was obviously too large for its personal use. The seller was charged with reason to know that the seeds would be resold.

---

[85]   Because of the requirement that the buyer rely on the seller's expertise, cases in which the seller is not a merchant are relatively rare.

[86]   UCC §§ 2–315; 2A–213.

[87]   UCC § 2–315, Comment 1.

[88]   595 F. Supp. 1495, 40 UCC Rep. Serv. 49 (E.D.N.Y. 1984). *See also* Neilson Business Equipment Center, Inc. v. Italo Monteleone, M.D., P.A., 524 A.2d 1172, 3 UCC Rep. Serv. 2d 1721 (Del. 1987) (seller who agreed to customize computer equipment to meet buyer's processing needs gave warranty of fitness).

[89]   551 F.2d 1057, 21 UCC Rep. Serv. 443 (6th Cir. 1977).

The implied warranty of fitness does not arise when the buyer fails to communicate his or her needs and the seller is unable to infer those needs from the surrounding circumstances.[90]

[2]   Particular Purpose

The Code drafters intended that the implied warranty of fitness apply only when the goods are used for a "particular purpose." If the goods are to be used for any of their ordinary purposes, the buyer should be limited to the implied warranty of merchantability, if any. The following statement from the Comments makes this distinction clear:

> A "particular purpose" differs from the ordinary purpose for which the goods are used in that it envisages a specific use by the buyer which is peculiar to the nature of his business whereas the ordinary purposes for which goods are used are those envisaged in the concept of merchantability and go to uses which are customarily made of the goods in question. For example, shoes are generally used for the purpose of walking upon ordinary ground, but a seller may know that a particular pair was selected to be used for climbing mountains.[91]

Lewis v. Mobil Oil Corp.[92] is one of the leading cases on the "particular purpose" doctrine. The seller recommended that the buyer, a sawmill operator, use a nonadditive mineral oil in the hydraulic system of the sawmill. Even though the oil was not defective, the buyer recovered because it failed to remedy the problem for which it had been selected. Another example of a particular purpose can be found in *Fiddler's Inn, Inc. v. Andrews Distributing Co., Inc.*[93] The buyer purchased heating units that failed to keep the rooms in its inn warm. The heaters were of merchantable quality, but they were too small for the rooms. Although use of the heaters in the large rooms qualified as a particular purpose, the seller avoided liability because the buyer had selected the heaters.

The implied warranty of fitness should not be invoked when goods are being used for an ordinary purpose, and most courts have understood this point. For example, in *Crysco Oilfield Services, Inc. v. Hutchison-Hayes International, Inc.*,[94] the court held that no implied warranty of fitness arose when shale

---

[90]   *See, e.g.*, Hickham v. Chronister, 792 S.W.2d 631, 13 UCC Rep. Serv. 2d 132 (Mo. Ct. App. 1990) (seller of orthodontic molds not liable when orthodontist supplied the plans and specifications).

[91]   UCC § 2–315, Comment 2.

[92]   438 F.2d 500, 8 UCC Rep. Serv. 625 (8th Cir. 1971).

[93]   612 S.W.2d 166, 31 UCC Rep. Serv. 1277 (Tenn. Ct. App. 1980).

[94]   913 F.2d 850, 12 UCC Rep. Serv. 2d 1019 (10th Cir. 1990). *See also* Fernandes v. Union Bookbinding Co., Inc., 400 Mass. 27, 507 N.E.2d 728, 5 UCC Rep. Serv. 2d 959 (1987) (warranty of fitness not breached when spacer ply cutting press being used for its ordinary

shakers were used in oil fields for precisely those tasks for which they were manufactured.

A number of courts, undoubtedly influenced by the buyer's reliance on the seller's expertise, have incorrectly merged the implied warranty of merchantability and the implied warranty of fitness. *Renze Hybrids, Inc. v. Shell Oil Co.*,[95] for example, involved an insecticide that had been designed for use against a variety of insects. The buyer purchased the product for use against one of these insects, and the court held that this constituted a particular purpose. Similarly, the court in *Great Dane Trailer Sales, Inc. v. Malvern Pulpwood, Inc.*[96] stated explicitly that when the buyer's particular purpose in purchasing the goods happens to be one of the ordinary purposes for which the goods were manufactured, the two warranties merge and the buyer can enforce either. And in *Soaper v. Hope Industries, Inc.*,[97] the buyer of a film processor recovered for breach of the implied warranty of fitness when the product failed while processing film. The court reasoned that a product that is unfit for any purpose is also unfit for a particular purpose.

Courts should resist any analysis that merges the concepts of merchantability and fitness. If goods are being used for an ordinary purpose, only the implied warranty of merchantability is at issue. Of course, in many cases the distinction will be irrelevant. If the buyer has relied on the seller to select the goods, the seller will have likely stated expressly that the goods will do the job. If so, the buyer can claim breach of an express warranty and need not rely on the implied warranty of fitness.

[3]   Reliance by the Buyer

In addition to having reason to know of the buyer's particular purpose, the seller must have reason to know that the buyer is relying on the seller's expertise in selecting the goods. In *Light v. Weldarc Co., Inc.*,[98] for example, the buyer was blinded in one eye when his safety glasses slipped and he was struck by a flying object. The buyer admitted that he had been aware when he made the purchase that safety glasses are prone to slip, and he had accepted the pair in

---

purpose caused personal injury); Van Wyk v. Norden Laboratories, Inc., 345 N.W.2d 81, 37 UCC Rep. Serv. 1489 (Iowa 1984) (warranty of fitness not breached where cattle vaccine made the cattle ill).

[95]   418 N.W.2d 634, 5 UCC Rep. Serv. 2d 1331 (Iowa 1988).

[96]   301 Ark. 436, 785 S.W.2d 13, 11 UCC Rep. Serv. 2d 875 (1990). *See also* Filler v. Rayex Corp., 435 F.2d 336, 8 UCC Rep. Serv. 323 (7th Cir. 1970) (young baseball player injured when flip-up baseball sunglasses shattered on being struck by a baseball).

[97]   424 S.E.2d 493, 20 UCC Rep. Serv. 2d 101 (S.C. 1992).

[98]   569 So. 2d 1302, 14 UCC Rep. Serv. 2d 431 (Fla. Ct. App. 1992).

question even though they did not have a headstrap. Under the circumstances, the reliance was insufficient to invoke the implied warranty of fitness.[99]

Other buyers have lost because their own expertise negated any reliance. In *O'Keefe Elevator Co., Inc. v. Second Avenue Properties, Ltd.*,[100] the buyer of a wheelchair lift was found to have relied on its own knowledge rather than that of the seller. *Sylvia Coal Co. v. Mercury Coal & Coke Co.*[101] is another example. The buyer claimed that the coal it had purchased was unfit for making coke. The seller prevailed when it demonstrated that it had no knowledge of the process for making coke and that the buyer was experienced in that regard.

[D]   The Warranties of Title and Against Infringement [2–312; 2A–211]

In a contract for the sale of goods, the seller impliedly warrants to the buyer that the seller has good title. This warranty provides that:

(a) the title conveyed shall be good, and its transfer rightful; and
(b) the goods shall be delivered free from any security interest or other lien or encumbrance of which the buyer at the time of contracting has no knowledge.[102]

The seller need not be a merchant to breach the implied warranty of title. If the buyer loses the goods because of an adverse claim of ownership (as when the goods were stolen) or an enforceable security interest, the warranty has been breached.

There is an exception for sales made in circumstances "which give the buyer reason to know that the person selling does not claim title in himself or that he is purporting to sell only such right or title as he or a third person may have."[103] Thus, the warranty of title does not arise for goods that are purchased at a sheriff's execution sale or a secured party's foreclosure sale.[104]

Has the implied warranty of title been breached when a third party asserts a colorable claim to the goods that is ultimately defeated by the buyer? The Comments indicate that Article 2 has abolished any implied warranty of quiet possession,[105] suggesting that the seller is not liable for costs the buyer incurs in successfully defending against the claim. The Comments also state, however,

---

[99] The court did not address whether the buyer's use constituted a particular purpose.
[100] 216 Neb. 170, 343 N.W.2d 54, 37 UCC Rep. Serv. 1100 (1984).
[101] 151 W. Va. 818, 156 S.E.2d 1, 4 UCC Rep. Serv. 650 (1967).
[102] UCC § 2–312(1).
[103] UCC § 2–312(2).
[104] UCC § 2–312, Comment 5.
[105] UCC § 2–312, Comment 1.

that "[d]isturbance of quiet possession, although not mentioned specifically, is one way, among many, in which the breach of the warranty of title may be established"[106] and that one of the purposes of the implied warranty of title is to ensure that the buyer "not be exposed to a lawsuit in order to protect [title]."[107] These statements suggest that the implied warranty of quiet possession still exists and has been merged into the implied warranty of title. The few cases on point indicate that assertion of a claim that casts a substantial cloud on the buyer's title gives rise to a cause of action[108] but assertion of a frivolous claim does not.[109]

There is no implied warranty of title in Article 2A because the lessor does not deliver title to the goods to the lessee. Article 2A does, however, expressly recognize the implied warranty of quiet possession.[110] The Comments explain the warranty as follows:

> Inherent in the nature of the limited interest transferred by the lease—the right to possession and use of the goods—is the need of the lessee for protection greater than that afforded to the buyer. Since the scope of the protection is limited to claims or interests that arose from acts or omissions of the lessor, the lessor will be in position to evaluate the potential cost, certainly a far better position than that enjoyed by the lessee.[111]

Articles 2 and 2A protect the buyer and lessee from claims of patent infringement when the seller or lessor is a merchant.[112] Liability, of course, does not extend to cases in which the buyer or lessee furnishes the specifications for the goods.[113]

---

[106] Id.

[107] Id.

[108] See, e.g., American Container Corp. v. Hanley Trucking Corp., 111 N.J. Super. 322, 268 A.2d 313, 7 UCC Rep. Serv. 1301 (1970); Maroone Chevrolet, Inc. v. Nordstrom, 587 So. 2d 514, 15 UCC Rep. Serv. 2d 759 (Fla. Ct. App. 1991). Contra, Cochran v. Horner, 121 Ga. App. 297, 173 S.E.2d 448, 7 UCC Rep. Serv. 707 (1970).

[109] See, e.g., Maroone Chevrolet, Inc. v. Nordstrom, 587 So. 2d 514, 15 UCC Rep. Serv. 2d 759 (Fla. Ct. App. 1991) (whether claim is substantial is an objective test, not predicated on the baseless anxiety of a hypersensitive buyer).

[110] UCC § 2A–211(1).

[111] UCC § 2A–211, Comment.

[112] UCC §§ 2–312(3), 2A–211(2). The warranty is not made by a finance lessor. Because the finance lessor does not participate in selection of the goods, it does not have any way to ensure that the goods in the lease do not infringe on patents of third parties.

[113] UCC §§ 2–312(3), 2A–211(3).

§ 5.03   WARRANTY DISCLAIMERS [2–316; 2A–214]

Warranty disclaimers are among the most frequent problems encountered by dissatisfied buyers. Effective language can eliminate both express and implied warranties. Warranty disclaimers must be contrasted with limited-remedy clauses, which are discussed in the next section.[114] With a limited-remedy clause, the warranty exists but the buyer's choice of remedies is restricted. With an effective disclaimer, there is no warranty, so the buyer lacks any remedy whatsoever.

[A]   Disclaiming Express Warranties

There is something inherently suspicious when a seller who has made an express warranty attempts to disclaim responsibility. The disclaimer is inconsistent with the words or conduct that created the warranty and, unless the seller is somehow able to reconcile the conduct or language negating the warranty with the conduct or language that gave rise to it, the disclaimer is inoperative.[115] The Comments indicate that this rule protects the buyer "from unexpected or unbargained language of disclaimer by denying effect to such language when inconsistent."[116]

On occasion, a seller has been able to synthesize language in a way that affords protection from the buyer's claim. In *Consolidated Papers, Inc. v. Dorr-Oliver, Inc.*,[117] for example, the seller warranted that a wood-processing machine was free from defects but also stated that decomposition by chemical action and wear did not qualify as a defect. Reading the language together, the court held that the seller had not warranted that the machine would not fail due to corrosion. A similar result was reached in *Alan Wood Steel Co. v. Capital Equipment Enterprises, Inc.*,[118] where the seller described the product as a "75 ton, 40 foot boom Brownhoist Steam Locomotive Crane" but also stated that all descriptions were approximations. The court held that the seller had not expressly warranted that the crane would lift 75 tons.

Doubtful cases are construed in the buyer's favor, and when reconciliation is impossible the disclaimer is inoperative. For example, a written statement that an irrigation system was trouble-free was held to negate a blanket disclaimer of express warranties in *Whitaker v. Farmhand, Inc.*[119] Similarly, in

---

[114] See § 5.04, *infra.*
[115] UCC § 2–316(1). Article 2A is comparable.
[116] UCC § 2–316, Comment 1.
[117] 153 Wis. 2d 589, 451 N.W.2d 456, 11 UCC Rep. Serv. 2d 492 (Ct. App. 1989).
[118] 39 Ill. App. 3d 48, 349 N.E.2d 627, 19 UCC Rep. Serv. 1310 (1976).
[119] 173 Mont. 345, 567 P.2d 916, 22 UCC Rep. Serv. 375 (1977).

Fundin v. Chicago Pneumatic Tool Co.,[120] a blanket disclaimer was insufficient to protect a seller who had expressly warranted that a drilling rig could drill to a specified depth. In numerous other cases, courts have found blanket disclaimers or phrases like "as is" insufficient to disclaim express warranties.[121]

Unfortunately for many buyers, the rule rendering disclaimers ineffective is expressly made subject to the parol evidence rule.[122] Thus the buyer may be unable to introduce evidence of language or conduct supporting the existence of an express warranty. In *Investors Premium Corp. v. Burroughs Corp.*,[123] for example, the buyer alleged that the seller had made express warranties prior to consummation of the sale. The court found that the parties had reduced their agreement to a final and complete writing and granted summary judgment for the seller. The application of the parol evidence rule to express warranties is not different from its general application, and the rule is discussed at length elsewhere in this book.[124]

[B]   Disclaiming the Implied Warranties of Merchantability and Fitness

The Code provides a number of mechanisms for disclaiming the implied warranties of merchantability and fitness. The warranties can be disclaimed by the use of certain "magic" words, by other language that is appropriate to the circumstances, by the buyer's conduct in inspecting the goods, or by a course of dealing or usage of trade. These mechanisms are discussed in the ensuing subsections.

[1]   Disclaimers Using "Safe-Harbor" Language

To exclude or modify the implied warranty of merchantability in a sale or lease, the word "merchantability" must be used.[125] To exclude or modify the implied warranty of fitness in a sale, the Code suggests language like "There are no warranties which extend beyond the description on the face hereof."[126] In a lease, the suggested language is the following: "There is no warranty that

---

[120] 152 Cal. App. 3d 951, 199 Cal. Rptr. 789, 38 UCC Rep. Serv. 55 (1984).

[121] *See, e.g.,* Perfection Cut, Inc. v. Olsen, 470 N.E.2d 94, 39 UCC Rep. Serv. 1237 (Ind. Ct. App. 1984).

[122] UCC §§ 2–316(1), 2A–214(1).

[123] 389 F. Supp. 39, 17 UCC Rep. Serv. 115 (D.S.C. 1974).

[124] *See* § 4.02 *supra.*

[125] UCC §§ 2–316(2), 2A–214(2).

[126] UCC § 2–316(2). The quoted language is given as an example, and phrases like "there is no warranty of fitness" should also be effective. More general language may suffice, but its use is risky. *See, e.g.,* § 2–316, Comment 4; Thorman v. Polytemp, Inc., 2 UCC Rep. Serv. 772 (N.Y. County Ct. 1965) (statement that express warranties were given "in lieu of all statutory or implied warranties" held sufficient).

the goods will be fit for a particular purpose."[127] The Code thus creates a "safe harbor" for the seller or lessor who uses the suggested words.

For sales transactions, the implied warranty of merchantability can be disclaimed orally, although only a foolish seller would attempt to do so. If the disclaimer is in writing, it must be conspicuous. Any disclaimer of the implied warranty of fitness must be by a conspicuous writing. The more stringent requirement for disclaiming the implied warranty of fitness is undoubtedly predicated on the fact that the warranty cannot arise without reliance by the buyer, whereas the implied warranty of merchantability arises without regard to reliance. Article 2A does not make such a fine distinction. Disclaimers of both warranties must be made by way of a conspicuous writing.[128]

Much of the litigation has centered on the conspicuousness requirement. The term "conspicuous" is defined as follows:

> A term or clause is conspicuous when it is so written that a reasonable person against whom it is to operate ought to have noticed it. A printed heading in capitals (as: NON-NEGOTIABLE BILL OF LADING) is conspicuous. Language in the body of a form is "conspicuous" if it is in larger or other type or color. But in a telegram any stated term is "conspicuous." Whether a term or clause is "conspicuous" is for decision by the court.[129]

This provision creates an objective test, but the court must take into consideration the relative sophistication of the parties. This approach is dictated by the "reasonable person *against whom it is to operate*" language.[130] More should be required to set off a disclaimer when the buyer is a consumer than when the buyer is a merchant.[131] Indeed, when the contract has been negotiated in detail by the attorneys for two relatively sophisticated commercial entities, the court should find[132] that each term is conspicuous.[133]

Disclaimers have been found to be inconspicuous in a variety of contexts.[134] For some courts, inconspicuous disclaimers are ineffective as a matter of law.[135]

---

[127] UCC § 2A–214(2). As with § 2–316(2), the quoted language is given as an example.

[128] UCC § 2A–214(2).

[129] UCC § 1–201(10).

[130] *Id.* (emphasis supplied).

[131] *See, e.g.*, Ellmer v. Delaware Mini-Computer Systems, Inc., 665 S.W.2d 158, 38 UCC Rep. Serv. 751 (Tex. Civ. App. 1983) (citing buyer sophistication as a factor in deciding whether a term is conspicuous).

[132] The issue, although one of fact, is to be decided by the court. UCC § 1–201(10).

[133] *See, e.g.*, American Elec. Power Co. v. Westinghouse Elec. Corp., 418 F. Supp. 435, 19 UCC Rep. Serv. 1009 (S.D.N.Y. 1976).

[134] *See, e.g.*, Office Supply Co., Inc. v. Basic/Four Corp., 538 F. Supp. 776, 34 UCC Rep. Serv. 857 (E.D. Wis. 1982) (italicized disclaimer not conspicuous); Blankenship v. Northtown

In some instances, however, a court has upheld an inconspicuous disclaimer because the buyer was aware of it at the time of contracting. In *Cates v. Dover Corp.*,[136] for example, the buyer of automotive lifts was denied summary judgment even though the disclaimer was inconspicuous, because there was a genuine issue regarding his knowledge of the disclaimer. This approach is troubling when the buyer is a merchant who is unsophisticated relative to the seller, or is a consumer. Making a disclaimer conspicuous is not difficult, and applying a rigorous enforcement standard provides a strong deterrent value. Unless the buyer is a relatively sophisticated commercial entity, the court should invalidate an inconspicuous disclaimer.

A number of decisions deal with disclaimers located on the reverse sides of standardized forms. In *Hunt v. Perkins Machinery Co., Inc.*[137] for example, the front of the form made no reference to the reverse side. Moreover, the form was attached to a pad and until the contract was signed, the buyer had no opportunity to examine the reverse side. The court had no difficulty invalidating the disclaimer. A reverse-side disclaimer will be upheld when the front of the form contains a conspicuous reference to the reverse side and the disclaimer itself is set off from the rest of the text.[138] A conspicuous reference on the front of the form will not salvage an inconspicuous disclaimer on the back,[139] and conspicuous print on the reverse side will not help if the reference on the front is in the same color and type as the other provisions.[140]

[2]   Disclaimers Using Other Language

Section 2–316(2), which creates the safe-harbor language referred to in the preceding subsection, is expressly subject to section 2–316(3). This latter

---

Ford, Inc., 95 Ill. App. 3d 303, 420 N.E.2d 167, 31 UCC Rep. Serv. 480 (1981) (disclaimer contained within section entitled "Factory Warranty" not conspicuous since the heading suggested the creation of warranties rather than their disclaimer); Stauffer Chemical Co. v. Curry, 778 P.2d 1083, 10 UCC Rep. Serv. 2d 342 (Wyo. 1989) (disclaimer printed on bottom half of sack in type half the size of the other type on the sack not conspicuous).

[135] *See, e.g.*, Walter E. Heller & Co. v. Convalescent Home of First Church of Deliverance, 49 Ill. App. 3d 213, 365 N.E.2d 1285, 22 UCC Rep. Serv. 574 (1977); Rhurek v. Chrysler Credit Corp., 262 So. 2d 452, 10 UCC Rep. Serv. 988 (Fla. Ct. App. 1972), *cert. denied*, 267 So. 2d 833 (Fla. 1972).

[136] 790 S.W.2d 559, 12 UCC Rep. Serv. 2d 47 (Tex. Ct. Civ. App. 1990). *See also* Office Supply Co., Inc. v. Basic/Four Corp., 538 F. Supp. 776, 34 UCC Rep. Serv. 857 (E.D. Wis. 1982) (inconspicuous disclaimer effective because buyer's president was aware of it).

[137] 352 Mass. 535, 226 N.E.2d 228, 4 UCC Rep. Serv. 281 (1967).

[138] *See, e.g.*, Childers & Venters, Inc. v. Sowards, 460 S.W.2d 343, 8 UCC Rep. Serv. 433 (Ky. 1970).

[139] *See, e.g.*, Norm Gershman's Things to Wear, Inc. v. Mercedes Benz of North America, Inc., 558 A.2d 1066, 9 UCC Rep. Serv. 2d 541 (Del. 1989).

[140] Massey-Ferguson v. Utley, 439 S.W.2d 57, 6 UCC Rep. Serv. 51 (Ky. Ct. App. 1969).

provision states that unless the circumstances indicate otherwise, the seller can disclaim all implied warranties by using expressions like " 'as is,' 'with all faults' or other language that in common understanding calls the buyer's attention to the exclusion of warranties and makes plain that there is no implied warranty."[141] The suggested phrases are not safe harbors: a clause using alternative language is not effective if, under the circumstances, the buyer could not be expected to understand that it was intended to operate as a disclaimer.

The use of the "as is" term is common in the sale of used goods, particularly automobiles, but not in the sale of new goods. Thus the court in *Gindy Manufacturing Corp. v. Cardinale Trucking Corp.*[142] held that the phrase did not disclaim the implied warranty of merchantability in a sale of new trucks. Even with used goods, a seller cannot be certain that an "as is" clause will be effective. In *Knipp v. Weinbaum*,[143] for example, the court reversed summary judgment for a seller who used such a clause in connection with the sale of a used motorcycle. The fact that the buyer was an ordinary consumer might have convinced a jury that, under the circumstances, the buyer did not understand the meaning of the phrase.

Article 2 does not explicitly require that clauses containing alternative language be in writing or that they be conspicuous, although most of the cases have imposed such requirements.[144] Article 2A explicitly requires a conspicuous writing.[145]

[3]   Inspection of the Goods

If the buyer or lessee, before entering into the contract, has inspected the goods or has refused a request that they be inspected, there is no implied warranty with respect to defects the examination ought in the circumstances to have revealed.[146] The Code does not expressly provide for the same result in the case of express warranties, but the Comments suggest that a seller may be able to rely on an inspection in that context as well:

> Application of the doctrine of "caveat emptor" in all cases where the buyer examines the goods regardless of statements made by the seller is, however, rejected by this Article. Thus, if the offer of examination is accompanied by words as to their merchantability or specific attributes

---

[141] UCC §§ 2–316(3)(a), 2A–214(3)(a).

[142] 111 N.J. Super. 383, 268 A.2d 345, 7 UCC Rep. Serv. 1257 (1970).

[143] 351 So. 2d 1081, 22 UCC Rep. Serv. 1141 (Fla. Ct. App. 1977).

[144] *See, e.g.,* Fernandez v. Western R.R. Builders, Inc., 112 Idaho 907, 736 P.2d 1361, 5 UCC Rep. Serv. 2d 347 (1987); Board of Directors of Harriman v. Southwest Petroleum Corp., 757 S.W.2d 669, 7 UCC Rep. Serv. 2d 386 (Tenn. Ct. App. 1988).

[145] UCC § 2A–214(3)(a).

[146] UCC §§ 2–316(3)(b); 2A–214(3)(b).

and the buyer indicates clearly that he is relying on those words rather than on his examination, they give rise to an "express" warranty. In such cases the question is one of fact as to whether a warranty of merchantability has been expressly incorporated in the agreement. Disclaimer of such an express warranty is governed by subsection (1) of the present section.

Thus when the buyer has made an inspection, the seller can argue that express warranties did not become part of the basis of the bargain.

For the seller to avoid liability, the buyer must have actually inspected the goods as fully as he or she desired, or must have refused to inspect them. Refusal requires that the seller demand an inspection, not merely give the buyer an opportunity for one.[147] Moreover, the inspection or refusal must occur prior to contracting. If the contract has already been formed, an inspection that occurs upon delivery will not operate to exclude warranty liability.[148]

The seller cannot prevail on this theory unless the defect is one that the buyer ought in the circumstances to have discovered. Two factors are relevant to this issue: the buyer's expertise and the obviousness of the defect.[149] Accordingly, professionals are held to a higher standard than buyers who have no expertise with regard to the goods.[150]

[4] Post-Contracting Disclaimers

Sellers sometimes deliver disclaimers to buyers after the contract for sale has been consummated. The disclaimer may be located on an invoice, or it might be printed in a warranty booklet that is not turned over to the buyer until the goods are delivered.[151] Courts have routinely invalidated such disclaimers

---

[147] *See, e.g.,* Calloway v. Manion, 572 F.2d 1033 (5th Cir. 1978); Agricultural Services Ass'n v. Ferry-Morse Seed Co., 551 F.2d 1057 (6th Cir. 1977); UCC § 2–316, Comment 8.

[148] *See, e.g.,* Murray v. Kleen Leen, Inc., 41 Ill. App. 3d 436, 354 N.E.2d 415, 20 UCC Rep. Serv. 298 (1976) (examination of pigs on delivery).

[149] UCC § 2–316, Comment 8.

[150] *See, e.g.,* Hall Truck Sales, Inc. v. Wilder Mobile Homes, Inc., 402 So. 2d 1299, 32 UCC Rep. Serv. 440 (Fla. Dist. Ct. App. 1981) (buyer of earth-moving machine should have discovered machine's inability to grade soil); Twin Lakes Mfg. Co., Inc. v. Coffey, 222 Va. 467, 281 S.E.2d 864, 32 UCC Rep. Serv. 770 (1981) (consumer buyer could not be expected to discover defect in mobile home's frame).

[151] Occasionally the disclaimer is located in a security agreement that is executed after the contract for sale has been consummated. UCC § 9–206(2) makes it clear that Article 2 governs the sales aspects of the transaction, and Comment 3 to that section states that it "prevents a buyer from inadvertently abandoning his warranties by a 'no warranties' term in the security agreement when warranties have already been created under the sales arrangement."

on the ground that they represent unilateral attempts to modify existing contracts.[152]

Sellers frequently request that buyers return postcards after the sale to register the product for express warranty purposes. The seller may then attempt to use the postcard to show the buyer's assent to a contract modification. This argument was unsuccessful in *Van der Broeke v. Bellanca Aircraft Corp.*[153] The buyer, a commercial crop duster, ordered an airplane manufactured by the defendant and received a warranty booklet containing a disclaimer several months after placing the order. The buyer subsequently returned the warranty-registration postcard to the manufacturer. The postcard was not signed by the buyer, and it did not make reference to the disclaimer. The court held that there was insufficient evidence to support a modification since the postcard did not indicate the buyer's assent to the disclaimer. Even if there had been a modification, the lack of a signature would have rendered it unenforceable under the Statute of Frauds.[154]

A post-contract disclaimer contained in an invoice was upheld in *Tolmie Farms, Inc. v. Stauffer Chemical Co.*[155] The court noted that such clauses are generally ineffective, but the parties had engaged in similar transactions over a long period of time and on each occasion the buyer had received an invoice containing the disclaimer. According to the court, a course of dealing was created pursuant to which the buyer had acquiesced in the seller's terms. This analysis is troubling. There was no evidence that the buyer had been aware of the earlier disclaimers and since post-contract terms are generally ineffective, the buyer was justified on each occasion in not reading the invoice. It is difficult to see how a term that was ineffective in each instance could become effective through cumulative use unless the buyer had at some point become aware of it. The Code does provide for disclaimers through course of dealing, course of performance, or usage of trade,[156] but a course of dealing requires a common basis of understanding in order to be effective.[157] Since the buyer was unaware of the earlier disclaimers, that common basis was lacking in *Tolmie Farms.*

---

[152] *See, e.g.,* Sanco v. Ford Motor Co., Inc., 771 F.2d 1081, 41 UCC Rep. Serv. 766 (7th Cir. 1985); Bowdoin v. Showell Growers, Inc., 817 F.2d 1543, 3 UCC Rep. Serv. 2d 1366 (11th Cir. 1987); Gold-Kist, Inc. v. Citizens & Southern Nat'l Bank, 286 S.C. 272, 333 S.E.2d 67, 41 UCC Rep. Serv. 327 (S.C. Ct. App. 1985). *But see* Hahn v. Ford Motor Co., Inc., 434 N.E.2d 943, 33 UCC Rep. Serv. 1277 (Ind. Ct. App. 1982) (jury justified in finding post-contracting disclaimer effective when buyer conceded that he had understood at time of sale that manufacturer limited its warranty to 12 months).

[153] 576 F.2d 582, 24 UCC Rep. Serv. 594 (5th Cir. 1978).

[154] UCC § 2–209(3). The Statute of Frauds provision governing modifications is discussed in § 2.06[B][1] *supra.*

[155] 124 Idaho 607, 862 P.2d 299, 23 UCC Rep. Serv. 2d 65 (1993).

[156] UCC §§ 2–316(3)(c); 2A–214(3)(c). These concepts are discussed generally in § 4.03 *supra.*

[157] UCC § 2–205(1).

[C] Disclaimers and Unconscionability

Can a disclaimer provision that is properly drafted to meet the requirements of section 2–316 nevertheless be invalidated under the unconscionability doctrine?[158] Several of the illustrations in the Comments to section 2–302, the general unconscionability section, involve warranty disclaimers.[159] Their inclusion suggests that mere mechanical compliance with the Code's language and conspicuousness requirements is not enough to insulate disclaimers from attack. On the other hand, section 2–316 does not expressly mention unconscionability as does its counterpart, section 2–719, dealing with limited-remedy clauses. Further, the requirements of section 2–316 are precise and relatively easy to police, suggesting the absence of any need for the more general policing doctrine of unconscionability.[160]

A majority of courts have concluded that disclaimer clauses are subject to the unconscionability doctrine,[161] although there are a number of decisions to the contrary.[162] Quite a few states have resolved the issue by enacting nonuniform legislation forbidding disclaimers of implied warranties in consumer transactions.[163]

§ 5.04 MODIFICATION OR IMPAIRMENT OF RIGHTS AND REMEDIES [2–719; 2A–503]

[A] Substituted Remedy Clauses

A seller who does not wish to disclaim warranties may nonetheless seek to limit exposure for their breach. The Code facilitates this approach by permitting the agreement to provide for remedies that are in addition to or in substitution for those that would otherwise be available, and to limit or alter the

---

[158] Unconscionability is discussed in § 4.06[A] *supra*.

[159] UCC § 2–302, Comment 1.

[160] The policy arguments are articulated in Leff, *Unconscionability and the Code—The Emperor's New Clause*, 115 U. Pa. L. Rev. (1967) (arguing that UCC § 2–316 preempts application of the unconscionability doctrine), and Phillips, *Unconscionability and Article 2 Implied Warranty Disclaimers*, 62 Chi.-Kent L. Rev. 199 (1985) (arguing that unconscionability should be used aggressively to invalidate disclaimers).

[161] *See, e.g.*, Rottinghaus v. Howell, 35 Wash. App. 99, 666 P.2d 899, 37 UCC Rep. Serv. 42 (1983); FMC Fin. Corp. v. Murphree, 632 F.2d 413, 30 UCC Rep. Serv. 496 (5th Cir. 1980).

[162] *See, e.g.*, Ohio Savings Bank v. H. L. Vokes Co., 54 Ohio App. 3d 68, 560 N.E.2d 1328, 13 UCC Rep. Serv. 2d 92 (1989) (UCC § 2–302 inapplicable to warranty disclaimers in a commercial setting); Ford Motor Co. v. Moulton, 511 S.W.2d 690, 14 UCC Rep. Serv. 312 (Tenn. 1974), *cert. denied*, 419 U.S. 870 (1974).

[163] *See, e.g.*, Md. Com. Law Ann. § 2–316 (1982); Mass. Ann. Laws ch. 106, § 2–316A (1984); Kan. Stat. Ann. § 50–636(a) (1983).

ordinary measure of damages.[164] Without a substituted-remedy clause, the buyer might reject nonconforming goods or, in an appropriate case, revoke acceptance of them,[165] or keep the goods and recover direct, consequential, and incidental damages proximately caused by the breach.[166]

A common technique used by sellers is to create an express warranty that the goods will be free from defects in material and workmanship for a stated duration and then to specify that the exclusive remedy for breach of this warranty is repair or replacement of the defective part or the defective product. The typical writing then goes on to disclaim all other express warranties and all implied warranties. In transactions governed by the federal Magnuson–Moss Warranty—Federal Trade Commission Improvement Act,[167] the seller is precluded from disclaiming implied warranties but in some cases can shorten their duration to coincide with that of the express warranty.[168]

For the buyer to be limited to the substituted remedy, there must be express agreement that the remedy be exclusive[169] and the remedy must not fail its essential purpose.[170] Failure to satisfy either of these requirements means that the buyer has access to all of the ordinary Code remedies in addition to the substituted remedy.

[1]   "Expressly Agreed to Be Exclusive"

Although the courts have not required that the writing use the word "exclusive," most have required that the language make clear that the stated remedy is the sole remedy and is not optional. In *Ralston Purina Co. v. Hartford Accident and Indemnity Co.*[171] the contract provided that if the goods, which included a flock of chickens, materially decreased in value prior to delivery the buyer "may either" proceed with the purchase at a mutually agreeable new price or terminate the contract. Many of the chickens were found to be contaminated prior to delivery and had to be destroyed, and the buyer asserted a claim for damages for breach of warranty. The buyer settled with the seller, which sought indemnification from its insurer. The insurer defended on the ground

---

[164] UCC §§ 2–719(1); 2A–503(1).

[165] Rejection and revocation of acceptance are discussed in §§ 7.04, 7.05 *infra*.

[166] Monetary damages for breach of warranty are discussed in § 8.05[B] *infra*.

[167] Act of 1975, Pub. L. No. 93–637, 88 Stat. 2183, 15 U.S.C. § 2301 *et seq.* (1988). The Act applies primarily but not exclusively to purchases by consumers.

[168] Under the Act, sellers must designate written warranties as either "full" or "limited." If the warranty is "limited," the duration of the implied warranties can be shortened. 15 U.S.C. § 2308 (1988).

[169] UCC §§ 2–719(1)(b); 2A–503(2).

[170] UCC §§ 2–719(2); 2A–503(2).

[171] 540 F.2d 914, 19 UCC Rep. Serv. 1348 (8th Cir. 1976).

that the seller had agreed to a settlement that went beyond its contractual responsibilities. Noting that the word "may" is permissive rather than mandatory, the court concluded that the stated remedies were optional and found for
the seller.

When the buyer is a commercial entity, the courts have sometimes been
willing to construe ambiguous language in the seller's favor. At the extreme is
Dravo Corp. v. M. L. Barge Operating Corp.,[172] where the court concluded that a
substituted remedy was exclusive despite the total absence of language to that
effect. Although the decision goes too far, it is not the only example of a court
ignoring the plain language of the Code to find against a commercial buyer.[173]

Other courts have strained to find a remedy optional when the buyer is a
consumer. In *Ford Motor Co. v. Reid*,[174] for example, the contract contained a
clause setting out an express warranty and providing for repair or replacement
in the event of breach. The contract then stated that the *warranty* was "in lieu
of any other express or implied warranty." The court held that the quoted language referred to the warranty itself, not the remedy. To be safe, the seller must
make it clear that the *remedy* is exclusive.

[2]   Failure of Essential Purpose

If an exclusive remedy fails its essential purpose, the buyer's right to
pursue other remedies is restored. Most of the cases involve sellers who either
fail to honor the substituted remedy or try but cannot effectuate the remedy in
a timely fashion. In *Select Pork, Inc. v. Babcock Swine, Inc.*,[175] the substituted
remedy specified return of the purchase price in the event of nonconformity.
When the seller delivered the wrong kind of pigs and then refused to refund
the purchase price, the buyer's ordinary Code remedies were restored. In *Great
Dane Trailer Sales, Inc. v. Malvern Pulpwood, Inc.*,[176] the court held that a substituted repair-or-replacement remedy failed its essential purpose when the seller's shoddy repair work left the buyer's trailer in an unsafe condition.[177]

---

[172] 35 UCC Rep. Serv. 1180 (W.D. Pa. 1982).

[173] *See also* Veath v. Specialty Grains, Inc., 190 Ill. App. 3d 787, 546 N.E.2d 1005, 10 UCC Rep.
Serv. 2d 771 (1989) (remedy exclusive despite lack of language to that effect).

[174] 250 Ark. 176, 465 S.W.2d 80, 8 UCC Rep. Serv. 985 (1971).

[175] 640 F.2d 147, 30 UCC Rep. Serv. 839 (8th Cir. 1981). The contract also contained a clause
excluding consequential damages, which the court found unconscionable under UCC §
2–719(3).

[176] 301 Ark. 436, 785 S.W.2d 13, 11 UCC Rep. Serv. 2d 875 (1990).

[177] For another case holding that a substituted remedy fails its essential purpose if the buyer
is substantially deprived of the benefit of the bargain, *see* Fargo Mach. & Tool Co. v.
Kearney & Trecker Corp., 428 F. Supp. 364, 21 UCC Rep. Serv. 80 (E.D. Mich. 1977).

The rationale that underlies the essential-purpose doctrine is that it is deceptive for a seller to give a warranty without providing the buyer with at least a minimally adequate remedy for its breach.[178] If the seller does not want to give a remedy, he or she should forthrightly disclaim all warranties.

Numerous cases have dealt with "lemons." A lemon is a product the seller is unable to repair despite repeated attempts. In some cases, the same problem repeats itself; in others, the product manifests a series of unrelated defects. In the typical case, the buyer eventually becomes frustrated and attempts either to revoke acceptance or to recover direct and consequential damages. The seller, of course, insists on additional repair opportunities. The decisions in this area exhibit a disturbing lack of uniformity.[179] Clearly, the remedy will fail at some point, but the buyer must guess as to when that will occur.[180] Generally, a consumer buyer will be afforded more protection than a commercial buyer, and a seller will be given more repair opportunities when the goods are complex pieces of machinery.

In a few cases, the substituted remedy has failed its essential purpose even though the seller was willing to abide by it in a timely fashion. In *Rudd Construction Equipment Co. v. Clark Equipment Co.*,[181] for example, a parts manufacturer's repair-or-replacement remedy failed its essential purpose when the part caused the machine in which it was installed to catch fire. The court held that merely replacing the part would not provide the buyer with a "fair quantum" of a remedy. This approach finds support in the Comments, which state:

[I]t is of the very essence of a sales contract that at least minimum adequate remedies be available. If the parties intend to conclude a contract for sale within this Article they must accept the legal consequences that there be at least a fair quantum of remedy for breach of the obligations or duties outlined in the contract.[182]

---

[178] UCC § 2–719, Comment 1.

[179] *Contrast* Liberty Truck Sales, Inc. v. Kimbrel, 548 So. 2d 1379, 9 UCC Rep. Serv. 2d 908 (Ala. 1989) (repair remedy failed its essential purpose when new trucks needed four repairs) *with* Belcher v. Versatile Farm Equip. Co., 443 So. 2d 912, 37 UCC Rep. Serv. 706 (Ala. 1983) (repair remedy did not fail its essential purpose despite four attempts to repair).

[180] A number of states have resolved this problem for consumers buying new motor vehicles. The typical "lemon law" expands the buyer's remedies after a stated number of repair attempts or cumulative days in the repair shop. *See, e.g.,* Rev. Stat. Mo. § 407.560 *et seq.* (1986).

[181] 735 F.2d 974, 38 UCC Rep. Serv. 873 (6th Cir. 1984). *See also* Andover Air Ltd. Partnership v. Piper Aircraft Corp., 7 UCC Rep. Serv. 2d 1494 (D. Mass. 1989) (remedy worth $10 failed its essential purpose when buyer's losses exceeded $100,000).

[182] UCC § 2–719, Comment 1.

A few courts have invoked the essential-purpose doctrine to invalidate clauses that give the buyer an unreasonably short period of time to assert a claim for breach of warranty. In *Wilson Trading Corp v. David Ferguson, Ltd.*,[183] for example, a contract for the sale of yarn stated that no claims could be asserted more than 10 days after receipt of the yarn. But the buyer could not discover the yarn's tendency to fade unevenly until after the yarn had been knitted into sweaters and washed. Enforcement of the 10-day provision would have left the buyer without a remedy, and the court held that the provision failed its essential purpose. Of course, it was not really the remedy that failed; it was the time limitation that was unreasonable. A more appropriate basis for the holding, and one mentioned by the court, is section 1–204(1), which provides, "Whenever this Act requires any action to be taken within a reasonable time, any time which is not manifestly unreasonable may be fixed by agreement." Given the nature of the goods and the defect, the 10-day limitation in *Wilson Trading* was manifestly unreasonable.

[B]   Clauses Limiting or Excluding Consequential Damages

Sellers often seek to avoid liability through clauses that limit or exclude consequential damages. The Code expressly sanctions such clauses but subjects them to an unconscionability test.[184] When the consequential loss takes the form of personal injuries caused by consumer goods, a clause precluding the consumer from recovering is prima facie unconscionable.[185] This presumption is virtually impossible to overcome, but the seller managed to prevail in *Mullan v. Quickie Aircraft Corp.*[186] The buyer, who was generally knowledgeable about airplane kits, was a certified pilot and an experienced woodworker. He purchased a wooden-airplane kit and later suffered personal injuries when the airplane crashed. Given his unusually high level of expertise, the court upheld the manufacturer's clause excluding consequential damages.

When the product causes personal injury to someone other than a consumer, the presumption of unconscionability does not apply. Thus in *Schlenz v. John Deere Co.*,[187] the court correctly placed the burden of establishing unconscionability on the buyer, a farmer who was injured while using farm machinery.

Even without the presumption of unconscionability, a consumer buyer may be able to avoid the impact of a clause excluding consequential damages. In *Fischer v. General Electric Hotpoint*,[188] for example, the buyer of a refrigerator

---

[183] 23 N.Y.2d 398, 297 N.Y.S.2d 108, 244 N.E.2d 685, 5 UCC Rep. Serv. 1213 (1968).
[184] UCC §§ 2–719(3); 2A–503(3).
[185] *Id.*
[186] 797 F.2d 845, 1 UCC Rep. Serv. 2d 1540 (10th Cir. 1986).
[187] 511 F. Supp. 224, 31 UCC Rep. Serv. 1020 (D. Mont. 1981).
[188] 108 Misc. 2d 683, 438 N.Y.S.2d 690, 31 UCC Rep. Serv. 849 (Sup. Ct. 1981).

recovered for food that spoiled when the refrigerator failed, notwithstanding the presence of an exclusionary clause. By contrast, the seller in *Lobianco v. Property Protection, Inc.*[189] prevailed when the buyer's home burglar alarm failed. The court emphasized the fact that the buyer had chosen not to insure against the risk of burglary.

When the buyer is a commercial entity, most courts have routinely upheld clauses limiting consequential damages,[190] although a few decisions favor the buyer. In *Oldham's Farm Sausage Co. v. Salco, Inc.,*[191] for example, the buyer suffered over $200,000 in consequential losses when sausage-processing equipment failed to operate properly. The court held that the clause, which was buried in fine print, was unconscionable.[192]

[C]   Substituted Remedy Clauses and Clauses Limiting Consequential Damages in Combination

Sellers frequently use substituted-remedy clauses and clauses limiting consequential damages in combination. The rationale for this approach is that it provides two lines of defense. If the substituted-remedy clause fails its essential purpose, the limit on consequential damages will still reduce the seller's overall exposure.

Some courts have confounded the seller's expectations by holding that a failure of the substituted-remedy clause's essential purpose also renders unenforceable the clause limiting consequential damages.[193] A majority of the decisions, including most recent ones, have analyzed the two clauses separately.

---

[189] 292 Pa. Super. 346, 437 A.2d 417, 33 UCC Rep. Serv. 281 (1981).

[190] *See, e.g.,* Jim Dan, Inc. v. O. M. Scott & Sons Co., 785 F. Supp. 1196, 17 UCC Rep. Serv. 2d 788 (W.D. Pa. 1992) (limitation conscionable in sale of chemicals to farming corporation); Canal Elec. Co. v. Westinghouse Elec. Corp., 973 F.2d 988, 18 UCC Rep. Serv. 2d 391 (1st Cir. 1992) (limitation conscionable in contract for sale of power generators entered into by two large electric companies).

[191] 633 S.W.2d 177 (Mo. Ct. App. 1982).

[192] A few courts have read a conspicuousness requirement into UCC § 2–719. *See, e.g.,* Moscatiello v. Pittsburgh Contractors Equip. Co., 407 Pa. Super. 363, 595 A.2d 1190, 16 UCC Rep. Serv. 2d 71 (1991) (substituted-remedy clause); Stauffer Chem. Co. v. Curry, 778 P.2d 1083, 10 UCC Rep. Serv. 2d 342 (Wyo. 1989) (substituted-remedy clause). A majority of courts, contrasting § 2–719 with § 2–316, have refused to impose a conspicuousness requirement. *See, e.g.,* McCrimmon v. Tandy Corp., 202 Ga. App. 233, 414 S.E.2d 15, 17 UCC Rep. Serv. 2d 1134 (1992) (limitation on consequential damages); Island Creek Coal Co. v. Lake Shore, Inc., 832 F.2d 274, 4 UCC Rep. Serv. 2d 1067 (4th Cir. 1987) (limitation on consequential damages). A limitation on consequential damages must be conspicuous to be effective under the Magnuson–Moss Warranty—Federal Trade Commission Improvement Act, 15 U.S.C. §§ 2304, 2311 (1988).

[193] *See, e.g.,* Matco Mach. & Tool Co. v. Cincinnati Milacron Co., 727 F.2d 777, 37 UCC Rep.

For example, *American Electric Power Co. v. Westinghouse Electric Corp.*[194] involved the sale of a $12 million generator to a public utility. The court treated the two limitation clauses separately because they were stated in separate sections of the contract, the transaction was between two large commercial entities, the machinery was complex and somewhat experimental, and after the substituted-remedy clause was struck, the buyer was still able to recover the purchase price.

The *American Electric* decision is conceptually correct. The Code specifies that the essential-purpose doctrine applies to substituted-remedy clauses.[195] Deciding whether such a clause has failed its essential purpose is a jury question, and it is based on the seller's post-contracting behavior. The test for determining the effectiveness of a clause limiting consequential damages is unconscionability.[196] This issue is for the court, and it is based on the precontractual conduct of the seller and the status of the parties.

The current trend is to approach the issue on a case-by-case basis. As long as the contract adequately represents the parties' real understandings regarding the allocation of risks, the clause limiting consequential damages will be enforced even if the substituted-remedy clause is stricken.[197] When the consequential damages are caused by the seller's willful or dilatory conduct in failing to effectuate the substituted remedy, however, the court is likely to strike both clauses.[198]

§ 5.05 DEFENSES BASED ON THE CLAIMANT'S CONDUCT

The defendant in a breach of warranty action may be able to demonstrate that the losses incurred were the result of the plaintiff's own conduct in using the goods. In approaching this issue, many courts have borrowed from the law

---

Serv. 1577 (8th Cir. 1984); Ehlers v. Chrysler Motor Corp., 88 S.D. 612, 226 N.W.2d 157, 16 UCC Rep. Serv. 737 (1975).

[194] 418 F. Supp. 435, 19 UCC Rep. Serv. 1009 (S.D.N.Y. 1978).

[195] UCC §§ 2–719(2); 2A–503(2).

[196] UCC §§ 2–719(3), 2A–503(3).

[197] *See, e.g.,* Colonial Life Ins. Co. of America v. Electronic Data Systems Corp., 817 F. Supp. 235, 20 UCC Rep. Serv. 2d 753 (D.N.H. 1993); Smith v. Navistar Int'l Transportation Corp., 957 F.2d 1439, 17 UCC Rep. Serv. 2d 84 (7th Cir. 1992).

[198] *See, e.g.,* Employers Ins. Co. of Wausau v. Suwannee River Spa Lines, Inc., 866 F.2d 752, 8 UCC Rep. Serv. 2d 659 (5th Cir. 1989).

of torts, particularly the doctrine of strict liability.[199] The Restatement (Second) of Torts provides:

> Contributory negligence of the plaintiff is not a defense when such negligence consists merely in a failure to discover the defect in the product, or to guard against the possibility of its existence. On the other hand the form of contributory negligence which consists in voluntarily proceeding to encounter a known danger, and commonly passes under the name of assumption of risk, is a defense under this Section as in other cases of strict liability. If the user or consumer discovers the defect and is aware of the danger, and nevertheless proceeds unreasonably to make use of the product and is injured by it, he is barred from recovery.[200]

The Code does not use terms like "contributory negligence" and "assumption of risk." The Comments suggest that the issue should be treated as one of causation. That is, the breach of warranty is not the proximate cause of the damages if the plaintiff engages in a certain level of misconduct. The relevant Comment states:

> In an action based on breach of warranty, it is of course necessary to show not only the existence of the warranty but the fact that the warranty was broken and that the breach of warranty was the proximate cause of the loss sustained. In such an action an affirmative showing by the seller that the loss resulted from some action or event following his own delivery of the goods can operate as a defense. . . . Action by the buyer following an examination of the goods which ought to have indicated the defect complained of can be shown as matter bearing on whether the breach itself was the cause of the injury.[201]

This Comment is consistent with the standard established by the Restatement (Second) of Torts. The following Comment, however, appears to expand the defense:

> Where the injury involved follows the use of goods without discovery of the defect causing the damage, the question of "proximate" cause turns on whether it was reasonable for the buyer to use the goods without such inspection as would have revealed the defects. If it was not reasonable for him to do so, or if he did in fact discover the defect

---

[199] *See, e.g.*, Monsanto Co. v. Logisticon, Inc., 763 S.W.2d 371, 9 UCC Rep. Serv. 2d 934 (Mo. Ct. App. 1989) (permitting assumption of risk to be used as a defense); Wallace v. Owens-Illinois, Inc., 300 S.C. 518, 389 S.E.2d 155, 11 UCC Rep. Serv. 2d 835 (Ct. App. 1989) (rejecting contributory negligence as a defense based on analogy to rules governing strict liability in tort).

[200] Restatement (Second) of Torts § 402A, Comment n.

[201] UCC § 2–314, Comment 13.

prior to his use, the injury would not proximately result from the breach of warranty.[202]

The failure to inspect would be considered contributory negligence and would not be a defense to an action for strict liability in tort.

The Comments notwithstanding, courts that have adopted the Code's proximate causation terminology have generally not considered a mere failure to inspect a sufficient defense. In *Upjohn Co. v. Rachelle Laboratories, Inc.*,[203] for example, the court concluded that the buyer's loss was proximately caused by the breach, even though an inspection by the buyer would have revealed the defect.

Even if the buyer has not inspected the goods, misuse of the product can rise to the level of assumption of the risk. In *Hoelter v. Mohawk Services, Inc.*,[204] for example, the plaintiff was precluded from recovering in tort when his defective tires sustained a blowout while he was speeding. Surely the result would have been the same had the action been predicated on breach of the implied warranty of merchantability.

Courts are increasingly using a comparative fault approach when presented with evidence of the buyer's assumption of the risk. In *Signal Oil & Gas Co. v. Universal Oil Products*,[205] for example, a refinery discovered two months before it caused a fire that a piece of equipment had been improperly assembled. The court held that the jury should be instructed to allocate the loss between the parties based on their comparative fault. Since the behavior must rise to the level of assumption of risk to constitute a defense, contributory negligence should not be used to reduce a buyer's damages.[206]

The courts are still in the process of sorting out the rationale for applying comparative fault to warranty actions. The doctrine springs, of course, from the law of torts,[207] and strict liability in tort is generally unavailable when the plaintiff's loss is purely economic, as opposed to personal injury or certain kinds of

---

[202] UCC § 2–715, Comment 5.

[203] 661 F.2d 1105, 32 UCC Rep. Serv. 747 (6th Cir. 1981). *See also* Coulter v. American Bakeries Co., 530 So. 2d 1009, 7 UCC Rep. Serv. 2d 49 (Fla. Dist. Ct. App. 1988) (contributory negligence rejected as partial defense in state adopting comparative fault for breach of warranty actions).

[204] 170 Conn. 495, 365 A.2d 1064 (1976).

[205] 572 S.W.2d 320, 24 UCC Rep. Serv. 555 (Tex. 1978).

[206] *See, e.g.,* Coulter v. American Bakeries Co., 530 So. 2d 1009, 7 UCC Rep. Serv. 2d 49 (Fla. Dist. Ct. App. 1988).

[207] Some states have statutes making comparative fault applicable to all products liability actions involving personal injury or property damage. Citing such a statute, the court in Little Rock Elec. Contractors, Inc. v. Okonite Co., 294 Ark. 399, 744 S.W.2d 381, 5 UCC Rep. Serv. 2d 978 (1988), declined to apply comparative fault to a case involving purely

property damage. Reasoning by analogy, the court in *Broce O'Dell Concrete Products, Inc. v. Mel Jarvis Construction Co., Inc.*[208] declined to apply comparative fault when breach of an express warranty led to a loss that was purely economic. As the trend toward application of comparative fault continues, the courts are increasingly likely to take the next step and apply the doctrine to cases of economic loss.

§ 5.06   PRIVITY

At common law, lack of privity of contract created an impenetrable barrier for a party with a breach of warranty claim.[209] This barrier meant that only a buyer could bring a warranty action, and only against that buyer's immediate seller. The Uniform Sales Act, the Code's predecessor, was generally interpreted in accordance with this common-law tradition.

Privity problems are usually divided into two classes—horizontal and vertical. Horizontal privity addresses the question of who qualifies as a proper plaintiff. A buyer is always a proper plaintiff, but what about the buyer's guest or employee, or an innocent bystander? Vertical privity addresses the question of who constitutes a proper defendant. If a manufacturer sells a product to a retailer, which then sells it to a consumer, can the consumer recover from the manufacturer? If the consumer's spouse is injured by the product and seeks to recover from the manufacturer, both horizontal and vertical privity issues are involved.

[A]   Strict Liability in Tort: A Brief Comparison

Under Restatement (Second) of Torts, a merchant seller is liable for personal injury or property damage caused by a product which is sold in a defective condition that renders it unreasonably dangerous to the ultimate user or consumer.[210] Liability attaches even though the seller has exercised the highest level of care in preparing and selling the product, thus creating a standard similar to that created by the Code's implied warranty of merchantability.[211] Lack

---

economic loss. *Cf.* Correia v. Firestone Tire & Rubber Co., 388 Mass. 342, 446 N.E.2d 1033 (1983) (declining to apply comparative fault statute that spoke of "damages for negligence" to a warranty action). In other states, the courts have adopted comparative fault in the absence of a statute. *See, e.g.,* Frazer v. A. F. Munsterman, Inc., 123 Ill. 2d 245, 527 N.E.2d 1248, 7 UCC Rep. Serv. 2d 121 (1988).

[208] 634 P.2d 1142, 32 UCC Rep. Serv. 762 (Kan. Ct. App. 1981).

[209] *See generally* Prosser, *The Fall of the Citadel (Strict Liability to the Consumer),* 50 Minn. L. Rev. 791 (1966).

[210] Restatement (Second) of Torts § 402A.

[211] *See* discussion in § 5.02[B] *supra.*

of privity is not a defense to strict liability in tort.[212] Disclaimers are never effective if the product causes personal injury, although some courts have upheld disclaimers between merchants of relatively equal bargaining strength when only property damage was involved.[213]

A party with a product dissatisfaction claim can often bring an action under either a warranty or tort theory. Because of the elimination of the privity, notice, and disclaimer defenses, strict liability in tort is generally seen as the preferred theory. Sometimes, however, the strict tort theory is not available. The statute of limitations for torts might have expired, leaving the claimant with warranty as the only possibility.[214] Further, strict liability in tort is not available except for physical injury to a person or to property. Tort claims often involve damage to property other than the product itself. The damage usually occurs as the result of a violent interaction between the product and the other property. For example, the plaintiff in *Star Furniture Co. v. Pulaski*[215] recovered in tort when the product, an electric clock, malfunctioned and burned down his store. When the damage to the other property occurs passively, the courts are split, although the trend is to relegate the matter to contract law. The leading case on this topic, *Brown v. Western Farmers Association*,[216] involved a claim that chicken feed caused the chickens' eggs to taste bad. Although they were not physically harmed, the chickens had to be replaced. The court refused to allow a recovery in tort, emphasizing that the chicken feed was not sold in an unreasonably dangerous condition.

The courts have also split on loss involving violent injury to the product itself. Many courts view the problem as one of risk allocation and conclude that it is more appropriately handled by contract law,[217] but substantial authority

---

[212] The notice requirement imposed by the Code is also not required in strict tort liability. UCC § 2–607(3). *See* discussion in § 7.03[B][3] *infra*.

[213] *See, e.g.,* Keystone Aeronautics Corp. v. R. J. Enstrom Corp., 499 F.2d 146, 14 UCC Rep. Serv. 1087 (3d Cir. 1974).

[214] The Code's statute of limitations is discussed in § 5.07 *infra*.

[215] 297 S.E.2d 854 (W. Va. 1982).

[216] 268 Or. 470, 521 P.2d 537 (1974). *See also* Myers v. A. O. Smith Harvestore Products, Inc., 114 Idaho 432, 757 P.2d 695, 6 UCC Rep. Serv. 2d 1467 (Ct. App. 1988) (when feed storage and delivery system caused feed to deteriorate and resulted in illness to cattle, the claim involved commercial expectations and did not sound in tort). *But see* Tony Spychalla Farms, Inc. v. Hopkins Agricultural Chemical Co., 151 Wis. 2d 431, 444 N.W.2d 743, 10 UCC Rep. Serv. 2d 734 (Ct. App. 1989) (tort recovery permitted when crop dust caused seed potatoes to become petrified); Board of Education v. A, C, & S, Inc., 131 Ill. 2d 428, 546 N.E.2d 580, 10 UCC Rep. Serv. 2d 90 (1989) (while passive injury cases should usually be decided under a warranty theory, tort recovery was appropriate when asbestos fibers caused damage to buildings because the fibers also created a serious health risk).

[217] Damin Aviation Corp. v. Sikorsky Aircraft, 705 F. Supp. 170, 9 UCC Rep. Serv. 2d 491 (S.D.N.Y. 1989); Sharp Bros. Contracting Co. v. American Hoist & Derrick Co., 703 S.W.2d 901, 42 UCC Rep. Serv. 1246 (Mo. 1986).

to the contrary persists.[218] With passive damage to the product itself, the vast majority of courts have held that the issues should be tried under contract law.[219] When the injury amounts to a "secondary" economic loss, such as lost profits, preclusion of the availability of tort law is virtually unanimous.

When strict liability in tort is unavailable, either because of the statute of limitations or because the damages will not support a recovery, the claimant is left with only a claim for breach of warranty. Although it has suffered serious erosion in recent years, the privity doctrine then may still operate to shield the seller from liability.

[B]   Horizontal Privity

The Code addresses the issue of who can be a proper plaintiff by giving the states the following alternatives:

Alternative A. A seller's warranty whether express or implied extends to any natural person who is in the family or household of his buyer or who is a guest in his home if it is reasonable to expect that such person may use, consume or be affected by the goods and who is injured in person by breach of the warranty. A seller may not exclude or limit the operation of this section.

Alternative B. A seller's warranty whether express or implied extends to any natural person who may reasonably be expected to use, consume or be affected by the goods and who is injured in person by breach of the warranty. A seller may not exclude or limit the operation of this section.

Alternative C. A seller's warranty whether express or implied extends to any person who may reasonably be expected to use, consume or be affected by the goods and who is injured by breach of the warranty. A seller may not exclude or limit the operation of this section with respect to injury to the person of an individual to whom the warranty extends.[220]

A claimant who comes within the applicable alternative is treated as a third-party beneficiary of the seller's warranties.

---

[218] *See, e.g.,* Russell v. Ford Motor Co., 281 Or. 587, 575 P.2d 1383 (1978); Fordyce Concrete, Inc. v. Mack Trucks, Inc., 535 F. Supp. 118, (D. Kan. 1982); Vaughan v. General Motors Corp., 102 Ill. 2d 431, 466 N.E.2d 195, 38 UCC Rep. Serv. 1619 (1984).

[219] The best discussion is in *East River S.S. Corp. v. Transamerica Delaval, Inc.,* 476 U.S. 858, 106 S. Ct. 2295, 90 L. Ed.2d 865, 1 UCC Rep. Serv. 2d 609 (1986). *See also* Flintkote Co. v. Dravo Corp., 678 F.2d 942 (11th Cir. 1982). *But see* Northern Power & Engineering Corp. v. Caterpillar Tractor Co., 623 P.2d 324 (Alaska 1981) (tort theory available if product created risk of violent injury even though actual injury occurred passively).

[220] UCC § 2–318. § 2A–216 is comparable.

A majority of states have adopted Alternative A, the most restrictive alternative. Lack of privity still operates as a defense if the plaintiff does not have personal injuries or is not a member of the described class. Notably, the class excludes bystanders, employees, and guests outside the home.

The most important issue under Alternative A is whether the defined class should be treated as a floor or as a ceiling. That is, are the courts free to extend protection to persons outside the class? Although somewhat ambiguous, the Comments can be read as supporting the idea that the alternative merely establishes a minimum.[221] The Code's Permanent Editorial Board, however, concluded that the alternative creates a ceiling and that persons outside the class lack standing.[222] This position is the more logical, since the states that adopted Alternative A were free to expand the class by adopting one of the other alternatives. As might be expected, the courts have divided on the issue.[223] Of course, in most cases a party who has suffered personal injuries but stands outside the defined class will be able to recover in strict liability in tort, which has dispensed with all privity barriers.

Like Alternative A, Alternative B encompasses only personal injuries, but it is significantly less restrictive as to the class of potential plaintiffs. The class includes any natural person "who may reasonably be expected to use, consume or be affected by" the product. Alternative C is the most liberal. As with Alternative B, the class is broadly defined. Unlike Alternatives A and B, the claimant's recovery is not limited to personal injuries, so business entities are granted standing.

Even a proper plaintiff has only the rights of a third-party beneficiary, and his or her rights rise no higher than those of the buyer. Thus if the seller has effectively disclaimed all warranties, the plaintiff cannot recover. The last sentence of each alternative does not preclude sellers from disclaiming warranties or from effectively limiting the available remedies.[224] It simply precludes them from contractually providing that their warranties do not run to the protected

---

[221] UCC § 2–318, Comment 3; § 2–313, Comment 2.

[222] Permanent Editorial Board for the Uniform Commercial Code, Report No. 3, at 13 (1967).

[223] For cases holding that Alternative A cannot be expanded beyond the defined class, *see* Curlee v. Mock Enterprises, Inc., 41 UCC Rep. Serv. 63 (Ga. Ct. App. 1985) (guest on houseboat lacked standing); Thompson v. Rockford Mach. Tool Co., 744 P.2d 357, 4 UCC Rep. Serv. 2d 1418 (Wash. Ct. App. 1987) (employee lacked standing); Crews v. W. A. Brown & Son, Inc., 106 N.C. App. 324, 416 S.E.2d 924, 18 UCC Rep. Serv. 2d 112 (1992) (13-year-old church member severely injured by freezer lacked standing).

For a case expanding Alternative A's protection beyond the defined class, see Whitaker v. Lian Feng Mach. Co., 156 Ill. App. 3d 316, 509 N.E.2d 591, 4 UCC Rep. Serv. 2d 444 (1987) (employee).

[224] UCC § 2–318, Comment 1.

class. Alternative C implicitly permits sellers to limit the rights of third-party beneficiaries with claims that are not based on personal injuries.

[C]   Vertical Privity

Vertical privity is not involved when the last seller in the chain of distribution is being sued. That seller, however, may have gone out of business, may lack adequate resources to compensate the claimant, or may have effectively disclaimed its warranty liability. The Code is silent on a claimant's right to pursue a remote seller. The Comments to the horizontal privity provisions state:

> The first alternative expressly includes as beneficiaries within its provisions the family, household and guests of the purchaser. Beyond this, the section is neutral and is not intended to enlarge or restrict the developing case law on whether the seller's warranties, given to his buyer who resells, extend to other persons in the distributive chain.[225]

Like horizontal privity, vertical privity is rarely an issue when personal injury is involved because of the ready availability of strict liability in tort. When the tort alternative is not available, as when the statute of limitations has run in tort but not in contract, most courts applying the Code have dropped the vertical privity barrier.[226] Others, however, have maintained the privity defense.[227] The latter courts have reasoned that since the plaintiff could have brought the claim in tort, there is no need to modify traditional contract doctrine.

The courts are more divided when the plaintiff's claim is for economic loss. In the leading case of *Morrow v. New Moon Homes, Inc.*,[228] the buyers of a mobile home sued the manufacturer when the product proved seriously defective. The court permitted the action, observing that:

> A number of courts recently confronting this issue have declined to overturn the privity requirement in warranty actions for economic loss. One principal factor seems to be that these courts simply do not find the social and economic reasons which justify extending enterprise liability to the victims of personal injury or property damage equally

---

[225] UCC § 2–318, Comment 3.

[226] *See, e.g.*, Roberts v. General Dynamics, Convair Corp., 452 F. Supp. 688, 21 UCC Rep. Serv. 565 (S.D. Tex. 1977); Williams v. West Penn Power Co., 467 A.2d 811, 36 UCC Rep. Serv. 107 (Pa. Super. 1983).

[227] *See, e.g.*, Baughn v. Honda Motor Co., Ltd., 107 Wash.2d 127, 727 P.2d 655, 2 UCC Rep. Serv. 2d 445 (1986); Kramer v. Piper Aircraft Corp., 520 So. 2d 37, 5 UCC Rep. Serv. 2d 301 (Fla. 1988).

[228] 548 P.2d 279, 19 UCC Rep. Serv. 1 (Alaska 1976).

compelling in the case of a disappointed buyer suffering "only" economic loss. There is an apparent fear that economic losses may be of a far greater magnitude in value than personal injuries, and being somehow less foreseeable these losses would be less insurable, undermining the risk spreading theory of enterprise liability.

Several of the courts which have recently considered this aspect of the privity issue have found those arguments unpersuasive. We are in agreement and hold that there is no satisfactory justification for a remedial scheme which extends the warranty action to a consumer suffering personal injury or property damage but denies similar relief to the consumer "fortunate" enough to suffer only direct economic loss.[229]

Morrow involved "primary" economic loss—loss of value of the product itself. "Secondary" economic loss means, in essence, consequential damages. Many recent decisions have differentiated between primary and secondary economic loss. With primary economic loss, the recent trend is toward allowing recovery,[230] although there continue to be cases to the contrary.[231] With secondary economic loss, the split is more profound. A number of decisions have permitted the plaintiff to recover,[232] although at least as many decisions are to the contrary.[233] The issue is not an easy one, but in the final analysis the courts should refrain from exposing sellers to losses for which they are unable to plan and against which they may be unable to insure.

[D]   Express Warranties

The vertical privity defense is rarely successful when the claimant has relied on promises or affirmations of fact in a remote seller's advertising. Allowing a seller to use advertising to induce buyers to purchase its product and then to assert lack of privity when one of them brings a product dissatisfaction claim would be incongruous. In the leading case on this issue, *Randy Knitwear,*

---

[229] 548 P.2d at 290–91, 19 UCC Rep. Serv. at 17–18.

[230] *See, e.g.,* Spagnol Enterprises, Inc. v. Digital Equip. Corp., 390 Pa. Super. 372, 568 A.2d 948, 11 UCC Rep. Serv. 2d 49 (1990); Consumers Power Co. v. Mississippi Valley Structural Steel Co., 636 F. Supp. 1100, 1 UCC Rep. Serv. 2d 402 (E.D. Mich. 1986).

[231] *See, e.g.,* Pronti v. DML of Elmira, Inc., 103 A.D.2d 918, 478 N.Y.S.2d 156, 39 UCC Rep. Serv. 455 (Sup. Ct. 1984); Wellcraft Marine v. Zarzour, 577 So. 2d 414, 15 UCC Rep. Serv. 2d 109 (Ala. 1991).

[232] *See, e.g.,* Crest Container Corp. v. R. H. Bishop Co., 111 Ill. App. 3d 1068, 445 N.E.2d 19, 35 UCC Rep. Serv. 1498 (1982); Spagnol Enterprises, Inc. v. Digital Equip. Corp., 390 Pa. Super. 372, 568 A.2d 948, 11 UCC Rep. Serv. 2d 49 (1990).

[233] *See, e.g.,* Mt. Holly Ski Area v. U.S. Electrical Motors, 666 F. Supp. 115, 4 UCC Rep. Serv. 2d 715 (1987); Professional Lens Plan, Inc. v. Polaris Leasing Corp., 234 Kan. 742, 675 P.2d 887, 38 UCC Rep. Serv. 69 (1984).

Inc. v. American Cyanamid Co.,[234] the defendant produced a resin that was sold to textile firms to make their products shrink-resistant. The plaintiff purchased from a textile firm cloth that had been treated with the resin and brought suit after the cloth shrank. The court, noting that it was unrealistic to allow a manufacturer to avoid liability after engaging in a heavy advertising campaign, overruled its prior decisions requiring privity.

[E]   Finance Lessee as Beneficiary of Supply Contract [2A–209]

In a statutory finance lease, the finance lessor acquires the goods from the supplier, by either sale or lease, and then leases them to the finance lessee.[235] The finance lessor does not make the implied warranties of merchantability or fitness and only rarely makes an express warranty. Accordingly, the finance lessee must look to the supplier for warranty protection. By operation of law, Article 2A makes the finance lessee the beneficiary of all warranties, express or implied, that the supplier has made to the finance lessor.[236]

The extension of warranty protection to the finance lessee does not modify the rights and obligations of the finance lessor and the supplier under the supply contract, nor does it create an inference that the finance lessee has assumed any of the finance lessor's obligations.[237] Once the supplier receives notice that the goods are subject to a finance lease, the supply contract cannot be modified or rescinded. If the supplier and the finance lessor modify or rescind the supply contract before the supplier receives notice, the modification or rescission is effective against the finance lessee. In such a case, the finance lessor is deemed to have assumed liability for any warranties that would have run to the finance lessee had the modification or rescission not occurred.[238]

The finance lessee's remedies are limited by the nature of the leasehold interest.[239] For example, if the goods are defective, the finance lessee can reject them and recover damages from the supplier, but the right to recover any money already paid accrues to the finance lessor. Nothing in Article 2A prevents the supplier from disclaiming warranties or limiting the available remedies.

---

[234] 11 N.Y.2d 5, 226 N.Y.S.2d 363, 181 N.E.2d 399 (1962). *See also* Fundin v. Chicago Pneumatic Tool Co., 152 Cal. App. 3d 951, 199 Cal. Rptr. 789, 38 UCC Rep. Serv. 55 (1984). *But see* Stewart v. Gainesville Glass Co., 233 Ga. 578, 212 S.E.2d 377 (1975) (manufacturer of special glass windows not liable to homeowner since its express warranties did not run to a clearly identified person).

[235] Finance leases are discussed generally in § 1.05[B] *supra.*

[236] UCC § 2A–209(1).

[237] UCC § 2A–209(2).

[238] UCC § 2A–209(3).

[239] UCC § 2A–209(1).

§ 5.07   THE STATUTE OF LIMITATIONS [2–725, 2A–506]

The statute of limitations for both sales and leases expires four years after the cause of action accrues, although the period can be shortened to as little as one year by agreement of the parties.[240] In sales transactions, a cause of action accrues when the breach occurs, regardless of the aggrieved party's knowledge of the breach.[241] Ordinarily, a breach of warranty occurs when the seller tenders delivery,[242] thus making it possible for the limitations period to run before the buyer becomes aware of the defect. In *Beckmire v. Ristokrat Clay Products Co.*,[243] for example, bricks that the buyer had purchased for the exterior of his home began to deteriorate after only six years. The buyer argued that the nature of bricks is such that the implied warranty of merchantability should run beyond six years. The court did not disagree, but even though the implied warranty may have been breached, the statute of limitations had run.

Certain events will operate to extend the statutory period. For example, while repairs alone will not toll the running of the statute,[244] the court in *Coakley & Williams, Inc. v. Shatterproof Glass Corp.*[245] held that the period begins anew if the seller tenders replacement goods. When the seller undertakes to install the goods, several courts have held that the cause of action does not accrue until the installation is complete.[246]

The Code does not alter the common-law rules governing tolling of the statute.[247] For example, in *Balog v. Center Art Gallery—Hawaii, Inc.*,[248] the seller's constant reiterations to the buyer that a painting was genuine prevented the buyer from discovering that it was a forgery, and this gave rise to an estoppel that tolled the running of the statute. Of course, fraud or concealment of a defect by the seller will also toll the statute.[249]

---

[240] UCC §§ 2–725(1), 2A–506(1).

[241] UCC § 2–725(2).

[242] *Id.* There is authority that a cause of action for a default other than a breach of warranty accrues when the default occurs. *See, e.g.*, Frank Novak & Sons, Inc. v. Sommer & Maca Indus., Inc., 182 Ill. App. 3d 781, 538 N.E.2d 700, 9 UCC Rep. Serv. 2d 53 (1989) (in suit by seller to recover the price, cause of action did not accrue until the bill first became due).

[243] 36 Ill. App. 3d 411, 343 N.E.2d 530, 18 UCC Rep. Serv. 1218 (1976).

[244] *See, e.g.*, Poppenheimer v. Bluff City Motor Homes, 658 S.W.2d 106, 38 UCC Rep. Serv. 167 (Tenn. Ct. App. 1983).

[245] 706 F.2d 456, 36 UCC Rep. Serv. 87 (4th Cir. 1983).

[246] *See, e.g.*, Westinghouse Elec. Corp. v. Carolina Power & Light Co., 12 UCC Rep. Serv. 2d 127 (W.D. Pa. 1990); City of Willmar v. Short-Elliot-Hendrickson, Inc., 498 N.W.2d 766, 15 UCC Rep. Serv. 2d 912 (Minn. Ct. App. 1993).

[247] UCC §§ 2–725(4), 2A–506(4).

[248] 745 F. Supp. 1556, 12 UCC Rep. Serv. 2d 962 (D. Haw. 1990).

[249] Freiberg v. Atlas-Turner, Inc., 37 UCC Rep. Serv. 1592 (D. Minn. 1984).

If the warranty explicitly extends to future performance and the defect cannot be discovered until the time for performance arrives, the statutory period does not begin to run until the defect is or should be discovered.[250] In *Perry v. Augustine*,[251] for example, the new furnace that the buyer purchased for his home was expressly warranted to heat the home to 75 degrees when the outside temperature fell to 20 degrees below zero. The court held that the limitations period did not begin to run until conditions arose that allowed the promise to be tested.

Sellers frequently warrant that their products will be free from defects for a stated period of time, and such promises clearly extend to future performance.[252] By contrast, a statement that the seller will repair any defects that appear within a stated period does not extend to future performance because the seller's promise focuses on the remedy and does not state explicitly that no defects will occur.[253] Since the reference to future performance must be explicit, none of the implied warranties can fall within the "future performance" exception.[254]

Courts have split on whether to apply Article 2's statute of limitations to claims for indemnification. The typical case involves a manufacturer who sells goods to a retailer, who then resells them to the ultimate buyer. If the ultimate buyer sues the retailer for breach of warranty, the retailer will try to throw the loss back onto the manufacturer. Although the retailer's suit can be seen as a warranty action in its own right, it is more properly viewed as an indemnification action. A right to indemnification arises when one party discharges a debt that should have been paid by another. Should Article 2's four-year provision apply to such actions, or should a state's general statute of limitations, which is typically longer, control?[255]

---

[250] UCC § 2–725(2).

[251] 37 Pa. D.&C.2d 416, 3 UCC Rep. Serv. 735 (Pa. Ct. Com. Pl. 1965). *See also* Hillcrest Country Club v. N.D. Judds Co., 236 Neb. 233, 461 N.W.2d 55, 12 UCC Rep. Serv. 2d 990 (1990) (express warranty that acrylic finish on roofing material would last for 20 years extended to future performance).

[252] *See, e.g.*, Black Leaf Prods. Co. v. Chemisco, Inc., 678 S.W.2d 827, 39 UCC Rep. Serv. 508 (Mo. Ct. App. 1984).

[253] *See, e.g.*, Poppenheimer v. Bluff City Motor Homes, 658 S.W.2d 106, 38 UCC Rep. Serv. 167 (Tenn. Ct. App. 1983); Crouch v. General Elec. Co., 699 F. Supp. 585, 7 UCC Rep. Serv. 2d 1113 (S.D. Miss. 1988). *But see* Long Island Lighting Co. v. Transamerica Delaval, Inc., 646 F. Supp. 1442, 2 UCC Rep. Serv. 2d 1333 (S.D.N.Y. 1986) (applying future performance exception to repair-or-replace remedy).

[254] *See, e.g.*, Murphy v. Spelts-Schultz Lumber Co. of Grand Island, 240 Neb. 275, 481 N.W.2d 422, 17 UCC Rep. Serv. 2d 467 (1992).

[255] The drafters of Article 2A resolved this issue by providing that "[a] cause of action for indemnity accrues when the act or omission on which the claim for indemnity is based is

A number of courts, promoting a policy of repose, have applied the four-year provision.[256] Others, however, concerned about the fact that the retailer's suit could be precluded before the ultimate buyer's suit even commenced, have applied the general statute of limitations.[257] The best approach is a compromise position articulated in *Sheehan v. Morris Irrigation, Inc.*[258] The court in *Sheehan* concluded that Article 2 applied because the indemnitee had sufficient time to bring its action before the four-year period expired. The court made it clear, however, that it would have opted for the general statute of limitations had that not been the case.

Suppose the goods remain on the retailer's shelf for more than four years, and the ultimate buyer later brings a suit for breach of warranty against the remote manufacturer. The few courts that have ruled on this issue have reached different conclusions. In *Patterson v. Her Majesty Industries, Inc.*,[259] the court sided with the ultimate buyer, a consumer, and held that the cause of action accrued when the goods were purchased from the retailer. This approach, which is consistent with the drafters' intention that there be minimally adequate remedies available for breaches of warranty, makes sense. The need to protect the consumer is particularly acute when the retailer disclaimed its own warranties at the time of sale and the consumer relied on the apparent existence of the manufacturer's warranty. Some decisions, however, have rejected the *Patterson* approach.[260]

Because of the differing nature of lease transactions, Article 2A deviates from the statutory analogue with respect to the statute of limitations. Many lease transactions have a duration in excess of four years, and it is not uncommon for the lessor in a long-term lease to be responsible for maintenance and repairs. Accordingly, Article 2A provides that a cause of action for breach of warranty accrues when the lessee should have discovered the breach rather than upon tender of the goods.[261]

---

or should have been discovered by the indemnified party, whichever is later." UCC § 2A–506(2).

[256] *See, e.g.,* Farmers Nat'l Bank v. Wickham Pipeline, 114 Idaho 565, 759 P.2d 71 (1990).

[257] *See, e.g.,* City of Wood River v. Geer-Melkus Constr. Co., 233 Neb. 179, 444 N.W.2d 305, 9 UCC Rep. Serv. 2d 957 (1989).

[258] 460 N.W.2d 413, 13 UCC Rep. Serv. 2d 145 (S.D. 1990).

[259] 450 F. Supp. 425, 23 UCC Rep. Serv. 1198 (E.D. Pa. 1978).

[260] *See, e.g.,* Thomas v. King Ridge, Inc., 771 F. Supp. 478, 16 UCC Rep. Serv. 2d 127 (D.N.H. 1991); Heller v. United States Suzuki Motor Co., 64 N.Y.2d 407, 488 N.Y.S.2d 132, 477 N.E.2d 434, 37 UCC Rep. Serv. 156 (1985).

[261] UCC § 2A–506(2).

§ 5.08   CUMULATION AND CONFLICT OF WARRANTIES [2–317; 2A–215]

Occasionally, warranties will be in conflict. If possible, they should be construed in a way that makes them consistent with one another and that gives the buyer the maximum cumulative protection.[262] The presumption that warranties are cumulative can be an important aid to the buyer. For example, suppose the seller gives an express warranty that the product will be free from defects but limits it in duration. If a defect arises after the stated period, the buyer may still be able to prevail under an implied warranty theory.[263]

When warranties are in such conflict that any attempt to harmonize them would be unreasonable, the intention of the parties governs.[264] The Code creates the following presumptions to assist in ascertaining that intent:

(a) Exact or technical specifications displace an inconsistent sample or model or general language of description.
(b) A sample from an existing bulk displaces inconsistent general language of description.
(c) Express warranties displace inconsistent implied warranties other than an implied warranty of fitness for a particular purpose.[265]

Application of these presumptions is similar to application of the Code's hierarchy of terms, discussed elsewhere in this book.[266]

---

[262] UCC § 2–317, § 2A–215. *See, e.g.,* Singer Co. v. E.I. DuPont de Nemours & Co., 579 F.2d 433, 24 UCC Rep. Serv. 276 (8th Cir. 1978) (express warranty that paint would pass lab tests did not negate implied warranty of fitness).

[263] *See, e.g.,* Koellmer v. Chrysler Motors Corp., 6 Conn. Cir. Ct. 478, 276 A.2d 807, 8 UCC Rep. Serv. 668 (1970) (express warranty not inconsistent with implied warranty of merchantability). *But see* Mountain Fuel Supply Co. v. Central Engineering & Equip. Co., 611 P.2d 863, 29 UCC Rep. Serv. 817 (Wyo. 1980) (express warranty of limited duration negated implied warranty of merchantability).

Under the Magnuson–Moss Warranty—Federal Trade Commission Improvement Act, sellers of consumer goods who give written warranties must designate whether those warranties are "full" or "limited." In neither case can implied warranties be disclaimed, but if the written warranty is limited, the duration of the implied warranties can be shortened to coincide with that of the written warranty. 15 U.S.C. § 2308 (1988).

[264] UCC §§ 2–317, 2A–215.

[265] *Id.*

[266] See § 4.03[D] *supra.*

CHAPTER

6

Risk of Loss

§ 6.01 INTRODUCTION

A variety of calamities may befall specific goods that are the subject of a contract for sale or lease. These events can result in loss, damage, or destruction. They can occur at any time, including during the manufacture, storage, or transit of the goods, or after they have been delivered into the possession of the buyer or lessee. The transit and delivery stage is often the period of greatest exposure to loss because the goods are being moved from one location to another and third parties, such as carriers, are often involved. When a loss occurs without the fault of either party to the sale or lease, a method of loss allocation is required.

Although the Uniform Sales Act tied most of the rights and duties of parties, including loss allocation principles, to the location of title,[1] the Code greatly reduced the significance of the concept. Title had proven to be an unworkable concept in several contexts of sales transactions. It was largely dependent on the intentions of the parties, which were unclear in many cases, leaving the results of those cases in doubt. Articles 2 and 2A therefore abandon title as a pivotal concept for the resolution of issues like loss allocation.[2]

---

[1] Uniform Sales Act § 22.

[2] "Each provision of this Article with regard to the rights, obligations and remedies of the seller, the buyer, purchasers or other third parties applies irrespective of title to the goods except where the provision refers to such title." UCC § 2–401. Article 2A includes a comparable provision, adding that the provisions of the Article apply without respect to who has possession of the goods. UCC § 2A–302. Martin v. Mellands, 27 UCC Rep. Serv. 94 (N.D. 1979) (trial court's use of title as relevant indicium for risk of loss was erroneous).

Articles 2 and 2A allocate losses only between the seller and buyer or the lessor and lessee, respectively. Other persons or entities may face the ultimate liability with respect to a particular loss. A carrier or storer of goods may incur liability for the high duty of care it owes with respect to goods in its possession. A third party may incur liability for negligence that causes the loss. An insurer may have to pay for a particular loss. Separate relationships and bodies of law determine the liabilities of such third parties. Articles 2 and 2A allocate the loss only between the parties to a sales or lease contract.

Allocation of the risk of loss affects the duties of the parties. If the goods are lost or destroyed after risk of their loss has passed to the buyer, the buyer is obligated to pay for them.[3] On the other hand, if the risk has not yet passed to the buyer when the goods are lost or destroyed, the seller must make a substitute, conforming tender in order to avoid liability for nondelivery.[4]

Part A: Sales

§ 6.02   In the Absence of Breach [2–509]

Article 2 provides a set of rules that governs the allocation of the risk of loss when neither party has breached the sales contract.[5] Another provision determines the effect, if any, that a breach by either party has upon the risk allocation.[6]

[A]   Express Agreement

The parties to a sales contract can agree between themselves on when the risk of loss should pass to the buyer.[7] Pursuant to the principle of freedom of contract, the parties can include provisions in their agreement addressing loss.[8]

---

3   The buyer's obligation is to pay for the goods. UCC § 2–301; UCC § 2–709(1)(a) (seller cause of action for price in the risk-of-loss context). *See* § 9.04[A][2] *supra*. Rheinberg Kellerei GmbH v. Brookfield Nat'l Bank of Commerce, 901 F.2d 481, 11 UCC Rep. Serv. 2d 1214 (5th Cir. 1990) (seller entitled to recover for wine that deteriorated after remaining exposed at a harbor).

4   The seller's obligation is to transfer and deliver the goods. UCC § 2–301. On measures of damages for nondelivery, *see* §§ 8.03[B], 8.04 *infra*.

5   UCC § 2–509.

6   UCC § 2–510.

7   UCC § 2–509(4).

8   Forest Nursery Co., Inc. v. I.W.S., Inc., 141 Misc. 2d 661, 534 N.Y.S.2d 86, 8 UCC Rep. Serv. 2d 923 (N.Y. Dist. Ct. 1988) (risk of loss passed to buyer through terms stating "No Risk to Supplier" and "NOTICE: ALL SHIPMENTS TRAVEL AT RISK AND COST OF PURCHASER").

They should be careful to articulate their intentions clearly, however, as courts have sometimes held that the language employed was not sufficient to pass the risk of loss. For example, in *Caudle v. Sherrard Motor Co.*[9] the court held that a contract clause that no loss or destruction of a house trailer would release the buyer from his or her obligation did not place the risk of loss on the buyer when the trailer was stolen from the dealer's lot before the buyer took possession. The court interpreted the clause as fixing responsibility on the buyer after possession was transferred. Passing the risk to the buyer before delivery is so uncommon, in the view of the court, that the seller should be required to articulate such an intention more clearly.[10]

When goods are to be shipped by carrier, the parties often include express terms that consist of abbreviations that comprise a form of business shorthand designed to specify various requirements for the transaction.[11] The use of an F. O.B. designation carries consequences for risk-of-loss allocation. The term F.O.B. means "free on board" at the named place, and it can be used simply in connection with a stated price.[12]

For example, assume that a seller in San Francisco enters into a contract with a buyer in New York and that the goods are to be shipped by rail. Considerably different consequences would result depending on whether the contract specified "F.O.B. San Francisco $15,000" or "F.O.B. New York $15,000." The first version of the express term creates a shipment contract; the latter version represents a destination contract. Each version determines when the seller has tendered delivery, which party is responsible for the costs of transit, and when the risk of loss passes to the buyer.

Under the shipment contract,[13] the seller will tender in San Francisco by complying with the requirements of section 2–504. Essentially the seller must put conforming goods into the carrier's possession, make an appropriate contract for their transport, and notify the seller that the goods have been sent. The seller is responsible for any costs incurred in getting the goods into the possession of the carrier, but the cost responsibility ends there, which means that the buyer must pay the carrier's charge for transporting the goods. The seller's

---

[9] 525 S.W.2d 238, 17 UCC Rep. Serv. 754 (Tex. Ct. App. 1975).

[10] *See also* Hayward v. Postma, 31 Mich. App. 720, 188 N.W.2d 31, 9 UCC Rep. Serv. 379 (1971) (clause in agreement that required the buyer to carry insurance on the goods at all times was insufficient to prove risk of loss on an uninsured boat destroyed in a fire on the seller's premises).

[11] *See* UCC §§ 2–319 (F.O.B. and F.A.S terms), 2–320 (C.I.F. and C. & F. terms), 2–321 (same).

[12] UCC § 2–319(1). A. M. Knitwear Corp. v. All America Export–Import Corp., 41 N.Y.2d 14, 390 N.Y.S.2d 832, 359 N.E.2d 342, 20 UCC Rep. Serv. 581 (1976) (the meaning of an F.O.B. term must be the ordinary and well-understood meaning in the absence of a contrary intention of the parties).

[13] UCC § 2–319(1)(a).

risk also ends when it puts the goods into possession of the carrier. Thus, if the goods were destroyed in a traffic accident in San Francisco while the seller was carrying them across town to the rail terminal, the loss would be on the seller. A loss incurred in a rail mishap during cross-country transit, however, would occur after the risk of loss passed to the buyer.[14]

The buyer attains more for the stated $15,000 purchase price under destination contract terms.[15] The seller would be required to transport the goods to New York and tender delivery for them there by making them available to the buyer's disposition.[16] The seller would also incur the expense of transporting the goods across country to New York and bear the risks associated with such transit. An F.O.B. term in a contract thus includes a risk allocation component.

F.O.B. terms can be much more specific than simply designating the relevant city. For example, the designation could be "F.O.B. seller's plant." The designation can even be directed toward a specific vehicle or vessel. When, in addition to a term indicating either the place of shipment or the place of destination, the term is also F.O.B. vessel, car, or other vehicle, "the seller must in addition at his own expense and risk load the goods on board."[17]

[B]   Shipment by Carrier

Article 2 includes provisions that allocate risk of loss when the contract "requires or authorizes the seller to ship the goods by carrier."[18] The loss allocation under this provision is comparable to the results attained through use of an F.O.B. provision.[19] A consistent approach thus applies irrespective of whether the parties create a shipment or a destination contract through the use of F.O.B. terms, through other express terms, or through commercial understanding derived from trade usage or course of dealing. If shipment by carrier is at least authorized, the risk-of-loss provisions also apply, even though the shipment contract or destination contract variant is not designated. The shipment contract is presumed, unless the seller agrees otherwise.[20] The Comments

---

14   Black Prince Distillery, Inc. v. Home Liquors, 148 N.J. Super. 286, 372 A.2d 638, 21 UCC Rep. Serv. 1037 (1977) (buyer of liquor liable for purchase price of goods that were hijacked from the carrier's truck).

15   UCC § 2–319(1)(b).

16   UCC § 2–503(1),(3).

17   UCC § 2–319(1)(c). Consolidated Bottling Co. v. Jaco Equip. Corp., 442 F.2d 660, 8 UCC Rep. Serv. 966 (2d Cir. 1971) (the term "f.o.b. purchaser's truck" left the risk of loss on the seller until the truck was loaded).

18   UCC § 2–509(1).

19   See § 6.02[A] supra.

20   La Casse v. Blaustein, 93 Misc. 2d 572, 403 N.Y.S.2d 440, 23 UCC Rep. Serv. 907 (1978);

explain that "[t]he seller is not obligated to deliver at a named destination and bear the concurrent risk of loss until arrival, unless he has specifically agreed so to deliver or the commercial understanding of the terms used by the parties contemplates such delivery."[21]

Section 2–509(1) reads in full as follows:

Where the contract requires or authorizes the seller to ship the goods by carrier
   (a) if it does not require him to deliver them at a particular destination, the risk of loss passes to the buyer when the goods are duly delivered to the carrier even though the shipment is under reservation (Section 2–505); but
   (b) if it does require him to deliver them at a particular destination and the goods are there duly tendered while in the possession of the carrier, the risk of loss passes to the buyer when the goods are there duly so tendered as to enable the buyer to take delivery.

The first of these two rules deals with shipment contracts, as the seller is not required to deliver the goods at a particular destination. Of course, even in a shipment contract, the seller must enter into a contract with the carrier that enables the goods to be sent to the correct destination.[22] The key distinction is the delivery concept. In a shipment contract, the seller tenders delivery upon full compliance with the requirements of section 2–504.[23] Tender thus occurs when the seller puts conforming goods into the possession of the carrier, makes an appropriate contract for their delivery, forwards any necessary documents to the buyer, and notifies the buyer.[24] In the terminology of section 2–509(1)(a),

---

Ninth St. East, Ltd. v. Harrison, 5 Conn. Cir. Ct. 597, 259 A.2d 772, 7 UCC Rep. Serv. 171 (1968).

[21] UCC § 2–503, Comment 5.

[22] Eberhard Mfg. Co. v. Brown, 61 Mich. App. 268, 232 N.W.2d 378, 17 UCC Rep. Serv. 978 (1975) ("ship to" term in contract did not create a destination contract even in the absence of an F.O.B. provision). *See also* Pestana v. Karinol Corp., 367 So. 2d 1096, 25 UCC Rep. Serv. 1306 (Fla. Ct. App. 1979) (shipment contract created in the absence of delivery terms).

[23] UCC § 2–503(2). Montana Seeds, Inc. v. Holliday, 178 Mont. 119, 582 P.2d 1223, 24 UCC Rep. Serv. 884 (1978) (because risk of loss passed to buyer on delivery of goods to the carrier, any cause of action in the buyer for misdelivery of part of the shipment to the wrong address was against the carrier).

[24] Rheinberg-Kellerei GmbH v. Vineyard Wine Co., Inc., 53 N.C. App. 560, 281 S.E.2d 425, 32 UCC Rep. Serv. 96 (1981) (seller's failure to notify buyer directly or by forwarding shipping documents until after loss of shipment at sea did not facilitate buyer's protecting its interest by insurance and left the risk of loss on the seller).

the contract does not require the seller to deliver the goods "at a particular destination."[25]

The risk of loss in a contract that requires or authorizes the seller to ship the goods by carrier passes to the buyer when the seller tenders delivery. In the shipment contract, risk of loss passes when the seller duly delivers the goods to the carrier.[26] In the destination contract, tender occurs and risk of loss passes when the carrier enables the buyer to take delivery.[27] Tender of delivery requires the seller to put and hold conforming goods at the buyer's disposition, to provide any necessary notification to the buyer, and to tender any necessary documents.[28]

[C]   Goods Held by a Bailee

Section 2–509(2) provides in its entirety as follows:

Where the goods are held by a bailee to be delivered without being moved, the risk of loss passes to the buyer
  (a) on his receipt of a negotiable document of title covering the goods; or
  (b) on acknowledgment by the bailee of the buyer's right to possession of the goods; or
  (c) after his receipt of a non-negotiable document of title or other written direction to deliver, as provided in subsection (4)(b) of Section 2–503.

These three subsections cover the three possible scenarios with respect to goods that the seller has entrusted to a third-party bailee. Subsection (a) covers cases in which the bailee issues a negotiable document for the goods. Because the document represents title to the goods, risk of loss between the seller and the buyer should pass when the buyer receives the negotiable document, and subsection (a) so provides.[29]

---

[25] Morauer v. Deak & Co., Inc., 26 UCC Rep. Serv. 1142 (D.C. Super. 1979) (agreement that seller was to ship gold coins to buyer at his home was not a destination contract, so risk of loss passed on delivery of the packages to the post office).

[26] UCC §§ 2–509(1)(a), 2–503(2), 2–504.

[27] UCC § 2–509(1)(b).

[28] UCC § 2–503(1), (3), (5). Baumgold Bros., Inc. v. Allan M. Fox Co., East, 375 F. Supp. 807, 14 UCC Rep. Serv. 580 (N.D. Ohio 1973) (held nonperformance of tender obligations when seller sent a package containing diamonds by registered mail that disappeared after the postman left it on the counter of buyer's unattended store).

[29] Henry Heide, Inc. v. Atlantic Mut. Ins. Co., 80 Misc. 2d 485, 363 N.Y.S.2d 515, 16 UCC Rep. Serv. 701 (Sup. Ct. 1975) (delivery of 3,200 bags of sugar was tendered via the warehouse receipt).

Rather than issuing a negotiable document, the bailee might give the seller a nonnegotiable document, the scenario contemplated in subsection (c). This document does not represent title to the bailed goods, but rather functions as a receipt for the goods bailed. The seller's delivery of the nonnegotiable document to the buyer does not establish the buyer's right to obtain the goods from the bailee unless the buyer is named in the document as a person entitled to receive delivery. If the document names the seller, the seller can facilitate the buyer's right to take possession by giving the buyer a written delivery order. This order, when given to the bailee, establishes the buyer's right to possession of the goods.[30] Risk of loss does not pass to the buyer until the buyer receives a writing establishing the right to possession and the buyer has a reasonable opportunity to present this writing to the bailee.[31] If the bailee refuses to honor the writing, the seller's tender is defeated.[32]

In the final scenario, the bailee might not give any type of document to the seller. Subsection (b) provides the functional equivalent of subsection (c) by indicating that risk of loss will pass from the seller to the buyer when the bailee acknowledges the buyer's right to possession of the goods. For example, in *Whately v. Tetrault*,[33] the seller of a motorboat and trailer accompanied the buyer to the place where they were stored and informed the bailee that the goods had been sold and would be picked up the following day by the buyer's agent. The court held that the agent's arrangement with the bailee to pick up the goods constituted the bailee's acknowledgment of the buyer's right to the goods and passed the risk of loss.

An occasional seller has tried to apply the literal language of subsection (b) to cases that do not involve a bailment. For example, in *Caudle v. Sherrard Motor Co.*,[34] the buyer was called away on business before being able to take delivery of a house trailer that he had just purchased. The seller indicated that the buyer could return at his convenience for the trailer, but in the interim the trailer was stolen from the seller's premises. The seller contended that the risk of loss had passed to the buyer under section 2–509(2)(b) because prior to the theft the seller had acknowledged the buyer's right to possession of the trailer. The seller contended that it was acting merely as a bailee in holding the goods for the buyer.

---

[30] UCC § 7–403(1),(4).

[31] UCC §§ 2–509(2)(c), 2–503(4)(b). Commonwealth Propane Co. v. Petrosol Int'l, Inc., 818 F.2d 522, 3 UCC Rep. Serv. 2d 1778 (6th Cir. 1987) (written delivery direction for stored propane).

[32] UCC § 2–503(4)(b).

[33] 29 Mass. App. Dec. 112, 5 UCC Rep. Serv. 838 (1964).

[34] 525 S.W.2d 238, 17 UCC Rep. Serv. 754 (Tex. Ct. App. 1975).

The court properly rejected the seller's position.[35] The bailee characterization is technical at best. The seller had simply agreed to postpone the time at which the buyer would take delivery of the goods.[36] Allowing sellers to pass the risk of loss to buyers simply by acknowledging the buyer's right to take possession of the goods would defeat an underlying rationale of the risk-of-loss allocation under the Code. The Comments are clear in specifying that the drafters intended to leave the risk of loss on a merchant who is to make physical delivery at his or her own place of business until the buyer actually receives the goods.[37] The seller who remains in possession of the goods continues to exert control over them and can be expected to insure them.[38]

[D] All Other Cases

A residual provision governs when risk of loss shifts in the absence of default in all cases in which none of the other rules apply.[39] Its two separate rules are distinguished on the basis of whether the seller is a merchant. When the seller is a merchant, risk of loss does not pass to the buyer until the buyer actually receives the goods.[40] "Receipt" of goods is defined in Article 2 to mean "taking physical possession of them."[41] This definition eliminates the possibility of arguments based on constructive or symbolic possession. The merchant continues to exert control over the goods and prudently would continue to insure his or her interest in them. The risk of loss thus remains on the merchant seller who delivers goods at his or her place of business until the buyer takes physical possession of them.[42]

---

[35] For similar holdings, *see* Conway v. Larsen Jewelers, Inc., 104 Misc. 2d 872, 429 N.Y.S.2d 378, 29 UCC Rep. Serv. 842 (Civ. Ct. 1980) (no bailment created with respect to piece of jewelry purchased on a lay-away plan); Courtin v. Sharp, 280 F.2d 345 (5th Cir. 1960), *cert. denied,* 365 U.S. 814, 81 S. Ct. 693, 5 L. Ed. 2d 692 (1961) (seller of colt did not qualify as bailee for purposes of § 2–509(2)(b) by agreeing to board colt for the buyer).

[36] Silver v. Wycombe Meyer Co., Inc., 124 Misc. 2d 717, 477 N.Y.S.2d 288, 39 UCC Rep. Serv. 467, (Civ. Ct. 1984), *aff'd,* 130 Misc. 2d 227, 498 N.Y.S.2d 334 (1985).

[37] UCC § 2–509, Comment 3. The applicable rule that allocates the risk of loss in this circumstance is UCC § 2–509(3). For discussion of this rule, *see* § 6.02[D] *infra.*

[38] *Id.*

[39] UCC § 2–509(3).

[40] National Plumbing Supply Co. v. Castellano, 118 Misc. 2d 150, 460 N.Y.S.2d 248, 36 UCC Rep. Serv. 814 (Just. Ct. 1983) (delivery of goods to unnamed individuals on a job site not under the control of the buyer did not pass the risk of loss).

[41] UCC § 2–103(1)(c). Ron Mead T.V. & Appliance v. Legendary Homes, Inc., 746 P.2d 1163, 6 UCC Rep. Serv. 2d 117 (Okla. Ct. App. 1987) (leaving appliances in unlocked garage from which they were stolen did not constitute buyer's physical possession necessary for "receipt").

[42] UCC § 2–509, Comment 3. Hayward v. Postma, 31 Mich. App. 720, 188 N.W.2d 31, 9 UCC Rep. Serv. 379 (1971).

A different rule applies when the seller is not a merchant. Risk of loss passes to the buyer in these cases on tender of delivery, which occurs when the seller puts and holds conforming goods at the buyer's disposition. Assume for example that an individual agrees to buy several pieces of furniture from a neighbor who does not qualify as a merchant. If the neighbor agrees to hold the goods for the buyer while the buyer arranges to rent a trailer to move them, the risk of loss passes to the buyer even though the buyer has not yet taken possession.

§ 6.03   IN THE EVENT OF BREACH [2–510]

A breach by either party to a sales contract may influence the risk-of-loss allocation. Section 2–510 includes three rules that govern the effect of a breach on risk of loss. Two of these rules concern breach by the seller; the last covers breach by the buyer. A breach may or may not affect the risk of loss.

[A] Buyer's Right to Reject

The risk-of-loss allocation is affected when the seller's tender gives the buyer a right to reject. The applicable provision states that "[w]here a tender or delivery of goods so fails to conform to the contract as to give a right of rejection the risk of their loss remains on the seller until cure or acceptance."[43] When this provision is invoked, it leaves the risk of loss on the seller.

Because the buyer has a right to reject at such a low threshold, this provision will be invoked whenever the seller makes a nonconforming tender or delivery of goods. A buyer can reject if the tender or delivery of goods fails in any respect to conform to the contract.[44] Although a buyer must purposefully implement a rejection for it to be effective,[45] the risk allocation provision is based on the buyer's *right* to reject. It thus is not dependent on the buyer's actually rejecting.[46]

---

[43] UCC § 2–510(1).

[44] UCC § 2–601. For discussion of this standard, *see* § 7.04[A] *infra.* Jakowski v. Carole Chevrolet, Inc., 180 N.J. Super. 122, 433 A.2d 841, 31 UCC Rep. Serv. 1615 (1981) (buyer entitled to reject new car that was delivered without undercoating and polymer finish, so risk of loss remained on the seller).

[45] UCC § 2–602(1). *See* discussion in § 7.04[B] *infra.*

[46] T. J. Stevenson & Co., Inc. v. 81,193 Bags of Flour, 629 F.2d 338, 30 UCC Rep. Serv. 865 (5th Cir. 1980) (delivery of unmerchantable flour gave buyer the right to reject and thus left the risk of loss on seller).

Consider, for example, a shipment contract that calls for the seller to ship goods by rail from one coast to a city in the Midwest. If the seller ships conforming goods in accordance with the terms of the contract, the risk of loss passes to the buyer when the seller properly ships the goods.[47] If the seller ships defective goods, however, the risk of their loss remains on the seller, because the buyer has a right to reject the tendered goods. A buyer located in the Midwest will probably be unaware of the defect, and thus not even in a position to consider rejection yet. The defect nevertheless will preclude the risk of loss from passing.

Even though a tender or delivery of goods does not conform to the contract, the buyer may nevertheless decide to accept them. Acceptance in this circumstance is the event that transfers risk of loss from the breaching seller to the buyer. Acceptance can result from the buyer's positive indication of willingness to take the goods or the buyer's failure to reject them within a reasonable time.[48] In neither instance can the buyer be held to an acceptance without a prior opportunity to inspect the tendered goods.[49] The buyer can preclude acceptance, and the transfer of risk of loss of goods tendered by a breaching seller, by making an effective rejection.[50]

Sometimes a breaching seller can suspend a buyer's rejection by giving the aggrieved buyer a seasonable notification of an intention to cure the nonconformity in the original tender. The Code includes a limited right of cure for the seller, and the seller sometimes attains the right through consensual agreement with the buyer.[51] When a cure is made with respect to the goods that were originally tendered, as by repairing a defect, the risk of loss with respect to those goods passes when the cure is accomplished. If the cure consists of replacing the original goods with a conforming tender, the risk of loss is not affected with respect to the nonconforming goods that were originally tendered.[52]

[B]   Buyer's Revocation of Acceptance

The second rule that applies in a case of breach by the seller involves buyer revocation of acceptance. It provides that "[w]here the buyer rightfully revokes acceptance he may to the extent of any deficiency in his effective insurance coverage treat the risk of loss as having rested on the seller from the beginning."[53]

---

[47]   UCC § 2–509(1)(a).

[48]   Acceptance of goods is covered in UCC § 2–606. *See* discussion § 7.03 *infra*.

[49]   Inspection rights are covered in UCC § 2–513. *See* discussion § 7.03[A][1] *infra*.

[50]   One of the consequences of an acceptance is that it terminates any prior right of the buyer to reject. UCC § 2–607(1). *See* discussion § 7.03[B][1] *infra*.

[51]   UCC § 2–508. For discussion of the cure concept, *see* § 7.04[C] *infra*.

[52]   UCC § 2–510, Comment 2.

[53]   UCC § 2–510(2).

Unlike the first rule, which was based on the buyer's right to reject, the aggrieved buyer must actually revoke in order to invoke this rule.[54]

This distinction can be particularly significant in light of the provision that requires a revocation to be made "before any substantial change in condition of the goods which is not caused by their own defects."[55] For example, if goods are destroyed because of a fire caused by defective wiring in the goods themselves, the buyer may still be entitled to revoke the acceptance and pass the loss back to the seller. If the goods are destroyed by a fire unrelated to a defect in the goods, the risk of loss will remain on a buyer who has not yet revoked, even if the buyer had the right to do so.

Any case that is governed by the second rule (buyer's rightful revocation of acceptance) will have already passed through the first rule (buyer's right of rejection). Although the seller will have made a nonconforming tender or delivery, entitling the aggrieved buyer to reject, the buyer will have accepted the goods. Thus, based on the first rule, the risk of loss will have passed to the buyer on acceptance. The second rule then determines whether an effective revocation of that acceptance will reallocate the risk of loss to the seller. A buyer entitled to invoke the second rule can treat the risk of loss as though it had always remained on the seller.

Another distinction between the rule based on a buyer's right to reject and a buyer's rightful revocation of acceptance is that the latter rule may or may not reallocate the loss to the seller because of the seller's breach. Risk of loss can be passed back to the breaching seller only to the extent that the buyer's effective insurance coverage is deficient.[56] If the loss is fully covered by the buyer's insurance, the risk of loss remains on the buyer. If the buyer has no insurance coverage, the entire loss can be passed to the breaching seller. Partial insurance coverage results in the buyer's retaining the risk of loss for the insured portion of the loss, with the loss for the remainder being passed to the seller.

The limitation that permits reallocation of risk of loss to the breaching seller only to the extent of a deficiency in the buyer's effective insurance coverage

---

[54] Revocation of acceptance is covered by UCC § 2–608. For a discussion of the concept, *see* § 7.05 *infra*.

[55] UCC § 2–608(2).

[56] "The word 'effective' as applied to insurance coverage in those subsections is used to meet the case of supervening insolvency of the insurer. The 'deficiency' referred to in the text means such deficiency in the insurance coverage as exists without subrogation." UCC § 2–510, Comment 3.

operates as an antisubrogation provision.[57] Upon paying the buyer for loss or damage to the goods, an insurer might be inclined to recoup that payment from the seller by subrogating itself to the buyer's cause of action against the seller for breach of contract. The insurance contract with the buyer might even include a provision that entitles the insurer to subrogate itself to any claims the buyer would have against third parties with respect to a loss for which the insurer compensates the buyer. The Code's antisubrogation provision defeats any opportunity for the insurer to assert a successful claim against the seller by leaving on the buyer the risk of any loss for which the buyer is effectively insured. The buyer thus does not have any claim against the breaching seller with respect to the paid loss, eliminating any claim to which the insurance company can subrogate.

[C]   Breach by the Buyer

Section 2–510 includes one rule about the effect of a breach by the buyer on risk-of-loss allocation. The rule provides that "[w]here the buyer as to conforming goods already identified to the contract for sale repudiates or is otherwise in breach before risk of their loss has passed to him, the seller may to the extent of any deficiency in his effective insurance coverage treat the risk of loss as resting on the buyer for a commercially reasonable time."[58] This rule should be scrutinized when a buyer breaches before risk of loss would otherwise pass to the buyer under the applicable rule of section 2–509. The seller may or may not be able to use the occasion of the buyer's breach to shift the risk of loss to the buyer sooner.

The rule on the effect of a buyer's breach will pass the risk of loss to the buyer only if three conditions are satisfied: (1) the goods must conform to the contract, (2) they must have been identified to the contract before the buyer breaches, and (3) the seller must have a deficiency in its insurance coverage. If the goods are nonconforming, the seller would have breached by tendering them and the buyer could have rejected. Until the goods are identified to the contract,[59] the buyer does not even have an insurable interest in them.[60] The third condition is an antisubrogation provision that operates the same as the comparable provision that applies when a buyer rightfully revokes its acceptance.[61]

---

[57] "This section merely distributes the risk of loss as stated and is not intended to be disturbed by any subrogation of an insurer." UCC § 2–510, Comment 3.

[58] UCC § 2–510(3).

[59] For discussion of the concept of identification, *see* § 1.03[B].

[60] UCC § 2–501(1).

[61] *See* § 6.03[B] *supra*.

When these three conditions are met, the aggrieved seller is entitled to pass the risk of loss to the buyer, but only for a commercially reasonable time. This provision has been construed to allow the seller, upon learning of the buyer's breach, to secure an insurance rider to cover the affected goods.[62] In *Multiplastics, Inc. v. Arch Industries, Inc.*,[63] the court upheld a transfer of the risk of loss to the breaching buyer for slightly longer than one month, during which time the seller did not secure any insurance coverage. The court based its decision on principles of estoppel, however, because the buyer had repeatedly indicated that it would transmit delivery instructions to the seller and accept deliveries of the goods.

Part B: Leases

§ 6.04   GENERAL RULE [2A–219(1)]

Determining the risk of loss is much easier under the general rule of Article 2A. This rule provides that "risk of loss is retained by the lessor and does not pass to the lessee."[64] It reflects the general practice in personal property leasing[65] and is based on considerations of which party is more likely to insure the goods against loss. The most sensible approach generally is for the lessor to insure the goods and pass through the applicable portion of the cost to the lessee in the form of higher rent, particularly if the rental term is relatively short. Otherwise the lessor might have to insure the goods, drop the insurance on leasing them, and then reinsure at the termination of a given lease term.

§ 6.05   EXCEPTIONS

[A] Applicability

Article 2A recognizes two exceptions to the general rule on risk-of-loss allocation. The parties can expressly agree to a different risk allocation scheme. The general rule also does not apply to finance leases.

---

[62] Multiplastics, Inc. v. Arch Indus., Inc., 348 A.2d 618, 14 UCC Rep. Serv. 573 (Conn. 1974).
[63] *Id.*
[64] UCC § 2A–219(1).
[65] UCC § 2A–219, Comment.

[1]   Express Agreement

The parties are free to determine risk-of-loss allocation pursuant to the principle of freedom of contract. Article 2 includes a specific provision that recognizes this right in the risk-of-loss context.[66] The drafters of Article 2A felt that an explicit provision was unnecessary because Article 2A is founded on the freedom of contract principle.[67] The parties to a lease thus can decide which party ought to bear the risk of loss and when, if at all, it will pass to the lessee. Passing the loss to the lessee might be sensible in a longer-term lease in which the lessee assumes the responsibility for care and maintenance of the goods.

Article 2A includes a unique provision on agreements concerning insurance: "The parties by agreement may determine that one or more parties have an obligation to obtain and pay for insurance covering the goods and by agreement may determine the beneficiary of the proceeds of the insurance."[68] This provision recognizes that an agreement that requires the lessee to obtain insurance can be construed not to allocate the risk of loss to the lessee.[69] Although not shifting the risk of loss to the lessee, such an agreement places the responsibility and the cost of insuring the goods on the lessee. Failure to comply would be a default by the lessee, entitling the lessor to the resulting damages.

[2]   Finance Leases [2A–219(1)]

Article 2A allocates the risk of loss differently in a finance lease. It provides that "[i]n the case of a finance lease, risk of loss passes to the lessee."[70] This loss allocation is based on the role that the finance lessor plays in a finance lease transaction. The finance lessor is not involved in selecting or supplying the goods, but rather acts as a financing conduit enabling the finance lessee to acquire use of the goods.[71] Although a finance lessor can take possession of the goods,[72] generally they are delivered directly from the manufacturer or supplier to the finance lessee. Finance leases also tend to be of relatively long duration. Therefore, in the absence of a contrary agreement, the risk of loss in a finance lease is passed to the finance lessee.

---

[66]   UCC § 2–509(4). *See* § 6.02[A] *supra.*

[67]   UCC § 2A–219, Comment.

[68]   UCC § 2A–218(5).

[69]   The issue has been litigated in the Article 2 context. Hayward v. Postma, 31 Mich. App. 720, 188 N.W.2d 31, 9 UCC Rep. Serv. 379 (1971) (language in secured sales agreement that buyer must "at all times keep the goods fully insured" held not to be sufficient to apprise the buyer that risk of loss had passed on goods the buyer had not yet received); Lynch Imports, Ltd. v. Frey, 200 Ill. App. 3d 781, 558 N.E.2d 484, 13 UCC Rep. Serv. 2d 750 (1990) (rider in parties' contract that buyers would obtain insurance held not conclusive on its face to pass risk of loss to buyers).

[70]   UCC § 2A–219(1).

[71]   *See* § 1.05[B] *supra.*

[72]   UCC § 2A–103, Comment (g).

[B]   When Risk Passes

If the risk of loss is to pass to the lessee in a particular lease agreement, the time at which the risk passes must be ascertained. This timing issue is not relevant to most bipartite lease transactions because the risk of loss remains on the lessor. If the parties expressly agree that the risk will be borne by the lessee, the timing issue is left open if their agreement does not also indicate when the risk is incurred by the lessee. Similarly, timing issues can arise when Article 2A shifts the risk of loss to the finance lessee under a finance lease.

Article 2A therefore provides rules that apply if "risk of loss is to pass to the lessee and the time of passage is not stated."[73] These rules are patterned on the Article 2 statutory analogue.[74] Thus, a distinction is drawn between cases in which a party defaults and those in which neither party defaults. These Article 2A provisions apply, however, only to cases in which the parties have agreed to transfer the risk of loss to the lessee and to finance leases, and then only if the time for making the transfer is not included in the parties' agreement.

[1]   In the Absence of Default [2A–219(2)]

The first rules that determine when risk of loss passes in the absence of breach apply to cases in which the lessor is required or authorized to ship the goods by carrier.[75] They duplicate precisely the comparable Article 2 rules.[76] Thus, in a shipment contract the risk of loss passes to the lessee when the goods are duly delivered to the carrier, whereas in a destination contract the risk of loss does not pass until the goods are duly tendered to enable the lessee to take delivery.[77]

Article 2A does not incorporate several of the Article 2 provisions that are needed to amplify these delivery concepts in order for the risk-of-loss provisions to work. It does not include the sections on F.O.B. provisions,[78] manner of tender of delivery,[79] or shipment by a carrier.[80] These provisions simply do not play a sufficient role in the leasing context to justify their inclusion in Article 2A, even in the context of risk allocation. Lease agreements commonly include express terms that determine the risk of loss, which narrows considerably the role of the Code's rules on shipment and destination contracts. The typical practice in finance leases in which the goods will be shipped directly by the

---

[73] UCC § 2A–219(2).

[74] *See* UCC §§ 2–509, 2–510.

[75] UCC § 2A–219(2)(a).

[76] UCC § 2–509(1)(a). *See* § 6.02[B] *supra*.

[77] For an explanation of shipment and destination contracts, *see* § 6.02[A] *supra*.

[78] UCC § 2–319.

[79] UCC § 2–503.

[80] UCC § 2–504.

supplier to the finance lessee is particularly relevant. The finance lease agreement generally requires the finance lessee to certify in writing that the goods have been received in good condition.

The additional Code provisions that are needed to apply the Article 2A rules on determining when risk passes in a lease where the goods are shipped by carrier and the parties have not agreed on when the risk passes still probably do not need to be included in Article 2A in order to be available. The meaning of the F.O.B. provisions was established through business usage prior to their inclusion in Article 2. Custom or usage thus can provide consistent meanings for these terms. In the relatively few cases in which a court will be required to determine whether a tender of delivery has occurred under an Article 2A transaction, it can easily apply the Article 2 provisions by analogy. The omission of these provisions from Article 2A does not support any inference that the drafters thereby intended to abrogate those provisions for lease transactions.

The second rule on when risk of loss passes to the lessee in the absence of a default applies when the goods are held by a bailee and are to be delivered without being moved. It provides that "the risk of loss passes to the lessee on acknowledgment by the bailee of the lessee's right to possession of the goods."[81] This rule also mirrors a provision of Article 2.[82] The other two options in this context that are included in Article 2—dealing with the issuance of negotiable and nonnegotiable documents by the bailee—were omitted from Article 2A as they are not relevant to lease transactions.[83]

The final rule is the residual provision, and it is likewise comparable to the Article 2 provision.[84] Thus, when the lessor is a merchant, the risk of loss passes to the lessee upon his or her receipt of the goods.[85] In the case of a finance lease, the same rule applies when the supplier is a merchant. Receipt of goods means "taking physical possession of them."[86] When the lessor is not a merchant, risk of loss passes to the lessee on tender of delivery.

[2]   In the Event of Default [2A–220]

Article 2A follows the Article 2 format of stating additional rules on risk-of-loss allocation that apply when either party is in default.[87] Precisely the same Article 2 rules are incorporated. Thus the rules are based on the lessee's right

---

81 UCC § 2A–219(2)(b).
82 UCC § 2–509(2)(b). *See* § 6.02[C] *supra.*
83 UCC § 2A–219, Comment.
84 UCC § 2A–219(2)(c). *See* UCC § 2–509(3) and § 6.02[D] *supra.*
85 UCC § 2A–219(2)(c).
86 UCC § 2–103(1)(c). This section is cross-referenced by UCC § 2A–103(3).
87 UCC § 2A–220. *See* UCC § 2–510.

to reject, proper revocation by the lessee, and default by the lessee.[88] Again, these rules apply only when the risk of loss is to pass to the lessee and the time for its passage is not stated by the parties.

The rules stated in Article 2A do require some care in their application to finance leases. The Comments caution that the reallocation rule based on revocation does not "allow the lessee under a finance lease to treat the risk of loss as having remained with the supplier from the beginning."[89] A lessee can use the revocation provision only upon making an effective revocation of acceptance, and Article 2A strictly limits that right with respect to a finance lessee. For the most part, the obligations undertaken by a finance lessee become irrevocable upon acceptance of the goods.[90] Any attempt to revoke in this context would not be rightful and thus would not invoke a risk reallocation.

---

[88] *See* § 6.03 *supra*.
[89] UCC § 2A–220, Comment.
[90] UCC § 2A–407(1). *See* § 7.05[G] *supra*.

CHAPTER

7

Performance and Breach

§ 7.01 OBLIGATIONS OF THE PARTIES [2–301]

Article 2 states the general obligations of sellers and buyers as follows: "The obligation of the seller is to transfer and deliver and that of the buyer is to accept and pay in accordance with the contract."[1] The applicable methods of tender of delivery by a seller are explained in Chapter 4.[2] Because a sale "consists in the passing of title from the seller to the buyer for a price,"[3] the seller must also transfer title in the goods to the buyer. Although most of the provisions of Article 2 apply without regard to the nexus of title to the goods at any particular moment,[4] the essence of a sale is ultimately tied to a transfer of title. The requirement for the seller to transfer and deliver in accordance with the contract means that execution of the seller's obligations must comply with the terms of the contract and with applicable Code provisions.

The buyer's obligations must similarly be read within the context of other sections of Article 2. The next section of this chapter addresses the responses available to a buyer following tender of delivery by the seller. If the tender conforms to the contract, the buyer is obligated to accept it. This concept and the consequences that follow its occurrence are explained, as well as the options

---

[1] UCC § 2–301.
[2] *See* § 4.05[B][1]–[3] *supra*.
[3] UCC § 2–106(1).
[4] UCC § 2–401.

available when tender is nonconforming. The time, place, and method of payment are governed by contract terms, or in their absence, by the gap-filler provisions on payment that were covered in Chapter 4.[5]

Part A: Buyer Responses to Tender of Delivery

§ 7.02   OVERVIEW

Once a seller tenders delivery of goods, a buyer has a choice.[6] Following a reasonable opportunity to inspect the goods, the buyer can either accept the goods or reject them. If the goods conform to the contract, the duty is to accept them. A rejection under these circumstances constitutes breach by the buyer, but it also precludes an acceptance by essentially returning the goods to the seller. Alternatively, if the goods are nonconforming, the buyer has the right to reject them. The buyer may nevertheless accept the nonconforming goods and rely upon breach of warranty damages for a remedy. So the buyer has the choice to accept or to reject. Furthermore, a buyer who accepts may also have a limited right to revoke the acceptance. Like a rejection, revocation precludes acceptance and throws the goods back onto the seller.

Acceptance, rejection, and revocation are thus three inconsistent buyer responses to a seller's tender.[7] Acceptance is the pivotal concept. It constitutes a basic contract obligation of the buyer. It is also relevant to a determination of both rejection and revocation. Rejection is pre-acceptance behavior by the buyer, meaning that it must occur before acceptance. Revocation is post-acceptance behavior. It undoes the legal effectiveness of the buyer's previous acceptance. Because of its pivotal role, the concept of acceptance is discussed first.

§ 7.03   ACCEPTANCE

[A]   Methods of Acceptance [2–606; 2A–515]

A buyer accepts tendered goods whenever any of the events listed in section 2–606 occur. This section provides:

Acceptance of goods occurs when the buyer

---

5   *See* § 4.05[B][4], [5] *supra.*
6   The same choice and concepts apply to a lessee upon tender by the lessor.
7   One commentator has dubbed these concepts the UCC's TARR Baby. *See* Whaley, *Tender, Acceptance, Rejection and Revocation—The UCC's TARR Baby,* 24 Drake L. Rev. 52 (1974).

(a) after a reasonable opportunity to inspect the goods signifies to the seller that the goods are conforming or that he will take or retain them in spite of their non-conformity; or

(b) fails to make an effective rejection (subsection (1) of Section 2–602), but such acceptance does not occur until the buyer has had a reasonable opportunity to inspect them; or

(c) does any act inconsistent with the seller's ownership; but if such act is wrongful as against the seller it is an acceptance only if ratified by him.[8]

[1]   Statement

The first of these methods of acceptance generally involves a statement by the buyer to the seller. For example, after examining the goods, the buyer might indicate to the seller that the goods conform to the contract.[9] Alternatively, the buyer might describe a discovered flaw in the goods but nevertheless state an intention to take them anyway.[10] The positive manifestation of the intention to take the goods, whether a defect has been discovered or not, is the basis for this method of acceptance.

The stated intention alone is not sufficient, however, because it operates as an acceptance only after the buyer has had a reasonable opportunity to inspect the goods. The parties can specifically agree to the buyer's inspection rights;[11] otherwise inspection is at a reasonable time and place, and in a reasonable manner.[12] The inspection right is important because it gives the buyer an opportunity to determine whether the seller has tendered in accordance with the

---

8   UCC § 2–606(1).

9   In re L&M Fabricators, 114 B.R. 100 (Bankr. W.D. Pa. 1990) (message to seller noting that 2,214 delivered steel U-bolts were ready for heat treating).

10   International Commodities Export Corp. v. North Pacific Lumber Co., 764 F. Supp. 608, 15 UCC Rep. Serv. 2d 825 (D. Or. 1991) (buyer aware that beans would not meet import standards); Plateq Corp. v. Machlett Laboratories, 189 Conn. 433, 456 A.2d 786, 35 UCC Rep. Serv. 1162 (1983) (on being assured that some remaining minor deficiencies would be corrected, buyer indicated it would send its truck to pick up custom-made steel tanks).

11   The agreement of the parties in *Bevel-Fold, Inc. v. Bose Corp.*, 9 Mass. App. 576, 402 N.E.2d 1104, 28 UCC Rep. Serv. 1333 (1980), allowed the buyer of stereo cabinets to make a final quality inspection of the goods during its own production process. *See* UCC § 2–513(4) (place or method of inspection fixed by the parties presumed to be exclusive). The parties also can agree that the buyer does not have a right to inspect prior to payment or to acceptance. *See* UCC § 2–513(3).

12   Unless otherwise agreed and subject to subsection (3), where goods are tendered or delivered or identified to the contract for sale, the buyer has a right before payment or acceptance to inspect them at any reasonable place and time and in any reasonable manner. When the seller is required or authorized to send the goods to the buyer, the inspection may be after their arrival.

terms of the contract. The buyer, however, need not actually inspect the goods before acceptance can occur. The buyer must be afforded a reasonable opportunity to inspect, but if that opportunity is not exercised, the inspection right is waived.[13]

Before allowing the buyer to take possession of the goods, the seller may require the buyer to sign a form indicating that the buyer has inspected the goods and found them to be conforming. The effectiveness of the purported acceptance will depend on the nature of the goods and the inspection opportunity actually afforded the buyer. The proverbial inspection of kicking the tires of a new car and taking it for a spin around the block is unlikely to convince most courts that the buyer had a reasonable opportunity to inspect with respect to mechanical difficulties that were not readily apparent.[14]

[2]   Silence

Many acceptances by buyers result from their inactivity and silence. Under the second method of acceptance, a buyer who does not make an effective rejection is held to have accepted, again subject to a reasonable opportunity to inspect the goods.[15] The buyer must initiate affirmative action in order to reject tendered goods.[16] Failure to do so results in an automatic acceptance.[17]

UCC § 2–513(1). HCI Chemicals (USA), Inc. v. Henkel KGaA, 966 F.2d 1018, 18 UCC Rep. Serv. 2d 436 (5th Cir. 1992) (provision in contract giving buyer right to inspect at place of delivery to carrier did not supplant UCC § 2–513(1)).

[13] G & H Land & Cattle Co. v. Heitzman & Nelson, Inc., 102 Idaho 204, 628 P.2d 1038, 31 UCC Rep. Serv. 541 (1981).

[14] Zabriskie Chevrolet, Inc. v. Smith, 99 N.J. Super. 441, 240 A.2d 195, 5 UCC Rep. Serv. 30 (1968) (held buyer had not completed inspection of a new car when a latent defect in the transmission made the car inoperable a short distance from the dealer's place of business). *See also* Moses v. Newman, 658 S.W.2d 119, 37 UCC Rep. Serv. 461 (Tenn. Ct. App. 1983) (access to mobile home on seller's sales lot and during installation on his own lot held not sufficient as reasonable opportunity to inspect); Shelton v. Farkas, 30 Wash. App. 549, 635 P.2d 1109, 32 UCC Rep. Serv. 1421 (1981) (inspection by music teacher revealed crack in violin purchased two days earlier). *But see* Rozmus v. Thompson's Lincoln-Mercury Co., 209 Pa. Super. 120, 224 A.2d 782, 3 UCC Rep. Serv. 1025 (1966) (buyer signed acceptance form for new car).

[15] DiDomenico Packaging Corp. v. Nails Again, Inc., 139 Misc. 2d 525, 527 N.Y.S.2d 676, 6 UCC Rep. Serv. 2d 119 (Civ. Ct. 1988) (acceptance resulted when buyer held shipment of paper cartons for several months without making a simple inspection that would have shown they were nonconforming because they did not include a printed customer guarantee).

[16] UCC § 2–602(1). *See* § 7.04[B] *infra*.

[17] EPN-Delaval, S.A. v. Inter-Equip, Inc., 542 F. Supp. 238, 34 UCC Rep. Serv. 130 (S.D. Tex. 1982) (failure for 65 days to inspect and reject goods with defects that would be obvious to the buyer's quality control staff resulted in acceptance); Fablok Mills, Inc. v. Cocker Machine & Foundry Co., 125 N.J. Super. 251, 310 A.2d 491, 13 UCC Rep. Serv. 449 (1973)

[3]   Conduct

The final method of acceptance is based on the buyer's conduct with respect to the goods. A buyer is held to an acceptance by doing an act that is inconsistent with the seller's ownership. Thus, a buyer who has actually rejected tendered goods can be held nevertheless to accept them if the buyer's actions are inconsistent with rejection.

This last method of acceptance has proven particularly difficult to construe. The language chosen by the drafters has contributed to this problem. Technically, any use of the goods would be inconsistent with the seller's ownership. Yet certainly not all use by the buyer should be sufficient to indicate an acceptance by the buyer. Some use, for example, can be necessary for the buyer to inspect the goods effectively. The problem is furthered by the provision in section 2–602 that "after rejection any exercise of ownership by the buyer with respect to any commercial unit is wrongful as against the seller."[18] This provision suggests that use of the goods after rejection results in a subsequent acceptance of the goods. This perspective contributed to pre-Code cases that held that any use of goods precluded rescission as inconsistent with the revesting of title in the seller.[19]

The problems in construing this method of acceptance are demonstrated by the cases in which a buyer continues to use the goods following rejection or revocation of acceptance.[20] One line of cases has evolved that preserves the effectiveness of the rejection or revocation so long as subsequent use of the goods is "reasonable" and the seller is compensated for the value of the continued use.[21] This approach recognizes the difficulties associated with a buyer whose financing is committed to the delivered product[22] or who cannot promptly cover in the marketplace.[23] The opposing line of cases reflects pre-Code law by

---

(purchaser notified seller of problems with knitting machines, but having not rejected was held to an acceptance); Hudspeth Motors, Inc. v. Wilkinson, 238 Ark. 410, 382 S.W.2d 191, 2 UCC Rep. Serv. 273 (1964) (buyer held truck with defects for five months without any attempt to reject).

[18] UCC § 2–602(2)(a).

[19] *See* Comer v. Franklin, 53 So. 797, 799 (Ala. 1910).

[20] *See generally* R. J. Robertson, Jr., *Rights and Obligations of Buyers with Respect to Goods in Their Possession After Rightful Rejection or Justifiable Revocation of Acceptance*, 60 Ind. L.J. 663 (1985).

[21] On awarding of compensation for post-revocation use, *see* Erling v. Homera, Inc., 298 N.W.2d 478, 30 UCC Rep. Serv. 181 (N.D. 1980); *see also* § 7.05[F] *infra*.

[22] McCullough v. Bill Swad Chrysler-Plymouth, Inc., 449 N.E.2d 1289, 36 UCC Rep. Serv. 513 (Ohio 1983) (buyer's financial position was limited); Mobile Homes Sales Management, Inc. v. Brown, 562 P.2d 1378, 21 UCC Rep. Serv. 1040 (Ariz. Ct. App. 1977) (most of the buyers' savings were tied up in the mobile home purchase).

[23] Computerized Radiological Servs. v. Syntex Corp., 595 F. Supp. 1495, 40 UCC Rep. Serv. 49 (E.D.N.Y. 1984) (one year required to obtain another X-ray scanner); Minsel v. El

providing that any substantial use of goods following their rejection or revocation of acceptance is wrongful against the seller and precludes the buyer from effectively claiming the rejection or revocation.[24]

This third method of acceptance was deleted from the Article 2A designations of acceptance. The Comments to Article 2A state that the provision was omitted "as irrelevant given the lessee's possession and use of the leased goods."[25] This reasoning is certainly dubious in the context of a purported rejection or revocation. Although a lease gives a lessee possession and use of the leased goods for the duration of the lease term, rejection or revocation by the lessee ends these interests of the lessee and the residuary interest of the lessor predominates, just as rejection or revocation by a buyer ends the buyer's interest in the goods purchased.

The drafters of Article 2A also changed the first method of acceptance. In addition to signifying an intent to the lessor that the goods are conforming or that the lessee will take or retain them in spite of their nonconformity, an acceptance results when the lessee "acts with respect to the goods in a manner that signifies" a comparable intent.[26] This provision is sufficient to deal with cases in which the lessee claims to have rejected or revoked but subsequently acts inconsistently with respect to the goods. On the other hand, it is balanced enough to allow appropriate cases to be distinguished. For example, a lessee who rejects or revokes acceptance, but continues to use the goods in order to mitigate damages[27] or permit cure,[28] or because cover is not immediately

---

Rancho Mobile Home Ctr., Inc., 188 N.W.2d 9, 9 UCC Rep. Serv. 448 (Mich. Ct. App. 1971) (buyers continued to occupy mobile home for six weeks following revocation because of their inability to find alternative housing). *But see* Computerized Radiological Services v. Syntex Corp., 786 F.2d 72, 42 UCC Rep. Serv. 1656 (2d Cir. 1986) (use of CAT scanner for 22 months following a letter of revocation held to constitute a reacceptance, as use continued longer than reasonably necessary to acquire another scanner).

[24] George v. Fannin, 588 N.E.2d 195, 17 UCC Rep. Serv. 113 (Ohio Ct. App. 1990); Waltz v. Chevrolet Motor Div., 307 A.2d 815, 12 UCC Rep. Serv. 874 (Del. Super. Ct. 1973); F. W. Lang Co. v. Fleet, 165 A.2d 258, 1 UCC Rep. Serv. 177 (Pa. Super. Ct. 1960).

[25] UCC § 2A–515, Comment.

[26] UCC § 2A–515(1)(a).

[27] Romy v. Picker Internat'l, Inc., 18 UCC Rep. Serv. 2d 771 (E.D. Pa. 1992) (unpublished) (doctor's continued use of MRI system necessary to continue in business); Johannsen v. Minnesota Valley Ford Tractor Co., 304 N.W.2d 654, 31 UCC Rep. Serv. 558 (Minn. 1981) (continued use of tractor to complete farming operation mitigated damages).

[28] CPC Internat'l, Inc. v. Techni-Chem, Inc., 660 F. Supp. 1509, 4 UCC Rep. Serv. 2d 485 (N.D. Ill. 1987) (10 months of effort by seller to remedy plus a list of suggestions for further remedial efforts); The Software House, Inc., 32 Ohio App. 3d 61, 513 N.E.2d 1372, 4 UCC Rep. Serv. 2d 1400 (1986) (six months of futile efforts by seller to correct defects in computer software).

available,[29] has not acted with respect to the goods in a manner that signifies a willingness to retain them.

The approach in Article 2A provides insight into the appropriate construction of the third method of acceptance in Article 2. The Comments indicate that under this method, "any action taken by the buyer, which is inconsistent with his claim that he has rejected the goods, constitutes an acceptance."[30] Not all use of goods following a rejection is inconsistent with the claim of rejection. In essence, the third method of acceptance is directed toward buyer conduct that is sufficient to indicate the buyer's intention to retain the goods.

The variety of fact patterns makes generalizations in this area particularly inappropriate. Consider actions taken by the buyer with respect to the goods that cannot be reversed. In *La Villa Fair v. Lewis Carpet Mills, Inc.*,[31] the court recognized that the buyer had to cut into three or four rolls of carpet in order to determine deficiencies. Cutting some of the carpet was necessary to exercise the buyer's inspection rights. Compare *Intervale Steel Corp. v. Borg & Beck Division of Borg-Warner Corp.*,[32] in which the buyer promptly made "blanks" from all of the steel delivered by the buyer and did not discover the defect until later when it tried to work the blanks in filling an order for a finished product. The court held that the third method of acceptance was inapplicable, based on an argument advanced by two commentators that the section should not apply when the buyer is ignorant of the defect.[33] Although this proposition can be helpful, it should not be considered inviolate. The buyer in *Intervale Steel* irrevocably altered the form of the tendered goods. The court found acceptance under section 2–606(1)(b), positing that the three-month delay was too long for rejection. The primary basis for its holding, however, was that the buyer had finished its inspection of the goods and manufactured them into parts. That basis for the holding, which seems correct, is better based on the buyer's conduct signifying an acceptance than on the buyer's failure to reject.

A sampling of cases demonstrates several circumstances in which courts have determined that a buyer has accepted by acting inconsistently with the ownership rights of the seller. Buyers thus have accepted by commingling 10

---

[29] Hospital Computer Systems, Inc. v. Staten Island Hospital, 788 F. Supp. 1351, 18 UCC Rep. Serv. 2d 140 (D. N.J. 1992) (continued use of customized computer billing and accounting system for 18 months while replacement system was developed).

[30] UCC § 2–606(1)(c).

[31] 219 Kan. 395, 548 P.2d 825, 19 UCC Rep. Serv. 120 (1976).

[32] 578 F. Supp. 1081, 38 UCC Rep. Serv. 805 (E.D. Mich. 1984).

[33] J. White & R. Summers, *Handbook of the Law Under the Uniform Commercial Code* 351–53 (student 3d ed. 1988).

loads of grain with other grain,[34] destroying defective grass-catcher bags,[35] authorizing repairs to a boat,[36] adding shoes to inventory and selling nearly half of them,[37] denying seller's request to return the goods after a purported rejection,[38] installing kitchen units with readily apparent defects,[39] installing a hoist and dump bed on a truck,[40] processing potatoes into flakes and selling them,[41] removing plants from their containers and planting them in a landscaping contract,[42] and driving, repairing, painting, and attempting to sell an automobile.[43] Circumstances that have been held insufficient to constitute an acceptance include using a machine with the objective of making it work rather than in production,[44] blanching peanuts in a process that did not substantially change them,[45] transshipping uninspected goods in their original, unopened packaging to another location,[46] and continuing to use carpet that had been affixed to the floor.[47]

[B]   Consequences of Acceptance [2–607; 2A–516]

Several consequences are tied to an acceptance. A buyer who accepts will still have remedies for any nonconformities in the seller's tender, but, as is

---

34 Veath v. Specialty Grains, Inc., 190 Ill. App. 3d 787, 546 N.E.2d 1005, 10 UCC Rep. Serv. 2d 771 (1989).

35 C. R. Daniels, Inc. v. Yazoo Mfg. Co., Inc., 641 F. Supp. 205, 2 UCC Rep. Serv. 2d 481 (S.D. Miss. 1986).

36 Tonka Tours, Inc. v. Chadima, 354 N.W.2d 519, 39 UCC Rep. Serv. 122 (Minn. Ct. App. 1984).

37 Lorenzo Banfi di Banfi Renzo & Co. v. Davis Congress Shops, Inc., 568 F. Supp. 432, 36 UCC Rep. Serv. 1183 (N.D. Ill. 1983).

38 JL Clark Mfg. Co. v. Gold Bond Pharmaceutical Corp., 669 F. Supp. 40, 5 UCC Rep. Serv. 2d 93 (D. R.I. 1987).

39 Cervitor Kitchens, Inc. v. Chapman, 82 Wash.2d 694, 513 P.2d 25, 13 UCC Rep. Serv. 458 (1973).

40 Park Co. Implement Co. v. Craig, 397 P.2d 800, 2 UCC Rep. Serv. 379 (Wyo. 1964).

41 Borges v. Magic Valley Foods, Inc., 102 Idaho 204, 616 P.2d 273, 29 UCC Rep. Serv. 1282 (1980).

42 Oda Nursery, Inc. v. Garcia Tree & Lawn, Inc., 708 P.2d 1039, 42 UCC Rep. Serv. 164 (N.M. 1985).

43 Fiat Auto U.S.A., Inc. v. Hollums, 185 Ga. App. 113, 363 S.E.2d 312, 5 UCC Rep. Serv. 2d 969 (1987).

44 Distco Laminating, Inc. v. Union Tool Corp., 81 Mich. App. 612, 265 N.W.2d 768, 24 UCC Rep. Serv. 129 (1978).

45 Stratton Industries, Inc. v. Northwest Georgia Bank, 191 Ga. 683, 382 S.E.2d 721, 10 UCC Rep. Serv. 2d 387 (1989).

46 Columbia Can Co. of J.J., Inc. v. Africa-Middle East Marketing, Inc., 188 N.J. Super. 45, 455 A.2d 1143, 36 UCC Rep. Serv. 137 (1983).

47 Garfinkel v. Lehman Floor Covering Co., 60 Misc. 2d 72, 302 N.Y.S.2d 167, 6 UCC Rep. Serv. 915 (Dt. Ct. 1969).

explained below, the buyer's options will be more severely limited. With one exception discussed elsewhere with respect to finance leases,[48] the same consequences apply to acceptance in both sale and lease contexts.

[1]   Rejection and Revocation

Acceptance precludes rejection of accepted goods.[49] Even if the buyer had the right to reject nonconforming goods, the failure to make an effective rejection automatically results in acceptance and terminates any further right to reject.[50] Consequently the buyer is left with goods that it could quite easily have thrown back onto the seller by implementing a rejection.

The only further opportunity to return the goods to the seller is through revocation—a right considerably more restricted than rejection[51]—and it too may be affected by acceptance. If the goods were accepted by a buyer who knew they were nonconforming, the buyer cannot revoke unless the acceptance was based on a reasonable assumption that the nonconformity would be reasonably cured.[52] A buyer who accepts goods without any reasonable expectation that discovered nonconformities will be cured lacks an equitable basis for returning the goods to the lessor, and is therefore denied a right of revocation.

[2]   Obligation to Pay

A buyer who accepts goods must pay for them at the contract rate.[53] This requirement, operating together with the provisions that preclude rejection and revocation, effectively binds the buyer to complete its contract obligations following an acceptance. Acceptance of the goods thus often means that an aggrieved buyer cannot cancel the contract.

In a falling market, the buyer is particularly well-advised to reject goods that do not conform to the contract. By accepting the goods, the buyer must pay the full contract price. The buyer can recover damages, but they are measured only by the difference in value of the goods as warranted and as delivered.[54]

---

[48] UCC § 2A–516(2). *See* § 7.05[G] *infra*.

[49] UCC § 2–607(2).

[50] UCC §§ 2–606(1)(b); 2–607(2).

[51] *See* § 7.05[A][1] *infra*.

[52] UCC § 2–607(2).

[53] UCC § 2–607(1). Articles 2 and 2A differ to the extent that a seller and a lessor can enforce this obligation. *See* §§ 9.04[A][1], 9.04[B] *supra*.

[54] UCC § 2–714(2). Upon notifying the seller, the buyer can set off damages resulting from the seller's breach of contract. UCC § 2–717. Adam Metal Supply Inc. v. Electrodex, Inc., 386 So. 2d 1316, 30 UCC Rep. Serv. 178 (Fla. Ct. App. 1980).

This difference might be measured, for example, by the cost of replacing a defective component part in the goods.[55] By rejecting the goods, the buyer avoids paying the purchase price and can recover any of the price already paid.[56] The buyer can then purchase comparable goods on the open market at a lower price than the contract required. The seller's breach would be fortuitous for the buyer, but only if the buyer effectively rejects the tendered goods.

[3] Notification

Another consequence of acceptance concerns notification requirements. The most significant requirement is to notify the seller within a reasonable time after the buyer discovers or should have discovered any breach. Failure to comply is severe—the buyer is barred from any remedy.[57] The nature of the notice, however, need not be elaborate: "The content of the notification need merely be sufficient to let the seller know that the transaction is still troublesome and must be watched."[58] Notification is required to protect the interests of the seller. Notice may enable the seller to correct defects, prepare for negotiations and litigation, and guard against stale claims that it cannot investigate.[59]

The dire consequences of failing to provide the requisite notice suggest that careful attention should be given to providing the notice as promptly as possible. Commercial standards apply to determine a reasonable time for notification by a buyer who qualifies as a merchant.[60] The notice should also be complete, as illustrated in *Industrial Fiberglass v. Jandt*.[61] The buyer in that case purchased portable fiberglass tanks to lease to its customers. Although the seller/manufacturer corrected several problems that had been discovered with

---

[55] *See* § 8.05[B][1] *infra*.

[56] UCC § 2–711(1).

[57] UCC 2–607(3)(a). Massey v. Thomaston Ford Mercury, 196 Ga. App. 278, 395 S.E.2d 663, 14 UCC Rep. Serv. 2d 129 (1990) (waiting one year before notifying seller that truck did not have a radio, air conditioning, and power steering precluded breach of contract claim); Fleet Maintenance, Inc. v. Burke Energy Midwest Corp., 11 Kan. App.2d 523, 728 P.2d 408, 2 UCC Rep. Serv. 2d 904 (1986) (failure to notify seller of defective condition of engine barred buyer from any remedy, including revocation of acceptance and action for damages for breach of an implied warranty).

[58] UCC 2–607, Comment 4.

[59] Church of the Nativity of Our Lord v. WatPro, Inc., 474 N.W.2d 605, 15 UCC Rep. Serv. 2d 830 (Minn. Ct. App. 1991).

[60] Philip A. Feinberg, Inc. v. Bernstein & Sparber Corp., 8 UCC Rep. Serv. 190 (N.Y. Sup. Ct. 1970) (buyer's failure to inspect goods and find patently evident nonconformity within period fixed in the contract precluded remedies).

[61] 40 UCC Rep. Serv. 133 (N.D. 1985).

the tanks, the seller was never notified that the insides of the tanks were bub-
bling and cracking. The buyer's failure to give this notification prevented the
buyer from recovery for breach of warranty with respect to this problem.

The Code does not provide a special rule with respect to consumer transactions. A Comment, however, indicates that a more liberal standard is appropriate for consumer buyers: " 'A reasonable time' for notification from a retail
consumer is to be judged by different standards so that in his case it will be
extended, for the rule of requiring notification is designed to defeat commercial
bad faith, not to deprive a good-faith consumer of his remedy."[62] This Comment has influenced the courts in sales cases.[63]

[4]   Burden of Proof

Another effect of acceptance of goods is that the buyer bears the burden to
establish any breach with respect to the goods accepted.[64] The significance of
this allocation can be overstated. A buyer who rejects the goods and seeks
money damages will also bear the burden with respect to establishing breach
by the seller. If the buyer rejects and is content to simply cancel the contract,
the seller will have to establish breach by the buyer in order to prevail.

The burden of proof allocation was significant in *Miron v. Yonkers Raceway,
Inc.*[65] Because the buyer's claims of rejection and revocation were not successful, the buyer was held to an acceptance and relegated to an action for
breach of warranty. Money damages from such a claim would have protected
the buyer because the sale involved a racehorse that was discovered to have a
hairline fracture in a leg bone. The unfortunate buyer also lost on the warranty
claim, however, because he was unable to show that the defective condition
existed at the time of acceptance. The horse itself could have caused this injury,
particularly during transport or while located in unfamiliar new surroundings.
The expert witnesses differed in their interpretations of the time of injury based
on X-rays of the horse's leg. The buyer thus could not meet the burden of establishing a crucial element of its claim for warranty damages.

---

[62]   UCC § 2–607, Comment 4.
[63]   Riley v. Ken Wilson Ford, Inc., 109 N.C. App. 163, 426 S.E.2d 717, 20 UCC Rep. Serv. 2d
       74 (1993) (adequate notice from consumer from filing of complaint); Hansen v. FMC
       Corp., 32 UCC Rep. Serv. 828 (D. Kan. 1981) (injured employee of buyer not required to
       give notice). *But see* Allen v. G. D. Searle & Co., 708 F. Supp. 1142, 8 UCC Rep. Serv. 2d
       983 (D. Or. 1989) (consumer's failure to notify manufacturer of IUD of personal damages
       suffered in breach of warranty barred the claim).
[64]   UCC 2–607(4).
[65]   400 F.2d 112, 5 UCC Rep. Serv. 673 (2d Cir. 1968). *See also* Alliance Wall Corp. v. Ampat
       Midwest Corp., 17 Ohio App. 3d 59, 477 N.E.2d 1206, 41 UCC Rep. Serv. 377 (1984) (buyer
       unable to establish whether damage to aluminum panels occurred in manufacturing pro-
       cess or in transit).

§ 7.04   REJECTION

[A]   Perfect Tender Rule [2–601; 2A–509(1)]

A buyer of goods is entitled to reject the seller's performance "if the goods or the tender of delivery fail in any respect to conform to the contract."[66] With a rightful rejection, the buyer can cancel the contract, recover any of the purchase price paid, and receive damages for total breach.[67] This standard is clearly distinguishable from the general contract-law requirement of a material breach before the aggrieved party is entitled to cancel and recover total damages.[68] With a tender of anything less than exact performance by the seller, the buyer is entitled to reject.[69] The standard of exact compliance with the seller's contract obligations is commonly referred to as the perfect tender rule.

The buyer has three options upon a seller's nonconforming tender. The buyer can reject all of the goods or accept them all. Alternatively, the buyer can accept any commercial units and reject the rest.[70] A commercial unit is defined as "such a unit of goods as by commercial usage is a single whole for purposes of sale and division of which materially impairs its character or value on the market or in use."[71]

The reasoning that supports limiting an aggrieved party's right to cancel the contract does not justify applying the material breach doctrine to a buyer's right to reject.[72] Common-law implementation of the concept of constructive

---

[66] UCC § 2–601. A lessee's right to reject is patterned precisely on this provision. UCC § 2A–509(1).

[67] UCC § 2–711(1).

[68] E. A. Farnsworth, *Contracts* § 8.15 (2d ed. 1990). Printing Center of Texas, Inc. v. Supermind Pub. Co., Inc., 669 S.W.2d 779, 39 UCC Rep. Serv. 127 (Tex. Ct. App. 1984) (complete performance rather than substantial performance required).

[69] Ramirez v. Autosport, 88 N.J. 277, 440 A.2d 1345, 33 UCC Rep. Serv. 134 (1982); Moulton Cavity & Mold, Inc. v. Lyn-Flex Indus., Inc., 396 A.2d 1024, 25 UCC Rep. Serv. 1026 (Me. 1979). Some courts have ignored the Article 2 perfect tender rule in favor of a substantial nonconformity test. D. P. Technology Corp. v. Sherwood Tool, Inc., 751 F. Supp. 1038, 13 UCC Rep. Serv. 2d 686 (D. Conn. 1990) (holding that the Connecticut Supreme Court would require that a delay in delivery of specially manufactured goods must be substantial in order for the buyer to reject under § 2–601, and remanding for determination of whether 16-day delay was substantial); Clark v. Zaid, Inc., 282 A.2d 483, 9 UCC Rep. Serv. 1014 (Md. 1971) (holding that in determining the right of a buyer to reject furniture the court must consider factors such as the nature and extent of damage and whether it could be repaired).

[70] *But see* Salinas Lettuce Farmers Coop. v. Larry Ober Co., Inc., 28 UCC Rep. Serv. 684 (USDA 1980) (acceptance of part and rejection of part of a commercial unit is not an effective rejection and constitutes acceptance of the entire unit).

[71] UCC § 2–105(6).

[72] For more detailed elaboration on the rationales underlying the perfect tender rule *see*

conditions to order the performance of contract promises[73] created a harshness that had to be ameliorated. The creation of the implied-in-law condition greatly enhanced the risk of forfeiture because the party required to proceed could lose all rights on the contract by tendering anything less than complete performance. The forfeiture risk is particularly poignant in situations like construction contracts, in which labor and materials expended in a performance that falls short of complete performance cannot be returned to the contractor.[74]

This potentially harsh impact was mitigated by establishment of a less demanding standard for satisfying constructive conditions.[75] Substantial performance, rather than exact performance, is sufficient to satisfy the constructive condition; the less-than-perfect tender constitutes a nonmaterial breach but the constructive condition is satisfied, preventing cancellation of the contract by the aggrieved party.[76] The reasoning does not extend to contracts for the sale of goods, however, because the ability to return the goods to the breaching seller avoids most forfeiture in these cases. The rights of an aggrieved party are better protected under the perfect tender rule because the standard provides more certainty in its appropriate application than is possible under the material breach rule.[77]

[B] Procedural Aspects [2–602; 2A–509(2)]

Rejection never occurs automatically. In fact, it is acceptance that is automatic if the buyer does not act. The failure to reject after a reasonable opportunity to inspect the goods results in acceptance of the goods,[78] with the attendant consequence of terminating the right of rejection.[79] The right of rejection must be exercised to prevent its waiver.[80]

Lawrence, *Appropriate Standards for a Buyer's Refusal to Keep Goods Tendered by a Seller*, 35 William & Mary L. Rev. 1635 (1994); Lawrence, *The Prematurely Reported Demise of the Perfect Tender Rule*, 35 U. Kan. L. Rev. 557 (1987). For a different perspective *see* Sebert, *Rejection, Revocation, and Cure Under Article 2 of the Uniform Commercial Code: Some Modest Proposals*, 84 Nw. U. L. Rev. 375 (1990).

[73] *See* Jones v. Barkley, 99 Eng. Rep. 434, 437–38 (K.B. 1781) (paraphrasing the opinion of *Kingston v. Preston*). *See generally* Patterson, *Constructive Conditions in Contracts*, 42 Colum. L. Rev. 903 (1942).

[74] E. A. Farnsworth & W. Young, *Cases and Materials on Contracts* 695 (4th ed. 1988).

[75] Boone v. Eyre, 126 Eng. Rep. 160(a) (K.B. 1777).

[76] Jacob & Youngs, Inc. v. Kent, 129 N.E. 889 (N.Y. 1921).

[77] Multiple criteria must be considered in deciding whether a breach is material. Restatement (Second) of Contracts § 241 (1979). An aggrieved party who errs in balancing these criteria and proceeds to cancel the contract will thereby commit a material breach. Walker & Co. v. Harrison, 81 N.W.2d 352 (Mich. 1957).

[78] UCC § 2–606(1)(b). *See* § 7.03[A][2] *supra*.

[79] UCC § 2–607(2). *See* § 7.03[B][1] *supra*.

[80] Robinson v. Jonathan Logan Fin., 277 A.2d 115, 9 UCC Rep. Serv. 57 (D.C. Ct. App. 1971)

The basic procedural requirements for rejection include two elements: "Rejection of goods must be within a reasonable time after their delivery or tender" and "is ineffective unless the buyer seasonably notifies the seller."[81] The Code thus distinguishes between the right to reject and the effectiveness of rejection. The right to reject is waived if it is not effectively exercised by meeting these procedural requirements. Alternatively, exercising these procedures creates a rejection that is effective. In the absence of a right to reject, such action by the seller results in breach, but it nevertheless precludes acceptance.[82]

[1]   Timeliness

The rejection of goods must occur within a reasonable time of tender or delivery to be effective. The Code provides the broad guideline that "[w]hat is a reasonable time for taking any action depends on the nature, purpose and circumstances of such action."[83] The circumstances of a rejection are based on the facts presented in each case. The other two factors in the guideline—nature and purpose—are inherent in the policies that underlie a lessee's right to reject. Rejection throws the goods back onto the seller and precludes acceptance by the buyer. Its effectiveness is tied to timely assertion in order to create an incentive for vigilance and prompt action following tender by the seller. Prompt detection of deficient tender is generally desirable because the nature and extent of the problem can be investigated sooner, responsibility for the deficiency can be ascertained more readily, and the adverse consequences of a breach can be more easily minimized. Seasonable notification of rejection is needed to protect the seller's interests, as the seller must make a decision on how to respond.

The reasonable time during which to reject was very short in *Miron v. Yonkers Raceway, Inc.*[84] The buyer sought to reject a racehorse after discovering a fracture in one of its legs less than 24 hours after taking delivery. The rejection was not effective because more than a reasonable time had passed. The court noted that a spirited animal could have injured itself after delivery was taken by the buyer. In addition, the injury could have been easily ascertained in an inspection by a veterinarian, and such an inspection is customarily made prior to taking delivery of a racehorse.

(legal right to reject and intention to reject are irrelevant if buyer fails to comply with requirements for rejection).

[81]   UCC § 2–601. The Article 2A provision on leases is comparable. UCC § 2A–509(2).

[82]   Integrated Circuits Unlimited v. E. F. Johnson Co., 875 F.2d 1040, 8 UCC Rep. Serv. 2d 695 (2d Cir. 1989).

[83]   UCC 1–204(2).

[84]   400 F.2d 112, 5 UCC Rep. Serv. 112 (2d Cir. 1968).

Comparing cases provides a sense of how courts have resolved the time-liness issue. In *Hartz Seed Co. v. Colman*,[85] the court held that rejection of soy-beans after one month was timely because testing was required to discover the defect and the time for testing was reasonable. On the other hand, seven weeks to reject undersized steel was held unreasonable in *Michael M. Berlin & Co. v. T. Whiting Mfg., Inc.*[86] because of the ease with which the steel could have been measured. Notice of rejection within a month and a half was timely in *Badger Produce Co., Inc. v. Prelude Foods International, Inc.*[87] because the rejected frozen crabmeat was kept in cold storage and was only semiperishable. Rejection of pork roasts for excessive fat only three hours after inspection was untimely, however, in *Max Bauer Meat Packer, Inc. v. United States*[88] because placing the meat in a deep freeze during the delay froze it too much to permit reworking or reinspection. In *La Villa Fair v. Lewis Carpet Mills, Inc.*,[89] rejection of carpeting nine months after delivery was held to be reasonable because the seller knew the carpeting would be stored until needed for installation in an apartment con-struction project delayed by strike. Delay caused rejection to be untimely in *Wakeman Leather Co. v. Irvin B. Foster Sportswear Co., Inc.*[90] when rejection was made beyond the five days specified in the contract term and the 10 days rec-ognized through trade usage.

[2]   Notice Contents

The buyer's notice to the seller must be specific enough to indicate that the buyer is rejecting the goods. Several courts have invalidated purported rejec-tion notices because they merely advised the seller about a problem.[91] Such a brief notice is generally sufficient to preserve the buyer's breach of warranty claim,[92] but it is not enough to support a rejection. The seller is entitled to know that the buyer is not just dissatisfied with the transaction but rather is actually rejecting the goods. The seller can then determine an appropriate response to the buyer's position.

The specific reasons for rejecting have to be stated only in specified circum-stances. Section 2–605(1) provides as follows:

The buyer's failure to state in connection with rejection a particular

---

[85]   271 Ark. 756, 612 S.W.2d 91, 30 UCC Rep. Serv. 944 (1981).

[86]   5 UCC Rep. Serv. 357 (N.Y. Sup. Ct. 1968).

[87]   130 Wis. 2d 230, 387 N.W.2d 98, 1 UCC Rep. Serv. 2d 422 (Wis. Ct. App. 1986).

[88]   458 F.2d 88, 10 UCC Rep. Serv. 1056 (Ct. Cl. 1972).

[89]   219 Kan. 395, 548 P.2d 825, 19 UCC Rep. Serv. 120 (1976).

[90]   308 N.Y.S.2d 103, 7 UCC Rep. Serv. 710 (1970).

[91]   Integrated Circuits Unlimited, Inc. v. E. F. Johnson Co., 875 F.2d 1040, 8 UCC Rep. Serv. 2d 695 (2d Cir. 1989); CMI Corp. v. Leemar Steel Co., 733 F.2d 1410, 38 UCC Rep. Serv. 798 (10 Cir. 1984).

[92]   *See* UCC 2–607(3), Comment 4.

defect which is ascertainable by reasonable inspection precludes him from relying on the unstated defect to justify rejection or to establish breach

> (a) where the seller could have cured it if stated seasonally; or
> (b) between merchants when the seller has after rejection made a request in writing for a full and final written statement of all defects on which the buyer proposes to rely.[93]

A buyer's failure to state the grounds for objection could impair the seller's right to cure a nonconforming tender.[94] A formal demand for a specification of defects enables merchants in commercial transactions to rely on a final statement of objections by another merchant. In cases that fall beyond the scope of the two enumerated circumstances, however, the buyer is not bound solely by the content of the notice. The drafters chose a policy of "permitting the buyer to give a quick and informal notice of defects in a tender without penalizing him for omissions in his statement."[95]

[3]   Rights and Duties of Buyer

All buyers who effectively reject with respect to goods of which they have taken physical possession incur a basic responsibility. The buyer must "hold them with reasonable care at the seller's disposition for a time sufficient to permit the seller to remove them."[96]

If the seller does not provide instructions on disposition within a reasonable time following rejection, the buyer generally is entitled to "store the rejected goods for the seller's account or reship them to him or resell them for the seller's account."[97] The buyer generally has no further duties if the goods were rejected rightfully.[98]

Additional duties sometimes are imposed on buyers who are merchants. If the rejected goods are in the possession or control of the buyer, and if the seller has neither an agent nor a place of business in the market where the rejection occurs, the merchant buyer must follow any reasonable instructions from the

---

[93] The comparable provision for lease transactions is UCC § 2A–514(1).

[94] For discussion of the seller's right to cure following rejection, see § 7.04[C] infra.

[95] UCC § 2–605, Comment 1.

[96] UCC § 2–602(2)(b). Section 2A–512(1)(a) is comparable. Graybar Elec. Co. v. Shook, 17 N.C. App. 81, 193 S.E.2d 392, 11 UCC Rep. Serv. 1189 (1973).

[97] UCC § 2–604. Section 2A–512(1)(b) is comparable. Broglie v. Mackay-Smith, 26 UCC Rep. Serv. 87 (4th Cir. 1979) (buyer's sale of horse); Pacific Marine Schwabacher, Inc. v. Hydroswift Corp., 525 P.2d 615, 15 UCC Rep. Serv. 354 (Utah 1974).

[98] UCC § 2–603(2)(c). Section 2A–512(1)(c) is comparable.

seller regarding the goods.[99] Instructions from the seller are not reasonable if the seller does not provide indemnity for expenses after the buyer demands it. When the seller does not provide instructions under the circumstances described above, the merchant buyer must proceed unilaterally "to make reasonable efforts to sell them [the goods] for the seller's account if they are perishable or threaten to decline in value speedily."[100]

A buyer who complies with the Code obligations is entitled to reimbursement from the seller for reasonable expenses incurred in caring for the goods or in selling them, including a reasonable sales commission.[101] Reimbursement can come from the seller or can be taken directly out of sales proceeds.[102] A buyer who executes the imposed obligations in good faith is protected against any liability based on acceptance or conversion.[103]

Article 2A adds a provision that does not appear in the statutory analogue.[104] It protects the interest of a purchaser who purchases in good faith from a lessee who disposes of the goods following a rightful rejection. The purchaser "takes the goods free of any rights of the lessor and the supplier even though the lessee fails to comply" with some of the requirements of Article 2A.

[C]   The Cure Limitation [2–508; 2A–513]

One of the most significant limitations on a buyer's right to reject is the seller's right to cure.[105] Cure following rejection is not an absolute right, but when properly invoked by a qualifying seller, it suspends the effectiveness of the buyer's rejection. Cure rights thus afford the breaching seller a second opportunity to tender a conforming performance. Section 2–508 provides in its entirety as follows:

(1) Where any tender or delivery by the seller is rejected because nonconforming and the time for performance has not yet expired, the

---

[99] UCC § 2–603(1).

[100] UCC § 2–603(1). Traynor v. Walters, 342 F. Supp. 455, 10 UCC Rep. Serv. 965 (M.D. Pa. 1972) (Christmas trees).

[101] UCC §§ 2–603(2); 2–604. Askco Engineering Corp. v. Mobil Chemical Corp., 535 S.W.2d 893, 19 UCC Rep. Serv. 1119 (Tex. Ct. App. 1976) (buyer recovered for freight, warehousing, loading and unloading charges, and disposal charges for plastic that buyer unsuccessfully shipped back to seller, stored for one year, and ultimately buried).

[102] Eska Kleiderfabrik v. Peters Sportswear Co., Inc., 483 F. Supp. 1228, 29 UCC Rep. Serv. 534 (E.D. Pa. 1980) (buyer could retain payment for expenses incurred in handling, storage, and sale of rightfully rejected goods but was liable to the seller for the remainder).

[103] UCC §§ 2–603(3); 2–604.

[104] UCC § 2A–511(4).

[105] UCC § 2–508. Cure rights for a lessor are comparable. UCC § 2A–513.

seller may seasonally notify the buyer of his intention to cure and may then within the contract time make a conforming delivery.

(2) Where the buyer rejects a non-conforming tender which the seller had reasonable grounds to believe would be acceptable with or without money allowance the seller may if he seasonally notifies the buyer have a further reasonable time to substitute a conforming tender.

The elements necessary to qualify for cure are explained below.[106]

[1]   Time During Which to Cure

The application of the two subsections to section 2–508 differs depending on whether the contract time for the seller's performance has expired. The first subsection can apply only when the seller performs early so that additional time for performance remains.[107] For example, a seller may deliver a refrigerator on Wednesday under a contract that requires its delivery no later than Friday. If the buyer rejects the tender because the refrigerator is the wrong color, the seller can preserve a right to cure within the remaining contract time by promptly notifying the buyer of that intention. A subsequent conforming tender within the contract time for performance will still give the buyer the precise bargained-for performance.[108] Invocation of the cure right with time remaining for performance under the terms of the contract essentially precludes the buyer from treating the early defective tender as an anticipatory breach of contract.[109]

If the parties do not specify a time for the seller's performance, the gap-filler provision of section 2–309(1) must be used. This section provides that in

---

[106] Section 2–508 is not the only relevant source of cure rights in a contract for the sale of goods, although too many courts and commentators have tried to force most cure issues into the format of this section. Additional aspects of cure are found in § 2–607(2), § 2–612(2), the express terms of the sales contract, and separate consensual cure agreements. Each is discussed in the relevant sections of this text. More extensive analysis of cure under § 2–508 is provided in Lawrence, *Cure Under Article 2 of the Uniform Commercial Code: Practices and Prescriptions*, 21 UCC L.J. 138 (1988). Analysis of cure in additional contexts is provided in Lawrence, *Cure in Contracts for the Sale of Goods: Looking Beyond Section 2–508*, 21 UCC L.J. 333 (1989).

[107] Marlowe v. Argentine Naval Comm'n, 808 F.2d 120, 2 UCC Rep. Serv. 2d 1226 (D.C. Cir. 1986) (failure to cure within the remaining time for contract performance).

[108] Meads v. Davis, 22 N.C. App. 479, 206 S.E.2d 868, 15 UCC Rep. Serv. 40 (1974) (problem discovered during installation of carpet, but contract included installation).

[109] When a seller actually does make an anticipatory repudiation, on the other hand, § 2–508(1) does not give the seller an opportunity to cure. The section applies only after the buyer's rejection of the seller's tendered performance. *See* Neptune Research & Dev., Inc. v. Teknics Indus. Sys., Inc., 235 N.J. Super. 522, 563 A.2d 465, 10 UCC Rep. Serv. 2d 107 (1989).

the absence of agreement, the time for delivery is to be a reasonable time. The comments to the section indicate that when the time for delivery is reasonable, either party must notify the other party of an actual proposed performance date before being able to establish a breach based on delay.[110] In the absence of any prior notification of a proposed delivery date, the buyer cannot reject on the ground that more than a reasonable time for delivery has passed because the delivery date is construed as being too indefinite. Arguably, however, the term becomes fixed under these circumstances when a seller proposes the date through a tender of delivery. Under this interpretation, the seller could no longer qualify for cure under section 2–508(1) because the time for contract performance would expire with tender of delivery.

Even if the parties establish a fixed date for the seller's delivery, they may subsequently modify that date. The case of *Traynor v. Walters*[111] illustrates the effect of such a modification on the applicability of section 2–508(1). After setting a date in the contract for the delivery of Christmas trees, the parties modified the date. After a rightful rejection and the receipt of an intention to cure the nonconforming tender, the buyer waived the time set in the modification by agreeing to accept additional trees at a later date. Thus, the tender of delivery of the cure was held to be within the time for the seller's performance.

Section 2–508(2) will be of greater importance to most sellers. It allows a qualifying seller a further reasonable time beyond the contract period for performance to cure a nonconforming tender. Successful invocation of this cure right thus extends the time allowed for the breaching seller to tender a proper performance. The additional time is not indefinite, but rather only a "further reasonable time." Although the standard necessarily is worded broadly to apply to a myriad of potential fact patterns, the context for its application suggests that courts should consider time to be of the essence.

Allowing additional time for a seller to cure is based on balancing the interests of both parties to the contract. The seller, under the high standard imposed by the perfect tender rule, is protected against a forfeiture of contract rights by an extended opportunity to cure a nonconforming tender. The buyer's right to perfect tender suffers only marginal interference because an effective cure must conform to the contract in all respects except the time of the seller's performance.[112] A seller's additional time for cure should be viewed as granting the seller a second chance, while providing the aggrieved buyer with performance that is still at least close to perfect tender.

---

[110] UCC § 2–309, Comment 5.

[111] 342 F. Supp. 455, 10 UCC Rep. Serv. 455 (M.D. Pa. 1972).

[112] *See* § 7.04[C][5] *infra* on the requirements for an effective cure tender.

Based on the need to achieve this balance, a breaching seller who is granted a further reasonable time to substitute a conforming tender must act expeditiously. A seller cannot lock the disappointed buyer into an extended waiting period, but rather should apply the necessary attention and effort to correct the deficiency promptly. Delay in investigating and correcting the problem should cause the cure effort to fail.[113] The opportunity to cure should also be contingent on the seller's ability to accomplish it. Repeated unsuccessful cure efforts should terminate further cure rights,[114] as should impossibility of initiating a prompt cure.[115]

A few courts have inappropriately tied the additional time for cure under section 2–508(2) to a determination of whether the buyer changed position following rejection but before the attempted cure.[116] Notification of intent to cure by a qualifying seller precludes the buyer's right to change position. The buyer is required to allow an opportunity to cure during further reasonable time. Use of a changed-position criterion to measure the seller's time to cure has the undesirable tendency, on the one hand, of prompting buyers to act both precipitously and improperly to infringe upon the cure opportunity and, on the other hand, of allowing sellers to retain cure rights indefinitely unless buyers take additional affirmative steps to cut them off.

[2] Seasonable Notification

The statutory right to cure following rejection by the buyer must be implemented by the seller. The seller must provide the buyer with seasonable notification of the intent to cure. As long as the original time frame is still available to the seller, the right to cure is subject only to the seller providing this seasonable notification.[117] Although additional criteria qualify the availability of cure after the contract time for performance has passed, seasonable notification of an intent to cure is still required.[118]

---

[113] Mobile Housing, Inc. v. Stone, 490 S.W.2d 611, 12 UCC Rep. Serv. 235 (Tex. Ct. App. 1973) (no repair work commenced on mobile home until nearly two months after rejection).

[114] General Motors Acceptance Corp. v. Grady, 27 Ohio App. 3d 321, 501 N.E.2d 68, 2 UCC Rep. Serv. 2d 887 (1985) (court found support for trial court's judgment that reasonable time to cure had passed when seller's response to numerous attempts to have new car repaired indicated unwillingness or inability to cure promptly).

[115] Johannsen v. Minnesota Valley Ford Tractor Co., 304 N.W.2d 654, 31 UCC Rep. Serv. 558 (Minn. 1981) (dealer indicated to buyer on August 3 that he could not fix hydraulic leak problem on new tractor until replacement parts became available the following April).

[116] Ramirez v. Autosport, 88 N.J. 277, 440 A.2d 1345, 33 UCC Rep. Serv. 134 (1982); Bartus v. Riccardi, 55 Misc. 2d 3, 284 N.Y.S.2d 222, 4 UCC Rep. Serv. 845 (N.Y. Sup. Ct. 1967).

[117] Clark Oil Trading Co. v. Amerada Hess Trading Co., 1993 WL 300039 (S.D.N.Y.) (unpublished) (notification of intent to cure during time remaining for contract performance gave seller right to cure that was interfered with by buyer).

[118] National Fleet Supply, Inc. v. Fairchild, 450 N.E.2d 1015, 36 UCC Rep. Serv. 480 (Ind. Ct.

Seasonable notification by the buyer should mean prompt notification. Notification is important to the buyer because it is the mechanism that suspends the effectiveness of a properly invoked rejection.[119] The aggrieved buyer should not be required to speculate long concerning whether the seller will attempt a cure. The notice requirement promotes vigilance with respect to claiming the seller's cure right, prompts the seller to ascertain the extent and correctability of the asserted deficiency, and apprises the buyer of the seller's position concerning the transaction.

The requirement of a seasonable notification of an intent to cure following rejection by the buyer necessarily implies a reasonable opportunity for the seller to ascertain promptly the existence and extent of any defect alleged by the buyer and to decide on a response. The facts of *Wilson v. Scampoli*[120] are illustrative. The color television delivered by the seller had a reddish tinge that the service representative could not adequately diagnose while examining the set in the buyer's home. Rather than allowing the chassis to be removed for examination at the seller's shop, the buyer's daughter insisted on receiving a different set. The appellate court reversed a grant of rescission and awarded the seller the purchase price. The seller qualified for the cure right, but the buyer impaired the opportunity for the seller to make a reasonable inspection to determine the cause and correctability of the red tinge. The seller was willing to adjust the set to achieve its proper picture quality or replace it if repairs proved necessary following an expedited examination of the set, but the buyer's response precluded the seller from the opportunity to establish a definite position on the cure method and to notify the buyer of it.[121]

[3] Reasonable Grounds to Believe

When the contract time for seller performance has passed, the seller does not have an automatic statutory right to cure. The buyer must have rejected a nonconforming tender that the seller had reasonable grounds to believe would be acceptable to the buyer. In the absence of such reasonable grounds, the Code does not give the seller a cure right.

App. 1983) (seller who indicated a full refund would be given on return of nonconforming truck engine did not provide seasonable notification of intent to cure).

[119] *See* Wolfes v. Terrel, 173 Ga. App. 835, 328 S.E.2d 569, 41 UCC Rep. Serv. 837 (1985) (court properly rejected seller's motion for directed verdict on grounds that buyer had failed to pursue a cure remedy under § 2–508).

[120] 228 A.2d 848, 4 UCC Rep. Serv. 178 (D.C. Ct. App. 1967).

[121] Another apt illustration is *Uchitel v. F. R. Tripler & Co.*, 107 Misc. 2d 310, 434 N.Y.S.2d 77, 30 UCC Rep. Serv. 933 (N.Y. Sup. Ct. 1980). The buyer rejected custom-made garments, but would not try them on for the seller to determine whether any alterations were necessary.

The Comments show that the drafters included this requirement to balance the interests of the seller and the buyer.

> Subsection (2) seeks to avoid injustice to the seller by reason of a surprise rejection by the buyer. However, the seller is not protected unless he has "reasonable grounds to believe" that the tender would be acceptable.[122]

The right to cure protects the seller against surprise rejections, and the reasonable-grounds limitation protects the buyer against improper allegations of surprise. The limitation can be appreciated in the context of the aim of alleviating the increased forfeiture that could accompany use of the perfect tender rule. Cure allows a second chance to provide the necessary perfect tender, but its availability is conditioned on the seller's bona fide initial effort to comply. Sellers are not entitled to automatic extensions in the time for their contract performance simply by forcing buyer rejection through incomplete or other nonconforming tenders.

A seller cannot qualify for this statutory cure right in the absence of adequate grounds to believe that the tender is perfect or that commercially legitimate reasons justify the belief that the tender nevertheless will not cause the buyer to complain.[123] The rejection that the seller subsequently faces must be a surprise in the sense that it reasonably expected that the buyer would accept the tendered delivery. When sellers know or should know that a rejection will follow their imperfect tender, they are not entitled to claim surprise at the buyer's response or to assert cure rights under section 2–508(2).

A seller can satisfy this limitation on the cure remedy when a tender made without knowledge of a nonconformity is made in good faith and is consistent with commercially reasonable standards.[124] One of the landmark opinions in this area, *Wilson v. Scampoli*,[125] illustrates the point well. The merchandise had been delivered to the customer in a factory-sealed carton. The court specifically found that the seller had "reasonable grounds to believe that merchandise like color television sets, new and delivered as crated at the factory, would be acceptable as delivered . . . ."[126]

---

[122] UCC § 2–508, Comment 2.

[123] Unfortunately, too many courts applying § 2–508(2) have simply ignored the "reasonable grounds to believe" requirement. *See* Schmitt & Frisch, *The Perfect Tender Rule—An "Acceptable" Interpretation*, 13 U. Tol. L. Rev. 1375, 1380 (1980) (suggesting that more cases have ignored this element than have addressed it).

[124] *Accord*, J. White & R. Summers, *Uniform Commercial Code* 381 (3d student ed. 1988) (good faith).

[125] 228 A.2d 848, 4 UCC Rep. Serv. 178 (D.C. Ct. App. 1967).

[126] *Id.* at 849.

Overgeneralizations should be avoided, however. The stated assumption would not be so well founded if the seller had received a recall order on the delivered set or if similar sets delivered to customers had resulted in a significant number of subsequent complaints. In the *Wilson* case, the seller's expert witness testified that removal of a television chassis was frequently necessary with new sets to determine the cause of color malfunction (the buyer's complaint) and the extent of adjustment or correction needed to achieve full operational efficiency. Depending on the degree of frequency involved, the seller reasonably might have been expected to check the color quality prior to delivery.

A seller tendering with knowledge of a deficiency in the tender can still qualify if it has a commercially reasonable basis to assume the tender will be acceptable to the buyer.[127] One of the better-reasoned opinions in this regard is *Joc Oil USA, Inc. v. Consolidated Edison Co.*[128] The seller's tender of crude oil with a sulfur content of 0.92% under a contract specifying 0.5% maximum sulfur content did not preclude the seller's right to cure. The court held that the seller was justified in believing that the initial tender would be acceptable to the buyer because the oil, which was en route to the United States at the time of contract formation, had been certified for a sulfur content of 0.52% by an Italian refinery. Furthermore, the court found that "although it had no predelivery knowledge of the .92% sulfur content . . . [the seller] would still have believed that such a shipment would have been acceptable to Con Ed based upon its prior knowledge of Con Ed purchase and use practices [burning fuel with up to 1% sulfur content] during this period of oil scarcity and volatile pricing."[129]

In the well-known case of *Zabriskie Chevrolet, Inc. v. Smith,*[130] the court held the seller to a standard that is too high. The buyer of a new automobile

---

[127] *Accord,* J. White & R. Summers, *Uniform Commercial Code* 381 (3d student ed. 1988) (reason to believe the goods would be acceptable).

[128] 434 N.Y.S.2d 623, 30 UCC Rep. Serv. 426 (Sup. Ct. 1980), *aff'd sub nom.,* T. W. Oil, Inc. v. Consolidated Edison Co., 84 A.D.2d 970, 447 N.Y.S.2d 572 (1981), *aff'd,* 57 N.Y.2d 574, 457 N.Y.S.2d 458, 443 N.E.2d 932, 35 UCC Rep. Serv. 12 (1982).

[129] *Id.* at 630. Comparable reasoning was applied to reach a different result in McKenzie v. Alla-Ohio Coals, Inc., 29 UCC Rep. Serv. 852 (D.C. C.D. 1979), in which the seller delivered coal with an ash content ranging between 13.5% and 16% under a purchase order specifying that the ash content was not to exceed 7.5%. Addressing the reasonableness of the seller's belief, the court noted that "it is unlikely that a reasonable seller in plaintiff's position would be ignorant of such drastic variances in the quality of the coal . . . [and] similarly, no evidence of trade custom in the record indicate[d] that coal with such high ash content would be suitable for use as metallurgical coal, the purpose for which it was purchased." *Id.* at 857.

[130] 99 N.J. Super. 441, 240 A.2d 195, 5 UCC Rep. Serv. 30 (1968).

experienced major problems with the vehicle only a short distance from the seller's place of business. The dealer subsequently determined that the transmission was defective. The court ruled that the seller did not qualify under the reasonable-grounds requirement for a right to cure because the seller's mechanics either knew or should have known about substantial defects in the cars sold. The court specifically noted that the transmission was one of the items required to be inspected on the seller's inspection and adjustment schedule.

The *Zabriskie* court's position is simply too sweeping. Certain types of latent defects are beyond the capacity of a dealer–seller to discover, yet the court ignored the discoverability of the defect that plagued the transmission in this case. The court's holding on the seller's belief of acceptability of the product is sustainable only if the transmission defect was a type that should have been discovered through a reasonable dealer inspection of the component.

Some courts and commentators have improperly applied a magnitude-of-the-defect test in assessing the reasonableness of the seller's belief that the goods will be acceptable to the buyer.[131] This test precludes availability of cure when the seller's tender involves a major deficiency. Use of this test constitutes an unwarranted rewriting of the statutory standard. It substitutes a standard based on the nature of the breach for the statutory requirement of a seller's belief in the acceptability of the tender. A seller's right to cure under section 2–508(2) is not eliminated just because the defect in the tender is material; nor is the seller automatically entitled to cure just because the defect is relatively minor.

[4]   Money Allowance

Cure under section 2–508(2) is available when the buyer rejects a tender that the seller reasonably believed would be acceptable "with or without money allowance." If the seller had reasonable grounds to believe that the buyer would agree to a price allowance for the nonconforming aspect of the seller's tender, a rejection by the buyer would legitimately surprise the seller. The seller thus could qualify for an opportunity to cure the tender by providing seasonable notification of an intent to cure.

The case of *Joc Oil USA, Inc. v. Consolidated Edison Co.*[132] illustrates the appropriate application of the price allowance provision. After certification tests

---

[131] Johannsen v. Minnesota Valley Ford Tractor Co., 304 N.W.2d 654, 31 UCC Rep. Serv. 558 (Minn. 1981); Jones v. Abriani, 169 Ind. App. 556, 350 N.E.2d 635, 19 UCC Rep. Serv. 1102 (1967).

[132] 434 N.Y.S.2d 623, 30 UCC Rep. Serv. 426 (Sup. Ct. 1980), *aff'd sub nom.*, T. W. Oil, Inc. v. Consolidated Edison Co., 84 A.D.2d 970, 447 N.Y.S.2d 572 (1981), *aff'd*, 57 N.Y.2d 574, 457 N.Y.S.2d 458, 443 N.E.2d 932, 35 UCC Rep. Serv. 12 (1982).

showed that sulfur content of the oil tendered by the seller was too high, the parties met in an unsuccessful attempt to negotiate a price agreement pursuant to a contract clause that provided for price adjustment negotiations. The seller then offered to cure by substituting a conforming delivery, but the buyer refused to allow this cure. The court determined that the contract term providing for price negotiations supported the reasonableness of the seller's belief that the tender would be acceptable to the buyer. That belief was further buttressed by the buyer's indicated willingness to keep and use nonconforming oil if an appropriate price adjustment could be arranged. The buyer's interference with the seller's right to cure thus was wrongful.

Contrary to the position indicated by some commentators,[133] the seller cannot force a price settlement on the buyer. A price adjustment is not an appropriate method to cure a nonconforming tender. It would deprive the buyer of the right to receive perfect tender by requiring the buyer to accept nonconforming goods and monetary compensation for their deficiencies. It would also unduly dilute the requirement that sellers have a reasonable basis to believe that their tender will be acceptable to the buyer. Eliminating these controls would remove desirable incentives for sellers to take measures to assure that the goods they supply meet their buyers' needs.

[5]   Conforming Tender

A seller who invokes the right to cure an improper tender or delivery (whether with time remaining for seller performance or not) has the applicable time period to provide a tender or delivery that is conforming. Goods and any part of a performance are "conforming" to a contract "when they are in accordance with the obligations under the contract."[134] This concept determines the adequacy of the seller's cure. The seller's cure tender must be perfect tender in all aspects of the contract specifications, except that an additional reasonable time is allowed when cure is made pursuant to section 2–508(2).[135] The perfect tender rule is the standard against which the cure tender is measured.

Following a notification of intent to cure, one of three things will happen: the seller will not go forward with a cure within the time allowed; the seller will provide a conforming tender; or the seller will provide another nonconforming tender. In the first instance, the buyer's original rejection will become

---

[133] J. White & R. Summers, *Uniform Commercial Code* 384 (3d student ed. 1988) (despite modest violence to statutory language, should allow price allowance as cure for nonsubstantial nonconformities).

[134] UCC § 2–106(2).

[135] Travelers Indem. Co. v. MAHO Mach. Tool Corp., 952 F.2d 26, 16 UCC Rep. Serv. 2d 369 (2d Cir. 1991) (seller's insistence that buyer incur transportation costs between Singapore and Germany for replacement of defective machine precluded finding of adequate cure).

effective again upon the seller's failure to make a timely cure. The seller would have announced the intent to cure but not followed through by exercising the right, and further action will not be necessary for an effective rejection. In the second case, a new conforming tender will cure the original nonconformity and terminate the buyer's right to reject. Continuing to reject would be wrongful and would constitute a breach by the buyer. In the third situation, the seller's second tender, like the first, is nonconforming, but the buyer's initial rejection covers only the first tender. The buyer must respond to the subsequent tender of ineffectual cure; failure to do so after a reasonable time to inspect the newly tendered goods will result in their acceptance by the buyer. Since the purported cure does not conform in all respects to the contract, however, section 2–601 gives the aggrieved buyer the right to reject the new tender.

The issue of adequacy of cure is often raised in the context of whether the seller must replace nonconforming goods or is entitled to repair them. Repair should be allowed, provided that it will result in goods that conform to the contract. If the quality of the product is not degraded and it is as acceptable as a product that never had the deficiency, cure in the form of repair is adequate. The buyer should not be required, on the other hand, "to accept patchwork goods or substantially repaired articles in lieu of flawless merchandise."[136] In essence, the repaired product must comply with all of the applicable warranties for the repair to satisfy the perfect tender rule and to constitute an adequate cure.

The standard was not met in *Worldwide RV Sales & Serv. v. Brooks*.[137] The contract specifications called for "dual roof air conditioning," but the mobile home was tendered and rejected with only one roof air conditioner. The offer to cure would have placed air conditioning units properly at the front and back of the vehicle, but by removing the single unit from the center, the "cure" would have left a hole in the roof. The court easily concluded that this proposal was not a cure because it was not a substitute conforming tender.

The case that is probably cited most often for adequacy of repair under section 2–508 is overly restrictive. In refusing to uphold the seller's cure by repair, the court in *Zabriskie Chevrolet, Inc. v. Smith* noted that cure "does not, in the court's opinion, contemplate the tender of a new vehicle with a substituted transmission, not from the factory and of unknown lineage from another vehicle in plaintiff's possession.[138] The facts of that case, however, show that the dealer replaced the defective transmission with one that was removed from another vehicle on the dealer's showroom floor. The substituted transmission did

---

[136] Wilson v. Scampoli, 228 A.2d 848, 850, 4 UCC Rep. Serv. 178 (D.C. Ct. App. 1967).
[137] 534 N.E.2d 1132, 8 UCC Rep. Serv. 2d 386 (Ind. Ct. App. 1989).
[138] 99 N.J. Super. 441, 458, 240 A.2d 195, 205 (1968).

not appear to have been old or defective, nor did the value of the vehicle appear to have been lessened.

The *Zabriskie* court also introduced what has become known as the "shaken-faith" doctrine. It considers the effect that knowledge of the original defect and repair has on the disappointed buyer. The court states:

> For a majority of people the purchase of a new car is a major investment, rationalized by the peace of mind that flows from its dependability and safety. Once their faith is shaken, the vehicle loses not only its real value in their eyes, but becomes an instrument whose integrity is substantially impaired and whose operation is fraught with apprehension.[139]

The shaken-faith doctrine is an appropriate consideration, provided it is not applied as a subjective standard. The right to reject arises only on a nonconforming tender, and the objective criterion of warranty obligations applies in determining whether the goods conform to the contract. The acceptability of the repair as a cure should thus be determined from the perspective of a reasonable buyer. When knowledge of the circumstances of a repair would leave a reasonable buyer sufficiently apprehensive about the reliability or quality of the purchased product, the buyer does not receive what was bargained for and the repair is not an adequate cure.[140]

The *Zabriskie* court, however, appears to yield excessively to the buyer's subjective complaints. Shaken faith was assumed, and its reasonableness was not explored. The buyer urged that what he bargained for was "a new car with factory new parts, which would operate perfectly as represented."[141] The tendered cure appears to have provided that consideration. The seller did not rebuild the defective transmission, giving the buyer patchwork goods; rather, it completely replaced the part. The case does not indicate that the defect in the buyer's auto was anything more than an isolated instance, that its replacement would not enable the vehicle to perform as represented, that any other components in the auto were defective, or that the events that led to the discovery of the defective transmission in any way changed any of the performance capabilities of the rest of the car.

Better reasoning under the shaken-faith doctrine is provided in *Bayne v. Nall Motors, Inc.*[142] The court stressed the "lack of positive knowledge that there

---

[139] *Id.*

[140] Hemmert Agric. Aviation, Inc. v. Mid-Continent Aircraft Corp., 663 F. Supp. 1546, 4 UCC Rep. Serv. 2d 726 (D. Kan. 1987) (discomfort and fear from the handling of a crop-dusting aircraft and repeated efforts to correct the problem).

[141] 99 N.J. Super. at 451, 240 A.2d at 200.

[142] 12 UCC Rep. Serv. 1137 (Iowa Dist. Ct. 1973).

was not other damage done" in holding that replacement of the differential after its parts welded and locked the drive train was not an adequate cure.[143] The court further supported its position by noting:

> The fact that the dealer and manufacturer and their employees strongly believe in the quality of the repaired auto does not make this vehicle as acceptable as a similar automobile that has not experienced the same tremendous internal impact and a reasonable buyer could not be expected to be satisfied under the facts herein.[144]

The *Bayne* case is an excellent example of circumstances in which the shaken-faith doctrine operates to exclude repairs or the replacement of component parts as an adequate cure. Some courts unwittingly have allowed the doctrine to be used improperly as leverage to extract another form of cure that the buyer prefers.[145]

[6]   Consensual Cure

Even though Article 2 does not provide a breaching seller with any statutory cure rights, the right can be attained with the buyer consensually. The seller might offer to correct the deficiency and receive an affirmative response from the buyer, or the buyer might request or even demand a cure. Neither party can force the other to acquiesce, but when they do so, cure rights are created beyond any that are provided in Article 2 or the original terms of the contract. Their mutual consent serves to modify the original contract.

Consensual cure can arise at any time following the seller's initial tender. In *Havas v. Love*,[146] the purchaser of a motor bus observed smoke coming from the air-conditioning unit. He allowed the seller an opportunity to fix the unit, but on noticing smoke and fumes coming from the motor, he rejected. The court did not address the basis for the cure opportunity, but clearly it was consensual cure prior to rejection.

---

[143] *Id.* at 1140.

[144] *Id.* at 1141. Two additional well-reasoned cases on this point are Champion Ford Sales, Inc. v. Levine, 49 Md. App. 547, 433 A.2d 1218, 32 UCC Rep. Serv. 108 (Ct. Spec. App. 1981) (difference between a car with a new factory-built and installed engine and a repaired car with a shop-rebuilt engine), and Ford Motor Co. v. Mayes, 575 S.W.2d 480, 24 UCC Rep. Serv. 1057 (Ky. Ct. App. 1978) (pickup truck frame was twisted and "diamonded," which would cause unusual stress and wear to various moving parts of the truck).

[145] *See* Asciolla v. Manter Oldsmobile-Pontiac, Inc., 117 N.H. 85, 370 A.2d 270, 21 UCC Rep. Serv. 112 (1977) (court upheld buyer insistence on replacement of automobile rather than just the transmission).

[146] 89 Nev. 458, 514 P.2d 1187, 13 UCC Rep. Serv. 466 (1973).

Buyers should require prompt agreement with the seller in this context. Otherwise their failure to reject within a reasonable time might be held to be an acceptance, which, in turn, would preclude a right of rejection. A seller who does not qualify for a right to cure following rejection under section 2–508 might nevertheless be afforded a consensual right to cure.[147] The buyer might also make an acceptance that is expressly conditioned upon a defined cure.[148] If the condition fails, the acceptance is ineffectual and the buyer is entitled to reject.[149]

Parties who reach a cure agreement can shape their cure arrangement as they please on terms concerning the nature of the corrective action or the length of time that will be allowed for cure. The agreement becomes a modification that replaces the original contract requirements. Neither party can then revert unilaterally to the original terms of the contract.[150] In essence, the modification agreement on cure redefines the seller's required performance under the contract.

[D]   The Good-Faith Limitation [1–203]

Rejection is not a self-executing right of an aggrieved buyer. Rather, the buyer is required to take action in order to enforce the right.[151] Consequently, the right to reject is limited by the obligation to act in good faith. Section 1–203 provides, "Every contract or duty within this Act imposes an obligation of good faith in its performance or enforcement." The cure right must be exercised in good faith.

The good-faith limitation is an important mechanism for just application of the perfect tender rule. The primary complaint about the perfect tender rule is

---

[147] See Art Metal Prod. Co. v. Royal Equip. Co., 670 S.W.2d 152, 38 UCC Rep. Serv. 1202 (Mo. Ct. App. 1984) (school district rejected nonconforming athletic lockers but allowed additional time in which to correct the deficiencies); Great Am. Music Mach., Inc. v. Mid-South Record Pressing Co., 393 F. Supp. 877, 17 UCC Rep. Serv. 381 (M.D. Tenn. 1975) (after buyer rejected tendered records because they were warped, pitted, and blistered, the parties agreed that the records should be repressed).

[148] North Am. Steel Corp. v. Siderius, 75 Mich. App. 391, 254 N.W.2d 899, 22 UCC Rep. Serv. 62 (1977) (subject to price adjustment).

[149] Christopher v. Larson Ford Sales, Inc., 557 P.2d 1009, 20 UCC Rep. Serv. 873 (Utah 1976) (seller's promise that buyers could return motor home if problems persisted entitled buyers to reject when the condition to their acceptance failed).

[150] Cardwell v. International Housing, 282 Pa. Super. 498, 423 A.2d 355, 359, 31 UCC Rep. Serv. 512 (1980) (buyer who agreed to delivery of a mobile home model different from the one specified in the written contract "abandoned rights to reject the mobile home as nonconforming to the original contract").

[151] UCC § 2–602(1). See § 7.04[B] supra.

that it affords an opportunity for a buyer who has become dissatisfied with the bargain to nitpick the seller's tender to find an inconsequential defect that can be used as an excuse to cancel the contract. The good-faith limitation is the tool to counter such buyer abuse of the rejection right.

Contract performance should fulfill the legitimate expectations of the contracting parties.[152] A buyer that receives the full measure of what was bargained for, in the sense of fulfilling these expectations, has no right to reject, despite some insignificant deviation from the precise contract specifications. The perfect tender rule is not intended to empower buyers to seize upon slight contract deviations of no actual importance to them as a pretext for discontinuing the contract. A buyer acts dishonestly by feigning dissatisfaction with the seller's performance when the true motive for rejecting the goods is based on some other factor,[153] such as the desire to avoid the contract obligation during a falling market.[154] The good-faith obligation is the Code mechanism that precludes such behavior and thereby limits application of the perfect tender rule to instances in which it is invoked honestly.

[E]   The Installment Contract Exception [2–612; 2A–510]

Section 2–612 governs nonconforming deliveries made under installment contracts.[155] This section does not incorporate the perfect tender rule. Subsection (3) allows the buyer to cancel the contract only when the nonconformity of one or more installments "substantially impairs the value of the whole contract."[156] Cancellation of an entire installment contract affects performance that is not yet due, rather than just rejection of a tendered installment. The drafters'

---

[152] E. A. Farnsworth, *Contracts* 562 (2d ed. 1990).

[153] At a minimum, "good faith" means "honesty in fact in the conduct or transaction concerned." UCC 1–201(19).

[154] Neumiller Farms, Inc. v. Cornett, 368 So. 2d 272, 26 UCC Rep. Serv. 61 (Ala. 1979) (claim of dissatisfaction with subsequent deliveries of chipping potatoes after the market price declined substantially below the contract price was held to be made in bad faith, making the refusal to accept a breach). For a study on buyer attempts to reject during a falling market, *see generally* Eno, *Price Movement and Unstated Objections to the Defective Performance of Sales Contracts*, 44 Yale L.J. 782 (1935).

[155] "An 'installment contract' is one which requires or authorizes the delivery of goods in separate lots to be separately accepted, even though the contract contains a clause 'each delivery is a separate contract' or its equivalent." UCC § 2–612(1).

[156] Subsection 2–612(3) provides in its entirety as follows:

Whenever non-conformity or default with respect to one or more installments substantially impairs the value of the whole contract there is a breach of the whole. But the aggrieved party reinstates the contract if he accepts a non-conforming installment without seasonably notifying of cancellation or if he brings an action with respect only to past installments or demands performance as to future installments.

approach in subsection (3) is consistent with other provisions involving prospective impairment of expectations.[157] Subsection (3) is therefore explained
within the discussion of prospective impairment.[158]

The second subsection of section 2–612 governs a buyer's right to reject an
individual nonconforming installment. It also uses the substantial impairment
test in lieu of the perfect tender rule. The substantial impairment test is comparable to the material breach standard of common law.[159] The Comments to
another section that applies the substantial impairment test clearly tie it to the
materiality concept.[160]

Section 2–612(2) provides as follows:

> The buyer may reject any installment which is non-conforming if the
> non-conformity substantially impairs the value of that installment and
> cannot be cured or if the non-conformity is a defect in the required doc-
> uments; but if the non-conformity does not fall within subsection (3)
> and the seller gives adequate assurance of its cure the buyer must
> accept that installment.

The provision deals with only a single installment already tendered by the
seller, a circumstance that is much more comparable to rejection in a nonin-
stallment case than it is to prospective impairment of the buyer's expectations.
Nevertheless, the drafters applied the substantial impairment test to this context as well.

The seller in an installment contract has a more generous right to cure the
deficiencies than the seller in a contract calling for a single delivery. Unlike the
general section 2–508 rights on cure, the installment section does not differentiate between cases in which the contract time for performance has and has
not expired. The cure section applies only on a buyer's rejection, but the installment section precludes the buyer from rejecting if cure is possible. Sellers
must seasonably notify buyers of their intent to cure under the general section,
whereas installment contract sellers must give adequate assurance of the cure
of a nonconforming installment. In the latter case, the buyer must accept the
tendered installment solely on the strength of the assurance of cure, whereas under section 2–508, the buyer has already rejected the nonconforming
tender and can await the seller's cure effort before responding further. Section

---

[157] UCC §§ 2–609; 2–610.

[158] See § 7.09[D] infra.

[159] See Restatement (Second) of Contracts § 241.

[160] "The most useful test of substantial value is to determine whether material inconvenience
or injustice will result if the aggrieved party is forced to wait and receive an ultimate
tender minus the part or aspect repudiated." UCC § 2–610, Comment 3 (addressing anticipatory repudiation).

2–612(2) omits all reference to the section 2–508(2) condition that the seller have reasonable grounds to believe that the nonconforming tender will be acceptable to the buyer. The sections even differ as to the nature of a cure, since the Comments to the installment recognize a price allowance as appropriate, but section 2–508 does not. The extent of these inconsistencies shows that the two sections establishing the seller's right to cure do not interact.[161]

The absolute right to cure given to sellers under section 2–612(2) is sensible. The installment contract creates a continuing relationship between the buyer and seller that extends beyond the single nonconforming delivery, and the buyer is not entitled to cancel that contractual relationship. The parties must continue to deal with each other in the future, so preconditions for allowing the seller an opportunity to correct a curable tender are less desirable. Assurances by the seller that the nonconforming installment will be cured are particularly appropriate given the continuing nature of the contractual relationship.

[F]   The Shipment Contract Exception [2–504]

Section 2–504 establishes the proper manner for a seller's tender of delivery in a shipment contract.[162] The section imposes obligations on the seller in three respects: placing goods in possession of a carrier and contracting for their transport; tendering necessary documents; and notifying the buyer of the shipment. The final sentence of the section eliminates the perfect tender rule as the measure for rejection in two of these obligations. It provides that, "[f]ailure to notify the buyer . . . or to make a proper contract . . . is a ground for rejection only if material delay or loss ensues."

This exception to the perfect tender rule probably was adopted as a reaction to earlier case law in which buyers rejected because of some noncompliance with shipping arrangements, even though they did not suffer any perceivable injury. One of two cases marking recognition of the perfect tender rule in the United States presented just such circumstances. The seller in *Filley v. Pope*[163] shipped pig iron from Leith, Scotland, under a contract calling for shipment from Glasgow as soon as possible. The seller shipped from Leith because the only ship available was discharging her cargo there and, due to a scarcity of

---

[161] Many courts addressing cure rights with respect to installment contracts have failed to perceive these distinctions. Bodine Sewer, Inc. v. Eastern Ill. Precast, Inc., 143 Ill. App. 3d 920, 493 N.E.2d 705, 1 UCC Rep. Serv. 2d 1480 (1986); Continental Forest Products, Inc. v. White Lumber Sales, Inc., 256 Or. 466, 474 P.2d 1, 8 UCC Rep. Serv. 178 (1970).

[162] A "shipment contract" is one in which "the seller is required or authorized to send the goods to the buyer and the contract does not require him to deliver them at a particular destination." UCC § 2–504. Article 2A has no comparable provision.

[163] 115 U.S. 213 (1885).

ships at the time, a vessel would not be available from Glasgow for several weeks. The Supreme Court upheld the buyer's refusal to accept the tendered iron upon its arrival in New Orleans, considering itself "bound to give effect to the terms which the parties have chosen for themselves" and to have "neither the means, nor the right, to determine why the parties in their contract specified 'shipment from Glasgow.' "[164]

Greater concern for the seller developed in cases of nonconformity because of delay and shipping arrangements, however, particularly when the buyer did not suffer damages or rejected in the face of a falling market. Following the general postwar price collapse in the 1920s, the Supreme Court sought to mitigate the rigor of the *Filley* decision. In *Lamborn v. National Bank of Commerce*,[165] the Court engaged in an exercise of interpretation of contract language to reverse the lower court that had upheld, on the basis of the *Filley* opinion, a buyer's rejection on the grounds that precisely conforming shipping orders had not been issued, despite the fact that the actual voyage of the vessel complied. The inclusion of the material breach standard in section 2–504 reflects the desire to preclude decisions like *Filley v. Pope*.

Section 2–504, on the other hand, carefully preserves the perfect tender standard in relation to the seller's obligation to obtain and promptly tender any necessary documents. This part of the codification of section 2–504 is consistent with the drafting of section 2–612(2). Section 2–612(2) generally limits the right to reject an installment to a case of nonconformity that "substantially impairs the value of that installment," but also leaves the perfect tender rule applicable "if the non-conformity is a defect in the required documents." These provisions reflect the mercantile custom requiring strict compliance in documentary transactions.[166] Scholars have long recognized the justifications for preserving the free marketability of documents and precluding buyers in cash sales from incurring the greater credit risks associated with securing a refund from the seller.[167]

§ 7.05   REVOCATION OF ACCEPTANCE [2–608; 2A–517]

The end result of a rightful revocation of acceptance[168] is comparable to the effect of a rightful rejection: the buyer is not held to an acceptance and thus

---

[164] *Id.* at 220.

[165] 276 U.S. 469 (1928).

[166] *See* Honnold, *Buyer's Right of Rejection*, 97 U. Pa. L. Rev. 457, 467 (1949).

[167] *Id.* at 478–79; Llewellyn, *On Warranty of Quality and Society: I*, 36 Colum. L. Rev. 699, 730–31 (1936).

[168] UCC § 2–608. With the exception of some specialized provisions dealing with finance

does not incur the consequences of an acceptance. Essentially, the goods are thrown back on the seller. The procedural aspects of a revocation are also quite comparable to rejection. The right to revoke, however, differs significantly from the right to reject. As the following discussion explains, the right to revoke is much more constrained.

[A] The Right

[1] Limited Circumstances

Buyers are entitled to revoke only in certain limited circumstances that depend on whether they accepted with awareness of a nonconformity in the accepted goods. When they discover a defect prior to accepting, revocation of the acceptance is possible only if they proceed on the reasonable assumption that the defect will be cured and it is not seasonably cured.[169] Buyers who know of defects but accept the goods anyway without any expectation that their sellers will correct the defects do not have any equitable basis later to insist on revocation.

When buyers accept without having discovered nonconformities in the goods, revocation is available in only two circumstances.[170] The acceptance must have been reasonably induced either by the difficulty of discovering the defect or by assurances from the seller. These limitations on the availability of revocation create an incentive for vigilance by buyers of goods. Buyers are not bound to an acceptance until they have been afforded a reasonable opportunity to inspect,[171] but failure to exercise the opportunity results in waiver of the right to inspect.[172] With acceptance of tendered goods, buyers are precluded not only from rejecting but also from revoking for nonconformities that should

---

leases, which are covered separately in this text, the provisions for leases are comparable. UCC § 2A–517.

[169] UCC § 2–608(1)(a). Adams v. Grant, 358 S.E.2d 142, 2 UCC Rep. Serv. 2d 1307 (S.C. Ct. App. 1986) (after promising to cure, seller refused to repair some defects and attempted other repairs unsuccessfully).

[170] UCC § 2–608(1)(b).

[171] UCC 2–606(1)(a),(b). See § 7.03[A] supra.

[172] In re Barney Schogel, Inc., 12 B.R. 697, 34 UCC Rep. Serv. 29 (Bankr. S.D. N.Y. 1981) (buyer who did not discover defect in specially manufactured windows until after installation because of failure to inspect them upon delivery was precluded from revoking acceptance).

have been revealed by reasonable inspection.[173] Essentially, any right to reject based on discoverable defects that is lost because of inspection delay cannot subsequently be reinstated in the form of revocation of acceptance.

Revocation of acceptance made without prior discovery of nonconformities is permitted in two instances in which buyers are excused for not having made the discovery. Buyers are not prevented from revoking for defects that are too difficult to detect through a reasonable pre-acceptance inspection.[174] The other special circumstance involves assurances by a seller concerning the conformity of the goods. Such assurances can allay a buyer's vigilance in inspecting the goods and thereby discovering a defect.[175]

[2]   Subjective Standard of Substantial Impairment

Even when a buyer can establish one of the limited circumstances under which a right of revocation may be preserved, the buyer still does not necessarily have the right. A buyer who qualifies under one of the required circumstances "may revoke his acceptance of a lot or commercial unit whose non-conformity substantially impairs its value to him."[176] Unlike the right to reject, which is governed by the perfect tender rule, the right to revoke is controlled by a standard comparable to the common-law doctrine of material breach.

Two noted commentators have identified several cogent reasons why buyers are required to meet this higher standard before being allowed to throw nonconforming goods back onto their sellers after having accepted the goods.[177] Goods tend to depreciate more in the buyer's possession. Chances also increase that the defect was either caused or exacerbated by the buyer. The buyer can

---

[173] Hummel v. Skyline Dodge, Inc., 589 P.2d 73, 26 UCC Rep. Serv. 46 (Colo. Ct. App. 1978) (holding that there is no revocation for defects unknown at time of acceptance that could have been discovered through reasonable inspection). *See also* Herbert v. Harl, 757 S.W.2d 585, 7 UCC Rep. Serv. 2d 740 (Mo. 1988) (buyers of used car who took it to body shop to inspect for evidence of prior collisions and engine operation before they purchased it had no basis for revocation of acceptance).

[174] Atlantic Industries, Inc. v. O.E.M., Inc., 555 F. Supp. 184, 35 UCC Rep. Serv. 795 (W.D. Okla. 1983) (buyer required to undertake only the inspection tests common in the industry); Kesner v. Lancaster, 378 S.E.2d 649, 9 UCC Rep. Serv. 2d 122 (W. Va. 1989) (test for revocation of acceptance satisfied when buyer makes reasonable inspection and defect is not reasonably apparent or buyer does not have some special expertise).

[175] Alpert v. Thomas, 643 F. Supp. 1406, 2 UCC Rep. Serv. 2d 99 (D. Vt. 1986) (seller's assurances that a horse was breeding sound and that the seller would have the necessary breeding soundness evaluation performed induced buyer to accept the horse without discovering the nonconformity).

[176] UCC § 2–608(1).

[177] J. White & R. Summers, *Uniform Commercial Code* 368–69 (3d student ed. 1988).

also benefit from use of the goods. These arguments justify deviating from the perfect tender rule once a buyer accepts goods and subsequently seeks to revoke that acceptance.

The substantial impairment standard for purposes of revocation of acceptance is based on the buyer's personal circumstances. Section 2–608(1) provides in part that the buyer may revoke the acceptance of goods "whose nonconformity substantially impairs their value to him." The subjective nature of the standard is emphasized in the Comments: "The test is not what the seller had reason to know at the time of contracting; the question is whether the nonconformity is such as will in fact cause a substantial impairment of value to the buyer though the seller had no advance knowledge as to the buyer's particular circumstances."[178]

The inclusion of the subjective standard is consistent with the drafters' desire to make it easier for aggrieved buyers to determine their legal response to sellers' nonconforming tenders. The buyer must assume the higher burden of showing substantial impairment to justify a revocation of acceptance, but the showing need be made only in relation to the buyer's own circumstances. Undoubtedly, a case in which the goods substantially conformed on an objective basis, but were substantially defective to the particular plaintiff, would be unusual. The focus of the aggrieved buyer's response, nevertheless, is narrowed to the buyer's own case, making a decision on how to proceed easier. Buyers can rely more confidently upon their own circumstances when determining whether to revoke; in the event of litigation, they can focus the attention of the court and the jury on how the breach impacted on their specific needs.

The subjective nature of the substantial impairment standard does not apply to the determination of whether a breach exists, but rather to the impact of the breach on the buyer. The seller's breach results from the nonconformity of tendered goods, and the warranty provisions of Article 2, not any idiosyncratic tastes or needs of the buyer, govern that determination. When the seller's tender conforms to the contract specifications, the seller has performed properly and the buyer has neither the right to reject nor the right to revoke acceptance.

The distinction can be illustrated through the facts of *Fullerton Aircraft Sales & Rentals, Inc. v. Page Avjet Corp.*[179] The buyer complained of vibrations in a purchased aircraft but was not permitted to revoke acceptance because other pilots did not notice excessive vibration. In addition, however, the court based

---

[178] UCC § 2–608, Comment 2.
[179] 3 UCC Rep. Serv. 2d 1393 (4th Cir. 1987) (unpublished).

its holding on the fact that the buyer could not demonstrate that he was particularly sensitive to ordinary levels of vibration. This latter consideration was not applied correctly. The tendered aircraft complied with express warranties and the implied warranty of merchantability, and the seller did not extend an implied warranty of fitness based on the buyer's apparent heightened sensitivity to vibration. The tender thus conformed to the contract requirements, and the buyer did not have a basis to revoke, irrespective of his sensitivity level. Had a warranty been breached by the seller, the determination of whether it impaired the value of the aircraft to the buyer would then be determined in light of any idiosyncratic sensitivity level of the particular buyer, perhaps allowing revocation for vibration levels that would not impair the value of the aircraft to buyers with normal tolerance levels.

[B]   Procedural Aspects

Revocation, like rejection, is never self-executing. The aggrieved buyer must take action to invoke the right. Revocation is not effective until the buyer notifies the seller of it.[180] The relationship to other Article 2 notification requirements is detailed in Comment 5 to section 2–608 as follows:

> The content of the notice under subsection (2) is to be determined in this case as in others by considerations of good faith, prevention of surprise, and reasonable adjustment. More will generally be necessary than the mere notification of breach required under the preceding section.[181] On the other hand the requirements of the section on waiver of buyer's objections do not apply here.[182] The fact that quick notification of trouble is desirable affords good ground for being slow to bind a buyer by his first statement. Following the general policy of this Article, the requirements of the content of notification are less stringent in the case of a non-merchant.[183]

The notification must indicate to the seller that the buyer does not intend to retain the goods,[184] although it does not require the buyer to offer to return the

---

[180] UCC § 2–608(2). *Accord* UCC § 2A–517(4).

[181] *See* § 7.03[B][3] *supra.*

[182] UCC § 2–605. *See* § 7.04[B][2] *supra.*

[183] *See* § 7.03[B][3] *supra.*

[184] Solar Kinetics Corp. v. Joseph T. Ryerson & Son, Inc., 488 F. Supp. 1237, 29 UCC Rep. Serv. 85 (D. Conn. 1980).

goods to the seller.[185] More is required than simply the notification of breach that is necessary for a buyer to preserve remedies.[186]

A revocation "must occur within a reasonable time after the buyer discovers or should have discovered the ground for it."[187] The reasons for requiring timeliness are comparable to the policies that underlie timely notice of rejection.[188] A "reasonable time" in the revocation context, however, generally extends beyond the comparable standard of timeliness required in other contexts: "Since this remedy will be generally resorted to only after attempts at adjustment have failed, the reasonable time period should extend in most cases beyond the time in which notification of breach must be given, beyond the time for discovery of non-conformity after acceptance, and beyond the time for rejection after tender."[189]

Revocation must also occur "before any substantial change in the condition of the goods which is not caused by their own defects."[190] The seller essentially is entitled to have the goods returned without their deterioration in the hands of the buyer. If the deterioration is a result of defects in the goods as tendered, such as spoilage that spreads to additional fruit included as part of a lot, this limitation on revocation does not apply.

A buyer who revokes an acceptance has the same rights and responsibilities with respect to the goods as one who rejects them.[191] These rights and duties have been discussed already.[192]

[C] Cure

A statutory right to cure does not extend to sellers following revocation. Despite the limitation of section 2–508(2) to cases of rejection, a number of

---

[185] CPC Internat'l, Inc. v. Techni-Chem, Inc., 660 F. Supp. 1509, 4 UCC Rep. Serv. 2d 485 (1987).

[186] *But see* Performance Motors, Inc. v. Allen, 280 N.C. 385, 186 S.E.2d 161, 10 UCC Rep. Serv. 568 (1972) (complaints about mobile home together with cessation of payment held sufficient).

[187] UCC 2–608(2). Article 2A is comparable on the requirements of timeliness of revocation. UCC § 2A–517(4).

[188] *See* § 7.04[B][1] *supra.*

[189] UCC § 2–608, Comment 4. Zoss v. Royal Chevrolet, Inc., 11 UCC Rep. Serv. 527 (Ind. Super. Ct. 1972) (unsuccessful repair efforts by seller of Corvette made subsequent revocation timely).

[190] UCC § 2–608(2).

[191] UCC § 2–608(3). *Accord,* UCC § 2A–517(5).

[192] *See* § 7.04[B][3] *supra.*

courts have indicated that the cure rights of that section apply following a buyer's acceptance of a nonconforming tender.[193] Several other courts have properly denied the availability of a statutory right to cure following revocation.[194]

A statutory right to cure should not be extended to sellers following revocation because the perfect tender rule does not cover the right to revoke. A buyer who otherwise qualifies can revoke only if a nonconformity in the goods substantially impairs their value to the buyer. Consistent with cure following a rejection, the revocation would be suspended upon notification of the seller's intent to cure. Unlike the rejection cases, however, cure would be sufficient to thwart a revocation if it eliminates the substantial impact of the impairment but nevertheless leaves the buyer with a nonconforming tender. The buyer's expectation in a sales case is to receive goods that conform to the contract. Cure following revocation may leave a buyer with goods that do not conform in some respect and only a right to money damages for the deficiency.

The cure approach incorporated in the *Restatement* (Second) of Contracts has precisely this latter effect: a cure that raises the level of performance enough to avoid a material breach is sufficient to preclude the aggrieved party from canceling the contract. The different treatment of a construction contract is again justified, however, by the significant possibility of forfeiture. Even a party who materially breaches can face substantial forfeiture in a construction contract because the material and labor applied in performing cannot be returned upon cancellation of the contract. The opportunity to cure addresses that risk of forfeiture, giving the breaching party a second chance to raise its performance to the nonmaterial breach level required under these contracts.

On the other hand, cure in Article 2 is limited in order to alleviate the impact of the perfect tender rule and allow a second chance to meet buyer expectations of receiving a conforming tender. Because the goods themselves are returned to the breaching seller, sellers faced with a rightful revocation of acceptance do not face a forfeiture risk comparable to that faced by construction contractors.

Extending the cure right in one class of revocation cases clearly would be unjustified. A buyer who accepts goods while aware of a nonconformity is entitled to revoke only if the buyer accepted the goods "on the reasonable assumption that its non-conformity would be cured and it has not been seasonably cured."[195] The buyer is allowed to revoke in this situation only after

---

[193] A.F.L. Flack, S.p.A. v. E. A. Karay Co. 639 F. Supp. 314, 1 UCC Rep. Serv. 2d 1500 (S.D. N.Y. 1987); Conte v. Dwan Lincoln-Mercury, Inc., 374 A.2d 144, 20 UCC Rep. Serv. 899 (Conn. 1976).

[194] Bonebrake v. Cox, 499 F.2d 951, 14 UCC Rep. Serv. 1318 (8th Cir. 1974); Gappelberg v. Landrum, 666 S.W.2d 88 (Tex. 1984).

[195] UCC § 2–608(1)(a).

the cure effort has already failed. Sellers in these cases surely should not be afforded a second cure opportunity.

In respect to these cases, many courts and commentators have failed to recognize the implicit right to cure that is included in sections 2–607 and 2–608.[196] A buyer who accepts nonconforming goods under the assumption that the seller will cure them can revoke due to the defects only if cure does not follow seasonably. Therefore, the buyer implicitly grants the seller in these cases an opportunity to cure *after* acceptance by the buyer but *before* revocation.[197]

[D]   Wrongful Revocation

If a buyer who is not entitled to reject nevertheless follows applicable procedures by seasonably notifying the seller of its rejection promptly after tender of the goods, the buyer generally is considered to have rejected. The rejection is wrongful, making the buyer liable for breach. But the rejection is nevertheless effective, which precludes the consequences of an acceptance.[198]

The rationale that underlies recognition of a wrongful but nevertheless effective rejection is based on economic efficiency. The seller is generally in a better position than the buyer to dispose of the rejected goods and to minimize damages. With even a wrongful return through rejection, the seller is required to utilize its superior resale position and to satisfy itself with damages against the breaching buyer.

The same rationale has some merit in the context of wrongful revocation, but it is outweighed by other considerations that justify treating revocation differently from rejection.[199] The goods are more likely to have deteriorated or depreciated in a revocation context. The seller's superior ability to dispose of the goods might diminish when the nature or quality of the goods changes. Furthermore, the policy reasons that support making revocation of acceptance less readily available than rejection to an aggrieved buyer[200] also justify a refusal to recognize the effectiveness of a wrongful revocation. Article 2 does not

---

[196] Jensen v. Seigel Mobile Homes Group, 668 P.2d 65, 69, 35 UCC Rep. Serv. 804 (Idaho 1983) ("A right to cure is relevant only when a buyer has rejected the goods prior to a formal acceptance and the Uniform Commercial Code does not allow a seller the right to cure defects following a buyer's acceptance of the goods").

[197] Champion Ford Sales, Inc. v. Levine, 433 A.2d 1218, 1222, 32 UCC Rep. Serv. 108 (Md. Ct. Spec. App. 1981) (seller has right to cure when "buyer accepts nonconforming goods with the expectation that the nonconformity will be remedied").

[198] Integrated Circuits Unlimited v. E. F. Johnson Co., 875 F.2d 1040, 8 UCC Rep. Serv. 2d 695 (2d Cir. 1989).

[199] *See* J. White & R. Summers, *Uniform Commercial Code* 291–92, 295–97 (3d student ed. 1988).

[200] *See* § 7.05[A] *supra*.

stipulate the consequences of a wrongful revocation, however, thus leaving the issue in considerable doubt.[201]

[E]   Revocation and Privity

Courts traditionally have required privity between the parties before the buyer is entitled to revoke.[202] Thus, buyers have generally not been entitled to revoke their purchase of goods and recover their payments from a distant manufacturer with whom they did not contract. This limitation on revocation is based upon the Code use of the term "seller" in the provisions dealing with acceptance and revocation.[203]

A few courts have shown a willingness to extend the traditional bounds by allowing revocation against a manufacturer of the goods. Most of these cases involve the breach of an express warranty extended by the manufacturer.[204] An occasional court has also allowed revocation against the manufacturer when the dealer who sold the goods became insolvent following the sale.[205]

[F]   Compensation for Use of Goods

A buyer who has successfully revoked may be held to have reaccepted the goods by continuing to use them. The varied responses of courts with respect to continued use have been discussed already in the context of buyer use following a purported rejection.[206] Several courts now recognize circumstances in which continued use of the goods will not bind the buyer to a reacceptance.[207]

A buyer who accepts goods, revokes the acceptance, and continues to use the goods may benefit considerably from the extended use of the seller's

---

[201] Akron Brick & Block Co. v. Moniz Engineering Co., Inc., 365 Mass. 92, 310 N.E.2d 128, 14 UCC Rep. Serv. 563 (1974) (relying on statement in Comment 2 that revocation is "possible" only when limitations to the section are met). *But see* UCC § 2–703 ("[w]here the buyer wrongfully rejects or revokes"); UCC § 2–709(3) (same).

[202] Voytovich v. Bangor Punta Operations, Inc., 494 F.2d 1208, 15 UCC Rep. Serv. 45 (6th Cir. 1974); Seekings v. Jimmy GMC of Tucson, Inc., 131 Ariz. 1, 638 P.2d 210, 32 UCC Rep. Serv. 1450 (1981).

[203] "Seller" means "a person who sells or contracts to sell goods." UCC § 2–103(1)(d).

[204] Gochey v. Bombardier, Inc., 153 Vt. 607, 572 A.2d 921, 11 UCC Rep. Serv. 870 (1990); Durfee v. Rod Baxter Imports, Inc., 262 N.W. 349, 22 UCC Rep. Serv. 945 (Minn. 1977).

[205] Ford Motor Credit Co. v. Harper, 671 F.2d 1117, 33 UCC Rep. Serv. 921 (8th Cir. 1982).

[206] *See* § 7.04[B][3] *supra.*

[207] Some courts have focused on problems related to financing the delivered product or the practical problems of effecting a cover.

goods.[208] This use of the goods can occur prior to the actual revocation,[209] as well as after notification of revocation in appropriate circumstances.[210] To the extent that use confers a benefit on the buyer, the buyer should be required to compensate the seller.

Even though Article 2 does not refer to a duty to compensate sellers in these cases, an expanding number of courts have imposed such a duty.[211] Because the Code does not displace the applicable principles of common law in this context,[212] these courts appropriately rely on such principles, most notably restitution. Under this approach, the compensation should be based on the benefit received by the buyer rather than on application of the contract terms or calculations based on cost to the seller.

[G] Irrevocable Promises in Finance Leases [2A–407]

The right to revoke an acceptance is severely constrained in the finance lease context. The finance lessor acts merely as a financing conduit to facilitate the lessee's acquisition of the goods from the manufacturer or the supplier. The warranties of the manufacturer or supplier are extended to the finance lessee, so in the event of a problem with the goods, the finance lessee's remedy is to pursue the manufacturer or the supplier. The finance lessee generally does not have an option to revoke the acceptance or even to set off rental payments due under the lease. Article 2A provides that in a finance lease that is not also a consumer lease "the lessee's promises under the lease contract become irrevocable and independent upon the lessee's acceptance of the goods."[213] This provision is a statutory enactment having the effect of a "hell or high water" clause commonly included in finance leases.[214] This clause is so named (the term was

---

[208] Stroh v. American Recreation & Mobile Home Corp., 530 P.2d 989, 16 UCC Rep. Serv. 726 (Colo. Ct. App. 1975) (one year of occupancy before revocation and another 17 months of subsequent occupancy).

[209] Pavesi v. Ford Motor Co., 382 A.2d 954, 23 UCC Rep. Serv. 929 (N.J. Sup. Ct., Ch. Div. 1978).

[210] Johannsen v. Minnesota Valley Ford Tractor Co., 304 N.W.2d 654, 31 UCC Rep. Serv. 558 (Minn. 1984).

[211] North River Homes, Inc. v. Bosarge, 594 So. 2d 1153, 17 UCC Rep. Serv. 2d 121 (Miss. 1992); Johnson v. General Motors Corp., 668 P.2d 139, 36 UCC Rep. Serv. 1089 (Kan. 1983); Jorgensen v. Presnall, 545 P.2d 1382, 18 UCC Rep. Serv. 1206 (Or. 1976); Stroh v. American Recreation & Mobile Home Corp., 530 P.2d 989, 16 UCC Rep. Serv. 726 (Colo. Ct. App. 1975). Cases that have not allowed compensation for use include *Zoss v. Royal Chevrolet, Inc.*, 11 UCC Rep. Serv. 527 (Ind. Super. Ct. 1972).

[212] UCC § 1–103.

[213] UCC § 2A–407(1).

[214] Stewart v. United States Leasing Corp., 702 S.W.2d 288 (Tex. Ct. App. 1985) (lessee who signed acceptance certificate held liable to lessor despite nondelivery of equipment from supplier).

originally used in ship charter agreements) to indicate the lessee's responsibility to continue making payments under the lease after accepting the goods, regardless of subsequent events.

The provision in Article 2A that a finance lessee's promises are irrevocable upon acceptance cannot be taken literally. The provision on revocation preserves the right for a finance lessee, but only when acceptance was induced by assurances of the finance lessor.[215] The finance lessee's reliance on assurances from the finance lessor can reduce the lessee's vigilance in inspecting the goods and is thus the basis for granting the finance lessee the right to revoke. Revocation is precluded for finance lessees in the other two circumstances in which revocation is generally allowed for lessees and buyers.[216] The finance lessee cannot look to the finance lessor for cure, so the finance lessee is not allowed to revoke an acceptance that was induced on the assumption that the nonconformity would be cured. Since the finance lessor did not participate in selection of the goods, the finance lessee is not allowed to revoke due to a nonconformity in the goods that was difficult to discover prior to acceptance.

Part B: Breach or Default

§ 7.06   SALE OF GOODS

[A]   Breach by Seller [2–711]

Although Article 2 states that the seller's obligation is to transfer and deliver,[217] it is more specific with respect to the circumstances that lead to breach by the seller. Section 2–711 in Article 2 provides an index of the Code remedies available to an aggrieved buyer. The significance of the provision is easily overlooked, however, because the applicable section focuses on remedies. The preamble language of this section articulates the circumstances of breach by the seller that are sufficient to entitle the buyer to invoke the Code remedies.

The section 2–711 index identifies four instances of seller breach. Two of them are consistent with general contract-law analysis. A seller who fails to deliver in accordance with the terms of the contract has not fulfilled the

---

[215] UCC § 2A–517(1)(b).
[216] See § 7.05[A][1] supra.
[217] UCC § 2–301. See § 7.01 supra.

contract obligation and thus breaches.[218] Similarly, a seller who makes an anticipatory repudiation breaches the contract and thereby entitles the buyer to the stated remedies. The remaining two instances of seller breach are based on actions taken by the buyer. Breach sufficient to invoke the statutory remedies also results when the buyer rightfully rejects or justifiably revokes acceptance.

[B] Breach by Buyer [2–703]

The comparable index provision for breach by the buyer is section 2–703. The preamble provision also identifies four instances of breach by the buyer. Article 2 states that a buyer is obligated to accept conforming goods and to pay for them. The stated instances of breach naturally are tied to these obligations. Consequently, a buyer breaches by wrongfully rejecting tendered goods or wrongfully revoking acceptance of goods, as these actions violate the duty to accept. Failure to pay is another identified form of breach. The fourth instance is anticipatory repudiation.

§ 7.07   LEASE OF GOODS

[A] Default

Article 2A follows some of the Article 2 approach described above, but it also incorporates some differences. Similar to sections 2–711 and 2–703 on general remedies for buyers and sellers, sections 2A–508 and 2A–523 identify the range of remedies available to lessees and lessors. Whereas Article 2 ties the availability of these remedies to specific instances of breach by the seller or the buyer, Article 2A is stated in terms of default by the lessor or the lessee. The reference to default uses the concept as applied in Article 9.

The initial section of Part 5 of Article 2A states fundamental provisions concerning default under a lease agreement. Part 5 covers the remedies available to aggrieved parties following default. The initial section of Part 5 is patterned after section 9–501 of Article 9 on secured transactions. Following a default by the lessor or the lessee, the aggrieved party has the rights and remedies provided in Article 2A and in the lease agreement.[219] Article 9 provides rights and remedies predominantly in favor of secured parties against their defaulting debtors. Article 2A departs from this approach by providing an extensive array

---

[218] The index provision is not as complete as it ought to be because it does not index the section 2–714 remedy for breach of warranty that applies when a buyer accepts nonconforming goods. *See* § 8.05 *infra*. The breach of warranty remedy should have also been indexed, in which case breach includes both nondelivery and improper delivery.

[219] UCC § 2A–501(2).

of remedies for both lessors and lessees. The addition of substantial remedies for both parties was required because the nature of the obligations in a lease contract is more bilateral than under a secured transaction.[220] In this respect, the remedies approach is again comparable to Article 2.

Also in keeping with the general default approach of Article 9, Section 2A–501(3) establishes that on default by the lessor or the lessee, "the party seeking enforcement may reduce the party's claim to judgment, or otherwise enforce the lease contract by self-help or any available judicial procedure or nonjudicial procedure, including administrative proceeding, arbitration, or the like." This provision is simply an expanded statement of Section 9–501(1), which reflects the procedures available to a foreclosing secured party. Consequently, some of the options, particularly self-help, have the greatest relevance in cases of lessors' remedies.

In determining what constitutes default, Article 2A resembles Article 9 in some respects but differs substantially in others. Neither article specifically defines default. Article 9 does not address the matter at all, leaving it to the parties to determine in their security agreement what events will be sufficient to establish the debtor's default.[221] Courts have held that, in the absence of a clause in the security agreement defining events of default, the only implicit basis for default is nonpayment by the debtor.[222] Article 2A goes further, providing in section 2A–501 that "[w]hether the lessor or the lessee is in default under a lease contract is determined by the lease agreement and this Article."[223]

Although Article 2A includes indexes that state statutory forms of default, the lease agreement itself can designate other bases of default. For example, it may impose specified obligations on the lessee, such as a requirement to insure the goods or to provide regular maintenance service. Alternatively, the lease agreement may impose specified obligations on the lessor, such as the duty to maintain or repair the goods. Failure to comply with any of these additional obligations can be made the basis for default.

Any additional methods that may constitute a default must be identified in the lease agreement before Article 2A remedies are available. Like the secured transactions approach under Article 9, an agreement creating an obligation of the lessee or prohibiting certain actions by the lessee is not alone sufficient to invoke the statutory remedies. A separate default clause is required to specify

---

[220] UCC § 2A–101, Comment.
[221] *See* B. Clark, *The Law of Secured Transactions Under the Uniform Commercial Code* ¶ 4.02 (1988).
[222] Whisenhunt v. Allen Parker Co., 119 Ga. App. 813, 168 S.E.2d 827, 6 UCC Rep. Serv. 969 (1969).
[223] UCC § 2A–501(1).

the various actions required or prohibited elsewhere in the lease. Often, however, a general default provision is simply added, making the breach of any covenant in the agreement an event of default.[224] If the lease imposes additional obligations on the lessee, but does not specifically consider their breach a default, the lessor's remedy is for common-law damages for breach of contract.

[B] Default by Lessor [2A–508]

Article 2A is comparable to Article 2 in listing specific instances of statutory default and including them in the index of remedies for each party. The index of lessee remedies is provided in section 2A–508(1) and includes four instances of lessor default. These four instances reflect the same instances of breach by a seller under Article 2. They are failure of the lessor to deliver goods in conformity with the contract, anticipatory repudiation by the lessor, rightful rejection of the goods by the lessee, and justifiable revocation of acceptance by the lessee.

[C] Default by Lessee [2A–523]

The index of lessor remedies in section 2A–523 also includes the four standard instances of default by a lessee. A lessee defaults statutorily by wrongfully rejecting, wrongfully revoking acceptance, failing to pay as required, or anticipatorily repudiating.

Part C: Prospective Impairment of Expectations

§ 7.08 GENERAL

In addition to the basic obligations imposed on buyers and sellers to perform their respective duties when they become due under the contract, Article 2 is consistent with common law in recognizing obligations that arise immediately upon contract formation: "A contract for sale imposes an obligation on each party that the other's expectation of receiving due performance will not be impaired."[225] Protection of the reasonable expectations of parties to a contract requires, in addition to timely execution of the promised performance, that neither party prospectively impair the reasonable expectations of the other party. Provisions on anticipatory repudiation and the right to demand adequate assurance of performance address problems associated with prospective

---

[224] UCC § 2A–303, Comment 1.
[225] UCC § 2–609(1). Section 2A–401(1) is comparable.

impairment. A provision that determines when an aggrieved party can cancel the executory portion of an installment contract is also relevant.

§ 7.09   ANTICIPATORY REPUDIATION [2–610; 2A–402]

The provision on anticipatory repudiation follows the common-law concept very closely. The doctrine of anticipatory repudiation was recognized in the famous case of *Hochster v. De La Tour*,[226] in which an employee was permitted to sue his employer for repudiation even though the time for the employee to start work had not yet commenced. The doctrine of anticipatory repudiation provides the aggrieved party with immediate remedies even when the promised performance of the repudiating party is not yet due.

[A]   What Constitutes Repudiation

Article 2 provides remedies "[w]hen either party repudiates the contract with respect to a performance not yet due the loss of which will substantially impair the value of the contract to the other."[227] The determination that a repudiation has occurred is consistent with the approach of common law.[228] The Comments indicate that "anticipatory repudiation centers upon an overt communication of intention or an action which renders performance impossible or demonstrates a clear determination not to continue with performance."[229]

In addition to a definite and unequivocal indication of repudiation prior to the time for performance, an anticipatory repudiation must "substantially impair the value of the contract to the other."[230] The Comments provide an indication of when this standard has been met: "whether material inconvenience or injustice will result if the aggrieved party is forced to wait and receive

---

[226] 2 El. & B. 678, 118 Eng. Rep. 922 (Q.B. 1853).

[227] UCC § 2–610. Section 2A–402 is comparable.

[228] Pillsbury Co. v. Ward, 250 N.W.2d 35, 21 UCC Rep. Serv. 118 (Iowa 1977) (buyer's delay of delivery date was substantial impairment, which was comparable to common-law material breach).

[229] UCC § 2–610, Comment 1. Barclays Am. Business Credit Inc., v. E & E Enters., Inc., 697 S.W.2d 694, 42 UCC Rep. Serv. 706 (Tex. Ct. App. 1985) (statement by seller/assignor to buyer/account debtor that the plant was closing and it would not deliver orders was a repudiation); Red River Commodities, Inc. v. Eidsness, 459 N.W.2d 811, 13 UCC Rep. Serv. 2d 1084 (N.D. 1990) (sale of harvested sunflower to a third party was repudiation). *But see* Gatoil (USA), Inc. v. Washington Metro. Area Transit Auth., 801 F.2d 451, 2 UCC Rep. Serv. 2d 151 (D.C. Cir. 1986) (communications to buyer about difficulties obtaining a supplier did not constitute repudiation).

[230] UCC § 2–610.

an ultimate tender minus the part or aspect repudiated."[231] Substantial impairment is similar to the common-law standard of material breach.[232]

[B]   Options of the Aggrieved Party

The aggrieved party has several options following an anticipatory repudiation. One option is to waive the right to proceed against the repudiating party and instead await a retraction of the repudiation.[233] This enables the repudiating party to retract and thereby reinstate the contract.[234] The aggrieved party can pursue this course only for a commercially reasonable time and exercise of this alternative is also subject to the mitigation-of-damages principle.

For example, in *Oloffson v. Coomer*[235] a farmer was under contract to grow and deliver in October a specified quantity of corn to a grain merchant. The season had been too wet for planting, so on June 3 the farmer told the merchant to obtain corn from other sources. Rather than trying to cover following this repudiation, the merchant kept insisting on delivery from the farmer. The court determined that the merchant's awaiting performance by the farmer and not covering under these circumstances were not reasonable. The court limited the merchant's damages to the losses sustained on the date of repudiation rather than basing them on the date of actual cover following the scheduled delivery dates.

---

[231] UCC 2–610, Comment 3.

[232] Neptune Research & Dev., Inc. v. Teknics Indus. Sys., Inc., 235 N.J. Sup. 522, 563 A.2d 465, 10 UCC Rep. Serv. 2d 107 (1989). This court applied the criteria of Section 214 of the Restatement (Second) of Contracts to determine if a breach is material. These criteria are as follows:

(a) the extent to which the injured party will be deprived of the benefit which he reasonably expected;

(b) the extent to which the injured party can be adequately compensated for the part of that benefit of which he will be deprived;

(c) the extent to which the party failing to perform or to offer to perform will suffer forfeiture;

(d) the likelihood that the party failing to perform or to offer to perform will cure his failure, taking account of all the circumstances including any reasonable assurances;

(e) the extent to which the behavior of the party failing to perform or to offer to perform comports with standards of good faith and fair dealing.

[233] Fredonia Broadcasting Corp. v. RCA Corp., 481 F.2d 781, 12 UCC Rep. Serv. 1088 (5th Cir. 1973).

[234] *See* § 7.09[C] *infra.*

[235] 11 Ill. App. 3d 918, 296 N.E.2d 871, 12 UCC Rep. Serv. 1082 (1973).

An aggrieved party also has the right to demand adequate assurances of performance from the repudiating party.[236] The aggrieved party always has this right when reasonable expectations of performance by the other party are prospectively impaired.[237] This right is provided in section 2–609 and is discussed in the next section of this text. It allows the aggrieved party, rather than simply waiting on the repudiating party, to take action that is still short of invoking the doctrine of anticipatory repudiation. It allows the repudiating party a second chance to perform under the contract, but only if timely assurance of that performance is forthcoming.

An aggrieved party that decides to invoke the doctrine can do so by invoking a remedy for breach. Applicable remedies for buyers and sellers are indexed in sections 2–711 and 2–703 respectively. These provisions both recognize anticipatory repudiation as a form of breach that makes the remedies available for an aggrieved party. The applicable remedies include recovery of money damages and cancellation of the contract.[238]

An anticipatory repudiation also justifies an aggrieved party who is currently performing to suspend that performance.[239] Continuation of performance is not necessary following the other party's unequivocal refusal to perform under the contract. Thus, in *Unique Systems, Inc. v. Zotos International, Inc.*,[240] a seller whose contract required it to develop and manufacture hairspray systems for the buyer was entitled to suspend its efforts on the contract after the buyer repudiated by indicating that it would not proceed until market tests that were not required in the contract were conducted with results satisfactory to the buyer.

[C]   Retraction [2–611; 2A–403]

A repudiating party can sometimes retract the repudiation and thereby reinstate the contract. The retraction must occur before the next performance is due and before the aggrieved party has "canceled or materially changed his

---

[236] Hudson Feather & Down Prods., Inc. v. Lancer Clothing Corp., 513 N.Y.S.2d 173, 3 UCC Rep. Serv. 2d 1804 (1987) (repudiation creates reasonable grounds for insecurity, thus entitling the aggrieved party to demand assurances).

[237] UCC § 2–609.

[238] A difficult statutory construction issue is posed when an aggrieved buyer seeks damages measured on the contract price/market price differential following an anticipatory repudiation. For discussion of this issue, *see* § 8.04[B][2] *infra*.

[239] Created Gemstones, Inc. v. Union Carbide Corp., 417 N.Y.S.2d 905, 391 N.E.2d 987, 26 UCC Rep. Serv. 712 (1979) (repudiation by seller entitled buyer to suspend payments on gems previously delivered).

[240] 622 F.2d 373, 28 UCC Rep. Serv. 1340 (8th Cir. 1980).

position or otherwise indicated that he considers the repudiation final."[241] The occurrence of any of these events prior to retraction terminates the right to retract.[242] Aggrieved parties have been found to have materially changed their position, for example, by purchasing the goods from another source[243] and by ceasing to advertise the seller's products.[244] When these events have not occurred, allowing a retraction is sensible because it enables the repudiating party to reinstate the contract under circumstances in which the interests of the aggrieved party are not prejudiced. The aggrieved party may actually be waiting to see if a retraction will be forthcoming. The aggrieved party's interests, even with respect to delay resulting from the repudiation, are protected when rights are reinstated under the contract "with due allowance to the aggrieved party for any delay occasioned by the repudiation."[245]

A retraction can be made "by any method which clearly indicates to the aggrieved party that the repudiating party intends to perform."[246] The intention can be manifested through words or conduct.[247] It will be insufficient if it includes conditions to which the repudiating party is not entitled.[248] The aggrieved party can make justifiable demands for assurances of performance.

[D] Installment Contracts [2–612(3); 2A–510(2)]

In determining whether an aggrieved party can treat a nonconformity or default in delivery under an installment contract as a default with respect to the entire contract, the Code uses the same test applied to a default based on an anticipatory repudiation. Section 2–612(3) provides, "Whenever nonconformity or default with respect to one or more installments substantially impairs the value of the whole contract there is a breach of the whole." With

---

[241] UCC § 2–611(1). Section 2A–403 is comparable.

[242] Neptune Research & Dev., Inc. v. Tecknics Indus. Sys., Inc., 235 N.J. Super. 522, 563 A.2d 465, 10 UCC Rep. Serv. 2d 107 (1989) (attempted retraction later the same day as repudiation was too late because buyer canceled the contract in the interim).

[243] Bonebrake v. Cox, 499 F.2d 951, 14 UCC Rep. Serv. 1318 (8th Cir. 1974) (bowling alley equipment).

[244] Record Club of Am., Inc. v. United Artists Records, Inc., 643 F. Supp. 925, 2 UCC Rep. Serv. 2d 1310 (S.D. N.Y. 1986).

[245] UCC § 2–611(3).

[246] UCC § 2–611(2).

[247] Gibbs, Nathaniel (Can.) Ltd. v. International Multifoods Corp., 804 F.2d 450, 2 UCC Rep. Serv. 2d 1312 (8th Cir. 1986) (agreement by buyer to accept subsequent delivery); Fast v. Southern Offshore Yachts, 587 F. Supp. 1354, 38 UCC Rep. Serv. 1569 (D. Conn. 1984) (buyer's execution and signature of proposed escrow agreement for balance due on sale served as retraction).

[248] Pittsburgh-Des Moines Steel Co. v. Brookhaven Manor Water Co., 532 F.2d 572, 18 UCC Rep. Serv. 931 (7th Cir. 1976) (seller indicated it would begin construction of a large water tank on receipt of personal guarantee of payment by buyer's president).

substantial impairment to the whole contract, the aggrieved party is entitled to treat the default on a particular installment like an anticipatory repudiation of the entire contract. Substantial impairment of the value of the whole lease contract allows the aggrieved party to pursue remedies for default for all of the goods under the installment lease contract.

The Comments direct the focus to the appropriate standard. They state that "[w]hether the non-conformity in any given installment justifies cancellation as to the future depends, not on whether such non-conformity indicates an intent or likelihood that the future deliveries will also be defective, but whether the non-conformity substantially impairs the value of the whole contract."[249]

The distinction is drawn neatly in *Holiday Manufacturing Corp. v. BASF Systems, Inc.*,[250] a case involving a contract for the manufacture of 6 million cassettes to be delivered at the rate of 500,000 per month. The initial deliveries contained substantial defects, but the court nevertheless found that the non-conformities did not substantially impair the value of the contract to the buyer. The court reached its conclusion based on the buyer's ability to cure the defects and the buyer's lack of protest about the delays required for the cures. By way of contrast in *SJ Groves & Sons Co. v. Warner Co,*[251] the court found that substantial impairment resulted from the seller's failure to deliver adequate supplies of concrete at the scheduled times because this caused delays in construction that resulted in heavy overtime expenses.[252]

Several cases involve the refusal of sellers to ship any more goods under an installment contract because their buyers have failed to make timely payments for earlier installments. The Comments also provide helpful insight to these cases: "If only the seller's security in regard to future installments is impaired, he has the right to demand adequate assurances of proper performance but has not an immediate right to cancel the entire contract."[253] The applicable test is substantial impairment of the value of the whole contract. Sellers generally must first demand assurances of performance.[254] If such reassurances are not forthcoming within a commercially reasonable time, the impairment can

---

[249] UCC § 2–610. Comment 6.

[250] 380 F. Supp. 1096, 15 UCC Rep. Serv. 820 (D.C. Neb. 1974).

[251] 576 F.2d 524, 24 UCC Rep. Serv. 1 (3d Cir. 1978).

[252] *See also* Graulich Caterer Inc. v. Hans Holterbosch, Inc., 101 N.J. Super. 61, 243 A.2d 253, 5 UCC Rep. Serv. 440 (1968) (substantial impairment when seller could not deliver quality food comparable to samples used to form the contract and buyer needed the food daily for its World's Fair pavilion).

[253] UCC § 2–610, Comment 6.

[254] Cassidy Podel Lynch, Inc. v. SnyderGeneral Corp., 944 F.2d 1131, 15 UCC Rep. Serv. 2d 1225 (3d Cir. 1991) (failure to demand assurance).

ripen into anticipatory repudiation.[255] Withholding further shipments without a prior demand for assurances can constitute a breach by the seller.[256]

As the case of *Cherwell-Ralli, Inc. v. Rytman Grain Co.*[257] demonstrates, however, a demand for adequate assurances is not required in all cases. The buyer contended incorrectly that a seller in an installment contract may never cancel, even though the buyer is repeatedly in default on payment, without first demanding adequate assurances of performance. The buyer was substantially behind on its payments and, becoming concerned about future deliveries, it sought assurances from the seller. The seller indicated it would continue to deliver if the buyer paid for prior shipments. The buyer sent a check, but stopped payment when concerned again about deliveries. The court upheld the seller's cancellation of the contract. The Comments provide support for the result: "It is clear under this Article, however, that defects in prior installments are cumulative in effect, so that acceptance does not wash out the defect 'waived.' "[258]

§ 7.10 DEMAND FOR ASSURANCES OF PERFORMANCE [2–609; 2A–401]

[A] The Right

If the reasonable expectations of a party to a sales contract are impaired, but not sufficiently to allow the aggrieved party to invoke the doctrine of anticipatory repudiation, another response is available under Article 2. The aggrieved party can demand adequate assurance of performance from the other party to remove the impairment.[259] Failure of the other party to provide an adequate response causes the impairment to ripen into a full-blown anticipatory repudiation.[260] The Code approach allows the aggrieved party to take a more assertive stance than is available under the traditional common-law doctrine of prospective inability to perform.[261]

The right to make a demand for assurances is provided in the first subsection of section 2–609: "When reasonable grounds for insecurity arise with respect to the performance of either party the other may in writing demand

---

[255] *See* § 7.10[B] *infra*.

[256] Gulf Chem. & Metallurgical Corp. v. Sylvan Chem. Corp., 122 N.J. Super. 499, 300 A.2d 878, 12 UCC Rep. Serv. 117 (1973) (no showing by seller that buyer's failure to pay for first installment substantially impaired value of contract to seller).

[257] 433 A.2d 984, 29 UCC Rep. Serv. 513 (Conn. 1980).

[258] UCC § 2–612, Comment 6.

[259] UCC § 2–609. Section 2A–401 is comparable.

[260] *See* UCC § 2–609(4).

[261] *See* J. Calamari & J. Perillo, *The Law of Contracts* § 12–2 (3d ed. 1987); Robertson, *The Right to Demand Adequate Assurance of Due Performance under UCC Section 2–609 and Restatement (Second) of Contracts Section 251*, 38 Drake L. Rev. 305 (1989).

adequate assurance of due performance and until he receives such assurance may if commercially reasonable suspend any performance for which he has not already received the agreed return." The demand must be in writing.[262] The Comments clarify that a significant degree of impairment is generally required: "If either the willingness or the ability of a party to perform declines materially between the time of contracting and the time for performance, the other party is threatened with the loss of a substantial part of what he has bargained for."[263]

Decided cases provide a contextual basis for understanding the relevant types of impairment. Courts have found adequate grounds for insecurity in the following: a seller failed to provide roof trusses on a regular basis as required on a construction project,[264] a high percentage of goods delivered in a prior installment were defective,[265] a seller indicated its intention to alter the terms of the contract unilaterally,[266] a buyer was known to be in financial difficulties,[267] a buyer breached on another grain contract with the seller,[268] and a buyer learned that similar goods sold by the seller to other buyers had proved to be defective.[269] Courts have found that reasonable grounds for insecurity were not present, however, in the following cases: a buyer's concerns about future performance based on its subjective evaluations and unsupported assumptions about the market and not on objective, identifiable conduct of the seller,[270] a merchant's delay in forwarding papers in a sale of heifers,[271] a buyer's uncertainty about performance by its principal supplier when the buyer had several other suppliers available who could deliver,[272] and a low cash balance in the bank account of a buyer with substantial assets.[273]

---

[262] Continental Grain Co. v. McFarland, 628 F.2d 1348, 29 UCC Rep. Serv. 512 (4th Cir. 1980); USX Corp. v. Union Pac. Resources Co., 753 S.W.2d 845, 7 UCC Rep. Serv. 2d 100 (Tex. Ct. App. 1988).

[263] UCC 2–609, Comment 1.

[264] Universal Builders Corp. v. United Methodist Convalescent Homes of Conn., 7 Conn. App. 318, 508 A.2d 819, 1 UCC Rep. Serv. 2d 763 (1986).

[265] T&S Brass & Bronze Works, Inc. v. Pic-Air, Inc., 790 F.2d 1098, 1 UCC Rep. Serv. 2d 433 (4th Cir. 1986).

[266] Copylease Corp. of Am. v. Memorex Corp., 403 F. Supp. 625, 18 UCC Rep. Serv. 317 (S.D. N.Y. 1975).

[267] Lubrication & Maintenance, Inc. v. Union Resources Co., 522 F. Supp. 1078, 32 UCC Rep. Serv. 1117 (S.D. N.Y. 1981).

[268] National Farmers Org. v. Bartlett & Co., 560 F.2d 1350, 22 UCC Rep. Serv. 658 (8th Cir. 1977).

[269] Creusot-Lorie Int'l, Inc. v. Coppus Eng'g Corp., 585 F. Supp. 45, 39 UCC Rep. Serv. 186 (S.D. N.Y. 1983).

[270] Universal Resources Corp. v. Panhandle Eastern Pipe Line Co., 813 F.2d 77, 3 UCC Rep. Serv. 2d 988 (5th Cir. 1987).

[271] Cole v. Melvin, 441 F. Supp. 193, 22 UCC Rep. Serv. 1154 (D. S.D. 1977).

[272] In re Coast Trading Co., Inc, 26 B.R. 737, 35 UCC Rep. Serv. 1180 (D. Or. 1982).

[273] Pittsburgh-Des Moines Steel Co. v. Brookhaven Manor Water Co., 532 F.2d 572, 18 UCC Rep. Serv. 931 (7th Cir. 1976).

The Code does not provide guidance on the form of the demand for assurances. The cases show, however, that it should be specific enough to communicate to the other party that the party is suspending performance while awaiting assurances or that a failure to provide assurances will be treated as a repudiation. The courts have found the following to be inadequate: a request for information,[274] an indication that the buyer wished to meet with the seller,[275] and a request for acceleration of payment for the first shipment of goods.[276]

An aggrieved party should not make a demand for excessive assurances. The right extends to demand adequate assurances only, but not more.[277] Some courts have unduly restricted the scope of proper demand by limiting the aggrieved party to demand only what it is entitled to under the terms of the contract.[278] A mere verbalized response indicating that performance will be forthcoming will not be sufficient in some cases to remove an impairment to the aggrieved party's expectations. Courts have sustained demanded assurances in the form of an escrow deposit,[279] correction of quantity and quality control problems,[280] confirmation of intent to receive shipments,[281] and a guarantee and a letter of credit.[282]

[B]   Effect of the Demand

After receiving a justified demand, a party has a reasonable time not exceeding 30 days in which to provide adequate assurances.[283] When adequate

---

[274] SPS Indus., Inc. v. Atlantic Steel Co., 186 Ga. App. 94, 366 S.E.2d 410, 6 UCC Rep. Serv. 2d 122 (1988) (letter requesting information as to why shipment was late).

[275] Penberthy Electromelt Int'l, Inc. v. U.S. Gypsum Co., 38 Wash. App. 514, 686 P.2d 1138, 39 UCC Rep. Serv. 891 (1984).

[276] National Ropes, Inc., v. National Diving Serv., Inc., 513 F.2d 53, 16 UCC Rep. Serv. 1376 (5th Cir. 1975).

[277] U.S. v. Great Plains Gasification Assocs., 819 F.2d 831, 4 UCC Rep. Serv. 2d 1442 (8th Cir. 1987) (purchaser of natural gas could not seek assurances of long-term sales under contract that allowed seller to abandon services in good faith).

[278] Scott v. Crown, 765 P.2d 1043, 7 UCC Rep. Serv. 2d 464 (Colo. Ct. App. 1988).

[279] Kunian v. Development Corp. of Am., 165 Conn. 300, 334 A.2d 427, 12 UCC Rep. Serv. 1125 (1973) (insecurity based on failure to make payments or abide by subsequent promises to pay).

[280] LNS Inv. Co., Inc. v. Phillips, 66 Co., 731 F. Supp. 1484, 12 UCC Rep. Serv. 2d 113 (D. Kan. 1990) (insecurity based on unacceptable quantity and quality of goods ordered).

[281] USX Corp. v. Union Pac. Resources Co., 753 S.W.2d 845, 7 UCC Rep. Serv. 2d 100 (Tex. Ct. App. 1988).

[282] Creusot-Lorie Int'l, Inc. v. Coppus Eng'g Corp., 585 F. Supp. 45, 39 UCC Rep. Serv. 186 (S.D. N.Y. 1983) (insecurity based on similar goods failing when provided to other buyers).

[283] UCC § 2–609(4).

assurances are provided, the impairment is eliminated, and the aggrieved party must continue with its performance.[284] Failure to provide adequate assurances of due performance causes an impairment that initially created only reasonable grounds for insecurity to escalate to a full-fledged repudiation.[285] Thus a demand for assurances is a tool available to the aggrieved party to address uncertainty about the other party's performance: adequate assurances must be forthcoming to alleviate the uncertainty, or else the contract can be treated as repudiated.

Part D: Excuse

§ 7.11   FUNDAMENTAL VERSUS INCIDENTAL

Even though a sales or lease contract imposes fixed obligations on the parties, the Code recognizes defenses based on contingencies that were unforeseen at the time of contract formation. The defense of excuse is recognized because unanticipated difficulties intervene to make performance considerably more difficult or even impossible.[286] The Code defenses reflect the common-law doctrine of impossibility of performance,[287] and extend beyond common law in embracing the doctrine of commercial impracticability.[288]

The sales provisions on excuse cover casualty to identified goods, substituted performance, and failure of presupposed conditions. Section 2–613 provides excuse when identified goods suffer casualty. Section 2–614 permits

---

[284] American Bronze Corp v. Streamway Prods., 8 Ohio App. 3d 223, 456 N.E.2d 1295, 37 UCC Rep. Serv. 687 (1982) (buyer responded to demand concerning payment by tendering a check for all outstanding accounts and agreeing to the demand to make prompt payment of new accounts).

[285] UCC § 2–609(4). Cassidy Podel Lynch, Inc., v. SnyderGeneral Corp., 944 F.2d 1131, 15 UCC Rep. Serv. 2d 1225 (3d Cir. 1991) (failure to provide adequate assurances held to be a breach).

[286] See generally Wladis, *Impracticability as Risk Allocation: The Effect of Changed Circumstances Upon Contract Obligations for the Sale of Goods*, 22 Ga. L. Rev. 503 (1988).

[287] See Taylor v. Caldwell, 122 Eng. Rep. 309 (1963).

[288] The leading pre-Code case on commercial impracticability is *Mineral Park Land Co. v. Howard*, 172 Cal. 289, 156 P. 458 (1916). The doctrine has never gained much favor at common law. The related common-law doctrine of frustration of purpose is not recognized by the Code, but since it was not abrogated, it can apply to contracts for the sale or lease of goods. UCC § 1–103.

substituted performance when the agreed manner of delivery becomes impracticable or the agreed means or manner of payment fails because of governmental regulation. Section 2–615 excuses a seller's performance that becomes commercially impracticable because of a contingency whose nonoccurrence was a basic assumption of the contract or because of good-faith compliance with a governmental regulation. Comparable provisions cover lease transactions.[289]

The Code provisions on excuse assume that the courts can distinguish between the essential features of the contract and the incidental or subsidiary aspects.[290] Generally, the essential features of the agreement are the transfer of specified goods from the seller or lessor and payment by the buyer or lessee. The incidental aspects deal with the manner and means by which these fundamental purposes are to be achieved. Events that make performance of the essential purposes of the transaction commercially impractical can result in excused performance. In contrast, events that impinge on the parties' ability to carry out the incidental aspects do not excuse all performance. Rather, they excuse the parties from using the methods set forth in the contract, but they also impose on the parties an obligation to find commercially reasonable substitute means to achieve the essential purposes of the sale or lease.

§ 7.12   CASUALTY TO IDENTIFIED GOODS [2–613; 2A–221]

Article 2 includes a provision that reflects the common-law approach of excusing performance when the subject matter of the contract has been destroyed without the fault of either party.[291] Several requirements must be satisfied, however, for the defense of excuse to apply. The first requirement is that the goods destroyed must have been identified when the contract was made. Excuse is based on the premise that goods whose continued existence is presupposed by the agreement are destroyed, making performance impossible.[292] Thus, destruction of the seller's soybean crop by weather did not excuse the seller in *Bunge Corp. v. Recker*[293] because the contract terms did not identify the goods except by kind and amount. Since the contract was not specifically for the beans that the seller was growing, the destruction of his crop simply meant

---

[289] UCC §§ 2A–221, 2A–404, 2A–405.

[290] UCC § 2–614, Comment 1.

[291] UCC § 2–613. Section 2A–221 is comparable.

[292] UCC 2–613, Comment 1. Emery v. Weed, 494 A.2d 438, 41 UCC Rep. Serv. 115 (Pa. Super. 1985) (existence of Corvettes similar to the one stolen was irrelevant since the one stolen had been identified in the contract).

[293] 519 F.2d 449, 17 UCC Rep. Serv. 400 (8th Cir. 1975).

that the seller had to acquire beans for his contract from another source to avoid breaching the contract.[294]

The second requirement for excuse based on casualty to identified goods is that the loss must have occurred without the fault of either party. Fault is a "wrongful act, omission or breach";[295] it includes negligence as well as willful wrong conduct.[296] The third requirement is that the loss must have occurred before the risk of loss passed to the buyer.[297] Buyer assumption of the consequences for casualties that afflict the purchased goods is a primary aspect of passing the risk of loss.[298]

When these requirements are met, the contract is avoided if the loss from the casualty is total. The seller then must only return any payments that have been made.[299] If the loss is partial, the buyer is entitled to inspect the goods and elect to treat the contract as avoided or accept the goods. Under the latter option, the only right allowed against the seller is a reduction in the contract price to reflect the lessened quantity or quality of the goods.

§ 7.13   SUBSTITUTED PERFORMANCE [2–614; 2A–404]

The excuse permitted in the substituted-performance provision is quite limited. It excuses exact compliance with the incidental aspects of the contract when they have failed or become commercially impracticable.[300] The rationale behind substituted performance is that delivery and payment can normally be performed in another manner without seriously jeopardizing the reasonable expectations of either party. If delivery of the goods or payment for them can

---

[294] *See also* Valley Forge Flag Co., Inc. v. New York Dowel & Moulding Import Co., Inc., 395 N.Y.S.2d 138, 21 UCC Rep. Serv. 1320 (N.Y. Civ. Ct. 1977) (UCC § 2–613 not applicable to shipboard loss of dowels during a heavy storm while in transit from Malaysia because the goods were not identified at time of contracting).

[295] UCC § 1–201(16).

[296] UCC § 2–613, Comment 1.

[297] Salines v. Flores, 26 UCC Rep. Serv. 1159 (Tex. Civ. App. 1979) (in sale of watermelons "by the patch" risk of loss passed to the buyer at time of contracting, so contract was not avoided by destruction of the watermelons in hailstorm). For the applicable provisions on risk of loss, *see* §§ 2–509 and 2–510 and the discussion in § 6.02 *supra*.

[298] The buyer is liable for purchase price of such goods. UCC § 2–709(1)(a).

[299] Conway v. Larsen Jewelers, Inc., 429 N.Y.S.2d 378, 29 UCC Rep. Serv. 842 (Civ. Ct. N.Y.C. 1980) (claimant not entitled to increased market value of necklace purchased on layaway plan that was subsequently stolen from seller's store).

[300] UCC §§ 2–614; 2A–404.

be attained through reasonable substituted means, it must be tendered and accepted.

Substituted performance becomes applicable with respect to delivery when "without fault of either party the agreed berthing, loading, or unloading facilities fail or an agreed type of carrier becomes unavailable or the agreed manner of delivery otherwise become commercially impracticable."[301] Under these circumstances, if a commercially reasonable substitute is available, it must be tendered and accepted. If a commercially reasonable substitute is not available, the seller may be excused from performing under the section on excuse by failure of a presupposed condition.[302]

The Code provisions do not allocate the increased costs that may be associated with a substitute manner of delivery. The issue was addressed in *Jon-T Farms, Inc. v. Goodpasture, Inc.*,[303] in which the court imposed these costs on the seller. The parties agreed that the seller should ship some of the grain to the buyer in trucks once it became clear that a rail-car shortage would delay shipments. The court reasoned that under the contract the seller would have to incur the cost of transporting the grain to the railhead for loading and the contract did not impose any obligation on the buyer for increased costs.

When governmental regulation precludes the means or manner of payment agreed on by the parties, the provision on substituted performance again applies. If the contract is still fully executory, the seller is permitted to withdraw from the transaction unless the buyer can provide a substantially equivalent payment. If the buyer has already taken delivery, the buyer is entitled to pay in accordance with the terms of the regulation, unless the regulation is discriminatory, oppressive, or predatory.

§ 7.14 COMMERCIAL IMPRACTICABILITY [2–615; 2A–405]

[A] Excuse

Section 2–615 provides, in part, as follows:

Delay in delivery or non-delivery in whole or in part by a seller who complies with paragraphs (b) and (c) is not a breach of his duty under a contract for sale if performance as agreed has been made impracticable by the occurrence of a contingency the non-occurrence of which

---

[301] UCC § 2–614(1).

[302] UCC § 2–615. *See* § 7.14[A][1] *infra.*

[303] 554 S.W.2d 743, 21 UCC Rep. Serv. 1309 (Tex. Ct. App. 1977).

was a basic assumption on which the contract was made or by compliance in good faith with any applicable foreign or domestic governmental regulation or order whether or not it later proves to be
invalid.[304]

Two distinct elements must be established to invoke this defense successfully:
(1) either (a) the failure or nonoccurrence of a basic assumption or (b) an intervening governmental regulation, and (2) resulting commercial impracticability.

[1] Nonoccurrence of a Basic Assumption

The determination of whether an unexpected occurrence is sufficient to
allow excuse has turned generally on the more traditional concept of foreseeability.[305] If a particular event is foreseeable, but the parties do not do anything
to address its occurrence, the basic assumption is that it is not the basis for an
excuse of either party. The Comments specifically state that excuse of a seller
results "where his performance has become commercially impracticable because of unforeseen supervening circumstances not within the contemplation
of the parties at the time of contracting."[306] Courts quite consistently have
denied excuse of performance when the contingency complained of was foreseeable at the time of contracting.

The court's decision in *Eastern Air Lines, Inc. v. Gulf Oil Corp.*[307] is illustrative. Eastern and Gulf extended a long-term supply contract for aviation fuel
at several locations. In order to pass through increased costs of crude oil, the
contract included an escalation clause, using an indicator based on domestic
supply that would make Eastern's costs per gallon for jet fuel directly propor-
tional to Gulf's costs per barrel for crude oil. Gulf claimed excuse from its contract obligations based on the escalated increases in crude oil prices imposed
by OPEC nations for oil they produced and the embargo imposed on several
nations that resulted in the so-called energy crisis in the United States. The
court, however, determined that the defense was unavailable because the
events leading up to the price increases were reasonably foreseeable at the time

---

[304] UCC § 2–615(a). § 2A–405 is comparable. Although § 2–615(a) is written in terms of sellers,
the Comments add that "the reason of the present section may well apply and entitle the
buyer to the exemption." UCC § 2–615, Comment 9. The courts have recognized this approach. Lawrence v. Elmore Bean Warehouse, Inc., 108 Idaho 892, 702 P.2d 930, 41 UCC
Rep. Serv. 358 (1985); Hancock Paper Co. v. Champion Int'l Corp., 424 F. Supp. 285, 21
UCC Rep. Serv. 132 (E.D. Pa. 1976).

[305] *See* Farnsworth, *Disputes over Omissions in Contracts*, 68 Colum. L. Rev. 860 (1968). Waldinger Corp. v. CRS Group Engineers, Inc., Clark Dietz Div., 775 F.2d 781, 42 UCC Rep.
Serv. 172 (7th Cir. 1985).

[306] UCC § 2–615, Comment 1. Comment 4 also refers to unforeseen contingencies.

[307] 415 F. Supp. 429, 19 UCC Rep. Serv. 721 (S.D. Fla. 1975).

the contract was executed. The court pointed to prior use of oil as a political weapon by oil-producing nations, repeated interruptions in the crude oil trade, and volatility in the foreign oil market.[308]

A milk supplier in *Maple Farms, Inc. v. City of Elmira*[309] sought to be excused from a milk supply contract with a school district. The supplier attributed the 23 percent increase in market price over the contract price for the milk to unexpected crop failures and the sale of grain to Russia. The court determined, however, that the price increases were foreseeable. Milk prices had risen significantly prior to this contract. The court also noted the general inflation of the times.

A case that allowed the impracticability defense was *Florida Power & Light v. Westinghouse Electric Corp.*[310] Westinghouse agreed to provide uranium for nuclear power plants to Florida Power for a period of 10 years at a fixed price and, under an option selected by Florida Power, agreed to dispose of the spent fuel. The parties anticipated that the spent fuel would be sent to a reprocessing plant. Government policy changed, however, and reprocessing plants were not built. The court relieved Westinghouse of its obligation to take the spent fuel, which effectively passed the cost of storage to Florida Power.[311]

The courts have considered several cases involving crop failure.[312] The Comments provide the following guidelines:

> The case of a farmer who has contracted to sell crops to be grown on designated land may be regarded as falling either within the section on casualty to identified goods or this section, and he may be excused, when there is a failure of the specific crop, either on the basis of the destruction of identified goods or because of the failure of a basic assumption of the contract.[313]

---

[308] For another decision holding that the consequences of the oil situation in the Middle East were foreseeable, *see* Publicker Indus. v. Union Carbide Corp., 17 UCC Rep. Serv. 989 (E.D. Pa. 1975).

[309] 76 Misc. 2d 1080, 352 N.Y.S.2d 784, 14 UCC Rep. Serv. 722 (Sup. Ct. 1974).

[310] 826 F.2d 239 (4th Cir. 1987). *See generally* Joskow, *Commercial Impossibility, the Uranium Market and the Westinghouse Case,* 6 J. Legal Stud. 119 (1977).

[311] Another case in which a change in government policy afforded a basis for relief is *Eastern Air Lines, Inc. v. McDonnell Douglas Corp.,* 532 F.2d 957, 19 UCC Rep. Serv. 353 (5th Cir. 1976) (*force majeure* clause provided basis for excuse of delay in delivery of aircraft occasioned by Department of Defense demands for Vietnam war efforts).

[312] *See generally* Bugg, *Crop Destruction and Forward Grain Contracts: Why Don't Sections 2–613 and 2–615 of the UCC Provide More Relief?,* 12 Hamline L. Rev. 669 (1989).

[313] UCC § 2–615, Comment 9.

Following this approach, the court in *Dunavant Enterprises, Inc. v. Ford*[314] allowed excuse due to flooding of the land on which the contract-designated cotton is to be grown. When the contract does not specify the land on which the crop is to be grown, as in *Wickliffe Farms, Inc. v. Owensboro Grain Co.*,[315] the courts generally have refused to allow relief. The underlying assumption is that the parties did not contract for a specific source of crops, so the seller's obligation is broader and must include acquiring them from somewhere other than initially intended. The same reasoning has generally been applied to suppliers other than persons engaged in farming operations.[316]

When the event upon which excuse is premised causes an exclusive source of supply to fail, as in the cases of crops to be grown on designated land, the event that causes failure must be beyond the control of the seller, in addition to being unforeseeable. The Comments identify the requirement as follows: "There is no excuse under this section, however, unless the seller has employed all due measures to assure himself that his source will not fail."[317] Thus, in *Nissho-Iwai Co. v. Occidental Crude Sales, Inc.*,[318] the seller was not excused because its failure to pay taxes and other fees to the government of Libya resulted in the embargo that left it unable to deliver oil. Similarly, the court in *Roth Steel Products v. Sharon Steel Corp.*[319] did not excuse a seller that caused its own problems by accepting too many purchase orders for raw materials that it knew were in short supply.

[2]   Governmental Regulation

A special type of unanticipated intervening event that can also be used as the basis to invoke commercial impracticability is a government regulation that precludes performance. Excuse has been allowed under this provision when the excused party had to comply with newly promulgated environmental regulations.[320] A contract obligation to accept plaintiff's city's sewage was excused in *Kansas City, Missouri v. Kansas City, Kansas*[321] because the Federal Water Pollution Control Act Amendments of 1972 were enacted. Compliance with the

---

[314] 294 So. 2d 788, 20 UCC Rep. Serv. 667 (Miss. 1974).

[315] 684 S.W.2d 17, 39 UCC Rep. Serv. 195 (Ky. Ct. App. 1984) (drought adversely affected corn crop).

[316] Bliss Produce Co. v. AE Albert & Sons, Inc., 35 Agri. Dec. 742, 20 UCC Rep. Serv. 917 (1976).

[317] UCC § 2–615, Comment 5.

[318] 729 F.2d 1530, 38 UCC Rep. Serv. 1237 (5th Cir. 1984).

[319] 705 F.2d 134, 35 UCC Rep. Serv. 1435 (6th Cir. 1983).

[320] International Minerals & Chem. Corp. v. Llano, Inc., 770 F.2d 879, 41 UCC Rep. Serv. 347 (10th Cir. 1985), *cert. denied*, 475 U.S. 1015, 106 S. Ct. 1196, 89 L. Ed. 2d 310 (1986).

[321] 393 F. Supp. 1 (W.D. Mo. 1975).

new treatment requirements of the federal law would have imposed a substantial, unreasonable burden on the defendant.

On the other hand, the enactment of relevant government regulations is not alone sufficient. The court in *Sabine Corp. v. ONG Western, Inc.*[322] did not allow a government regulation that effected a price rise for natural gas as a basis for excuse because such regulation is foreseeable in the industry.

[3] Resulting Commercial Impracticability

A seller who can establish the nonoccurrence of a basic assumption of the contract or an intervening governmental regulation must also show commercial impracticability in order to claim excuse successfully. This element generally translates into the increased financial hardship that continued performance will impose. One court stated the issue as follows: "Whether 'grave injustice' would result from failure to excuse performance is merely an inquiry used to assess whether the cost to the contracting party of performing the contract is so excessive and unreasonable as to warrant the conclusion that performance has become impracticable."[323] The Comments address the impact of increased costs as a basis for the defense.

> Increased cost alone does not excuse performance unless the rise in cost is due to some unforeseen contingency which alters the essential nature of the performance. Neither is a rise or a collapse in the market in itself a justification, for that is exactly the type of business risk which business contracts made at fixed prices are intended to cover. But a severe shortage of raw materials or of supplies due to a contingency such as war, embargo, local crop failure, unforeseen shutdown of major sources of supply or the like, which either causes a marked increase in cost or altogether prevents the seller from securing supplies necessary to his performance, is within the contemplation of this section.[324]

The common factor the courts have addressed in assessing assertions of commercial impracticability is the extent of the hardship imposed by the unforeseen contingency. The courts consistently have taken a strict view.[325] The loss or expense must be severe, extreme, excessive, or unreasonable. Few sellers

---

[322] 725 F. Supp. 1157, 11 UCC Rep. Serv. 2d 83 (W.D. Okla. 1989).

[323] Sabine Corp. v. ONG Western, Inc., 725 F. Supp. 1157, 1176, 11 UCC Rep. Serv. 2d 83 (W.D. Okla. 1989).

[324] UCC § 2–615, Comment 4.

[325] Although many commentators believe § 2–615 was devised to improve the availability of the law on excuse, the courts have not pursued such a course. *See* Hurst, *Freedom of Contract in an Unstable Economy: Judicial Reallocation of Contractual Risks under UCC Section 2–615*, 54 N.C. L. Rev. 545, 555 (1976).

have been successful in establishing the requisite degree of hardship. In *Louisiana Power & Light Co. v. Allegheny Ludlum Indus., Inc.*,[326] for example, the seller sought excuse from a contract to supply condenser tubing for construction of a nuclear plant because shortages of critical raw materials and increased labor costs increased its costs of performing by about 38 percent. The court was unsympathetic, noting that both the division that was to supply the tubing and the overall corporate structure of Allegheny would make profits that year. The court noted that the deprivation of an anticipated profit and the loss resulting from contracting performance are not pleasant, but they are facts of life in commercial transactions and not sufficient to invoke the doctrine of commercial impracticability.[327]

In addition to finding that price increases related to the Arab oil embargo were foreseeable, the court in *Eastern Air Lines, Inc. v. Gulf Oil Corp.*[328] found that Gulf did not carry its burden to show that the increased costs resulted in the requisite hardship. Gulf did not present evidence that showed its real costs, but rather costs that had been inflated by internal profits added on at various stages of the importation and manufacturing process. The year the energy crisis began in this country proved to be Gulf's most profitable year, and the following year was even better.

The most dramatic application of commercial impracticability came in *Aluminum Co. of America v. Essex Group, Inc.*[329] The parties entered into a long-term contract under which Alcoa converted raw material supplied by Essex into molten aluminum.[330] The contract included carefully negotiated price-escalator provisions, but they proved to be inadequate in the face of substantial increases related to the energy crisis and pollution control requirements. Alcoa contended that it would lose $75 million in performing the remainder of the contract and sought relief. The court found commercial impracticability. Rather than excusing any further performance by Alcoa, however, the court established a new price for the services.[331]

---

[326] 517 F. Supp. 1319, 32 UCC Rep. Serv. 847 (E.D. La. 1981).

[327] *See also* Iowa Elec. Light & Power Co. v. Atlas Corp., 467 F. Supp. 129, 23 UCC Rep. Serv. 1171 (N.D. Iowa 1978) (rather than focusing on a nearly sevenfold increase in market price of uranium, the court addressed seller's costs of production and found that a 50–80 percent increase was not sufficient for excuse on grounds of commercial impracticability).

[328] 415 F. Supp. 429, 19 UCC Rep. Serv. 721 (S.D. Fla. 1975).

[329] 499 F. Supp. 53, 29 UCC Rep. Serv. 1 (W.D. Pa. 1980).

[330] The case is not within the scope of Article 2 because Alcoa was simply processing goods that Essex already owned.

[331] For differing perspectives of the *Alcoa* decision, *see* Dawson, *Judicial Revision of Frustrated Contracts: The United States*, 64 B.U. L. Rev. 1 (1984) (sharply critical); Speidel, *Court-Imposed Price Adjustments under Long-Term Supply Contracts*, 76 Nw. U. L. Rev. 369 (1981) (approves court adjustments).

[B] Duties of the Seller

A seller must comply with the remaining provisions of section 2–615 in order to be able to rely on an excuse allowed under that section. One of the duties imposed on the seller applies when only a portion of the seller's capacity to perform has been affected.[332] Production and deliveries then must be allocated among the seller's customers under a plan that is fair and reasonable.[333] This plan can include regular customers who are not then under contract, as well as the seller's own requirements.[334] The seller is also required to give the buyer seasonable notification of delay or nondelivery, and an estimated quota that it will make available to the buyer when allocation of partial capacity is required.[335] Upon receiving notification, a buyer has the option to terminate the executory portion of the contract or acquiesce and thereby modify the contract.[336]

---

[332] See generally White, Allocation of Scarce Resources under Section 2–615 of the UCC: A Comparison of Some Rival Models, 12 U. Mich. J. L. Ref. 503 (1979).

[333] UCC § 2–615(b). Cosden Oil & Chem. Co. v. Karl O. Helm Aktiengesellschaft, 736 F.2d 1064, 38 UCC Rep. Serv. 1645 (5th Cir. 1984) (failure of seller of polystyrene to include buyer made allocation plan unfair); Terry v. Atlantic Richfield Co., 72 Cal. App. 3d 962, 140 Cal. Rptr. 510, 22 UCC Rep. Serv. 669 (1977) (allocation plan based on percentage of prior purchases upheld because it was fairly drawn with respect to customers as a whole). See Note, Uniform Commercial Code § 2–615(b): Duty to Allocate in a Shortage Economy, 14 Suffolk U. L. Rev. 1136 (1980).

[334] Roth Steel Products v. Sharon Steel Corp., 705 F.2d 134, UCC Rep. Serv. 134 (6th Cir. 1983) (allocation invalid with inclusion of a subsidiary of seller that had not been a previous customer of seller).

[335] UCC § 2–615(c). Bunge Corp. v. Miller, 381 F. Supp. 176, 15 UCC Rep. Serv. 384 (W.D. Tenn. 1974).

[336] UCC § 2–616. Section 2A–406 is comparable, except that the modification option is not available in any finance lease that is not also a consumer lease.

CHAPTER

8

Remedies of Buyers and Lessees

§ 8.01 GENERAL

Articles 2 and 2A include indexes of applicable remedy provisions available to aggrieved parties in sale and lease transactions.[1] These remedy provisions are available in cases of breach in a sale transaction, whereas lease transactions are determined in terms of default.[2] The reference to default in Article 2A reflects the closer correlation of Article 2A to Article 9 on secured transactions.[3] Both monetary and nonmonetary remedies are available under both Articles.

This chapter focuses primarily on the monetary remedies available to buyers. The applicable nonmonetary remedies are highlighted at the end of the chapter. The principal differences with respect to lessee remedies are integrated into the discussion of buyer remedies. Two relevant concepts also are explained at the outset. The initial explanation covers the cumulative nature of the applicable remedies. The second explanation addresses a concept that is unique to lease transactions. Although the Article 2A formulas for monetary damages are patterned closely on provisions of Article 2, each of the leasing formulas must adjust for the time value of money. Because it affects all of the Article 2A formulas, it is explained at the outset.

---

[1] UCC §§ 2–703, 2–711, 2A–508, 2A–523.
[2] See §§ 7.06, 7.07 supra.
[3] See § 7.07[A] supra.

[A]   Cumulation of Remedies

The rights and remedies stated in Articles 2 and 2A are cumulative.[4] The parties to a sale or lease transaction are thus not required to elect a particular remedy with the result of foreclosing other rights and remedies. The Comments to Article 2 state: "This Article rejects any doctrine of election of remedy as a fundamental policy and thus the remedies are essentially cumulative in nature and include all of the available remedies for breach."[5] The Comments to Article 2A also indicate a rejection of the doctrine of election of remedy.[6]

The cumulative approach is consistent with the Code's objective that "remedies provided shall be liberally administered to the end that the aggrieved party may be put in as good a position as if the other party had fully performed."[7] As the Comments state:

> Therefore, cumulation of, or selection among, remedies is available to the extent necessary to put the aggrieved party in as good a position as it would have been in had there been full performance. However, cumulation of, or selection among, remedies is not available to the extent that the cumulation or selection would put the aggrieved party in a better position than it would have been in had there been full performance by the other party.[8]

[B]   Time Value of Money

Monetary damages in lease cases must be reduced to present value. An award of damages is reduced to a single amount, even though in a lease transaction the performance of the parties would extend over a period of time, perhaps even a number of years. The time value of money thus must be reflected in the determination of damages. A successful litigant will receive current payment for damages, whereas if performance had continued, payments would be made over the term of the lease with dollars of gradually decreasing value. Earlier payment in the form of damages enables the successful litigant to earn a present rate of return on that money.

Thus, in order to reflect the time use of money, the lease formulas reduce damages awards to present value. "Present value" is defined to mean "the

---

4   UCC § 2–703, Comment 1; UCC § 2A–501(4).
5   UCC § 2–703, Comment 1.
6   UCC § 2A–508, Comment 2; UCC § 2A–523, Comment 1.
7   UCC § 1–106(1).
8   UCC § 2A–501, Comment 4.

amount as of a date certain of one or more sums payable in the future, discounted to the date certain."[9] The damages formulas in Article 2A include the necessary dates for their application of the discount. Reducing each element to present value essentially determines the amount of money that would have to be invested now at the applicable rate of return to produce an indicated amount at the stated time in the future.

Calculating present value requires the use of a discount rate. The Article 2A definition of present value includes the following provision concerning selection of a discount rate:

> The discount is determined by the interest rate specified by the parties if the rate was not manifestly unreasonable at the time the transaction was entered into; otherwise, the discount is determined by a commercially reasonable rate that takes into account the facts and circumstances of each case at the time the transaction was entered into.

Plaintiffs will benefit from lower discount rates because these will increase the recovery; higher discount rates will lower the recovery.

Part A: Monetary Remedies

§ 8.02   RECOVERY OF PAYMENTS MADE [2–711(1); 2A–508(1)(b)]

When an aggrieved buyer does not receive or retain goods from the seller, the buyer is entitled to recover any of the purchase price that has been paid.[10] This remedy is thus available when the seller fails to deliver goods[11] or anticipatorily repudiates,[12] and when the buyer rightfully rejects tendered goods[13] or justifiably revokes an acceptance of them.[14] Because the buyer will not keep the seller's goods following the seller's breach, the buyer is entitled to recover any amount previously paid for the goods. If the buyer accepts the seller's

---

[9] UCC § 2A–103(1)(u).

[10] UCC § 2–711(1).

[11] June G. Ashton Interiors v. Stark Carpet Corp., 142 Ill. App. 3d 100, 491 N.E.2d 191, 2 UCC Rep. Serv. 2d 74 (1986).

[12] Government of Republic of China v. Compass Communications Corp., 473 F. Supp. 1306, 28 UCC Rep. Serv. 393 (D. D.C. 1979).

[13] Hollingsworth v. The Software House, Inc., 32 Ohio App. 3d 61, 513 N.E.2d 1372, 4 UCC Rep. Serv. 2d 1400 (1986).

[14] S&R Metals, Inc. v. C. Itoh & Co. (America), Inc., 859 F.2d 814, 7 UCC Rep. Serv. 2d 61 (9th Cir. 1988).

goods, even though they are defective, the buyer is obligated to pay the purchase price for those goods.[15] Consistent with this obligation, the aggrieved buyer is not entitled to the return of any of the price that has been paid for accepted goods.[16]

The comparable remedy is not as absolute in the lease context. In cases in which an aggrieved lessee does not retain the goods of the lessor for the full lease term, the lessee may "recover so much of the rent and security as has been paid and is just under the circumstances."[17] The added limitation on recovery under the "justness" standard recognizes that a lessee might be able to cancel a lease contract after having used the goods for a considerable period of time.[18] For example, a lessee entitled to revoke acceptance of the goods after having used them successfully for most of the lease term covered by the paid rent might not be entitled to much, if any, of the rent paid.[19] Alternatively, the lessee generally could recover all or most of the prepaid rent for goods that are not delivered or for goods he or she promptly rejects.

§ 8.03   COVER [2–712; 2A–518]

The preferred monetary recovery for a buyer who does not receive goods from the seller, or who properly rejects or revokes tendered goods, is cover.[20] The buyer "covers" simply by purchasing comparable goods from another seller and using any increase in the cost of the cover as the basis for calculating damages. This remedy is preferred because it comes closest to meeting the contract remedies objective of placing the aggrieved party in the same economic position as if the contract been performed. Cover facilitates this objective because it is based on the actual costs incurred by the buyer to acquire the goods from a substitute source.

[A]   The Substitute

Article 2 places some constraints on which substitute purchase transactions can qualify for use of the cover measure of damages. It provides as

---

15 UCC § 2–607(1). *See* § 7.03[B][2] *supra*.
16 Acceptance also affects the measure of damages available to the buyer. *See* § 8.05 *infra*.
17 UCC § 2A–508(1)(b).
18 UCC § 2A–508, Comment 2.
19 A comparable issue has been raised in the sales context when buyers use the goods for a long period of time before revoking. Article 2 does not provide for any compensation to the seller for such use, but several courts have required payment based on principles of restitution. *See* § 7.05[F] *supra*.
20 The cover measure of damages has not been recognized as a traditional remedy at common law. Farnsworth, *Legal Remedies for Breach of Contract*, 70 Colum. L. Rev. 1145, 1191–92 (1970).

follows: "After a breach within the preceding section the buyer may 'cover' by making in good faith and without unreasonable delay any reasonable purchase of or contract to purchase goods in substitution for those due from the seller."[21] The aggrieved buyer thus must (1) cover in good faith, (2) act without unreasonable delay, and (3) make a reasonable substitute purchase.

The standards of good faith and without unreasonable delay are basically controls to ensure that aggrieved buyers do not increase the amount of damages unnecessarily. Buyers cannot intentionally select the most expensive means of cover available or a means that will advance their own special interests.[22] Because inflationary pressure tends to cause prices to rise over time, lengthy delays are likely to increase the cost of a cover. These two standards thus protect the interest of the seller against excessive recoveries.[23]

Two caveats are critical in applying these two standards. The first is to recognize that both standards are highly sensitive to surrounding circumstances. Appropriate action in one context may not be acceptable in a situation with differing circumstances. For example, waiting 38 days to cover in a rapidly rising market would not generally satisfy the standards. Such action was sustained in *Dangerfield v. Markel*,[24] however, because the buyer could not cover any sooner.[25] The facts of each case must be analyzed carefully.

The other caveat is that the restraint on the extent of recovery is applied only in general terms. The Comments make this point clear: "The test of proper cover is whether at the time and place the buyer acted in good faith and in a reasonable manner, and it is immaterial that hindsight may later prove that the

---

21 UCC § 2–712(1).
22 In *Oloffson v. Coomer*, 11 Ill. App. 3d 918, 296 N.E.2d 871, 12 UCC Rep. Serv. 1082 (1973), the seller notified the buyer he could not plant corn because the ground was too wet. Rather than covering on the organized market, the buyer waited until the contract delivery date several months later. The court justifiably did not allow the cover. The delay would enable the buyer to speculate at the expense of the seller in hopes that the market price would drop below the contract price.
23 The absence of impairment of this objective led the court in *American Carpet Mills v. Gunny Corp.*, 649 F.2d 1056, 31 UCC Rep. Serv. 964 (5th Cir. 1981), to uphold covers made during a period extending from March to September. Prices on the spot market for the goods declined steadily during this period, so any delay in initiating cover accrued to the seller's benefit.
24 278 N.W.2d 364, 26 UCC Rep. Serv. 419 (N.D. 1979).
25 *See also* Erie Casein Co., Inc. v. Anric Corp., 217 Ill. App. 3d 602, 577 N.E.2d 892, 15 UCC Rep. Serv. 2d 1240 (1991)(not covering until prices had risen significantly was justified because buyer encountered the same problems as seller in attempting to obtain the goods).

method of cover was not the cheapest or most effective."[26] Thus, a school district in *Huntington Beach Union High School Dist. v. Continental Information Systems Corp.*[27] that allowed other bids to expire, which ultimately led to higher cover costs, had acted reasonably and thus could include the cover cost in its measure of damages.[28]

One issue that has been litigated is whether the buyer can cover by providing the goods itself rather than acquiring them from a third party. In *Dura-Wood Treating Co. v. Century Forest Industries, Inc.*,[29] the seller argued unsuccessfully that the Code does not contemplate the buyer covering by purchasing from itself. The court upheld the cover because the buyer had taken price quotations and ultimately determined that it could produce the goods at a lower price.[30] On the other hand, the court determined in *Kiser v. Lemco Industries, Inc.*[31] that merely stating that it had purchased a quantity of its own wheat at a stated price, without more, did not establish the good faith of the cover transaction.

The buyer must also make a reasonable purchase in substitution for the goods under contract in order to use the cover remedy as a measure of damages. This requirement poses no difficulty when the buyer purchases goods that are identical to those described in the contract. Buyers, however, might be inclined or even forced by circumstances to purchase goods that differ in some respect. The Comments clarify that the cover provision envisions "goods not identical with those involved but commercially usable as reasonable substitutes under the circumstances of the particular case."[32] The closer a buyer's cover transaction is to the original contract specifications, the more likely it is to withstand scrutiny.[33] The question remains, however, as to the considerations that

---

[26] UCC § 2–712, Comment 2.

[27] 621 F.2d 353, 29 UCC Rep. Serv. 112 (9th Cir. 1980).

[28] *See also* Farmer's Union Co-op Co. of Mead, Nebraska v. Flamme Bros., 196 Neb. 699, 245 N.W.2d 464, 20 UCC Rep. Serv. 77 (1976)(co-op purchase of corn from its regular customers over two-week period at varying prices rather than immediate purchase on open market was upheld as cover in good faith and without unreasonable delay).

[29] 675 F.2d 745, 33 UCC Rep. Serv. 1201 (5th Cir. 1982).

[30] *See also* Cives Corp. v. Callier Steel Pipe & Tube, Inc., 482 A.2d 852, 39 UCC Rep. Serv. 1705 (Me. 1984)(did not appear that buyer profited from in-house manufacture of substitute tubular steel).

[31] 536 S.W.2d 585, 19 UCC Rep. Serv. 1134 (Tex. Civ. App. 1976).

[32] UCC § 2–712, Comment 1.

[33] *Compare* Goodell v. KT Enters., Ltd., 394 So.2d 1087, 31 UCC Rep. Serv. 129 (Fla. Ct. App. 1981)(purchase of belt conveyor system for use in pizza-freezing business constituted cover because it was of same general type as unit first ordered), *with* Valley Die Cast Corp. v. A. C. W., Inc., 25 Mich. App. 321, 181 N.W.2d 303, 8 UCC Rep. Serv. 488 (1970)(buyer did not cover by purchasing a more expensive car-wash system that operated on entirely different principle from pressure system purchased under original contract).

should guide the courts in determining how to accommodate covers that differ from the original contract.

If the cover transaction is for goods that are either superior or inferior to the goods under the original contract, the court should be willing to adjust the value in accordance with these features, provided that the valuation can be made with a sufficient degree of certainty.[34] Not all courts have followed this course, however. The court in *Martella v. Woods*[35] held that the purported cover of heifers of superior weight and quality was not a reasonable substitute. The purchase of a boat with smaller engines and 10 percent fewer features was held to qualify as a cover in *Meshinsky v. Nichols Yacht Sales, Inc.*[36] because the buyer had not improved its economic position with the replacement. The buyer also received less than it had bargained for, and that part of the loss was not compensated.

Even if a qualifying cover transaction provides goods with higher quality and the value of that additional quality can be calculated, the court should not adjust the value of the improvement from the cover remedy unless the buyer will benefit from the improved quality. In the case of *In re Lifeguard Industries, Inc.*,[37] the buyer entered into a cover contract for aluminum siding with the only other manufacturer who produced the type of siding required, but the cover siding had some superior features. If the buyer could have realized a monetary benefit by charging more for installing the substitute improved product, the cover price should be adjusted to reflect this benefit. On the other hand, if the buyer were already contractually committed to install a product at a fixed price, the additional quality would not benefit the buyer and an adjustment would not be appropriate.

[B]   The Cover Formula

The measure of cover damages for an aggrieved buyer is stated as follows:

The buyer may recover from the seller as damages the difference between the cost of cover and the contract price together with any incidental or consequential damages as hereinafter defined (section 2–715), but less expenses saved in consequence of the seller's breach.[38]

---

[34] The court in *Kanzmeier v. McCoppin*, 398 N.W.2d 826, 4 UCC Rep. Serv. 2d 1084 (Iowa 1987), held that a buyer who bought 358 "lighter steers" after seller breach of contract to buy 360 "big steers" did not cover because fact-finder had no way to determine whether higher price paid was due to rising market or difference in weight.

[35] 715 F.2d 410, 36 UCC Rep. Serv. 1200 (8th Cir. 1983).

[36] 110 N.J. 464, 541 A.2d 1063, 6 UCC Rep. Serv. 2d 1144 (1988).

[37] 42 B.R. 734 (E.D. Ohio 1983).

[38] UCC § 2–712(2).

The formula thus uses the actual cost of cover that the buyer incurred. Adjustments are made for additional costs, such as those related to procuring a cover contract.[39] Expenses saved because of the breach are deducted. These expenses include savings like cheaper costs incurred for transportation of the goods on the substitute contract compared to the original contract terms.[40]

[C] Leases

The Article 2A provisions on the cover remedy are based on the Article 2 analogue, but some changes were made to reflect special considerations raised by lease transactions. Article 2A specifically authorizes the buyer to cover through purchase or lease,[41] but only substitute lease agreements can qualify for use of the cover formula for measuring damages.[42] The payment obligation incurred in a purchase agreement cannot be compared appropriately with the payment obligation in an original lease because of the inherently different nature of the two transactions.

Lease transactions also can have significantly different terms—such as length, insurance coverage, maintenance requirements—that can affect their payment obligations. Thus, in addition to the requirements that the lessee cover in good faith and in a commercially reasonable manner, the lease remedy requires that the new lease agreement be "substantially similar to the original lease agreement."[43] Cover made in the form of a purchase or a lease that does not qualify relegates the lessee to the same measure of damages as if the lessee elects not to cover.[44]

Although the Comments indicate that the "substantially similar" criterion is not a familiar one, it is certainly comparable to the Article 2 requirement that a qualifying cover be a "reasonable purchase" that is "in substitution [of goods] due from the seller." The terms themselves may differ, but they promote precisely the same objective. Ultimately, in both sales and leases, the terms that affect cost and value under the original contract and the cover transaction must be sufficiently comparable to legitimize calculating damages based on the actual terms of both agreements.[45]

---

[39] For discussion of incidental and consequential damages, see § 8.06 *infra*.

[40] Melms v. Mitchell, 266 Or. 208, 512 P.2d 1336, 13 UCC Rep. Serv. 223 (1973)(expenses saved by buyers not having to cut the dry wood they purchased in cover had to be deducted).

[41] UCC § 2A–518(1). This authorization reflects the Article 9 principle of allowing the secured party to dispose of the collateral as it sees fit following default. *See* UCC § 9–504.

[42] UCC § 2A–518(2).

[43] UCC § 2A–518(2).

[44] *See* UCC § 2A–519(1); *See* § 8.04 *infra*.

[45] The Comments suggest this focus.

   [T]he various elements of the new lease agreement should also be examined. Those

Because the variables among leases are so likely, the Comments in Article 2A are much more explicit in articulating the need for courts to make necessary adjustments to the amounts that would otherwise be produced through the cover formula. They state that "[i]f the differences between the original lease and the new lease can be easily valued, it would be appropriate for a court to adjust the difference in rental to take account of the difference between the two leases, find that the new lease is substantially similar to the old lease, and award cover damages under this section."[46]

Lease terms can present a particularly troublesome issue because a substitute lease can never cover precisely the same period as the original lease, unless the lessor repudiates before its commencement of performance. The Comments therefore identify two tests that courts should apply in determining whether the substitute lease is substantially similar: the lease terms must be commercially comparable and the court must be able to make fair apportionments.[47]

The difference between the term of the original lease and that of the substitute lease also affects the cover damages formula for leases. Rent under the original lease contract is deducted from rent under the new lease agreement, but only for the period of time that performance under the two lease terms coincides.[48] The Comments clarify that the lessee is entitled to consequential damages to compensate for the loss of use of the goods during the period between default on the original lease and commencement of the cover lease transaction.[49]

§ 8.04 MARKET PRICE/CONTRACT PRICE DIFFERENTIAL [2–713; 2A–519(1),(2)]

An alternative to cover is provided for buyers and lessees who have not accepted goods from their sellers or lessors. This measure awards the difference

---

elements include the presence or absence of options to purchase or release; the lessor's representations, warranties and covenants to the lessee, as well as those to be provided by the lessee to the lessor; and the services, if any, to be provided by the lessor or by the lessee. All of these factors allocate cost and risk between the lessor and the lessee and thus affect the amount of rent to be paid.
UCC § 2A–518, Comment 5.

[46] UCC § 2A–518, Comment 5.

[47] UCC § 2A–518, Comment 7.

[48] The Article 2A general measure for cover damages is
the present value, as of the date of the commencement of the term of the new lease agreement, of the rent under the new lease agreement applicable to that period of the new lease term which is comparable to the then remaining term of the original lease agreement minus the present value as of the same date of the total rent for the then remaining lease term of the original lease agreement.
UCC § 2A–518(2).

[49] UCC § 2A–518, Comment 2.

between the market price for the goods and the contract price.[50] Reflecting prevailing market prices, rather than an actual cost incurred by the aggrieved buyer or lessee, this measure of damages is comparable to the damages approach of common law. Even though it does not measure damages as accurately as the cover measure of damages, its inclusion is necessary because the cover measure may be unavailable, if the buyer or lessee does not cover or if the substitute transaction does not qualify.[51] In the absence of cover, the drafters had to rely on the marketplace to determine a measure of damages.[52]

[A]   Election

One issue that has persisted under Article 2 is whether a buyer who does cover can choose to ignore the cover remedy in favor of measuring damages by the market price/contract price differential. Obviously a buyer would be motivated to follow this course only when the differential would exceed cover damages. Commentators have disagreed on this issue,[53] but few courts have confronted it directly.[54] The better choice, based on policy reasons, would be to deny to a buyer who has made a qualifying cover the opportunity to choose the alternative measure. Contract remedies are designed to place the aggrieved party in the same position as performance would have. When implemented, the cover remedy meets that objective with precision. Allowing the buyer to ignore the actual cover damages and elect the market price/contract price differential simply enables the buyer to obtain overcompensation. This

---

[50] UCC 2–713(1). Gawlick v. American Builders Supply, Inc., 519 P.2d 313, 13 UCC Rep. Serv. 1031 (N.M. Ct. App. 1974)(buyer entitled not only to return of purchase price of vehicle with defective title, but also to difference between purchase price and market value of vehicle with clear title). The Article 2A formula is stated in terms of the difference between the present value of market rent less the present value of the original rent. UCC § 2A–519(1). Under both formulas, incidental and consequential damages are added, and expenses saved are deducted. Ralston Purina Co. v. McFarland, 550 F.2d 967, 21 UCC Rep. Serv. 136 (4th Cir. 1977)(incorrect holding that seller could not introduce evidence of buyer expenses saved because buyer did not introduce evidence of incidental or consequential damages).

[51] Interior Elevator Co. v. Limmeroth, 278 Or. 589, 565 P.2d 1074, 22 UCC Rep. Serv. 69 (1977)(§ 2–713 damages available to buyer who did not cover).

[52] See generally Childres, Buyer's Remedies: The Danger of 2–713, 72 Nw. U. L. Rev. 837 (1978).

[53] J. White & R. Summers, Uniform Commercial Code 262–63 (3d. ed. 1988)(buyer who covers should be held to the cover remedy); Peters, Remedies for Breach of Contract Relating to the Sale of Goods under the Uniform Commercial Code: A Roadmap for Article Two, 73 Yale L.J. 199, 260 (1963)(buyer should be able to choose between 2–712 and 2–713 remedies).

[54] Cosden Oil & Chem. Co. v. Karl O. Helm Aktiengesellschaft, 736 F.2d 1064, 38 UCC Rep. Serv. 1645 (5th Cir. 1984)(buyer not allowed to seek higher damages under § 2–713 than are available under § 2–712, but jury found that buyer had in fact not covered); Flood v. MP Clark, Inc., 335 F. Supp. 970 (E.D. Pa. 1971)(§ 2–713 not applicable when buyer has covered).

issue is resolved for lease transactions because Article 2A explicitly provides that the choice of the higher recovery is not available once a lessee has made a qualifying cover.[55]

Neither Article 2 nor Article 2A, on the other hand, requires an aggrieved buyer or lessee to elect to cover. Provisions in both Articles specifically preserve the other Code remedies for parties who do not make an effective cover.[56] The Comments stress that cover is not a mandatory remedy.[57] Whether to cover is essentially a business judgment.[58]

[B] Selecting the Market

With market price an essential element in the damages formula that is based on market price/contract price differential, there must be a means to identify the applicable market. Market identity can become more complex in sales and lease transactions because tender of the goods and their receipt can occur at different times and places. Consequently, the drafters had to provide a means to designate the applicable market for use with this formula. The drafters had to provide a means to identify the appropriate place and time at which to determine market price.

[1] Place

The location for market price under both Articles 2 and 2A is "the place for tender or, in cases of rejection after arrival or revocation of acceptance, . . . the place of arrival."[59] The reasoning behind this choice is stated in the Comments: "The general baseline adopted in this section uses as a yardstick the market in which the buyer would have obtained cover had he sought that relief."[60] The drafters thus drew assumptions about where a buyer would have covered had that option been pursued. When the goods are rejected, when an acceptance is revoked, or when a seller fails to ship goods under a destination contract, the assumption is that the buyer would cover in the buyer's local market because the buyer would not have time to allow for a reshipment of goods from the

---

[55] The section on market rent/contract rent differential recovery limits its availability to cases in which "a lessee elects not to cover or a lessee elects to cover and the cover is by a lease agreement that for any reason does not qualify for treatment under Section 2A–518(2) [the cover provision], or is by purchase or otherwise." UCC § 2A–519(1).

[56] UCC § 2–712(3); 2A–518(3). Neal-Cooper Grain Co. v. Texas Gulf Sulphur Co., 508 F.2d 283, 16 UCC Rep. Serv. 7 (7th Cir. 1974)(failure by buyer to cover does not bar any remedy except consequential damages that could have been prevented).

[57] UCC § 2–712, Comment 3; UCC § 2A–518, Comment 1.

[58] "The decision to cover is a function of commercial judgment, not a statutory mandate replete with sanctions for failure to comply." UCC § 2A–518, Comment 1.

[59] UCC §§ 2–713(2); 2A–519(2).

[60] UCC § 2–713, Comment 1.

more distant market. On the other hand, the assumption when a seller breaches by not shipping goods under a shipment contract or by anticipatory repudiation, is that with the time for shipment still available, the buyer would most likely return to the same marketplace for a cover transaction.

The court in *Bliss Produce Co. v. A. E. Albert & Sons, Inc.*[61] applied as the standard the reference in the Comments to the market in which the buyer would most likely have covered. Even though the contract provided for a shipment contract for potatoes from Arizona to North Carolina, the court used the North Carolina market as a reasonable market from which cover could have been obtained because potatoes were unobtainable in Arizona. The standard stated in the Code is fixed, however, and clearly leaves the presumed cover market in Arizona. The reference in the Comments simply provides the rationale by which the drafters fixed the assumptions that they chose.

These assumptions can affect more than simply determination of the market price for the goods. They can also affect determination of transportation costs, perhaps requiring an adjustment in the form of expenses saved from the general measure of the market price/contract price differential. A buyer who rejects or revokes with respect to goods shipped under a shipment contract, but who would presumably cover in the local market, is deemed to have saved the expense of transporting the goods from the distant market. However, a buyer who would presumably cover in the same market in which the goods were tendered is not considered to have saved any transportation expenses, and a deduction would not be made.[62]

The validity of the assumptions used to determine marketplace is certainly questionable. On the one hand, they are based on actions that the aggrieved buyer or lessee either could not or did not want to pursue. Furthermore, a buyer or lessee who does cover is not limited by the choices on which the assumptions are based, and those choices may or may not be relevant in any given transaction. On the other hand, the drafters had to devise some guiding principles to prevent aggrieved parties from simply "market" shopping. Because the cover measure is the preferred remedy, the drafters sought to approximate, to the extent possible, the same measure of damages based on market price that would have been realized had the buyer or the lessee made a qualifying cover.

---

[61]   35 Agric. Dec. 742, 20 UCC Rep. Serv. 917 (1976).

[62]   The court in *Productora E Importadora De Papel, S.A. De C.V. v. Fleming*, 376 Mass. 826, 383 N.E.2d 1129, 25 UCC Rep. Serv. 729 (1979), misapplied this provision by deducting transportation costs for goods that were not shipped under a shipment contract.

[2]   Time

Article 2 provides that market price is to be determined "at the time when the buyer learned of the breach."[63] This determination of time for fixing the price in the applicable market is also based on tying this measure of damages to approximate the damages available under the cover remedy. A buyer cannot proceed to cover on account of a seller's breach until the buyer is aware of the breach.

Considerable confusion has resulted from application of the section 2–713 measure of damages in cases of anticipatory repudiation.[64] The language is unclear with respect to determining the time to select the market price. Specifically, does a buyer learn of the breach at the time of learning of the repudiation, or are the terms "breach" and "repudiation" used differently in this context?

Section 2–723 suggests that, in cases of anticipatory repudiation, drafters had different times in mind. The section provides:

> If an action based on anticipatory repudiation comes to trial before the time for performance with respect to some or all of the goods, any damages based on market price (Section 2–708 or Section 2–713) shall be determined according to the price of such goods prevailing at the time when the aggrieved party learned of the repudiation.[65]

This section becomes superfluous if the term "learned of the breach" in section 2–713 is interpreted as when the buyer learned of the repudiation. Furthermore, to be consistent with the seller's analogous remedy, which is stated in section 2–708, section 2–713 should be interpreted as the time for the seller's performance.[66] Few courts have adopted this interpretation, however.[67]

Many courts have held that "learned of the breach" means the same as "learned of the repudiation."[68] Although this interpretation is problematic

---

[63] UCC § 2–713(1).

[64] *See generally* Jackson, *Anticipatory Repudiation and the Temporal Element of Contract Law: An Economic Inquiry into Contract Damages in Cases of Prospective Nonperformance*, 31 Stan. L. Rev. 69, 104–06 (1978); Sebert, *Remedies under Article Two of the Uniform Commercial Code: An Agenda for Review*, 130 U. Pa. L. Rev. 360, 372–73 (1981).

[65] UCC § 2–723(1).

[66] Section 2–708(1) measures the market price for the seller's damages at the time and place for tender. *See* § 9.02[B][1] *infra*.

[67] Cargill, Inc. v. Stafford, 533 F.2d 1222 (10th Cir. 1977)(in the absence of clearer statutory intent, interpretation that corresponds to common-law approach is appropriate). *See also* Roth Steel Prods. v. Sharon Steel Corp., 705 F.2d 134 (6th Cir. 1983). This is also the interpretation favored by two noted commentators. J. White & R. Summers, *Uniform Commercial Code* 278–83 (3d ed. 1988). They advance several arguments against interpreting the two terms as synonymous. *Id.*

[68] Neal-Cooper Grain Co. v. Texas Gulf Sulphur Co., 508 F.2d 283, 16 UCC Rep. Serv. 7 (7th Cir. 1974); Fredonia Broadcasting Corp., Inc. v. RCA Corp., 481 F.2d 781, 12 UCC Rep.

with respect to section 2–723, it is conceptually sound. Section 2–609(1) provides that a contract for sale imposes an obligation not to impair the expectations of the other party. An anticipatory repudiation constitutes a breach of this obligation, and a buyer learns of this breach on learning of the repudiation.

Yet a third interpretation has evolved in some courts. It measures the market at a commercially reasonable time after the buyer learns of the repudiation.[69] This interpretation is consistent with Article 2 principles of mitigation. Following an anticipatory repudiation, an aggrieved party is entitled for a commercially reasonable period of time to await performance by the repudiating party.[70] This delay in responding affords the repudiating party an opportunity to retract the repudiation and reinstate the contract. Additionally, buyers are given a commercially reasonable time to determine how to effectuate a cover,[71] and they are ultimately precluded from recovering consequential damages for any loss they could have prevented by covering.[72]

§ 8.05 DAMAGES WHEN BUYER ACCEPTS THE GOODS [2–714; 2A–519(3),(4)]

Damages measured by cover and by the market price/contract price differential are alternative measures of damages to protect the buyer's expectation interest in cases in which the buyer has not accepted the goods. A buyer will not have accepted either because the seller did not tender any goods, or because the buyer has effectively rejected the tender or revoked an acceptance of the tender. In any of these circumstances, the buyer does not retain the seller's goods.

The remedies differ when the buyer accepts the goods. One of the legal consequences of an acceptance, even if the seller's tender is deficient, is that the buyer must pay for the goods at the contract rate.[73] Obviously, the buyer is not entitled in these cases to recover any of the purchase price that has been paid.

Serv. 1088 (5th Cir. 1973); Burgess v. Curly Olney's, Inc., 198 Neb. 153, 251 N.W.2d 888, 21 UCC Rep. Serv. 794 (1977); Sawyer Farmers Coop. Assoc. v. Linke, 231 N.W.2d 791, 17 UCC Rep. Serv. 102 (N.D. 1975).

69 Cosden Oil & Chem. Co. v. Karl O. Helm Aktiengesellschaft, 736 F.2d 1064, 38 UCC Rep. Serv. 1645 (5th Cir. 1984). This interpretation is favored by another group of noted commentators. R. Hillman, J. McDonnell, & S. Nickles, *Common Law and Equity under the Uniform Commercial Code* ¶ 8.04[4][b] (1985).

70 UCC § 2–610(a).

71 UCC § 2–712(1). *See* § 8.03[A] *supra*.

72 UCC § 2–715(2)(a). *See* § 8.06[B] *infra*.

73 UCC § 2–607(1). *See* § 7.03[B][2] *supra*.

Articles 2 and 2A also provide different measures of recovery for a seller's breach and a lessor's default with respect to goods that the buyer nevertheless accepts.

[A] Recovery of Ordinary Loss

One of the measures of damages in cases in which the buyer has accepted the goods is very broad and provides as follows:

> Where the buyer has accepted goods and given notification (subsection (3) of Section 2–607) he may recover as damages for any non-conformity of tender the loss resulting in the ordinary course of events from the seller's breach as determined in any manner which is reasonable.[74]

Incidental and consequential damages are also recoverable.[75]

This measure covers any type of nonconformity that constitutes a breach under a sales contract in which the buyer retains the goods. For example, a seller's failure to make a timely delivery of the goods would be a nonconforming tender, as would the seller's failure to comply with shipping instructions. A tender of nonconforming goods would also be within the scope of this provision. Another remedy provision based on breach of warranty is more likely to be applied in these cases, however, because it states the standard measure of recovery in such cases.[76]

[B] Breach of Warranty

[1] The Standard Formula

The formula for a buyer's recovery based on the seller's breach of warranty is stated as follows:

> The measure of damages for breach of warranty is the difference at the time and place of acceptance between the value of the goods as accepted and the value they would have had if they had been as warranted, unless special circumstances show proximate damages of a different amount.[77]

---

[74] UCC § 2–714(1). The Article 2A provision is comparable. UCC § 2A–519(3).
[75] UCC § 2–714(3).
[76] See § 8.05[B][1] infra.
[77] UCC § 2–714(2). Article 2A is comparable. UCC § 2A–519(4).

This measure is essentially the difference in the value of the goods as warranted and their value as accepted. The aggrieved buyer is also entitled to incidental and consequential damages.[78]

The value of the goods as warranted is often determined by their contract price. The contract price provides evidence of such value, but it is not conclusive.[79] A buyer who can establish that the value of the goods would exceed the contract price is entitled to the benefit of that bargain. Thus, in *Chatlos Systems, Inc. v. National Cash Register Corp.*,[80] the court affirmed an award of damages that was more than four times the total contract price of $46,020. The market value of the computer that would have performed as warranted was established at $207,826.50, while the computer in its defective condition was worth only $6,000. Damages were based on the difference.

If the value of the goods would be less than the contract price, the buyer is better off to reject the seller's tender than to accept the goods. Rejection enables the buyer to use the fortuity of the seller's breach to escape a bad bargain, whereas the measure of damages following acceptance of the goods will be based on an actual value that is less than the contract price.

A common method for establishing the difference in value between the goods as warranted and as delivered is to prove the cost to repair the deficient aspects of the goods.[81] Some courts have qualified the admission of evidence on cost of repairs based on the difficulty of otherwise proving the value of the goods.[82] Alternatively, some courts have limited recovery to the cost of repair.[83] Proof of the cost of repairs shows the expenditure needed to give the buyer goods that conform to the contract.

Adjustments in this approach will sometimes be necessary, however, to achieve the aim of placing the buyer in the same position that performance by

---

[78] UCC § 2–714(3).
[79] Canterra Petroleum, Inc. v. Western Drilling & Mining Supply, 418 N.W.2d 267, 5 UCC Rep. Serv. 2d 1002 (N.D. 1987)(purchase price may be strong but not conclusive evidence of value of goods); Bendix Home Sys., Inc. v. Jessop, 644 P.2d 843, 33 UCC Rep. Serv. 1686 (Alaska 1982).
[80] 670 F.2d 1304, 33 UCC Rep. Serv. 934 (3d Cir. 1982).
[81] Nelson v. Logan Motor Sales, Inc., 370 S.E.2d 734, 7 UCC Rep. Serv. 2d 116 (W. Va. 1988)(buyer's repair bills admitted); Jones v. Abriani, 169 Ind. App. 556, 350 N.E.2d 635, 19 UCC Rep. Serv. 1102 (1976)(estimated cost of repairs).
[82] Winchester v. McCullough Bros. Garage, Inc., 388 So. 2d 927, 30 UCC Rep. Serv. 212 (Ala. 1980).
[83] Tarter v. MonArk Boat Co., 430 F. Supp. 1290, 22 UCC Rep. Serv. 33 (E.D. Mo. 1977), aff'd, 574 F.2d 984 (8th Cir. 1978)(damages limited to $37,000 cost of repairing boat rather than estimated $100,000 differential between value of boat as warranted and as delivered).

the seller would have done. If repair will not suffice to make the goods equivalent to conforming, unrepaired goods, damages measured solely by the cost of repair would undercompensate the buyer. The buyer should be entitled to an additional amount that reflects the difference in value between conforming and repaired goods.[84] A buyer might also be overcompensated through repair. If used goods are repaired with new parts, the ultimate life of the goods may be extended, thereby increasing their value. Adjustments should then be made to depreciate this additional benefit garnered by the buyer through repair.[85]

Sometimes the cost-to-repair method of valuation will not be available because the goods cannot be repaired. When their deficiencies are so extensive that the goods are unrepairable, determining their salvage value can establish the value of the goods as delivered.[86] If the tendered goods have greater value, that value can be established through a resale of the goods by the buyer.[87]

[2] Time and Place to Measure Value

The standard formula for measuring breach of warranty damages provides that the values to be applied in the differential are to be determined "at the time and place of acceptance."[88] These designations are the ones that are relevant to the buyer, because the buyer then gains control over and use of the goods. A considerable time can pass between the time a buyer enters into a contract and the time it accepts the seller's tender. As the court in *Chatlos Systems, Inc. v. National Cash Register Corp.*[89] perceptively pointed out, the difference in the value of the goods as warranted and as accepted can be due to an increase in their value from the time they were ordered until they were delivered, as well as to an initially favorable contract price negotiated by the buyer.

[3] Special Circumstances

The standard formula for breach of warranty damages makes the differential between the value of goods as warranted and their value as accepted

---

[84] Hartzell v. Justius Co., Inc., 693 F.2d 770, 34 UCC Rep. Serv. 1594 (A1982); Soo Line Ry. Co. v. Fruehauf Corp., 547 F.2d 1365, 20 UCC Rep. Serv. 1181 (8th Cir. 1977).

[85] Tennessee Carolina Transp., Inc. v. Strick Corp., 283 N.C. 423, 196 S.E.2d 711, 12 UCC Rep. Serv. 1055 (1973)(court should instruct jury that damages under § 2–714 should be reduced by the amount, if any, by which repairs enhanced value of goods).

[86] Massey-Ferguson Credit Corp. v. Webber, 841 F.2d 1245, 6 UCC Rep. Serv. 2d 63 (4th Cir. 1988).

[87] ITT-Industrial Credit Co. v. Mile Concrete Co., Inc., 31 N.C. App. 450, 229 S.E.2d 814, 20 UCC Rep. Serv. 1067 (1976)(resale price constituted some evidence of value of goods). *But see* Uganski v. Little Giant Crane & Shovel, Inc., 35 Mich. App. 88, 192 N.W.2d 580, 10 UCC Rep. Serv. 57 (1971)(resale came too late to serve as evidence of value of goods as accepted).

[88] UCC § 2–714(2).

[89] 670 F.2d 1304, 33 UCC Rep. Serv. 934 (3d Cir. 1982).

subject to the proviso: "unless special circumstances show proximate damages of a different amount."[90] This provision has been used by courts most frequently to deviate from the times that are stipulated for determining the applicable values. For example, if the defect in the goods is not detected by the buyer until some time after their acceptance, some courts have determined that the value of the goods as accepted should be measured at the time the buyer detected or should have detected the breach.[91] This approach generally increases the buyer's recovery because the goods usually depreciate in value.

Courts have also found "special circumstances" in cases of breach of the warranty of title. In these cases, the value of the goods as warranted is generally measured as of the time the buyer has to give up the goods.[92] This approach measures damages based on the actual loss to the buyer. If the goods have depreciated after acceptance, the buyer has enjoyed their use until relinquishment and is compensated only for the remaining value lost.[93] If the goods have appreciated in value, as often happens with art objects, the buyer is compensated based on actual value and is thus protected.[94]

§ 8.06   INCIDENTAL AND CONSEQUENTIAL DAMAGES [2–715; 2A–520]

Incidental and consequential damages can be added to the basic measure of recovery for a buyer's damages. Although the basic measure actually used is dictated by whether the buyer accepted the goods or made a qualifying cover for substitute goods, each of the three basic measures of damages also allows for recovery of incidental and consequential damages.[95] Sometimes these elements will be the most important facet of recovery because they may far exceed any of the general measures of damages.

---

[90] UCC § 2–714(2).

[91] Harlan v. Smith, 507 So. 2d 943, 4 UCC Rep. Serv. 2d 1452 (Ala. Ct. App. 1986)(value of mobile home at time buyer discovered defects).

[92] Itoh v. Kimi Sales, 74 Misc. 2d 402, 345 N.Y.S.2d 416, 13 UCC Rep. Serv. 64 (Cir. Ct. 1973)(value of automobile at time it was taken from buyers by police).

[93] Metalcraft, Inc. v. Pratt, 65 Md. Ct. App. 281, 500 A.2d 329, 42 UCC Rep. Serv. 14 (1985)(value of goods on date of dispossession even though effects of depreciation made goods less valuable than when accepted).

[94] Jeanneret v. Vichey, 541 F. Supp. 80, 34 UCC Rep. Serv. 56 (S.D. N.Y. 1982)(proper to fix damages based on appreciated value of painting at time of trial); Menzel v. List, 24 N.Y.2d 91, 298 N.Y.S.2d 979, 246 N.E.2d 742, 6 UCC Rep. Serv. 330 (1969)(buyer forced to give up painting entitled to $22,500 as the value of the painting at time of trial rather than the $4,000 paid for it more than 10 years earlier).

[95] UCC § 2–712(2)(cover), 2–713(1)(market price/contract price differential), 2–714(3)(accepted goods).

[A] Incidental

Article 2 provides for incidental damages as follows:

Incidental damages resulting from the seller's breach include expenses reasonably incurred in inspection, receipt, transportation and care and custody of goods rightfully rejected, any commercially reasonable charges, expenses or commissions in connection with effecting cover and any other reasonable expense incident to the delay or other breach.[96]

This list is not exhaustive but is rather illustrative of the types of recoverable damages.[97]

Incidental damages concern rights and obligations under the contract. They cover costs that a party incurs in fulfilling obligations under the contract. For example, a buyer must assume specific duties with respect to tendered goods following a rejection or a revocation of acceptance.[98] The buyer can recover as incidental damages any of the reasonable expenses incurred in carrying out those duties.[99] Incidental damages also include the payments that a buyer must make in order to exercise its own rights under the contract. Good illustrations include the costs of inspecting the goods or of arranging for a cover lease agreement.[100]

[B] Consequential

Article 2 provides for consequential damages as follows:

Consequential damages resulting from the seller's breach include

(a) any loss resulting from general or particular requirements and needs of which the seller at the time of contracting had reason to know and which could not reasonably be prevented by cover or otherwise; and

---

[96] UCC § 2–715(1). Article 2A is comparable. UCC § 2A–520(1).

[97] UCC § 2–715, Comment 1.

[98] UCC § 2–602(2)(general duties); UCC § 2–603 (merchant buyer). *See* § 7.04[B][3], 7.05[B] *supra*.

[99] Lanners v. Whitney, 247 Or. 223, 429 P.2d 398, 4 UCC Rep. Serv. 369 (1967)(buyer who revoked acceptance of airplane entitled to recover money spent to preserve it).

[100] Happy Dack Trading Co. Ltd. v. Agro-Indus., Inc., 602 F. Supp. 986, 41 UCC Rep. Serv. 1718 (S.D. N.Y. 1984)(inspection costs included travel and testing expenses incurred by buyers); Consolidated Data Terminals v. Applied Digital Data Sys., Inc., 708 F.2d 385, 36 UCC Rep. Serv. 59 (9th Cir. 1983)(expenses incurred in inspecting, shipping, handling, and storing defective computer terminals).

(b) injury to person or property proximately resulting from any. breach of warranty.[101]

Consequential damages essentially are the additional costs and injuries tied causally to the default, even though they are not part of the benefit expected to be conferred by the other party's performance and are not incurred through performance by the affected party or in the exercise of rights under the contract. Recovery for lost profits is the consequential damages claim that is most frequently litigated.[102] Courts in sales cases have also allowed recovery on claims for the cost of wasted labor in processing nonconforming goods,[103] restoration of a roof after removal of defective solar panels,[104] the cost of leasing software for use with a defective bookkeeping machine,[105] loss of corollary sales,[106] and the cost of substitute accommodations during delay in delivery of a mobile home.[107]

The Code is consistent with common law in placing limitations on the extent of liability for consequential damages. The foreseeability element stemming from *Hadley v. Baxendale*[108] is stated explicitly. Sellers are liable only for the consequential damages of which they had reason to know at the time of contracting. They need not have the potential damages within their actual contemplation: "It is not necessary that there be a conscious acceptance of an insurer's liability on the seller's part, nor is his obligation for consequential damages limited to cases in which he fails to use due effort in good faith."[109] The foreseeability test is satisfied when sellers either know or have reason to know of the special damages that could flow from a breach.[110]

---

[101] UCC § 2–715(2). Article 2A is comparable. UCC § 2A–520(2).

[102] Burrus v. Itek Corp., 46 Ill. App. 3d 350, 360 N.E.2d 1168, 21 UCC Rep. Serv. 1009 (1977)(lost profits established based on decrease in printing work following purchase of printing press); Franklin Grain & Supply Co v. Ingram, 44 Ill. App. 3d, 385 N.E.2d 922, 21 UCC Rep. Serv. 53 (1976)(loss of buyer's wheat crop due to late delivery of fertilizer).

[103] Atlantic Indus., Inc. v. O.E.M., Inc., 555 F. Supp. 184, 35 UCC Rep. Serv. 795 (W.D. Okla. 1983).

[104] Lanham v. Solar Am. of Cincinnati, Inc., 28 Ohio App. 3d 55, 501 N.E.2d 1245, 2 UCC. Rep. Serv. 2d 1545 (1986)(characterized by the court as incidental damages).

[105] Acme Pump Co., Inc. v. National Cash Register Co., 32 Conn. Supp. 69, 337 A.2d 672, 16 UCC Rep. Serv. 1242 (1974).

[106] Migerobe, Inc. v. Certina USA, Inc., 924 F.2d 1330, 14 UCC Rep. Serv. 2d 59 (5th Cir. 1991).

[107] Long v. Quality Mobile Home Brokers, Inc., 248 S.E.2d 311, 25 UCC Rep. Serv. 470 (S.C. 1978).

[108] 156 Eng. Rep. 145 (Ex. 1854).

[109] UCC § 2–715, Comment 3.

[110] Sun Maid Raisin Growers v. Victor Packing Co., 146 Cal. App. 3d 787, 194 Cal. Rptr. 612, 37 UCC Rep. Serv. 148 (1983); Adams v. J.I. Case Co., 125 Ill. App. 2d 388, 261 N.E.2d 1, 7 UCC Rep. Serv. 1270 (1970).

In one of the better-known cases dealing with consequential damages, *Lewis v. Mobil Oil Corp.*,[111] the seller was held to have breached an implied warranty of fitness for a particular purpose by supplying an inappropriate oil for the buyer's hydraulic sawmill machinery. Problems resulted with the machinery over a long period before the correct oil was prescribed. The court allowed the buyer to recover its lost profits during this period.

A buyer must also prove consequential damages with reasonable certainty. The requirement is not stated specifically in the text of section 2–715, but it also is not abrogated by the Code and thus is applicable through common law.[112] The Comments clarify that a technical standard of precise exactitude is not intended:

> The burden of proving the extent of loss incurred by way of consequential damage is on the buyer, but the section on liberal administration of remedies rejects any doctrine of certainty which requires almost mathematical precision in the proof of loss. Loss may be determined in any manner which is reasonable under the circumstances.[113]

The issue is most likely to be relevant in claims for lost profits, for the courts will not allow the buyer simply to speculate.[114] The established business rule, under which recovery for lost profits is generally available only for businesses that have past experiences from which prospective profits can be extrapolated, has also been applied under Article 2.[115] Most courts by now, however, have rejected the established business rule as an absolute bar to recovery of lost profits in favor of an approach that assesses whether a rational basis is available to infer an appropriate measure.[116]

The provision on consequential damages also limits buyer recovery to loss "which could not reasonably be prevented by cover or otherwise."[117] This

---

[111] 438 F.2d 500, 8 UCC Rep. Serv. 625 (8th Cir. 1971).

[112] UCC § 1–103.

[113] UCC § 2–715, Comment 4.

[114] General Supply & Equip. Co. v. Phillips, 490 S.W.2d 913, 12 UCC Rep. Serv. 35 (Tex. Ct. App. 1972)(florist estimated lost profits based on greater production and earnings per unit than he had ever realized). Courts have also generally denied recovery for factors like mental suffering. Carpel v. Saget Studios, Inc., 326 F. Supp. 1331, 9 UCC Rep. Serv. 82 (E.D. Pa. 1971)(no recovery for mental suffering for photographer's failure to deliver wedding pictures).

[115] Gerwin v. Southeastern Cal. Ass'n of Seventh Day Adventists, 14 Cal. App. 3d 209, 92 Cal. Rptr. 111, 8 UCC Rep. Serv. 643 (1971).

[116] Hardesty v. Andro Corp.-Webster Div., 555 P.2d 1030, 20 UCC Rep. Serv. 352 (Okla. 1976)(established profit experience of similar businesses); Computer Sys. Eng'g, Inc. v. Qantel Corp., 740 F.2d 59 (1st Cir. 1984)(buyer of computer software established lost profits through expert testimony).

[117] UCC § 2–715(2)(a). *See generally* Hillman, *Keeping the Deal Together after Material Breach— Common Law Mitigation Rules, the UCC, and the Restatement (Second) of Contracts*, 47 Colo. L. Rev. 553 (1976).

provision reflects the basic contract principle of avoidability under which an aggrieved party is not entitled to recover damages that could have been avoided through mitigation. The avoidability principle does not impose a duty on the buyer to mitigate, such as by entering a cover transaction. It simply prevents the buyer from recovering consequential damages for any of those damages that could have been mitigated through cover.[118] The avoidability principle has also been invoked successfully in contexts other than the failure of a buyer to cover.[119]

A different standard is applied to consequential damages in the form of personal or property injury. These injuries are recoverable if they are "proximately resulting from any breach of warranty."[120] The Comments explain as follows:

> Where the injury involved follows the use of goods without discovery of the defect causing the damage, the question of "proximate" cause turns on whether it was reasonable for the buyer to use the goods without such inspection as would have revealed the defects. If it was not reasonable for him to do so, or if he did in fact discover the defect prior to his use, the injury would not proximately result from the breach of warranty.[121]

Claims based on injury to person or property do not require the showing of foreseeability that claims for other forms of consequential damages require. The application of the proximate causation form of limitation of liability for personal and property injury cases is consistent with the strict liability approach that underlies warranty liability.[122]

---

[118] Hayes v. Hettinga, 228 N.W.2d 181, 16 UCC Rep. Serv. 983 (Iowa 1975)(buyer failed to establish lost profits as consequential damages by failing to show the loss could not have been prevented by cover).

[119] *See, e.g.,* Chatlos Sys., Inc. v. National Cash Register Corp., 479 F. Supp. 738, 27 UCC Rep. Serv. 647 (D. N.J. 1979), *aff'd on other grounds,* 635 F.2d 1081 (3d Cir. 1980)(buyer refusal to allow seller further access to computer to attempt to program it properly); R.I. Lampus Co. v. Neville Cement Products. Corp., 232 Pa. Super. 242, 336 A.2d 397, 16 UCC Rep. Serv. 996 (5th Cir. 1982)(use of goods that buyer should have known would not meet its needs); Erdman v. Johnson Bros. Radio & Television Co., Inc. 260 Md. 190, 271 A.2d 744, 8 UCC Rep. Serv. 656 (1970)(buyer could not recover for loss from house fire caused by defective television when buyer left set plugged in after it smoked and emitted sparks).

[120] UCC § 2–715(2)(b).

[121] UCC § 2–715, Comment 5. Erdman v. Johnson Bros. Radio & TV Co., 260 Md. 190, 271 A.2d 744, 8 UCC Rep. Serv. 656 (1970)(buyer who had seen television set smoke and give off sparks but nevertheless left it plugged in could not hold seller liable for value of his house when set caught fire and burned the house).

[122] *See* discussion in § 5.06[A] *supra.*

Part B: Nonmonetary Damages

§ 8.07　CANCELLATION [2–711(1), 2A–508(1)(a)]

An aggrieved buyer is entitled to cancel the contract in any of the circumstances of seller breach that allow the buyer to recover any of the purchase price that has been paid.[123] The applicable circumstances include all of the cases in which the buyer will not retain the seller's goods: when the seller fails to deliver or anticipatorily repudiates, or when the buyer rightfully rejects or justifiably revokes. The buyer cannot cancel for goods that have been accepted, or for subsequent installments of an installment contract in which the breach does not go to the whole contract.[124]

Article 2 provides that " '[c]ancellation' occurs when either party puts an end to the contract for breach by the other."[125] It has the same effect as a termination, "except that the cancelling party also retains any remedy for breach of the whole contract or any unperformed balance."[126] An aggrieved buyer may both cancel the contract and recover money damages.[127]

§ 8.08　SPECIFIC PERFORMANCE [2–716; 2A–521]

Rather than monetary damages, buyers and lessees are sometimes entitled to delivery of the goods themselves through a decree of specific performance. Courts, in their discretion, may award specific performance under Articles 2 and 2A if "the goods are unique or in other proper circumstances."[128]

By requiring that the goods be unique, the Code perpetuates the traditional basis for granting a decree of specific performance. The remedy is equitable in nature and has not generally been granted when monetary damages would

---

[123] UCC §§ 2–711(1), 2A–508(1)(b). *See* § 8.02 *supra*.

[124] *See* § 8.02 *supra*.

[125] UCC § 2–106(4). Article 2A is comparable. UCC § 2A–103(1)(b).

[126] *Id.* " 'Termination' occurs when either party pursuant to a power created by agreement or law puts an end to the contract otherwise than for its breach." UCC § 2–106(3). Article 2A is comparable. UCC § 2A–103(1)(z). *See* Vending Credit Corp. v. Trudy Toys Co., 5 Conn. Cir. Ct. 629, 260 A.2d 135 (1969)(lessee required to exercise option to terminate lease agreement within time stipulated in lease agreement).

[127] Lanners v. Whitney, 247 Or. 223, 428 P.2d 398, 4 UCC Rep. Serv. 369 (1969).

[128] UCC § 2–716(1); UCC § 2A–521(1).

enable the aggrieved buyer to obtain comparable goods elsewhere. The Code, however, also expands the meaning of "unique." The Comments explain:

> In view of this Article's emphasis on the commercial feasibility of re-placement, a new concept of what are "unique" goods is introduced under this section. Specific performance is no longer limited to goods which are already specific or ascertained at the time of contracting. The test of uniqueness under this section must be made in terms of the total situation which characterizes the contract.[129]

The drafters thus clearly rejected pre-Code cases in which the courts, perpet-uating a meaning of unique that is consistent with one-of-a-kind heirlooms,[130] denied specific performance for goods in cases of market shortages.[131] The intent is to make market realities a relevant consideration in requests for spe-cific performance. Consequently, the court in *Sedmak v. Charlie's Chevrolet, Inc.*[132] awarded specific performance in ordering delivery of an "Indy Pace Car" Corvette because it had been produced in a limited edition.[133]

The Code goes further by authorizing specific performance in "other proper circumstances." The liberalizing intent of the drafters is explicit in the following comment: "[W]ithout intending to impair in any way the exercise of the court's sound discretion in the matter, this Article seeks to further a more liberal attitude than some courts have shown in connection with the specific performance of contracts of sale."[134] The only suggestion, however, of what constitutes "other proper circumstances" for purposes of specific performance is the cryptic indication that "inability to cover is strong evidence of 'other proper circumstances.' "[135]

Perhaps the most expansive application of the standard was made in *Ste-phan's Machine & Tool, Inc. v. D & H Machinery Consultants, Inc.*[136] The seller promised to deliver a replacement for defective machinery, but did not keep the promise. The buyer had made financing commitments for the purchase and

---

[129] UCC § 2–716, Comment 2.

[130] An Article 2 case consistent with this standard is *Gay v. Seafarer Fiberglass Yachts, Inc.*, 14 UCC Rep. Serv. 1335 (N.Y. Sup. Ct. 1974)(yacht with special hull design manufactured exclusively by defendant was unique).

[131] McAllister v. Patten, 214 Ark. 293, 215 S.W.2d 701 (1948)(dealer refusal to deliver prom-ised new car during period of critical market shortages due to the war effort).

[132] 622 S.W.2d 694, 31 UCC Rep. Serv. 851 (Mo. Ct. App. 1981).

[133] *See also* Copylease Corp. of Am. v. Memorex Corp., 408 F. Supp. 758 (S.D. N.Y. 1976)(product may be unique if other brands available are "distinctly inferior" in quality).

[134] UCC § 2–716, Comment 1.

[135] UCC § 2–716, Comment 2.

[136] 65 Ohio App. 2d 197, 417 N.E.2d 579 (1979).

could not finance the purchase of a replacement. The court awarded specific performance because of the buyer's financial situation.

In a case that arose out of the energy crisis, *Laclede Gas Co. v. Amoco Oil Co.*,[137] the parties had agreed to a long-term supply contract for propane. The buyer successfully enjoined the seller from breaching. The court was persuaded that the acknowledged impossibility for the buyer to negotiate another contract of comparable duration made the case one of other proper circumstances for a decree of specific performance.

Although an order for specific performance is within the discretion of the court, buyers are also granted a limited right to replevy goods in a sales contract. The applicable provision states: "The buyer has a right to replevin for goods identified to the contract if after reasonable effort he is unable to effect cover for such goods or the circumstances reasonably indicate that such effort will be unavailing. . . . "[138] The discretion of courts to deny the buyer access to a seller's goods is thus limited in cases in which the buyer cannot cover, but only if the seller's goods have been identified to the contract.

---

[137] 522 F.2d 33, 17 UCC Rep. Serv. 447 (8th Cir. 1975).
[138] UCC § 2–716(3). Article 2A is comparable. UCC § 2A–521(3).

CHAPTER
9

Remedies of Sellers and Lessors

Part A: Monetary Remedies

§ 9.01   RESALE [2–706, 2A–527]

[A]   Sales

When a buyer breaches by repudiating, by failing to pay, or by wrongfully rejecting or revoking, the seller can sell the goods to another buyer and use the resale price as the basis for recovery of damages.[1] The resale must qualify under criteria that are explained below. When it does qualify, the seller's measure of damages is "the difference between the resale price and the contract price."[2] Incidental damages incurred by the seller are added, and any expenses saved as a result of the buyer's breach are subtracted.

This measure of damages is the preferred monetary remedy for an aggrieved seller because it best meets the objective of contract remedies, which is to place the seller in the same economic position that would have resulted had the contract been performed. This measure uses the exact amount realized by the seller in the substitute disposition of the goods. By using actual resale price, this measure of damages reflects the seller's injuries precisely. Damages based on a seller's resale are comparable to a buyer's damages based on cover.[3]

---

[1]   UCC § 2–703(d).
[2]   UCC § 2–706(1).
[3]   *See* § 8.03 *supra.*

In order for the seller's resale transaction to qualify for damages based on the resale, the resale must be made in good faith and in a commercially reasonable manner.[4] These criteria operate as limiting factors that protect the interests of the breaching buyer. The seller cannot simply resell at a purposely reduced price with the intent to increase damages or even sell at any price offered assuming that any loss can be passed through to the breaching buyer. The seller must provide enough attention and effort to the resale transaction to enhance the amount received. Sellers who sell goods on their own behalf are motivated by their own economic self-interest to bargain for a fair purchase price. Because the economic interest of the breaching buyer is at stake in the resale transaction, these limiting criteria are imposed to motivate the seller to continue to strive for a fair bargain.

Article 2 grants sellers considerable leeway in determining particular aspects of a resale transaction, but it makes the determination of every one of them subject to the standard of commercial reasonableness. Particulars addressed in the Code provisions include the choice of a public or private sale, sale through one or more contracts, sale in a single unit or in parcels, and choice as to time and place of sale.[5] The overarching guideline on resale, however, is that "every aspect of the sale including the method, manner, time, place and terms must be commercially reasonable."[6] The intended interplay between seller discretion and the "commercially reasonable" restriction is made explicit in the Comments: "Subsection (2) frees the remedy of resale from legalistic restrictions and enables the seller to resell in accordance with reasonable commercial practices so as to realize as high a price as possible in the circumstances."[7] Another part of the Comments states that the objective is "to enable the seller to dispose of the goods to the best advantage."[8] Thus, the seller must make reasonable efforts to attain as high a price as possible.

The Second Circuit in *Apex Oil Co. v. Belcher Co. of New York, Inc.*[9] properly overturned the district court's award of resale damages. The seller sold the oil that was subject to the original contract on the day after the buyer breached.

---

[4] UCC § 2–706(1).

[5] UCC § 2–706(2).

[6] UCC § 2–706(2). Coast Trading Co. v. Cudahy Co., 592 F.2d 1074, 25 UCC Rep. Serv. 1037 (9th Cir. 1978)(fictitious "wash" sale was designed to inflate damage claim); McMillan v. Meuser Material & Equip. Co., 60 Ark. 422, 541 S.W.2d 911, 20 UCC Rep. Serv. 110 (1976)(14-month delay in resale held unreasonable); California Airmotive Corp. v. Jones, 415 F.2d 554, 6 UCC Rep. Serv. 1007 (6th Cir. 1969)(material issue of fact when ad for resale gave incorrect date and location).

[7] UCC § 2–706, Comment 4.

[8] UCC § 2–706, Comment 6.

[9] 855 F.2d 997, 6 UCC Rep. Serv. 2d 1025 (2d Cir. 1988).

Six weeks later, the seller sold the same amount of a comparable grade of oil to another buyer at a price substantially below the contract price. The Second Circuit held that the second sale could not be used to fix the breaching buyer's damages. Due to the volatility of the market for such oil, the delay before the purported resale was clearly unreasonable. In addition, the resale of the oil immediately following breach fixed the value of those goods.

The provisions on resale also include directives concerning public and private sales. The directives are minimal with respect to a private sale: the seller must give the buyer reasonable notification of the intent to resell the goods.[10] In addition to buyer notification of the time and place of the resale,[11] public sales involve several more requirements.[12] The sale must be at a place or market that is usual for a public sale, provided that one is available.[13] With respect to goods that are not available to be viewed by persons attending the sale, the seller must provide notice to prospective bidders as to where the goods are located and must allow reasonable inspection of the goods. The seller is entitled to bid on the goods at the resale. Except for sales in an established market for sales of futures, only identified goods can be sold through a public resale.

The requirement for identification of the goods does not require that they have been identified to the contract before breach by the buyer. The goods need not even have been in existence at the time of breach.[14] Thus, for example, a seller is not deprived of resale just because the buyer anticipatorily repudiates before the seller completes manufacture of the goods.

Another Article 2 provision facilitates the seller's opportunity to utilize the resale measure of damages.[15] A seller who learns of the buyer's breach with respect to conforming goods in the seller's possession or control can identify the goods to the contract. The seller can also exercise commercial judgment as to whether to complete the manufacture of goods that are intended for the contract but unfinished.[16] If loss can be avoided, the seller is well advised to

---

[10] UCC § 2–706(3). Alco Standard Corp. v. F & B Mfg. Co., 51 Ill. 2d 186, 281 N.E.2d 652, 10 UCC Rep. Serv. 639 (1972)(notice need only indicate intention to resell).

[11] Cole v. Melvin, 441 F. Supp. 193, 22 UCC Rep. Serv. 1154 (D. S.D. 1977)(failure to notify buyer prior to public and private resales precluded use of resale prices to fix damages). Notification is excused if the goods are perishable or threaten to decline in value speedily. UCC § 2–607(4)(b).

[12] UCC § 2–706(4).

[13] Public sale means a sale by auction. UCC § 2–607, Comment 4.

[14] UCC § 2–706(2).

[15] UCC § 2–704.

[16] Young v. Frank's Nursery & Crafts, Inc., 58 Ohio St. 3d 242, 569 N.E.2d 1034, 14 UCC Rep.

complete the goods to enhance the resale price that can be recovered.[17] The right to identify goods to the contract after breach by the seller facilitates the availability of the seller's primary remedy of resale.[18]

[B]   Leases

Following a default by the lessee, the lessor is entitled to dispose of the goods by a subsequent lease, sale, or other method of disposition.[19] The right to dispose of the goods can apply to goods the lessor refuses to deliver, goods the lessor claims by taking possession, and even goods remaining in the lessee's possession. The lessor often will want to reacquire possession of the goods prior to disposing of them due to practical aspects affecting their disposal.

The lessor can use the proceeds of the disposition transaction as a basis to measure damages from the buyer's breach only if the disposition qualifies. Like the Article 2 requirements, the disposition must be made in good faith and in a commercially reasonable manner. Under Article 2A, however, the disposition can be by lease only, and the substitute lease agreement must be substantially similar to the original lease agreement. These requirements are the same ones that Article 2A uses to determine the qualification of a substitute lease as a valid cover for determining damages by an aggrieved lessee.[20] The original agreement and the substitute agreement must be comparable enough to justify comparing them for purposes of fixing damages.[21] Precise correlation on all terms is unlikely in the lease context. The primary guiding premise, therefore, is that the courts should adjust the damages formula to reflect the value of the

---

Serv. 2d 463 (1991)(burden on buyer to establish that seller's decision not to complete preparation of goods was commercially unreasonable).

[17] Superior Derrick Services, Inc. v. Anderson, 831 S.W.2d 868, 18 UCC Rep. Serv. 2d 706 (Tex. Ct. App. 1992)(following repudiation by buyer, seller simply stopped production, so mast never became identified to the contract).

[18] UCC § 2–704, Comment 1. Servbest Foods, Inc. v. Emessee Indus., Inc., 82 Ill. App. 3d 662, 403 N.E.2d 1, 29 UCC Rep. Serv. 518 (1980)(held that subsequent identification of truly fungible goods to the resale contract is appropriate even though other conforming goods had been identified originally).

[19] UCC § 2A–527(1).

[20] See § 8.03[C] supra.

[21] In most lease cases decided before Article 2A, the courts required the proceeds of a disposition by the lessor to be deducted from the amounts due under the lease. Fisher Trucking, Inc. v. Fleet Lease, Inc., 304 Ark. 451, 803 S.W.2d 888, 14 UCC Rep. Serv. 2d 887 (1991); Deutz-Allis Credit Corp. v. Jensen, 458 N.W.2d 163, 12 UCC Rep. Serv. 2d 512 (Minn. Ct. App. 1990). The dispositions in these cases, however, were by sale of the goods. A sale covers not only the value of the remaining lease term but the lessor's residual value in the goods as well. A sale is not sufficiently comparable to the original lease to provide a valid basis for comparison.

differences and thus enable the substitute lease to qualify as substantially similar, provided that the differences can be valued with reasonable certainty.[22]

The damages formula for a substitute lease transaction is stated in terms of three elements, as follows:

> [T]he lessor may recover from the lessee as damages (i) accrued and unpaid rent as of the date of the commencement of the term of the new lease agreement, (ii) the present value, as of the same date, of the total rent for the then remaining lease term of the original lease agreement minus the present value, as of the same date, of the rent under the new lease agreement applicable to that period of the new lease term which is comparable to the then remaining term of the original lease agreement, and (iii) any incidental damages allowed under Section 2A–530, less expenses saved in consequence of the lessee's default.[23]

The first element gives the lessor all of the rent that has accrued and remains unpaid up until the date the substitute lease commences. The second element awards the differential between the remaining rental under the original lease agreement and the rental for the comparable term under the new lease agreement. These future rents covered under the second element are reduced to present value. The third element adds incidental damages and deducts expenses saved as a result of the breach.

The demarcation between the first two elements is appropriately fixed at the time that the new lease commences. The lessor will need some time to negotiate a new lease agreement following default by the lessee. The lessor thus should be entitled to recover rent under the original lease until the new lease commences. Ending recovery under the first element at the moment of default would reduce damages based on the new lease even though that lease was not yet effective.

[C] Comparing Sales, Leases, and Secured Transactions

Some significant similarities accompany the disposition of goods under sales, leases, and secured transactions. On the other hand, substantial differences also affect dispositions in these three basic types of transactions. In any of the transactions, the disposing party has the discretion to select the method of disposal. Sellers and lessors must enter into a qualifying sale or qualifying lease, respectively, in order to measure damages based on the new transaction;[24] otherwise they are relegated to damages based on the market/contract

---

[22] UCC § 2A–527, Comment 5.
[23] UCC § 2A–527(2).
[24] UCC §§ 2–706(1), 2A–527(2).

differential.[25] Secured lenders can use any method of disposal that will enhance the recovery,[26] but failure to adhere to the standard of commercial reasonableness will subject them to liability.[27] In any of the three types of transactions, the party taking in good faith under the disposition takes free of the interest of the other party under the original agreement, even if the party making the disposition fails to comply with some of the Code requirements governing the disposition.[28]

Although sellers and lessors are entitled to dispose of the goods following an applicable breach or default, they are never obligated to do so.[29] If they prefer, they can retain possession of the goods for their own use. Article 9, however, generally requires a secured party who takes possession of collateral to dispose of it in a commercially reasonable manner.[30]

A secured party has an interest in the collateral only to secure the extent of the outstanding indebtedness. The secured lender thus must account for any proceeds from the disposition after deducting expenses and the unpaid debt, with the debtor receiving any ultimate surplus.[31] The debtor has equity in the collateral and has the right to redeem the collateral prior to its disposition by the secured party.[32] To protect the debtor and other secured party interests, Article 9 imposes rules concerning notification for public and private sales.[33]

A lessor holds a residual interest in leased goods. Consequently, a lessor need not account to the lessee for any profit made on a disposition.[34] The lessee does not have any equity of redemption in the goods.[35] The basic rules concerning public and private sales and notification to the defaulting party are deleted in the lease context. A sale can never serve as a sufficiently comparable transaction for purposes of using the proceeds as a basis for measuring damages to a lessor. Recognizing that lessors using a substitute lease transaction for

---

[25] UCC § 2–706, Comment 2. Foxco Indus., Ltd. v. Fabric World, 595 F.2d 976, 26 UCC Rep. Serv. 694 (5th Cir. 1979)(failure to notify buyer of private sale). UCC § 2A–527(3).

[26] UCC § 9–504(1).

[27] UCC § 9–507.

[28] UCC §§ 2–706(5), 2A–527(4), 9–504(4).

[29] UCC §§ 2–703, 2–706(1). UCC § 2A–527, Comment 1.

[30] The strict foreclosure rights of a secured party are quite limited. *See* UCC §§ 9–504, 9–505.

[31] UCC §§ 9–504(1),(2).

[32] UCC § 9–506.

[33] UCC § 9–504(3). These rules are similar in many respects to the rules applicable to sellers who wish to use the resale transaction as the basis to measure damages. *See* § 9.01[A] *supra*.

[34] UCC § 2A–527(5).

[35] UCC § 2A–527, Comment 10.

damages purposes have multiple variables to negotiate and often face rapid change in the market place, the drafters determined not to draft with specificity.[36]

A seller of goods also is not required to account to the breaching party for any profit realized upon resale of the goods.[37] Article 2 divorces the seller's right to resell and the consequences of resale from the question of when title to the goods passes.[38] Essentially, however, when a seller properly utilizes the resale provision, the sale will not be consummated and the seller, as "owner" of the goods, is not accountable for any profit. The sole purpose of the regulation of public and private sales and the notice requirements is to protect the breaching buyer's interest in having as high a resale price as possible in order to minimize the damages that will result from using resale price as the basis for their determination. Failure to adhere relegates the aggrieved seller to damages measured by contract price/market price differential. Comparable failure by a secured party, on the other hand, can lead to liability of the secured party.[39]

The situation differs when buyers or lessees exercise the right to dispose of goods in a sales or lease transaction. When buyers or lessees properly reject or revoke tendered goods, they are granted security interests in the goods in their possession or control. They are entitled to dispose of these goods in the same manner as an aggrieved seller or lessor to cover any expenses they incur for inspection, receipt, transport, or care and custody of the goods.[40] The interests of such buyers and lessees extend, however, only to the recovery of expenses they have incurred. As a result, they must account for any amount recovered in excess of these expenses.[41]

§ 9.02   CONTRACT PRICE/MARKET PRICE DIFFERENTIAL [2–708(1); 2A–528(1)]

[A] The Measure

The Code also retains the traditional method of fixing seller damages based on the difference between contract price and market price.[42] Incidental

---

[36] UCC § 2A–527, Comment 4.
[37] UCC § 2–706(6). Mott Equity Elevator v. Svihovec, 236 N.W.2d 900, 18 UCC Rep. Serv. 388 (N.D. 1975).
[38] UCC § 2–401; UCC § 2–706, Comment 11.
[39] UCC § 9–507 (subject to being ordered or restrained, liable for causal loss, and subject to penalty when the collateral is consumer goods).
[40] UCC §§ 2–711(3), 2A–508(5). Bevel-Fold, Inc. v. Bose Corp., 9 Mass. App. 576, 402 N.E.2d 1104, 28 UCC Rep. Serv. 1333 (1980).
[41] UCC § 2–706(6). Texpor Traders, Inc. v. Trust Co. Bank, 720 F. Supp. 1100, 10 UCC Rep. Serv. 2d 1227 (S.D. N.Y. 1989). UCC § 2A–527(5).
[42] UCC § 2–708(1).

damages are also added to this difference, and expenses saved in consequence of the buyer's breach are deducted. This alternative measure is necessary, despite being a less precise measure of actual damages than the measure based on resale. Sellers are not required to enter a resale transaction following breach by a buyer. Furthermore, only resale transactions that satisfy the standard of commercial reasonableness can even qualify for use in fixing damages. An alternative measure is needed to govern those cases in which a reliable resale price is not available.

The differential in the lease context is based on the total of three elements. A lessor is entitled to recover

(i) accrued and unpaid rent as of the date of default if the lessee has never taken possession of the goods, or, if the lessee has taken possession of the goods, as of the date the lessor repossesses the goods or an earlier date on which the lessee makes a tender of the goods to the lessor, (ii) the present value as of the date determined under clause (i) of the total rent for the then remaining lease term of the original lease agreement minus the present value as of the same date of the market rent at the place where the goods are located computed for the same lease term, and (iii) any incidental damages allowed under Section 2A–530, less expenses saved in consequences of the lessee's default.[43]

The first two elements award the lessor unpaid rent that has accrued under the lease plus the present value of the difference between the original rent and the market rent for the remainder of the lease term.

[B]   Determining the Market

[1]   Sales

Although the contract/market differential is comparable to the buyer's remedy based on market/contract differential,[44] the drafters were not consistent in establishing the method of determining the applicable market price. The buyer's remedy ascertains market time based on when the buyer learned of the breach and establishes market place based on the market in which the buyer most likely would have covered had that option been pursued.[45] The provision for the seller's remedy, however, stipulates that market price is determined "at the time and place for tender."[46] This approach neither conforms with the selection factors for the buyer's remedy nor reflects the market in which the seller

---

[43]   UCC § 2A–528(1).
[44]   *See* UCC § 2–713 and § 8.04 *supra*.
[45]   *See* § 8.04[B] *supra*.
[46]   UCC § 2–708(1).

would have been most likely to resell the goods. For example, a California seller would most likely resell in California upon learning of a breach prior to shipment to a New York buyer, whereas destination contract terms would have tender occurring in New York.[47] Similarly, under shipment contract terms, the tender would occur in California. If the goods are wrongfully rejected after their arrival in New York, the seller most surely would attempt to resell them in New York. The drafters do not provide guidance concerning their selection of market identification criteria.

[2] Leases

The drafters of Article 2A provide a much more reasoned approach to the issue. The aggrieved lessor is entitled to recover unpaid rent that has accrued under the lease until the lessor was in a position to undertake a disposition. At that relevant point in time, the differential between original rent and market rent applies to the remainder of the lease term. The opportunity to re-lease is thus the primary factor that controls the designation of the market date for purposes of the remedy.

The demarcation point between recovery of accrued rent under the lease and of the differential depends on whether the lessee has taken possession of the goods. If the lessee has taken possession, the rental obligation under the lease continues until the lessor repossesses the goods or until the lessee tenders them back to the lessor, whichever is earlier. The differential represents the principle of mitigation, giving the defaulting lessee the benefit of the market value that the lessor could have attained by entering into a substantially similar lease. Without reacquiring possession of the goods, the lessor is not in a position to re-lease them to another party. A lessee could delay repossession for a considerable period of time following default, through resistance or litigation. During this time the lessee would continue to have possession and use of the lessor's goods. Consequently, the date of lessor repossession determines the market date in these cases. The lessor cannot extend recovery of rent simply by delaying repossession. The lessee can fix the market date by simply retendering the goods to the lessor.

If the lessee has not taken possession of the goods, the demarcation point is the date of default. A lessor in possession or control of the goods could commence mitigation through a substitute lease immediately upon the lessee's default. As a result, the market rent is determined at this earlier date.

Article 2A establishes the market place as the place where the goods are located when the lease rent/market rent differential is determined under the

---

[47] For discussion of tender of delivery, see § 4.05[B] supra.

formula. The premise is that the designated location generally will be the most economically efficient place to dispose of the goods.

§ 9.03   Lost Profits [2–708(2); 2A–528(2)]

Article 2 provides a different formula when the measure based on market rent "is inadequate to put the seller in as good a position as performance would have done."[48] Article 2A includes the same provision for lessors.[49] The basic measure of recovery is then the profit (including reasonable overhead) that the seller or lessor would have realized from full performance of the breaching party.[50] In addition to incidental damages, the formula provides for "due allowance for costs reasonably incurred and due credit for payments or proceeds of [disposition]."[51]

Application of the provision has evolved into recognition of certain categories of sellers who will not be adequately protected by other measures of damages. The most readily apparent of these is generally referred to as the "lost-volume seller."[52] This seller, like many retailers, has a ready supply of goods available to meet the demand from buyers.[53] Particular goods will be sold to another buyer following breach, but if the goods are standard-priced, the seller will not be awarded any damages under the contract/market differential. The seller's true interest is the profit associated with each sale. If the original buyer had not breached, the seller would have earned the profit from the additional sale. That profit becomes the measure of recovery for the lost-volume seller.[54]

Pre-Article 2A cases recognized the appropriateness of awarding damages based on lost profits to a lessor who lost volume business through breach by the lessee. In *Locks v. Wade*,[55] for example, the lessor could acquire as many

---

[48] UCC § 2–708(2).

[49] UCC § 2A–528(2).

[50] Vitex Mfg. Co. v. Caribtex Corp., 377 F.2d 795, 4 UCC Rep. Serv. 182 (3d Cir. 1967) (allowable overhead held to include pro rata share of fixed costs).

[51] UCC §§ 2–708(2), 2A–528(2).

[52] *See generally* Harris, *A Radical Restatement of the Law of Seller's Damages: Sales Act and Commercial Code Results Compared*, 18 Stan. L. Rev. 66 (1965).

[53] *See* Ragen Corp. v. Kearney & Trecker Corp., 912 F.2d 619, UCC Rep. Serv. (3d Cir. 1990)(seller not entitled to lost-profit recovery because it could not have supplied a second buyer).

[54] Islamic Republic of Iran v. Boeing Co., 771 F.2d 1279, 41 UCC Rep. Serv. 1178 (9th Cir. 1985); Snyder v. Herbert Greenbaum & Assocs., 38 Md. App. 144, 380 A.2d 618, 22 UCC Rep. Serv. 1104 (1977).

[55] 36 N.J. Super. 128, 114 A.2d 875 (App. Div. 1955).

jukeboxes as it could lease in its business. The defaulting lessee argued that the lessor's damages claim should be reduced by the amount realized in a new lease of the goods. The court disagreed, however, and awarded damages based on the difference between the lease rent and the cost the lessor would have incurred in performing.[56]

A case that could become influential in this area is *R. E. Davis Chemical Corp. v. Diasonics, Inc.*[57] After the buyer repudiated a contract for the purchase of a magnetic resonance imager, the seller resold the equipment to a third party at the same purchase price. The seller counterclaimed for lost profits when the buyer sued for the return of its down payment. The buyer contended that the seller's failure to introduce evidence to identify the third-party buyer defeated its claim for lost profits. The Seventh Circuit disagreed, and established the following three-part test to determine when a seller qualifies as a lost-volume seller: (1) the seller must possess the capacity to make an additional sale, (2) the additional sale would have been profitable for the seller, and (3) the seller probably would have made the additional sale even if the breach had not occurred. Under this test, the seller qualified for recovery of lost profits.

In the case of a lost-volume seller or lessor, the formula for the measure based on lost profits cannot be applied literally. The formula requires a credit for proceeds of resale or other disposition. Deduction of a lost-volume seller's resale proceeds would defeat the whole purpose of allowing recovery for lost profits. Courts generally have ignored the deduction in cases of lost-volume sellers in favor of advancing the underlying remedies policy of placing the seller in as good a position as if the buyer had performed.[58]

Another class of parties for whom the lost-profits measure of recovery is available is the components manufacturer, a seller who manufactures or assembles the goods subject to a sale or lease. If the buyer or lessee repudiates before the goods have been completed, the manufacturer has to decide whether to complete them.[59] When the decision is justifiably made not to complete the goods, the manufacturer's loss of the anticipated profit from the transaction cannot be recouped from a substitute transaction. The manufacturer of uncompleted goods is thus entitled to recover lost profits.[60] The entire damages formula operates properly with this class of seller or lessor. Both reasonable

---

[56] *See also* Honeywell, Inc. v. Lithonia Lighting, Inc., 317 F. Supp. 406 (N.D. Ga. 1970).

[57] 826 F.2d 678 (7th Cir. 1991).

[58] Teradyne, Inc. v. Teledyne Indus., Inc., 676 F.2d 865, 33 UCC Rep. Serv. 1669 (1st Cir. 1982); Neri v. Retail Marine Corp., 30 N.Y.2d 393, 334 N.Y.S.2d 165, 285 N.E.2d 311, 10 UCC Rep. Serv. 950 (1972).

[59] UCC §§ 2–704(2), 2A–524(2). *See* § 9.01[A] *supra*.

[60] Bead Chain Mfg. Co. v. Saxton Prods., Inc., 183 Conn. 266, 439 A.2d 314, 31 UCC Rep. Serv. 91 (1981)(manufacturer granted lost profits on incomplete electrical components for

overhead and costs reasonably incurred in manufacturing and incidental damages are added to the lost profit, and the payments or proceeds received from sale or salvage are deducted.[61]

§ 9.04   ACTION FOR PRICE OR RENT [2–709; 2A–529]

In certain circumstances a seller can bring an action for the price of the goods that the buyer has failed to pay. This remedy is analogous to an aggrieved buyer's action for specific performance, and like specific performance, the availability of the remedy is limited. The remedy is generally not available on the premise that sellers of goods are often in the business of selling such goods and are thus better situated than the buyer to make an alternate disposition of the goods. Article 2 stipulates the circumstances in which this advantage does not apply to the seller and limits the seller's action for the price to those circumstances.

A seller who sues the buyer for the price of the goods must hold for the buyer any of the goods that have been identified to the contract and that are still within the seller's control.[62] Payment of the judgment entitles the buyer to the goods.[63] Any time before collection of the judgment, however, the seller can resell the goods and credit the proceeds to the buyer.[64]

[A]   Limited Applicability

[1]   Accepted Goods

One of the consequences of buyer acceptance of tendered goods is that the buyer must pay for them at the contract rate.[65] The requirement makes sense because the buyer has taken and retained goods of the seller. The remedies provision on action for the price thus recognizes a cause of action in the seller with

---

which no resale market existed); Timber Access Industries Co. v. U.S. Plywood-Champion Papers, Inc., 263 Or. 509, 503 P.2d 482, 11 UCC Rep. Serv. 994 (1972)(same for undelivered logs).

[61] More extensive analysis of the lost-profits recovery and several controversies that have developed can be found in Goetz & Scott, *Measuring Seller's Damages: The Lost Profits Puzzle*, 31 Stan. L. Rev. 323 (1979); Harris, *A General Theory for Measuring Seller's Damages for Total Breach of Contract*, 60 Mich. L. Rev. 577 (1962); Speidel & Clay, *Seller's Recovery of Overhead under UCC Section 2–708(2): Economic Cost Theory and Contract Remedial Policy*, 57 Cornell L. Rev. 681 (1972).

[62] UCC § 2–709(2).

[63] *Id.*

[64] *Id.*

[65] UCC § 2–607(1). *See* § 7.03[B][2] *supra.*

respect to accepted goods "when the buyer fails to pay the price as it becomes due."[66] Article 2 generally denies an action for price when the buyer has not accepted the goods.[67] The seller who retains possession of or control over the goods will generally be in a superior position to dispose of the goods elsewhere. These sellers must use the other Code measures to calculate damages.

An action for the price of goods accepted can require a proper application of the concepts of rejection and revocation.[68] For example, in *Integrated Circuits Unlimited v. E.F. Johnson Co.*,[69] the buyer wrongfully rejected some of the lots of electronic parts shipped by the seller. Even though the buyer did not have the right to reject, the rejection was procedurally effective. The rejection precluded acceptance, and the seller did not have an action for the price of the rejected goods. The court in *McClure Oil Corp. v. Murray Equipment, Inc.*[70] held that the buyer's letter indicating that it was "having problems" with delivered pumps was not a rejection. Having accepted the goods, the buyer was liable for the contract price. In *Solar Kinetics Corp. v. Joseph T. Ryerson & Sons, Inc.*,[71] the court held that the buyer's failure to comply with the procedural requirements of a revocation meant that the buyer was still held to have accepted the goods. The seller thus was entitled to recover the unpaid balance of the purchase price.[72]

[2] Goods Lost or Damaged

One exception to the general principle of limiting a seller's cause of action for price to buyer acceptance of tendered goods applies when "conforming goods [are] lost or damaged within a commercially reasonable time after risk of their loss has passed to the buyer."[73] Loss or destruction of goods after risk

---

[66] UCC § 2–709(1)(a). Lupofresh, Inc. v. Pabst Brewing Co., Inc., 505 A.2d 37, 42 UCC Rep. Serv. 1651 (Del. Super. 1985).

[67] Hayes v. Hettinga, 228 N.W.2d 181, 16 UCC Rep. Serv. 983 (Iowa 1975)(court properly entered judgment against seller in action for price because evidence did not show buyer had accepted the goods).

[68] For explanations of rejection and revocation, *see* §§ 7.04, 7.05 *supra*.

[69] 875 F.2d 1040, 8 UCC Rep. Serv. 2d 695 (2d Cir. 1989).

[70] 515 N.E.2d 546, 5 UCC Rep. Serv. 2d 1354 (Ind. Ct. App. 1987).

[71] 488 F. Supp. 1237, 29 UCC Rep. Serv. 85 (D. Conn. 1980).

[72] The effectiveness of a wrongful revocation is less certain. Section 2–709(3) appears to recognize it, but the comments indicate that the action for price for goods accepted "include only goods as to which there has been no *justified* revocation of acceptance, for such a revocation means that there has been a default by the seller which bars his rights under this section." UCC § 2–709, Comment 5 (emphasis added). Although the drafting is unclear, the preferable position is to deny the effectiveness of a wrongful revocation. *See* § 7.05[D] *supra*.

[73] UCC § 2–709(1)(a).

of their loss has passed to the buyer means that the buyer is liable under the contract to pay for the goods.[74] The seller does not have a significantly enhanced opportunity to dispose of the goods in this context. The seller cannot dispose of goods that have been lost, and goods that have been damaged or destroyed are different from the goods the seller sells.

The availability of this exception requires proper application of the Code provisions on risk of loss allocation.[75] Most of the cases concerning risk of loss and actions for price have involved goods shipped by common carrier. For example, the buyer in *Montana Seeds, Inc. v. Holliday*[76] was liable for the purchase price of seed delivered to the buyer at the wrong location because under the contract, the goods were to be delivered to the buyer without specification of a particular destination.[77] Similarly, in *Ninth St. East, Ltd. v. Harrison*,[78] the contract terms provided F.O.B. the seller's location. Risk of loss passed to the buyer upon proper shipment by the seller,[79] so that despite the subsequent loss of the goods, the buyer was liable for their price. Risk of loss passed to the buyer in *Rheinberg Kellerei GmbH v. Brooksfield Nat'l Bank of Commerce Bank*[80] after tendered wine arrived at the harbor and was available for the buyer to take delivery.[81] The wine deteriorated substantially when it remained exposed at the harbor because of the buyer's failure to pay the amount due upon presentment of a letter of collection, and the buyer was liable for the purchase price. The entire risk of loss passed to the buyer with respect to goods still in the seller's possession in *Multiplastics, Inc. v. Arch Industries*[82] because the buyer had breached and the seller's insurance did not cover the loss.[83] The seller thus was entitled to the full purchase price.

[3]   Goods Not Readily Resalable

The other exception to limiting the seller to an action for price of goods accepted by the buyer entitles the seller to recover the price "of goods identified to the contract if the seller is unable after reasonable effort to resell them at a reasonable price or the circumstances reasonably indicate that such effort will

---

[74] For discussion on allocation of the risk of loss under Articles 2 and 2A, and the legal consequences of the allocation, *see* Chapter 6.

[75] *See* §§ 2–509, 2–510.

[76] 178 Mont. 119, 582 P.2d 1223, 24 UCC Rep. Serv. 884 (1978).

[77] *See* UCC § 2–509(1)(a). Any claim on behalf of the buyer would be against the carrier or the buyer's insurance company.

[78] 5 Conn. Cir. Ct. 597, 259 A.2d 772, 7 UCC Rep. Serv. 171 (1968).

[79] *See* UCC §§ 2–319(1)(a); 2–509(1)(a).

[80] 901 F.2d 481, 11 UCC Rep. Serv. 2d 1214 (5th Cir. 1990).

[81] *See* UCC § 2–509(1)(b).

[82] 166 Conn. 280, 348 A.2d 618 (1974).

[83] *See* UCC § 2–510(3).

be unavailing.''[84] This exception simply states the opposite of the premise on which the action for price is generally excluded. A seller who is unable to resell goods is not better placed to dispose of them. Furthermore, relegating a seller in these circumstances to damages based on market price would allocate an unfair burden to establish market value.

Sellers would be well advised to make and document efforts toward resale. The seller in *Continental-Wirt Electronics Corp. v. Sprague Electric Co.*[85] successfully recovered the purchase price after making several unsuccessful efforts to resell. In *Multi-Line Manufacturing, Inc. v. Greenwood Mills, Inc.*,[86] however, the appellate court overturned summary judgment in favor of a seller that provided only the opinion of its merchandise manager on the reasonableness of its not reselling fabric.

[B]   Recovery of Rent

The drafters of Article 2A originally followed the statutory analogue precisely in allowing a limited opportunity for a lessor to recover the rent that the lessee promised to pay under the lease.[87] They ultimately adhered to the sales model with respect to lost or damaged goods and goods that the lessor cannot dispose of, but they made a significant change regarding accepted goods.[88]

Allowing a lessor to recover rent for any accepted goods posed problems with respect to mitigation of damages. A lessor could take possession of the goods and still recover the present value of future rent, as long as the lessor held the goods for the lessee. The approach failed to recognize a fundamental distinction between sales and lease transactions. A seller cannot retake possession of goods that a buyer has accepted in an unsecured sales transaction. If the sale is secured, the secured party can repossess the goods, but it must dispose of them in a commercially reasonable manner and apply the proceeds to the outstanding indebtedness, remitting any surplus to the debtor/buyer.

In a lease, however, the lessor is entitled to take possession of the goods following a default by the lessee,[89] but the lessor is not required to dispose of

---

[84] UCC § 2–709(1)(b).

[85] 329 F. Supp. 959, 9 UCC Rep. Serv. 1049 (E.D. Pa. 1971).

[86] 123 Ga. App. 372, 180 S.E.2d 917, 9 UCC Rep. Serv. 80 (1971).

[87] UCC § 2A–529(1)(1987).

[88] Article 2A also includes provisions comparable to Article 2 concerning the lessor's holding goods available to the lessee, the lessee's right to use of the goods for the remaining lease term on payment of the judgment, and the lessor's right to dispose of the goods prior to collection of the judgment. UCC § 2A–529(3),(4).

[89] UCC § 2A–525.

them.[90] Allowing the lessor to recover the rent after repossessing the goods eliminates any incentive for the lessor to mitigate damages.

The Supreme Court of Idaho stated the nature of the problem in the pre-Code case of *Industrial Leasing Corp. v. Thomason*.[91]

> If Industrial Leasing were allowed to collect the rentals for the full term of the lease, while the equipment was sitting idle and not in use, it would still retain the farm equipment in a relatively new condition and would then be able to rent it out for substantially another period similar to the lease in question, thereby reaping a windfall to the extent that the property was not physically or economically depreciated during the course of the lease with appellant Thomason.[92]

The drafters subsequently decided that "it is not economically sound to both allow recovery of the full rent and the goods to go unused."[93] They amended the provision so that future rent can be recovered by a lessor for goods accepted only if the lessor has not repossessed them or the lessee has not tendered them back to the lessor.[94] "The rule in Article 2 that the seller can recover the price of accepted goods is rejected" in Article 2A.[95] When the lessor leaves the lessee in possession of the goods following a default, and the lessee chooses to retain them, the lessor is entitled to recover rent, since the lessee is continuing to enjoy the beneficial use of the goods. If either party chooses to terminate lessee possession, however, the lessor cannot recover future rent just because the lessee initially accepted the goods. The damages of the lessee will be mitigated to the extent of the rent the lessor attains through a qualifying substitute lease or of the market rent through the contract rent/market rent differential.

§ 9.05 INCIDENTAL DAMAGES [2–710; 2A–530]

Each of the four seller's damages provisions specifically provides that the seller may also recover incidental damages. Sellers' incidental damages are described as follows:

> Incidental damages to an aggrieved seller include any commercially reasonable charges, expenses or commissions incurred in stopping delivery, in the transportation, care and custody of goods after the buyer's

---

90 UCC § 2A–527, Comment 1.
91 96 Ida. 574, 532 P.2d 916 (1974).
92 *Id.* at 919.
93 National Conference of Commissioners on Uniform State Law, Amendments to Uniform Commercial Code Article 2A, Leases § 2A–529, Drafting Note (July 13, 1990).
94 UCC § 2A–529(1)(a).
95 UCC § 2A–529, Comment 1.

breach, in connection with return or resale of the goods or otherwise resulting from the breach.[96]

This description is intended only as a nonexhaustive list of the major additional elements of damage that follow breach by the buyer.[97] Article 2A includes a comparable provision for lessors.[98]

The courts have readily recognized commercially reasonable expenditures by the seller as incidental damages. The seller in *Afram Export Corp. v. Metallurgiki Halyps, S.A.*[99] recovered incidental damages for freight charges, inspection, and certification on resale of the goods. In *Lee Oldsmobile, Inc. v. Kaiden*[100] the seller recovered commissions on the resale of the automobile and transportation charges for delivering it to the place of resale. The court in *Servbest Foods, Inc. v. Emessee Industries, Inc.*[101] awarded incidental damages for the cold storage of meat.

Neither Article 2 nor Article 2A includes a provision that recognizes consequential damages for sellers or lessors. Admittedly, consequential damages generally are less crucial to sellers and lessors than they are to buyers and lessees, as the latter parties often need additional recovery to compensate them for lost profits or for injuries resulting from defective products.[102] The general measures of damages usually protect sellers and lessors adequately. These parties nevertheless still can suffer consequential damages.[103] One of the most readily apparent forms of these damages is the lost value of money that has not been paid. An aggrieved seller or lessor might even be required to incur debt to meet its own obligations that would be unpaid following breach.[104]

In the absence of a specific provision authorizing their recovery, sellers and lessors have had to be more resourceful in trying to attain consequential damages. One approach that has met with significant success is to bring the claim within the scope of the incidental damages provision.[105] Some support for this

---

[96] UCC § 2–710.

[97] UCC § 2–710, Comment.

[98] UCC § 2A–530.

[99] 592 F. Supp. 446, 40 UCC Rep. Serv. 911 (E.D. Wis. 1984).

[100] 56 Md. App. 556, 363 A.2d 270, 20 UCC Rep. Serv. 117 (1976).

[101] 82 Ill App. 3d 662, 403 N.E.2d 1, 29 UCC Rep. Serv. 518 (1980).

[102] *See* § 8.06[B] *supra.*

[103] Nobs Chem., USA, Inc. v. Koppers Co., Inc., 616 F.2d 212, 28 UCC Rep. Serv. 1039 (5th Cir. 1980)(no recovery for seller's loss of volume discount).

[104] SC Gray, Inc. v. Ford Motor Co., 92 Mich. App. 789, 286 N.W.2d 34, 29 UCC Rep. Serv. 417 (1979)(no recovery allowed for interest seller paid on loans taken out to maintain its business when buyer did not pay).

[105] Masters Mach. Co., Inc. v. Brookfield Athletic Shoe Co., Inc., 4 UCC Rep. Serv. 2d 749 (1st Cir. 1986)(interest on loan in connection with the contract that was actually paid by seller

approach can be found in the statutory section because it includes reference to "any commercially reasonable charges . . . otherwise resulting from the breach."[106] The approach does violence, however, to the true distinction between incidental and consequential damages.

Alternatively, consequential damages might be allowed through the general Code provision that recognizes that general principles of common law supplement the Code.[107] Section 1–106(1) provides that "neither consequential or special nor penal damages may be had except as specifically provided in this Act or by other rule of law." Consequential damages for the seller are recognized under common law.[108] Many courts, however, have simply refused to allow sellers to recover damages that would be properly characterized as consequential.[109]

§ 9.06   INJURY TO LESSOR'S RESIDUAL INTEREST [2A–532]

Article 2A adds a right of recovery to protect a lessor's residual interest. It provides that "[i]n addition to any other recovery permitted by this Article or other law, the lessor may recover from the lessee an amount that will fully compensate the lessor for any loss of or damage to the lessor's residual interest in the goods caused by the default of the lessee."[110] A lessee might fail to return the goods to the lessor at the end of the lease term, or the goods might be returned in damaged condition beyond normal wear and tear that would be permitted from the lessee's use. This provision in Article 2A entitles the lessor to compensation for such impairment of the residual interest.

---

held recoverable as incidental damages); Bulk Oil (USA), Inc. v. Sun Oil Trading Co., 697 F.2d 481, 35 UCC Rep. Serv. 23 (2d Cir. 1983)(post-breach interest payments on bank loan incurred by seller to finance acquisition of goods allowed as incidental damages); Commonwealth Edison Co. v. Decker Coal Co., 3 UCC Rep. Serv. 2d 601 (N.D. Ill. 1987)(loss of use of money awarded as incidental damages).

[106] UCC § 2–710. *See also* UCC § 2A–530.

[107] UCC § 1–103. Wallace Steel, Inc. v. Ingersoll-Rand Co., 739 F.2d 112, 38 UCC Rep. Serv. 1665 (2d Cir. 1984); Associated Metals & Minerals Corp. v. Sharon Steel Corp., 590 F. Supp. 18, 39 UCC Rep. Serv. 892 (S.D. N.Y. 1983), *aff'd*, 742 F.2d 1431 (2d Cir. 1983).

[108] Restatement (Second) of Contracts § 351.

[109] Petroleo Brasileiro, SA v. Ameropan Oil Corp., 372 F. Supp. 503, 14 UCC Rep. Serv. 661 (E.D. N.Y. 1974)(no recovery allowed for banking charges suffered as a result of breach); Sprague v. Sumitomo Forestry Co., Ltd., 144 Wash. 2d 751, 709 P.2d 1200, 42 UCC Rep. Serv. 202 (1985)(loss of logging time proximately caused by buyer's breach was not compensable).

[110] UCC § 2A–532.

Part B: Nonmonetary Remedies

§ 9.07   CANCELLATION [2–703(f), 2A–523(1)(a)]

Sellers or lessors are entitled to cancel the contract when their buyers or lessees wrongfully reject or revoke acceptance or fail to make payments due or repudiate.[111] Executory rights on both sides are discharged upon cancellation.[112] The rights and remedies of the seller or lessor, however, are retained.[113]

§ 9.08   WITHHOLDING DELIVERY [2–703(a), 2A–523(1)(c)]

Although the contract obligations of a seller are to transfer and deliver goods to the buyer,[114] the seller is authorized in a number of circumstances to withhold delivery. Comparable rights are provided for a lessor. The right is allowed generally whenever a buyer or lessee breaches or defaults by wrongfully rejecting or revoking, by failing to make payment due on or before delivery, or by repudiating.[115] In addition, a seller can refuse to deliver except for cash upon discovering that the buyer is insolvent.[116] The lessor's right is similar, except a lessor does not even have to deliver the goods for a cash payment.[117] Placing goods into the hands of an insolvent lessee who could somehow manage a cash payment for the first term of the lease would greatly impair the lessor's prospects for subsequent payments. An insolvent lessee would also lack the financial capability to satisfy any lease requirements such as insuring the goods or providing repair and maintenance services.

When a buyer or lessee is insolvent, the seller or lessor also has the right to stop delivery of goods that are in the possession of a carrier or other bailee.[118] If the goods have been shipped to the buyer or lessee, the shipper may still have time to change the delivery instructions to the carrier. Timely instructions to a warehouseman can also prevent the delivery of stored goods.

---

[111] UCC §§ 2–703(f), 2A–523(1)(a). Goldstein v. Stainless Processing Co., 465 F.2d 392, 11 UCC Rep. Serv. 522 (7th Cir. 1972)(failure to pay); Pillsbury Co. v. Ward, 250 N.W.2d 35, 21 UCC Rep. Serv. 118 (Iowa 1977)(repudiation).

[112] UCC §§ 2–106(3),(4); 2A–505(1).

[113] UCC §§ 2–106(3),(4); 2–720; 2A–505(1),(3).

[114] UCC § 2–301.

[115] UCC §§ 2–703(a), 2A–523(1)(c). As a practical matter, a seller or lessor usually will have already delivered prior to a rejection or revocation.

[116] UCC § 2–702(1).

[117] UCC § 2A–525(1).

[118] UCC §§ 2–705(1), 2A–526(1).

Even when a buyer or lessee is not insolvent, delivery of goods by a bailee can be stopped if the buyer or lessee has repudiated or failed to make a payment due before delivery or if the seller or lessor for any other reason has a right to withhold or reclaim the goods.[119] The right to stop delivery under these circumstances, however, is limited to shipments the size of a carload, truckload, planeload, or larger. The drafters considered that the imposition of stop-delivery orders for small shipments would impose an undue burden on carriers.[120] When the buyer or lessee is known to be insolvent, the burden on the carrier is not considered sufficient to overcome the interest of the seller or lessor in withholding the goods.

Articles 2 and 2A specify time limitations on the effectiveness of an order to stop delivery of goods in transit or storage. The seller or lessor must stop delivery before the buyer receives the goods and before negotiation to the buyer of any negotiable document covering the goods.[121] A stop-delivery order must also be made before a bailee other than a carrier acknowledges to the buyer or lessee that the bailee holds the goods for the buyer or lessee.[122] In the case of a carrier, the stoppage must occur before the carrier makes a comparable acknowledgment by reshipment or as a warehouseman.[123]

The notification to stop delivery must be sufficient to enable the bailee through the exercise of reasonable diligence to prevent delivery of the goods.[124] The bailee is obligated, after such a notification, to hold the goods and to deliver them according to the directions of the seller or lessor. The seller or lessor, however, is liable to the bailee for any charges or damages that result.[125]

§ 9.09 RETAKING POSSESSION [2–702(2), 2A–525]

[A] Seller

A seller generally does not have the right to repossess the goods following a breach by the buyer. Even if the buyer refuses to pay, the seller cannot reclaim

---

[119] UCC §§ 2–705(1), 2A–526(1). Amoco Pipeline Co. v. Admiral Crude Oil Corp., 490 F.2d 114, 13 UCC Rep. Serv. 1019 (10th Cir. 1974)(buyer's check for crude oil dishonored by drawee bank).

[120] UCC § 2–705, Comment 1.

[121] UCC §§ 2–705(2)(a),(d); 2A–526(2)(a)(a negotiable document of title would not be issued to a lessee). Amoco Pipeline Co v. Admiral Crude Oil Corp., 490 F.2d 114, 13 UCC Rep. Serv. 1019 (10th Cir. 1974)(oil in possession of pipeline company had not been delivered to buyer).

[122] UCC §§ 2–705(2)(b); 2A–526(2)(b).

[123] UCC §§ 2–705(2)(c); 2A–526(2)(c).

[124] UCC §§ 2–705(3)(a); 2A–526(3)(a).

[125] UCC §§ 2–705(3)(b); 2A–526(3)(b).

the goods. The unpaid seller is simply a general creditor for the purchase price. The seller must reduce its claim to judgment and, if necessary, execute on the judgment. A seller who wants the right to reclaim the goods must retain a purchase-money security interest in the goods.[126] Even then, the security interest is a limited form of property interest that will not serve to reconvey title in the goods back to the seller. Rather, the seller must dispose of the goods and is entitled to retain from the proceeds only an amount sufficient to cover its expenses and the outstanding balance on the debt.[127]

Article 2 recognizes only a narrowly circumscribed right for a seller on credit to reclaim goods. Usually the seller must demand recovery of the goods within 10 days of the buyer's receipt, but the right is available only when the seller learns that the buyer received the goods on credit while insolvent.[128] Buyer receipt of goods on credit while insolvent is considered to be a tacit misrepresentation of solvency and fraudulent as against the seller.[129] The 10-day limitation is inapplicable if the buyer gave the seller a written misrepresentation of solvency within three months before delivery of the goods.[130] Successful reclamation of the goods excludes all other remedies with respect to the goods.[131]

The reclamation rights of a cash seller basically recognize continuation of the common-law cash-sale doctrine.[132] Article 2 provides, "Where payment is due and demanded on the delivery to the buyer of goods or documents of title, his right as against the seller to retain or dispose of them is conditional upon his making the payment due."[133] The comments indicate that this provision codifies the cash seller's right of reclamation.[134] The comments were amended

---

[126] "A security interest is a 'purchase money security interest' to the extent that it is—
(a) taken or retained by the seller of the collateral to secure all or part of its price." UCC § 9–107.

[127] UCC § 9–504(1),(2).

[128] UCC § 2–702(2).

[129] UCC § 2–702, Comment 2.

[130] Section 2–702(2) is the exclusive source for a seller's right of reclamation based on fraud or misrepresentation of solvency or intent to pay. "Except as provided in this subsection the seller may not base a right to reclaim goods on the buyer's fraudulent or innocent misrepresentation of solvency or of intent to pay." UCC § 2–702(2).

[131] UCC § 2–702(3).

[132] A cash sale involves a contemporaneous exchange of goods for cash or a check. "[P]ayment by check is conditional and is defeated as between the parties by dishonor of the check on due presentment." UCC § 2–511(3). See also UCC § 3–802(1)(b)(original version); UCC § 3–310(b)(revised version).

[133] UCC § 2–507(2).

[134] UCC § 2–507, Comment 3.

in 1990 to address the question of whether the seller's right was subject to a time limitation, an issue that had been frequently litigated.

> There is no specific time limit for a cash seller to exercise the right of reclamation. However, the right will be defeated by delay causing prejudice to the buyer, waiver, estoppel, or ratification of the buyer's right to retain possession. Common law rules and precedents governing such principles are applicable (Section 1–103).[135]

[B] Lessor

A lessor's right to take possession of the goods is patterned more on the rights of a secured party than of a seller. Like the debtor's position in a secured transaction, default terminates the right of a lessee to retain possession of the goods.[136] The lessor's right to possession, however, is based on protection of the lessor's residual interest in the goods. Thus, once the lessor reclaims possession, the similarity to a secured transaction ends. The lessor is not required to dispose of the goods or to pay to the lessee any of the proceeds of a disposition.

A lessor has several options following default by the lessee:

> If the lessor or the lessee is in default under the lease contract, the party seeking enforcement may reduce the party's claim to judgment, or otherwise enforce the lease contract by self-help or any available judicial procedure or nonjudicial procedure, including administrative proceeding, arbitration, or the like, in accordance with this Article.[137]

Judicial action to enforce a lessor's right to take possession of the goods can lead to injunctive relief.[138] In most jurisdictions, a lessor can proceed through a summary approach like a replevin action.

A lessor can avoid the use of any judicial action to repossess goods following default by the lessee, provided that the repossession can be accomplished without a breach of the peace.[139] The lessor has a superior right to possession of the goods following default, but society has a predominant interest in avoiding confrontations that might escalate into violence. If breach of the peace is threatened, the lessor must proceed by judicial action. The lessor

---

[135] UCC § 2–507, Comment 3.

[136] UCC § 2A–525.

[137] UCC § 2A–501(3) (based on UCC § 9–501(1),(2)).

[138] UCC § 2A–525, Comment 3, citing Clark Equip. Co. v. Armstrong Equip. Co., 431 F.2d 54 5th Cir. 1970), *cert. denied*, 402 U.S. 909 (1971).

[139] UCC § 2A–525(3).

is also well advised to proceed by judicial action if the grounds for lessee default are subject to challenge. Taking possession in the absence of a default establishing the right to possession leaves the lessor vulnerable to claims of breach of the lease contract and conversion. The latter action opens the prospect for a demand for punitive damages.[140]

Part C: Liquidated Damages

§ 9.10 SALES [2–718(1)]

Parties to a sales contract may choose to avoid the uncertainty of measuring damages in the event of a breach by including a liquidated damages clause in their contract. A valid liquidated damages clause determines the amount of damages, thereby removing their assessment from the purview of the court and the jury. A liquidated damages clause provides an efficient means of establishing damages and serves to inform the contracting parties about the extent of their liability in the event of their breach.

Despite inherent advantages to liquidated damages, the courts historically have been concerned about their potential for abuse. Article 2 reflects this concern by authorizing an agreement on liquidation but subjecting it to limitations. The applicable provision states:

> Damages for breach by either party may be liquidated in the agreement but only at an amount which is reasonable in the light of the anticipated or actual harm caused by the breach, the difficulties of proof of loss, and the inconvenience or nonfeasibility of otherwise obtaining an adequate remedy. A term fixing unreasonably large liquidated damages is void as a penalty.[141]

The first of these requirements expands the approach followed at common law.[142] The reasonableness of the liquidated amount was scrutinized at common law only prospectively—based on the harm that was anticipated to result in the event of breach. Article 2 allows reasonableness to be tested either

---

[140] See Mitchell v. Ford Motor Credit Co., 688 P.2d 42, 38 UCC Rep. Serv. 1812 (Okla. 1984)(award of only $1,000 actual damages but an additional $60,000 punitive damages against a secured party who converted the collateral).

[141] UCC § 2–718(1).

[142] Equitable Lumber Corp. v. I.P.A. Land Development Corp., 38 N.Y.2d 516, 381 N.Y.S.2d 459, 344 N.E.2d 391, 18 UCC Rep. Serv. 273 (1976). See generally Comment, Liquidated Damages: A Comparison of the Common Law and the Uniform Commercial Code, 45 Fordham L. Rev. 1349 (1977).

by the harm anticipated at the time of contracting or by the harm that actually resulted following breach. For example, in *California & Hawaiian Sugar Co. v. Sun Ship, Inc.*,[143] the court upheld liquidated damages totaling $4.4 million dollars for an eight-month delay in building a barge because the damages were reasonable in light of the anticipated harm that could result from the loss of charter opportunities.[144] In *Lafayette Stabilizer Repair, Inc. v. Machinery Wholesalers Corp.*,[145] the court focused on the harm that actually resulted in holding that a contract provision limiting recoverable damages to a $6,900 allowance for repairs was not reasonable when the goods proved to be unusable and beyond repair.

The alternative application of either test was demonstrated in *Equitable Lumber Corp v. I.P.A. Land Development Corp.*[146] A contract provision required that, in the event of breach, the buyer would be required to pay reasonable attorneys' fees, which were defined as 30 percent of any amount collected. The court said that the reasonableness of the provision could be determined either (1) in light of the anticipated damages, which would require an assessment of its relationship to the fee that an attorney would normally charge for collection of the seller's claim, or (2) based on a comparison with the actual fee arrangement agreed upon by the seller and its attorney.

Although most cases that fail under this criterion involve liquidated damages that are excessive, an occasional court has refused to uphold a clause because the damages are too low. The major case is *Varner v. BL Lanier Fruit Co.*[147] The buyer of fruit breached after picking only some of the crop from the seller's trees, and the seller could not sell the remainder of the fruit. The contract provided as liquidated damages that the seller would retain the advance payment that the buyer had made for some of the fruit. The court was concerned that the buyer would not have to pay damages for any of the unpicked fruit and thus held that the liquidated damages clause was unconscionable.

The second requirement for a liquidated damages provision under Article 2 is that the amount stipulated must be reasonable in light of the difficulties of

---

[143] 794 F.2d 1433, 1 UCC Rep. Serv. 2d 1211 (9th Cir. 1986).

[144] The actual damages proved by the buyer at trial were only $368,000 spent by the buyer for a different means of shipping its crop. The buyer also suggested that it had lost more than $3 million from lost charter opportunities, but the evidence was not sufficient to support such a finding.

[145] 750 P.2d 1290, 40 UCC Rep. Serv. 122 (5th Cir. 1985).

[146] 38 N.Y.2d 516, 381 N.Y.S.2d 459, 344 N.E.2d 391, 18 UCC Rep. Serv. 273 (1976).

[147] 370 So.2d 61, 26 UCC Rep. Serv. 716 (Fla. Dist. Ct. App. 1979).

proving the loss.[148] This requirement appears to follow the common-law approach of determining difficulty of estimation as of the time of contract formation. It tends to preclude the use of liquidated damages provisions when actual damages can be reasonably estimated at the time of contract formation.[149]

Article 2 also provides that liquidated damages are to be measured against the inconvenience or nonfeasibility of otherwise obtaining an adequate remedy. Apparently this requirement extends the focus beyond simply the difficulty of estimating money damages to a consideration of other available remedies as well. For example, availability of the remedy of specific performance in the event of a breach might be used to preclude enforceability of a liquidated damages clause.

Finally, Article 2 indicates that unreasonably large liquidated damages are penalties and not enforceable. Several courts have decided cases under this provision, often without indicating whether this characterization is an independent test or the consequence of applying the other requirements.[150] The court in *Equitable Lumber Corp. v. I.P.A. Land Development Corp.*[151] stated that even though a liquidated damages provision meets the initial requirements of the Article 2 provision, it may still fail if its effect is to serve as a penalty rather than as a legitimate attempt to estimate damages. The liquidated damages clause in that case made the buyer liable for attorneys' fees of 30 percent of any amount collected. The court indicated that even if that provision were reasonable in the sense of actual damages based on the agreement entered into between the seller and its attorney, it would still be void as a penalty if the stipulated amount was grossly disproportionate to the loss the seller would

---

[148] Baker v. International Record Syndicate, Inc., 812 S.W.2d 53, 15 UCC Rep. Serv. 2d 875 (Tex. Ct. App. 1991)(liquidated damages clause of $1,500 per negative in photographer's suit was reasonable given the difficulty of determining value of a work of art, potential for fame, and long-term earning power of photographs).

[149] Lee Oldsmobile, Inc. v. Kaiden, 32 Md. App. 556, 363 A.2d 270, 20 UCC Rep. Serv. 117 (1976) (liquidated damages provision held inapplicable because actual damages were capable of accurate estimation at time of contract formation).

[150] Welch v. K-Beck Furniture Mart, Inc., 3 Ohio App. 3d 171, 444 N.E.2d 48, 35 UCC Rep. Serv. 474 (1981)(terms of furniture layaway agreement, under which a buyer who defaulted could forfeit over 40 percent of the price, held unenforceable as a penalty); Hertz Commercial Leasing Corp. v. Dynatron, Inc., 37 Conn. Supp. 7, 427 A.2d 872, 30 UCC Rep. Serv. 770 (1980)(lease case decided under Article 2 held that liquidated damages provision was harsh and penal and subjected the lessee to a forfeiture). *But see* Coast Trading Co., Inc. v. Parmac, Inc., 21 Wash. App. 896, 587 P.2d 1071, 25 UCC Rep. Serv. 1047 (1978)(demonstration by defendant that actual damages exceeded 15 percent of purchase price disposed of plaintiff's contention that 15 percent cancellation fee was a penalty).

[151] 38 N.Y.2d 516, 381 N.Y.S.2d 459, 344 N.E.2d 391, 18 UCC Rep. Serv. 273 (1976).

have incurred in the absence of the buyer's agreement to pay attorney's fees. The court essentially concluded that the reasonableness of the seller's actual damages would be measured not only by the contract terms with its attorney but by external market criteria as well.

§ 9.11   Leases [2A–504]

The Article 2A provision on liquidated damages is based on Article 2, but it deletes most of the requirements in the sales provision. The Article 2A provision states:

> Damages payable by either party for default, or any other act or omission, including indemnity for loss or diminution of anticipated tax benefits or loss or damages to lessor's residual interest, may be liquidated in the lease agreement but only at an amount or by a formula that is reasonable in light of the then anticipated harm caused by the default or other act or omission.[152]

The sole standard is reasonableness of the damages, determined prospectively with respect to the anticipated harm.

Liquidated damages provisions have traditionally been included in lease agreements, particularly addressing the potential default of a lessee. The drafters desired to encourage the continuation of this practice in personal property leasing. They eliminated the remaining standards to facilitate the use of liquidated damages in recognition of general leasing practices.[153]

Article 2A also eliminates the Article 2 provision that "[a] term fixing unreasonably large liquidated damages is void as a penalty."[154] The Comments explain the reason for this deletion:

> Further, . . . the expansion of subsection (1) to enable the parties to liquidate the amount payable with respect to an indemnity for loss or diminution of anticipated tax benefits resulted in another change: the last sentence of Section 2–718(1), providing that a term fixing unreasonably large liquidated damages is void as a penalty, was also not incorporated. The impact of local, state and federal tax laws on a leasing transaction can result in an amount payable with respect to the tax indemnity many times greater than the original purchase price of the

---

[152] UCC § 2A–504(1).

[153] UCC § 2A–504, Comment, states: "Thus, consistent with the common law emphasis upon freedom to contract with respect to bailments for hire, this section has created a revised rule that allows greater flexibility with respect to leases of goods."

[154] UCC § 2–718(1). See § 9.10 supra.

goods. By deleting the reference to unreasonably large liquidated damages the parties are free to negotiate a formula, restrained by the rule of reasonableness in this section. These changes should invite the parties to liquidate damages.[155]

The deletion of the reference to unenforceable penalty provisions is not likely to alter pre-Article 2A case law significantly, even though a number of cases concerning leases of personal property have held unenforceable liquidated damages provisions that were deemed to create penalties.[156] The courts likely will simply conclude that a liquidated damages provision that would have been deemed to constitute a penalty is unenforceable because it is excessive and thus does not meet the requirement that liquidated damages must be reasonable relative to the anticipated harm. Earlier cases also struck down the enforceability of liquidated damages clauses on these grounds.[157]

The Article 2A provision also reflects prior law in authorizing the use of a formula to establish liquidated damages. The Comments include several formulas that have been used in personal property leases.[158] One formula, for example, adds overdue lease payments, accelerated future lease payments, and the estimated residual value, from which it deducts the net proceeds from the lessor's disposal of the goods by sale or re-lease. Tax indemnities, costs, interest, and attorneys' fees are also often added. Any formula that entitles the lessor to recover for accelerated future lease payments should require mitigation by the lessor through sale or re-lease of the goods.[159] Future rents should also be reduced to present value.[160]

---

[155] UCC § 2A–504, Comment.

[156] Taylor v. Commercial Credit Equip. Corp., 170 Ga. App. 332, 316 S.E.2d 788 (1984)(acceleration of rental payments without reduction to present value bears no reasonable relationship to probable actual damages and is an unenforceable penalty).

[157] Walter Implement, Inc. v. Focht, 107 Wash.2d 553, 730 P.2d 1340 (1987)(addition of 20 percent of future rent held to have no relation to estimated damages).

[158] UCC § 2A–504, Comment.

[159] Frank Nero Auto Lease v. Townsend, 64 Ohio App. 2d 65, 411 N.E.2d 507 (1979)(agreement allowing lessor to repossess vehicle and accelerate future rents but with no provision to mitigate damages allows double payment and is contrary to public policy). *But see* Citicorp. Indus. Credit, Inc. v. Roundtree, 185 Ga. App. 417, 364 S.E.2d 65 (1987)(lessor's failure to mitigate by selling or re-leasing equipment for benefit of lessees irrelevant because express terms of lease agreement provided otherwise).

[160] Pre-Article 2A cases generally overlook the concept of present value. Cases that address the issue consider it relevant. Adams v. D&D Leasing Co. of Ga., Inc., 191 Ga. App. 121, 381 S.E.2d 94 (1989)(acceleration of remaining rental payments without reduction to present value cannot constitute reasonable estimate of probable loss); CHR Equip. Fin., Inc. v. C&K Transport, Inc., 448 N.W.2d 693 (Iowa Ct. App. 1989)(not error for trial court to reduce future lease payments to present value).

CHAPTER

10

Third-Party Interests

§ 10.01 ASSIGNMENT AND DELEGATION

[A] Sales [2–210]

Under modern law, most rights can be assigned and most duties can be delegated.[1] Article 2 confirms these general principles with respect to sales of goods by recognizing "both delegation of performance and assignability as normal and permissible incidents of a contract for the sale of goods."[2] All rights of either a seller or a buyer thus are generally assignable,[3] and, as a general proposition, a party to a sales contract can perform his or her duty through a delegate.[4]

Both common law and Article 2 recognize certain limitations on these general principles. Assignments that might materially alter the nature of the duty undertaken or that subject the obligor to some new risk are not assignable.[5] Thus, for example, a promise to care for a person for that person's life would

---

[1] Restatement (Second) of Contracts, §§ 317(2), 318(1) (1979).
[2] UCC § 2–210, Comment 1. First Nat'l Bank of Milltown v. Schrader, 375 N.E.2d 1124, 24 UCC Rep. Serv. 219 (Ind. Ct. App. 1978)(error for trial court to dismiss assignee's action to recover balance of purchase price on grounds that assignor/seller was the real party in interest because seller's contract rights were assignable).
[3] UCC § 2–210(2).
[4] UCC § 2–210(1).
[5] Restatement (Second) of Contracts § 317(2)(a).

305

not be assignable because the duty undertaken by the promisor could be materially altered.[6] Similarly, Article 2 precludes assignability "where the assignment would materially change the duty of the other party, or increase materially the burden or risk imposed on him by his contract, or impair materially his chance of obtaining return performance."[7]

Several of the Article 2 cases concerning the materiality issue have involved assignments of seller warranties.[8] Only Georgia has held that an assignment of Code warranties as a matter of law materially alters the risks and burdens of the seller,[9] but even in that state, an existing claim for breach of warranty is assignable.[10] In other contexts, courts have held material changes in duties or burdens of the parties did not result from a seller's assignment of a defendant's account for the purchase of carpeting[11] or from a buyer's assignment of a contract for the sale of cotton.[12]

With respect to delegation of a duty, Article 2 entitles a party to perform the duty through a delegate "unless the other party has a substantial interest in having his original promisor perform or control the acts required by the contract."[13] The language in the Restatement (Second) of Contracts is nearly identical.[14] Thus, for example, the duty to sing at a scheduled performance is not delegable because of the personal nature of the promised performance.[15] By comparison, the court in *Buckeye Ag-Center, Inc. v. Babchuk*[16] held that a seller's duty to supply a specified quantity of corn was delegable.[17]

---

[6]   Restatement (Second) of Contracts § 317, Comment d, Illustration 3.

[7]   UCC § 2–210(2). The language in the Restatement (Second) of Contracts provision is comparable.

[8]   Sharrard, McGee & Co., P.A. v. Suz's Software, Inc., 100 N.C. App. 428, 396 S.E.2d 815, 12 UCC Rep. Serv. 2d 1006 (1990)(warranty claim assignable); Collins Co., Ltd. v. Carboline Co., 125 Ill. 2d 498, 532 N.E.2d 834, 7 UCC Rep. Serv. 2d 616 (1988)(warranty rights assignable).

[9]   Kaiser Aluminum & Chemical Corp. v. Ingersoll-Rand Co., 519 F. Supp. 60, 32 UCC Rep. Serv. 1369 (S.D. Ga. 1981).

[10]   Irvin v. Lowe's of Gainesville, Inc., 165 Ga. App. 828, 302 S.E.2d 734, 36 UCC Rep. Serv. 450 (1983).

[11]   Trust Co. Bank v. Barrett Distributors, Inc., 459 F. Supp. 959, 25 UCC Rep. Serv. 986 (S.D. Ind. 1978).

[12]   Tennell v. Esteve Cotton Co., 546 S.W.2d 346, 21 UCC Rep. Serv. 978 (Tex. Ct. App. 1977).

[13]   UCC § 2–210(1).

[14]   Restatement (Second) of Contracts § 318 (1979).

[15]   Restatement (Second) of Contracts § 318, Comment c, Illustration 6.

[16]   533 N.E.2d 179, 9 UCC Rep. Serv. 2d 76 (Ind. Ct. App. 1989).

[17]   *Compare* the following illustration from the Restatement (Second): "A contracts with B that A will personally cut the grass on B's meadow. A cannot effectively delegate performance of the duty to C, however competent C may be." Restatement (Second) of Contracts § 318, Comment c, Illustration 7 (referencing *Union Bond and Trust Co. v. M and M Wood Working Co.*, 256 Or. 384, 474 P.2d 339 (1970)).

A delegation of performance to another party does not relieve the delegating party of its duty to perform or of liability for its breach.[18] An effective delegation is sufficient to substitute another party to perform the duty, but the obligation on the original party remains until it is discharged by performance or otherwise.[19] This legal consequence of delegation is illustrated nicely in *Midwest Precision Services, Inc. v. PTM Industries Corp.*[20] The supplier of a machine sued the buyer, but the buyer relied on a provision in the contract that delegated to its intended lessee the buyer's duties with respect to accepting the tendered goods and permitting any applicable cure rights. The appellate court affirmed the district court's holding that the provision did not insulate the buyer from resulting liability when the lessee wrongfully rejected the goods. Similarly, in *Tarter v. MonArk Boat Co.*[21] an assignment of a contract to build a houseboat, which included delegation of the duty to construct the boat, did not relieve the defendant assignor of liability for breaches that resulted from the assignee's efforts.

Another exception to the general principle that rights can be assigned and duties can be delegated with respect to contracts for the sale of goods is contrary agreement of the parties.[22] The preclusion is overridden, however, with respect to an assignment of certain rights that are no longer executory, specifically the right to damages for breach of the whole contract or of a right resulting from full performance by the assignor.[23] These rights can be assigned effectively even when their assignment is specifically prohibited in the agreement. Following breach of the whole contract, the aggrieved party can cancel the contract and the breaching party is left without any equitable basis to assert the validity of the clause prohibiting assignment of the damages claim. If the assignor has fully performed its obligations under the contract, the other party should not be concerned about tendering its performance to the assignee. Assignment contrary to the express agreement is justified because in the absence of any executory obligations of the assignor, the assignment does not involve any question of delegation.[24]

The desire to leave assignments of rights less fettered than delegations of duties is also reflected in the Article 2 provision that a broad prohibition against

---

[18]   UCC § 2–210(1). *See also* Restatement (Second) of Contracts § 318(3). *See also* C.I.T. Corp. v. Jonnet, 3 UCC Rep. Serv. 321 (Pa. Ct. Com. Pl. 1965), *aff'd*, 419 Pa. 435, 214 A.2d 620, 3 UCC Rep. Serv. 968 (1965)(buyer's assignment of its rights to goods purchased under installment sales contract does not relieve buyer of its contract liability).

[19]   Restatement (Second) of Contracts § 316, Comment c.

[20]   887 F.2d 1128, 9 UCC Rep. Serv. 2d 1169 (1st Cir. 1989).

[21]   430 F. Supp. 1290, 22 UCC Rep. Serv. 33 (E.D. Mo. 1977).

[22]   UCC § 2–210(1)(delegation), § 2–210(2)(assignment). The Restatement (Second) of Contracts is comparable. *See* §§ 317(2)(c)(assignment), § 318(1)(delegation of duty).

[23]   UCC § 2–210(2).

[24]   UCC § 2–210, Comment 3.

assignment of "the contract" must be construed only as a bar against delegation of the assignor's duties, unless the circumstances of the transaction indicate to the contrary.[25] In the absence of an explicit prohibition, an assignment of "the contract" or other comparably general terms is an assignment of the assignor's rights and a delegation of performance of the assignor's duties.[26] This latter consequence with respect to delegation is subject to language or circumstances that indicate otherwise, with the most predominant example being an assignment for security.[27]

The assignee's acceptance of the delegation constitutes a promise on the part of the assignee to perform the duties and is enforceable by both the assignor and the other party to the contract with the assignor.[28] Thus, in *McKinnie v. Milford*[29] the original seller of a horse and his buyer could both enforce an obligation in their contract against a subsequent buyer/assignee. The original sales contract entitled the seller to use the horse for two breedings each year for as long as the horse lived. This duty was delegated to the subsequent buyer, who purchased the horse with full awareness of the original seller's breeding rights.

[B]   Leases [2A–303]

Article 2A reflects principles embodied in Article 2 with respect to the alienability of interests under a lease agreement. Assignability and delegation are thus considered also to be normal incidents of a lease contract, provided that the burdens and risks to the other party are not materially increased. In a lease transaction, for example, a lessor's burden would be increased if the lessee's interest was assigned to a sublessee who would subject the leased goods to considerably more wear and tear.

Article 2A deviates substantially from Article 2 with respect to the legal consequences that follow from certain classes of transfers of contract interests. A transfer that "materially impairs the prospect of obtaining return performance by, materially changes the duty of, or materially increases the burden or risk imposed on, the other party to the lease" subjects the transferor under

---

25 UCC § 2–210(3).

26 UCC § 2–210(4).

27 *Id.* Richter, S.A. v. Bank of America N.T.S.A., 939 F.2d 1176, 16 UCC Rep. Serv. 2d 681 (5th Cir. 1991)(bank that accepted assignment of wine purchase agreement as security for loan did not assume assignor's obligations).

28 *Id.* De La Rosa v. Tropical Sandwiches, Inc., 298 So. 2d 471, 15 UCC Rep. Serv. 595 (Fla. Ct. App. 1974)(purchaser of restaurant's assets did not assume obligation of promissory note given in previous transaction and was therefore not liable for any of balance due on note).

29 597 S.W.2d 953, 29 UCC Rep. Serv. 430 (Tex. Ct. App. 1980).

Article 2A to liability for damages that are caused by the transfer and cannot be reasonably mitigated.[30] Such material effects would preclude assignability under Article 2.

The consequence of a provision in the parties' agreement prohibiting transfers also differs substantially between Articles 2 and 2A. Assignments of rights in a sales transaction are effective, even though assignment is expressly prohibited in the agreement, whenever assignment is based on a right to damages for breach of the whole contract or a right arising out of due performance of the assignor's entire obligation.[31] Article 2A also recognizes these categories of prohibitions,[32] as well as specified prohibitions concerning the creation or enforcement of a security interest.[33] The Article 2A provisions, however, are not directed toward neutralizing an express prohibition in the parties' agreement, but rather toward precluding damages that would otherwise be available to the aggrieved party when a transfer that has been prohibited is nevertheless made.

These distinctions are necessary because Articles 2 and 2A establish different general rules with respect to the effectiveness of express prohibitions against transfers. Article 2 generally upholds the effectiveness of a prohibition, but Article 2A makes a transfer effective notwithstanding a lease provision to the contrary.[34] The consequence of ignoring the prohibition in a lease agreement is to subject the transferor to liability for damages,[35] unless the prohibition falls within one of the exceptional categories discussed above.

Although Article 2A deviates from Article 2 with respect to the general rule concerning the consequences of violating a prohibition against transfers, it is consistent with the approach of Article 9. A debtor who grants a security interest in collateral still has a disposable interest that can be subjected to the claims of creditors. Article 9 thus includes a provision that maintains the alienability of a debtor's rights in collateral that is subject to a security interest.[36]

---

[30] UCC § 2A–303(5)(b).

[31] UCC § 2–210(2).

[32] UCC § 2A–303(4).

[33] UCC § 2A–303(3).

[34] UCC § 2A–303(2).

[35] The measure of the damages depends on whether the transfer is simply prohibited or is made an event of default under the lease agreement. In the former circumstance, damages are based on damages caused by the transfer, the same measure that is applied to transfers that materially change the position of the other party in the absence of an express prohibition against transfer. UCC § 2A–303(5)(b). When a transfer is also made an event of default, damages are measured under the full array of Article 2A remedies, as well as any provided in the lease agreement. UCC § 2A–303(5)(a). For discussion on the significance of the default concept in Article 2A, *see* § 7.07[A] *supra*.

[36] ''The debtor's rights in collateral may be voluntarily or involuntarily transferred (by way

The alienability of a party's interest under the lease or of the lessor's residual interest is similarly maintained despite prohibitions to the contrary. Like Article 9, the provisions reach both involuntary and voluntary transfers.[37]

§ 10.02   PRIORITIES

Even though sales and leases are both essentially two-party transactions, a wide array of third parties might claim competing interests in affected goods. A buyer of goods might resell them to someone else, or a lessee might sublease the goods. A party might grant a security interest in the interest that it holds under a sale or lease agreement. A third party might obtain a lien on the goods by operation of law or an unsecured creditor might assert a claim against a party's interest. Articles 2, 2A, and 9 include provisions that govern conflicting claims by these third-party claimants and parties to sales and lease transactions. The broad contours of these priorities are provided in the remainder of this chapter.

[A]   Subsequent Buyers or Lessees [2–403, 2A–304, 2A–305]

[1]   Derivative Title

A long-standing principle of Anglo-Saxon jurisprudence has been the protection of ownership in property. This principle was pervasive for much of the history of common law. Initially acquired property rights prevailed over subsequent acquisition as a method of allocating the loss between two innocent parties. The historical protection of ownership extended even to defeating subsequent parties who could qualify as bona fide purchasers.

This traditional approach to the ownership of property is reflected in the rule of derivative title, a rule based on the fundamental property law tenet that title is derived. A transferee of property acquires whatever rights the transferor has in the property. This rule is the basis for the colorful maxim that an assignee

---

of sale, creation of a security interest, attachment, levy, garnishment or other judicial process) notwithstanding a provision in the security agreement prohibiting any transfer or making the transfer constitute a default." UCC § 9–311.

[37] The concept of transfer is quite broad, including dispositions "by sale, sublease, creation or enforcement of a security interest, or attachment, levy, or other judicial process." UCC § 2A–303(2).

stands in the shoes of the assignor.[38] Articles 2 and 2A both state the rule of derivative title as the general rule governing transfers of goods.[39]

[2] Bona Fide Purchasers

The sacrosanct protection of established property interests began to erode with the development of mercantile interests that inevitably accompanied the expansion of marketplaces. Owners of goods began to rely on agents to execute their transactions and to represent their interests in distant markets. Dishonest actions by agents created an impetus for the development of exceptions to the rule of derivative title. Owner culpability became the conceptual basis to favor transferees over prior owners of goods. An owner who allows goods to enter into the stream of commerce without taking adequate steps to protect his or her interests is considered to have less compelling equities when faced by an subsequent innocent purchaser of the goods.

One of the exceptions to the rule of derivative title is thus based on the concept of voidable title.[40] It represents a middle ground between the extreme cases of a transferee receiving the owner's title through a sale of the property by the owner but receiving nothing through a sale by a thief who has stolen the owner's property. The doctrine of voidable title applies when a person acquires possession of an owner's goods by defrauding the owner.[41] The person who acquires the goods cannot defeat the owner's claim, but a subsequent bona fide purchaser can. The owner's entrustment of the goods to the fraudulent party enables that party to deceive subsequent transferees and has become the conceptual basis to allocate the loss to the owner when the subsequent transferee is innocent and has paid value for the goods.

Both Articles 2 and 2A include the doctrine of voidable title: "A person with voidable title has power to transfer a good title to a good faith purchaser for

---

[38] "The right of an assignee is subject to any defense or claim of the obligor which accrues before the obligor receives notification of the assignment. . . ." Restatement (Second) of Contracts § 336(2) (1981). *See also* UCC § 9–318(1).

[39] "A purchaser of goods acquires all title which his transferor had . . . ." UCC § 2–403(1). *See also* UCC § 2A–304(1) (rights of subsequent lessee from lessor of goods under existing lease contract); UCC § 2A–305(1) (rights of buyer or sublessee from lessee of goods under existing lease contract).

[40] *See generally* Weber, *The Extension of the Voidable Title Principle Under the Code*, 49 Ky. L.J. 437 (1961).

[41] Articles 2 and 2A include specific instances in which the voidable title doctrine applies. These instances include the transferor's being deceived as to the identity of the purchaser, the lessor, or the lessee, and the procurement of delivery through fraud that is punishable as larcenous under criminal law. Delivery in a cash sale or in exchange for a check that is subsequently dishonored is also included, as such transactions are presumed to be fraudulent. UCC §§ 2–403(1), 2A–304(1), 2A–305(1).

value."[42] The doctrine of voidable title is thus an exception to the rule of derivative title because it recognizes circumstances under which a transferee can acquire rights greater than the rights of the transferor.[43]

[3]   Ordinary Course of Business

Entrusting possession of goods to a merchant who deals in goods of the same kind empowers the merchant to transfer all of the entrustor's rights to a subsequent buyer or lessee in the ordinary course of business. Thus, an owner of an appliance who gives it to a merchant for repairs will lose to a subsequent buyer in the ordinary course of business who purchases the appliance after the merchant wrongfully adds it to the store's inventory.[44] Similarly, a subsequent lessee in the ordinary course of business will take free of an initial lease contract if the initial lessee entrusts the goods to the lessor's possession.[45]

The culpability rationale also applies in favor of this exception. The entrustment places the goods in the hands of the only entity that can transfer them to a buyer in ordinary course of business or a lessee in ordinary course of business.[46] In addition to exemplifying the basic qualities of bona fide purchasers, the subsequent transferees must acquire the goods from the inventory of a person engaged in selling or leasing goods of that kind.[47] By entrusting goods to such a merchant, the entrustor creates in the merchant the indicia of apparent authority to sell or lease that the subsequent buyer or lessee is justified in relying upon.[48]

[B]   Secured Parties [9–307(1); 9–301(1)(c); 2A–307]

Article 9 includes priority rules that govern conflicts between secured parties and a number of possible competing claimants, including buyers of goods.

---

[42]   UCC § 2–403(1). *See also* §§ 2A–304(1), 2A–305(1).

[43]   *See generally* Dolan, *The UCC Framework: Conveyancing Principles and Property Interests*, 59 B.U. L. Rev. 811 (1979).

[44]   UCC § 2–403(2).

[45]   UCC § 2A–304(2). If a thief steals goods from an owner and entrusts them to a merchant, a subsequent buyer in ordinary course or a subsequent lessee in ordinary course will not defeat the owner because the subsequent party in ordinary course receives only the interest of the entrustor.

[46]   " 'Entrusting' includes any delivery and any acquiescence in retention of possession regardless of any condition expressed between the parties to the delivery or acquiescence and regardless of whether the procurement of the entrusting or the possessor's disposition of the goods have been such as to be larcenous under the criminal law." UCC § 2–403(3). This provision is cross-referenced in Article 2A. UCC § 2A–103(3).

[47]   UCC §§ 1–201(9), 2A–103(1)(o).

[48]   For a discussion of the relationship of agency law principles to the entrustment concept of commercial law, *see* Lawrence, *The "Created by His Seller" Limitation of Section 9–307(1): A Provision in Need of an Articulated Policy*, 60 Ind. L.J. 73 (1984).

Consistent with the principles concerning entrustment just discussed, a buyer in ordinary course of business takes free of a security interest created by his or her seller, even if the security interest has been perfected.[49] The secured party is financing the inventory of a merchant, thereby entrusting the goods to the possession of the merchant and creating apparent authority for the merchant to sell the goods in due course. A secured party can defeat any other buyer by perfecting the security interest before the buyer's interest arises.[50] The buyer can defeat the secured party, however, to the extent that the buyer, prior to perfection of the security interest, gives value and receives delivery of the goods without knowledge of the existence of the security interest.[51]

The provisions on priorities between secured parties and parties to lease transactions properly belong in Article 9. Their inclusion would be consistent with the approach of stating priority provisions with respect to security interests in Article 9. The drafters of Article 2A did not have a mandate to make any additions to Article 9, however, so they included the priority provisions in Article 2A.

Article 2A provides general rules that make creditors of lessees and creditors of lessors subject to the lease contract.[52] The rule with respect to creditors of lessees does not allow any exceptions for secured parties. A secured creditor's interest thus can attach only to the remainder of the lessee's leasehold interest in the goods. The rule with respect to creditors of lessors does provide some exceptions. A secured creditor will have priority if the security interest was perfected before the lease contract became enforceable or if the lessee does not give value and receive delivery of the goods without knowledge of the security interest.[53]

[C]   Other Creditors [2–403(2); 2A–306; 2A–307(2)(c); 2A–308]

If a buyer or lessee enters into an agreement but then leaves the goods in the possession of the seller or lessor, subsequent parties might be deceived by the retention of possession. Continued possession of the goods provides indicia of ownership that might lead a lender into extending credit. Articles 2 and 2A therefore provide that a creditor of such a seller or lessor can treat the sale or lease transaction as void if the retention of possession is fraudulent under any rule of law in the applicable state.[54]

---

[49] UCC § 9–307(1).
[50] UCC § 9–301(1)(c).
[51] Id.
[52] UCC § 2A–307(1),(2).
[53] UCC § 2A–307(2)(b),(c).
[54] UCC §§ 2–403(2), 2A–308(1). Additional provisions enable a creditor to attack a fraudulent transfer or voidable preference that becomes enforceable in satisfaction or as security for a pre-existing claim for money. UCC §§ 2–402(3)(b), 2A–308(2).

Article 2A includes some additional priority provisions with respect to creditors. A lien that is given by statute or rule or law on services or materials provided by a person in the ordinary course of his or her business takes priority over any interest of the lessor or lessee.[55] This priority is the only exception recognized with respect to the general rule that a creditor of a lessee takes subject to the lease contract.[56] In addition to this exception, a creditor of a lessor has priority when the creditor holds a lien that attached to the goods before the lease contract became enforceable.[57]

---

[55] UCC § 2A–306.
[56] UCC § 2A–307(1).
[57] UCC § 2A–307(2)(a).

TABLE OF CASES

(References are to sections.)

A

A & G Constr. Co. v. Reid Bros. Logging Co. ....3.03[B]; 4.03[C]

A.F.L. Flack, S.p.A. v. E.A. Karay Co. ..7.05[C]

A.M. Knitwear Corp. v. All America Export-Import Corp. .... 6.02[A]

Ace Supply, Inc. v. Rocky-Mountain Mach. Co. ....4.02[E], [G][3]

Acme Pump Co., Inc. v. National Cash Register Co. ....8.06[B]

Adam Metal Supply, Inc. v. Electrodex, Inc. ....5.02[A][2]

Adam Metal Supply Inc. v. Electrodex, Inc. .... 7.03[B][2]

Adams v. Petrade Int'l, Inc. 3.06

Adams v. Grant ....7.05[A][1]

Adams v. J.I. Case Co. ....8.06[B]

Adams v. D&D Leasing Co. of Ga., Inc. 9.11

Advance Concrete Forms, Inc. v. McCann Constr. Specialties Advent Sys., Ltd. v. Unisys Corp. .... 3.03[D]

Afram Export Corp. v. Metallurgiki Halyps, S.A. 9.05

Agricultural Services Association v. Ferry-Morse Seed Co. ....5.02[C][1]

Agricultural Services Ass'n v. Ferry-Morse Seed Co. ....5.02[B][2], [3]

Airstream, Inc. v. CIT Financial Services, Inc. ....4.02[B]

Akron Brick & Block Co. v. Moniz Engineering Co., Inc. .... 7.05[D]

Alabama Great Southern R.R. Co. v. McVay .... 3.03[D]

Alamo Clay Prods., Inc. v. Gunn Tile Co. .... 4.05[A]

Alan Wood Steel Co. v. Capital Equip. Enterprises, Inc. ....5.02[A][4]; 5.03[A]

Alaska Northern Dev., Inc. v. Alyeska Pipeline Serv. Co. ....4.02[D][2], [E]

Alco Standard Corp. v. F & B Mfg. Co. .... 9.01[A]

Allen M. Campbell Co. v. Virginia Metal Indus. 3.06

Allen v. Nicole, Inc. .... 5.02[B][1]

Allen v. G.D. Searle & Co. .... 7.03[B][3]

Alliance Wall Corp. v. Ampat Midwest Corp. .... 2.05[B][1]

Alliance Wall Corp. v. Ampat Midwest Corp. .... 2.05[B][1]; 7.03[B][4]

Alpert v. Thomas ....7.05[A][1]

Aluminum Co. of America v. Essex Group, Inc. ....7.14[A][3]

American Elec. Power Co. v. Westinghouse Elec. Corp. .... 5.03[B][1]

American Container Corp. v. Hanley Trucking Corp. .... 5.02[D]

American Parts Co., Inc. v. American Arbitration Ass'n .... 2.05[A]

American Plastic Equip., Inc. v. CBS, Inc. ....3.04[B]

American Honda Motor Co., Inc. v. Boyd ....5.02[A][2]

American Home Improvement, Inc. v. MacIver ....4.06[A][1]

American Carpet Mills v. Gunny Corp. .... 8.03[A]

American Bronze Corp. v. Streamway Prods. ....7.10[B]

American Electric Power Co. v. Westinghouse Electric Corp. ....5.04[C]

Amoco Pipeline Co. v. Admiral Crude Oil Corp. 9.08

Andover Air Ltd. Partnership v. Piper Aircraft Corp. ....5.04[A][2]

Anthony v. Tidwell ....3.05[B]

AP Propane, Inc. v. Sperback 3.03

Apex Oil Co. v. Belcher Co. of New York, Inc. .... 9.01[A]

ARB, Inc. v. E-Sys., Inc. ....4.02[E]

Arcuri v. Weiss ....3.03[C]

Art Metal Prod. Co. v. Royal Equip. Co. ....7.04[C][6]

Asciolla v. Manter Oldsmobile-Pontiac, Inc. ....7.04[C][5]

Askco Engineering Corp. v. Mobil Chemical Corp. .... 7.04[B][3]

Associated Metals & Minerals Corp. v. Sharon Steel Corp. 9.05

Atlan Industries, Inc. v. O.E.M., Inc. ....7.05[A][1]; 8.06[B]

Automotive Spares Corp. v. Archer Bearings Co. ....3.03[B]

Autzen v. John C. Taylor Lumber Sales, Inc. ....5.02[A][2], [4]

[References are to sections.]

B

Badger Produce Co., Inc. v. Prelude Foods
  International, Inc. .... 7.04[B][1]
Baker v. City of Seattle .... 1.03[A][2]
Baker v. Compton .... 1.03[C]
Baker v. International Record Syndicate,
  Inc. 9.10
Balog v. Center Art Gallery—Hawaii,
  Inc. .... 5.02[A][1]; 5.07
Banner Iron Works, Inc. v. Amax Zinc
  Co. .... 4.06[B]
Barber & Ross Co. v. Lifetime Doors,
  Inc. .... 3.03[B], [C]
Barclays Am. Business Credit Inc., v. E & E
  Enters., Inc. .... 7.09[A]
Bartus v. Riccardi .... 7.04[C][1]
Baughn v. Honda Motor Co., Ltd. .... 5.06[C]
Baumgold Bros., Inc. v. Allan M. Fox
  Co. .... 6.02[B]
Bayne v. Nall Motors, Inc. .... 7.04[C][5]
Bazak International Corp. v. Mast Industries,
  Inc. .... 3.04[A], [C]
Bead Chain Mfg. Co. v. Saxton Prods.,
  Inc. 9.03
Beckmire v. Ristokrat Clay Products Co. ..5.07
Belcher v. Versatile Farm Equip.
  Co. .... 5.04[A][2]
Beldengreen v. Ashinsky 3.02
Bendix Home Sys., Inc. v. Jessop ..... 8.05[B][1]
Best Buick, Inc. v. Welcome .... 5.02[A][2]
Best v. United States Nat'l Bank .... 4.06[A][3]
Bevel-Fold, Inc. v. Bose
  Corp. .... 7.03[A][1]; 9.01[C]
Bigelow v. Agway, Inc. .... 5.02[A][4]
Black Prince Distillery, Inc. v. Home
  Liquors .... 6.02[A]
Black Leaf Prods. Co. v. Chemisco, Inc. 5.07
Blankenship v. Northtown Ford,
  Inc. .... 5.03[B][1]
Bliss Produce Co. v. A.E. Albert & Sons,
  Inc. .... 7.14[A][1]; 8.04[B][1]
Blockhead, Inc. v. Plastic Forming Co.,
  Inc. .... 5.02[A][3]
BNE Swedbank, S.A. v. Banker .... 4.02[B]
Board of Directors of Harriman v. Southwest
  Petroleum Corp. .... 5.03[B][2]
Board of Control v. Burgess 2.04
Board of Education v. A, C, & S, Inc. ... 5.06[A]
Bodine Sewer, Inc. v. Eastern Ill. Precast,
  Inc. .... 7.04[E]

Boese-Hilburn Co. v. Dean Mach.
  Co. .... 2.05[C][1]
Bona v. Graefe .... 1.03[A][1]
Bonebrake v. Cox .... 1.03[C]; 7.05[C]; 7.09[C]
Boone v. Eyre .... 7.04[A]
Bowdoin v. Showell Growers, Inc. ... 5.03[B][4]
Broce O'Dell Concrete Products, Inc. v. Mel
  Jarvis Construction Co., Inc. 5.05
Broges v. Magic Valley Foods, Inc. ..7.03[A][3]
Broglie v. Mackay-Smith .... 7.04[B][3]
Brown Mach. v. Hercules, Inc. 2.02
Brown v. Western Farmers
  Association .... 5.06[A]
Buckeye Ag-Center, Inc. v. Babchuk .. 10.01[A]
Bulk Oil (USA), Inc. v. Sun Oil Trading
  Co. 9.05
Bunge Corp. v. Recker 7.12
Bunge Corp. v. Miller .... 7.13[B]
Burbic Constr. Co., Inc. v. Cement Asbestos
  Prod. Co., Inc. .... 2.05[C][1]
Burgess v. Curly Olney's, Inc. .... 8.04[B][2]
Burk v. Emmick .... 4.05[B][5]
Burrus v. Itek Corp. .... 8.06[B]
Busby, Inc. v. Smoky Valley Bean,
  Inc. .... 3.04[A]

C

C. Itoh & Co. v. Jordan Int'l Co. .... 2.05[D][2]
C.I.T. Corp. v. Jonnet .... 2.06[B][3]; 10.01[A]
C.R. Daniels, Inc. v. Yazoo Mfg.
  Co. .... 7.03[A][3]
California Airmotive Corp. v. Jones .... 9.01[A]
California & Hawaiian Sugar Co. v. Sun Ship,
  Inc. 9.10
Calloway v. Manion .... 5.03[B][3]
Canal Elec. Co. v. Westinghouse Elec.
  Corp. .... 5.04[B]
Canterra Petroleum, Inc. v. Western Drilling
  & Mining Supply .... 8.05[B][1]
Carboni v. Arrospide .... 4.06[A]
Cardwell v. International Housing ..7.04[C][6]
Carey v. Woburn Motors, Inc. .... 5.02[B][2]
Cargill, Inc. v. Stafford .... 8.04[B][2]
Carnes Constr. Co. v. Richards & Conover
  Steel & Supply Carpel v. Saget Studios,
  Inc. .... 8.06[B]
Cassidy Podel Lynch, Inc., v. SnyderGeneral
  Corp. .... 7.09[D]; 7.10[B]
Cates v. Dover Corp. .... 5.03[B][1]
Caudle v. Sherrard Motor Co. .... 6.02[A], [C]

[References are to sections.]

Century Ready-Mix Co. v. Lower &
Co. ....4.02[D][2]

Cervitor Kitchens, Inc. v.
Chapman ....7.03[A][3]

Chambers Steel Engraving Corp. v.
Tambrands, Inc. .... 3.05[A]

Champion Ford Sales, Inc. v. Levine ....7.05[C]

Chatlos Systems, Inc. v. National Cash
Register Corp. .... 8.05[B][1], [2]; 8.06[B]

Cherwell-Ralli, Inc. v. Rytman Grain
Co. .... 7.09[D]

Chicopee Concrete Serv., Inc. v. Hart Eng'g
Co. .... 2.03[B]

Childers & Venters, Inc. v.
Sowards .... 5.03[B][1]

CHR Equip. Fin., Inc. v. C&K Transport,
Inc. 9.11

Christopher v. Larson Ford Sales,
Inc. ....7.04[C][6]

Church of the Nativity of Our Lord v.
WatPro, Inc. .... 7.03[B][3]

Ciba-Geigy Corp. v. Alter ....5.02[A][4]

Citicorp. Indus. Credit, Inc. v.
Roundtree 9.11

Citizens Bank v. Taggart .... 4.05[B][5]

Cives Corp. v. Callier Steel Pipe & Tube,
Inc. .... 8.03[A]

Clark v. Zaid, Inc. .... 7.04[A]

Clark Oil Trading Co. v. Amerada Hess
Trading Co. ....7.04[C][2]

Clark Equip. Co. v. Armstrong Equip.
Co. ....9.09[B]

CMI Corp. v. Leemar Steel Co. .... 7.04[B][2]

Coakley & Williams, Inc. v. Shatterproof Glass
Corp. 5.07

Coast Trading Co., Inv. v. Parmac, Inc. 9.10

Coast Trading Co. v. Cudahy Co. .... 9.01[A]

Cochran v. Horner .... 5.02[D]

Cohen v. Hathaway .... 5.02[B][1]

Cole v. Melvin ....7.10[A]; 9.01[A]

Coleman v. Dupree .... 4.03[A]

Collins Co., Ltd. v. Carboline Co. ...... 10.01[A]

Colonial Life Ins. Co. of America v. Electronic
Data Systems Corp. ....5.04[C]

Columbia Nitrogen Corp. v. Royster
Co. .... 4.03[D]

Columbia Can Co. of J.J., Inc. v. Africa-Middle
East Marketing ....7.03[A][3]

Columbus Trade Exch., Inc. v. AMCA Int'l
Corp. ....3.03[D]; 3.06

Comer v. Franklin ....7.03[A][3]

Commonwealth Propane Co. v. Petrosol Int'l,
Inc. .... 6.02[C]

Commonwealth Edison Co. v. Decker Coal
Co. 9.05

Computer Network Ltd. v. Purcell Tire &
Rubber Co. 2.01

Computer Sys. Eng'g, Inc. v. Qantel
Corp. .... 8.06[B]

Computerized Radiological Services v. Syntex
Corp. ....5.02[B][2], [C][1]; 7.03[A][3]

Conaway v. 20th Century Corp. ....3.03[C]

Consolidated Foods Corp. v. Roland Foods,
Inc. 3.02

Consolidated Papers, Inc. v. Dorr-Oliver,
Inc. .... 5.03[A]

Consolidated Bottling Co. v. Jaco Equip.
Corp. .... 6.02[A]

Consolidated Data Terminals v. Applied
Digital Data Sys., Inc. .... 8.06[A]

Construction Aggregates, Inc. v. Hewitt-
Robins, Inc. ....2.05[D][1]

Consumers Power Co. v. Mississippi Valley
Structural Steel Co. .... 5.06[D]

Conte v. Dwan Lincoln-Mercury, Inc. ..7.05[C]

Continental Grain Co. v. McFarland .... 7.10[A]

Continental Forest Products, Inc. v. White
Lumber Sales, Inc. ....7.04[E]

Continental-Wirt Electronics Corp. v. Sprague
Electric Co. ....9.04[A][3]

Conway v. Larsen Jewelers, Inc. ..6.02[C]; 7.12

Cooley v. Big Horn Harvestore Sys.,
Inc. .... 2.06[B][1]

Copylease Corp. of Am. v. Memorex
Corp. ....7.10[A]; 8.08

Corinthian Pharmaceutical Systems, Inc. v.
Lederle Laboratories .... 2.02; 2.03[B]

Cork Plumbing Co. v. Martin Bloom
Associates, Inc. ....1.03[C]

Correia v. Firestone Tire & Rubber Co. 5.05

Cosden Oil & Chem. Co. v. Karl O. Helm
Aktiengesellschaft ...7.14[B]; 8.04[A], [B][2]

Costilla v. Aluminum Co. of
America .... 5.02[B][2]

Coulter v. American Bakeries Co. 5.05

Courtin v. Sharp ....6.02[C]

Cowin Equip. Co. v. General Motors
Corp. ....4.06[A][3]

CPC Internat'l, Inc. v. Techni-Chem,
Inc. .... 7.03[A][3]; 7.05[B]

Created Gemstones, Inc. v. Union Carbide
Corp. .... 7.09[B]

[References are to sections.]

Crest Container Corp. v. R.H. Bishop
Co. ....5.02[A][1]; 5.06[C]
Creusot-Lorie Int'l, Inc. v. Coppus Eng'g
Corp. .... 7.10[A]
Crews v. W.A. Brown & Son, Inc. ....5.06[B]
Crouch v. General Elec. Co. 5.07
Crysco Oilfield Services, Inc. v. Hutchison-
Hayes International ....5.02[C][2]
Cumberland Farms, Inc. v. Drehan Paving &
Flooring Co. ....1.03[C]
Curlee v. Mock Enterprises, Inc. ....5.06[B]
Czarnecki v. Roller .... 5.02[B][1]

D

D.P. Technology Corp. v. Sherwood Tool,
Inc. .... 7.04[A]
D.R. Curtis Co. v. Mathews .... 4.05[A]
Dairyland Fin. Corp. v. Federal Intermediate
Credit Bank 3.02
Daitom, Inc. v. Pennwalt Corp. ....
.....................................2.05[A], [B][1], [D][2]
Dale R. Hornung Co. v. Falconer Glass
Industries, Inc. .... 2.05[C][1]
Damin Aviation Corp. v. Sikorsky
Aircraft .... 5.06[A]
Dangerfield v. Markel .... 8.03[A]
Daughtrey v. Ashe ....5.02[A][1]
De La Rosa v. Tropical Sandwiches,
Inc. .... 10.01[A]
Deck House, Inc. v. Scarborough, Sheffield &
Gaston, Inc. ....4.02[G][3]
Dehahn v. Innes ....1.03[C]
Delano Growers' Cooperative Winery v.
Supreme Wine Co., Inc. .... 5.02[B][2]
Deutz-Allis Credit Corp. v. Jensen ....9.01[B]
Diamond Fruit Growers, Inc. v. Krack
Corp. .... 2.05[D][2]
DiDomenico Packaging Corp. v. Nails Again,
Inc. ....7.03[A][2]
Distco Laminating, Inc. v. Union Tool
Corp. ....7.03[A][3]
Division of Triple T Services, Inc. v. Mobil Oil
Corp. .... 4.03[D]
Dorton v. Collins & Aikman Corp. ..2.05[D][1]
Dotts v. Bennett .... 5.02[B][1]
Double-E Sportswear Corp. v. Girard Trust
Bank .... 2.06[B][3]
Downie v. Abex Corp. ....5.02[A][4]
Dravo Corp. v. White Consolidated
Industries, Inc. ....1.03[C]

Dravo Corp. v. M. L. Barge Operating
Corp. ....5.04[A][1]
Drennan v. Star Paving Co. ....2.03[B]
Dresser Industries, Inc. v. The Gradall
Co. ....2.05[D][2]
Dubrofsky v. Messer .... 2.05[B][1]
Dunavant Enterprises, Inc. v. Ford ..7.14[A][1]
Dura-Wood Treating Co. v. Century Forest
Industries, Inc. .... 8.03[A]
Durfee v. Rod Baxter Imports, Inc. ....7.05[E]

E

Earl of Chesterfield v. Janssen .... 4.06[A]
East River S.S. Corp. v. Transamerica Delaval,
Inc. .... 5.06[A]
Eastern Air Lines, Inc. v. McDonnell Douglas
Corp. ....7.14[A][1]
Eastern Air Lines, Inc. v. Gulf Oil
Corp. .... 7.14[A][1], [3]
Eberhard Mfg. Co. v. Brown .... 6.02[B]
Ehlers v. Chrysler Motor Corp. ....5.04[C]
Ellis Canning Co. v. Bernstein ....3.03[B]
Ellmer v. Delaware Mini-Computer Systems,
Inc. .... 5.03[B][1]
Emery v. Weed 7.12
Empire Gas Corp. v. American Bakeries
Co. ....4.05[C]
Employers Ins. Co. of Wausau v. Suwannee
River Spa Lines, Inc. ....5.04[C]
EPN-Delaval, S.A. v. Inter-Equip,
Inc. ....7.03[A][2]
Epprecht v. IBM Corp. .... 3.05[A]
Equitable Lumber Corp. v. I.P.A. Land
Development Corp. 9.10
Erdman v. Johnson Bros. Radio & TV
Co. ....8.06[B]
Erie Casein Co., Inc. v. Anric Corp. ..... 8.03[A]
Erling v. Homera, Inc. ....7.03[A][3]
Eska Kleiderfabrik v. Peters Sportswear Co.,
Inc. .... 7.04[B][3]

F

F.W. Lang Co. v. Fleet ....7.03[A][3]
Fablok Mills, Inc. v. Cocker Machine &
Foundry Co. ....7.03[A][2]
Fargo Mach. & Tool Co. v. Kearney & Trecker
Corp. ....5.04[A][2]
Farmer's Union Co-op Co. of Mead, Nebraska
v. Flamme Bros. .... 8.03[A]

[References are to sections.]

Farmers Union Coop. Gin v. Smith ..5.02[A][4]
Farmers Nat'l Bank v. Wickham
    Pipeline 5.07
Farmland Service Coop., Inc. v. Klein ..3.05[B]
Fast v. Southern Offshore Yachts ....7.09[C]
Fear Ranches, Inc. v. Berry .... 5.02[B][1]
Federal Express Corp. v. Pan American World
    Airways, Inc. ....1.03[C]
Fernandez v. Western R.R. Builders,
    Inc. .... 5.03[B][2]
Fernandes v. Union Bookbinding Co.,
    Inc. ....5.02[C][2]
Ferragamo v. Massachusetts Bay
    Transportation Authority .... 5.02[B][1]
Fiat Auto U.S.A., Inc. v. Hollums ....7.03[A][3]
Fiddler's Inn, Inc. v. Andrews Dist. Co.,
    Inc. ....5.02[B][2], [C][2]
Field v. Golden Triangle Broadcasting,
    Inc. ....1.03[C]
Filler v. Rayex Corp. .... 5.02[C][2]
Filley v. Pope .... 7.04[F]
First Valley Leasing, Inc. v. Goushy .....3.03[B]
First Nat'l Bank of Milltown v.
    Schrader .... 10.01[A]
Fischer v. General Electric Hotpoint .....5.04[B]
Fisher Trucking, Inc. v. Fleet Lease,
    Inc. ....9.01[B]
Fleet Maintenance, Inc. v. Burke Energy
    Midwest Corp. .... 7.03[B][3]
Flintkote Co. v. Dravo Corp. .... 5.06[A]
Flood v. MP Clark, Inc. .... 8.04[A]
Florida Power & Light v. Westinghouse
    Electric Corp. ....7.14[A][1]
FMC Fin. Corp. v. Murphree ....5.03[C]
Ford Motor Co. v. Mayes ....7.04[C][5]
Ford Motor Co. v. Reid ....5.04[A][1]
Ford Motor Co. v. Moulton ....5.03[C]
Ford Motor Credit Co. v. Harper ....7.05[E]
Fordyce Concrete, Inc. v. Mack Trucks,
    Inc. .... 5.06[A]
Forest Nursery Co., Inc. v. I.W.S.,
    Inc. .... 6.02[A]
Foster v. Colorado Radio Corp. ....1.03[C]
Foxco Indus., Ltd. v. Fabric World ....9.01[C]
Frank Novak & Sons, Inc. v. Sommer & Maca
    Indus., Inc. 5.07
Frank Nero Auto Lease v. Townsend 9.11
Franklin County Coop. v. MFC
    Services ....3.05[B]
Franklin Grain & Supply Co. v.
    Ingram ....8.06[B]
Frazer v. A.F. Munsterman, Inc. 5.05

Fredonia Broadcasting Corp., Inc. v. RCA
    Corp. ....7.09[B]; 8.04[B][2]
Fredrick v. Dryer .... 5.02[B][2]
Freiberg v. Atlas-Turner, Inc. 5.07
Fullerton Aircraft Sales & Rentals, Inc. v. Page
    Avjet Corp. ....7.05[A][2]
Fundin v. Chicago Pneumatic Tool
    Co. ....5.03[A]; 5.06[D]
Funding Systems Leasing Corp. v. King Louie
    International, Fuquay v. Revels Motors,
    Inc. .... 5.02[B][2]
Futch v. James River—Norwalk, Inc. 3.06

G

G & H Land & Cattle Co. v. Heitzman &
    Nelson, Inc. ....7.03[A][1]
Gappelberg v. Landrum ....7.05[C]
Gardner Zemke Co. v. Dunham Bush,
    Inc. .... 2.05[B][1]
Garfinkel v. Lehman Floor Covering
    Co. ....7.03[A][3]
Gatoil (USA), Inc. v. Washington Metro. Area
    Transit Auth. .... 7.09[A]
Gawlick v. American Builders Supply,
    Inc. 8.04
Gay v. Seafarer Fiberglass Yachts, Inc. 8.08
Geldermann & Co. v. Lane Processing,
    Inc. ....4.06[A][2]
General Plumbing & Heating, Inc. v.
    American Air Filter Co., Inc. ....4.02[H]
General Matters, Inc. v. Penny Products,
    Inc. ....3.03[C]
General Motors Acceptance Corp. v.
    Grady ....7.04[C][1]
General Supply & Equip. Co. v.
    Phillips ....8.06[B]
George v. Fannin ....7.03[A][3]
Geotech Energy Corp. v. Gulf States
    Telecommunications & Information
    Systems. ....1.03[C]
Gerwin v. Southeastern Cal. Ass'n of Seventh
    Day Adventists ....8.06[B]
Gibbs, Nathaniel (Can.) Ltd. v. International
    Multifoods Corp. ....7.09[C]
Gillman v. Chase Manhattan Bank,
    N.A. ....4.06[A][1]
Gindy Manufacturing Corp. v. Cardinale
    Trucking Corp. .... 5.03[B][2]
Glenn Dick Equipment Co. v. Galey
    Construction, Inc. ....1.03[A][2]
Gochey v. Bombardier, Inc. ....7.05[E]

[References are to sections.]

Gold-Kist, Inc. v. Citizens & Southern Nat'l
Bank .... 5.03[B][4]
Golden Plains Feedlot, Inc. v. Great W. Sugar
Co. 3.06
Goldman v. Barnett ....5.02[A][1]
Goldstein v. Stainless Processing Co. 9.07
Goodell v. KT Enters., Ltd. .... 8.03[A]
Goodman v. Wenco Management .... 5.02[B][2]
Government of Republic of China v. Compass
Communications Corp. 8.02
Graham Hydraulic Power, Inc. v. Stewart &
Stevenson Power ....2.05[B][1], [C][1]
Graulich Caterer Inc. v. Hans Holterbosch,
Inc. .... 7.09[D]
Graybar Elec. Co. v. Shook .... 7.04[B][3]
Great Am. Music Mach., Inc. v. Mid-South
Record Pressing Co. ....7.04[C][6]
Great Dane Trailer Sales, Inc. v. Malvern
Pulpwood, Inc. .... 5.02[C][2]; 5.04[A][2]
Great Northern Packaging, Inc. v. General
Tire and Rubber Co. .... 3.03[D]
Gulf Chem. & Metallurgical Corp. v. Sylvan
Chem. Corp. .... 7.09[D]

H

Hadley v. Baxendale .... 8.06[B]
Hahn v. Ford Motor Co., Inc. .... 5.03[B][4]
Hall Truck Sales, Inc. v. Wilder Mobile
Homes, Inc. .... 5.03[B][3]
Hall v. T.L. Kemp Jewelry, Inc. ....5.02[A][1]
Hancock Paper Co. v. Champion Int'l
Corp. .... 7.14[A]
Hansen v. FMC Corp. .... 7.03[B][3]
Happy Dack Trading Co. Ltd. v. Agro-Indus.,
Inc. .... 8.06[A]
Hardesty v. Andro Corp.-Webster
Div. ....8.06[B]
Harlan v. Smith .... 8.05[B][3]
Hartz Seed Co. v. Colman .... 7.04[B][1]
Hartzell v. Justius Co., Inc. .... 8.05[B][1]
Harvey v. McKinney ....3.05[B]
Havas v. Love .... 7.04[C][6]
Hayes v. Ariens Co. .... 5.02[B][2]
Hayes v. Hettinga .... 8.06[B]; 9.04[A][1]
Hayward v. Postma .....6.02[A], [D]; 6.05[A][1]
HCI Chemicals (USA), Inc. v. Henkel
KGaA ....7.03[A][1]
Heggblade-Marguleas-Tenneco, Inc. v.
Sunshine Biscuit, Inc. .... 4.03[D]
Heller v. United States Suzuki Motor
Co. 5.07

Hemmert Agric. Aviation, Inc. v. Mid-
Continent Aircraft Corp. ....7.04[C][5]
Henry Heide, Inc. v. Atlantic Mut. Ins.
Co. ....6.02[C]
Hertz Commercial Leasing Corp. v. Dynatron,
Inc. 9.10
Hickham v. Chronister .... 5.02[C][1]
Hill Aircraft & Leasing Corp. v.
Simon ....5.02[A][2]
Hillcrest Country Club v. N.D. Judds
Co. 5.07
Hochster v. De La Tour .... 7.09[A]
Hoelter v. Mohawk Services, Inc. ....5.05[C]
Hoffman v. Boone 3.06
Holiday Manufacturing Corp. v. BASF
Systems, Inc. .... 7.09[D]
Holiday Rambler Corp. v. First Nat'l Bank &
Trust .... 4.05[B][5]
Hollingsworth v. The Software House,
Inc. ....7.03[A][3]; 8.02
Honeywell, Inc. v. Lithonia Lighting,
Inc. 9.03
Horn & Hardart Co. v. Pillsbury Co. ... 3.03[A]
Hospital Computer Systems, Inc. v. Staten
Island Hospital ....7.03[A][3]
Howard Construction Co. v. Jeff-Cole
Quarries, Inc. ....3.03[C]; 3.05[C]
Hrosik v. J. Keim Builders ....5.02[A][4]
Hudson Feather & Down Prods., Inc. v.
Lancer Clothing Corp. ....7.09[B]
Hudspeth Motors, Inc. v.
Wilkinson ....7.03[A][2]
Hummel v. Skyline Dodge, Inc. ....7.05[A][1]
Hunt Foods & Industries v.
Doliner ....4.02[E], [G][3]
Hunt v. Perkins Machinery Co.
Inc. .... 5.03[B][1]
Huntington Beach Union High School Dist. v.
Continental Information
Systems .... 8.03[A]

I

Impossible Elec. Techniques, Inc. v.
Wackenhut Protective
Systems .... 3.03[C]; 3.05[A]
In re Atkins .... 2.06[B][1]
In re Barney Schogel, Inc. ....7.05[A][1]
In re Bicoastal Corp. 3.02
In re BTS, Inc. .... 4.05[A]
In re Coast Trading Co. .... 7.10[A]
In re L&M Fabricators ....7.03[A][1]

[References are to sections.]

In re Lifeguard Industries, Inc. .... 8.03[A]
Industrial Fiberglass v. Jandt .... 7.03[B][3]
Industrial Leasing Corp. v. Thomason ...9.04[B]
Insul-Mark Midwest, Inc. v. Modern
    Materials, Inc. ....1.03[C]
Integrated Circuits Unlimited v. E.F. Johnson
    Co. .... 7.04[B], [B][2]; 7.05[D]; 9.04[A][1]
Interco, Inc. v. Randustrial Corp. .....5.02[A][1]
Interior Elevator Co. v. Limmeroth 8.04
International Commodities Export Corp. v.
    North Pacific Lumber ....7.03[A][1]
International Minerals & Chem. Corp. v.
    Llano, Inc. ....7.14[A][2]
Intershoe, Inc. v. Bankers Trust Co. ..... 4.02[H]
Interstate Plywood Sales Co. v. Interstate
    Container Corp. .... 4.05[A]
Intervale Steel Corp. v. Borg & Beck Division
    of Borg-Warner Corp. ....7.03[A][3]
Investors Premium Corp. v. Burroughs
    Corp. ...., 5.03[A]
Iowa Elec. Light & Power Co. v. Atlas
    Corp. ....7.14[A][3]
Irvin v. Lowe's of Gainesville, Inc. .... 10.01[A]
Islamic Republic of Iran v. Boeing Co. 9.03
Island Creek Coal Co. v. Lake Shore,
    Inc. ....5.04[B]
Itoh v. Kimi Sales .... 8.05[B][3]
ITT-Industrial Credit Co. v. Mile Concrete
    Co., Inc. .... 8.05[B][1]
Ivey's Plumbing & Electric Co. v. Petrochem
    Maintenance, Inc. ....2.04; 3.03[D]

J

Jackson v. Meadows ....3.05[B]
Jacob & Youngs, Inc. v. Kent .... 7.04[A]
Jaffray v. Davis .... 2.06[A]
Jakowski v. Carole Chevrolet, Inc. .... 6.03[A]
James Baird Co. v. Gimbel Bros. ....2.03[B]
Jeanneret v. Vichey .... 8.05[B][3]
Jenkins & Boiler Co., Inc. v. Schmidt Iron
    Works, Inc. ....2.03[B]
Jensen v. Seigel Mobile Homes
    Group ....5.02[A][4]; 7.05[C]
Jim Dan, Inc. v. O. M. Scott & Sons
    Co. ....5.04[B]
JL Clark Mfg. Co. v. Gold Bond
    Pharmaceutical Corp. ....7.03[A][3]
Jo-Ann, Inc. v. Alfin Fragrances, Inc. ... 3.03[D]
Joc Oil USA, Inc. v. Consolidated Edison
    Co. ....7.04[C][3][4]

Johannsen v. Minnesota Valley Ford Tractor
    Co. ....7.03[A][3]; 7.04[C][1], [3]; 7.05[F]
John P. Saad & Sons v. Nashville Thermal
    Transfer Corp. ....4.03[C]
John H. Wickersham Eng'g & Constr., Inc. v.
    Arbutus Steel Co. ....3.03[C]
Johnson v. CFM, Inc. .... 5.02[B][2]
Johnson v. Mobil Oil Corp. .... 4.06[A], [A][2]
Johnson v. General Motors Corp. .... 7.05[F]
Jon-T Farms, Inc. v. Goodpasture, Inc. 7.13
Jones v. Wide World of Cars, Inc. .... 3.05[A]
Jones v. Star Credit Corp. .... 4.06[A][1], [3]
Jones v. Abriani .... 7.04[C][3]
Jones v. Barkley .... 7.04[A]
Jones v. Abriani .... 8.05[B][1]
Jorgensen v. Presnall .... 7.05[F]
Joseph Heiting & Sons v. Jacks Bean
    Co. ....3.05[C]
June G. Ashton Interiors v. Stark Carpet
    Corp. 8.02

K

Kaiser Aluminum & Chemical Corp. v.
    Ingersoll-Rand Co. .... 10.01[A]
Kansas City, Missouri v. Kansas City,
    Kansas ....7.14[A][2]
Kanzmeier v. McCoppin ....8.3[A][3]
Keith v. Buchanan ....5.02[A][1]
Keller v. A.O. Smith Harvestore Products,
    Inc. ....1.02[G][2]
Kern Oil & Refining Co. v. Tenneco Oil
    Co. ....4.03[C]
Kesner v. Lancaster ....7.05[A][1]
Keystone Aeronautics Corp. v. R.J. Enstrom
    Corp. .... 5.06[A]
Kiser v. Lemco Industries, Inc. .... 8.03[A]
Klein v. Sears Roebuck & Co. ....5.02[A][2]
Kleinschmidt Division of SCM Corp. v.
    Futuronics, Inc. 2.01
Kline Iron & Steel Co., Inc. v. Gray
    Communications Consultant Inc. ... 3.04[A]
Knipp v. Weinbaum .... 5.03[B][2]
Knoxville Rod & Bearing, Inc. v. Bettis Corp.
    of Knoxville, Inc. .... 2.06[B][2]
Koellmer v. Chrysler Motors Corp. 5.08
Kopper Clo Fuel, Inc., v. Island Lake Coal
    Co. ....5.02[A][3]
Kramer v. Piper Aircraft Corp. ....5.06[C]
Kunian v. Development Corp. of Am. ...7.10[A]

[References are to sections.]

L

La Casse v. Blaustein ....6.02[B]
La Villa Fair v. Lewis Carpet Mills,
　Inc. ....7.03[A][3]; 7.04[B][1]
Laclede Gas Co. v. Amoco Oil Co. 8.08
Lafayette Stabilizer Repair, Inc. v. Machinery
　Wholesalers Corp. 9.10
Lamborn v. National Bank of
　Commerce ....7.04[F]
Lancaster Glass Corp. v. Phillips ECG,
　Inc. ....4.03[C]
Langemeier v. Nat'l Oats Co., Inc ....4.06[A][3]
Lanham v. Solar Am. of Cincinnati,
　Inc. ....8.06[B]
Lanners v. Whitney ....8.06[A]; 8.07
Latham & Associates, Inc. v. William Raveis
　Real Estate, Inc. ....4.02[G][2]
Lawrence v. Elmore Bean Warehouse,
　Inc. ....7.14[A]
Lee Oldsmobile, Inc. v. Kaiden 9.05; 9.10
Lewis v. Hughes ....3.05[B]
Lewis v. Mobil Oil Corp. .... 5.02[C][2]; 8.06[B]
Liberty Truck Sales, Inc. v. Kimbrel ...5.04[A][2]
Light v. Weldare Co., Inc. ....5.02[C][3]
Lingenfelder v. Wainwright Brewery
　Co. ....2.06[A]
Little Rock Elec. Contractors, Inc. v. Okonite
　Co. 5.05
LNS Inv. Co., Inc. v. Phillips ....7.10[A]
Lobianco v. Property Protection, Inc. ...5.04[B]
Lockwood v. Smigel ....3.05[C]
Long Island Lighting Co. v. Transamerica
　Delaval, Inc. 5.07
Long v. Quality Mobile Home Brokers,
　Inc. ....8.06[B]
Loranger Plastics Corp. v. Incoe Corp. 2.04
Loranger Constr. Corp. v. E.F.
　Hauserman ....2.03[B]
Lorenzo Banfi di Banfi Renzo & Co. v. Davis
　Congress Shop Inc. ....7.03[A][3]
Louisiana Power & Light Co. v. Allegheny
　Ludlum Indus., Inc. ....7.14[A][3]
Lowenstern v. Stop & Shop Companies 2.04
Lubrication & Maintenance, Inc. v. Union
　Resources Co. ....7.10[A]
Lupofresh, Inc. v. Pabst Brewing Co.,
　Inc. ....9.04[A][1]
Luther Williams, Jr., Inc. v.
　Johnson .... 4.02[F], [G][3]
Lynch Imports, Ltd. v. Frey ....6.05[A][1]

M

Madison Industries, Inc. v. Eastman Kodak
　Co. ....4.02[G][1]
Maple Farms, Inc. v. City of Elmira ...7.14[A][1]
Marion Square Corp. v. Kroger Co. ..... 3.03[D]
Marlowe v. Argentine Naval
　Comm'n ....7.04[C][1]
Maroone Chevrolet, Inc. v. Nordstrom ..5.02[D]
Martella v. Woods ....8.03[A]
Martin v. Mellands 6.01
Massey v. Hardcastle 3.06
Massey v. Thomaston Ford
　Mercury ....7.03[B][3]
Massey-Ferguson v. Utley ....5.03[B][1]
Massey-Ferguson, Inc. v. Laird ....5.02[A][4]
Massey-Ferguson Credit Corp. v.
　Webber ....8.05[B][1]
Master Palletizer Sys., Inc. v. T.S. Ragsdale
　Co. 2.02
Masters Mach. Co., Inc. v. Brookfield Athletic
　Shoe Co. 9.05
Matco Mach. & Tool Co. v. Cincinnati
　Milacron Co. ....5.04[C]
Max Bauer Meat Packer, Inc. v. United
　States .... 7.04[B][1]
Maxon Corp. v. Tyler Pipe Indus.,
　Inc. .... 4.06[A], [A][2]
McAllister v. Patten 8.08
McCarty v. Verson Allsteel Press Co. 2.02
McClanahan v. American Gilsonite
　Co. ....1.03[C]
McClure v. Duggan ....3.03[C]
McClure Oil Corp. v. Murray Equipment,
　Inc. ....9.04[A][1]
McCrimmon v. Tandy Corp. ....5.04[B]
McCullough v. Bill Swad Chrysler-Plymouth,
　Inc. ....7.03[A][3]
McJunkin Corp. v. Mechanicals,
　Inc. ....2.05[D][2]
McKenzie v. Alla-Ohio Coals, Inc. ...7.04[C][3]
McMillan v. Meuser Material & Equip.
　Co. .... 9.01[A]
Mead Corp. v. McNally-Pittsburgh Mfg.
　Corp. ....2.05[B][1], [C][2]
Meads v. Davis ....7.04[C][1]
Melms v. Mitchell ....8.03[B][3]
Menzel v. List ....8.05[B][3]
Meshinsky v. Nichols Yacht Sales,
　Inc. .... 8.03[A]
Metalcraft, Inc. v. Pratt .... 8.05[B][3]

[References are to sections.]

Michael M. Berlin & Co. v. T. Whiting Mfg.,
   Inc. .... 7.04[B][1]
Mid-South Packers, Inc. v. Shoney's, Inc. ..2.04
Midwest Precision Services, Inc. v. PTM
   Industries Corp. .... 10.01[A]
Migerobe, Inc. v. Certina USA,
   Inc. ....3.03[A]; 3.05[B]; 8.06[B]
Mileham & King, Inc. v. Fitzgerald ..5.02[A][3]
Miles v. Kavanaugh ....5.02[A][2]
Milltex Industries Corp v. Jacquard Lace Co.,
   Ltd. 3.04
Mineral Park Land Co. v. Howard 7.11
Minsel v. El Rancho Mobile Home Ctr.,
   Inc. ....7.03[A][3]
Miron v. Yonkers Raceway, Inc. .... 7.03[B][4]
Mitchell v. Ford Motor Credit Co. .... 9.09[B]
Mitchill v. Lath .... 4.02[D][1], [2]
Mobile Housing, Inc. v. Stone ....7.04[C][1]
Mobile Homes Sales Management, Inc. v.
   Brown ....7.03[A][3]
Modern Mach. v. Flathead County .... 3.03[B]
Modine Mfg. Co. v. North E. Indep. School
   Dist. .... 4.03[D]
Monarco v. Lo Greco 3.06
Monetti, S.P.A. v. Anchor Hocking
   Corp. ....1.03[C]; 3.03[C]
Monsanto Co. v. Logisticon, Inc. ....5.05[C]
Montana Seeds, Inc. v.
   Holliday .... 6.02[B]; 9.04[A][2]
Montgomery Indus. Int'l v. Thomas Constr.
   Co. .... 2.03[B]
Morauer v. Deak & Co., Inc. .... 6.02[B]
Morgan v. Stokely-Van Camp, Inc. .... 4.02[F]
Morrison's Cafeteria of Montgomery, Inc. v.
   Haddox .... 5.02[B][2]
Morrow v. New Moon Homes, Inc. ......5.06[C]
MortgageAmerica Corp. v. American Nat'l
   Bank .... 4.03[A]
Moscatiello v. Pittsburgh Contractors Equip.
   Co. .... 5.04[B]
Moses v. Newman ....7.03[A][1]
Mott Equity Elevator v. Svihovec ....9.01[C]
Moulton Cavity & Mold, Inc. v. Lyn-Flex
   Indus., Inc. .... 7.04[A]
Mountain Fuel Supply Co. v. Central
   Engineering & Equip. Co. 5.08
Mt. Holly Ski Area v. U.S. Electrical
   Motors ....5.06[C]
Mullan v. Quickie Aircraft Corp. ....5.04[B]
Multi-Line Manufacturing, Inc. v. Greenwood
   Mills, Inc. ....9.04[A][3]

Multiplastics, Inc. v. Arch Industries,
   Inc. ....6.03[C]; 9.04[A][2]
Murphy v. McNamara .... 1.03[A][1]; 4.06[A][1]
Murphy v. Spelts-Schultz Lumber Co. of
   Grand Island 5.07
Murray v. Kleen, Inc. .... 5.03[B][3]
Musil v. Hendrich .... 5.02[B][1]
Myers v. A.O. Smith Harvestore Products,
   Inc. .... 5.06[A]

N

Nanakuli Paving & Rock Co. v. Shell Oil
   Co. ....4.03[A], [B], [D]
Nat'l Utility Service, Inc. v. Whirlpool
   Corp. .... 2.06[B][3]
National Heater Co., Inc. v. Corrigan Co.
   Mechanical Contractor Inc. .... 4.05[B][3]
National Fleet Supply, Inc. v.
   Fairchild .... 7.04[C][2]
National Ropes, Inc., v. National Diving Serv.,
   Inc. .... 7.10[A]
National Farmers Org. v. Bartlett &
   Co. .... 7.10[A]
National Plumbing Supply Co. v.
   Castellano .... 6.02[D]
Neal-Cooper Grain Co. v. Texas Gulf Sulphur
   Co. ....8.04[A], [B][2]
Nebraska Builders Prods. Co. v. Industrial
   Erectors, Inc. .... 3.03[A]
Neibarger v. Universal Cooperatives,
   Inc. ....1.03[C]
Neilson Business Equipment Center, Inc. v.
   Italo Monteleone ....5.02[C][1]
Nelson v. Logan Motor Sales, Inc. ... 8.05[B][1]
Neptune Research & Dev., Inc. v. Tecknics
   Indus. Sys., Inc. ...... 7.04[C][1]; 7.09[A], [C]
Neri v. Retail Marine Corp. 9.03
Neumiller Farms, Inc. v. Cornett .....7.04[D][6]
Ninth St. East, Ltd. v. Harrison ....
   .... 6.02[B]; 9.04[A][2]
Nissho-Iwai Co. v. Occidental Crude Sales,
   Inc. ....7.14[A][1]
Nobs Chem., USA, Inc. v. Koppers Co.,
   Inc. 9.05
Norm Gershman's Things to Wear, Inc. v.
   Mercedes Benz of North America
   Inc. .... 5.03[B][1]
North River Homes, Inc. v. Bosarge .....7.05[F]
North Am. Steel Corp. v. Siderius ...7.04[C][6]

[References are to sections.]

Northern Power & Engineering Corp. v.
Caterpillar Tractor Co. .... 5.06[A]
Northwest Cent. Pipeline Corp. v. JER
Partnership ....4.02[D][2]

O

Oakley v. Little ....3.03[C]
Oda Nursery, Inc. v. Garcia Tree & Lawn,
Inc. ....7.03[A][3]
Office Supply Co., Inc. v. Basic/Four
Corp. .... 5.03[B][1]
Ohio Savings Bank v. H.L. Vokes Co. ...5.03[C]
O'Keefe Elevator Co., Inc. v. Second Avenue
Properties, Ltd. .... 5.02[C][3]
Oldham's Farm Sausage Co. v. Salco,
Inc. ....5.04[B]
Oloffson v. Coomer ....7.09[B]; 8.03[A]
Olympic Juniors, Inc. v. David Crystal,
Inc. 3.02
Orange and Rockland Utilities v. Amerada
Hess Corp. ....4.05[C]
Osborn v. Custom Truck Sales and
Serv. .... 5.02[B][2]
Oskey Gasoline & Oil Co. v. Continental Oil
Co. ....3.05[B]
Owens v. Patent Scaffolding Co. ....1.03[A][1]
Ozier v. Haines 3.06

P

Pacific Gas and Electric Co. v. G.W. Thomas
Drayage & Rigging Co. .... 4.04[A]
Pacific Western Resin Co. v. Condux Pipe
Sys., Inc. 3.04
Pacific Marine Schwabacher, Inc. v.
Hydroswift Corp. .... 7.04[B][3]
Palmer v. Idaho Peterbilt, Inc. ....4.03[B]
Paragon Resources, Inc. v. Nat'l Fuel Gas
Distr. Corp. .... 4.04[A]
Park Co. Implement Co. v. Craig .....7.03[A][3]
Patterson v. Her Majesty Industries, Inc. ..5.07
Pavesi v. Ford Motor Co. .... 7.05[F]
Penberthy Electromelt Int'l, Inc. v. U.S.
Gypsum Co. .... 7.10[A]
Perfection Cut, Inc. v. Olsen .... 5.03[A]
Performance Motors, Inc. v. Allen ....7.05[B]
Perry v. Augustine 5.07
Pestana v. Karinol Corp. .... 6.02[B]
Petroleo Brasileiro, SA v. Ameropan Oil
Corp. 9.05
Philip A. Feinberg, Inc. v. Bernstein & Sparber
Corp. .... 7.03[B][3]

Pillsbury Co. v. Ward ....7.09[A]; 9.07
Pittsburgh-Des Moines Steel Co. v.
Brookhaven Manor Water Co. ....
.... 7.09[C]; 7.10[A]
Plateq Corp. v. Machlett
Laboratories ....7.03[A][1]
Poel v. Brunswicke-Balke-Collender
Co. .... 2.05[A]
Poppenheimer v. Bluff City Motor
Homes 5.07
Printing Center of Texas, Inc. v. Supermind
Pub. Co., Inc. .... 7.04[A]
Procyon Corp. v. Components Direct,
Inc. ....3.03[B]
Productora E Importadora de Papel, S.A. de
C.V. v. Fleming ....8.04[B]
Professional Lens Plan, Inc. v. Polaris Leasing
Corp. ....5.06[C]
Pronti v. DML of Elmira, Inc. ....5.06[C]
Publicker Indus. v. Union Carbide
Corp. ....7.14[A][1]

Q

Quaney v. Tobine ....3.05[B]

R

R.A. Weaver & Assocs. v. Asphalt
Construction, Inc. ....4.05[C]
R.E. Davis Chemical Corp. v. Diasonics,
Inc. 9.03
R.I. Lampus Co. v. Neville Cement Products
Corp. ....8.06[B]
R.S. Bennett & Co. v. Economy Mechanical
Industries, Inc. 3.06
Ragen Corp. v. Kearney & Trecker Corp. ..9.03
Ralston Purina Co. v. McFarland 8.04
Ralston Purina Co. v. Hartford Accident &
Indemnity Co. ....5.04[A][1]
Ramirez v. Autosport ....7.04[A], [C][1]
Randy Knitwear, Inc. v. American Cyanamid
Co. .... 5.06[D]
Ray Martin Painting, Inc. v. Ameron,
Inc. .... 4.02[F]
Reaction Molding Technologies,
Inc. ....2.05[D][1]
Record Club of Am., Inc. v. United Artists
Records, Inc. ....7.09[C]
Red River Commodities, Inc. v.
Eidsness .... 7.09[A]
Regina Grape Prods. Co. v. Supreme Wine
Co. ....5.02[A][3]

[References are to sections.]

Renfroe v. Ladd 3.06

Rennie & Laughlin, Inc. v. Chrysler
Corp. .... 2.06[B][3]

Renze Hybrids, Inc. v. Shell Oil
Co. ....5.02[C][2]

Rheinberg Kellerei GmbH v. Brooksfield Nat'l
Bank of Commerce .... 6.01; 6.02[B]

Rhurek v. Chrysler Credit Corp. ...... 5.03[B][1]

Richter, S.A. v. Bank of America
N.T.S.A. .... 10.01[A]

Riegle Fiber Corp. v. Anderson Gin
Co. .... 3.03[D]

Riley v. Ken Wilson Ford, Inc. .... 7.03[B][3]

Roberts v. General Dynamics, Convair
Corp. ....5.06[C]

Robinson v. Jonathan Logan Fin. ....7.04[B]

Romy v. Picker Internat'l, Inc. ....7.03[A][3]

Ron Mead T.V. & Appliance v. Legendary
Homes, Inc. .... 6.02[D]

Roth Steel Products v. Sharon Steel
Corp. ....7.14[A][1], [B]

Roth Steel Prods. v. Sharon Steel
Corp. .... 8.04[B][2]

Roto-Lith, Ltd. v. F.P. Bartlett & Co.,
Inc. .... 2.05[D][1], [2]

Rottinghaus v. Howell ....5.03[C]

Royal Indem. Co. v. Westinghouse Elec.
Co. ....4.06[A][2]

Rozmus v. Thompson's Lincoln-Mercury
Co. ....7.03[A][1]

Rudd Construction Equipment Co. v. Clark
Equipment Co. ....,..5.04[A][2]

Russell v. Ford Motor Co. .... 5.06[A]

S

S&R Metals, Inc. v. C. Itoh & Co. (America),
Inc. 8.02

Sabine Corp. v. ONG Western,
Inc. .... 7.14[A][2], [3]

Sacred Heart Farmers Cooperative v.
Johnson 3.06

Salinas Lettuce Farmers Coop. v. Larry Ober
Co., Inc. .... 7.04[A]

Salines v. Flores 7.12

Sanco v. Ford Motor Co., Inc. .... 5.03[B][4]

Sawyer Farmers Coop. Assoc. v.
Linke .... 8.04[B][2]

SC Gray, Inc. v. Ford Motor Co. 9.05

Schlenz v. John Deere Co. ....5.04[B]

Schmaltz v. Nissen ....5.02[A][4]

Schwartzreich v. Bauman-Basch, Inc. .. 2.06[A]

Scott v. Crown .... 7.10[A]

Seaman's Direct Buying Service v. Standard
Oil Co. .... 3.03[D]

Sebasty v. Perschke .... 3.03[A]

Sedmak v. Charlie's Chevrolet,
Inc. ....3.05[C]; 8.08

Seekings v. Jimmy GMC of Tucson,
Inc. .... 7.05[E]

Seibel v. Layne & Bowler, Inc. .... 4.02[F]

Seigel v. Giant Food, Inc. .... 5.02[B][2]

Select Pork, Inc. v. Babcock Swine,
Inc. ....5.04[A][2]

Servbest Foods, Inc. v. Emessee Indus.,
Inc. ....9.01; 9.05[A]

Sessa v. Riegle ....5.02[A][1]

Sharp Bros. Contracting Co. v. American
Hoist & Derrick Co. .... 5.06[A]

Sharrard, McGee & Co., P.A. v. Suz's
Software, Inc. .... 10.01[A]

Sheenan v. Morris Irrigation, Inc. 5.07

Shelton v. Farkas ....7.03[A][1]

Siemen v. Alden .... 5.02[B][1]

Sierra Diesel Injection Serv., Inc. v. Burroughs
Corp. .... 4.02[F]

Signal Oil & Gas Co. v. Universal Oil
Products 5.05

Silver v. Wycombe Meyer Co., Inc. ....6.02[C]

Singer Co. v. E.I. DuPont de Nemours &
Co. 5.08

SJ Groves & Sons Co. v. Warner Co. .... 7.09[D]

Slyman v. Pickwick Farms ....5.02[A][1]

Smith Packing Co. v. Quality Pork
International, Inc. ....3.03[C]

Smith v. Navistar Int'l Transportation
Corp. ....5.04[C]

Smith-Scharff Paper Co. v. P.N. Hirsch & Co.
Stores, Inc. .... 3.05[A]

Snyder v. Herbert Greenbaum &
Associates .... 4.02[E]; 9.03

Soaper v. Hope Industries, Inc. .... 5.02[C][2]

Solar Kinetics Corp. v. Joseph T. Ryerson &
Sons, Inc. .... 7.05[B]; 9.04[A][1]

Songbird Jet Ltd., Inc. v. Amax, Inc. .... 3.03[A]

Soo Line Ry. Co. v. Fruehauf
Corp. .... 8.05[B][1]

Southern Idaho Pipe & Steel Co. v. Cal-Cut
Pipe & Supply, Inc. .... 2.05[B][1]

Southwest Concrete Prod. v. Gosh Constr.
Corp. .... 2.05[C][1]

Southwest Eng'g Co. v. Martin Tractor
Co. .... 3.03[B]

Spagnol Enterprises, Inc. v. Digital Equip.
Corp. ....5.06[C]

Sparks v. Stich .... 5.02[B][1]

Spartan Grain & Mill Co. v. Ayers .... 4.05[A]

[References are to sections.]

Sprague v. Sumitomo Forestry Co., Ltd. ...9.05

SPS Indus., Inc. v. Atlantic Steel Co. .... 7.10[A]

Standard Brands Chemical Indus., Inc. v. Pilot Freight Carriers, Inc. .... 5.02[B][2]

Standard Structural Steel Co. v. Debron Corp. ....1.03[C]

Stang v. Hertz Corp. ....5.02[A][4]

Star Furniture Co. v. Pulaski .... 5.06[A]

Starry Construction Co., Inc. v. Murphy Oil USA, Inc. .... 2.06[B][1]

Stauffer Chemical Co. v. Curry ....5.03[B][1]; 5.04[B]

Step-Saver Data Sys., Inc. v. Wyse Technology .... 2.05[D][1], [2]

Stephan's Machine & Tool, Inc. v. D & M Machinery Consultants, Inc. 8.08

Stephens v. G.D. Searle & Co. .... 5.02[B][2]

Stephenson v. Ketchikan Spruce Mills, Inc. .... 4.02[H]

Stewart v. Gainesville Glass Co. .... 5.06[D]

Stewart v. United States Leasing Corp. .... 7.05[G]

Storey v. Day Heating & Air Conditioning Co. .... 5.02[B][1]

Stratton Industries, Inc. v. Northwest Georgia Bank ....7.03[A][3]

Stroh v. American Recreation & Mobile Home Corp. .... 7.05[F]

Sun Maid Raisin Growers v. Victor Packing Co. ....8.06[B]

Superior Derrick Services, Inc. v. Anderson .... 9.01[A]

Sylvia Coal Co. v. Mercury Coal & Coke Co. ....5.02[A][4], [C][3]

Symbol Technologies, Inc. v. Sonco, Inc. .... 2.06[B][1]

Szabo v. Vinton Motors .... 4.05[B][5]

T

T.J. Stevenson & Co., Inc. v. 81, 193 Bags of Flour .... 5.02[B][2]; 6.03[A]

T.W. Oil, Inc. v. Consolidated Edison Co. ....7.04[C][3], [4]

T&S Brass & Bronze Works, Inc. v. Pic-Air, Inc. .... 7.10[A]

Tacoma Boatbuilding Co., Inc. v. Delta Fishing Co., Inc. .... 4.06[A][1]; 5.02[A][2]

Taller & Cooper v. Illuminating Elec. Co. .... 4.05[A]

Tarter v. MonArk Boat Co. .... 8.05[B][1]; 10.01[A]

Taylor v. Caldwell 7.11

Taylor v. Commercial Credit Equip. Corp. 9.11

Technographics, Inc. v. Mercer Corp. .... 2.05[B][1]

Tennell v. Esteve Cotton Co. .... 10.01[A]

Tennessee Carolina Transp., Inc. v. Strick Corp. .... 8.05[B][1]

Teradyne, Inc. v. Teledyne Indus., Inc. 9.03

Terry v. Moore ....5.02[A][4]

Terry v. Atlantic Richfield Co. ....7.14[B]

Testo v. Dunmire Oldsmobile, Inc. .. 5.02[B][2]

Texpor Traders, Inc. v. Trust Co. Bank ....9.01[C]

Thomas v. Amway Corp. ....5.02[A][4]

Thomas v. King Ridge, Inc. 5.07

Thomas Knutson Shipbuilding Corp. v. George W. Rogers Constr. Co. .... 2.06[B][3]

Thompson v. Rockford Mach. Tool Co. ....5.06[B]

Thompson Printing Mach. Co. v. B.F. Goodrich Co. 3.04

Thorman v. Polytemp, Inc. .... 5.03[B][1]

Timber Access Industries Co. v. U.S. Plywood-Champion Papers, Inc. 9.03

Tolmie Farms, Inc. v. Stauffer Chemical Co. .... 5.03[B][4]

Tonka Tours, Inc. v. Chadima ....7.03[A][3]

Tony Spychalla Farms, Inc. v. Hopkins Agricultural Chemical Co. .... 5.06[A]

Trans-Aire International, Inc. v. Northern Adhesive Co., Inc. ..... 2.05[C][1]; 5.02[A][3]

Transamerica Oil Co. v. Lynes, Inc. .... 2.05[C][1]

Travelers Indem. Co. v. MAHO Mach. Tool Corp. ....7.04[C][5]

Traynor v. Walters ....7.04[B][3], [C][1]

Triangle Mkt'g, Inc. v. Action Indus. ....3.05[B]

Trident Center v. Connecticut General Life Insurance .... 4.04[A]

Trilco Terminal v. Prebilt Corp. .... 3.04[A]

Trust Co. Bank v. Barrett Distributors, Inc. 10.01

Twin Disc, Inc. v. Big Bud Tractor, Inc. .... 2.05[B][1]

Twin Lakes Mfg. Co., Inc. v. Coffey .... 5.03[B][3]

Tymon v. Linoki ....3.03[C]

[References are to sections.]

U

U.S. v. Great Plains Gasification
Assocs. .... 7.10[A]
Uchitel v. F.R. Tripler & Co. .... 7.04[C][2]
Uganski v. Little Giant Crane & Shovel,
Inc. .... 8.05[B][1]
Union Carbide Corp. v. Oscar Mayer Foods
Corp. .... 2.05[C][1]
Unique Systems, Inc. v. Zotos
International .... 7.09[B]
Universal Builders, Inc. v. Moon Motor
Lodge, Inc. .... 2.06[B][3]
Universal Builders Corp. v. United Methodist
Convalescent Homes of Conn. .... 7.10[A]
Universal Resources Corp. v. Panhandle
Eastern Pipe Line Co. .... 7.10[A]
Upjohn Co. v. Rachelle Laboratories,
Inc. 5.05
Urban Indus. of Ohio, Inc. v. Tectum,
Inc. ....1.03[C]
USEMCO, Inc. v. Marbro Co., Inc. ...2.05[C][1]
USX Corp. v. Union Pac. Resources
Co. .... 7.10[A]

V

Valley Datsun v. Martinez .... 5.02[B][2]
Valley Iron & Steel Co. v.
Thorin ....5.02[B][1], [2]
Valley Die Cast Corp. v. A. C. W.,
Inc. .... 8.03[A]
Valley Forge Flag Co., Inc. v. New York
Dowel & Moulding Import Co., Inc. 7.12
Valmont Indus., Inc. v. Mitsui & Co. (USA),
Inc. .... 2.05[C][1]
Van der Broeke v. Bellanca Aircraft
Corp. .... 5.03[B][4]
Van Wyk v. Norden Laboratories,
Inc. ....5.02[C][2]
Varner v. BL Lanier Fruit Co. 9.10
Vaughan v. General Motors Corp. .... 5.06[A]
Veath v. Specialty Grains,
Inc. ....5.04[A][1]; 7.03[A][3]
Vending Credit Corp. v. Trudy Toys Co. ..8.07
Villalon v. Vollmering ....5.02[A][4]
Vitex Mfg. Co. v. Caribtex Corp. 9.03
Vlases v. Montgomery Ward & Co., Inc. 501
Vockner v. Erickson ....4.06[A][3]
Voytovich v. Bangor Punta Operations,
Inc. ....7.05[E]

W

W.E. Johnson Equip. Co. v. United Airlines,
Inc. ....1.03[A][2]
W.I. Snyder Corp. v. Caracciolo ....3.05[C]
W.R. Weaver Co. v. Burroughs
Corp. ....1.03[A][1]
Wakeman Leather Co. v. Irvin B. Foster
Sportswear Co., Inc. .... 7.04[B][1]
Waldinger Corp. v. CRS Group Engineers,
Inc., Clark Dietz Walker & Co. v.
Harrison .... 7.04[A]
Wallace v. Owens-Illinois, Inc. ....5.05[C]
Wallace Steel, Inc. v. Ingersoll-Rand Co. ...9.05
Walter E. Heller & Co. v. Convalescent Home
of First Church of Deliverance .... 5.03[B][2]
Walter Implement, Inc. v. Focht 9.11
Waltham Truck Equip. Corp. v. Massachusetts
Equip. Co. .... 3.03[A]
Waltz v. Chevrolet Motor Div. ....7.03[A][3]
Weaver v. American Oil Co. ....4.06[A][2]
Webster v. Blue Ship Tea Room .... 5.02[B][2]
Welch v. K-Beck Furniture Mart, Inc. 9.10
Wellcraft Marine v. Zarzour ....5.06[C]
West Central Packing, Inc. v. A.F. Murch
Co. .... 3.03[A]
Western Beef, Inc. v. Compton Inv.
Co. .... 4.04[A]
Western Indus., Inc. v. Newcor Canada,
Ltd. .... 4.03[A]
Western Int'l Forest Prods., Inc. v. Boise
Cascade Corp. .... 4.03[A]
Westinghouse Elec. Corp. v. Carolina Power
& Light Co. 5.07
Whately v. Tetrault ....6.02[C]
Whisenhunt v. Allen Parker Co. .... 7.07[A]
Whitaker v. Farmhand, Inc. .... 5.03[A]
Whitaker v. Lian Feng Mach. Co. ....5.06[B]
Whittle v. Timesavers, Inc. .... 5.02[B][2]
Wickliffe Farms, Inc. v. Owensboro Grain
Co. ....7.14[A][1]
Wikler v. Mar-Van Indus., Inc. 3.02
Williams v. Beechnut Nutrition
Corp. ....5.02[A][4]
Williams v. Walker-Thomas Furniture
Co. ....4.06[A][1]
Williams v. West Penn Power Co. ....5.06[C]
Willmar, City of v. Short-Elliot-Hendrickson,
Inc. 5.07
Wilson v. Scampoli ....7.04[C][2], [3], [5]
Wilson Trading Corp v. David Ferguson,
Ltd. ....5.04[A][2]

[References are to sections.]

Winchester v. McCullough Bros. Garage,
Inc. .... 8.05[B][1]
Windsor Mills, Inc. v. Collins & Aikman
Corp. .... 2.05[C][1]
Winston Industries, Inc. v. Stuyvesant
Insurance Co., Inc. .... 5.02[A][4]
Wisconsin Knife Works v. National Metal
Crafters .... 2.06[B][3]
Wivagg v. Duquesne Light Co. .... 1.03[A][2]
Wolfes v. Terrel .... 7.04[C][2]
Wood River, City of v. Geer-Melkus Constr.
Co. 5.07
Worldwide RV Sales & Serv. v.
Brooks .... 7.04[C][5]

Y

Young & Cooper, Inc. v. Vestring ....5.02[A][4]
Young v. Frank's Nursery & Crafts,
Inc. .... 9.01[A]
Yuzwak v. Dygert ....5.02[A][1]

Z

Zabriskie Chevrolet, Inc. v.
Smith ....7.03[A][1]; 7.04[C][3], [5]
Zoss v. Royal Chevrolet, Inc. .... 7.05[B], [F]

TABLE OF STATUTES

(References are to sections.)

UNIFORM COMMERCIAL CODE

Sec. 1–102(2)(b) 2.01
Sec. 1–102(3) 4.06
Sec. 1–103 ..... 1.06; 2.05[D][2]; 2.06[B][3]; 3.06;
    7.05[F]; 7.11; 8.06[B]; 9.05
Sec. 1–103, Comment 3 ....1.06
Sec. 1–106(1) ....8.01[A]; 9.05
Sec. 1–201, Comment 1 ....4.04[B]
Sec. 1–201, Comment 39 ....3.03[B]
Sec. 1–201(3) .... 2.01; 2.05[C][1]; 4.01; 4.03[D]
Sec. 1–201(9) .... 10.02[A][3]
Sec. 1–201(10) .... 5.03[B][1]
Sec. 1–201(11) ....2.01; 4.01; 4.03[D]
Sec. 1–201(16) 7.12
Sec. 1–201(19) ....4.06[B]; 7.04[D]
Sec. 1–201(26) ....2.03[A]; 3.04
Sec. 1–201(37) ....1.05[A][3]
Sec. 1–201(39) ....3.03[B]
Sec. 1–201(42) ....4.02[G][3]
Sec. 1–203 .... 4.06[A],[B]; 7.04[D]
Sec. 1–204(1) ....5.04[A][2]
Sec. 1–204(2) .... 7.04[B][1]
Sec. 1–205, Comments .... 4.03[A]
Sec. 1–205, Comment 2 ....4.03[B]
Sec. 1–205, Comment 4 .... 4.03[A]
Sec. 1–205, Comment 5 .... 4.03[A]
Sec. 1–205, Comment 9 .... 4.03[A]
Sec. 1–205(1) ....4.03[B]
Sec. 1–205(2) .... 4.03[A],[B]
Sec. 1–205(3) ....4.03[D]; 4.04[B]
Sec. 1–205(4) ....4.02[E]; 4.03[D]
Sec. 1–206 ....3.02
Sec. 1–208 ....4.06[B]
Sec. 2–101 ....1.03[A][1]
Sec. 2–102 ....1.03[A][1]
Sec. 2–103(1)(a) ....1.03[A][1]
Sec. 2–103(1)(c) ......4.06[B]; 6.02[D]; 6.05[A][1]
Sec. 2–103(1)(d) .... 1.03[A][1]; 7.05[E]
Sec. 2–104, Comment 2 ....3.04[B]; 5.02[B][1]
Sec. 2–104(1) ....3.04[B]; 5.02[B][1]
Sec. 2–105(1) ....1.03[B]
Sec. 2–105(2) ....1.03[B]
Sec. 2–105(6) .... 7.04[A]
Sec. 2–106, Comment 1 ....1.03[A][1]
Sec. 2–106(1) .... 1.03[A][1]; 1.05[A][2]; 7.01
Sec. 2–106(2) ....7.04[C][5]

Sec. 2–106(3) 8.08; 9.07
Sec. 2–106(4) 8.07; 9.07
Sec. 2–201 ....2.06[B][1],][2]; 3.02; 3.04
Sec. 2–201, Comment 1 ....3.03[C],[D]
Sec. 2–201, Comment 2 ....3.05[C]
Sec. 2–201(1) ...3.02; 3.03; 3.03[B],[C],[D]; 3.04;
    3.04[A]; 3.05[A]
Sec. 2–201(2) ....2.05[C]; 2.06[B][1]; 3.04;
    3.04[A],[B]
Sec. 2–201(3) .... 2.06[B][1]
Sec. 2–201(3)(a) .... 3.05[A]
Sec. 2–201(3)(b) ....3.05[B]
Sec. 2–201(3)(c) .... 3.03[A]; 3.05[C]
Sec. 2–202 ....3.04; 4.02[B],[C],[D][2],[E];
    4.03[D]
Sec. 2–202, Comment 2 ....4.02[G][1]
Sec. 2–202, Comment 1(a) ....4.02[D][2]
Sec. 2–202, Comment 1(b) .... 4.04[B]
Sec. 2–202, Comment 1(c) ....4.04[B]
Sec. 2–202, Comment 3 ....4.02[D][2]
Sec. 2–202(a) ....4.02[E],[G][1]
Sec. 2–202(b) ....4.02[G][1]
Sec. 2–203 ....2.04
Sec. 2–204 ....2.01
Sec. 2–204(1) 2.01
Sec. 2–204(2) 2.01
Sec. 2–204(3) ....2.01; 4.05[A]
Sec. 2–205 ....2.04
Sec. 2–205, Comment 3 ....2.04
Sec. 2–205(1) .... 5.03[B][4]
Sec. 2–206, Comment 3 ....2.03A
Sec. 2–206(1) ....2.05[D][2]
Sec. 2–206(1)(a) ....2.01; 2.03[A]
Sec. 2–206(1)(b) ....2.03[B]
Sec. 2–206(2), Comment 3 .... 2.03[A]
Sec. 2–206(2) .... 2.03[A]
Sec. 2–207 ....2.01; 2.05[B][1],[C],[C][1],
    [D][1],[2]; 3.04; 4.02[B]
Sec. 2–207, Comment 3 ....2.05[B][1]; [C][2]
Sec. 2–207, Comment 4 ....2.05[B][1]; [C][1];
    [D][1]
Sec. 2–207, Comment 5 ....2.05[C][1]
Sec. 2–207, Comment 6 ....2.05[B][1]; [C][2]
Sec. 2–207(1) ....2.05[B][1],[B][2],[C][2],[D],
    [D][1],[D][2]
Sec. 2–207(2) ....2.05[B][1],[B][2],[C],
    [C][1],[C][2]
Sec. 2–207(2)(a) ....2.05[C]

[References are to sections.]

Sec. 2–207(2)(b) .... 2.05[B][1],[C]; 3.04
Sec. 2–207(2)(c) ....2.05[C],[C][2]
Sec. 2–207(3) ....2.01; 2.05[D][2]
Sec. 2–208 ....2.06[B][3]; 4.03[C],[D]
Sec. 2–208, Comments ....4.03[B]
Sec. 2–208, Comment 3 .... 2.06[B][3]
Sec. 2–208(1) ....4.03[D]; 4.04[B]
Sec. 2–208(2) ....4.02[E]; 4.03[D]
Sec. 2–208(3) ..... 2.06[B][3]; 4.02[G][1]; 4.03[D]
Sec. 2–209 .... 2.06[B][1],[B][3]; 5.02[A][4]
Sec. 2–209, Comment 2 .... 2.06[A]
Sec. 2–209, Comment 3 ....2.06[B],[B][1]
Sec. 2–209(1) ....2.06[A],[B][1]
Sec. 2–209(2) .... 2.06[B],[B][2],[B][3]
Sec. 2–209(3) ....2.06[B],[B][1],[B][3]; 5.03[B][4]
Sec. 2–209(4) ....2.06[B],[B][3]
Sec. 2–209(5) ....2.06[B],[B][3]
Sec. 2–210, Comment 1 .... 10.01[A]
Sec. 2–210, Comment 3 .... 10.01[A]
Sec. 2–210(1) .... 10.01[A]
Sec. 2–210(2) ....10.01[A],[B]
Sec. 2–210(3) .... 10.01[A]
Sec. 2–210(4) .... 10.01[A]
Sec. 2–301 ....4.05[B],[B][4]; 6.01; 7.01;
                                            7.06[A]; 9.08
Sec. 2–302 .... 4.06[A]; 5.03[C]
Sec. 2–302, Comment 1 ....4.06[A][1]; 5.03[C]
Sec. 2–302, Comment 3 .... 4.06[A]
Sec. 2–302(1) ....4.06[A][3]
Sec. 2–305 .... 4.05[A]
Sec. 2–305, Comment 5 .... 4.05[B][2]
Sec. 2–305(1)(b) .... 4.05[A]
Sec. 2–305(1)(c) .... 4.05[A]
Sec. 2–305(4) .... 4.05[A]
Sec. 2–306 ....4.05[C]
Sec. 2–306, Comment 2 ....4.05[C]
Sec. 2–306(1) ....4.05[C]
Sec. 2–307 ....2.03[B]
Sec. 2–308 .... 4.05[B][3]
Sec. 2–308, Comment 2 .... 4.05[B][1]
Sec. 2–308(a) .... 4.05[B][1]
Sec. 2–308(b) .... 4.05[B][1]
Sec. 2–309, Comment 1 .... 4.05[B][2]
Sec. 2–309, Comment 4 .... 4.05[B][2]
Sec. 2–309, Comment 5 ....4.05[B][2]; 7.04[C][1]
Sec. 2–309, Comment 6 .... 4.05[B][2]
Sec. 2–309(1) ....7.04[C][1]
Sec. 2–310(a) ....2.05[B][1]
Sec. 2–310(b) ....4.05[B][3]; 9.09[A]
Sec. 2–311(1) .... 4.05[B][3]
Sec. 2–311(2) .... 4.05[B][3]
Sec. 2–312, Comment 1 .... 5.02[D]
Sec. 2–312, Comment 5 .... 5.02[D]
Sec. 2–312(1) .... 5.02[D]

Sec. 2–312(2) .... 5.02[D]
Sec. 2–312(3) .... 5.02[D]
Sec. 2–313, Comment 2 ....5.06[B]
Sec. 2–313, Comment 3 ....5.02[A][4]
Sec. 2–313, Comment 4 ....5.02[A][2]
Sec. 2–313, Comment 6 ....5.02[A][3]
Sec. 2–313, Comment 7 ....5.02[A][4]
Sec. 2–313, Comment 8 ....5.02[A][4]
Sec. 2–313(1)(a) .... 5.02[A],[A][1]
Sec. 2–313(1)(b) .... 5.02[A]
Sec. 2–313(1)(c) .... 5.02[A]
Sec. 2–313(2) ....5.02[A][1]
Sec. 2–314 .....2.05[B][1]; 3.04[B]; 5.02[B],[B][2]
Sec. 2–314, Comment 3 ....5.02[B][1],[B][2]
Sec. 2–314, Comment 7 .... 5.02[B][2]
Sec. 2–314, Comment 10 .... 5.02[B][2]
Sec. 2–314, Comment 13 ....5.05
Sec. 2–314(2) .... 5.02[B][2]
Sec. 2–314(2)(a) .... 5.02[B][2]
Sec. 2–314(2)(b) .... 5.02[A][3],[B][2]
Sec. 2–314(2)(c) .... 5.02[B][2]
Sec. 2–314(2)(e) .... 5.02[B][2]
Sec. 2–314(2)(f) .... 5.02[A][4],[B][2]
Sec. 2–314(3) ....2.05[D][2]
Sec. 2–315 ....5.02[C]
Sec. 2–315, Comment 1 ....5.02[C][1]
Sec. 2–315, Comment 2 ....5.02[C][2]
Sec. 2–316 ....5.03[C]
Sec. 2–316, Comment ....5.03[A]
Sec. 2–316, Comment 8 .... 5.03[B][3]
Sec. 2–316(1) .... 5.03[A]
Sec. 2–316(2) ....1.03[A][2]; 5.03[B][1],[B][2]
Sec. 2–316(3) .... 5.03[B][2]
Sec. 2–316(3)(a) .... 5.03[B][2]
Sec. 2–316(3)(b) .... 5.03[B][3]
Sec. 2–316(3)(c) .... 5.03[B][4]
Sec. 2–317 ....5.08
Sec. 2–318 ....5.06[B]
Sec. 2–318, Comment 1 ....5.06[B]
Sec. 2–318, Comment 3 ....5.06[B],[C]
Sec. 2–319 .... 4.05[B]; 6.02[A]; 6.05[B][1]
Sec. 2–319(1)(a) ....6.02[A]; 9.04[A][2]
Sec. 2–319(1)(b) .... 6.02[A]
Sec. 2–319(1)(c) ....4.05[B][3]; 6.02[A]
Sec. 2–319(3) .... 4.05[B][3]
Sec. 2–320 ....4.05[B]; 6.02[A]
Sec. 2–321 .... 6.02[A]
Sec. 2–326 ....3.02
Sec. 2–401 ....1.03[A][1]; 6.01; 7.01; 9.01[C]
Sec. 2–403(1) ....10.02[A][1],[A][2]
Sec. 2–403(1)(b) .... 4.05[B][5]
Sec. 2–403(1)(c) .... 4.05[B][5]
Sec. 2–403(2) ....10.02[A][3],[C]
Sec. 2–403(3) ....10.02[A][3]

[References are to sections.]

Sec. 2–403(3)(b) ....10.02[C]
Sec. 2–501(1) ....6.03[C]
Sec. 2–501(1)(a) ....1.03[B]
Sec. 2–501(1)(b) ....1.03[B]
Sec. 2–503 .... 4.05[B][3]; 6.05[B][1]
Sec. 2–503, Comment 5 ....4.05[B][3]; 6.02[B]
Sec. 2–503(1) ....4.05[B][2],[B][3],[B][4];
6.02[A],[B]
Sec. 2–503(1)(a) .... 4.05[B][2]
Sec. 2–503(1)(b) .... 4.05[B][2]
Sec. 2–503(2) ....4.05[B][3]; 6.02[B]
Sec. 2–503(3) .... 4.05[B][3]; 6.02[A],[B]
Sec. 2–503(4)(b) ....6.03[C]
Sec. 2–503(5) ....6.02[B]
Sec. 2–504 ....4.05[B][3]; 6.02[B]; 6.05[B][1];
7.04[F]
Sec. 2–504, Comment 1 .... 4.05[B][3]
Sec. 2–507, Comment .... 4.05[B][5]; 9.09[A]
Sec. 2–507(1) .... 4.05[B][4]
Sec. 2–507(2) .... 9.09[A]
Sec. 2–508 ....4.06[B]; 6.03[A];
7.04[C],[C][1],[C][5],[E]
Sec. 2–508, Comment 2 .... 7.04[C][3]
Sec. 2–508(1) ....7.04[C][1]
Sec. 2–508(2) ....7.04[C][1],[C][3],[C][4],
[C][5],[E]; 7.05[C]
Sec. 2–509 ..... 6.02; 6.03[C]; 6.05[B]; 9.04[A][2]
Sec. 2–509, Comment 3 .... 6.02[C],[D]
Sec. 2–509(1) ....6.02[B]; 6.03[A]
Sec. 2–509(1)(a) .... 6.02[B]; 6.03[A]; 6.05[B][1];
9.04[A][?]
Sec. 2–509(1)(b) ....4.05[B][3]; 6.02[B];
9.04[A][2]
Sec. 2–509(2) ....6.02[C]
Sec. 2–509(2)(b) ....6.05[A][1]
Sec. 2–509(2)(c) ....6.03[C]
Sec. 2–509(3) ....6.02[C]; 6.05[A][1]
Sec. 2–509(4) ....6.02[A]; 6.05[A][1]
Sec. 2–510 .... 6.02; 6.03,[C]; 6.05[A][2],[B];
9.04[A][2]
Sec. 2–510, Comment 2 .... 6.03[A]
Sec. 2–510, Comment 3 ....6.03[B]
Sec. 2–510(2) ....6.03[B]
Sec. 2–510(3) ....6.03[C]; 9.04[A][2]
Sec. 2–511(1) .... 4.05[B][4]
Sec. 2–511(2) .... 4.05[B][5]
Sec. 2–511(3) .... 4.05[B][5]; 9.09[A]
Sec. 2–512(1) .... 4.05[B][3]
Sec. 2–512(2) .... 4.05[B][5]
Sec. 2–513 .... 6.03[A]
Sec. 2–513, Comment 5 .... 4.05[B][4]
Sec. 2–513(1) .... 4.05[B][3],[B][4]; 7.03[A][1]
Sec. 2–513(3) ....4.05[B][3]; 7.03[A][1]
Sec. 2–513(3)(a) .... 4.05[B][4]

Sec. 2–513(3)(b) .... 4.05[B][4]
Sec. 2–513(4) ....7.03[A][1]
Sec. 2–601 ....4.05[B][2]; 6.03[A];
7.04[A],[B],[C][5]
Sec. 2–602(1) .... 6.03[A]; 7.03[A][2]; 7.04[D]
Sec. 2–602(2) .... 8.06[A]
Sec. 2–602(2)(a) ....7.03[A][3]
Sec. 2–602(2)(b) .... 7.04[B][3]
Sec. 2–603 .... 8.06[A]
Sec. 2–603(1) .... 7.04[B][3]
Sec. 2–603(2) .... 7.04[B][3]
Sec. 2–603(2)(c) .... 7.04[B][3]
Sec. 2–603(3) .... 7.04[B][3]
Sec. 2–604 .... 7.04[B][3]
Sec. 2–605 ....7.05[B]
Sec. 2–605, Comment 1 .... 7.04[B][2]
Sec. 2–605(1) .... 7.04[B][2]
Sec. 2–606 ....6.03[A]; 7.03[A]
Sec. 2–606(1) ....7.03[A]
Sec. 2–606(1)(a) ....7.05[A][1]
Sec. 2–606(1)(b) ....7.03[A][3],[B][1]; 7.05[A][1]
Sec. 2–606(1)(c) ....7.03[A][3]
Sec. 2–607, Comment 4 .... 7.03[B][3]; 9.01[A]
Sec. 2–607(3), Comment 4 .... 7.04[B][2]
Sec. 2–607 ....7.05[C]
Sec. 2–607(1) ......6.03[A]; 7.03[B][2]; 8.02; 8.05;
9.04[A][1]
Sec. 2–607(2) .... 7.03[B][1]; 7.04[C]
Sec. 2–607(3) .... 5.06[A]
Sec. 2–607(3)(a) .... 7.03[B][3]
Sec. 2–607(4) .... 7.03[B][4]
Sec. 2–607(4)(b) .... 9.01[A]
Sec. 2–608 .... 6.03[B]; 7.05; 7.05[C]
Sec. 2–608, Comment 2 ....7.05[A][2]
Sec. 2–608, Comment 4 ....7.05[B]
Sec. 2–608, Comment 5 ....7.05[B]
Sec. 2–608(1) ....7.05[A][2]
Sec. 2–608(1)(a) ....7.05[A][1],[C]
Sec. 2–608(1)(b) ....7.05[A][1]
Sec. 2–608(2) .... 6.03[B]; 7.05[B]
Sec. 2–608(3) ....7.05[B]
Sec. 2–609 ....7.04[E]; 7.09[B]; 7.10[A]
Sec. 2–609, Comment 1 .... 7.10[A]
Sec. 2–609(1) ....7.08; 8.04[B][2]
Sec. 2–609(4) .... 7.10[A],[B]
Sec. 2–610 .... 4.05[B][4]; 7.04[E]; 7.09[A]
Sec. 2–610, Comment 1 .... 7.09[A]
Sec. 2–610, Comment 3 ....7.04[E]; 7.09[A]
Sec. 2–610, Comment 6 .... 7.09[D]
Sec. 2–610(a) .... 8.04[B][2]
Sec. 2–611(1) ....7.09[C]
Sec. 2–611(2) ....7.09[C]
Sec. 2–611(3) ....7.09[C]
Sec. 2–612 ....7.04[E]

[References are to sections.]

Sec. 2–612, Comment 6 .... 7.09[D]
Sec. 2–612(1) ....7.04[E]
Sec. 2–612(2) ....7.04[C],[E],[F]
Sec. 2–612(3) ....7.04[E]; 7.09[D]
Sec. 2–613 ....7.11; 7.12
Sec. 2–613, Comment 1 ....7.12
Sec. 2–614 ....7.11; 7.13
Sec. 2–614, Comment 1 ....7.11
Sec. 2–614(1) 7.13
Sec. 2–615 .... 4.06[B]; 7.11; 7.13;
                                                    7.14[A],[A][3],[B]
Sec. 2–615, Comment 1 ....7.14[A][1]
Sec. 2–615, Comment 4 ....7.14[A][1],[A][3]
Sec. 2–615, Comment 5 ....7.14[A][1]
Sec. 2–615, Comment 9 .... 7.14[A],[A][1]
Sec. 2–615(a) .... 7.14[A]
Sec. 2–615(b) ....7.14[B]
Sec. 2–615(c) ....7.14[B]
Sec. 2–616 ....7.14[B]
Sec. 2–702, Comment 2 .... 9.09[A]
Sec. 2–702(1) 9.08
Sec. 2–702(2) .... 4.05[B][5]; 9.09[A]
Sec. 2–702(3) .... 9.09[A]
Sec. 2–703 ....7.05[D]; 7.06[B]; 7.07[A]; 7.09[B];
                                                    8.01; 9.01[C]
Sec. 2–703, Comment 1 ....8.01
Sec. 2–703(a) 9.08
Sec. 2–703(d) .... 9.01[A]
Sec. 2–703(e) .... 3.05[A]
Sec. 2–703(f) 9.07
Sec. 2–704 .... 9.01[A]
Sec. 2–704, Comment 1 .... 9.01[A]
Sec. 2–704(2) 9.03
Sec. 2–705, Comment 1 ....9.08
Sec. 2–705(1) 9.08
Sec. 2–705(2)(a) 9.08
Sec. 2–705(2)(b) 9.08
Sec. 2–705(2)(c) 9.08
Sec. 2–705(2)(d) 9.08
Sec. 2–705(3)(a) 9.08
Sec. 2–705(3)(b) 9.08
Sec. 2–706 ....9.01[C]
Sec. 2–706, Comment 4 .... 9.01[A]
Sec. 2–706, Comment 6 .... 9.01[A]
Sec. 2–706, Comment 11 ....9.01[C]
Sec. 2–706(1) ....9.01[A],[C]
Sec. 2–706(2) .... 9.01[A]
Sec. 2–706(3) .... 9.01[A]
Sec. 2–706(4) .... 9.01[A]
Sec. 2–706(5) ....9.01[C]
Sec. 2–706(6) ....9.01[C]
Sec. 2–708 .... 8.04[B][2]
Sec. 2–708(1) ....8.04[B][2]; 9.02[A],[B][1]
Sec. 2–708(2) ....3.05[A]; 9.03

Sec. 2–709, Comment 5 ....9.04[A][1]
Sec. 2–709(1)(a) .... 6.01; 7.12; 9.04[A][1],[A][2]
Sec. 2–709(1)(b) ....3.05[A]; 9.04[A][3]
Sec. 2–709(2) 9.04
Sec. 2–709(3) ....7.05[D]; 9.04[A][1]
Sec. 2–710 ....9.05
Sec. 2–710, Comment 9.05
Sec. 2–711 ....7.06[A]; 7.07[A]; 7.09[B]; 8.01
Sec. 2–711(1) ....7.03[B][2]; 7.04[A]; 8.02; 8.07
Sec. 2–711(3) ....9.01[C]
Sec. 2–712, Comment 1 .... 8.03[A]
Sec. 2–712, Comment 2 .... 8.03[A]
Sec. 2–712, Comment 3 .... 8.04[A]
Sec. 2–712(1) .... 8.03[A]; 8.04[B][2]
Sec. 2–712(2) .... 8.03[B]; 8.06
Sec. 2–712(3) .... 8.04[A]
Sec. 2–713 .... 8.04[B][2]; 9.02[B][1]
Sec. 2–713, Comment 1 .... 8.04[B][1]
Sec. 2–713(1) ....8.04,[B][2]; 8.06
Sec. 2–713(2) .... 8.04[B][1]
Sec. 2–714 ....7.06[A]
Sec. 2–714(1) .... 8.05[A]
Sec. 2–714(2) ....7.03[B][2]; 8.05[B][1],[B][2],[B][3]
Sec. 2–714(3) .... 8.05[A],[B][1]; 8.06
Sec. 2–715, Comment 1 .... 8.06[A]
Sec. 2–715, Comment 3 ....8.06[B]
Sec. 2–715, Comment 4 ....8.06[B]
Sec. 2–715, Comment 5 .... 5.05; 8.06[B]
Sec. 2–715(1) .... 8.06[A]
Sec. 2–715(2) ....8.06[B]
Sec. 2–715(2)(a) ....8.04[B][2]; 8.06[B]
Sec. 2–715(2)(b) .... 8.06[B]
Sec. 2–716, Comment 1 ....8.08
Sec. 2–716, Comment 2 ....8.08
Sec. 2–716(1) 8.08
Sec. 2–716(3) 8.08
Sec. 2–717 .... 7.03[B][2]
Sec. 2–718(1) 9.10; 9.11
Sec. 2–719 ....5.03[C]; 5.04[B]
Sec. 2–719, Comment 1 ....5.04[A][2]
Sec. 2–719(1) .... 5.04[A]
Sec. 2–719(1)(b) .... 5.04[A]
Sec. 2–719(2) .... 5.04[A],[C]
Sec. 2–719(3) ....1.03[A][2]; 5.04[A][2],[B],[C]
Sec. 2–720 ....9.07
Sec. 2–725(1) 5.07
Sec. 2–725(2) 5.07
Sec. 2–725(4) 5.07
Sec. 2A–101, Comment ....1.04; 7.07[A]
Sec. 2A–102 ....1.05[A][1]
Sec. 2A–102, Comment ....1.05[A][1]
Sec. 2A–103, Comment(g) ..1.05[B]; 6.05[A][2]
Sec. 2A–103(1)(b) 8.07
Sec. 2A–103(1)(e) ....1.05[C]

[References are to sections.]

Sec. 2A–103(1)(g) ....1.05[B]
Sec. 2A–103(1)(g)(ii) ....1.05[B]
Sec. 2A–103(1)(j) ....1.05[A][1]
Sec. 2A–103(1)(o) ....10.02[A][3]
Sec. 2A–103(1)(u) ....8.01[B]
Sec. 2A–103(1)(z) 8.07
Sec. 2A–103(2) ....4.06[B]
Sec. 2A–103(3) .... 6.05[A][1]; 10.02[A][3]
Sec. 2A–108(1) .... 4.06[A],[A][3]
Sec. 2A–108(2) ....4.06[A][4]
Sec. 2A–108(3) .... 4.06[A]
Sec. 2A–108(4)(a) ....4.06[A][4]
Sec. 2A–108(4)(b) ....4.06[A][4]
Sec. 2A–201, Comment ....3.04; 3.05[C]
Sec. 2A–201(1) 3.03
Sec. 2A–201(1)(a) 3.02
Sec. 2A–201(1)(b) ....3.03,[C],[E]
Sec. 2A–201(2) .... 3.03[E]
Sec. 2A–201(3) ....3.03[D],[E]
Sec. 2A–201(4)(a) .... 3.05[A]
Sec. 2A–201(4)(b) ....3.05[B]
Sec. 2A–201(4)(c) ....3.05[C]
Sec. 2A–201(5) 3.05
Sec. 2A–202 ....4.02[B]
Sec. 2A–203 ....2.04
Sec. 2A–204(1) 2.01
Sec. 2A–204(2) 2.01
Sec. 2A–205 ....2.04
Sec. 2A–206(1) .... 2.03[A]
Sec. 2A–206(2) .... 2.03[A]
Sec. 2A–207(1) ....4.03[C]
Sec. 2A–209(1) .... 1.05[B]; 5.06[E]
Sec. 2A–209(2) ....5.06[E]
Sec. 2A–209(3) ....5.06[E]
Sec. 2A–210(1)(a) .... 5.02[A],[A][1]
Sec. 2A–210(1)(b) .... 5.02[A]
Sec. 2A–210(1)(c) .... 5.02[A]
Sec. 2A–210(2) ....5.02[A][1]
Sec. 2A–210, Comment .... 5.02[D]
Sec. 2A–211(1) .... 5.02[D]
Sec. 2A–211(2) .... 5.02[D]
Sec. 2A–211(3) .... 5.02[D]
Sec. 2A–212 ....5.02[B]
Sec. 2A–213 ....5.02[C]
Sec. 2A–214(1) .... 5.03[A]
Sec. 2A–214(2) .... 5.03[B][1]
Sec. 2A–214(3)(a) .... 5.03[B][2]
Sec. 2A–214(3)(b) .... 5.03[B][3]
Sec. 2A–214(3)(c) .... 5.03[B][4]
Sec. 2A–215 ....5.08
Sec. 2A–216 ....5.06[B]
Sec. 2A–218(5) ....6.05[A][1]
Sec. 2A–219, Comment .... 6.01[A][1]; 6.04;
                                                              6.05[A][1]

Sec. 2A–219(1) ....6.04; 6.05[A][2]
Sec. 2A–219(2) ....6.05[B]
Sec. 2A–219(2)(a) .... 6.05[B][1]
Sec. 2A–219(2)(b) ....6.05[A][1]
Sec. 2A–219(2)(c) ....6.05[A][1]
Sec. 2A–220 ....6.05[A][2]
Sec. 2A–220, Comment ....6.05[A][2]
Sec. 2A–221 ....7.11; 7.12
Sec. 2A–302 ....6.01
Sec. 2A–303, Comment 1 .... 7.07[A]
Sec. 2A–303(2) ....10.01[B]
Sec. 2A–303(3) ....10.01[B]
Sec. 2A–303(4) ....10.01[B]
Sec. 2A–303(5)(a) .... 10.01[B]
Sec. 2A–304(1) ....10.02[A][1],[A][2]
Sec. 2A–304(2) ....10.02[A][3]
Sec. 2A–305(1) ....10.02[A][1],[A][2]
Sec. 2A–306 ....10.02[C]
Sec. 2A–307(1) ....10.02[B],[C]
Sec. 2A–307(2) ....10.02[B]
Sec. 2A–307(2)(a) ....10.02[C]
Sec. 2A–307(2)(b) ....10.02[B]
Sec. 2A–307(2)(c) ....10.02[B]
Sec. 2A–308(1) ....10.02[C]
Sec. 2A–308(2) ....10.02[C]
Sec. 2A–401 .... 7.10[A]
Sec. 2A–401(1) 7.08
Sec. 2A–402 .... 7.09[A]
Sec. 2A–403 ....7.09[C]
Sec. 2A–404 ....7.11; 7.13
Sec. 2A–405 ....7.11; 7.14[A]
Sec. 2A–406 ....7.14[B]
Sec. 2A–407(1) ....1.05[B]; 6.05[A][2]; 7.05[F]
Sec. 2A–501 .... 7.07[A]
Sec. 2A–501(1) .... 7.07[A]
Sec. 2A–501(2) .... 7.07[A]
Sec. 2A–501(3) ....7.07[A]; 9.09[B]
Sec. 2A–503(1) .... 5.04[A]
Sec. 2A–503(2) ....5.04[A],[C]
Sec. 2A–503(3) ....5.04[B],[C]
Sec. 2A–504, Comment 9.11
Sec. 2A–504(1) 9.11
Sec. 2A–505(1) 9.07
Sec. 2A–505(3) 9.07
Sec. 2A–506(1) 5.07
Sec. 2A–506(2) 5.07
Sec. 2A–506(4) 5.07
Sec. 2A–508 .... 7.07[A]
Sec. 2A–508(1) ....7.07[B]
Sec. 2A–509(1) .... 7.04[A]
Sec. 2A–509(2) ....7.04[B]
Sec. 2A–511(4) .... 7.04[B][3]
Sec. 2A–512(1)(a) .... 7.04[B][3]
Sec. 2A–512(1)(b) .... 7.04[B][3]

[References are to sections.]

Sec. 2A–512(1)(c) .... 7.04[B][3]
Sec. 2A–513 ....7.04[C]
Sec. 2A–514(1) .... 7.04[B][2]
Sec. 2A–515, Comment ....7.03[A][3]
Sec. 2A–515(1)(a) ....7.03[A][3]
Sec. 2A–516(2) ....7.03[B]
Sec. 2A–517 ....7.05
Sec. 2A–517(1)(b) .... 7.05[G]
Sec. 2A–517(4) ....7.05[B]
Sec. 2A–517(5) ....7.05[B]
Sec. 2A–521(3) 8.08
Sec. 2A–523 .... 7.07[A],[C]
Sec. 2A–523(1)(a) 9.07
Sec. 2A–523(1)(c) 9.08
Sec. 2A–524(2) 9.03
Sec. 2A–525 .... 9.04[B]; 9.09[B]
Sec. 2A–525, Comment 3 ....9.09[B]
Sec. 2A–525(1) 9.08
Sec. 2A–525(2) ....1.05[A][3]
Sec. 2A–525(3) ....9.09[B]
Sec. 2A–526(1) 9.08
Sec. 2A–526(2)(a) 9.08
Sec. 2A–526(2)(b) 9.08
Sec. 2A–526(2)(c) 9.08
Sec. 2A–526(3)(a) 9.08
Sec. 2A–526(3)(b) 9.08
Sec. 2A–527 ....1.05[A][3]
Sec. 2A–527, Comment 1 ....9.01[B]; 9.04[C]
Sec. 2A–527, Comment 4 ....9.01[C]
Sec. 2A–527, Comment 5 ....9.01[B]
Sec. 2A–527, Comment 10 ....9.01[C]
Sec. 2A–527(1) ....9.01[B]
Sec. 2A–527(2) ....9.01[B],[C]
Sec. 2A–527(3) ....9.01[C]
Sec. 2A–527(4) ....9.01[C]
Sec. 2A–527(5) ....9.01[C]
Sec. 2A–528(1) .... 9.02[A]
Sec. 2A–528(2) 9.03
Sec. 2A–529, Comment 1 ....9.04[B]
Sec. 2A–529(1) ....9.04[B]
Sec. 2A–529(1)(a) ....9.04[B]
Sec. 2A–529(3) ....9.04[B]
Sec. 2A–529(4) ....9.04[B]
Sec. 2A–530 ....9.05
Sec. 2A–532 ....9.06
Sec. 3–310(b) .... 9.09[A]
Sec. 3–802(1)(b) .... 9.09[A]
Sec. 5–104 ....3.02
Sec. 7–303(1)(a) .... 4.05[B][4]

Sec. 7–403(1) .... 4.05[B][4]; 6.02[C]
Sec. 7–403(4) ....6.03[C]
Sec. 8–319 ....3.02
Sec. 9–107 ....9.09[A]
Sec. 9–110 ....3.03[E]
Sec. 9–203 ....3.02
Sec. 9–203(1)(a) ....3.03[E]
Sec. 9–206(2), Comment 3 .... 5.03[B][4]
Sec. 9–206(2) .... 5.03[B][4]
Sec. 9–301(1)(c) ....10.02[B]
Sec. 9–307(1) ....10.02[B]
Sec. 9–311 ....10.01[B]
Sec. 9–318(1) ....10.02[A][1]
Sec. 9–501 .... 7.07[A]
Sec. 9–501(1) ....7.07[A]; 9.09[B]
Sec. 9–501(2) ....9.09[B]
Sec. 9–503 ....1.05[A][3]
Sec. 9–504 ....8.03[C]; 9.01[C]
Sec. 9–504(1) .... 1.05[A][3]; 9.01[C]; 9.09[A]
Sec. 9–504(2) .... 1.05[A][3]; 9.01[C]; 9.09[A]
Sec. 9–504(3) ....9.01[C]
Sec. 9–504(4) ....9.01[C]
Sec. 9–505 ....9.01[C]
Sec. 9–506 ....9.01[C]
Sec. 9–507 ....9.01[C]

CONSUMER LEASING ACT
(15 U.S.C.)

Sec. 1667(1) ....1.05[C]

MAGNUSON-MOSS ACT
(15 U.S.C.)

Sec. 2301 *et seq.* .... 5.04[A]
Sec. 2304 ....5.04[B]
Sec. 2308 ....5.04[A]; 5.08
Sec. 2311 ....5.04[B]

RESTATEMENT
OF CONTRACTS

Sec. 178, Comment f 3.06
Sec. 207 ....3.03
Sec. 237 ....4.02[A]
Sec. 240 ....4.02[A]

[References are to sections.]

RESTATEMENT (SECOND) OF CONTRACTS

Sec. 20 .... 4.04[B]
Sec. 24 ....2.02
Sec. 27 .... 3.04[A]
Sec. 39 .... 2.05[A]
Sec. 45 .... 2.03[A]
Sec. 54(2) .... 2.03[A]
Sec. 56 .... 2.03[A]
Sec. 62(2) .... 2.03[A]
Sec. 63 .... 2.03[A]
Sec. 69(2) .... 2.05[A]
Sec. 84(1) .... 2.06[B][3]
Sec. 87(1) 2.04
Sec. 87(2) .... 2.03[A]
Sec. 89 .... 2.06[A]
Sec. 110 ....3.01
Sec. 129 ....3.05[A],[C]
Sec. 131 ....3.03
Sec. 131, Comment f ....3.03[C]
Sec. 133, Illustration 2 ....3.03[C]
Sec. 138 ....3.07
Sec. 139(2)(a) 3.06
Sec. 139(2)(b) 3.06
Sec. 143, Comment a, Illustration 1 ....3.07
Sec. 201 .... 4.04[B]
Sec. 201(2) .... 4.04[B]
Sec. 201(3) .... 4.04[B]
Sec. 202(3) .... 4.04[B]
Sec. 203(b) .... 4.04[B]
Sec. 206 .... 4.04[B]
Sec. 207 .... 4.04[B]
Sec. 209(2) ....4.02[C]
Sec. 209(2) Comment c ....4.02[C]
Sec. 210 .... 4.02[A]
Sec. 210(1) .... 4.02[A]
Sec. 210(2) .... 4.02[A]
Sec. 210, Comment b ....4.02[D][1]
Sec. 212, Comment b .... 4.04[A]
Sec. 213 .... 4.02[A]
Sec. 214 .... 7.09[A]
Sec. 214(d) ....4.02[G][2]
Sec. 214, Comment c, Illustration 6 .. 4.02[G][2]
Sec. 215, Comment b ....4.02[E]
Sec. 217 ....4.02[G][3]
Sec. 241 .... 7.04[A],[E]
Sec. 316, Comment c .... 10.01[A]
Sec. 317, Comment d, Illustration 6 .. 10.01[A]
Sec. 317(2) .... 10.01[A]
Sec. 317(2)(a) .... 10.01[A]

Sec. 317(2)(c) .... 10.01[A]
Sec. 318 .... 10.01[A]
Sec. 318(1) .... 10.01[A]
Sec. 318(3) .... 10.01[A]
Sec. 318, Comment c, Illustration 6 ... 10.01[A]
Sec. 318, Comment c, Illustration 7 ... 10.01[A]
Sec. 336(2) ....10.02[A][1]
Sec. 351 ....9.05
Sec. 375 ....3.07

RESTATEMENT OF RESTITUTION

Sec. 108 ....3.07

RESTATEMENT (SECOND) OF TORTS

Sec. 402A .... 5.02[B][2]; 5.06[A]
Sec. 402A, Comment n 5.05

UNIDROIT (CONVENTION OF INTERNATIONAL FINANCIAL LEASING)

Generally 1.04

UNIFORM CONSUMER CREDIT CODE

Generally ....1.05[C]
Sec. 5.108(1) ....4.06[A][4]
Sec. 5.108(2) ....4.06[A][4]
Sec. 5.108(6) ....4.06[A][4]

UNIFORM PERSONAL PROPERTY LEASING ACT

Generally 1.04

UNIFORM SALES ACT

Generally ....3.05[C]; 5.06
Sec. 12 ....5.02[A][4]
Sec. 22 ....1.03[A][1]; 6.01

INDEX

(References are to sections)

A

ACCEPTANCE OF GOODS
(See also REVOCATION OF
      ACCEPTANCE and STATUTE OF
      FRAUDS)
Action for price § 9.04[A]
Action for rent § 9.04[B]
Acts inconsistent with seller's
      ownership § 7.03[A][3]
Allocated part performance § 7.14[B]
Buyer obligation § 7.01
Casualty to goods § 7.12
Conduct as § 7.03[A][3]
Effect of
    Burden of proof § 7.03[B][4]
    Notification requirements § 7.03[B][3]
    Payment required § 7.03[B][2]
    Rejection precluded § 7.03[B][1]
    Revocation limited § 7.03[B][1]
Effect on risk of loss allocation § 7.03[B]
Failure to reject as § 7.03[A][2]
Inspection opportunity § 7.03[A][1],[2]
Installment contract § 7.09[D]
Methods § 7.03[A]
Precluded for disposal of rejected
      goods § 7.04[B][3]
Statement as § 7.03[A][1]
ACCEPTANCE OF OFFER
(See also BATTLE OF THE FORMS,
      FORMATION OF CONTRACTS
      and OFFER)
Generally § 2.03[A]
"Mailbox" rule § 2.03[A]
Medium of § 2.03[A]
Methods of
    Beginning performance § 2.03[A]
    Reasonable in the
      circumstances § 2.03[A]
    Return promise § 2.03[A]
Notice to offeror § 2.03[A]
Unilateral and bilateral
      contrasted § 2.03[A]

Unilateral contract trick
    Defined § 2.03[B]
    Nonconforming goods, shipment
      of § 2.03[B]
    Notice of accommodation § 2.03[B]
ACCRUAL OF ACTION (See STATUTE OF
      LIMITATIONS)
ADDITIONAL TERMS (See BATTLE OF
      THE FORMS)
ADEQUATE ASSURANCES
Cure, installment contract § 7.04[E]
Escalation to anticipatory
      repudiation § 7.10
Failure to make timely payments for
      installments § 7.09[D]
Failure to provide § 7.10[B]
Form of demand § 7.10[A]
Reasonable grounds for
      insecurity § 7.10[A]
Retraction of repudiation § 7.09[C]
Right to demand § 7.10[A]
Suspension of performance § 7.10[A]
Writing requirement § 7.10[A]
ADHESION CONTRACTS (See
      UNCONSCIONABILITY)
AFFIRMATION OF FACT (See EXPRESS
      WARRANTY)
AGREEMENT
Contract contrasted § 2.01
Defined § 2.01
AMBIGUOUS TERMS (See
      INTERPRETATION and PAROL
      EVIDENCE RULE)
ANTICIPATORY REPUDIATION
(See also ADEQUATE ASSURANCES and
      SUSPENSION)
Absence of cure rights § 7.04[C][1]
Breach § 7.06
Default § 7.07
Identification, of goods § 9.01[A]
Repudiation § 7.09[A]
Responses to § 7.09[B]
Retraction

Allowance for delay § 7.09[C]
Method § 7.09[C]
Timeliness § 7.09[C]
Waiting for § 7.09[B]
Substantial impairment § 7.09[A]
ASSUMPTION OF THE RISK (See CONTRIBUTORY FAULT)
ASSURANCES (See ADEQUATE ASSURANCES)
ATTORNEY'S FEES
Unconscionability claims in consumer leases § 4.06[A][4]

B

BAILEES (See RISK OF LOSS)
Stopping delivery by § 9.08
BASIS OF THE BARGAIN (See EXPRESS WARRANTY)
BATTLE OF THE FORMS
Additional terms §§ 2.05[B][1], 2.05[C][2]
"Between merchants" rule
    Generally § 2.05[C]
    Additional and different terms § 2.05[C][2]
    Materiality § 2.05[C][1]
        Arbitration clauses § 2.05[C][1]
        Disclaimers § 2.05[C][1]
        Surprise and hardship § 2.05[C][1]
    Objection to proposed terms § 2.05[C]
    Offer limiting acceptance to its terms § 2.05[C]
Counteroffer
    Common-law approach (the "mirror-image" rule) § 2.05[A]
    Expressly conditional expression of acceptance contrasted § 2.05[D][2]
    "Last-shot" rule § 2.05[A]
Expressions of assent § 2.05[B][1]
Dickered terms § 2.05[B][1]
Different terms §§ 2.05[B][1], [C][2]
Expressly conditional expression of acceptance
    Generally § 2.05[D]
    Counteroffer contrasted § 2.05[D][2]
    Contracts based on conduct (the "knock-out" rule) § 2.05[D][2]
    Language needed § 2.05[D][1]
"First-shot" rule defined § 2.05[B][1]
"Knock-out" rule § 2.05[D][2]
Proposals for addition to the contract § 2.05[B][1]

Written confirmations § 2.05[B][2]
BENEFICIARIES
Finance leases §§ 1.05[B], 5.06[E]
Reclamation claims of seller cut off by § 4.05[B][5]
BREACH
Buyer § 7.06[B]
Events of § 7.06
Seller § 7.06[A]
Statutory § 7.06
BREACH OF THE PEACE (See REPOSSESSION)
BREACH OF WARRANTY
Damages
    Cost to repair § 8.05[B][1]
    Measure § 8.05[B][1]
    Place to measure value § 8.05[B][2]
    Special circumstances § 8.05[B][3]
    Time to measure value § 8.05[B][2]
    Warranty of title § 8.05[B][3]
BURDEN OF PROOF
Course of dealing §§ 4.03[B], [C]
Course of performance § 4.03[C]
Effect of acceptance § 7.03[B][4]
Unconscionability § 4.06[A]
Usage of trade § 4.03[A]
BUYER
Breach § 7.06[B]
Defined § 1.03[A][1]
Obligations, basic § 7.01

C

CANCELLATION
Anticipatory repudiation, as response to § 7.09[B]
Defined § 8.07
Distinguished from termination § 8.07
Installment contracts §§ 7.04[E], 7.09[D]
Perfect tender rule § 7.04[A]
Remedy
    Buyer/lessee § 8.07
    Seller/lessor § 9.07
CARRIERS
Stopping delivery by § 9.08
CASH-SALE DOCTRINE (See RECLAMATION BY SELLER)
CASUALTY TO GOODS (See EXCUSE)
CAUSATION (See CONTRIBUTORY FAULT)
CHECK IN PAYMENT (See GAP-FILLERS and RECLAMATION BY SELLER)

"CERTAINLY" TEST (See PAROL
      EVIDENCE RULE)
COMMERCIAL IMPRACTICABILITY
Allocation of part production   § 7.14[B]
Buyer or lessee options after
      allocation   § 7.14[B]
Economic hardship   § 7.14[A][3]
Exclusive source of supply   § 7.14[A][1]
Excuse   § 7.11
Foreseeability   § 7.14[A][1]
Fundamental premise   § 7.11
Government regulation   § 7.14[A][2]
Nonoccurrence of a basic
      assumption   § 7.14[A][1]
Notification requirements   § 7.14[B]
Seller duty to allocate   7.14[B]
COMMERCIAL UNCONSCIONABILITY
      (See UNCONSCIONABILITY)
COMMERCIAL UNIT
Defined   § 7.04[A]
Perfect tender rule   § 7.04[A]
Revocation   § 7.05[A][1]
COMMERCIALLY REASONABLE
Cover   § 8.03[A],[C]
Resale   § 9.01[A]
COMPARATIVE FAULT (See
      CONTRIBUTORY FAULT)
COMPLETE WRITING (See PAROL
      EVIDENCE RULE)
COMPONENTS MANUFACTURER (See
      LOST PROFITS)
CONDITIONS PRECEDENT (See PAROL
      EVIDENCE RULE)
CONFIRMATIONS (See BATTLE OF THE
      FORMS, MODIFICATION OF
      CONTRACTS and STATUTE OF
      FRAUDS)
CONFLICT OF WARRANTIES (See
      CUMULATION AND CONFLICT
      OF WARRANTIES)
"CONFORMING"
Defined   § 7.04[C][5]
Standard for effective cure   § 7.04[C][5]
CONSEQUENTIAL DAMAGES
(See also SUBSTITUTED REMEDY
      CLAUSES)
Defined   § 8.06[B]
Exclusion or limitation
   Generally   § 5.04[B]
   Consumers, effect on   § 5.04[B]
   Effect of failure of essential
      purpose   § 5.04[C]
   Personal injury   § 5.04[B]
   Unconscionability   § 5.04[B]

Application of Prima facie   § 5.04[B]
Injury to person or property   § 8.06[B]
Lessor's generally precluded   § 9.05
Limitations   § 8.06[B]
Lost use until cover   § 8.03[C]
CONSIDERATION (See MODIFICATION
      OF CONTRACTS)
CONSISTENT TERMS (See
      INTERPRETATION and PAROL
      EVIDENCE RULE)
CONSUMER EXPECTATIONS TEST (See
      MERCHANTABILITY, IMPLIED
      WARRANTY OF)
CONSUMER LEASE
Defined   § 1.05[C]
Policy choice in drafting Article
      2A   § 1.05[C]
State legislation   § 1.05[C]
Unconscionability   § 4.06[A][4]
CONSUMERS
(See also CONSUMER LEASE)
Notice of breach or default   § 7.03[B][3]
CONTRACT
Agreement contrasted   § 2.01
Defined   § 2.01
For lease   1.05[A][1]
For sale   § 1.03[A][1]
CONTRACT FORMATION (See
      FORMATION OF CONTRACTS)
CONTRADICTORY TERMS (See
      INTERPRETATION and PAROL
      EVIDENCE RULE)
CONTRIBUTORY FAULT
Generally   § 5.05
Assumption of risk   § 5.05
Causation   § 5.05
Comparative fault   § 5.05
Proximate cause   § 5.05
Tort law contrasted   § 5.05
COUNTEROFFER (See BATTLE OF THE
      FORMS)
COURSE OF DEALING
(See also HIERARCHY OF TERMS,
      INTERPRETATION and PAROL
      EVIDENCE RULE)
Burden of proof   §§ 4.03[B],[C]
Defined   § 4.03[B]
Sequence of conduct   § 4.03[B]
COURSE OF PERFORMANCE
(See also HIERARCHY OF TERMS,
      INTERPRETATION and PAROL
      EVIDENCE RULE)
Burden of proof   § 4.03[C]
Defined   § 4.03[C]

COVER
Assumptions § 8.04[B][1]
Inability to
  Measure of damages § 8.04
  Replevin § 8.08
  Specific performance § 8.08
Incidental damages § 8.06[A]
Limitation on consequential
      damages § 8.06[B]
Measure of damages § 8.03[B]
Preferred remedy § 8.03
Reasonable purchase § 8.03[A]
Substantially similar
      requirement § 8.03[C]
Substitute lease § 8.03[C]
Substitute purchase § 8.03[A]
CREDIT SALE DOCTRINE (See
      RECLAMATION BY SELLER)
**CUMULATION AND CONFLICT OF
      WARRANTIES**
Generally § 5.08
Presumption that warranties are
      cumulative § 5.08
CURE
Ability to accomplish § 7.04[C][1]
Adequacy of § 7.04[C][5]
Consensual § 7.04[C][6]
Delay in effecting § 7.04[C][1]
Effect on rejection § 7.04[C][5]
Effect on risk of loss allocation § 7.03[B]
Failure to accomplish § 7.04[C][5]
Impairment of the right § 7.04[B][2]
Interference with the right § 7.04[C][2]
Installment contracts § 7.04[E]
Money allowance § 7.04[C][4]
Notification of intent § 7.04[C][2]
Reasonable grounds to believe § 7.04[C][3]
Replacement vs. repair § 7.04[C][5]
Shaken faith doctrine § 7.04[C][5]
Suspension of right to reject § 7.04[C]
Timing § 7.04[C][1]
CUSTOM
(See also USAGE OF TRADE)
After acceptance §§ 7.03[B][1]; 7.05[A][1]
After revocation § 7.05[C]
Early commercial law § 1.01

D

DAMAGES
(See also BREACH OF WARRANTY;
      CONSEQUENTIAL DAMAGES;
      MARKET VALUE; PENALTIES;

PRESENT VALUE; and specific
      subject headings, e.g., COVER and
      RESALE)
Breach of warranty § 8.05[B]
Consequential damages §§ 8.06[B]; 9.05
Cover § 8.03
Discount rate § 8.01[B]
Disposal of goods § 9.01[A],[B]
Expenses saved § 8.04[B][1]
Incidental §§ 8.06[A]; 9.05
Injury to residual interest § 9.06
Liquidated §§ 9.10, 9.11
Lost profits § 9.03
Market price § 9.02
Market rent § 9.02
Market value § 8.04[A],[B]
Measures of recovery
  Breach of warranty § 8.05[B][1]
  Cover § 8.03[B]
  Disposal of goods § 9.01[B]
  Lost profits § 9.03
  Market price § 8.04
  Market rent § 8.04
  Market value § 9.02[A]
  Ordinary loss § 8.05[A]
  Price recovery § 9.04[A]
  Rent recovery § 9.04[B]
  Resale § 9.01[A]
  Residual interest, injury to § 9.06
Ordinary loss § 8.05[A]
Payments made § 8.02
Present value § 8.01[B]
Price § 9.04[A]
Rent § 9.04[B]
Resale § 9.01[A]
DEFAULT
Clause § 7.07[A]
Events of § 7.07[B],[C]
Express designation § 7.07[A]
Lessee § 7.07[C]
Lessor § 7.07[B]
Requirement for Article 2A
      remedies § 7.07[A]
Statutory § 7.07[B],[C]
DEFECTIVE PRODUCTS (See
      MERCHANTABILITY, IMPLIED
      WARRANTY OF)
DELIVERY OF GOODS
(See also GAP-FILLERS)
Destination contract § 4.05[B][3];
      6.02[A],[B]
Excuse § 7.11
Failure of, default §§ 7.06[A], 7.07[B]

Receipt by buyer or lessee §§ 6.02[D]; 6.05[B][1]
Risk of loss under residual § 6.02[D]; 6.05[B][1]
Seller obligation § 7.01
Shipment contract §§ 4.05[B][3]; 6.02[A],[B]
Stopping
 Goods in possession of carrier or bailee § 9.08
 Insolvency of buyer or lessee § 9.08
Substituted performance § 7.13
Tender of
 Buyer response § 7.02
 Delivery, gap-filler § 4.05[B]
 Generally § 4.05[B][3]
 Perfect tender rule § 7.04[A]
 Place for § 8.04[B][1]
DELIVERY TERM (See GAP-FILLERS)
DEMAND FOR ADEQUATE ASSURANCES (See ADEQUATE ASSURANCES)
DESCRIPTION (See EXPRESS WARRANTY)
DESIGN DEFECTS (See MERCHANTABILITY, IMPLIED WARRANTY OF)
DESTINATION CONTRACT
Cost of shipment § 4.05[B][3]
Delivery to the buyer § 6.02[B]
"F.O.B." terms § 4.05[B][3], § 6.02[A]
Risk of loss § 4.05[B][3]
Seller's responsibilities § 4.05[B][3]
Tender § 4.05[B][3]
DIFFERENT TERMS (See BATTLE OF THE FORMS)
DISCLAIMER OF WARRANTY
Express warranty
 Construction to avoid inconsistency § 5.03[A]
 Inoperative if inconsistent with § 5.03[A]
 Parol evidence rule, effect on § 5.03[A]
Implied warranty
 Alternative language § 5.03[B][2]
 "As is" § 5.03[B][2]
 Conspicuousness § 5.03[B][1]
 Inspection as § 5.03[B][3]
 Oral disclaimers § 5.03[B][1]
 Post-contracting circumstances § 5.03[B][4]
 Refusal to inspect § 5.03[B][3]
 "Safe-harbor" language § 5.03[B][1]
 Unconscionability § 5.03[C]

Magnuson-Moss Act, effect on § 5.04[A]
Substituted remedy clauses contrasted § 5.03
DISPOSAL OF GOODS
Buyer remedy § 9.01[C]
Interest of subsequent transferee § 9.01[C]
Lessee remedy § 9.01[C]
Lessor remedy
 Measure of damages § 9.01[B]
 Sales distinguished § 9.01[C]
 Secured transactions distinguished § 9.01[C]
 "Substantially similar" requirement § 9.01[B]
 Substitute transaction requirements § 9.01[B]
Seller resale § 9.01[A]
DOCUMENTS
Of title § 6.02[C]
Payment against § 4.05[B][4]

E

ECONOMIC LOSS (See PRIVITY)
ELECTION
Casualty to goods § 7.12
Market damages § 8.04[A]
ESTOPPEL
(See also MODIFICATION OF CONTRACTS and STATUTE OF FRAUDS)
Option contracts created by § 2.03[A]
EXCUSE
(See also COMMERCIAL IMPRACTICABILITY)
Fundamental vs. incidental § 7.11
Casualty to goods §§ 7.11, 7.12
Commercial impracticability §§ 7.11, 7.14
Substituted performance §§ 7.11, 7.13
EXPRESS WARRANTY
(See also DISCLAIMER OF WARRANTY)
Affirmation of fact or promise
 Generally § 5.02[A][1]
 Basis of the bargain § 5.02[A][4]
 Contextual setting § 5.02[A][1]
 Empirically verifiable § 5.02[A][1]
 Opinion contrasted § 5.02[A][1]
 Promise § 5.02[A][1]
 Puffing § 5.02[A][1], 5.02[A][1],[4]
 Relative sophistication of parties § 5.02[A][1]

Value, statements
    regarding   §§ 5.02[A][1],
    5.02[A][4]
Words of promise not
    necessary   § 5.02[A][1]
Basis of the bargain
    Generally   § 5.02[A][4]
    Burden of proving reliance or
        nonreliance   § 5.02[A][4]
    Post-sale warranties
        As modifications   § 5.02[A][4]
        Bargain and contract
            contrasted   § 5.02[A][4]
    Reliance as a requirement   § 5.02[A][4]
Cumulation and conflict of
    warranties   § 5.08
Description
    As statement of quality   § 5.02[A][2]
    Basis of the bargain   § 5.02[A][4]
    Given to third party   § 5.02[A][2]
Disclaimers
    Construction to avoid
        inconsistency   § 5.03[A]
    Inoperative if inconsistent
        with   § 5.03[A]
    Parol evidence rule, effect on   § 5.03[A]
Future performance, statute of
    limitations   § 5.07
Model   § 5.02[A][3]
Privity   § 5.06[D]
Promise   § 5.02[A][1]
Sample or model
    Basis of the bargain   § 5.02[A][4]
    Sample and model
        contrasted   § 5.02[A][3]
EXPRESSION OF ASSENT (See BATTLE
    OF THE FORMS)
EXTRINSIC EVIDENCE (See
    INTERPRETATION and PAROL
    EVIDENCE RULE)

F

FAILURE OF ESSENTIAL PURPOSE (See
    SUBSTITUTED REMEDY
    CLAUSES)
FAILURE TO WARN (See
    MERCHANTABILITY, IMPLIED
    WARRANTY OF)
"FAIR QUANTUM" TEST (See
    SUBSTITUTED REMEDY
    CLAUSES)

FAULT
Casualty to goods   § 7.12
Defined   § 7.12
FINAL WRITING (See PAROL EVIDENCE
    RULE)
FINANCE LEASE
Beneficiary of supply
    agreements   §§ 1.05[B]; 5.06[E]
Defined   § 1.05[B]
"Hell or high water" clause   §§ 1.05[B];
    7.05[G]
Independent covenants   §§ 1.05[B]; 7.05[G]
Irrevocable promise   §§ 1.05[B]; 7.05[G]
Modification of supply
    agreement   § 5.06[E]
Parties   § 1.05[B]
Rescission of supply contract   § 5.06[E]
Revocation of acceptance
    Preclusions   §7.05[G]
    Right to revoke, limited   § 7.05[G]
Warranties inapplicable to finance
    lessors   § 1.05[B]
Warranty notification   § 1.05[B]
FINANCE LESSEE (See FINANCE LEASE)
FINANCE LESSOR (See FINANCE LEASE)
FIRM OFFER (See OFFER)
FIRST-SHOT RULE (See BATTLE OF THE
    FORMS)
FITNESS, IMPLIED WARRANTY OF
(See also DISCLAIMER OF WARRANTY)
Disclaimers
    Alternative language   § 5.03[B][2]
    "As is"   § 5.03[B][2]
    Conspicuousness   § 5.03[B][1]
    Inspection as   § 5.03[B][3]
    Post-contracting
        circumstances   § 5.03[B][4]
    Refusal to inspect   § 5.03[B][3]
    "Safe-harbor" language   § 5.03[B][1]
    Unconscionability   § 5.03[C]
Particular purpose   § 5.02[C][2]
Particular and ordinary purpose
    contrasted   § 5.03[C][2]
Reason to know buyer's use   § 5.03[C][1]
Reliance by buyer   § 5.03[C][1]
F.O.B. CONTRACT
Destination contracts   § 4.05[B][3]
Explained   § 6.02[A]
Risk allocation   § 6.02[A]
Shipment contracts   § 4.05[B][3]
Vehicle or vessel   § 6.02[A]
FOOD AND BEVERAGE SALES (See
    MERCHANTABILITY, IMPLIED
    WARRANTY OF)

"FOREIGN/NATURAL" TEST (See MERCHANTABILITY, IMPLIED WARRANTY OF)
FORMATION OF CONTRACT
(See also ACCEPTANCE OF OFFER, AGREEMENT, BATTLE OF THE FORMS, CONTRACT and OFFER)
Acceptance generally   § 2.03
Common-law approach   § 2.01
Conduct, formation by   § 2.01; 2.05[D][2]
Offer generally   § 2.02
"FOUR-CORNERS" DOCTRINE (See PAROL EVIDENCE RULE)
FRAUDS, STATUTE OF (See STATUTE OF FRAUDS)
FUTURE PERFORMANCE, WARRANTY AS TO (See STATUTE OF LIMITATIONS)

G

GAP-FILLERS
Delivery
   Place of   § 4.05[B][1]
   Tender of payment as concurrent condition   § 4.05[B][4]
   Time of
      Early delivery   § 4.05[B][2]
      Notification requirements   § 4.05[B][2]
      Reasonable time   § 4.05[B][2]
      Tender rules, effect on   § 4.05[B][2]
Output contract
   Good faith   § 4.05[C]
   Increase and decrease in demand contrasted   § 4.05[C]
   Indefiniteness as to quantity   § 4.05[C]
   Mutuality of obligation   § 4.05[C]
   Unreasonably disproportionate   § 4.05[C]
Payment
   Cash   § 4.05[B][4]
   Check, payment by
      Dishonor   § 4.05[B][5]
      Extension of time to obtain cash   § 4.05[B][5]
      Refusal by seller   § 4.05[B][5]
   Credit   § 4.05[B][4]
   Documents, payment against   § 4.05[B][4]
   Inspection by buyer   § 4.05[B][4]
   Time of   § 4.05[B][4]

Tender of delivery as concurrent condition   § 4.05[B][4]
Price
   Deferred term   § 4.05[A]
   Failure of pricing mechanism   § 4.05[A]
   Fixed by buyer   § 4.05[A]
   Fixed by seller   § 4.05[A]
   Intent to be bound   § 4.05[A]
   Open term   § 4.05[A]
   Reasonable price   § 4.05[A]
Requirement contract
   Good faith   § 4.05[C]
   Increase and decrease in demand contrasted   § 4.05[C]
   Indefiniteness as to quantity   § 4.05[C]
   Mutuality of obligation   § 4.05[C]
   Unreasonably disproportionate   § 4.05[C]
Time
   Cure following rejection   § 7.04[C][1]
GOOD FAITH
(See also MODIFICATION OF CONTRACTS)
Bad faith contrasted   § 4.06[B]
Defined
   Generally   § 4.06[B]
   Merchants   § 4.06[B]
Disposal of goods, lease   § 9.01[B]
Enforcement of contract, applicability to   § 4.06[B]
"Excluder" analysis   § 4.06[B]
Implied-in-law obligation   § 4.06[B]
Interest of transferee of goods   § 9.01[C]
Limitation on cure   § 7.04[D]
Merchants   § 4.06[B]
Negotiating contract, duty not applicable to   § 4.06[B]
Output contracts   § 4.05[C]
Performance of contract, applicability to   § 4.06[B]
Pervasive obligation   § 7.04[D]
Reasonable commercial standards of fair dealing   § 4.06[B]
Requirements contracts   § 4.05[C]
Resale   § 9.01[A]
Subjective honesty   § 4.06[B]
Unconscionability contrasted   § 4.06[A], [B]
GOODS
Defined   § 1.03[B]
Hybrid transactions   § 1.03[C]
Identification of   § 1.03[B]

H

"HELL OR HIGH WATER" CLAUSE (See FINANCE LEASE)
HISTORY
Commercial law prior to the U.C.C. § 1.01
DRAFTING PROCESS
Amending Article 2A § 1.04
Promulgation of the U.C.C. § 1.02
Promulgation of Article 2A § 1.04
Law Merchant § 1.01
HORIZONTAL PRIVITY (see PRIVITY)

I

IDENTIFICATION
Action for price § 9.04[A][3]
Casualty to goods § 7.12
Public sales § 9.01[A]
Replevin § 8.08
Risk of loss § 6.03[C]
Seller remedy § 9.01[A]
Time of occurrence § 1.03[B]
IMPAIRMENT OF EXPECTATIONS
(See also SUBSTANTIAL IMPAIRMENT)
Duty to avoid § 7.08
Prospective
    Anticipatory repudiation § 7.09
    Demand for adequate assurances § 7.10
IMPAIRMENT OF RIGHTS (See SUBSTITUTED REMEDY CLAUSES)
IMPLIED-IN-FACT TERMS (See COURSE OF DEALING, COURSE OF PERFORMANCE and USAGE OF TRADE)
IMPLIED-IN-LAW TERMS (See GAP-FILLERS)
IMPLIED WARRANTY OF FITNESS (See FITNESS, IMPLIED WARRANTY OF)
IMPLIED WARRANTY OF MERCHANTABILITY (See MERCHANTABILITY, IMPLIED WARRANTY OF)
IMPLIED WARRANTY OF TITLE AND AGAINST INFRINGEMENT (See TITLE, IMPLIED WARRANTY OF)
INCIDENTAL DAMAGES
Buyer's and lessee's § 8.06[A]
Seller's and lessor's § 9.05

INDEMNIFICATION (See STATUTE OF LIMITATIONS)
INFRINGEMENT (See TITLE, IMPLIED WARRANTY OF)
INSOLVENCY
Seller's right to take possession of goods § 9.09[A]
Stopping delivery § 9.08
INSPECTION
Casualty to goods § 7.12
Implied warranty disclaimers § 5.03[B][3]
Incidental damages §§ 8.06[A], 9.05
Payment duty, relationship to § 4.05[B][4]
Prerequisite for acceptance § 7.03[A][1],[2]
Public sales § 9.01[A]
Relevance to revocation of acceptance § 7.05[A][1]
Right to § 7.03[A][1]
Waiver of right § 7.03[A][1]
INSTALLMENT CONTRACTS
Anticipatory repudiation § 7.09[D]
Cancellation §§ 7.04[E], 7.09[D]
Cure § 7.04[E]
Rejection of single installment § 7.04[E]
Substantial impairment §§ 7.04[E], 7.09[D]
INSURANCE
Obligation to provide § 6.05[A][1]
Risk of loss § 6.03[B],[C]
INTERPRETATION
(See also PAROL EVIDENCE RULE)
Aids to § 4.04[B]
Ambiguous terms § 4.04[B]
Course of dealing § 4.04[B]
Course of performance § 4.04[B]
Extrinsic evidence, admissibility of § 4.04[B]
Intent of the parties
    Knowledge § 4.04[B]
    Reason to know § 4.04[B]
Plain meaning rule § 4.04[A]
Usage of trade § 4.04[B]
INVALIDATING CAUSES (See PAROL EVIDENCE RULE)
IRREVOCABLE OFFER (See OFFER)

K

KNOCK-OUT RULE (See BATTLE OF THE FORMS)

L

"LAST-SHOT" RULE (See BATTLE OF
    THE FORMS)
LAW MERCHANT (See HISTORY)
OF GOODS
(See also CONSUMER LEASE, FINANCE
    LEASE and STATUTE OF
    FRAUDS)
Defined § 1.05[A]
Disguised lease § 1.05[A][2]
Primary features § 1.05[A][1],[2]
Sales distinguished § 1.05[A][1]
"LEMONS" (See SUBSTITUTED REMEDY
    CLAUSES)
LESSEE
Default § 7.07[C]
Remedies (See REMEDIES)
LESSOR
Default § 7.07[B]
Remedies (See REMEDIES)
LIMITATIONS, STATUTE OF (See
    STATUTE OF LIMITATIONS)
LIMITED REMEDY CLAUSES (See
    SUBSTITUTED REMEDY
    CLAUSES)
LIQUIDATED DAMAGES
Generally § 9.01
Anticipated harm § 9.10, 9.11
Difficult proof of loss § 9.10
Formulas § 9.11
Leases § 9.11
Penalties § 9.10
Reasonableness §§ 9.10, 9.11
Sales § 9.10
LOSS ALLOCATION (See Risk of Loss)
LOST PROFITS
Alternative to market value
    damages § 9.03
Components manufacturer § 9.03
Consequential damages § 8.06[B]
Lost-volume sellers and lessors § 9.03
LOST-VOLUME SELLERS AND LESSORS
    (See LOST PROFITS)

M

MAGNUSON-MOSS ACT (See
    DISCLAIMER OF WARRANTY
    and SUBSTITUTED REMEDY
    CLAUSES)
MANUFACTURING DEFECTS (See
    MERCHANTABILITY, IMPLIED
    WARRANTY OF)

MARKET VALUE
Buyer/lessee damages
    Applicability § 8.04
    Election § 8.04[A]
    Market place § 8.04[B][1]
    Market time § 8.04[B][2]
    Measure § 8.04
Seller/lessor damages
    Market place, lease § 9.02[B][2]
    Market place, sale § 9.02[B][1]
    Market time, lease § 9.02[B][2]
    Market time, sale § 9.02[B][1]
    Measure § 9.02[A]
MATERIAL BREACH (See SUBSTANTIAL
    IMPAIRMENT)
MERCHANT
(See also BATTLE OF THE FORMS; GOOD
    FAITH DUTY;
    MERCHANTABILITY, IMPLIED
    WARRANTY OF; and STATUTE
    OF FRAUDS)
Between merchants in battle of the
    forms § 2.05[C]
Defined §§ 3.04[B], 5.02[B][1]
Disposal of rejected goods § 7.04[B][3]
Good faith duty § 4.06[B]
Implied warranty of merchantability given
    by § 5.02[B][1]
Risk of loss under residual
    rule §§ 6.02[D], 6.05[B][1]
Written confirmation rule in Statute of
    Frauds § 3.04[B]
MERCHANTABILITY, IMPLIED
    WARRANTY OF
(See also DISCLAIMER OF WARRANTY)
Adequately contained, packaged and
    labeled § 5.02[B][2]
Caveat emptor contrasted § 5.02[B][1]
Conformity to label § 5.02[B][2]
Consumer expectations test § 5.02[B][2]
Defect required for breach of § 5.02[B][2]
Defective instructions to
    buyer § 5.02[B][2]
Design defects § 5.02[B][2]
Disclaimers
    Alternative language § 5.03[B][2]
    "As is" § 5.03[B][2]
    Conspicuousness § 5.03[B][1]
    Inspection as § 5.03[B][3]
    Oral disclaimers § 5.03[B][1]
    Post-contracting § 5.03[B][4]
    Refusal to inspect § 5.03[B][3]
    "Safe-harbor" language § 5.03[B][1]
    Unconscionability § 5.03[C]

Failure to warn § 5.02[B][2]
Food and beverage sales § 5.02[B][2]
"Foreign/natural" test § 5.02[B][2]
Manufacturing defects § 5.02[B][2]
Merchant
    Defined § 5.02[B][1]
    Equipment sellers § 5.02[B][1]
    Farmers and ranchers § 5.02[B][1]
    Inventory sellers § 5.02[B][1]
    Manufacturers § 5.02[B][1]
Merchantability defined § 5.02[B][2]
Ordinary and particular purpose
        contrasted § 5.02[C][2]
Ordinary purpose § 5.02[B][2]
Passing without objection in the
        trade § 5.02[B][2]
Used goods, application to § 5.02[B][2]
MITIGATION OF DAMAGES
Lease-rent lessor remedy § 9.04[B]
Market-rent lessor remedy § 9.02[B][2]
Retraction of anticipatory
        repudiation § 7.09[B]
MODEL (See EXPRESS WARRANTY)
MODIFICATION OF CONTRACTS
(See also STATUTE OF FRAUDS and
        WAIVER)
Acceptance of allocated part
        performance § 7.14[B]
Consensual cure § 7.04[C][6]
Consideration
    Code approach § 2.06[A]
    Pre-existing duty rule § 2.06[A]
    Second Restatement
        approach § 2.06[A]
Good faith § 2.06[A]
Post-sale warranties § 5.02[A][4]
Statute of Frauds
    Application to modifications
        generally § 2.06[B][1]
    Estoppel § 2.06[B][3]
    Private statutes of frauds § 2.06[B][2]
    Statutory exceptions § 2.06[B][1]
    Waiver
        Modification contrasted § 2.06[B][3]
        Modification operating
            as § 2.06[B][3]
    Written confirmation rule § 2.06[B][1]
Supply agreement for finance
        lease § 5.06[E]
MODIFICATION OF RIGHTS (See
        SUBSTITUTED REMEDY
        CLAUSES)

N

NOMINAL CONSIDERATION (See
        SECURITY INTEREST)
NOTICE
Acceptance of offer § 2.03[A]
Breach or default § 7.03[B][3]
Excused performance § 7.14[B]
Intent to cure § 7.04[C][2]
Private sales § 9.01[A]
Public sales § 9.01[A]
Rejection § 7.04[B][2]
Revocation § 7.05[B]
Shipment contract §§ 4.05[B][3];
        6.02[A],[B]
Stopping delivery § 9.08
Warranties in a finance lease § 1.05[B]

O

OFFER
(See also ACCEPTANCE OF OFFER;
        BATTLE OF THE FORMS; FIRM
        OFFER and FORMATION OF
        CONTRACTS)
Generally § 2.02
Advertisements, circulars and price
        quotes § 2.02
Defined § 2.02
Firm offer
    Assurances that offer will be held
        open § 2.04
    Defined § 2.04
    Maximum period of
        irrevocability § 2.04
    Merchant requirement § 2.04
    Option contracts contrasted § 2.04
    Signed writing requirement § 2.04
Irrevocable offer
    Firm offers § 2.04
    Option contract created by
        estoppel § 2.03[A]
    Option contract supported by
        consideration § 2.04
Unilateral and bilateral
        contrasted § 2.03[A]
OPTION CONTRACT (See Offer)
OPTIONS (See SECURITY INTEREST)
ORDINARY LOSS (See DAMAGES)
ORDINARY PURPOSE (See
        MERCHANTABILITY, IMPLIED
        WARRANTY OF)
OUTPUT CONTRACT (See GAP-FILLERS)

P

PAROL EVIDENCE RULE
Ambiguous terms   § 4.02[G][4]
Complete writing (total integration)
   "Certainly included" test   § 4.02[D][2]
   Code test   § 4.02[D][2]
   Collateral contract doctrine   § 4.02[D][1]
   "Four-corners" doctrine   § 4.02[D][1]
   Intent of the parties   § 4.02[D][1]
   Merger clause, effect of   § 4.02[F]
   Mitchell test   § 4.02[D][1]
   "Naturally omitted" test   § 4.02[D][1]
   Second Restatement test   § 4.02[D][1]
Condition precedent   § 4.02[G][3]
Confirmatory memoranda   § 4.02[B]
Contradiction and consistency contrasted
   Hunt Foods test   § 4.02[E]
   Reasonable harmony test   § 4.02[E]
Contradictory terms generally   § 4.02[E]
"Explain" and "supplement"
      contrasted   § 4.02[B]
Express warranty, effect on   § 5.03[A]
Final writing (partial
      integration)   § 4.02[C]
Interpretation
   Generally   § 4.02[G][4]
   Supplementation
      contrasted   § 4.02[G][4]
Invalidating causes
   Generally   § 4.02[G][2]
   Condition precedent   § 4.02[G][3]
   Fraud   § 4.02[G][2]
   Illegality   § 4.02[G][2]
   Innocent misrepresentation   § 4.02[G][2]
   Negligent
      misrepresentation   § 4.02[G][2]
   Tort law, use of   § 4.02[G][2]
"Parol" defined   § 4.02[A]
Reformation   § 4.02[H]
Substantive law, rule of   § 4.02[A]
"Supplement" and "explain"
      contrasted   § 4.02[B]
Supplementation
   Generally   § 4.02[6]
   Course of dealing   § 4.02[G][1]
   Course of performance   § 4.02[G][1]
   Consistent additional terms   § 4.02[E]
   Interpretation contrasted   § 4.02[G][4]
   Usage of trade   § 4.02[G][1]
"Term" defined   § 4.02[G][3]
PARTICULAR PURPOSE (See FITNESS,
      IMPLIED WARRANTY OF)

PATENT INFRINGEMENT (See TITLE,
      IMPLIED WARRANTY OF)
PAYMENT
(See also GAP-FILLERS)
Adequate assurances   § 7.09[D]
Breach by buyer   § 7.06[B]
Buyer obligation   § 7.01
Compensation for disposal of rejected
      goods   § 7.04[B][3]
Compensation for use after
      revocation   § 7.05[F]
Consequence of acceptance   § 7.03[B][2]
Default by lessee   § 7.07[C]
Installment contract   § 7.09[D]
Substituted performance   § 7.13
PAYMENT ACCEPTED (See STATUTE OF
      FRAUDS)
PAYMENT TERM (See GAP-FILLERS)
PENALTIES (See LIQUIDATED
      DAMAGES)
PERFECT TENDER RULE
Generally   § 7.04[A]
Cure as second chance   § 7.04[C][3]
Installment contract exception   § 7.04[E]
Policy   § 7.04[A]
Shipment contract exception   § 7.04[F]
Standard for adequacy of cure   § 7.04[C][5]
PERSONAL PROPERTY (See STATUTE OF
      FRAUDS)
POSSESSION
Receipt   §§ 6.02[D], 6.05[B][1]
PRESENT VALUE
Breach of warranty   § 8.05[B][1]
Consequential damages, seller and
      lessor   § 9.05
Cover damages   § 8.03[C]
Defined   § 8.01[B]
Discount rate   § 8.01[B]
Market rent   § 8.04
PRICE, RECOVERY REMEDY
Buyer   § 8.02
Seller
   Accepted goods   § 9.04[A][1]
   Buyer entitled to goods   § 9.04
   Disposal impractical   § 9.04[A][3]
   Lost or damaged goods   § 9.04[A][2]
PRICE TERM (See GAP-FILLERS)
PRIMA FACIE UNCONSCIONABILITY
      (See SUBSTITUTED REMEDY
      CLAUSES)
PRIVATE STATUTES OF FRAUDS (See
      MODIFICATION OF
      CONTRACTS)

PRIVITY
Common-law approach § 5.06
Express warranty
    Seller's advertising § 5.06[D]
    Reliance of buyer § 5.06[D]
Finance lessees
    Modification or rescission of supply
        contract, effect of § 5.06[E]
    Third-party beneficiaries of supplier's
        warranties § 5.06[E]
Horizontal privity
    Alternative approaches § 5.06[B]
    Code alternatives as ceiling or
        floor § 5.06[B]
    Disclaimers, effect of § 5.06[B]
    Third-party beneficiary § 5.06[B]
Revocation of acceptance § 7.05[E]
Strict liability in tort compared § 5.06[A]
Vertical privity
    Economic loss generally § 5.06[C]
    Personal injury § 5.06[C]
    Primary economic loss § 5.06[C]
    Secondary economic loss § 5.06[C]
PROPOSALS (See BATTLE OF THE
        FORMS)
PROSPECTIVE IMPAIRMENT OF
        EXPECTATIONS (See
        ANTICIPATORY REPUDIATION
        and ADEQUATE ASSURANCES)
PROXIMATE CAUSE (see
        CONTRIBUTORY FAULT)
PUFFING (See EXPRESS WARRANTY)

Q

QUANTITY TERM
(See also GAP-FILLERS and STATUTE OF
        FRAUDS)
Output contract § 4.05[C]
Requirement contract § 4.05[C]
Statute of Frauds, writing
        requirement § 3.03[D]

R

RECEIPT (See POSSESSION)
RECLAMATION BY SELLER
(See also REPOSSESSION)
Bona fide purchasers from
        buyer § 4.05[B][5]
Cash sales
    Cash-sale doctrine § 9.09[A]
    Check equivalent to cash § 4.05[B][5]

Notice to buyer not
        required § 4.05[B][5]
    Sellers § 9.09[A]
    Title of buyer conditional § 4.05[B][5]
Credit sales
    Insolvency of buyer
        required § 4.05[B][5]
    Misrepresentation of
        solvency § 4.05[B][5]
    Notice to buyer required § 4.05[B][5]
Leases
    Lessors § 9.09[B]
    Protection of residual interest § 9.09[B]
REFORMATION (See PAROL EVIDENCE
        RULE and
        UNCONSCIONABILITY)
REJECTION
Action for price, precluded § 9.04[A][1]
Acts inconsistent with seller's ownership
        as § 7.03[A][3]
Breach § 7.06
Continued use of goods as § 7.03[A][3]
Cure limitation § 7.04[C]
Default § 7.07[B],[C]
Duties of buyers and lessees § 7.04[B][3]
Effective § 7.04[B]
Failure to exercise § 7.03[A][2]
Good faith limitation § 7.04[D]
Incidental damages § 8.06[A]
Installment contracts § 7.04[E]
Notification requirements § 7.04[B][2]
Perfect tender rule § 7.04[A]
Pre-acceptance behavior § 7.02
Procedures § 7.04[B]
Right to reject § 6.03[A]; 7.04[A]
Risk of loss, effect of right
        to on §§ 6.03[A], 6.05[B][2]
Security interest in goods § 9.01[C]
Timeliness § 7.04[B][1]
Waiver of right § 7.04[B]
Wrongful § 7.05[D]
REMEDIES
(See also CANCELLATION, DAMAGES
        and specific subject headings, e.g.,
        COVER; DISPOSAL OF GOODS;
        RESALE)
Breach of sale contract § 8.01
Buyer
    Breach of warranty damages § 8.05[B]
    Cancellation § 8.07
    Consequential damages § 8.06[B]
    Cover § 8.03[A],[B]
    Incidental damages § 8.06[A]
    Market damages § 8.04

Ordinary loss recovery § 8.05[A]
Purchase price paid recovery § 8.02
Replevin § 8.08
Specific performance § 8.08
Cumulative § 8.01[A]
Default on lease § 8.01
Indexes § 8.01
Lessee
  Breach of warranty damages § 8.05[B]
  Cancellation § 8.07
  Consequential damages § 8.06[B]
  Cover § 8.03[B],[C]
  Incidental damages § 8.06[A]
  Market damages § 8.04
  Ordinary loss recovery § 8.05[A]
  Rent paid recovery § 8.02
  Replevin § 8.08
  Specific performance § 8.08
Lessor
  Cancellation § 9.07
  Completion of unfinished
    goods § 9.01[B]
  Consequential damages, generally
    precluded § 9.05
  Disposal of goods § 9.01[B]
  Incidental damages § 9.05
  Identification of goods to lease
    contract § 9.01[B]
  Injury to residual interest § 9.06
  Lost profits § 9.03
  Market rent damages § 9.02[A]
  Rent recovery § 9.04[B]
  Repossession of goods § 9.09[B]
  Withholding delivery § 9.08
Liquidated damages §§ 9.10, 9.11
Seller
  Cancellation § 9.07
  Completion of unfinished
    goods § 9.01[A]
  Consequential damages, generally
    precluded § 9.05
  Identification of goods to sales
    contract § 9.01[A]
  Incidental damages § 9.05
  Lost profits § 9.03
  Market price damages § 9.02[A]
  Price recovery § 9.04
  Repossession, limited right § 9.09[A]
  Resale § 9.01[A]
  Withholding delivery § 9.08
REPAIR OR REPLACEMENT (See
    SUBSTITUTED REMEDY
    CLAUSES)

REPLEVIN
Buyer and lessee remedy § 8.08
Lessor remedy § 9.09[B]
REPOSSESSION
Breach of the peace § 9.09[B]
Cash-sale doctrine § 9.09[A]
Comparison, lessor and secured
    party § 9.09[B]
Judicial action § 9.09[B]
Self-help § 9.09[B]
Seller, limited right of § 9.09[A]
REPUDIATION (See ANTICIPATORY
    REPUDIATION)
REQUIREMENT CONTRACT (See GAP-
    FILLERS)
RESALE
Incidental damages § 9.01[A]
Lease distinguished § 9.01[C]
Measure of damages § 9.01[A]
Preferred remedy § 9.01[A]
Public and private § 9.01[A]
Secured transactions
    distinguished § 9.01[C]
Substitute transaction
    requirements § 9.01[A]
RESCISSION
Supply contract for finance lease § 5.06[E]
RESIDUAL INTEREST
Effect on lessor's disposition of
    goods § 9.01[C]
Injury to § 9.06
Protected by reclamation rights § 9.09[B]
Remedy for injury to § 9.06
Requirement of true lease § 1.05[A][2]
Sale, absence of § 1.05[A][1]
Two-part test § 1.05[A][2]
RETRACTION (See ANTICIPATORY
    REPUDIATION and WAIVER)
REVOCATION OF ACCEPTANCE
Action for price, precluded § 9.04[A][1]
Breach § 7.06
Compensation for use of goods § 7.05[F]
Cure, right to § 7.05[C]
Default § 7.07[B],[C]
Duties of buyers and lessees § 7.05[B]
Effect of continued use of
    goods § 7.03[A][3]
Effect on risk of loss § 6.03[B]; 6.05[B][2]
Finance lease
  Preclusion § 7.05[G]
  Right to revoke, limited § 7.05[G]
Incidental damages § 8.06[A]
Notification requirement § 7.05[B]
Post-acceptance behavior § 7.02

Privity   § 7.05[E]
Right to revoke   § 7.05[A]
Security interest in goods   § 9.01[C]
Substantial impairment   § 7.05[A][2]
Timeliness   § 7.05[B]
Wrongful   § 7.05[D]
RISK OF LOSS
Absence of breach in sales contract
Action for price   § 9.04[A][2]
   Bailed goods   § 6.02[C]
   Destination contract   § 6.02[A],[B]
   Express agreement   § 6.02[A]
   F.O.B. provisions   § 6.02[A]
   Merchant status   § 6.02[D]
   Residual provision   § 6.02[D]
   Shipment contract   §§ 4.05[B][3];
      6.02[A],[B]
Allocation, consequences of   § 6.01
Casualty to goods   § 7.12
Destination contract   § 4.05[B][3]
Leases
   Express agreement   § 6.05[A][1]
   Finance leases   § 6.05[A][2]
   General rule   § 6.04
   Time risk passes lease
      Absence of default   § 6.05[B][1]
      Bailee holding goods   § 6.05[B][1]
      Effect of default   § 6.05[B][2]
      Lessee default   § 6.05[B][2]
      Lessee revocation of
         acceptance   § 6.05[B][2]
      Lessee right to reject   § 6.05[B][2]
      Merchant status   § 6.05[B][1]
      Residual rule   § 6.05[B][1]
      Shipment contract   § 6.05[B][1]
Sales contract
   Buyer breach   § 6.03[C]
   Buyer revocation of
      acceptance   § 6.03[B]
   Buyer right to reject   § 6.03[A]
   Subrogation   § 6.03[B],[C]

S

SALE OF GOODS
Defined   § 1.03[A][1]
Hybrid transactions   § 1.03[C]
Lease distinguished   § 1.05[A][1]
Primary features   § 1.05[A][1]
SAMPLE (See EXPRESS WARRANTY)
SCOPE OF ARTICLE 2
Application by analogy   § 1.03[A][2]
Direct application   § 1.03[A][1]

SCOPE OF ARTICLE 2A
Consumer lease   § 1.05[C]
Finance lease   § 1.05[B]
Lease   § 1.05[A]
SECURED TRANSACTIONS
(See also SECURITY INTEREST)
Defined   § 1.05[A][2]
Disguised lease   § 1.05[A][2]
Lease distinguished   § 1.05[A][2]
Primary features   § 1.05[A][2]
SECURITY INTEREST
After rejection or revocation   § 9.01[C]
Economics of the transaction   § 1.05[A][2]
Lease distinguished   § 1.05[A][2]
Nominal consideration   § 1.05[A][2]
Options   § 1.05[A][2]
Residual interest   § 1.05[A][2]
SELLER
Breach   § 7.06[B]
Defined   § 1.03[A][1]
Obligations, basic   § 7.01
SERVICES
Sale of goods and   § 1.03[C]
SHAKEN FAITH DOCTRINE (See CURE)
"SHELF-LIFE" PROBLEM (See STATUTE
      OF LIMITATIONS)
SHIPMENT CONTRACT
Documents   § 7.04[F]
Exception to perfect tender rule   § 7.04[F]
F.O.B. terms   § 4.05[B][3]; 6.02[A];
      6.05[B][1]
Presumption   § 6.02[B]
Requirements
   Cost of shipment   § 4.05[B][3]
   Delivery to carrier   § 4.05[B][3]
   Notice to buyer   § 4.05[B][3]
   Selection of carrier   § 4.05[B][3]
   Shipment by carrier   § 6.02[B];
      6.05[B][1];   § 7.04[F]
   Shipping arrangements   § 7.04[F]
Risk of loss   § 4.05[B][3]
Tender   § 4.05[B][3]
SPECIALLY MANUFACTURED GOODS
      (See STATUTE OF FRAUDS)
SPECIFIC PERFORMANCE (See
      REMEDIES)
STATUTE OF FRAUDS
(See also MODIFICATION OF
      CONTRACTS)
Accepted goods
   Generally   § 3.05[C]
   Bailment or sale   § 3.05[C]
   Exclusion from Article 2A,
      rationale   § 3.05[C]

Payment made rule
  compared   § 3.05[C]
Admissions in judicial proceedings
  Involuntary admissions   § 3.05[B]
  "Laughing defendant" rule   § 3.05[B]
  Procedural admissions   § 3.05[B]
  Right to pursue discovery   § 3.05[B]
Dollar-amount thresholds   § 3.02
History of   § 3.01
Leases
  Description of the goods   § 3.03[E]
  Duration term   § 3.03[E]
Modifications, application to   § 2.06[B][1]
Noncompliance, effects of
  Affirmative defense   § 3.07
  Unenforceability   § 3.07
  Void and unenforceable
    contrasted   § 3.07
Nonstatutory exceptions
  Code as preemptive   § 3.06
  Equitable estoppel   § 3.06
  Promissory estoppel
    Definite and substantial
      reliance   § 3.06
    Unconscionable injury   § 3.06
Payment made
  Generally   § 3.05[C]
  Indivisible item   § 3.05[C]
Personal property other than goods
  Generally   § 3.02
  Amount or value of remedy   § 3.02
Private statutes of frauds   § 2.06[B][2]
Rationale for   § 3.01
Specially manufactured goods
  Not suitable for sale to others   § 3.05[A]
  Reliance, necessity of   § 3.05[A]
Statutory exceptions
  Accepted goods   § 3.05[C]
  Admissions in judicial
    proceedings   § 3.05[B]
  Application to
    modifications   § 2.06[B][1]
  Payment made   § 3.05[C]
  Specially manufactured
    goods   § 3.05[A]
  Written confirmation rule   § 3.04
Writing requirement
  Common-law approaches   § 3.03
  Multiple writings   § 3.03[A]
    Internal cross-references, necessity
      for   § 3.03[A]
  Quantity term, necessity for   § 3.03[D]
    Not enforceable beyond quantity
      shown   § 3.03[D]

Signature   § 3.03[B]
Sufficient to show contract   § 3.03[C]
Written confirmations
  Application to
    modifications   § 2.06[B][1]
  Between merchants   § 3.04[B]
  Contents generally   § 3.04[A]
  Contents not effective against
    recipient   § 3.04
  "Mailbox rule" not applicable   § 3.04
  "Merchant" defined   § 3.04[B]
  Receipt, time of   § 3.04
  Signature of sender effective against
    recipient   § 3.04
  Written notice of objection   § 3.04
STATUTE OF LIMITATIONS (See also
    TIME LIMITS)
Accrual of action   § 5.07
Future performance, warranty as to   § 5.07
Indemnification actions   § 5.07
Installation, effect on   § 5.07
"Shelf-life" problem   § 5.07
Tolling   § 5.07
Warranty actions   § 5.07
STOPPING DELIVERY (See DELIVERY OF
    GOODS)
SUBROGATION (See RISK OF LOSS)
SUBSTANTIAL IMPAIRMENT
Anticipatory repudiation   § 7.09[A]
Installment contract, cancellation
    of   § 7.04[E]
Material breach   § 7.04[E]
Rejection of installment   § 7.04[E]
Revocation of acceptance   § 7.05[A][2]
SUBSTANTIVE UNCONSCIONABILITY
    (See UNCONSCIONABILITY)
SUBSTITUTED PERFORMANCE (See
    EXCUSE)
SUBSTITUTED REMEDY CLAUSES
Additional remedies   § 5.04[A]
Consequential damages, exclusion or
    limitation of
  Generally   § 5.04[B]
  Consumers, effect on   § 5.04[B]
  Effect of failure of essential
    purpose   § 5.04[C]
  Personal injury   § 5.04[B]
  Unconscionability, applied *Prima
    facie*   § 5.04[B]
Disclaimers contrasted   § 5.03
"Expressly agreed to be
    exclusive"   § 5.04[A][1]
Failure of essential purpose
  Generally   § 5.04[A][2]

...ect on clauses excluding or limiting
 consequential damages § 5.04[C]
"Fair quantum" test § 5.04[A][2]
"Lemons" § 5.04[A][2]
Unconscionability contrasted § 5.04[C]
Optional remedies § 5.04[A]
Repair or replacement remedies § 5.04[A]
Magnuson-Moss Act, effect on § 5.04[A]
SUPEREMINENT PRINCIPLES (See GOOD
 FAITH and
 UNCONSCIONABILITY)
SUPPLEMENTATION (See PAROL
 EVIDENCE RULE)
SUPPLIER
Role in finance lease § 1.05[B]
SUSPENSION
Of performance
 Anticipatory repudiation § 7.09[B]
 Demand for adequate
 assurances § 7.10[A]
Of right to reject § 7.04[C][2]

T

THIRD-PARTY BENEFICIARIES (See
 PRIVITY)
TIME LIMITS (See also STATUTE OF
 LIMITATIONS)
Adequate assurances, providing § 7.10[B]
Awaiting retraction of anticipatory
 repudiation § 7.09[B]
Cash sales § 9.09[A]
Cover § 8.03[A]
Cure § 7.04[C][1]
Delivery, gap-filler § 4.05[B][2]
Inspection opportunity § 7.03[A][1]
Notice
 Breach or default § 7.03[B][3]
 Intent to cure § 7.04[C][2]
Payment § 4.05[B][4]
Rejection § 7.04[B][1]
Retraction of anticipatory
 repudiation § 7.09[C]
Revocation § 7.05[B]
Risk of loss passage § 6.03[C]
Seller right to take possession of
 goods § 9.09[A]
Shipment contract
 notification § 6.02[A],[B]
Stopping delivery of bailed goods § 9.08
Suspending performance because of
 insecurity § 7.10[A]

TIME VALUE OF MONEY (See PRESENT
 VALUE)
TITLE
Documents of § 6.02[C]
Relevance to sale of goods § 1.03[A][1]
Transfer § 7.01
Uniform Sales Act § 6.01
Uniform Commercial Code § 6.01
TITLE, IMPLIED WARRANTY OF
(See also DISCLAIMER OF WARRANTY)
Generally § 5.02[D]
Colorable claim § 5.02[D]
Exclusion by circumstances § 5.02[D]
Infringement § 5.02[D]
Lease contracts, no implied warranty of
 title § 5.02[D]
Patent infringement § 5.02[D]
Quiet possession
 Lease contracts § 5.02[D]
 Sales contracts § 5.02[D]
TOLLING (See STATUTE OF
 LIMITATIONS)
TRADE USAGE (See USAGE OF TRADE)
TRANSFER
Purchase from lessee disposing of rejected
 goods § 7.04[B][3]

U

UNCONSCIONABILITY
Adhesion contracts § 4.06[A]
Burden of proof § 4.06[A]
Commercial
 unconscionability § 4.06[A][2]
Consequential damages, exclusion or
 limitation of
 Consumers, effect on § 5.04[B]
 Personal injury § 5.04[B]
 Prima facie unconscionability § 5.04[B]
Consumer leases
 Attorney's fees recoverable § 4.06[A][4]
 Collection of claim § 4.06[A][4]
 Groundless claims § 4.06[A][4]
 Substantive unconscionability not
 required § 4.06[A][4]
Decision for judge § 4.06[A]
Defense § 4.06[A][3]
Good faith contrasted § 4.06[A], [B]
Disclaimer of warranty § 5.03[C]
Hearing, necessity for § 4.06[A]
Prima facie § 5.04[B]
Procedural and substantive § 4.06[A][1]

Procedural
  Inequality of bargaining
      power   § 4.06[A][1]
  Meaningful choice, lack of   § 4.06[A]
  Unfair surprise   § 4.06[A][1]
Remedies
  Defense procedurally   § 4.06[A][3]
  Reformation   § 4.06[A][3]
Sliding scale   § 4.06[A][1]
Standard-form contracts   § 4.06[A]
Status of parties   § 4.06[A][1], [C]
Substantive
  "Cross-collateral" clauses   § 4.06[A][1]
  Oppression   § 4.06[A][1]
  Price term   § 4.06[A][1]
Warranty disclaimers   § 5.03[C]
UNIFORM SALES ACT
Risk of loss   § 6.01
UNILATERAL CONTRACT TRICK (See
    ACCEPTANCE)
USAGE OF TRADE
(See also INTERPRETATION and PAROL
    EVIDENCE RULE)
Burden of proof   § 4.03[A]
Defined   § 4.03[A]
Regularity of observance   § 4.03[A]
Place of observance   § 4.03[A]
USED GOODS (See MERCHANTABILITY,
    IMPLIED WARRANTY OF)

V

VERTICAL PRIVITY (See PRIVITY)

W

WAIVER
(See also MODIFICATION OF
    CONTRACTS)
By election   § 2.06[B][3]
By estoppel   § 2.06[B][3]
Defined   § 2.06[B][3]
Inspection rights   § 7.03[A][1]
Modification contrasted   § 2.06[B][3]
Modification operating as   § 2.06[B][3]
Retraction of   § 2.06[B][3]
Right to reject   § 7.04[B]
WARRANTY (See CUMULATION AND
    CONFLICT OF WARRANTIES;
    EXPRESS WARRANTY; FITNESS,
    IMPLIED WARRANTY OF;
    MERCHANTABILITY, IMPLIED
    WARRANTY OF; TITLE,
    IMPLIED WARRANTY OF)
WARRANTY DISCLAIMER (See
    DISCLAIMER OF WARRANTY)
WARRANTY OF QUIET POSSESSION (See
    TITLE, IMPLIED WARRANTY
    OF)
WRITING REQUIREMENT (See
    ADEQUATE ASSURANCES and
    STATUTE OF FRAUDS)
WRITTEN CONFIRMATIONS (See
    BATTLE OF THE FORMS;
    MODIFICATION OF
    CONTRACTS and STATUTE OF
    FRAUDS)